THE STUDY OF EVANGELISM

THE STUDY OF EVANGELISM

Exploring a Missional Practice of the Church

Edited by

Paul W. Chilcote & Laceye C. Warner

William B. Eerdmans Publishing Company
Grand Rapids, Michigan / Cambridge, U.K.

Published 2008 by
Wm. B. Eerdmans Publishing Co.
2140 Oak Industrial Drive N.E., Grand Rapids, Michigan 49505 /
P.O. Box 163, Cambridge CB3 9PU U.K.

Printed in the United States of America

17 16 9 8 7 6

Library of Congress Cataloging-in-Publication Data

The study of evangelism: exploring a missional practice of the church /
edited by Paul W. Chilcote & Laceye C. Warner.
p. cm.
Includes bibliographical references.
ISBN 978-0-8028-0391-7 (pbk.: alk. paper)
1. Evangelistic work. I. Chilcote, Paul Wesley, 1954-
I. Warner, Laceye C.

BV3790.S888 2008
269.2 — dc22

2007044578

www.eerdmans.com

For

Rev. Janet Chilcote
and
Rev. Gaston Warner

Who live the gospel before us
on a daily basis

Contents

Contributors

William J. Abraham is Albert Cook Outler Professor of Wesley Studies and University Distinguished Professor at Perkins School of Theology, Southern Methodist University

Mortimer Arias is Bishop Emeritus of the Bolivian Methodist Church

David J. Bosch was Professor of Missiology and Head of the Department of Missiology at the University of South Africa

Carl E. Braaten is Professor Emeritus of Systematic Theology at Lutheran School of Theology, Chicago

Walter Brueggemann is William Marcellus McPheeters Professor Emeritus of Old Testament at Columbia Theological Seminary

Paul W. Chilcote is Visiting Professor of the Practice of Evangelism at Duke Divinity School

Orlando E. Costas was Judson Professor of Missiology and Dean at Andover-Newton Theological Seminary

Darrell L. Guder is Dean of Academic Affairs and Henry Winters Luce Professor of Missional and Ecumenical Theology at Princeton Theological Seminary

Stanley Hauerwas is Gilbert T. Rowe Professor of Theological Ethics at Duke Divinity School

George R. Hunsberger is Dean of Journey and Professor of Congregational Mission at Western Theological Seminary

Bill J. Leonard is Dean of the Divinity School and Professor of Church History at Wake Forest University

Walter L. Liefeld is Distinguished Professor Emeritus of New Testament at Trinity Evangelical Divinity School

Samuel Palma Manriquez is Institute Coordinator at Comunidad de Aprendizaje Puente, Chile

J. N. K. Mugambi is Professor of Philosophy and Religious Studies at the University of Nairobi and Professor Extraordinarius at the University of South Africa

Lesslie Newbigin was Bishop of the Church of South India

Mercy Amba Oduyoye is Director of the Insititute of Women in Religion and Culture and Professor of Religious Studies at the University of Ghana

Jerry Persha was formerly Associate Professor of Systematic Theology at Maryknoll School of Theology

Stephen K. Pickard is Head of The Charles Sturt University School of Theology and Director of the St. Mark's National Theological Centre, Australia

Dana L. Robert is Truman Collins Professor of World Christianity and History of Mission and Co-Director of the Center for Global Christianity and Mission at Boston University School of Theology

Letty M. Russell was Professor Emerita of Theology at Yale Divinity School

Ronald J. Sider is President and Founder of Evangelicals for Social Action

John Stott is Rector Emeritus of All Souls Church, Langham Place, London

Otis Turner is Associate for Racial Justice Policy Development in the National Ministries Division of the Presbyterian Church (USA).

J. Patrick Vaughn is Senior Pastor of Paoli Presbyterian Church, Paoli, Pennsylvania

Alexander Veronis is Priest Emeritus of Annunciation Greek Orthodox Church in Lancaster, Pennsylvania, and Founder and President Emeritus of the Orthodox Christian Mission Center Board

John H. Westerhoff is Professor Emeritus of Theology and Christian Nurture at Duke Divinity School

Hwa Yung is Director of the Centre for the Study of Christianity in Asia at Trinity Theological College, Singapore

Preface

The vision of this volume emerged in conversation over a meal. We both had contemplated the idea of a compilation of readings in the study of evangelism. Upon discovering this common interest, Dr. Chilcote suggested we join efforts. The Foundation for Evangelism, affiliated with the General Board of Discipleship of the United Methodist Church, had previously awarded Dr. Warner a grant to support two postdoctoral fellowships in evangelism at Duke Divinity School beginning in the fall of 2005. We therefore engaged in joint supervision of the post-doc fellows with Bishop Ken Carder and this program provided a context for the reading of major works of the discipline in the inaugural semester, with subsequent discussion of article-length essays related to the study of evangelism in the spring of 2006. This creative and collaborative process shaped the selection of material for this collection.

Our primary concern in the post-doc seminar was to introduce our students to classical texts and to discuss groundbreaking writing in the study of evangelism. We wanted our common reading to be representative, landmark, and global, including not only the research of major scholars in the field, but also work that reached out beyond the traditional boundaries constructed by denomination, culture, and ideology. What we thought would be a relatively easy task took us in directions we could hardly have imagined at the outset, leading to important discoveries at some turns and major disappointments at others. We were amazed by how much sifting was required to separate the wheat from the chaff and by how far we often had to go to locate landmark studies. The lacunae in the study of evangelism became immediately and sometimes painfully apparent. While writing and research seemed to abound in certain sectors of the Western church, even where passion for evangelism more generally had waned, locating English-language material from the non-Western world, where Christian vitality more generally reigns, proved to be an insurmountable challenge at times. Despite the fact that women predominate in the global Christian family (actually in all times and all places), studies by, for, and about women and evangelism remain in short supply. We are prepared to sympathize with every protest against almost any significant omission in this volume, and we commend to your attention the listing of books and monographs appended to it. These authors and titles are certain to lead you in directions and to discoveries that broaden your horizon concerning this ministry. Despite the difficulty of the task we set for ourselves, we are pleased with the outcome and hope that this journey through the study of evangelism — a missional practice of the church — informs and inspires all of our readers.

The production of a volume of this kind requires a genuine team effort. It has been a collaborative project from the beginning. The Foundation for Evangelism provided financial assistance that proved particularly helpful in the preparation of the final manuscript. Foundation funds supported the work of our research assistant, Amy Beth Hougland, whose primary tasks involved scanning, re-keying, and preparing clean texts from original articles. We express our appreciation first and foremost, therefore, to Paul Ervin, former executive director of the Foundation, and Amy Beth for their invaluable assistance. Gerry Warren of Duke Divinity School also provided technical assistance related to this detailed and often tedious work.

The influence of The Foundation for Evangelism also factored significantly in this project by virtue of a Postdoctoral Program in Evangelism founded in partnership with Duke Divinity School. The fellows mentioned above, Dr. Esther Chung and Dr. Roger Owens, and our faculty colleague, Bishop Ken Carder, met with us regularly during the spring semester of 2006, working through many of the essays included in this volume. Indeed, their input into the selection process helped us immeasurably with regard to the difficult question of exclusion or inclusion. Their observations and advice has shaped this anthology, and we are thankful to them for making it a more useful collection of writings. We have incurred a similar indebtedness to a large number of friends and colleagues, including Billy Abraham, Ron Crandall, Achim Härtner, Elaine Heath, George Hunsberger, Greg Jones, Randy Maddox, Ed Phillips, Dana Robert, Len Sweet, Bob Tuttle, David Lowes Watson, Lovett Weems, and David Wilkinson, who have given us helpful suggestions, examined drafts of this work in progress, and encouraged us in one way or another over these past months. Particular thanks are due to Don Kim and Joon-Sik Park for their assistance in the identification of pertinent materials related to the Asian context.

Unlike some disciplines, in which landmark research documents can be located easily in one or two scholarly journals, the materials collected here had to be culled from many different sources, some of which were much less accessible than others. Our initial survey of a relatively uncharted terrain, in fact, convinced us of the importance of this volume. We are grateful to those who permitted us to reprint these articles and to collect them in one place for the benefit of the church and academy. Particular thanks are due, of course, to the many authors whose careful study of evangelism, creative and innovative approaches to the practice, and passion about Christian witness are transparent in this volume. The original location of these publications and proper credits conclude this brief prefatory statement.

We are most grateful to Jon Pott, editor-in-chief of Wm. B. Eerdmans Publishing Company, for his immediate response to our proposal and for his enthusiasm for the project from the outset. Eerdmans has distinguished itself as a premier publisher of books related to mission and evangelism and we are honored to stand humbly in such a succession of important works. We offer our thanks as well to the editorial team, especially Linda Bieze who shepherded us through the process and produced such a handsome volume.

Many thanks also go to Steven Porter for his careful, persistent work compiling the indexes and offering editorial suggestions.

Finally, we thank our spouses, Rev. Janet Chilcote and Rev. Gaston Warner, for their support behind the scenes. Both of them are authentic "evangel bearers" and live the Good News before us on a daily basis. We dedicate this volume to them.

Acknowledgments

The essays in this volume were previously published in the journals and books listed below. They have undergone minor revision, and permission has been granted for their reprinting in this book.

The Asbury Journal

Paul W. Chilcote, "The Integral Nature of Worship and Evangelism: Insights from the Wesleyan Tradition," 61, no. 1 (Spring 2006): 7-23.

Church & Society

Otis Turner, "God's Justice and Good News: Looking at the Intertwined Dynamics of Evangelism and Antiracism," 92, no. 3 (January-February 2002): 109-16.

Ecumenical Review

Mercy Amba Oduyoye, "Unity and Mission: The Emerging Ecumenical Vision," 39, no. 3 (July 1987): 336-45.

Evangelical Missions Quarterly

Hwa Yung, "Strategic Issues in Missions — An Asian Perspective," 40, no. 1 (January 2004): 26-34.

Greek Orthodox Theological Review

Alexander Veronis, "Orthodox Concepts of Evangelism and Mission," 27, no. 1 (Spring 1982): 44-57.

International Bulletin of Missionary Research

David J. Bosch, "Evangelism: Theological Currents and Cross-Currents," 11, no. 3 (July 1987): 98-103.

Dana L. Robert, "Shifting Southward: Global Christianity Since 1945," 24, no. 2 (April 2000): 50-58.

International Review of Mission

Orlando E. Costas, "Evangelism and the Gospel of Salvation," 63, no. 1 (January 1974): 24-37.

Darrell L. Guder, "Incarnation and the Church's Evangelistic Mission," 83, no. 3 (July 1994): 417-28.

Samuel Palma Manriquez, "Religion of the People and Evangelism: A Pentecostal Perspective," 82, no. 3 (July 1993): 365-74.

J. N. K. Mugambi, "A Fresh Look at Evangelism in Africa," 87, no. 3 (July 1998): 342-60.

Ronald J. Sider, "Evangelism, Salvation, and Social Justice: Definitions and Interrelationships," 64, no. 3 (July 1975): 251-67.

John Stott, "The Significance of Lausanne," 64, no. 3 (July 1975): 288-94.

Interpretation

William J. Abraham, "A Theology of Evangelism: The Heart of the Matter," 48, no. 2 (April 1994): 117-30.

George R. Hunsberger, "Is there Biblical Warrant for Evangelism?" 48, no. 2 (April 1994): 131-44.

John H. Westerhoff, "Evangelism, Evangelization, and Catechesis," 48, no. 2 (April 1994): 156-65.

Journal of the Academy for Evangelism in Theological Education

Carl E. Braaten, "The Meaning of Evangelism in the Context of God's Universal Grace," 3 (1987-88): 9-19.

Journal of Pastoral Care

J. Patrick Vaughn, "Evangelism: A Pastoral Theological Perspective," 49, no. 3 (Fall 1995): 265-72.

Missiology

Mortimer Arias, "Centripetal Mission or Evangelization by Hospitality," 10 (January 1982): 69-81.

Walter L. Liefeld, "Women and Evangelism in the Early Church," 15, no. 3 (July 1987): 291-98.

Jerry Persha, "Toward Developing an Adequate and Comprehensive Understanding of Evangelization," 14, no. 3 (July 1986): 273-85.

Missionalia

Stephen K. Pickard, "Evangelism and the Character of Christian Theology," 21 (August 1993): 159-75.

Occasional Bulletin of Missionary Research

Mortimer Arias, "Contextual Evangelization in Latin America," 2, no. 1 (January 1978): 19-28.

Letty M. Russell, "Liberation and Evangelism — A Feminist Perspective," 2, no. 4 (October 1978): 128-30.

Review and Expositor

Bill J. Leonard, "Evangelism and Contemporary American Life," 77, no. 4 (Fall 1980): 493-506.

Word & World

Walter Brueggemann, "Evangelism and Discipleship," 24, no. 2 (Spring 2004): 121-35.

Wm. B. Eerdmans Publishing Company

David J. Bosch, "The Structure of Mission: An Exposition of Matt. 28:16-21," in *Exploring Church Growth*, ed. Wilbert R. Shenk, 1983, 218-48.

Lesslie Newbigin, "Evangelism in the Context of Secularization," in *A Word in Season: Perspectives on Christian World Missions*, ed. Lesslie Newbigin, 1994, 148-57.

Lesslie Newbigin, "Foolishness to the Greeks," in *Foolishness to the Greeks*, by Lesslie Newbigin, 1986, 1-10.

Brazos Press

Stanley Hauerwas, "Worship, Evangelism, Ethics: On Eliminating the 'And,'" in *A Better Hope*, 2000, 155-61.

Introduction

Growing Interest in Evangelism

By the turn of the new millennium, diverse communities of faith had rediscovered the importance of intentional, communal engagement in Christian practices. A growing interest developed with regard to the processes that engage, shape, nurture, and sustain persons and communities in their Christian faith. Concurrently, concern for evangelism emerged, not simply for the sake of institutional survival in increasingly post-Christian contexts, but as a constitutive part of the church — as a missional practice of the community of faith. Conceiving evangelism as an essential practice that engages the whole people of God, and not simply the peculiar vocation of elite specialists, many Christians have begun to embrace this calling afresh as a critical aspect of God's mission in the world. In the midst of this present foment, both teachers and practitioners recognize that evangelism has scholarly as well as programmatic dimensions. We hope that this collection of groundbreaking essays on the practice of evangelism will make a contribution to these new developments.

Books abound on evangelism. Many in the marketplace today tend to be "how-to" manuals — practical guides for the adoption of a specific strategy or articulations of a particular form or style of evangelism. These tend to be practice-oriented and often lack serious theological engagement and reflection. On the other hand, there are an increasing number of texts — especially as evangelism continues to "come of age" within the context of the theological academy — that attempt to plumb the depths of the biblical and theological heritage of the church with reference to evangelistic practice. Unfortunately, many of these studies offer little guidance with regard to application in life. As is true with regard to other so-called "practical disciplines," the need to help bridge this perennial, albeit false, dichotomy of theory and practice is critical. In addition to this holistic approach, interdisciplinarity must characterize the work of evangelism and inform its study. Scholars examine the practice of evangelism within existing fields, such as theological and historical studies, as well as in practical or pastoral areas of inquiry. Evangelism borrows and adapts methods, questions, and concerns intrinsic to established disciplines. This integral dynamic promises creative discoveries, new approaches, and distinctive ways of viewing the practice of evangelism. In addition to our concern that evangelism find its true place within the larger *missio Dei* as a Christian practice, we also hope that this volume contributes to the rediscovery of evangelism's essential place within the theological curriculum.

Through careful study of these essays biblical scholars will be challenged to reexamine texts related to evangelism and obtain insight that informs faithful practice. Students of evangelism have hardly begun to marshal the primary missiological texts of our global Christian heritage so that historians can interpret and translate the actions of the community into new forms that are effective in the spreading of God's rule and not destructive to culture or human dignity. The serious study of evangelism can lead practitioners both to discover appropriate classical paradigms of discipling and to experiment with new forms of evangelism that cross or push boundaries with integrity and authenticity. If this collection of essays provides an impetus for scholars and practitioners to search out connections across traditional academic and ecclesial boundaries, then it will have been well worth the effort.

We have not framed this volume around the illusion that answers to the questions related to evangelism in our time are clear or easily formulated. In fact, we confess that we still struggle to identify the questions we should be asking. The complexity of our world and the dynamism of the human story confront the Christian community at every turn, pressing us to reflect upon our faith more deeply, to engage in dialogue more seriously, and to respond to crises around us more compassionately. Our claim, quite simply, is that all of this action bears directly upon our understanding of evangelism as a missional practice of the church. We marvel at the energy and creativity that revolves around evangelism at this particular time, and we rejoice in the many signs of vitality emerging from conversations about this practice that direct us increasingly into the most central and sacred places in our lives. Engaging in the study of evangelism elicits the most difficult and worthwhile questions related to the life of faith. How does one come to know God in Christ? What is the role of the Holy Spirit in conversion? How does the disciple of Christ engage the culture in which he or she is immersed? What is the relationship between the worship of God and God's claim upon us as children? What is the relationship between moments of crisis and processes of spiritual discovery in the Christian journey? Growing interest in evangelism gives rise to these questions and many more.

It is clear to us that the integrity and vitality of evangelism beyond this time of growing interest will depend in large measure upon Christian leaders who are committed to the integral nature of evangelism and the reign of God. Current interest in evangelism pulls the community of faith in many directions, leading some into paths that honor God's vision of peace, justice, and beloved community and others into ways (and particularly means) that seem antithetical to God's end. Our Christian past provides clues about this dynamic tension.

An Overview of Late Twentieth-Century Developments

Committed Christians throughout the ages have devoted much energy to the study of how persons are "brought to Christ" or how "Christians are made." Regardless of whether they have used the language of evangelism, the practice of evangelism has remained central to the propagation of the Christian faith since the time of the Apostles. Since the God revealed to us in Jesus Christ is a missionary God, it is actually right, in our view, to claim the historical origins of evangelism in the gracious act of creation itself. But this is much too large a canvas, obviously, upon which to paint an introduction to the texts collected in this volume. Our purposes here demand something much more modest. Developments in the twentieth century, and particularly events in postwar Europe, contributed in large measure to the growing interest in evangelism today, and a survey of this period places many of the selections included in this volume in their proper context.

The World Missionary Conference held in Edinburgh in 1910, considered by most to be the symbolic birth of the modern ecumenical movement, signaled the important place that evangelism was to have throughout the course of the century. The watchword of this event, "the evangelization of the world in this generation," reflected the optimism of the age, even as the world stood on the brink of war, and inspired many to reconsider the missionary mandate of the gospel. The ensuing World Wars wreaked havoc among the nations of established Christendom, making the century one of the most bloody eras in human history, but also fueled concern for the witness of the gospel in such a broken world. The establishment of the World Council of Churches (WCC) in 1948 fanned the evangelistic flame that had been kindled at the outset of the century, and much of the interest in and controversy about evangelism revolved around the evolution of this conciliar Protestant movement and its counterpart, the International Missionary Council (IMC), birthed at the Edinburgh conference.

Several conferences sponsored by the IMC explored the interface of mission, evangelism, and ecumenism, with Jerusalem (1928), Tambaram (1938), and Whitby (1947) in particular paving the way for new thought and action. Following the Second World War and its aftermath, the first major conference on evangelism sponsored by the IMC was held at Willingen, in Germany, in 1952. This event proved to be a watershed and established a trajectory for much of the conversation around mission and evangelism in the decades to follow. Set amid the rubble of war — the tragic sign of human brokenness — the delegates rediscovered that mission depended first and foremost on God's own activity. The great ecumenical figures of the age located mission in the purpose and action of the Triune God, rather than in the weakness of human institutions. Willingen is rightly considered one of the conferences having had the most lasting influence upon contemporary missiology and provided the impetus for a renewed vision of the *missio Dei.* Within a decade, ecumenical leaders fully integrated the work of the WCC and IMC, establishing a Commission on World Mission and Evangelism when the two bodies consolidated at the 1961 Assembly in New Delhi.

The decade of the 1960s proved tumultuous in every imaginable way. With regard to matters related to evangelism it witnessed the birth of a parallel movement among evangelical Protestants contradistinguished from that of the ecumenically minded. Billy Graham, of course, had become an icon of revivalistic evangelism during these years, and he and other evangelical leaders, Carl F. H. Henry in particular, began to consolidate the energy of this movement. The first World Congress on Evangelism of Berlin in 1966 echoed the concerns of Edinburgh 1910 for global evangelization, but the participants distanced themselves significantly from the more sociopolitical concerns of the WCC. The stage was set for a confrontation between evangelicals, who emphasized the personal dimension of salvation in Christ, and the ecumenicals, who increasingly elevated God's work in the redemption of the social order. Over the course of the decade, a classic fissure developed along the fault line of evangelism.

The world mission conference of the WCC, held in Bangkok at the turn of the years 1972/1973, fanned the flame of controversy into white heat. Concerned about the complicity of the church with regard to the exploitation and injustice of Euro-American colonialism, sensitive to emerging post-colonial contextual theologies, and cognizant of the influence of cultural identity in the shaping of evangelistic practice, the delegates proposed a temporary "moratorium" of mission activity from the North. The evangelicals countered with the International Congress on World Evangelization, held in Lausanne, Switzerland, in 1974. The "Lausanne Covenant," the first of three monumental declarations on evangelism in the final decades of the twentieth century, disassociated itself from the ecumenical theological developments, emphasizing the priority of evangelism in mission and defining the necessity, responsibilities, and goals of spreading the gospel. The congress also established the Lausanne Committee for World Evangelization, which became the essential mouthpiece of this movement of evangelistic renewal. Ironically, although Lausanne helped to delineate two opposing camps within the Protestant community with regard to a theology of evangelism, it also marked the beginning of rapprochement, a spirit that had also been in the air for some time.

That spirit of reconciliation surfaced in surprising ways, not among Protestants, but between the Protestant and Roman Catholic communities by virtue of the Second Vatican Council. As Protestant Christians struggled with the concepts of mission and evangelism in the closing decades of the twentieth century, Catholic Christians were engaged in equally creative conversations that would reorient their thinking about mission. This dialogue came to a climax in the second declaration of enduring significance from this era, *Evangelii Nuntiandi* (Evangelization in the Modern World), promulgated by Pope Paul VI in 1975. This document reflects many of the same concerns brought forward by both sides of the Protestant debate. In this statement the pope confirmed that evangelism constitutes the essential mission of the church. But he also declared the need for the church itself to be re-evangelized so that the freshness, vigor, and strength of the gospel might be proclaimed and lived anew. Indeed, the primary means of evangelism, he claimed, is the witness of authentic Christian lives; evangelism is the mission of the whole people of God.

In 1982 the WCC published "Mission and Evangelism — An Ecumenical Affirmation," the third landmark declaration of critical import in the development of a theology of evangelism during this period. This affirmation remains the fundamental text on mission and evangelism for the WCC, reflecting the effort of ecumenical leaders to establish a balance between the enduring significance of the proclamation of the gospel and the prophetic challenge to manifest God's just purposes in human history. It is a convergence document characterized by commitment to evangelism as the heart of mission, personal conversion to Christ as the foundation of the Christian life, solidarity with the victims of unjust social and economic systems, and witness to the reign of God through word and deed. While significant differences still exist between evangelical and ecumenical theologians and practitioners of evangelism, the chasm between them has narrowed significantly and the distinctions tend to be more matters of emphasis than of substance. While subsequent events have kept this dialogue fresh (in particular, Lausanne II: International Congress on World Evangelization in Manila [1989] with its "Manifesto" and the WCC's World Mission and Evangelism Conference in Athens [2005], building upon its 2000 declaration, "Mission and Evangelism in Unity"), the Lausanne Covenant (1974), *Evangelii Nuntiandi* (1975), and "Mission and Evangelism — An Ecumenical Affirmation" (1982) form a corpus of documents defining the late twentieth-century quest for a theology of mission and evangelism.

As the study of evangelism advanced along these fronts, primarily engaging the mission community, church leaders, and practitioners in the field, visionaries within academia began to consider the importance of these developments for theological education. Prior to the critical decade of missiological reflection (1972-82) few seminaries had full-time, regular rank faculty dedicated to the study of evangelism. Responding to what they perceived as a critical need, therefore, denominational agencies, such as the Foundation for Evangelism within the United Methodist Church, to offer but one example, attempted to support the ministry of evangelism in both the church and the academy. Within a decade of its inception in 1949, the Foundation had established two endowed chairs of evangelism in high-profile seminaries. But these positions remained anomalies until the 1980s, when the vision of established positions in evangelism in all the denominational centers of ministerial training became a passionate goal of the leadership. It is important not to minimize the crossfire weathered by those who pioneered the study of evangelism in these positions, often amenable as they were, and continue to be, both to the academy and to the church.

Within the broader academic sphere, older, established scholarly guilds, such as the American Society of Missiology, exhibited interest in the study of evangelism from its inception, but within the parameters of a larger scholarly mandate. It was not until 1973 that a small group of scholars established the Academy for Evangelism in Theological Education. The purpose of the Academy was to facilitate the teaching of evangelism, to share pedagogical ideas and methods, to develop new resources, to examine new trends in the discipline, and to foster scholarly research in evangelism and related concerns. The Academy continues to disseminate its work through an annual journal. In similar fashion, the American Society for Church Growth, focusing its attention more particularly on the nature, function, and health of Christian churches, employs the insights of social and behavioral sciences and publishes its findings in a journal of its own inaugurated in 1991. Despite the fact that the study of evangelism is in a nascent stage of development, it is not only derivative from but exerts an influence upon the institutions in which it is carried out. It is our hope that the critical study of evangelism will provide the catalyst for the kinds of conversations that transform and renew communities, both academic and ecclesial. How it will contribute to the larger world of the academy remains to be seen, but there is no question that the role it plays as a missional practice in the life of the church will be increasingly critical.

Evangelism: Definitions and Observations

The valuation of this emergent discipline reflects both a deepening interest within the Christian community and a growing dis-ease within a pluralistic culture concerning the place of evangelism in the wider society. The critical study of evangelism is developing, in other words, in a lively context in which the broad exchange of ideas is laden with both promise and peril. In the mix of it all, a close but complex relationship exists between the scholars and practitioners of evangelism. A satisfactory exposition of the church's mission in the contemporary world requires the insights of both, in addition to an elevated awareness of contextual concerns. These are complex matters.

The reader will encounter a range of definitions and understandings of evangelism, therefore, in the pages ahead. Given the nature of these times this should come as no surprise. Although some progress has been made in identifying its contours and features, much work needs to be done to establish anything approaching a satisfactory cartography of evangelism. Especially given the diversity and momentum of the closing decades of the previous century, both the practices of evangelism and the disciplined reflection upon them are understandably in flux. We believe that the current situation makes a volume like this one all the more critical. It is important for us, as the editors of this volume, therefore, to locate ourselves within the terrain and to outline the preliminary conclusions we have drawn concerning the present state of evangelism — conclusions that figure prominently, of course, in the decisions we have made with regard to the composition of this anthology.

Both of us are ordained clergy of The United Methodist Church and John Wesley Fellows of A Foundation for Theological Education. Essentially, this places us within the evangelical range of the broad Methodist theological spectrum, but that evangelicalism, for both of us, has been shaped definitively by our serious study of the Wesleyan tradition. In this theological heritage we find much value for the life of the church today beyond the boundaries of Methodism. Of particular interest to us is the way in which John and Charles

Wesley found it possible to hold typical polarities together in living out their life in Christ — personal and social, physical and spiritual, missional and evangelistic aspects of the faith. While evangelical, therefore, we are also ecumenical and have drawn much inspiration with regard to mission theology and evangelism from the twentieth-century ecumenical legacy, both Protestant and Roman Catholic. Our tendency is to place greater weight on theological concerns linked to evangelism than social scientific models of church life. For this reason, some readers may encounter less church growth material in this volume than they may have anticipated. Finally, we are deeply committed both to the church and to the academy and seek to advocate the rediscovery of the centrality of evangelism in both worlds.

With regard to the thinking that has guided our collection of these essays, we offer six propositions concerning evangelism:

First, evangelism is a vital part of something larger than itself, namely, the *missio Dei.* While evangelism is but one part of God's larger mission in the world, it is the essence — the heart — of all Christian mission.

Second, although the goal of evangelism is conversion, often experienced in crisis moments in the lives of individuals, evangelism is a process. Church leaders gathered in Eastbourne, England, in 1999, for the International Consultation on Discipleship, concluded that making a Christian is a process that takes place over a long period of time. We concur. Evangelism is a process more than it is an event.

Third, evangelism is concerned with discipling people in Christ. The primary purpose of evangelism is not growing churches or recruiting members (although both may be its consequence). God forms people into authentic disciples of Jesus, and we participate in that process through evangelism.

Fourth, evangelism is oriented toward the reign of God. The ultimate goal toward which evangelism moves is the realization of God's reign in human life. While not unconcerned with the salvation of the individual in and through Christ, initiating persons into an alternative community of God's people who give themselves for the life of the world is its proper end. We embrace a "holistic" vision of evangelism that affirms both personal salvation and social justice.

Fifth, evangelism is a missional practice of the whole people of God. Evangelism is not simply an activity; it is a set of practices — a habituated way of being in community. While some persons may be particularly gifted as evangelists within the community of faith, God claims all of God's children as "evangel bearers" for the purpose of God's mission of shalom in the world.

Sixth, evangelism is inescapably contextual. Just as all Christianity is contextual, the culture of the practitioner shapes the practice of evangelism and the culture of those evangelized determines the nature of the relationship and the practice. Evangelism, in other words, engages the Christian community in a complex inter-relational dynamic in both intra- and cross-cultural experiences of evangel-sharing.

Some of the essays the reader will encounter here reflect the full range of these concerns; others do not. While wanting to be representative in the selection of material for this volume, and never wanting to be heavy-handed in terms of exclusion, we need to be honest in saying that you will not encounter conceptions of evangelism antithetical to our own vision among the authors we have included. We appreciate the diversity of the Body of Christ manifest in the world today and are captivated by a holistic vision of evangelism that refuses to dichotomize this vital practice of the church into personal or social, salvation or justice polarities. It should not be surprising that the contributors to this volume have been trained as biblical scholars, theologians, and historians of Christianity, as well as practitioners of evangelism. In their commitment to understand the mission of God's people, they bring a rich blend of their own methods and conclusions. We seek to offer, therefore, a richly textured vision of the practice of evangelism in a resource that is both accessible and relevant.

Overview of the Contents of This Book

The thirty essays gathered into this volume, originally published in more than fifteen scholarly journals and books by some of the discipline's leading scholars, offer groundbreaking explorations of the missional practice of evangelism. Arranged under six headings, these essays define the practice of evangelism, identify biblical and historical sources for its study, explore the relationship of evangelism to the world of theology and to other ecclesial practices, and discuss evangelistic theology and practice in diverse ecclesial, ecumenical, and cultural contexts. The primary purpose of this volume is to lay a solid, scholarly foundation for future discourse, speaking to all who practice and study evangelism from a vast array of Christian perspectives and encouraging reflective and open dialogue about this practice within the community of faith. We invite the reader to join in this conversation.

The first two sections address foundational issues. Part One focuses on matters of definition with regard to the theology and practice of evangelism. Scholars produced some of the most exciting work in this arena in the last quarter of the twentieth century, and the vision of David J. Bosch, William J. Abraham, Orlando E. Costas, and Lesslie Newbigin continues to dominate the landscape. These writers expand the vision of evangelism, breaking out of stale concepts that are myopic and truncated, discussing the relationship of evangelism to the *missio Dei,* to the gospel of salvation in its multiple dimensions, and to the context of secularization in the West. Part Two surveys biblical and historical sources for the study of evangelism, examining the primary biblical texts and themes that inform the practice (George R. Hunsberger and David J. Bosch), recovering the lost history of early Christian women in evangelism (Walter L. Liefeld), analyzing the origins of American populist understandings of evangelism (Bill J. Leonard), and prognosticating about the southward shift of Christianity in our time (Dana L. Robert).

One of our contentions is that evangelism has a rightful place in the world of theology (Part Three). The very character of Christian theology mandates a central place for evangelism (Stephen K. Pickard), the essential meaning of evangelism only being intelligible within the wider context of God's universal grace (Carl E. Braaten). Incarnation (Darrell L. Guder), salvation and social justice (Ronald J. Sider), and worship and ethics (Stanley Hauerwas) are all inseparable from the evangelistic ministry of the church. Evangelism is theology, not simply a sub-discipline of practical theology informed by it. Part Four focuses on the relationship between evangelism and other ecclesial practices, exploring the links that connect evangelism to discipleship (Walter Brueggemann), catechesis (John H. Westerhoff), Christian public worship (Paul W. Chilcote), and pastoral care (J. Patrick Vaughn).

The final two sections deal with contextual matters, both ecclesial and cultural. Often suffering from a vision of evangelism confined by the parameters of one's own denomination or theological tradition, it is necessary to expand the horizons of evangelistic practice by seeing it through the eyes of the "other." Part Five exposes the reader to the understanding of evangelism in a wide range of ecclesial traditions. The organization of the material in this section juxtaposes Orthodox (Alexander Veronis) and Pentecostal (Samuel Palma Manriquez) perspectives and surveys the late twentieth-century developments among evangelical Protestants associated with the Lausanne Covenant (John Stott), Roman Catholics shaped by Pope Paul VI's exhortation on "Evangelization in the Modern World" (Jerry Persha), and conciliar Protestants involved in the emerging ecumenical vision of evangelism (Mercy Amba Oduyoye). Part Six consists of essays reflecting different cultural contexts and the evangelistic praxis that has emerged from them. First, in an excerpt from one of his groundbreaking books, Lesslie Newbigin examines the perennial issue of how Christian people relate to the culture in which they are immersed, offering important guidance concerning the definition of both gospel and culture. The remaining essays explore evangelistic praxis on the continents of Africa (J. N. K. Mugambi) and Asia (Hwa Yung), and in Latin America (Mortimer Arias), regions of the world characterized by remarkable Christian vitality.

An Afterword provides a glimpse into the future, seeking to identify emerging issues and new trajectories in the study of evangelism. From among the many significant developments in this regard, three seem most promising and crucial in our view. These issues include race and racism in the world today (Otis Turner), the perspective and place of women in the practices of the church (Letty M. Russell), and the centrality of hospitality in the task of evangel-bearing (Mortimer Arias).

Since we have drawn the selections in this volume from a wide variety of sources, we have felt it necessary to make some minimal editorial changes in the texts so as to maintain a uniformity of style throughout the volume. This affects format in some cases, but most notably, the style of scholarly annotation. In three cases we decided to retain the original style of presentation. David J. Bosch makes multiple references to over seventy-five separate works in chapter 6 and the conversion of these citations into standard footnotes proved unsuitable. So we have retained his internal citations with his listing of resources at the close of the essay. In chapter 16, it seemed reasonable to retain Westerhoff's list of suggested readings as part of the article, despite the fact that most of these works are included in the Further Reading bibliography at the close of this volume. Because of the frequent references to ecumenical documents in her essay, we have also retained Mercy Amba Oduyoye's internal citations with her own abbreviations. In some instances we have silently corrected the original texts when we have encountered grammatical errors. Again, for the purposes of stylistic uniformity, we have adopted conventional American practice with regard to punctuation and quotation in the texts.

One of the issues we struggled to resolve to our own satisfaction is the pervasive use of gender-specific language with reference to humanity in some of the essays. Both of us are strongly committed to the use of inclusive language in all of our writing and teaching. Our decision in the end, however, was to retain the original language of the essays with reference to this issue so as to maintain the historical integrity of these documents. Our hope is that this will provide a learning experience of its own.

We intend this volume for a wide audience. Christians engaged in the practice of evangelism will find much food for thought in these essays. This material can serve to ground clergy, lay ministers, and religious more thoroughly in the biblical and theological foundations of their practice. Scholars, and particularly teachers, who are committed to the study of evangelism will appreciate the wide range of material brought together in this single volume. Hopefully, we have saved our colleagues an immense labor. Those who work in theological, biblical, and historical fields will find this collection invaluable in terms of describing critical historical developments, paradigm shifts, interpretive insights, and cultural perspectives. When we finished this book, we were well aware of the fact that this is only a beginning. We invite you — scholar, church leader, practitioner, disciple — to seriously consider evangelism as a missional practice of the church. Reflect upon the ways in which God is calling you to be an evangel-bearer in your own context. Unlike many books on evangelism, this one offers you no rules or recipes for success. Rather, it introduces you to people who discovered the centrality of evangelism in their lives and ministries and have sought to articulate their vision of faithfulness in this glorious task and gift. Enjoy the conversation. Embrace the unique opportunities God reveals to you for living the practice of evangelism.

PART ONE

Defining the Ecclesial Practice and Theology of Evangelism

The essays collected in this opening section inform much of the recent discussion about definition, methodology, and practice as it relates to the ministry of evangelism. Church leaders of every stripe have spilled much ink over these particular issues during the past half-century and have conducted local and global gatherings to engage the Christian community in discussion around them. The contemporary climate of mainline denominational decline and general malaise in North America clamors for the careful definition of evangelism and the construction of a coherent theology of this ecclesial practice. While an increasing number of practitioners flood the market with practical guidebooks for evangelistic practice or panhandle their own particular version of evangelism, rarely do these books afford a theologically and historically robust understanding of evangelism or evaluate its practice from a critical point of view. In the world of the academy, scholars have attempted to find a niche for evangelism, some setting it apart as an aspect of missiology or a crucial topic within ecclesiology in the theological curriculum, others viewing it as a sub-discipline of practical theology or as a discrete field in its own right. In the context of this ferment, the writers featured here help to refine our understanding of the nature, purpose, and function of evangelism within the larger *missio Dei.*

This volume opens, therefore, with questions of definition and theological vision. Both terms, "evangelism" and "mission," elude easy definition. Difficulties also surround any attempt to articulate the interface of these two distinct ministries in the life of the church. Conceptual boundaries shift as interest groups labor to claim sufficient space for agendas that begin more often than not from reactive starting points rather than constructive biblical and theological foundations. Whether originating in the twentieth-century Fundamentalist-Modernist controversy in the United States or related to the legacy of colonial imperialism in an African context, to illustrate with just two examples, polarities are often manifest in conversations about the meaning of evangelism. The essays in this section, representing diverse international but biblically grounded perspectives, provide fundamental insights for the purpose of mapping this varied and, at times, treacherous conceptual terrain.

At least two main themes pervade the following essays: (1) the need to articulate the relationship between evangelism and mission, and (2) the dual dynamic of personal salvation in Jesus Christ and social action related to the reign of God in the practice of evangelism.

David J. Bosch, former dean of the Faculty of Theology at the University of South Africa in Pretoria, demonstrates how scholars and practitioners articulate a wide range of meaning in their efforts to define evangelism and mission. In a masterful survey of the literature, he identifies six ways in which these terms are used as synonyms and four ways in which they are conceived as distinct realities. In an effort to redefine evangelism, he argues for mission as the wider and evangelism as the narrower concept. A biblical understanding of mission, in his view, involves the believer in a drama of cosmic redemption and the glorification of God. Evangelism aims at incorporating others into this vision by means of witness, invitation, and communal outreach, through risk-taking practices that offer salvation as a gift and enlist Christians into the service of God's comprehensive reign. While distinct but not separate from mission, "evangelism is the *core, heart,* or *center*" of it all.

William J. Abraham and Orlando E. Costas address the second theme — the unfortunate bifurcation of personal salvation and social action in many theologies of evangelism. In opposition to truncated theologies of this variety, Abraham — an Irish Methodist converted in young adulthood, at once a theologian, philosopher, and evangelist — argues for a robust ecclesiology to frame the church's ministry of evangelism. As in his classic study, *The Logic of Evangelism,* over against reductionist tendencies that view evangelism (in more "conservative" circles) simply as proclamation, or simply as ministries of justice (in more "liberal" traditions), he describes evangelism as "a polymorphous ministry aimed at initiating people into the kingdom of God." As a dynamic process, evangelism entails not only invitation into God's reign, but also catechesis, or instruction, that grounds the believer in a life devoted to God's vision for all humanity.

In similar fashion, Orlando Costas, a Puerto Rican evangelical who taught missiology and evangelization in both North and Central American settings, proclaims a holistic vision of mission and evangelism based upon a "gospel of salvation" rooted in the biblical text. According to Costas, the particularity of Christianity's history in the Latin American context presents a severely conflicted narrative characterized by colonialism and oppression. This history leaves many suspicious of the church's relevance for the contemporary context. For Costas, a biblical doctrine of salvation reveals a liberating and searching God. Evangelism involves testimony to the reality of the life of Jesus of Nazareth and affirmation of the truth with regard to his redemptive mission and the ultimate reality of God's way. This witness, however, only becomes meaningful as it relates to the struggles for economic justice, dignity, solidarity, and hope within concrete human communities. The gospel of salvation is both gift and demand, calling for relationships built on trust and actions that manifest God's rule over all aspects of life.

At the dawn of the new millennium, societies dominated by secularization, particularly in the Western hemisphere, pose one of the greatest challenges to Christianity. In the closing article, Lesslie Newbigin, one of the greatest ecumenical statesmen and missionary theologians of the twentieth century, tackles this complex issue. Despite the fact that many Christians hailed the rise of secularization as a positive development, the ultimate consequence has been a shift from secular to pagan societies in which "faithless" people give their allegiance to "no-gods." Newbigin argues that the presence of the new reality of God's reign, as alternative to the domestication of the gospel, manifests itself in a peculiar shared life, the actions that originate it, and words that explain it. Evangelism, in such a context, has little to do with increasing the size and importance of the church. Rather, the clue to evangelism in a secular society is the local congregation, the way these communities shape their members as agents of God's reign and equip them to explain the Christian story through word and deed in a compelling and winsome manner.

From varied perspectives around the world, these writers develop definitions and build theologies of evangelism that refuse the old dichotomies separating mission from evangelism — the gift of personal salvation from the call to live in and for God's just and peaceable rule. They demonstrate how this holistic vision shapes both the ecclesial practice and the theology of evangelism. While evangelism and mission are distinct concepts, they are inseparable. In short, evangelism emerges as a complex set of formational practices at the heart of God's mission for the church in the world.

CHAPTER 1

Evangelism: Theological Currents and Cross-Currents Today

David J. Bosch

My assignment is to provide a concise survey of the ways in which evangelism is being understood and practiced today. I assume that this does not preclude an attempt to give my own view on what I believe evangelism should be. One of the problems is that evangelism is understood differently by different people. Another problem is that of terminology. The older term, still dominant in mainline churches, is "evangelism." More recently, however, both evangelicals and Roman Catholics have begun to give preference to the term "evangelization." It does not follow that they give the same contents to the term, as I shall illustrate.

Yet another problem is that of the relationship between the terms "evangelism" and "mission." Perhaps the best way of attempting to clear the cobwebs is to begin by distinguishing between those who regard evangelism and mission as synonyms and those who believe that the two words refer to different realities.

Mission and Evangelism as Synonyms

It is probably true that most people use "mission" and "evangelism" more or less as synonyms. Those who do this do not necessarily agree on what mission/evangelism means. Perhaps one could say that the definitions of mission/evangelism range from a narrow evangelical position to a more or less broad ecumenical one.

Position 1: Mission/evangelism refers to the church's ministry of winning souls for eternity, saving them from eternal damnation. Some years ago a South African evangelist, Reinhard Bonnke, wrote a book with the title *Plundering Hell.* This is what the church's mission is all about: making sure that as many people as possible get "saved" from eternal damnation and go to heaven. According to this first position it would be a *betrayal* of the church's mission to get involved in any other activities. Most people subscribing to this view would be premillennialist in their theology. Typical of the spirit of premillennialism is Dwight L. Moody's most quoted statement from his sermons: "I look upon this world as a wrecked vessel. God has given me a lifeboat and said to me, 'Moody, save all you can.'"[1]

Position 2: This position is slightly "softer" than the first. It also narrows mission/evangelism down to soul-winning. It would concede, nevertheless, that it would be good — at least in theory — to be involved in some other good activities at the same time, activities such as relief work and education. On the whole, however, such activities tend to *distract* from mission as soul-winning. It should therefore not be encouraged. Involvement in society is, in any case, *optional.*

Position 3: Here also mission/evangelism is defined as soul-winning. However, in this view, service ministries (education, health care, social uplift) are important, since they may draw people to Christ. They may function as forerunners of, and aids to, mission. "Service is a means to an end. As long as service makes it possible to confront men with the gospel, it is useful."[2]

Position 4: Here mission/evangelism relates to other Christian activities in the way that seed relates to fruit. We first have to change individuals by means of the verbal proclamation of the gospel. Once they have accepted Christ as Savior, they will be transformed and become involved in society as a matter of course. In the words of Elton Trueblood, "The call to become fishers of men precedes the call to wash one another's feet."[3] Jesus did not come into the world to change the social order: that is part of the *result* of his coming. In similar fashion the church is not called to change the social order: redeemed individuals will do that.

Position 5: Mission and evangelism are indeed synonyms, but this task entails much more than just the proclamation of the gospel of eternal salvation. It involves the total Christian ministry to the world outside the church. This is, more or less, the traditional position in ecumenical circles. When the International Missionary Council merged with the World Council of Churches (WCC) at its New Delhi meeting in 1961, it became one of several divisions of the WCC and was renamed Commission on World Mission and

1. Quoted in G. M. Marsden, *Fundamentalism and American Culture: The Shaping of Twentieth-Century Evangelicalism, 1870-1925* (New York: Oxford University Press, 1980), p. 38.

2. Harold Lindsell, "A Rejoinder," *International Review of Mission* 54 (October 1965): 439.

3. Elton Trueblood, *The Validity of the Christian Mission* (New York: Harper and Row, 1972), p. 98.

Evangelism. Both words, "mission" and "evangelism," were thus included in the title, not because they meant different things but precisely because they were, by and large, understood to be synonyms. Another synonym was the word "witness," which is also often used in the New Delhi Report. Phillip Potter was correct when he wrote, in 1968, that "ecumenical literature since Amsterdam (1948) has used 'mission,' 'witness' and 'evangelism' interchangeably."[4] This task was classically formulated as the ministry of the "whole church taking the whole gospel to the whole world." This ministry would, in the classical ecumenical position, always include a call to conversion.

Position 6: This goes beyond the previous position in that it does not insist that mission/evangelism would under all circumstances include a call to repentance and faith in Christ. Gibson Winter, for instance, says, "Why are men not simply called to be human in their historical obligations, for this is man's true end and his salvation."[5] Here mission/evangelism is understood virtually exclusively in interhuman and this-worldly categories. In similar vein George V. Pixley defines the kingdom of God exclusively as a historical category. The Palestinian Jesus movement, which was, according to him, a wholly political movement, was completely misunderstood by Paul, John, and others, who spiritualized Jesus' political program.[6] In Pixley's thinking, then, salvation becomes entirely this-worldly, God's kingdom a political program, history one-dimensional, and mission/evangelism a project to change the structures of society.

Evangelism Distinguished from Mission

There are four ways in which evangelism and mission are distinguished from each other as referring to different realities:

1. The "objects" of mission and evangelism are different. In the view of Johannes Verkuyl, for instance, evangelism has to do with the communication of the Christian faith in Western society, while mission means communicating the gospel in the third world.[7] Evangelism has to do with those who are *no longer* Christians or who are nominal Christians. It refers to the calling

4. Phillip Potter, "Evangelism and the World Council of Churches," *Ecumenical Review* 20, no. 2 (1968): 176.

5. Quoted in Ron Sider, *Evangelism, Salvation, and Social Justice* (Bramcote: Grove Books, 1977), p. 6.

6. Cf. G. V. Pixley, *God's Kingdom* (Maryknoll, N.Y.: Orbis, 1981), pp. 88-100.

7. J. Verkuyl, *Contemporary Missiology* (Grand Rapids: Eerdmans, 1978), p. 9. See also his *Inleiding in die evangelistiek* (Kampen: Kok, 1978), pp. 11, 67-74.

back to Christ of those who have become estranged from the church. Mission, on the other hand, means calling to faith those who have always been strangers to the gospel. It refers to those who are *not yet* Christians.

This view is still generally held in continental European circles, in both Lutheran and Reformed churches. It is, in fact, also the traditional view in Roman Catholicism, even in Vatican II documents such as the Constitution on the Church *(Lumen Gentium)* and the Decree on Mission *(Ad Gentes).*

2. A second group of theologians, instead of distinguishing between evangelism and mission, have decided simply to drop the word "mission" from their vocabulary. The French Catholic theologian Claude Geffré prefers "evangelization" to "mission" because of the latter term's "territorial connotation . . . and its historical link with the process of colonization."[8] Other Roman Catholics appear to move in a similar direction. John Walsh, in his book *Evangelization and Justice,* calls everything the church is doing in the areas of "human development, liberation, justice and peace . . . *integral* parts of the ministry of evangelization."[9] In similar vein Segundo Galilea recently published a book in which the activities described in the Beatitudes of the Gospels of Luke and Matthew are designated "evangelism": *The Beatitudes: To Evangelize as Jesus Did.*[10] Once more a very comprehensive, almost all-embracing understanding of evangelism comes to the fore and the concept "mission" is dropped.

3. A third group of theologians offer a variation of the position just described. They hold onto both concepts, "mission" and "evangelism"; however, the way they do it is to regard "evangelism" as the wider term and "mission" as the narrower term. Evangelism is described as an umbrella concept "for the entire manner in which the gospel becomes a reality in man's life"; it includes proclamation, translation, dialogue, service, and presence. Mission, on the other hand, becomes a purely theological concept, "used for the origin, the motivation and the ratification" of the activities referred to above.[11]

4. The fourth way in which we could differentiate between mission and evangelism is, in effect, the obverse of the one just described. Here "mission" becomes the wider, more comprehensive concept and "evangelism" the narrower one. There are, however, different ways in which this can be under-

8. Claude Geffré, "Theological Reflections on a New Age in Mission," *International Review of Mission* 71 (October 1982): 479.

9. John Walsh, *Evangelization and Justice* (Maryknoll, N.Y.: Orbis, 1982), p. 92.

10. Segundo Galilea, *The Beatitudes: To Evangelize as Jesus Did* (Maryknoll, N.Y.: Orbis, 1984).

11. M. Geijbels, "Evangelization, Its Meaning and Practice," *Al-Mushir* 20, no. 2 (Summer 1978): 73-82.

stood: (a) John Stott, and to a lesser extent the Lausanne Covenant, defines mission as evangelism plus social action. These two parts or aspects of mission are both important; indeed, they are imperative. The Lausanne Covenant adds, however: "In the church's mission of sacrificial service *evangelism is primary*" (italics added). Stott defends this prioritization of evangelism over against social involvement, for "how can we seriously maintain that political and economic liberation is just as important as eternal salvation?"[12] When criticized by Ron Sider for holding this position, Stott says, "Well, if pressed, I would still stand by it on the grounds that, *if one has to choose,* eternal salvation is more important than temporal welfare. . . . But . . . one should not normally have to choose."[13] (b) A second variation in the approach that regards mission as consisting of evangelism and social involvement is to state that these two expressions of mission are indeed genuinely different aspects of mission, but since they are equally important we should never prioritize. We may also say that they are so intimately intertwined that it would be futile to try to unravel them. (c) Third, there are those who — while agreeing with Stott that mission is evangelism plus social action — would argue that in today's world there can be no doubt that social involvement should take precedence over evangelism.

Evangelism: Toward a Redefinition

Let me now attempt to respond to the bewildering variety of interpretations of evangelism. On the whole I would align myself with those who regard mission as the wider and evangelism as the narrower concept. I have problems, however, with those — and there are many — who, following John Stott, define mission as evangelism plus social involvement. Depicting evangelism and social action as two separate segments or components of mission is unsatisfactory, since it may — and often does — lead to a battle for supremacy. Stott himself maintains the primacy of evangelism, thereby willy-nilly relegating social involvement to a secondary position. To illustrate the problem, I refer to the Thailand Statement, produced by the Consultation on World Evangelization that was held in Pattaya, Thailand, in June 1980. The meeting was organized by the Lausanne Continuation Committee and there were fre-

12. John Stott, *Christian Mission in the Modern World* (London: Falcon Books, 1975), p. 35.

13. John Stott, in Sider, *Evangelism,* p. 21. See also the Grand Rapids Report (Lausanne Occasional Papers, no. 21), *Evangelism and Social Responsibility: An Evangelical Commitment* (Exeter: Paternoster, 1982), pp. 24-25.

quent references to the Lausanne Covenant of 1974. At one point the statement says that "nothing contained in the Lausanne Covenant is beyond our concern, *so long as it is clearly related to world evangelization*" (italics added). The problem with this statement lies in what it does not say. It does not also assert that "nothing contained in the Lausanne Covenant is beyond our concern, so *long as it is clearly related to social involvement*." In remaining silent on this aspect, the Thailand Statement is opting for a position of dualism. The moment you regard mission as consisting of two separate or separable components — evangelism and social action — you have, in principle, admitted that each of the two components has a life of its own. You are then suggesting that it is possible to have evangelism without a social dimension and Christian social action without an evangelistic dimension. Stott's "separate but equal" position is, in fact, dangerous. It is too easy, in this definition, for any one of the two components to make a unilateral declaration of independence, so to speak.

I therefore wish to introduce an important modification in Stott's definition. I accept — in broad outlines — his wider definition of mission as being the total task that God has set the church for the salvation of the world. In its missionary involvement, the church steps out of itself, into the wider world. It crosses all kinds of frontiers and barriers: geographical, social, political, ethnic, cultural, religious, ideological. Into all these areas the church-in-mission carries the message of God's salvation. Ultimately, then, mission means being involved in the redemption of the universe and the glorification of God.

If this is mission, what then is evangelism? Let us consider this under eight aspects.

1. Evangelism is the *core, heart,* or *center* of mission; it consists in the proclamation of salvation in Christ to nonbelievers, in announcing forgiveness of sins, in calling people to repentance and faith in Christ, in inviting them to become living members of Christ's earthly community and to begin a life in the power of the Holy Spirit. The apostolic exhortation *Evangelii Nuntiandi,* article 9, puts it in the following words: "As kernel and center of the Good News, Christ proclaims salvation, this great gift of God which is liberation from everything that oppresses people but which is, above all, liberation from sin and the Evil One, in the joy of knowing God and being known by him, of seeing him, and of being turned over to him." People are "being led into the mystery of God's love, who invites [them] to establish a personal relationship with him in Christ" (*Ad Gentes* 13).

This does not limit evangelism to soul-winning, as some argue. It is a biblically untenable position to take, as our ultimate concern in evangelism, the salvaging of a soul that must endure when all the world has perished. Lesslie Newbigin calls this a "Hindu solution," and adds; "In the sharpest possible contrast to this attempt, the Bible always sees the human person realistically as a living body-soul whose existence cannot be understood apart from the network of relationships that bind the person to family, tribe, nation, and all the progeny of Adam."[14]

A variant of the emphasis on soul-winning is the idea that evangelism is concerned primarily with the inward and spiritual side of people. As Harold Lindsell puts it: "The mission of the church is pre-eminently spiritual — that is, its major concerns revolve around the non-material aspects of life."[15] This is a gnostic interpretation of the Christian faith, however; it denies the corporateness of salvation as well as the incarnational character of the gospel.

If — in contrast to them — we describe evangelism in terms of calling people to faith in Christ, we refer to human beings of flesh and blood in *all* their relationships; we do not refer to evangelism as operative only in individual or spiritual categories. We do not believe, however, that the central dimension of evangelism as calling people to faith and a new life can ever be relinquished. I have called evangelism the "heart" of mission. If you cut the heart out of a body, that body becomes a corpse. With evangelism cut out, mission dies; it ceases to be mission.

2. Evangelism seeks to bring people into the visible community of believers (cf. *Ad Gentes* 13). In 1982 the Central Committee of the World Council of Churches published a very important document entitled *Mission and Evangelism — An Ecumenical Affirmation.* Paragraph 25 of this document states, inter alia: "It is at the heart of the Christian mission to foster the multiplication of local congregations in every human community. The planting of the seed of the gospel will bring forward a people gathered around the Word and sacrament. . . . This task of sowing the seed needs to be continued until there is, in every human community, a cell of the kingdom, a church confessing Jesus Christ." Even so, evangelism is not the same as recruitment of church members. As Paul Löffler puts it: "[Evangelism] is not a form of ecclesiastical propaganda. Its aim cannot be to enlarge the membership of a particular church or to promote a particular doctrine."[16]

There are two manifestations of the understanding of evangelism as church expansion. In the traditional Roman Catholic approach, evangelism is

14. Lesslie Newbigin, "Cross-Currents in Ecumenical and Evangelical Understandings of Mission," *International Bulletin of Missionary Research* 6, no. 4 (October 1982): 149.

15. Quoted in Waldron Scott, *Bring Forth Justice* (Grand Rapids: Eerdmans, 1980), p. 94.

16. Paul Löffler, "Evangelism," *One World* 29 (September 1977): 8.

defined as the road from the church to the church. Here the church is regarded as a divine institution franchised by God and stocked with a supply of heavenly graces, which the clergy can dispense to their customers. In Protestant circles, evangelism is frequently understood as "transferring" as many people as possible from the world into the church, for church and world are regarded as being in absolute antithesis to each other. Numerical church growth is frequently of the highest importance, and such growth is seen as the fruit of successful evangelism. Donald McGavran of the Church Growth movement, for instance, does not seem to experience much difficulty with the multiplication of denominations. In his major work we read, "Frequently a church splits and both sections grow,"[17] and he does not appear to be overly worried by this. Proselytizing evangelism also seems to be in order; McGavran euphemistically calls it "transfer growth" (as distinguished from "biological" and "conversion" growth).[18]

Such preoccupation with ecclesial ingathering may easily turn evangelism into a mechanism for institutional self-aggrandizement. In the face of this we have to emphasize that authentic evangelism may in fact cause people not to join the church, because of the cost involved.

3. Evangelism involves witnessing to what God has done, is doing, and will do. It therefore does not announce anything that we are bringing about but draws people's attention to what God has brought about and is still bringing about. Evangelism is not a call to put something into effect. It gives testimony to the fact that Christ has already conquered the powers of darkness (Col. 1:13) and has broken down the middle wall of partition (Eph. 2:14-17). The British Nationwide Initiative in Evangelism (in which "ecumenicals," "evangelicals," and Roman Catholics cooperated) put this in the following words: "Christians commend not themselves but the love of God as known in Jesus."[19]

This does not suggest that evangelism consists in verbal witness only. It consists in word *and* deed, proclamation *and* presence, explanation *and* example. The verbal witness indeed remains indispensable, not least because our deeds and our conduct are ambiguous; they need elucidation. The best we can hope for is that people will deduce from our behavior and our actions that we have "a hope within" us. Our lives are not sufficiently transparent for people to be able to ascertain whence our hope comes. So we must name the Name of

17. Donald A. McGavran, *Understanding Church Growth,* rev. ed. (Grand Rapids: Eerdmans, 1980), p. 3.

18. McGavran, *Understanding Church Growth,* p. 98.

19. *Evangelism: Convergence and Divergence* (London: Nationwide Initiative in Evangelism, 1980), p. 3.

him in whom we believe (1 Peter 3:15). But this does not mean that evangelism is only verbal. The biblical concept *euangelizesthai* refers to more than the English word "preach" does. Richard Cook has suggested that — at least in Paul's epistle to the Galatians — the Greek word *euangelizesthai* should not be rendered "preach the Gospel" but "embody the Gospel in their midst."[20]

4. Evangelism is invitation: it should never deteriorate into coaxing, much less into threat. Both these — coaxing and threat — are often used in so-called evangelistic campaigns. Sometimes evangelism is interpreted to mean inculcating guilt feelings in people. They have to be made to see how sinful they are so that they — in despair, as it were — will turn to Christ in order to be saved. They have to be shown that this is the only way out: like mice in a laboratory, the listeners are supposed to experience an electric shock each time they try a wrong solution, until they are persuaded to enter through the one and only safe door.

A variation of interpreting evangelism as the inculcating of guilt feelings is to scare people into repentance and conversion with stories about the horrors of hell. Lesslie Newbigin comments on this approach: ". . . to make the fear of hell the ultimate motivation for faith in Christ is to create a horrible caricature of evangelism. I still feel a sense of shame when I think of some of the 'evangelistic' addresses I have heard — direct appeals to the lowest of human emotions, selfishness and fear. One could only respect the tough-minded majority of the listeners who rejected the message."[21] Such an approach indeed degrades the gospel of free grace and divine love. People should turn to God because they are drawn to him by his love, not because they are pushed to him for fear of hell. Newbigin elaborates: "It is only in the light of the grace of God in Jesus Christ that we know the terrible abyss of darkness into which we must fall if we put our trust anywhere but in that grace." Furthermore, "[T]he grave and terrible warnings that the New Testament contains about the possibility of eternal loss are directed to those who are confident that they are among the saved. It is the branches of the vine, not the surrounding brambles, that are threatened with burning."[22]

5. Evangelism is possible only when the community that evangelizes — the church — is a radiant manifestation of the Christian faith and has a winsome lifestyle. Marshall McLuhan has taught us that the medium is the message. This is eminently true of the church-in-evangelism. If the church is to impart to the world a message of hope and love, of faith and justice, some-

20. Cf. Richard B. Cook, "Paul the Organizer," *Missiology* 10, no. 4 (October 1981): 491.

21. Newbigin, "Cross-Currents," p. 151.

22. Newbigin, "Cross-Currents," p. 151.

thing of this should become visible, audible, and tangible in the church itself. According to the book of Acts the early Christian community was characterized by compassion, fellowship, sharing, worship, service, and teaching (Acts 2:42-47; 4:32-35). Its conspicuously different lifestyle became in itself a witness to Christ. The Christians did not need to say, "Join us"; outsiders came to the church, drawn to it as if by a magnet. We, however, frequently have to push or pull people into the church. In the words of Michael Green: "Sometimes when a church has tried everything else — in vain — it comes reluctantly round to the idea that if it is to stay in business it had better resign itself to an evangelistic campaign."[23] Usually, however, this achieves precious little, because of the image that our churches have and because of their lack of relevance. They tend to be clubs for religious folklore. So what the churches often do get involved in is not evangelism, but propaganda; that is, they reproduce carbon copies of themselves and impart their own ghetto mentality to the people they "reach." In their evangelistic outreach, they often resemble a lunatic farmer who carries his harvest into his burning barn.

The German missiologist Hans-Werner Gensichen mentions five characteristics of a church involved in evangelism: (a) it lets outsiders feel at home; (b) it is not merely an object of pastoral care with the pastor having the monopoly: (c) its members are involved in society; (d) it is structurally flexible and adaptable; (e) it does not defend the interests of any select group of people.[24]

6. To evangelize is to take risks in at least two respects. In the first place, the evangelist or the church-in-evangelism has no control over how the gospel it proclaims will "come alive" in the hearers' context. The gospel may, and probably will, surprise and even upset them. There is no way, however, of avoiding this risk. Lesslie Newbigin puts it as follows: "The way in which the gospel will 'come alive' to every human person will be known in that person's experience and can not be determined *a priori*. The attempt so to determine it always ends in the legalistic distortion of the gospel — that is to say the distortion by which a free personal response to grace is replaced by a predetermined pattern of behaviour."[25]

Second, the evangelist is running a risk of getting changed in the course of the evangelistic outreach. Take the well-known story narrated in Acts 10 as

23. Michael Green, *Evangelism — Now and Then* (Downers Grove, Ill.: InterVarsity, 1982), p. 15.

24. H.-W. Genischen, *Glaube für die Welt* (Gütersloh: Gerd Mohn, 1971), pp. 170-72.

25. Lesslie Newbigin, "The Call to Mission — A Call to Unity?" in Peter Beyerhaus, ed., *The Church Crossing Frontiers: Essays on the Nature of Mission in Honour of Bengt Sundkler* (Lund: Gleerup, 1969), p. 260.

an example. We know it as the story of the conversion of Cornelius. It could, with equal justification, bear the title "The Conversion of Peter" or "The Conversion of an Evangelist." The person facing the toughest decisions here is not the pagan Cornelius but the Rev. Simon Peter. Walter Hollenweger comments correctly: "The real evangelist cannot help but take the risk that in the course of his evangelism his understanding of Christ will get corrected."[26] For this is precisely what happened to Peter. In Cornelius's house he did not just receive some additional theological insights. No, he began to understand Christ in a new way.

Usually, when the church sends out missionaries and evangelists, it is in the firm conviction that we, the believers, are in possession of the whole truth, whereas those to whom we go, the so-called pagans, sit in darkness and are doomed. Not for a moment does the church-in-evangelism and its evangelists expect that they themselves will change; all necessary change has to take place at the "receivers'" end. After all, we go out to help others get converted, not to be converted ourselves!

If, however, we are involved in authentic evangelism, things are indeed different. Look at Paul, for instance. José Comblin describes what happened to Paul. "When the Spirit sent Paul to the Greeks, it was not just to evangelize them; it was also to make it possible for Paul himself to see the real heart of his message. . . . The Spirit reveals to the Church through the mediation of new Christians . . . that many old things are not necessary, that they actually obscure the truth of Jesus Christ."[27]

7. Those who respond positively to evangelism receive salvation as a present gift and with it assurance of eternal blessedness. It is, however, not the primary purpose of evangelism to impart to people such guaranteed happiness, neither for this world nor the next. Some evangelists preach: "Are you lonely? Are you unhappy? Do you want peace of mind and personal fulfillment? Then come to Jesus!" Others say, as Francis Grim states in his book, *Die hemel en die hel:* the most important question facing every one of us is, "Where will I spend eternity?"[28]

Christ gives people joy, hope, trust, vision, relief, and courage in this life, as well as a blessed assurance for all eternity. But if the offer of all this gets center-stage attention in our evangelism, if evangelism becomes the offer of a psychological panacea, then the gospel is degraded to a consumer product and becomes the opiate of the people. Then evangelism fosters a self-centered

26. Walter Hollenweger, *The Meaning of Mission* (Belfast: Christian Journals, 1976), p. 17.
27. José Comblin, *The Meaning of Mission* (Maryknoll, N.Y.: Orbis, 1977), p. 107.
28. Reference in *Die Voorligter,* December 1985, p. 7.

and self-serving mindset among people and a narcissistic pursuit of fulfilled personhood. Then evangelism has become a television commercial where the call to conversion is presented in a Things-go-better-with-Jesus wrapping.

Karl Barth, in a penetrating excursus in his *Church Dogmatics* (IV/13), addressed himself to this issue.[29] Christian teaching, he says, has tended to regard Christians as enjoying an indescribably magnificent private good fortune. People's chief concern is then with their personal experiences of grace and salvation. Barth regards all this as thoroughly unbiblical and egocentric. The personal enjoyment of salvation, he argues, nowhere becomes the central theme of biblical conversion stories. Not that the enjoyment of salvation is wrong, unimportant, and unbiblical, but it is almost incidental and secondary. What makes a person a Christian is not primarily his or her personal experience of grace and redemption, but his or her ministry.

These comments of Barth have tremendous consequences for our understanding of evangelism. Evangelism that stops at calling people to accept Christ is incomplete and truncated. The church exists for the world, not the world for the church, as a reservoir from which the church draws. It is not simply to receive life that people are called to become Christians, but rather to *give* life.

8. Evangelism thus does not simply offer individuals personal bliss. Evangelism is calling people to become followers of Jesus. It is enlisting people for missions — a mission as comprehensive as that of Jesus. This hardly happens in most present-day evangelistic outreach. Often evangelists preach an entirely uncontextualized and disembodied gospel. They frequently employ all kinds of psychological and rhetorical devices to persuade people to accept their specific message. People are then indeed challenged to repent and come to faith, but often the challenge is issued in respect of those areas of life where conversion will not be too costly. That evangelism will take on these features is, in a sense, a foregone conclusion, in view of the fact that the churches into which new members are invited are usually compromised in the surrounding culture, particularly in societies where the pastor is considered to be in the employ of the congregation and thus dependent on the parishioners' goodwill and support.

This kind of evangelism calls upon people to adopt a lifestyle that is defined almost exclusively in micro-ethical and religio-cultic categories. A case in point is Bishop J. Waskom Pickett's classic, *Christian Mass Movements in India*. Pickett measures successful evangelism in terms of "attainments" in eleven areas: (1) knowledge of the Lord's Prayer, the Apostles' Creed, and the

29. Karl Barth, *Church Dogmatics* IV/3 (Edinburgh: T & T Clark, 1962), pp. 561-614.

Ten Commandments; (2) Sunday observance; (3) full membership in the church; (4) church attendance; (5) frequency of church services; (6) support of the church; (7) freedom from idolatry, charms, and sorcery; (8) abstention from participation in non-Christian festivals; (9) freedom from fear of evil spirits; (10) Christian marriage; (11) abstention from intoxicating beverages.[30] Where these characteristics manifest themselves in people, so the argument goes, evangelism has been successful. In similar vein Peter Wagner suggests that evangelism means calling people to "a code of life which includes positive behavior traits such as a daily Bible reading and prayer, grace before meals, and regular church attendance, as well as certain negative traits such as total abstinence from or extremely moderate use of tobacco, alcoholic beverages, and profanity in speech."[31] Note, however, that in this definition, as well as in Pickett's list of "attainments," all the positive elements have to do with narrowly defined religious and micro-ethical activities, and all the negative ones (those from which Christians should abstain) with the world. There is no reference whatsoever to any positive attitude to, or involvement in, the world. There is no indication that people's personal and spiritual liberation should have implications on the social and political front. There is a sharp break here; the liberation process is truncated.

To all this we must say that, whenever the church's involvement in society becomes secondary and optional, whenever the church invites people to take refuge in the name of Jesus without challenging the dominion of evil, it becomes a countersign of the kingdom. It is then not involved in evangelism but in counter-evangelism. When compassionate action is in principle subordinated to the preaching of a message of individual salvation, the church is offering cheap grace to people and in the process denaturing the gospel. The content of our gospel then is in the devastating formulation of Orlando Costas — "a conscience soothing Jesus, with an unscandalous cross, an otherworldly kingdom, a private, inwardly spirit, a pocket God, a spiritualized Bible, and an escapist church."[32] If the gospel is indeed the gospel of the kingdom, and if the kingdom is "the detailed expression of [God's] caring control of the whole of life," then we are concerned in our evangelism with a God whose "nature as king [is] to . . . uphold *justice and equity,* to *watch over the circumstances of strangers, widows and orphans,* and to liberate the poor and the prisoners."[33]

30. J. Waskom Pickett, quoted in McGavran, *Understanding Church Growth,* p. 174.

31. C. Peter Wagner, *Our Kind of People: The Ethical Dimensions of Church Growth* (Atlanta: John Knox, 1979), p. 3.

32. Orlando Costas, *Christ Outside the Gate* (Maryknoll, N.Y.: Orbis, 1982), p. 80.

33. Andrew Kirk, "The Kingdom, the Church, and a Distressed World," *Churchman* 94, no. 2 (1980): 139 (the italics are Kirk's).

In Conclusion

In summary, then, evangelism may be defined as that dimension and activity of the church's mission which seeks to offer every person, everywhere, a valid opportunity to be directly challenged by the gospel of explicit faith in Jesus Christ,[34] with a view to embracing him as Savior, becoming a living member of his community, and being enlisted in his service of reconciliation, peace, and justice on earth.

34. Cf. Thomas F. Stransky, "Evangelization, Missions, and Social Action: A Roman Catholic Perspective," *Review and Expositor* 78, no. 2 (Spring 1982): 343-50.

CHAPTER 2

A Theology of Evangelism: The Heart of the Matter

William J. Abraham

The central task of a theology of evangelism is to provide a clear and credible account of the ministry of evangelism that will foster and illuminate responsible evangelistic practices by the Christian church and its agents in the modern world. To date, very limited attention has been given to this crucial subject. The chief reason for this is that evangelism falls between a rock and a hard place. The rock is the extraordinary silence on the part of systematic theologians on the subject of evangelism. The hard place is the inability of practical theology to reach any sustained measure of internal self-criticism.

Evangelism as a topic of inquiry falls within both systematic and practical theology. Within systematic theology, it falls within the domain of ecclesiology; it is central to any comprehensive analysis of the mission and task of the church. Within practical theology, it has a space all to itself, although practical theology is in such conceptual disarray that this does not count for much.[1] Given the ambivalent status of evangelism as a subject of theological inquiry, evangelism as a ministry of the church can become everything and anything. The challenge is to mesh these two concerns into one coherent enterprise. The task is this: We need to spell out an account of evangelism that will be both serviceable in the actual practice of ministry and viable in its own right theologically. Beyond that, such an account must be suitably informed by historical considerations and true to the richness of the Christian gospel. We need an analysis of evangelism that will be at once historically grounded, theologically credible, and practically apt.

Despite the conceptual confusion and fog in the field, the last twenty

1. For an account of the place of evangelism in theology as a whole, see my "Athens, Aldersgate, and SMU: The Place of Evangelism in the Theological Encyclopedia," *Journal for the Academy of Evangelism in Theological Education* 40 (1990): 64-75.

years or so have seen an astonishing birthing of interests in evangelism. As part of this development, most mainline churches have become greatly enamored of church growth, owing in part to the fact that this permits its leaders to set aside the hard theological questions that have to be faced. In evangelical circles, Christians in this tradition have, for almost a century, seen themselves as the sole owners of evangelism, so much so that many find it difficult to distinguish between evangelism and evangelicalism.[2] For the most part, evangelicals have construed evangelism as essentially the proclamation of the gospel to unbelievers. In fact, church growth and proclamation constitute the two major visions of evangelism currently available to us. Converting people to God, making disciples, and saving souls make up the relevant minority reports. In what follows, I shall argue that we need to construe evangelism as a polymorphous ministry aimed at initiating people into the kingdom of God.

I.

Evangelism is a peculiarly Christian concept. It does not arise naturally in non-Christian contexts, although it can, of course, be stretched for usage in other religious traditions. Even in the Christian tradition it has had a very unstable usage down through the ages.[3] The seeds for evangelistic activity are very clearly rooted in the earlier Jewish tradition. Yet the early Christians had no developed theory of evangelism. Moreover, there was something of a division of the house when it came to evangelistic practice. Evangelism clearly took place within the Jewish circles that originally gave birth to Christianity, but the shift to Gentiles was accompanied by deep reluctance and enormous tension. The picture of the early Christians marching out to evangelize the Roman Empire in order to fulfill the Great Commission is a myth. It took determined leadership by figures like Stephen and Paul to carry the day on the issue. The apostle Peter, if Luke is right, needed nothing

2. Thus, the distinguished French historian Henri Daniel-Rops, speaking of evangelicals in the Church of England, writes: "The movement was called Evangelism, and it subsequently exercised a very real influence." See his *The Church in the Eighteenth Century,* trans. John Warrington (New York: Doubleday, 1960), p. 226.

3. For an older but still useful overview of the history of evangelism, see K. S. Latourette, "Pre-Nineteenth Century Evangelism: Its Outstanding Characteristics" and "Distinctive Features of the Protestant Missionary Methods of the Nineteenth and Twentieth Centuries," in *Evangelism,* ed. International Missionary Council (London: Oxford University Press, 1939), pp. 1-31.

less than a special divine revelation to convert him to evangelistic work among the Gentiles.[4] This whole story has yet to be adequately unraveled historically.

The language used to talk about evangelism is of limited value. Clearly the central verb used to cover the activity of evangelism, *euangelizomai,* is best translated by our verb "proclaim."[5] Hence, "to evangelize" basically meant the proclaiming of the good news of the gospel. Much has been made of this in the last century or so. Christians from very diverse backgrounds have argued that this provides sufficient warrant for construing evangelism today as proclamation.[6] This only succeeds, however, if the exclusive warrant for envisioning evangelism rests on biblical word-studies, and if the only relevant terms for evangelism focus on proclamation.

Neither of these assumptions can be sustained. The first does not hold because it is not at all clear that it is appropriate to derive a vision of evangelism merely from verbal considerations related to the etymology of "evangelism." One suspects that even the early Christians would have been wary of this, for they were not intentionally developing a theory of evangelism in their writings. The second assumption does not hold because not only do we have references to evangelistic activity, but we also learn of workers in evangelism, namely, "evangelists." The best way to construe these workers is to see them as second-generation apostles.[7] They represent those persons who did work similar to that of the apostles, that is, proclaimed the gospel and established converts in the faith in Christian communities, but they were naturally distinguished from the apostles in that they did not have that unique relationship to the risen Lord that was central to the work of the twelve and Paul. If we focus on this evidence, then it would be very misleading to restrict the work of evangelism in the early church to the activity of proclamation.

This is confirmed by the later history of evangelism, even though that history is far from uniform. It is clear that in the patristic period evangelism included the formation of Christians; it was not confined merely to proclamation. This is borne out by the actual work of evangelists when they traveled

4. Acts 10.

5. David Barrett provides an exhaustive account of the history of the concept in his *Evangelize! A Historical Survey of the Concept* (Birmingham, Ala.: New Hope, 1987). He begins by trying to restrict evangelism to proclamation, but in the end fails to sustain this analysis.

6. Especially noteworthy is David Lowes Watson, "The Church as Journalist: Evangelism in the Context of the Local Church in the United States," *International Review of Mission* 72 (1983): 56-74.

7. See Alastair Campbell, "Do the Work of an Evangelist," *Evangelical Quarterly* 64 (1992): 117-29.

into new territory.[8] It is also confirmed by the extensive use of individual and corporate spiritual direction focused on the incorporation of converts into the church and into the life of faith. Especially interesting, with respect to corporate spiritual direction, is the development of the catechumenate. Considerable care was taken to ensure that seekers really knew the gospel for themselves and to see that they were well grounded in the basic content and practices of the faith. This was a slow process, but it was absolutely essential if commitment was to be substantial and long-lasting. Not surprisingly, when Christianity became the official religion of the Roman Empire, this delicate component in the work of evangelism became eroded. It was well-nigh impossible for the church to cope with the hordes of uninstructed pagans who were shepherded en masse into the faith.

Even then, one can still see vestiges of this dimension of evangelism in the medieval period in the work to convert the heathen tribes of northern Europe. It would have been totally impractical and spiritually dangerous to restrict the work of evangelism to proclamation. It was absolutely essential that converts be baptized and minimally established in the faith. Exactly the same is true for the great burst of missionary activity that arose in the nineteenth century. With all its faults, this activity constitutes a brilliant episode in the history of evangelism; it bears ample testimony to the need to see evangelism as including the early phases of Christian initiation.

The missing link between the medieval and modern period is, of course, the Reformation and its aftermath. The Reformers had next to no interest in evangelism. Either they believed that this work was purely the responsibility of the first apostles, or they held that it had already been accomplished. Either way, the center of attention lay in reforming the church from its varied corruptions. In the Western church, it was the Roman Catholics and Pietists who first came to see that confining the work of evangelism to antiquity was both unbiblical and unrealistic. The debt we owe to the Pietists in recovering the ministry of evangelism in the modern period is incalculable. A crucial conduit for their approach to evangelism is visible in the life and work of John Wesley, one of the greatest evangelists in the history of the church. The Moravians helped Wesley to find a deep assurance of his own salvation and then provided him with both the stimulus and the initial model to work out the kind of evangelistic ministry that would be effective in his day and generation. What is especially significant is the creativity displayed by Wesley and his co-workers. He reluctantly launched forth into field preaching and carefully experimented with various sorts of small groups until he found a

8. Eusebius is an important witness to this. See *Ecclesiastical History* 5.10.2.

way to form the kind of Christian disciples who would act as salt and light in the world. All this was done, on the one hand, out of a deep theological appropriation of biblical and patristic sources and, on the other hand, out of a deep humility that forced him to depend constantly on the daily inspiration and guidance of the Holy Spirit.

Wesley's legacy in evangelism was ambivalent in the extreme. His anthropocentric focus and his tendency to depend rather naïvely on the narrow epistemologies of the Enlightenment left many of his later followers and admirers unprotected from the acids of modernity. One wing reduced his rich contribution to a focus on social action that is currently embodied in various schemes for social liberation. Influenced by Marxist suspicions of piety, there is virtually no interest in evangelism in this domain.[9] The more conservative wing of Wesley's followers developed his legacy into various schemes for revival. Initially, these kept intact the Wesleyan impulse for reform of the nation, but this did not last; in time, it gave birth to the tumultuous Pentecostal and Charismatic movements, which are only now receiving the historical and theological attention they deserve. The net result has been that evangelism has lost its moorings. It has been disconnected both intellectually and institutionally from the life of the church with disastrous results all around. Evangelism has been reduced to forms of social action among liberals and to manipulative schemes of conversion among conservatives. To be sure, this is exaggerated and oversimplified, but the work of binding up the wounds of our fathers and mothers in evangelism has scarcely begun.

The last decade or so has seen the beginnings of a truly substantive conversation. The origins of this are manifold. The collapse of Christendom in Europe, the intellectual and social failure of Communism, the internal disintegration of the Enlightenment obsession with science and epistemology, the burgeoning experiments in ecclesial renewal represented by the Charismatic movement, the surprising emergence of post-Christian forms of religion from within Christianity — all these and more have created space for a serious debate about evangelism. As yet, the points of convergence are few and far between. It is clear, for example, that evangelism must attend to the arrival

9. James Cone's comment is especially interesting: "Black theology must counsel blacks to beware of the Wesley brothers and their concern for personal salvation, the 'warm heart' and all the rest. What blacks do not need are warm hearts. Our attention must be elsewhere — political, social, and economic freedom!" See *A Black Theology of Liberation* (Maryknoll, N.Y.: Orbis, 1991), p. 206. For an exception to this general observation, see John W. De Gruchy, "No Other Gospel: Is Liberation Theology a Reduction of the Gospel?" in *Incarnational Ministry: The Presence of Christ in Church, Family, and Society*, ed. Christian D. Kettler and Todd H. Speidel (Colorado Springs: Helmers and Howard, 1990), pp. 176-90.

of the kingdom of God as absolutely constitutive of the gospel. It is also clear that evangelism is constitutive of apostolic identity. Any church that fails to reckon with this has missed a crucial component of apostolic Christianity, whatever else it may claim about its apostolic pedigree. Beyond this, it is obvious that serious renewal in evangelism will entail extensive conversation on deeply contested theological and practical issues. It will also entail a fresh encounter with the gospel embodied in the rich canonical traditions of the church.

II.

Any such encounter is likely to yield the following platitude: Whatever the gospel is, it centers on the inauguration of the kingdom of God in Jesus Christ, crucified and risen from the dead. Hence, the gospel is not first and foremost about a network of moral injunctions, nor about this or that kind of religious experience, nor about the arrival of the church, nor about some scheme of political liberation, nor about some magic formula to gain health and wealth, nor about a quick and easy way to find celestial fire-insurance. It is constituted by those extraordinary events in and through Jesus of Nazareth, through which God acted in history by his Holy Spirit to establish his rule in the world.

We owe this rediscovery to a revolutionary shift in New Testament studies brought about by Johannes Weiss and Albert Schweitzer. Not surprisingly, it has taken time to assimilate what the arrival of the kingdom means. Materially, Weiss and Schweitzer have not been the best of guides in this complex territory. We have stumbled through the various texts on the kingdom, lurching now to purely futuristic conceptions of the kingdom that have failed to materialize, and then to purely realized visions of the kingdom that dissolve any future dimension into a timeless, Platonic eternity. In the end, we cannot avoid a contested historical and theological judgment. The claim of the church is that God has come to us uniquely to establish his rule in and through Jesus Christ; what began there by the work of the Holy Spirit continues in the world today through the work of that same Spirit; in God's own time, that work will be brought to a fitting consummation. This is the heart of the gospel.[10]

To construe the gospel in this fashion in the contemporary situation is

10. I have argued for this account of the gospel in *The Logic of Evangelism* (Grand Rapids: Eerdmans, 1989), chap. 2.

to invite immediate challenge about its viability in the modern world. This is entirely natural, for Christians are deeply divided on both the content of the faith and on the norms to which we should appeal to settle disputes about its credibility. Christians, in other words, are in conflict about the status of their primary narrative.

On one end of the spectrum are those who encounter this classical rendering of the gospel narrative as strictly incomprehensible to the modern unbeliever. Contemporary proclamation of this narrative, therefore, requires its translation into the idiom of a favored philosophical tradition, such as existentialism or process metaphysics. This became something of a theological orthodoxy in the postwar generation.[11] Failure to reach agreement on the chosen philosophical idiom has undermined much of the enthusiasm for this option. It is also clear that this option owes much to a ready acceptance of crucial epistemological constraints imposed by the leading philosophers of the Enlightenment.

This option has also been rapidly supplanted among the cultural elites of the Christian tradition by a very different way of construing the incomprehensibility of the narrative. I refer, of course, to the tendency to interpret the account of the gospel outlined above as the product of patriarchal and hierarchical social forces that mask the intention to enslave and oppress. In this hermeneutical trajectory, the general strategy is to derive certain minimal moral concerns from the gospel stories and then construct from these concerns a new narrative of political liberation.[12] It is clear that this option owes much to the political aspirations of the Enlightenment in both its liberal and socialist forms.

Others see in both these options an inevitable reduction of the gospel to suit the intellectual requirements and unredeemed prejudices of the outsider. In fact, neither of these options can allow the gospel to be heard in all its radical particularity, beauty, and challenge. Both are tone-deaf to its richness. In both, the gospel is suffocated by attractive intellectual and political visions

11. I am confining my observations to the scene in North America. English theologians, given a characteristically more practical turn of mind, seem more content to settle for some kind of moralistic theism. For a recent example, see David Jenkins, "Evangelization and Culture," *Theology* 94 (1991): 5-10.

12. Influential examples of this can be found in Rosemary Radford Ruether, *Sexism and God-Talk: Toward a Feminist Theology* (Boston: Beacon Press, 1983) and Cone, *A Black Theology*. For an especially insightful evaluation of these kinds of proposals, see Ellen Charry, "Literature as Scripture: Privileged Reading in Current Religious Reflection," *Soundings* 54 (1991): 65-69. For my own analysis of the issues, see "The State of Christian Theology in North America," in *The Great Ideas Today* (Chicago: Encyclopaedia Britannica, 1991), pp. 242-86.

which are held as beyond intellectual challenge. These visions are threatened at their foundations by the gospel, that is, by eschatological events and actions that cannot be accommodated within the webs of conceivability and credibility out of which they are woven. Few theologians have seen this more clearly than the early Karl Barth, although figures as far apart as Søren Kierkegaard and John Henry Newman in the nineteenth century expressed this same insight with astute brilliance. In turn, the latter are the inspiration for two very different ways of resolving the difficulty before us. Both accept that the gospel narrative will appear on the surface to be incomprehensible or incredible to many moderns. The divergence arises from the different strategies deployed to deal with this.

One strategy is simply to accept that the gospel is absurd, given the standard canons of Enlightenment epistemologies. The gospel, however, has its own sources and norm. It is derived and founded on divine revelation. On this analysis the evangelist is called to present faithfully the good news of the kingdom, leaving it to God to supply such additional witness as is needed to bring conviction and conversion. Epistemological theories and systems are simply set aside as secondary or irrelevant.

Not surprisingly, it has been difficult to hold this line indefinitely. Thus, Barth's disciples have been driven in one way or another to provide some kind of backing for this posture at the level of critical reflection and epistemology. Others in the neighborhood of this tradition have taken the more radical course of developing a whole system of Reformed epistemology in order to undercut the Enlightenment critique of the gospel. Currently, philosophers such as Alvin Plantinga and Nicholas Wolterstorff are developing a brilliant network of epistemic proposals that at once make sense of the faith of the ordinary believer and equally provide a deep defense of the content of the classical Christian tradition.[13] The evangelist, on this analysis, is set free to preach and teach the gospel without first having to provide foundations constructed by this or that philosophy.

The other strategy currently being explored goes in a different direction. It begins, like the first strategy, by acknowledging that the gospel cannot be defended on the kind of ground staked out by the Enlightenment. The gospel narrative is, indeed, absurd when judged by the canons of rationalism and empiricism; Hume is essentially right about this. However, the problem lies

13. For a useful overview, see Kelly James Clark, *Return to Reason* (Grand Rapids: Eerdmans, 1990). The first two volumes of a three-volume work in this domain by Alvin Plantinga are available in *Warrant: The Current Debate* (New York: Oxford University Press, 1993), and *Warrant and Proper Function* (New York: Oxford University Press, 1993).

not in the gospel but in the narrow conception of reason and experience embodied in the norms of its critics, like Hume and his followers. Once these have been replaced by more appropriate canons of evaluation, then the Christian theologian is liberated both to teach the full wealth of Christian conviction and to offer a positive account of its epistemic status. Basil Mitchell, Richard Swinburne, Diogenes Allen, and William Alston have developed various proposals along this line.[14] In this case, the work of the evangelist is aided and abetted by sophisticated work in positive apologetics.

The crucial divide for evangelism lies not between those who favor a fideist, or a reliabilist, or an evidentialist, or a Reformed approach to the justification of religious belief. The deep issue is whether the Christian church does or does not have genuine and substantial good news of salvation for the world that can stand in deep continuity with its canonical traditions. Paul's warnings to the Galatians about the substituting of another gospel from that handed over in the tradition are especially pertinent at this juncture.[15] Modern revisionist and radical forms of the Christian tradition since Schleiermacher have generally failed on this count. Moreover, evangelism in any shape or form has rarely survived, let alone flourished, on this kind of soil for long.

The crucial schism in the church from this perspective stems, then, not from the break between East and West, nor in the break within the West between Roman Catholic and Protestant, but in the break at the Enlightenment represented by Schleiermacher. It is this third schism that is decisive.[16] In fact, the future of evangelism in the West may well depend on whether the deep wounds sustained from within that strike at the very core of the gospel narrative itself can ever by healed. In my judgment, the future lies in the hands of those who can reach across the divisions of the last millennium and retrieve with integrity the extraordinary narrative bequeathed in the canonical traditions of the early ecumenical traditions. Even though this is not the general consensus that one encounters in much academic theology nor the line one hears from the more visible leadership of the mainline churches, the pros-

14. See Basil Mitchell, *The Justification of Religious Belief* (Oxford: Oxford University Press, 1973); Richard Swinburne, *The Existence of God* (Oxford: Clarendon Press, 1979); Diogenes Allen, *Christian Belief in a Postmodern World* (Louisville: Westminster/John Knox, 1989); and William Alston, *Perceiving God* (Ithaca, N.Y.: Cornell University Press, 1992). This material is the tip of a deep iceberg that is only now beginning to have an impact on systematic theology. Also worth noting is Caroline Frank Davis, *The Evidential Value of Religious Experience* (Oxford: Clarendon Press, 1989).

15. Gal. 1:6-9.

16. I owe this way of expressing the matter to Dr. Andrew Walker in private conversation.

pects for this happening now are much greater than they were a generation ago. This is, in part, made possible by the fact that a deep defense for the gospel narrative can now be mounted at an intellectual and philosophical level that would have been unthinkable thirty years ago. The gospel narrative is a credible narrative.[17]

III.

Staking out the essentials of the gospel narrative, however, is a necessary but not sufficient condition for arriving at a viable conception of evangelism. We now need to think through the connection between evangelism and the evangel. How are the two to be linked? If the gospel centers on the arrival of the kingdom of God in Jesus Christ, how are we to construe the relation between evangelism and the kingdom of God? This is a pivotal matter.

The favored position for some time has been to insist that the natural connection is through some kind of speech act. Thus, evangelism has again and again been construed as the proclamation of the gospel. In some cases, this has been extended to include teaching the gospel or persuading someone to believe the gospel. In other cases, it has been expanded to the proclamation of the gospel in word and deed.[18] In this instance, it becomes natural for the actions of the church, say, in education, medical work, and social action, to be construed as evangelism every bit as much as does the verbal proclamation of the gospel. Moreover, it is surely this conception of evangelism that lies behind the enormous efforts currently being made to evangelize the world through radio and television. The warrant for the widely held conviction that the world can be evangelized through television is the claim that communication is of the essence of evangelism. Evangelism is just the verbal proclamation of the gospel; hence, in our situation the obvious tool for this is television.[19]

17. For my own contribution to this debate, see *An Introduction to the Philosophy of Religion* (Englewood Cliffs, N.J.: Prentice-Hall, 1985) and "Cumulative Case Arguments for Christian Theism," in *The Rationality of Religious Belief*, ed. William J. Abraham and Steven W. Holtzer (Oxford: Clarendon Press, 1987), pp. 17-38.

18. For example, the influential missiologist David J. Bosch writes, "It [evangelism] consists in word *and* deed, proclamation *and* presence, explanation *and* example." See his "Evangelism: Theological Currents and Cross-Currents," *International Bulletin of Missionary Research* (1987): 101 (emphasis is original). [Editors' note: Bosch's essay is also included in this volume; see p. 11 above.]

19. For a splendid analysis of so-called television evangelism, see Steve Bruce, *Pray TV: Televangelism in America* (New York: Routledge, 1990).

We have already seen that the attempt to base this on purely etymological considerations is precarious in the extreme. However, even if the argument about the origins of the term "evangelism" were to hold, that is, even if "evangelize" originally meant simply to "proclaim," this would not settle the matter. We also have to ask if this is the best way to construe evangelism in our situation today. We must explore how far it is appropriate to consider evangelism in these terms in our context. In my judgment, it is imperative that we enrich our conception of evangelism to the point where we move beyond mere proclamation to include within it the initial grounding of all believers in the kingdom of God. If we make this shift, then we actually come much closer to what evangelists, ancient and modern, have actually done; but, even at this, the argument is not advanced on purely historical grounds. The primary considerations revolve around the needs of our current situation in our modern Western culture. Here I shall be brief and make three points, one negative and two positive.

First, continuing to think of evangelism in terms of mere proclamation fosters the practice of disconnecting evangelism from the life of the local church. It nurtures the illusion that evangelism can be done by the religious entrepreneur who can simply take to the road and engage in this crucial ministry without accountability to the body of Christ. To be sure, there are lots of local churches who welcome this kind of evangelism. It allows them to ignore evangelism entirely as a constitutive element in the mission of the church, for it can hand this responsibility to the itinerating evangelist or it can keep evangelism to those seasons of the year in which it focuses on the proclamation of the gospel. However, this is not the acute problem here. The problem is that this way of construing evangelism has generally been used to cut evangelism loose from the life of the Christian community precisely because the responsibility of the evangelist has stopped once the proclamation has ceased. On this analysis, the evangelist need not belong to a church; indeed, if he does not like the church in which he was brought to faith, he can invent his own on the spot. Nor does the evangelist need to be accountable to the canonical traditions of the church; indeed, if she does not like the canonical narrative of the gospel, then she can invent her own narrative at will. Nor does the evangelist need to take any responsibility for the spiritual welfare of the seeker or convert; this can be conveniently left to others, in the field of Christian education, for example. In all, restricting evangelism to proclamation helps keep intact unhealthy evangelistic practices that should long ago have been abandoned. In a culture mesmerized by the power of the mass media, the church must recognize both the radical limits and the dangers of proclamation in our current situation.

Secondly, restricting evangelism in this manner cannot do the job that needs to be done in an increasingly pluralist and post-Christian culture. Evangelism needs to be expanded to include the early phases of Christian initiation. The gospel must to be handed over in such a way that those who receive it may be able to own it for themselves in a substantial way and have some sense of what they are embracing. Proclamation is but one part of the process that will make this possible. It will also require teaching and persuasion, spiritual direction, an introduction to the spiritual disciplines and the sacraments of the gospel, initiation into the basics of the Christian moral and doctrinal tradition, and some orientation on the kinds of religious experiences that may accompany entry into the kingdom of God. Without these, the new believer will not be able to survive spiritually, morally, or intellectually in the modern world. In short, an evangelistic church will take responsibility for the initial formation of Christian disciples as an integral component of its evangelism.

Thirdly, the wisdom of this strategy is borne out by a very significant, recent study of spiritual development in England. In that study careful attention was given to about five hundred people who had come to faith in recent years. The most pertinent piece of information to the issue at hand is that the majority of people studied came to faith over a relatively lengthy period of time.

> The gradual process is the way in which the majority of people discover God and the average time taken is about four years: models of evangelism which can help people along the pathway are needed. . . .
>
> Most "up-front" methods of evangelizing assume that the person will make a sudden decision to follow Christ. They may be asked to indicate this by raising a hand, making their confession, taking a booklet or whatever is the preferred method of the evangelist. The fact is that most people come to God much more gradually. Methods of evangelism which fit this pattern are urgently needed. The nurture group and the catechumenate are the best known at present, but others may need to be devised. The use of one-to-one conversations akin to some form of spiritual direction may be one possibility. Another may be a series of church services where people are introduced to the Christian faith over a period of time and given opportunity to respond at each stage. Even more urgently needed are means of helping non-churchgoers to discover God outside the church building in ways which enable a gradual response.[20]

20. John Finney, *Finding Faith Today: How Does it Happen?* (Swindon: British and Foreign Bible Society, 1992), p. 25. Finney's suggestions also fit the data that Thomas Albin has gleaned from the diaries of early Methodists. On Albin's analysis, it took on average about two years for early Methodists to move from showing interest in the gospel to where they had a mea-

A useful way to capture this vision of evangelism is to construe evangelism as directed fundamentally toward initiation into the kingdom of God. Achieving this will require both the activity of proclamation and the work of catechesis. More comprehensively, we might say that the ministry of evangelism will include effective evangelistic preaching, the active gossiping of the gospel in appropriate ways by all Christians everywhere, and the intentional grounding of new converts in the basics of the Christian faith.[21] This in fact comes close to what evangelism looked like in the early church.

In order to forestall possible misunderstanding, note that this proposal assumes that no evangelism is possible without the concurrent activity of the Holy Spirit. It also insists that evangelism must be rooted and grounded in the life of the local Christian congregation. Finally, it expects that evangelism will naturally result in the growth of local churches, but this is neither the goal nor focus of the ministry per se. The focus is the coming of God's kingdom in Jesus Christ, and the goal is to see people grounded in that kingdom here and now. In short, evangelism is simply the initial formation of genuine disciples of the Lord Jesus Christ.

IV.

In conclusion, it is worth reflecting briefly on the implications of our argument for recent discussions about the mission of the church. For almost a century there has been a noisy debate about how to conceive of the overall task of the church. Much of the energy spent on this has been devoted to the relative merits of evangelism, conceived as the verbal proclamation of the gospel, over against social action. The basic assumption has been that mission will consist exclusively of either gospel proclamation, or social action, or some combination of the two in which the status of one will be weighed as equal or inferior to the other.[22] Those who stress the importance of proclamation invariably point out that external salvation, in the divine scheme of things, must necessarily be construed as more important than temporal affairs; those who stress social action invariably stress the radical importance of God's involvement in Christ in the temporal scheme of things.

Independent observers of this debate must surely wonder if this way of

sure of assurance for themselves. Some took up to four years. See his proposed Ph.D. dissertation to be submitted to the University of Cambridge.

21. For an expanded account of this, see my *Logic of Evangelism,* chap. 8.

22. For a convenient summary, see Bosch, "Evangelism."

framing the issue begins to do justice to the richness of God's involvement in the world. For example, it trades on a strange silence about God's care for the natural order. Caring for the good creation God has given us cannot be subsumed under either proclamation or social action, yet this is surely an important task of the church in the modern world. Moreover, it is unduly restrictive to reduce the many things the church is called to do to proclamation and social action. Such reduction does not begin to touch the wider responsibility of the church to shape the whole tenor of a culture, something which cannot be limited to mere social action. Nor does it touch on the many responsibilities that the church must shoulder in the ongoing training, education, and nurture of its members. Worse still, this debate is silent on a simple and primary task of the church in rendering adequate praise and worship to the living God. Is not our first response to the gospel to gather together and celebrate all the wondrous things that God has done in the inauguration of his kingdom in our midst? Is this not a primary task of the church? And would not taking it seriously heal us of our moralistic egocentrism in both our evangelism and our social action?

This is not the place to resolve the issues these comments and questions raise. My point is more modest. The pertinent problem to identify is that this debate leaves out a crucial missing link between proclamation and social action It assumes that new believers can move naturally from hearing the gospel to social action. This is psychological and spiritual nonsense. A concrete example will make this clear. I began my ministry in a housing estate in Belfast, which at that time had the worst murder rate in Western Europe. Terrorism, then as now, was clearly one of the most serious social problems we encountered. In these circumstances, to construe the mission of the church exclusively in terms of proclamation and social action sounds initially attractive, but it would have been cruel in the extreme to accept this option. It omits the crucial need for adequate grounding in the faith. Certainly we can ask no less than that the new convert or believer pray for the coming of the kingdom of God here on earth as it is in heaven. An important principle then applies: The more we ask of the convert in social action, the more we must grapple with providing those intellectual, moral, and spiritual resources that will make possible such discipleship. My argument here is that evangelism should be so envisioned as to make this an integral part of its meaning. This major shift in perspective, were it to be adopted and implemented, would render obsolete the natural tendency to see evangelism and social action as somehow at odds or in competition with one another. It might also open up fresh ways to construe the wider and manifold mission of the church.

Finally, it permits us to see why social action is indeed an integral part of the overall mission of the church. Faithfulness to the gospel entails a fundamental acceptance of the kingdom of God now and in the future. For the individual, this clearly means that he or she has the chance to start all over again, to be "born again from above," to be baptized, and to be initiated into the church. Entry into the kingdom has its own inimitable grammar and content for the individual. However, the coming of the kingdom also has its own unique blessings and challenges for society as a whole. Nineteenth-century revivalists and twentieth-century liberals were absolutely right to insist on this and to grapple with what this meant for the social and political issues of the day. Anyone who takes the kingdom of God seriously must do so. In short, anyone who takes the gospel seriously must do so. So thinking of evangelism in the way proposed here will not only drive the church to get ahead with such actions as proclamation and initial catechesis, it will also drive us all to welcome God's merciful justice to roll across all of creation, society, and human history.

CHAPTER 3

Evangelism and the Gospel of Salvation

Orlando E. Costas

We are standing at the threshold of a new era in world evangelization. All over the world we see the church attempting to respond in different ways to her calling as God's witnessing community. World conferences on evangelization such as the recent Bangkok Conference on Salvation Today, Explo '72, the Urbana Conference on World Mission, and the International Congress on World Evangelization; the Jesus Revolution and the charismatic renewal movement; evangelistic movements such as "Christ the Only Way" and "Sodoin Dendo" in Asia; "New Life for All," "Christ for All" and other in-depth evangelistic efforts in Africa; the Evangelism in Depth programs in Latin America; and "Key '73" in the United States. These, plus the many spontaneous spiritual outbursts in other countries around the world, all point to the renewed interest of Christians around the world in giving witness to their faith in Jesus Christ.

As Christians endeavor to fulfill what the New Testament presents as one of their chief responsibilities, they must reflect critically and reverently on the nature of this task. The depth of one's commitment to a given enterprise is largely dependent on one's own understanding of that enterprise. Accordingly, if the renewed interest in evangelization is to have a lasting and profound effect, Christians will need to ponder seriously the meaning of their apostolate. Such a reflection must interact with the meaning of salvation. For the evangel is the announcement of the good news of salvation. It is a message about God's saving power made available to Jews and Gentiles through faith in Jesus Christ (cf. Rom. 1:16).

My purpose in the following pages will be, therefore, to inquire into the meaning of the salvation which the gospel announces and the implications for its communication to the world. To put it in question form: What does it mean to bring good news of salvation? I will attempt to respond to this question from a twofold perspective. The first is that of my own historical context.

I write as a Latin American evangelical. This means that behind my reflection the reader ought to bear in mind the situation of oppression and repression, imperialism and colonialism, starvation and poverty, power and powerlessness, frustration and despair which characterize Latin American society today. Such a situation forces me to reflect seriously on the meaning of the gospel for this captive and struggling continent. Thus I make no pretense of absolute objectivity. Rather, I approach the proposed question from the perspective of one who seeks to understand evangelism in the light of the concrete historical situation of mankind, and one for whom mankind is not an abstract concept but a concrete reality; that is, mankind is for me *first* and *foremost* contemporary Latin America. This may sound somewhat parochial, but it is a burden imposed upon me by my calling as an evangelist and my historical context. I am well aware of the fact that the world is much bigger than Latin America. But I insist that I can only understand the world from my own existential situation.

But note that I said that I write as a Latin American *evangelical.* My concern for the historical and the concrete must be seen in the light of one for whom the Christian faith implies a personal experience with Jesus Christ as Lord and Savior, one who makes no apologies as to his own personal experience of conversion and who is not ashamed to invite his fellowmen to repentance and faith in Christ.

Some may find such a perspective puzzling. They may wonder how I can reconcile such an apparent contradiction. My answer is that this is not without its historical precedent. There have been (and indeed still are!) thousands of Christians who have been committed to their historical situations with an equally zealous concern for the leading of their fellowmen to a personal experience with Jesus Christ. Moreover, such a view is congruent with the witness of Holy Scripture. For the latter portrays not an either/or, but a holistic, comprehensive message oriented to man in his multitudinous life situations.

This leads me to the second perspective from which I will attempt to respond to the proposed question, namely, that of biblical theology. In any discussion of evangelism, Scripture must play a normative role. This is substantiated by the fact that the Bible not only describes the context in the midst of which evangelism emerged, but explains how the early Christian community understood it. Scripture is thus a primary source of information about the nature of the gospel. Accordingly, an understanding of the meaning of evangelism is contingent upon the biblical understanding of the gospel and its implications for the whole world.

In my inquiry into the meaning of bringing good news of salvation from the perspective of biblical theology and through the eyeglasses of a Latin American evangelical, I am aiming at a twofold objective: (1) To clarify the depth of the evangelistic task in the light of the multitudinous situations of contemporary mankind; and (2) to attempt to outline a set of criteria for evaluating the theological integrity of the various ways by which contemporary Christians are seeking to fulfill their evangelistic vocation. These criteria are embedded in three propositions that define the nature of evangelism in relation to the totality of salvation.

Witnessing to a Liberating and a Searching God

In the first place, *to bring good news of salvation implies bearing witness to a liberating and a searching God.* For salvation is of God[1] and he actualizes it in the deliverance of the oppressed from bondage and captivity, in the quality of life which he demands from his creatures, and in his creative and providential deeds in the cosmos.

In the Old Testament, God is known as the Redeemer and Creator of Israel (Isa. 43:14-15, etc.). He delivered her from the bondage of Egypt and the Babylonian captivity. He created, redeemed, and called her in righteousness to be his own treasured possession as a kingdom of priests and set her up as "a covenant to the people, a light to the nations, to open the eyes that are blind, to bring out the prisoners from the dungeon, from the prison those who sit in darkness" (Isa. 42:6-7). Accordingly, he demanded from Israel a redemptive quality of life. The land was to be considered as belonging to God and thus could not be transferred. There was to be a periodic time of "liberation" wherein large landholdings would be annulled, slaves would be set free, and family debts would be cancelled (Lev. 25; Exod. 21, etc.). Provisions were to be made for the orphan and the widow, the stranger and the prisoner. Teachers were ordained to explain these laws, rulers called to make sure that

1. See, for example, the following passages, where salvation is explicitly attributed to God: Gen. 49:18; Exod. 14:13; 1 Sam. 2:1; 1 Chron. 16:23; Pss. 13:5; 27:1, 37:39; 50:23; 51:12; 70:4; 118:14; Isa. 12:2; Jer. 3:23; Lam. 3:26; Micah 7:7; Luke 1:69, 77; 2:30; 3:6; Acts 4:12; 28:28; Rom. 1:16; Eph. 1:13; 1 Thess. 5:9; Rev. 7:10; 12:10; 19:1. For a full and technical treatment of the biblical concept of salvation, see the following sources: Werner Foerster and Georg Fohrer, "sōzō, sōtēria, sōtēr, sōtērios," in *Theological Dictionary of the New Testament,* vol. 7, ed. Gerhard Friedrick, trans. Geoffrey W. Bromiley (Grand Rapids: Eerdmans, 1971), pp. 995-1024; Alan Richardson, "Salvation, Saviour," in *The Interpreter's Bible Dictionary,* R-Z, ed. George A. Buttrick (Nashville: Abingdon, 1962), pp. 169-81; G. Walters, "Salvation," in *The New Bible Dictionary,* 7, ed. D. Douglas (Grand Rapids: Eerdmans, 1962), pp. 1126-30.

the laws were kept and prophets raised to call attention to the people's deviation from the quality of life which God demanded and to remind them of their missionary responsibility to their neighbors.

In the Old Testament, God is also said to have revealed his liberating action in the creation and preservation of the cosmos. By "the word of the LORD the heavens were made, and all their host by the breath of his mouth," says the psalmist (Ps. 33:6). In giving origin to the cosmos, in making fruitful the empty and formless earth (Gen. 1:1-2) and imparting to man life and freedom (Gen. 2:7) God undertook his first liberating and saving act. Thus the psalmist could affirm that "from of old" he is "working salvation in the midst of the earth" (Ps. 74:12).

Having acted redemptively in the creation and preservation of the world and in the calling, deliverance, and guidance of Israel, he has spoken redemptively in his son (John 1:1-14; Heb. 1:2-3), thereby making it possible for all men to be liberated from the power of sin and death and for the whole creation to be set free "from its bondage to decay" (Rom. 8:21; 1-3; 1 Tim. 2:5-6).

> In the death and resurrection of Jesus Christ, a new world has erupted, a new age is inaugurated under the sign of liberation, from the world, from sin, from death, from the law, a liberation that is to be consummated in the Parousia. The Christian is [thus] called to liberty (Gal. 5:1, 13), a liberty which is both an anticipation of the definitive freedom to come and a stimulus for a new life (Rom. 8:15-27), a liberation that the whole creation desires and awaits (v. 22).[2]

To bear witness to the God of salvation is, consequently, to affirm the truth about his liberating deeds (cf. Isa. 42-44; 1 Peter 2:9). It is to affirm the reality of the gospel, which is the revelation of God (Rom. 1:1; 1 Cor. 1:1), and thus to point him out to all of mankind as a God of love and grace who became flesh, died on a cross, and descended unto the uttermost parts in search of a captive creation, and who continues this quest through his Spirit and the apostolate of his witnessing community.

The God of the gospel is, therefore, not only a liberating but a searching God. A God who is "not wishing that any should perish, but that all should reach repentance" (2 Peter 3:9). This is the rationale behind the command to evangelize the nations of the earth.

The whole creation has been imprisoned by man's moral and spiritual irresponsibility. Having been created in God's own image (Gen. 1:26ff.) to live

2. José Míguez-Bonino, "Theology and Liberation," *International Review of Mission* 61 (January 1972): 68.

in community (Gen. 2:18ff.) and to have dominion over the earth as God's vice-regent (Gen. 1:28-30), man has not lived up to his high calling. Accordingly, he has fallen into darkness, emptiness, and purposelessness and in so doing has affected the entire cosmos. But God, who is merciful and kind, has set out in Christ to deliver man from his captivity, and through his redemption, the entire creation. Thus he has purposed in the present age to have the great news of reconciliation communicated to "every creature which is under heaven" (Col. 1:23).

To bring good news of salvation is, therefore, to witness to the truthfulness of the gospel message. Such a witness has a threefold implication. First of all, it involves testifying to the *reality* of the life of Jesus of Nazareth (cf. Acts 10:39; Luke 1:2). Far from being merely concerned with the Christ of faith (who reveals himself as the risen and cosmic Christ), as Rudolf Bultmann and his school would have us believe, the early church witnessed to the life and ministry of Jesus. Little wonder that she preserved the sayings of Jesus, first in the form of an oral tradition and later in written form; that she saw the need for a canon of authorized writings to interpret his life and teachings; and that she incorporated these writings into her worship! In fact, so important was the life and ministry of our Lord to the early church that her worship services were rehearsals of the important periods of his life and ministry.[3]

Secondly, witnessing to the truth of the gospel implies affirming the truth with regard to the work of Christ. This is precisely the meaning of Luke's version of the Great Commission:

> Then he opened their minds to understand the Scriptures, and said to them, "Thus it is written, that the Christ should suffer and on the third day rise from the dead, and that repentance and forgiveness of sins should be preached in his name to all nations, beginning from Jerusalem. You are witnesses of these things." (Luke 24:44-48)

The "these things" of this passage are the basic facts about the Christ-event, namely, that Jesus came to suffer, that in the cross God's plan of salvation was

3. As far back as the end of the first century, two great moments can be identified in the church's worship, namely, the Galilean (or the service of the Word), which actualized the public ministry of Jesus through the proclamation of the Word, and the Jerusalemite (or the Eucharistic service), which actualized his private ministry among the disciples through the celebration of the Eucharist. For a good summary of these two moments and sound bibliographical references, see Jean-Jacques von Allmen, *Worship: Its Theology and Practice* (New York: Oxford University Press, 1965); Oscar Cullmann, *Early Christian Worship,* Studies in Biblical Theology no. 10 (London: SCM, 1951); William D. Maxwell, *An Outline of Christian Worship* (New York: Oxford University Press, 1936).

fulfilled, that Christ rose from the dead, and that through his death and resurrection the forgiveness of sins is now a possibility to all those who repent and put their trust in him. Elsewhere in the book of Acts, Luke records several statements in which the apostles bear witness to the reality of the work of Christ (cf. Acts 2:32; 3:15; 1:21-22). These statements further corroborate the claims of Luke 24:44-48.

Thirdly, to bear witness to the truth of the gospel implies affirming the veracity of God, for the gospel is a message about God (Rom. 1:1) and he is the ultimate reality of the universe. Consequently, to witness to the truth of the gospel is to affirm God as the truth.

But note: only they who have been with God, who have experienced him, can make such an affirmation. This is precisely the relevance of the Incarnation:

> And the Word became flesh and dwelt among us, full of grace and *truth*. . . . For the law was given through Moses; grace and *truth* came through Jesus Christ. No one has ever seen God; the only Son, who is in the bosom of the Father, he has made him known. (John 1:14, 17-18; emphasis added)

The Incarnation of Christ means, among other things, that we have an authentic witness to the reality of God, for he testifies of him with whom he has been and whom he has seen (cf. John 18:37). Thus he can claim to be *the* truth, for he is the ultimate revelation of truth (cf. John 14:6; 3:11, 32-33; 8:13ff.). Likewise, the Spirit can bear witness to the truth and is himself "the Spirit of truth" because he proceeds from the Father, represents and makes present the Son (John 14:26; 15:26). And not only does the Spirit bear witness to Christ as the truth, but also the believer, because he has been with him (cf. John 15:27); i.e., he has experienced him (John 20:20, 29-31) and has received his Spirit (Acts 1:8).

From this, it follows that only those who have experienced what John calls "the new birth" (John 3:3), i.e., conversion, can bear witness to the truth of the gospel. For a witness must testify of that which he knows. As R. K. Orchard has said,

> . . . the witness must be prepared to be cross-examined, and should not expect the process of cross-examination to be always controlled by judges' rules. In principle, he must be prepared to stake his life on the truth of that to which he testifies.[4]

4. R. K. Orchard, *Missions in a Time of Testing* (Philadelphia: Westminster, 1964), p. 80.

Only through a faith-encounter with Christ can men and women experience the truth, and only as they come to this knowledge are they qualified to bear witness to the truth of the gospel.

Interpreting Christ's Saving Work in the Light of the Struggles of Mankind

The Christian bears a tremendous responsibility. Since he has experienced the reality of God's liberating action in history, he must interpret the manifestation in time of this reality. Hence, the second proposition that defines the nature of evangelism in the context of the totality of salvation: *To bring good news of salvation is to interpret Christ's saving work in the light of the struggles of mankind.*

As a witness to the truth of the gospel, the Christian cannot be content simply with pointing to the historical facts about the life, ministry, and work of Christ. He must interpret the meaning of Christ for the here and now. He must relate Christ's saving work to all of life. Neither must the task of evangelism be understood as a mere sharing of one's personal experience with Christ. Of course, it includes this, but it also involves interpreting the comprehensiveness of God's salvation to all the peoples of the earth.

In the New Testament, salvation has at least a threefold meaning: (1) liberation from the power of sin and death (Rom. 8:1-2); (2) being born into the family of God (John 1:12; Rom. 8:16, 17, 29; Gal. 3:16, 26-29, 4:5b-7; 1 John 2:1-2); (3) participation in the reign of Christ (cf. Eph. 1:20ff.; 2:6; Rev. 1:5f.). Understood thus, salvation "offers a comprehensive wholeness in this divided life."[5] It has not only a personal but a collective, social quality; it not only has a future dimension but a present one as well.

> It is salvation of the soul and the body, of the individual and society, mankind and "the groaning creation" (Rom. 8:19). As evil works both in personal life and exploitative social structures which humiliate humankind, so God's justice manifests itself both in the justification of the sinner and in social and political justice. As guilt is both individual and corporate so God's liberating power changes both persons and structures. . . . This comprehensive notion of salvation demands of the whole of the people of God a matching comprehensive approach to their participation in salvation.[6]

5. "Salvation and Social Justice, Report of Section 11 of the Bangkok Conference," *International Review of Mission* 62 (April 1973): 199.

6. "Salvation and Social Justice," p. 199.

As members of the eschatological community of salvation, Christians are called to interpret Christ's saving work by actualizing in their everyday life the essential characteristics of salvation. Having been born into the family of God, they must actualize God's love in the fellowship of faith and in their relations with the rest of the world. Their experience of liberation from the power of sin and death requires of them the manifestation of God's *shalom*[7] in their life (i.e., a life of reconciliation, freedom, and fullness). Their participation in the life of God's kingdom demands of them a commitment to justice.

Salvation is operative not only in the realm of the spiritual, I-thou relationship, but also in the social and collective dimensions of life. As reported by Section II of the Bangkok Conference on Salvation Today, there are at least four social dimensions where we may see Christ's saving action at work.

1. Salvation works in the struggle for economic justice against the exploitation of people by people.
2. Salvation works in the struggle for human dignity against man's political oppression by his fellowmen.
3. Salvation works in the struggle for solidarity against the alienation of person from person.
4. Salvation works in the struggle of hope against despair in personal life.[8]

To be sure, the presence of salvation in each of these struggles is a relative one. Since Christ's saving action has not been revealed in its fullness, we cannot attribute an absolute character to each of its apparent manifestations in the struggles of life. Moreover, given the moral limitation and imperfection of mankind, each struggle is under the judgment of God. Nevertheless, Christians must recognize them as glimpses of the coming messianic salvation. For Christ, who is the Lord *and* Savior of the whole cosmos, *is* active in the conflicts of history. Accordingly, we ought not to limit the signs of the coming

7. At this point two remarks are in order. (1) The experience of *shalom* is possible through Christ who becomes "our peace" (Eph. 2:14ff.). This does not mean that only Christians can profit from its blessing. Obviously, when in society the church is able to bring about better living conditions these changes benefit every member of society. But it does mean that for the Christian *shalom* is possible in and through Christ inasmuch as *shalom* comes as a gift of God and Christ is God's peace made flesh. (2) The church has the obligation of actualizing in her everyday life God's *shalom*. If she cannot live a peaceful life with all of its implications, if she cannot provide the right conditions among her own for an authentic life style, she then has no right to proclaim to the world God's peace. What a lesson for the church of the twentieth century, which has much too often allowed her own to go unfed, to live in starvation and subhuman conditions while her leaders have lived in luxury and wealth!

8. "A Report of Section II," *International Review of Mission* 62 (April 1973): 200.

kingdom to the church. For the kingdom is larger than the church; it involves also God's sovereign rule over all principalities and powers. We ought, therefore, to look for signs of the kingdom in the struggles of people for justice, peace, solidarity, and hope. That these signs are not easily recognized by the world is undisputed. Even so, the church is called upon to discern them, under the guidance of the Holy Spirit, and interpret them to the world. This is part of the church's witnessing responsibility.

Just as God is present and active in the world of culture (understood in its wider sense as encompassing all of man's achievements), so he is in struggles against the oppressive, demonic forces of this world. Just as Christ's saving work extends to the world of nature, as a cosmic event, and the former looks forward to the redemption of the body, so mankind groans for a new world, and so God has in Christ pronounced himself in favor of man's total liberation from all that oppresses and dehumanizes him. Thus man's struggle for justice, peace, hope, and solidarity not only represents a legitimate aspiration, but one which is fed by God himself.

That man will never achieve a perfect, just, and peaceful world through himself is clearly taught in Scripture. But his search for justice, peace, hope, and solidarity is, nevertheless, a sign of the coming age which the church must relate to and interpret in the light of the gospel. Man's life struggles constitute, therefore, opportunities for the church to show forth and demonstrate prophetically Christ's saving power.

The church is faithful to her evangelistic imperative not only when she shows forth and actualizes in her life the marks of the coming salvation, but also when she participates in the conflicts of those who suffer and long to be liberated from their situations of oppression. The church is faithful to her witnessing vocation when she becomes a catalyst for God's liberating action in the world of poverty, exploitation, hunger, guilt, and despair by *standing* in *solidarity* with people, by *showing* them with *concrete actions* that God cares and wills to save them and by *helping them* to *understand* the material and moral roots of their situation. The church is faithful to her task of bringing good news of salvation when she relates the meaning of Christ to the history of mankind; when she interprets the history of the peoples of the various cultures of the earth in the light of the comprehensive meaning of the gospel; and when, specifically and concretely, she confronts each member of her surrounding neighboring communities with the claims of Christ upon his life and thus makes the gospel pertinent to his particular life situation.

Calling for a Commitment to Jesus Christ

This leads me to the third and final proposition: *To bring good news of salvation is to call for a commitment to Jesus Christ.*

An analysis of the evangelistic practice of the early church as described in the New Testament reveals that for the latter evangelism was not only a testimony to Christ's saving action and an interpretation of the meaning of salvation in the light of man's historical struggles, but a call to a life of commitment to the Lord. To evangelize was to call for a decision about God's liberating action in Jesus Christ, to invite people to confess him as the Lord and Savior of their lives, to recruit them for God's kingdom, to persuade them to be reconciled to God through his Son, to make them his disciples. This is made very clear not only in the Gospels and the sermons recorded in the book of Acts, but also in the epistles (2 Cor. 5:20b) and the book of Revelation (Rev. 3:20).[9]

But what does it mean to make a decision for Christ? What does confessing him as Lord and Savior involve? What are the implications of such a commitment? First, inviting people to commit their lives to Christ implies a simultaneous confrontation with the realities of their lives and the possibility which God makes available in Christ to enter into a new life. This is another way of saying that calling people to Christ involves an invitation to take a good hard look at themselves and their life situation — their selfishness and irresponsibility, their ambition, their ego weaknesses (inferiority complexes), their tendency to oppress their neighbor or to "sell themselves" to their neighbor, allowing him to oppress and domesticate them. Moreover, it involves a simultaneous offer to consider turning from themselves and putting their trust in the New Man, Christ Jesus, who is, at the same time, the way, the truth, and the life (John 14:6), and who consequently transforms them into a new creation (2 Cor. 5:17).

This is what is meant by the biblical concept of conversion. It implies at least two things: *repentance,* or a change of mind, and *faith* toward God. Effective evangelism must call for an "about face" from the ways of unrighteousness and a seeking after God through Jesus Christ our Lord (cf. Isa. 55:6-7).[10] Such a decision implies a commitment to everything to which Jesus Christ is himself committed. José Míguez-Bonino makes this exceedingly clear. He asks:

9. For a sound analysis of the evangelistic practice of the early church, see Michael Green, *Evangelism in the Early Church* (Grand Rapids: Eerdmans, 1970).

10. See also Acts 3:19, 26; 9:35; 11:21; 14:15; 15:3, 19; 26:18, 20.

> What happens when somebody is converted to Christ? He must know that he is not going into some sort of secluded soul fellowship, but that he is called to obedience to the One who said, "The Spirit of the Lord is upon me, because he has anointed me to preach good news to the poor. He has sent me to proclaim release to the captives and recovering of sight to the blind, to set at liberty those who are oppressed, to proclaim the acceptable year of the Lord." This is the Christ of the Gospel and there is no other Christ to be converted to.[11]

Unfortunately, this has not always been the case in the church's evangelizing enterprise. Instead of confronting men and women with their sin as manifested in their concrete social situations, the church has much too often confronted them with their abstract sinfulness, leaving their sinful relations to their particular life situations unaffected. Instead of confronting people with the demands of Christ, the church has accommodated the gospel to their own way of thinking and living. By failing to confront them with the claims and demands of the gospel, by failing to call them to a militant and responsible discipleship, the church has preached what Dietrich Bonhoeffer rightly called a "cheap grace."

Second, calling people to commit their lives to Christ implies inviting them to be incorporated into Christ. Hence the command to go and "make disciples of all nations, baptizing them in the name of the Father and of the Son and of the Holy Spirit, teaching them to observe all that I have commanded you" (Matt. 28:19-20).

In the New Testament, baptism is understood as the mark of incorporation into Christ, and thus, into his Body (cf. Rom. 6:3ff.; 1 Cor. 12:13). It is intimately related to conversion. Indeed it is the outward expression of conversion. Hence it is a public profession of repentance from sin and faith in Jesus.

Throughout church history, baptism has been considered the sacrament of initiation. It is a living witness to one's response to repentance, faith, and obedience to the gospel. Thus it signifies not only the believer's union with Christ, but also his entrance into the community of faith. For to be in Christ is not only to experience forgiveness and the indwelling presence of the Spirit, but also incorporation into Christ's Body.

Effective evangelism must, therefore, lead to incorporation into the church. For the new Christian, the church becomes a family in which he puts

11. José Míguez-Bonino, "The Present Crisis in Mission," quoted in E. M. Huenemann, "Evangelism and Renewal," General Assembly Issue Paper no. 2, Ninth Convention of the National Council of the Church of Christ, Dallas, Texas, December 3-8, 1972, 6. The article first appeared in *The Church Herald.*

into practice his experience of reconciliation through fellowship and communion with his brethren, a school in which he grows and is trained for mission, and a team through which he can fulfill his witnessing vocation.

Since the gospel is oriented toward change — a turning to Christ in repentance and faith, a transformation in one's way of thinking and acting through the enabling power of the Holy Spirit, a positive commitment to a new set of relationships, a new style of life, a new set of values and a new worldview — it must be adequately interpreted. The gospel must be expounded with clarity and precision. This is why Jesus commanded us to make disciples by teaching the peoples of the earth to observe all that he had commanded (Matt. 28:20a).

While the term *command* implies a set of rules to be kept, in Scripture a command is more than a rule; it is a life principle, a revelation of God's will (cf. Deut. 6:1ff.). The emphasis is thus not on the commandment but on the *commander.* Thus, the law of God is a revelation of *his* righteousness and perfect will, or to put it in more concrete terms, a revelation of God himself. The observance, therefore, of Christ's commandments implies an understanding of and commitment to his way of life. Likewise, the teaching of his commandments implies an interpretation of the meaning of his self-disclosure. To expound the gospel is to interpret the meaning of Christ in the light of his own teachings. These are the teachings which the Spirit committed to the apostles (John 14:26; Eph. 2:20) and which the apostles faithfully transmitted to their disciples and urged them diligently to transmit to other faithful men who would be able to teach others (1 Tim. 2:2; 6:20; 2 Tim. 1:8ff.; 4:1ff.).

One of the great tragedies in the church's evangelizing efforts has been the limited commitment of so many Christians to the aforementioned truth. This has led to a shallow evangelization, with very little content, a non-interpretative, distorted-beyond-recognition gospel. Indeed, as I have pointed out elsewhere, the crisis of contemporary evangelization is not methodological but theological. Lacking a sound theological foundation, the methods used can't help but produce shallow results. For when "the base is weak, the results are also weak, whether or not the best methods have been used in the process."[12]

If what has been said above about the nature of evangelism represents a faithful summary of the biblical understanding of the meaning of bringing good news of salvation, albeit through the eyeglasses of a Latin American evangelical, it must be asked, then, whether the various ways by which con-

12. Orlando Costas, "Hacia una evangelización pertinente," in *Hacia una teologia de la evangelización,* ed. Orlando Costas (Buenos Aires: La Aurora, 1973).

temporary Christians are seeking to fulfill their evangelistic vocation is a faithful fulfillment of the biblical mandate. For unless the evangelistic practice of the church corresponds to the biblical understanding of evangelism, unless the gospel which is witnessed to represents truly and indeed the comprehensiveness of Christ's saving work, unless it is interpreted in the light of the struggles of mankind and is accompanied by an uncompromising call to a life of commitment, evangelism becomes a frustrating experience and the gospel a truncated message. In this case, the renewed interest in evangelism that we witness in the church today will turn out to be no more than another fad.

CHAPTER 4

Evangelism in the Context of Secularization

Lesslie Newbigin

One must begin with some examination of the concept of secularization. Many sociologists now agree that the idea that has been dominant during the past half-century, namely that the progress of modern science and technology must increasingly eliminate religious belief, has proved to be false. The present century has in fact witnessed a marked growth in religiosity in Europe. It is true that this has not been expressed in Christian terms. But in the forms of many new religious movements, in the enthusiasm for Eastern types of religious belief and practice, in the revival of various ancient forms of pagan religion, and in the enormous popularity of astrology among European peoples, there is a luxuriant growth of religion in what is called the secular society. Moreover, in those parts of Europe where people have lived for forty years or more under the control of the Marxist ideology with its claim to replace religion completely by a "scientific" doctrine of human nature and history, the Christian churches have shown a power of survival and renewal much more impressive than what has been seen in the areas that called themselves the "free world."

And there is a further point to be made. Leaving aside movements that are recognizably religious in the sense that they affirm realities not available for investigation by the methods of empirical science, it is clear that there are, even in the most secularized societies, forces that have a religious character in the sense that they have the status of dogma and command total trust. In the great debates about secularization in the decade of the 1960s, when many Christians (such as Arend van Leeuwen) welcomed the process of secularization as a form of liberation made possible by the Christian gospel, it seemed to be taken for granted that secularization created a space free of all ideological or religious control. In this space, human beings (and Christians among them) would find the freedom to exercise their own rational and moral powers without coercion from any dominant belief system. The secular society was hailed as the free society. Writers such as Harvey Cox in the United States and Denis Munby in England encouraged the Christians of their day to welcome the process of secularization as a proper fruit of the Christian message and a further stage in human emancipation.

But a candid look at the societies that call themselves "secular" must surely dispel such illusions. Dogma does not vanish when the name is dropped. It is impossible to pretend that children in the state schools of Europe are not being taught to accept certain beliefs about human origins, human history, all shaped by certain assumptions. The loud complaints of Muslim parents that I hear in England are directed against precisely the claim that what their children are being taught to believe are simply "the facts," while everyone must know that they are in reality beliefs that a Muslim must reject. They quite rightly see that their children are being taught (not in the classes on "religious education" but in the classes on science, history, literature, and sociology) to believe that human life can be satisfactorily understood and managed without any reference to God. They protest against the arrogance that assumes that things taught in schools are simply "the facts," while religious beliefs are merely private opinion.

The apostles of secularization in the 1960s seemed to believe that human societies can flourish without any shared beliefs. But this is obviously not so. The societies we know in Europe share the belief that what human beings need to know in order to manage their lives is the body of assured knowledge that is available through the methods of science. Perhaps those critics are right to see Descartes as the key figure. The attempt to find a kind of certitude in the existence of the thinking self *(cogito ergo sum)* constitutes the deliberate choice of a position that is open to doubt. Why should we imagine that human beings should have available to them a basis for certitude other than the one provided by a trustful dependence on the Author of our being? Descartes' starting point already begs that question. But the secular societies that have developed in Europe since the seventeenth century share the common belief that reliable knowledge about human nature, and therefore about how human life is to be managed, is to be found not by reliance upon divine revelation and grace but by reliance upon the methods of empirical science. This, broadly speaking, is the dogma that controls public life, as distinct from private opinions that individuals are free to hold.

But the dogma does not measure up the realities of human nature. If there is no answer to the question "But why did this happen to me?" people will turn to astrology. If there is no answer to the question "What is human life really for? What is the purpose of human life and of whole creation?" people will seek to fill the void with the search for instant pleasure in drugs, in sex, in mindless violence through which one can express the sense of meaninglessness. We have to be endlessly entertained and we have to have idols to fill the empty space from which the living God has been removed. In the end, the society we have is not a secular society but a pagan society, a society in which men and women are giving their allegiance to no-gods. The rational part of us puts its trust in the findings of science but is left with no answer to the question of ultimate meaning. The way is open for the irrational part of us to develop a pantheon of idols.

The "secular" society is not a neutral area into which we can project the Christian message. It is an area already occupied by other gods. We have a battle on our hands. We are dealing with principalities and powers. What, then, is evangelism in this context?

To our "secular" contemporaries the answer to this question is quite simple. The Christian church is a voluntary association of people who wish to promote certain "values" for themselves and for society. These "values," like all others, are matters of personal choice. They are not matters of "fact" that everyone has to accept. It follows that the success of these "values" depends on the number of people who support them. There is a diminishing number of people who identify themselves with the Christian churches. The churches are therefore in danger of collapsing. Evangelism is an effort by the churches to avert this collapse and to recruit more adherents to their cause. It is even possible that this way of understanding evangelism may be in the minds of some church members. It then becomes impossible to conceal the element of anxiety that infects the enterprise. It becomes very important that *we* should succeed. The shadow of Pelagius hangs over the enterprise.

In contrast to this way of seeing things, it is a striking fact that nowhere in the letters of St. Paul does the apostle lay upon the church the duty of evangelism. The gospel is such a tremendous reality that he cannot possibly keep silent about it. "Woe is me if I do not preach the gospel" (1 Cor. 9:16). He seems to take it for granted that the same will be true for his readers. He is not slow to warn, persuade, rebuke his friends; it is a matter of life or death for him that they should be utterly faithful to Christ. But he never lays upon them the duty to go out and evangelize. Why should this be so?

The first evangelism in the New Testament is the announcement by Jesus that the kingdom of God is at hand. This, if one may put it so, is not ecclesiastical news but world news. It is not about "values" but about "facts." It is, strictly speaking, news, and it requires an immediate response in action. There is immediate excitement. People flock to hear. But it seems as if God's reign was not what we expected. There is both enthusiasm and rejection. In the end there is betrayal, condemnation, and death. God's reign has not appeared after all. There is despair and suicide. But what seemed to be the end is the new beginning. The tomb is empty, Jesus is risen, death is conquered, God does reign after all. There is an explosion of joy, news that cannot be kept secret. Everyone must hear it. A new creation has begun. One does not have to be summoned to the "task" of evangelism. If these things are really true, they have to be told. That, I suppose, is why St. Paul did not have to remind his readers about the duty of evangelism.

But can this have any relevance to the ordinary, comfortable, respectable Christian congregation in the suburbs of a contemporary European city? There is, let us admit, a big gulf between them. We have largely domesticated the gospel within our culture. We have quietly accepted, for practical purposes, the dogma that controls public life. We have accepted as the "real" history the story that is told in the school classrooms about the history of "civilization," which means the interpretation of the human story from the point of view of *this* moment and *this* place in the whole story. We have allowed the Bible to be inserted into this history as a very minor strand in the whole human story, one element in the history of religions, which is itself only one element in the whole fabric of human history. We have not had the boldness that, for example, our black-led churches in Birmingham show, to recognize the story that the Bible tells as the real story, the true story, the story that explains who we really are, where we come from, and where we are going. If we were faithful to our best traditions, if we took the Bible seriously over the years by the constant reading of it, expounding it, meditating on it, then we would see the story that is told in the schools as a story that misses the real point. What is the real point of the human story, in which my life is only a small part? It is not in the achievement, somewhere in the distant future, of a perfect human civilization. It is not in the achievement of my personal ambition, after which I decline into senility. The point of the whole story has been made once and for all in the events that the New Testament tells. If we believe that, then we live by a different story from the one that is told in our society. And the difference will become clear and will provoke questions. I have taken the example of St. Paul to suggest that we may be missing an essential point if we speak about evangelism as a duty. One could also point to the striking fact that almost all of the evangelistic sermons that are recorded in the Acts of the Apostles are responses to questions asked, rather than discourses given on the initiative of the speaker. It would seem that if the church is faithfully living the true story, the evangelistic dialogue will be initiated not by the church but by the one who senses the presence of a new reality and wants to inquire about its secret.

How will the presence of a new reality become known? I suggest by three things: by a certain kind of shared life, by actions, and by words that interpret actions. The first and fundamental one is a certain kind of shared life. At the heart of that life will be praise. St. Luke tells us that the first response of the first disciples to the resurrection of Jesus was that "they returned to Jerusalem with great joy and were continually in the Temple, praising God" (Luke 24:51). A community of people that, in the midst of all the pain and sorrow and wickedness of the world, is continually praising God is the first obvious result of living by another story than the one the world lives by. In our own century, we have the witness of the churches in the USSR, who for three generations were denied the opportunity of any kind of outward witness by word or action, but who sustained through those years a life of praise, reflecting in their worship the glory of the Triune God. It was that reality, the presence of something that by its very existence called into question the official story by which the nation was required to live, that drew men and women to faith in Christ through the darkest years of tyranny.

We know that the worship of a Christian congregation can become a dead and formal thing, having the outward form but lacking the inward joy of adoration. When that has happened, our duty is to pray for the reviving work of the Holy Spirit to kindle into flame the embers that are always there. We know that this prayer has been answered many times in ways beyond expectation. And where there is a praising community, there also will be a caring community with love to spare for others. Such a community is the primary hermeneutic of the gospel. All the statistical evidence goes to show that those within our secularized societies who are being drawn out of unbelief to faith in Christ say that they were drawn through the friendship of a local congregation. There is, of course, a kind of "loving" that is selfish — merely the desire to have more members for the congregation. This kind of "love" is quickly recognized. But a congregation that has at its heart a joyful worship of the living God and a constantly renewed sense of the sheer grace and kindness of God will be a congregation from which true love flows out to the neighbors, a love that seeks their good regardless of whether they come to church.

Second, the presence of a new reality will be made known by the acts that originate from it. Jesus' announcement of the gospel, that the kingdom of God is at hand, was immediately implemented by actions of healing and deliverance. These actions are portrayed as simple evidence that the power of God, his kindly rule over all powers, is present. They are acts of sheer compassion. A victim of leprosy, sensing the presence of this reality, says, "If you will you can make me clean." Jesus replies: "I will; be clean," touches him, and heals him (Mark 1:40-41). There are no conditions attached. Nothing is said about faith and repentance. It is the love of God in action. The reign of God has come near.

When the Christian congregation is filled with the Spirit and lives the true story, such actions will flow from it. Primarily they will be the actions of the members in their several vocations every day. While there are also actions that a congregation or a wider church body may undertake, these are secondary. The primary action of the church in the world is the action of its members in their daily work. The congregation may have no social action program and may yet be acting more effectively in secular society than a congregation with a big program of social action.

What is important in these actions — whether the personal actions of individual members or the corporate programs of a congregation — is that they spring out of the new life in Christ. It can be otherwise. They can be designed to attract new members, or to justify the congregation in the eyes of society by its good works. The Gospels make it clear that Jesus resolutely refused to make for himself a public reputation as a healer and a worker of miracles. His mighty works were indeed signs of the presence of the kingdom, but when he was asked for a sign he refused. When a multitude of people who had gathered around him were hungry, he fed them. But when they pursued him, he sternly told them that they must seek for the bread that does not perish with the eating (John 6:25). A program of church action may arise not from sheer compassion but from an ideological commitment to some vision of society shaped by the story that the world tells and not by the story that the Bible tells. The church then becomes one among a number of agencies for promoting justice and peace, rather than the sign and foretaste of the new reality where alone justice and peace embrace, the sign pointing to the crucified and risen Jesus in whom alone we can receive both God's justice and God's peace.

Third, then, the presence of the new reality will be attested to by words. The church has to speak, to announce the new reality, to preach. Here we have to reject two false positions. On the one hand there is the view that "actions speak louder than words," the view that the church will win people's allegiance to the gospel by good lives and good works and that preaching is unacceptable and unnecessary. The word "mission" is used to describe a range of activities in which explicit naming of the name of Jesus has no place. On this two things may be said. The first is that Jesus himself preached and instructed his disciples to preach. Not, as we have seen, that each act of healing or deliverance was accompanied by a sermon. Not at all. But the acts of healing and deliverance were not self-explanatory. They might even be the work of the devil (Mark 3:21ff.). And when Jesus sent out the Twelve with the authority to heal and deliver, he also told them to preach. It is clear that the preaching is an explanation of the mighty works, and that the mighty works are evidence that the preaching is true. They are not separable (Mark 6:7). Second, therefore, we have to say that the preaching of the church carries on weight if it does not come from a community in which the truth of what is preached is being validated (even though always imperfectly) in the life of the community. But the life of even the most saintly community does not by itself tell the story, the story in which the name of Jesus has the central place.

If these general affirmations are true, I would suggest that in thinking of evangelism in a secular society, and — in particular — in thinking of the re-evangelization of Europe, the following five points may be helpful.

1. Evangelism is not the effort of Christians to increase the size and importance of the church. It is the sharing of the good news that God reigns — good news for those who believe, bad news for those who reject. Evangelism must be rescued from a Pelagian anxiety, as though *we* were responsible for converting the world. God reigns and his reign is revealed and effective in the incarnation, ministry, death, and resurrection of Jesus. As we grow into a deeper understanding of this fact as we learn more and more to live by the other story, we become more confident in sharing this reality with those who have not yet seen it.

2. The clue to evangelism in a secular society must be the local congregation. There are many other things of which one could speak — mass evangelism of the Billy Graham type, Christian literature, radio and television, study and training courses, and so on. These are auxiliary. Many of them can be very valuable. But they are auxiliary to the primary center of evangelism, which is a local congregation. The congregation should live by the true story and center their life in the continual remembering and relating of the true story, and meditating on it and expounding it in its relation to contemporary events so that contemporary events are truly understood, and in sharing in the sacrament by which we are incorporated into the dying and rising of Jesus so that we are at the very heart of the story. The congregation that does this becomes the place where the new reality is present with its heart in the praise and adoration of God and in the sharing of the love of God among the members and in the wider society. And here, of course, an immense amount depends upon the leadership given through preaching, pastoral encouragement, and public action by those called to ministry in the congregation.

3. It will be a major part of the work of such congregations to train and enable members to act as agents of the kingdom in the various sectors of public life where they work. This kind of "frontier" work is very difficult, and although many promising starts have been made during the years since the last

war, there is still much to do. It must become a part of ordinary congregational life that members are enabled to think through and discuss the ways in which their Christian faith impinges on their daily life in their secular work. Here is the place where the real interface between the church and the world, between the new creation and the old, takes place. Here is where there ought to be a discernible difference in behavior between those who live by the old story and those who live by the story the Bible tells. It ought at many points to lead to differences in behavior, to dissent from current practice, to questioning. And this, of course, will be the place where the counterquestions arise. The Christian will be asked, "Why do you do this? Why do you behave like this?" Here is where the true evangelistic dialogue begins. At the present it is very rare to find this kind of situation because the churches have so largely accepted relegation to the private sector, leaving the public sector to be controlled by the other story.

4. From this it follows that it will also be the task of the local congregation to equip members to enter into this dialogue, to explain the Christian story and its bearing on daily life. And of course the explanation will not be complete without the invitation to become part of the community that lives by the other story and to learn there what it means to do so. Here is where the call to conversion comes, but it is not only a call addressed to the heart and the will, and not only concerned with personal and domestic life; it is also a call addressed to the mind, a call to a radically different way of seeing things, including all the things that make up daily life in the secular world.

5. If this approach is right, evangelism is not just the call to personal conversion, although it is that. It is not just a program for church growth, although it is that also. It is not just preaching, although it is that, and it is not just action for changing society, although it is that too. It is not a program for the reestablishment of the *Corpus Christianum* in Europe with the church in the supreme condition. Most certainly it is not that. But I believe it is possible to hope for and to work for something different — a Europe (a "common European home") that is a Christian society, not in the sense that it is ruled by the church, and not in the sense that everyone is a Christian, but in another sense, which I would indicate as follows. It is possible to envision a society in which Christians have engaged so seriously over several decades with the consequences of the Enlightenment (good and bad) and with the kind of society that has developed at the end of the twentieth century that those who achieve the highest standards of excellence in all the sectors of public life — politics, industry, learning, and the arts — may be shaped in their public work by the Christian story. Then the worship of the Triune God as he is made known to us in Jesus may again be the focus of ordinary life in our towns and villages.

Regardless of whether that is in the purpose of God for our continent, the main point is quite simple. We are entrusted with good news, the news that God reigns. That must be the starting point of all our thinking, and our evangelism will be an overflow of that joyful faith. Who knows, perhaps God has in store for our poor old secularized Europe a new birth of faith in the twenty-first century.

PART TWO

Biblical and Historical Sources for the Study of Evangelism

For the study of evangelism to have integrity it must be established upon solid biblical foundations and students of the church's mission must develop acute sensitivities with regard to historical contexts. A failure to take biblical and historical sources seriously can lead to truncated or deficient understandings of the mission of the church and its evangelistic ministry. There is ample evidence demonstrating how this has happened in the past. Critical, theological reflection upon the relationship between evangelistic practice and these particular sources demands much of the scholar and the community of faith. This kind of serious reflection is only in its beginning stages.

One of the purposes of this volume, therefore, is to encourage such dialogue. Interdisciplinary conversation that involves biblical exegetes, historians, and practitioners entails the development of relationships that have not always been natural. But the application of new hermeneutical lenses and methodologies to the study of evangelism engenders excitement with the creation of new perspectives and paradigms. Ideally, the construction of such a scholarly infrastructure builds upon itself dialectically.

A wide range of materials has been published over the years seeking to relate the Bible to evangelism and mission in one way or another. Some do little more than proof-text a particular vision of evangelism or seek to authenticate a peculiar understanding of mission. Some of this material, coming mostly out of American or European contexts, perpetuates unhealthy attitudes that are patronistic at best and imperialistic at worst. Still other works are limited by the narrowness of their scope historically or culturally. Over against the plethora of works attempting to interface biblical and evangelistic studies (albeit of mixed quality), historical analyses are rare indeed. It is virtually impossible to locate a "history of evangelism" per se. This deficiency is certainly linked to ambiguities and inconsistencies in language related to evangelism and mission. Regardless, it is not too much to claim that the "historical study" of evangelism has hardly begun. Until very recently, few studies have provided a depth of critical reflection informed by serious biblical/exegetical and historical/theological inquiry.

The emergence of the study of evangelism, alongside a whole spectrum of other ministry practices, we would like to argue, represents one of the greatest hopes for the resuscitation of genuine Christianity in the Western world and the United States in particular. Quick-fix remedies may ease the symptomatic sting of decline, but these will not address the deeper pathologies of the Christian community. Much of the difficulty faced by contemporary American mainline churches related to evangelism/mission can be better addressed through the rediscovery and careful study of biblical practices and better understood by means of attentiveness to the historical narrative, providing insight into the contemporary global context of the faith.

The essays in this section contribute to this expanding conversation between evangelists/missiologists and biblical/historical scholars. George R. Hunsberger, a professor of missiology at Western Theological Seminary, seeks to expand our understanding of evangelism by examining the traditional commissioning texts. He argues that Jesus' final words in the Gospels and at the beginning of Acts are not so much a "commission" to be obeyed as they are a "warrant" affirming the evangelistic mission in which the disciples already find themselves engaged. Building on the scholarship of other thoughtful scholars such as David J. Bosch, Darrell L. Guder, and Lesslie Newbigin, he identifies two primary problems in a traditional approach to these biblical texts, Matthew 28 in particular. First, by viewing the "Great Commission" as a command, obedience becomes the driving force of evangelism. Hunsberger challenges this command-and-obedience rationale for evangelism, pointing rather to the way in which evangelistic practice is not so much an assignment to be fulfilled as it is an identity, a promise, a gift to be received. Second, he questions modern reappropriations of the Great Commission, captive as they often are to Western notions of conquest and cultural dominance. Over against these misconceptions, and drawing upon the whole tenor of Scripture, he elevates the biblical concept of evangelism as it relates to the reign of God. Since God's rule is a new reality received and entered, not built or spread, in Hunsberger's view, he reconceives evangelism as companionship, the gospel as something given away, and evangelistic community as a company of those transformed through word and deed.

The biblical foundation established by Hunsberger squares fully with David Bosch's monumental exposition of Matthew 28:16-20. In his original article, after examining the literary form of the text, the missionary context in which it was written, and the relation of the Great Commission to the gospel as a whole, Bosch provides a detailed exegesis of this critical passage. The excerpt reprinted here focuses on the final two verses of the pericope (19-20). Bosch argues against contemporary theologies of mission that fixate on the verb "to go," thereby deflecting appropriate attention from the structural center of "making disciples." The twin practices of baptizing and teaching function as indissoluble aspects of this focal disciple-making task, rather than being viewed as sequential approaches to Christian assimilation. His guidelines for the structure of mission, including the biblical emphases of contextuality, servanthood, incarnation, and grace, among other important themes, inform evangelistic practice in the world today.

Walter L. Liefeld, a New Testament scholar and Lukan specialist associated with Trinity Evangelical Divinity School, combines biblical and historical studies in his examination of the place and role of women in the evangelistic ministries of the early church. Exploring one of the most neglected sources for the study of evangelism — the ministry of women — he argues that from its earliest days Christianity has been characterized by active female involvement in this ecclesial practice. Positing a holistic understanding of evangelism in the New Testament period, he elevates the proclamation of Anna, the testimony of the Samaritan woman, the confession of Martha, as well as the more overt ministries of Priscilla, Tryphena and Tryphosa, Phoebe, Lydia, and Syntyche. While acknowledging the complexity of the contextual dynamics and the limitations of evidence, Liefeld surveys women's contributions in the post-apostolic church through the fourth century, highlighting the remarkable witness of martyrs such as Vibia Perpetua and her slave Felicitas.

Bill J. Leonard's examination of "Evangelism and Contemporary American Life" describes those factors which have influenced evangelistic practice in this particular historical and cultural setting, namely, pluralism, revivalism, nationalism, and fundamentalism. This essay will help the North American reader, in particular, to understand the origins of popular views about evangelism that tended to dominate evangelical Christianity in the twentieth century. Pluralism, Leonard argues, fosters an aggressive and competitive style of evangelism; revivalism serves as "both the means and the technique for fulfilling the church's call to evangelize the masses"; nationalism illustrates the interconnectedness of Americanization, democracy, and millennialism in the minds of many evangelicals; and fundamentalism emphasizes personal conversion, non-negotiable doctrine, and anti-liberalism. After examining the connection between evangelism as a practice and evangelicalism as a theological orientation, Leonard demonstrates an appreciation for evangelistic practice and its development (and cherished place) in American culture, but also challenges the myopic vision and cultural arrogance that undergirds evangelism in this peculiar, albeit influential, setting.

Dana L. Robert, Truman Collins Professor of World Christianity and History of Mission at Boston University School of Theology, helps us turn the corner historically into the twenty-first century. One of the few in this volume that does not deal explicitly with the question of evangelism, her essay is critical to an understanding of global Christianity as it enters a new millennium. The second half of the twentieth century witnessed a seismic shift in Christian identity away from the Northern Hemisphere toward the South (African, Asian, and Latin American contexts). After examining the political and cultural contexts inherent to this change, Robert weaves a tapestry of emerging Christian movements and identifies some of the challenges posed by the realization of a truly global Christianity. Implications with regard to the concept and practice of evangelism radiate from her incisive study. For example, the crucial role played by indigenous evangelists in the global shift to the South points to the growing importance of contextual attentiveness in the evangelistic task. What will indigenous evangelism look like in the unfolding of the twenty-first century; how will the "interweaving of the warp of a world religion with the woof of local contexts" shape the evangelistic ministry of the church in the years to come?

CHAPTER 5

Is There Biblical Warrant for Evangelism?

George R. Hunsberger

It has become all too common, when attempting to ground evangelism in the New Testament, to resort to what we have called the Great Commission. The commissioning words of Jesus, variously reported at the end of each of the Gospels (Matt. 28:16-20; Mark 16:15-18; Luke 24:45-49; John 24:21-23) and at the beginning of Acts (1:6-8), are taken to be straightforward instructions, sufficient in their clarity to provide a rationale for evangelizing, no matter what the circumstances may be in which the church finds itself. But the need for a rationale — and the kind of rationale needed — is always shaped by the church's location in the social and cultural currents of its time and place, and by its character and life within those currents.

At the present time in North America, we in the churches find ourselves in a place rapidly ceasing to be a "churched culture."[1] Living in a post-Christian and pluralist society has sent shock waves through the psyche of our churches, shaking loose our long-accustomed security in the heritage of Christendom. This has brought us to the point of exploring the terrain in search of an identity beyond that of being merely a "vendor of religious services" for that niche of the population that exercises the private option to seek such services. We are thrust into a search for a sense of our mission in this new time and for the meaning of being witnesses to Christ in it.

The preachments and rationales of the past that do not specifically engage these new circumstances can only fail us. The growing disjuncture between the supposed clarity of Great Commission instructions and the practical behavior of large numbers of church members should alert us to this. In our situation, the instructions turn into an ever amplifying exhorta-

1. Cf. the use of this phrase by Kennon L. Callahan in *Effective Church Leadership* (San Francisco: Harper & Row, 1990).

tion to complete the assigned task. But what follows are either soft and fuzzy responses, in which anything that can be construed as lending influence in the direction of Christ "counts," or programmed schemes for structuring us all into activities that, by their very doing, are envisioned to achieve the task.

All of this is not to suggest that the commissioning words of Jesus have no relevance. It is to say that we must come to them in a new way, questioning what lies behind our tendency to focus on them and our way of seeing them as a rationale for evangelism. In this connection, two major problems present themselves.

(1) The first problem has to do with the way we tend to use the Great Commission as a rationale for evangelism. We appeal to it within a structure of thought oriented toward command and obedience. It is assumed, when we attempt to provide a biblical foundation for evangelism, that this is simply a matter of finding direct commands enjoining us to evangelize. It is further assumed that once such commands are found, evangelism is simply a matter of obedience. The presence of a command is thought to supply sufficient motivation for evangelism, and settling the issue of motivation is taken to be an adequate rationale.

This fails to ask questions about what lies beneath the command. Why was the command given? Why is it proper that, in a world with such a variety of other religious loyalties, we are thus commanded? How does the command make sense for us in Western societies today against the historical backdrop of cultural and religious imperialism? How can it be understood in a day when individual autonomy in matters of belief is asserted as a fundamental right?

More important, there are biblical reasons why our assumptions about a command-and-obedience rationale for evangelism ought to be questioned. In the first place, as missionary theologian Lesslie Newbigin suggests in his reflections on Acts 1:8, Jesus' statement that "you shall be my witnesses" is not so much a command as it is a promise, a promise linked with that of the coming Spirit. Newbigin urges: "Please note that it is a promise, not a command. It is not: 'You must go and be witnesses'; it is 'The Holy Spirit will come, and you will be witnesses.' There is a vast difference between these two."[2] It may be true that Newbigin pushes the grammatical point beyond what is warranted. But it is equally true that he has only touched lightly on a point of fundamental significance. Jesus' "prophetic promise," as Darrell Guder calls it, locates the accent in the text: Being witnesses is not our assignment; it is our identity. "When the Spirit comes to [the disciples] and gives them the gift of power, their very identity will be transformed into that of witnesses. As such, they will carry out the ministry of that witness throughout the world."[3]

That this is an important point is underscored by another of Newbigin's observations, this time on Paul:

> It is, is it not, a striking fact that in all his letters to the churches Paul never urges on them the duty of evangelism. He can rebuke, remind, exhort his readers about faithfulness to Christ in many matters. But he is never found exhorting them to be active in evangelism. . . . Mission, in other words, is gospel and not law; it is the overflow of a great gift, not the carrying of a great burden.[4]

Paul surely envisages that evangelism will continue to take place. He assumes it to be appropriate, given what the gospel is. But he never urges it as a duty. It may be added that neither in Paul's writings nor in any of the other New Testament documents outside the Gospels and the opening verses of Acts is there ever an appeal to Jesus' Great Commission. It might be argued that the reason for all this is that the churches at that time simply found themselves evangelizing spontaneously and therefore needed no exhortation in this regard. Even if this could be proved, which is doubtful, the question with which we are left is not, "How shall we motivate a contemporary church which does not evangelize spontaneously?" but, "Why is evangelizing not now happening as a matter of course?" In light of the twin promises of the Spirit's empowering and the transformation of our identity to be witnesses, the explanation must lie at a deeper level than can be answered by some strong reminder that a command to witness has been given. Something more fundamental to the integrity of the church is at stake.

Accordingly, the first problem with an approach oriented to command-and-obedience, aimed as it is at motivating evangelistic action by a sense of duty, is that this approach mitigates the sense that somehow evangelism ought to be a spontaneous expression, produced by the Spirit and born of the overflowing of what comes from knowing the good news. As Robert Henderson has put it, "When a person, or a congregation, understands and has experienced the joyous news of the kingdom of God, evangelization is natural and spontaneous. People cannot keep such news to themselves."[5] The

2. Lesslie Newbigin, *Mission in Christ's Way* (Geneva: WCC, 1987), p. 16.

3. Darrell Guder, *Be My Witnesses* (Grand Rapids: Eerdmans, 1985), p. 32.

4. Newbigin, *Mission in Christ's Way,* p. 21.

5. Robert T. Henderson, *Joy to the World: Spreading the Good News of the Kingdom* (Grand Rapids: Zondervan, 1991), p. 131.

use of command-and-obedience as a rationale for evangelism thwarts the expectation of spontaneity, which is born of promise, not requirement.

(2) The second major problem with our use of the Great Commission as the principal text for establishing our evangelistic mission is that its use for this purpose is a relatively recent development. Until the advent of the "modern missionary movement" and the important stimulus provided by William Carey in 1792, this text did not play this particular role. In fact, prior to Carey's reappropriation of the text, it had been interpreted in a way that did not urge explicit missionary obedience. The commission was understood to have been made to the first-century apostles, and they were believed to have accomplished it by going to all of the then-known world. Carey dared to challenge this notion in his tract entitled *An Enquiry into the Obligations of Christians to Use Means for the Conversion of the Heathen.* He argued that if the command to baptize and the promise of Christ's presence are still in force, then the commission to preach in all nations must also be binding.[6]

Although the modern missionary movement found support in a number of texts (David Bosch identifies Acts 16:9; Matt. 24:14; and John 10:10 as crucial ones), the chief text to which it appealed is Matthew 28:18-20. By the end of the nineteenth century, this became increasingly the case. Obedience to this final command of Jesus became "a kind of last line of defense" against challenges being made to the missionary cause.[7]

Bosch's major contribution in his magisterial work *Transforming Mission* is that he identifies the ways in which the church's understanding of its mission in various historical periods was shaped by the cultural currents of the period and place. He shows, for example, how John 3:16 is characteristic of the patristic understanding of mission, Luke 14:23 of the medieval Roman Catholic missionary efforts, and Romans 1:16-18 of the Protestant Reformation period.[8] In the case of the modern period, for which the Great Commission and the emphasis on obedience constituted the heart of the missionary paradigm, the major motifs in the church's thinking reflected the influence of the Enlightenment. The essential features of this influence include

> the undisputed primacy of reason, the separation between subject and object, the substitution of the cause-effect scheme for belief in purpose, the infatuation with progress, the unsolved tension between "fact" and

6. Cf. Harry R. Boer, *Pentecost and Missions* (Grand Rapids: Eerdmans, 1961), pp. 16-18.

7. David J. Bosch, *Transforming Mission: Paradigm Shifts in Theology of Mission* (Maryknoll, N.Y.: Orbis, 1991), pp. 340-41.

8. Bosch, *Transforming Mission*, p. 339.

> "value," the confidence that every problem and puzzle can be solved, and the idea of the emancipated, autonomous individual.[9]

In summary, Bosch concludes that

> The entire Western missionary movement of the past three centuries emerged from the matrix of the Enlightenment. On the one hand, it spawned an attitude of tolerance to all people and a relativistic attitude toward belief of any kind: on the other, it gave birth to Western superiority feelings and prejudice.[10]

Newbigin points out that the difficulty with post-Enlightenment use of the Great Commission was that the latter "could seem to validate a sort of triumphalist style of mission that accorded all too easily with the political and economic expansion of the European powers during this period, an expansion with which missions were (inevitably) so much connected."[11] An easy identification of missionary endeavor with the pride of enlightenment and progress lacks the critical principle for differentiating evangelism from an activity that merely underwrites the reigning values of the North American ethos. It fails to shape an evangelism capable of distinctive witness in a pluralist environment.

At a time when the church in North America finds that its social role has changed and that it is no longer the guardian of spirit and morality for the democratic experiment and that its faith is no longer the privileged option for understanding ultimate meanings and loyalties, it is essential that it acquire a new sense of what it is to evangelize. We in the church will need a new sense of missional identity that is more than the achievement of a mandated task. And we need to develop a missional lifestyle that does not aim at conquest and cultural dominance. Any proposed biblical grounding for evangelism must address these concerns if it is to have force and relevance.

In light of the problems attending our traditional way of interpreting Great Commission texts, we may imagine that it would be easiest simply to dismiss them and to look elsewhere for biblical grounding. But, in the end, they must be dealt with, no matter where we begin. It is better to explore whether they may be reappropriated in a way that is both truer to their original function and more useful to our present needs.

To explore the function of the Great Commission texts in the New Tes-

9. Bosch, *Transforming Mission,* p. 342.
10. Bosch, *Transforming Mission,* p. 344.
11. Newbigin, *Mission in Christ's Way,* p. 32.

tament is the place to begin. Before any of these texts had been written, the earliest church was already accustomed to sharing the "good news" with people in its social world. Certainly, this custom was not disconnected from the memory of Jesus' words, but it is far from certain that Jesus' words functioned as a command. Could it be that Jesus' words were intended for a different pastoral purpose?

Harry Boer concludes from his study of the early church's evangelizing behavior, as depicted in the New Testament, that "there is no evidence that consciousness of the Great Commission constituted an element in their motivation. . . . [T]here is no ground to believe that awareness of the Great Commission played a role in launching the Church on her missionary labors."[12]

Boer does not go far enough.[13] We must ask: If these texts did not launch the church on its missionary labors and did not provide it with conscious motivation, then what role did they play when they appeared in the Gospels and in Acts at the time they did? The central proposal of this essay is that we answer that question this way: *In the reporting of Jesus' final words in the Gospels and Acts we should see not a command for the early churches to obey but an affirmation of what they found themselves doing.* These texts are "evangelizing warrant," not "Great Commission." They do not mandate obedience to a mission; they validate the experience of being engaged in mission. Evangelism is not here required but authorized.

The predictive tone in Luke's two accounts is instructive. We have already noted the promissory character of Acts 1:8. In Luke 24, the missional warrant comes as an anticipation of the fulfillment of things long intended and already indicated in the Scriptures.

> Then he opened their minds to understand the Scriptures, and he said to them, "Thus it is written, that the Messiah is to suffer and to rise again from the dead on the third day, and that repentance and forgiveness of sins is to be proclaimed in his name to all nations, beginning from Jerusalem." (Luke 24:45-47)

Perceptions that, for the disciples, had been a long time coming are here expanded. The Synoptic Gospels share a structure that first shows how the

12. Boer, *Pentecost and Missions,* pp. 43-44.

13. Mortimer Arias, in his otherwise fine commentary on the varying forms of what he prefers to call the "last commission," appears also to have missed the importance of critiquing the structure of command-and-obedience assumed in words like "commission," "mandate," and "task." See Mortimer Arias and Alan Johnson, *The Great Commission: Biblical Models for Evangelism* (Nashville: Abingdon, 1992), pp. 11-16.

disciples gradually came to grasp the fact that Jesus was the Messiah. Their confession to this effect marked the turning point at which Jesus "began to show his disciples that he must go to Jerusalem and undergo great suffering at the hands of the elders and chief priests and scribes, and be killed, and on the third day be raised" (Matt. 16:21; cf. Mark 8:31 and Luke 9:22). For the disciples to accept this seemed impossible, and even after the resurrection Jesus still helped them grasp this point (cf. Luke 24:25-27). Now, as Jesus underscores it again, something new is added. Once the disciples have understood that the Messiah must suffer and rise from the dead, they will need to learn where all this will lead: It is written that "repentance and forgiveness of sins is to be proclaimed in his name to all nations" (Luke 24:46-47).

This prediction will have been no easier for the disciples to grasp than the other points in Jesus' curriculum. It would be naïve to assume that the disciples immediately understood it and went out to fulfill it. Rather, this prediction stands as the unfinished story that precipitated for Luke the writing of his sequel, Acts. Luke begins Acts with a restatement of Jesus' prediction because he intended to show how the early church learned in stages what this meant. It learned the latter as the Spirit fashioned the disciples into witnesses to the risen Christ among all the nations. Acts was written, as was the concluding part of Luke's Gospel, as a way to remind the church later in its history of Jesus' earlier prediction. The church, from its later vantage point, could remember and understand. It had lived its way into it. The memory of Jesus' prediction affirmed and authorized what became true for the church. Whatever fears or second thoughts had emerged for it, whatever distance it might have felt as a second generation of witnesses, here was the warrant inherited from Jesus. This is the way things were meant by God to be.

If these texts in which we discover how Jesus envisioned and anticipated the future mission of the church are present in the Gospels and Acts essentially as warrant and not command, then we may rightly search for, and expect to find, texts in the rest of the New Testament that display the ways in which such a sense of warrant took shape and root in the perceptions of the church and its leaders. We are not bound to look only for texts that bolster a sense of evangelistic duty but are free to find whatever texts respond to the questions that most press themselves on us in a pluralist environment. Is our impulse to evangelize, to announce that the reign of God is present and coming in Jesus Christ, legitimate? In a sea of opinions and proposals about the meaning and direction of things, is it proper to tell what we know about Jesus as though he is the power of creation and the word of truth? In the face of such questions, a search for warrant opens a new way for grounding evangelism in the whole fabric of the New Testament, not just in a few command-giving passages. It enables us to approach biblical foundations from more than a motivational viewpoint and in full view of our culture's critique. It allows us to explore what warrant exists for the fact that, in the church, evangelism continues to "happen," that somehow the Holy Spirit is the instigator, and that evangelism takes place as the overflow of the gospel among people captivated by the joy of the good news.

This way of exploring the New Testament needs more thorough treatment than I can provide here. But we can trace several themes so as to indicate the potential in such an approach. These themes show the kind of rationale for evangelism that lies implicit within the emerging mission of the early church and is embedded within the warranting and predictive words of Jesus prior to his ascension. Three themes will occupy our attention: the evangelizing attitude present in the pulse of the gospel itself; the evangelists' approach to people of a variety of cultures; and the modes of articulation experienced and expected in the early churches.

(1) At the center of the message Jesus proclaimed was the announcement of the reign of God. This theme has been increasingly recovered in recent reflections on the evangelizing mission of the church.[14] Still, as the phrase comes into the casual parlance of the church, it picks up untested assumptions about our relationship to God's reign. On the one hand, the reign of God becomes something we "extend." Especially among those with evangelical agendas, we imagine ourselves as those responsible to spread or expand the reign of God. On the other hand, those more concerned with the social implications of the gospel tend to speak about "building" the reign of God. Mission then has to do with establishing or fashioning the reign of God on earth.

There are problems with both assumptions. In the case of the first (to extend), the reign of God is conceived to be all "in here" and the church's mission is to be its CEOs, its sales promoters to extend it out to include more and more people. In the case of the second assumption (to build), the reign of God becomes a social project that we accomplish. It is conceived to be all "out there" awaiting construction by its architects, contractors, and carpenters.

It is noteworthy, however, that neither the expression "to extend" nor "to build" is ever used in the Bible to indicate the way we should see our responsibility regarding the reign of God. We find a parable about how the

14. Three books that are most helpful in this regard are Henderson, *Joy to the World;* Mortimer Arias, *Announcing the Reign of God: Evangelization and the Subversive Memory of Jesus* (Philadelphia: Fortress, 1984); and William J. Abraham, *The Logic of Evangelism* (Grand Rapids: Eerdmans, 1989). See also Monica Hill, ed., *Entering the Kingdom: A Fresh Look at Conversion* (Kent, U.K.: MARC Europe, 1984).

kingdom extends itself (Mark 4:30-32), but it is never said that we are to extend it. We find construction imagery having to do with the building of a congregation (1 Cor. 3:9-15), but the church is never equated with the reign of God, and we are never told to go out and build it.

What, then, are the appropriate verbs to use? In the Gospels, the most repeated and emphatic verbs directing our response to the reign of God are "to receive" and "to enter." They come, at times, intertwined: "Truly I say to you, whoever does not receive the kingdom of God like a child shall not enter it" (Luke 18:17). These verbs represent two image clusters that, taken together, provide a portrait of the identity of a Christian community and the stature of its mission. These clusters may be summarized as follows:

The reign of God may be said to be a gift we receive. It is something given (Luke 12:32). It is something that can be possessed (Luke 6:20; Matt. 5:9; Mark 10:14), but because it is yet coming, it is described as an inheritance to be possessed in the end (Matt. 5:5, 25:34; James 2:5; 1 Cor. 6:9-10; 15:50).

The reign of God may also be said to be a realm we enter. It meets us as God's welcome and invites us to come in. It is both a place to inhabit (Matt. 5:19; Col. 1:13) and a place yet coming that is to be inhabited (Matt. 7:21; 25:21, 23; 2 Peter 1:11). People can be "not far" from it (Mark 12:34). For some, it will be "very hard" to enter (Mark 10:23; Luke 18:24-25; Matt. 19:23-24). Some, in fact, "will not" enter at all (Matt. 5:20).

In a Christian consciousness shaped by these two images, there are serious dangers. On the one hand, there is the danger of presumption in so claiming to "possess" the reign of God that it becomes ours and not God's. On the other hand, there is the danger of pride in thinking ourselves to be securely "in." But it is by means of these very images that Jesus warns of these dangers: "I tell you, the kingdom of God will be taken away from you and given to a nation producing the fruits of it" (Matt. 21:43). "Truly, I say to you, the tax collectors and the harlots go into the kingdom of God before you" (Matt. 21:31).

It is in the dynamic present tense of these verbs "to receive" and "to enter" that there exists the greatest potential for a new way to conceive of our evangelism. The letter to the Hebrews uses the language instructively: "For we who have believed enter that rest. . . . Strive to enter that rest" (Heb. 4:3, 11). And again, "Therefore let us be grateful [since we are] receiving a kingdom that cannot be shaken" (Heb. 12:28). Here is a portrait of our conversion and its ongoing nature. We are those who, having been offered God's gift and God's welcome, daily receive and enter into the reign of God. This means that evangelism is construed in terms of companionship. We walk alongside others to whom the same gift is extended and to whom God offers the same welcome. We invite them to join us in the joy of daily receiving and entering into the reign of God. Evangelism, then, is not "to" or "at" people, it is "with" and "alongside" them. Evangelism as church growth or membership recruitment too easily serves our own personal or institutional interests. Evangelism consists rather in offering the gift of God and making welcome those whom God welcomes. The posture of invitation and initiation into a shared lifestyle then displaces the image of conquest and dominance. Evangelism in this posture is warranted by the nature of the gospel itself.[15]

(2) "If you wish to find the gospel, you must lose it." This loose and twisted version of Jesus' words may in fact provide the essential clue for understanding the struggle through which the church passed in its early years. At every point, the urging of the Spirit and the divinely appointed occasion of the moment pushed the church into an evangelizing beyond its understanding and challenged its assumptions about appropriate forms of belief, conversion, and worship. The first encounter for a church was with cosmopolitan Jews at Pentecost and then with Samaritans in the surrounding area. The conversions of an Ethiopian traveler, a god-fearing Roman soldier, and a diverse Gentile community in Antioch brought increasing pressure to bear on a church trying to figure out what it meant for people of a diversity of cultures to become captivated by the risen Lord. Jesus was very Jewish, but the mission into which the church had been thrust began to burst the wineskins with which these Jewish Christians were accustomed. Gradually, they became convinced that this was in fact what made their mission so universal and compelling.

Paul was the figure pushed to the front of these developments. His own sense of freedom from the law led him to the affirmation: "There is no longer Jew or Greek, there is no longer slave or free, there is no longer male or female; for all of you are one in Christ Jesus" (Gal. 3:28). But in an important sense, Paul also believed a variation on that language: "In Christ there is both Jew and Greek, there is both slave and free, there is both male and female." That is to say, Paul's affirmation of the essential oneness across hues of race, culture, class, and gender depended upon his affirmation of the integrity of the varieties of culture and heritage. Paul fought for the rights of Gentiles not to be forced into a

15. William Abraham has caught the heart of this approach in his book *The Logic of Evangelism.* He describes evangelism "as that set of intentional activities which is governed by the goal of initiating people into the kingdom of God for the first time" (p. 95), conceiving conversion as entry into the kingdom. Because he has seen the "enter" side but not the "receive" side, his approach may too easily identify entering the kingdom with entering the church. To keep both verbs in view would provide a corrective. For a fresh invitational approach, see Raymond Fung, *The Isaiah Vision: An Ecumenical Strategy for Congregational Evangelism* (Geneva: WCC, 1992).

Jewish mold. His experience of the grace of God was that it always moved beyond the ways in which it had thus far been grasped and embodied.

Nowhere does Paul more clearly articulate his missionary approach than in 1 Corinthians 9:14-23. Here he affirms that we only find the gospel, we only participate in it, in our evangelism (v. 23). And evangelism consists in losing the gospel, giving it away. Paul counted it to be his greatest reward to offer the gospel free of charge (v. 18). His greatest freedom in the gospel was to make himself a slave to all (v. 19). His greatest success for the gospel was found in becoming weak (v. 22). Paul's approach was in sharp contrast to the tendencies present in the Corinthian church at that time, tendencies not uncommon for the church in any time or place. The church there had impulses that cut the nerve of a missionary gospel and prevented them from being a missionary congregation. These people held the gospel in their grasp, in knowledge and strength. Their grip on the gospel was so tight that they refused to permit other responses to it or expressions of it. Others had to follow their particular leader (chaps. 1-3), exercise their spiritual gift (chaps. 12-14), and share their knowledge about meat offered to idols (chap. 8). At the height of contradiction, they required that others share their freedom! In other words, the Corinthians held a monopoly on the gospel. It had become domesticated in their hands.

Mission in such circumstances becomes religious egoism. Evangelism becomes recruitment. Paul's assertion that he offers the gospel free of charge draws the contrast. Is the gospel something required of people at the gate, or is it to be given away to people outside the gate? Are we to grab people to the gospel, or open up the gospel to them? Does the gospel bring people to us, or does it join us to other people?

Paul's own policy of identification with those among whom he offered the gospel free of charge opposes the tendency to restrict the gospel to a single cultural form. Of course, there is always the matter of the truth and integrity of the gospel; but this Paul preserved, while exhibiting his freedom to be enslaved to other cultural forms and styles. To those under the law he became like one under the law (although he was sure that in certain senses he was no longer "under" it). To those without God's law, he lived as they did (although he knew that he lived under Christ's law and dared not violate that). Paul's cultural identification was not uncritical, but he refined the path of cultural domination and imposition. He was willing to give the gospel away to new possessors of it and to lose it to their new styles, responses, and definitions. There he expected to see it sparkle, startle, surprise, and shine.

Paul was not unaware that there is a certain weakness in this strategy. But it is this very weakness that most validates the evangelizing mission of the church. We can be no less vulnerable than were those who brought the gospel to us and released it into our hands, or no less vulnerable than God has been to offer the divine reign as a gift and a welcome. For us as for Paul, it is in the weakness of giving the gospel away and losing our grasp on it as its sole possessors that we participate in it most fully. As we see something in the response of another that reveals our own blind spots, we hear again its call to repentance. As we watch the gospel affirm acceptance to others with idiosyncrasies of their own, we know more deeply that we, too, share in the gospel's accepting grace. In other words, we become evangelized by those to whom we give the gospel.

To Paul's way of thinking, particularity is not alien to the missionary impulse. It is the path along which the gospel travels as each receives from another the witness of the Spirit.[16] The gospel, which is always expressed within the terms of some particular culture, is intended for the peoples of all the nations. A consciousness of these cultural dynamics and an approach to people that envisions giving the gospel away to them are crucial for a warranted form of evangelism in our current pluralist environment. Lamin Sanneh has put it well that "[f]or all of us pluralism can be a rock of stumbling, but for God it is the cornerstone of the universal design."[17]

(3) In the New Testament literature, we observe Paul and we know that we see an evangelist at work. What he says about evangelizing is complemented by the ways we see him at work. We also catch the pulse of the work of the four "evangelists" in the written Gospels they have given us. The nature of the literature is such that these will be foremost as we explore the New Testament. Yet our perspectives will be skewed if we do not take note of the evangelists that did not write letters or Gospels. It is to the specific congregations that I refer. Clues about them may be fainter, but the substructure of living congregations bearing faith, love, and hope provides the foundational witness of the first-century church.

16. It is one of the major contributions of Lesslie Newbigin that he has fashioned a theology of cultural plurality that sees in our election to be bearers of the blessing the critical feature that unites particularity and universality. This is expounded most fully as the central theme of *Open Secret* (Grand Rapids: Eerdmans, 1978). For an exposition of his view, see George R. Hunsberger, "The Missionary Significance of the Biblical Doctrine of Election as a Foundation for a Theology of Cultural Plurality in the Missiology of J. E. Lesslie Newbigin," Ph.D. diss., Princeton Theological Seminary, 1987.

17. Lamin Sanneh, *Translating the Message: The Missionary Impact on Culture* (Maryknoll, N.Y.: Orbis, 1989), p. 27. Other important books on evangelism that attempt to take pluralism seriously include Lesslie Newbigin, *The Gospel in a Pluralist Society* (Grand Rapids: Eerdmans, 1989), and Donald C. Posterski, *Reinventing Evangelism: New Strategies for Presenting Christ in Today's World* (Downers Grove, Ill.: InterVarsity, 1989).

Especially intriguing is the portrait Paul gives of the newly formed community of believers at Thessalonica. Paul wrote 1 Thessalonians not many months after he first visited there and they first heard the gospel. Already, Paul affirms, they have proved to be imitators of him and his companions, who brought the gospel not only in word but in power, in the Holy Spirit, with full conviction, and with personal integrity (1 Thess. 1:5-6). In their willingness to believe openly, even against the pressure of direct persecution, the Thessalonians have already grown to be imitators of Jesus (1:6) and of the churches of God in Judea (2:14). In so short a time they have become examples of what believers are like (1:7); their faith — and the word of the Lord with it — has become known across their own province and the adjoining one (1:8). What has so profoundly demonstrated their faith is the visible change in their patterns of living: They have turned away from loyalty to idols, they serve a living and true God, and they live in hope, waiting for the risen Son of God to come from heaven at the time of justice (1:9-10). Of course, in the letter as a whole Paul matches these affirmations with encouragement to the Thessalonians to grow in these traits that already characterize them. All is not finished, but even at this embryonic point in the life of their church, their evangelizing quality is most evident.

It will not do to drive a wedge between actions and words and claim that Paul only affirms the lifestyle of the Thessalonians as though that were somehow sufficient. What Paul affirms about them could not have been observed had they been a silent group. The new orientation of their lives and the hope they held must certainly have found expression in language and confession. Word and deed were bound together in the way the congregation demonstrated — in living, embodied form — what the gospel is.

Whatever else may be said about modes of articulation appropriate to the gospel's announcement, embodiment is the essential feature of them all. Paul always invited his hearers to test his words against what they experienced him to be (e.g., 1 Cor. 2:1-5; 2 Cor. 1:12; 4:1-3; 6:3-10; 1 Thess. 2:1-8). In 1 Peter, the encouragement given to the churches rests on the same foundation: "Always be ready to make a defense to anyone who demands from you an accounting for the hope that is in you" (3:15). The assumption is that the presence of such a hope is an observable thing, demonstrable to public view by the community that embodies the gospel.

We are talking here about something much more substantial than the emphasis in evangelism training circles several decades ago. Then, the emphasis was more on encouraging consistent moral behavior because, otherwise, the gospel would be invalidated by violations of the accepted norms of the society everyone assumed the gospel affirms. Now, however, when such a correspondence of values no longer exists and announcing and living the gospel proposes a very different, alternate style of believing and living, demonstrating the gospel in life is not merely for the sake of keeping the way clear for a hearing of the gospel. The demonstration itself shows what the gospel is about. The congregation is the "hermeneutic of the gospel," the only lens through which people see and interpret what the gospel is about and how it may be embraced.[18] Donald Posterski stresses this when he says that in our modern pluralist setting "the gospel will be perceived as a feasible alternate when those who do not know God have some positive, personal experiences with people who do know him. Modern Christians have both the privilege of and the potential for becoming spiritual meaning-makers."[19]

A variety of modes of articulation of the gospel commend themselves as biblically warranted and contextually relevant today. One is the mode of the "witness," one who testifies on the witness stand in a trial and attests to what cannot be known in any other way.[20] Another is the "journalist," one who reports the public news that the reign of God is at hand.[21] Another model is that of "docent," in the sense of the way museums use docents. The evangelist as docent is one who interprets the meaning of what is experienced in the world. Finally, we may add the "rhetor," who makes the case that the gospel reveals the meaning of life and who urges the appropriate response. But it is required of all of these that they be grounded in an evangelistic commitment to a living embodiment of the gospel in tangible communities of faith, love, and hope.[22]

It is essential to the gospel that the gift of the reign of God and God's welcome to it not be withheld from but be genuinely offered to the world. It is essential to the church's mission that the gospel be given away to all to be embraced by them in their cultural particularity. And it is essential to the church's identity that it be a living embodiment of the gospel, demonstrating by word and deed what it means to believe and hope in the gospel. Taken together, these facets of the fabric of the New Testament link up with Jesus' warranting words to show how fundamentally valid and indispensable is the witnessing character and role of the church. The Spirit's persistent action to make the church such a witness is the confirming testimony.

18. Cf. Newbigin, *The Gospel in a Pluralist Society,* pp. 222-33.

19. Posterski, *Reinventing Evangelism,* p. 32.

20. Lesslie Newbigin, *The Light Has Come: An Exposition of the Fourth Gospel* (Grand Rapids: Eerdmans, 1982), p. 14.

21. David Lowes Watson, "The Church as Journalist: Evangelism in the Context of the Local Church in the United States," *International Review of Mission* 72 (1983): 57-74.

22. Darrell Guder's stress on an incarnational understanding of mission provides a valuable resource at this point. See his *Be My Witnesses.*

CHAPTER 6

The Structure of Mission: An Exposition of Matthew 28:16-20

David J. Bosch

The Great Commission in Matthew

The Great Commission in Christian Mission

The so-called Great Commission, particularly in its Matthean form (Matt. 28:19-20), has always been a powerful inspiration to Protestant missions. Truth to tell, there has been a tendency in more recent years, at least in some circles, to substitute Luke 4:16-20 for Matthew 28:16-20. Most evangelicals, however, continue to regard Matthew 28:18-20 as the major — if not sole — motivation for mission. Those who do so can at least look back upon a longer history than those who turn to Jesus' words in Nazareth (Luke 4:16-20) as the key missionary passage in Scripture. Matthew 28:16-20 has for many centuries played a crucial role in this regard. This creates an urgent need for a scholarly study of the history of the exegesis of this passage in relation to the church's worldwide mission.

In the early centuries of the Christian church the conviction developed that the apostles had subdivided the world among themselves and had completed the missionary task (see, for example, the Acts of Thomas and Eusebius).[1] Although Luther dismissed this as a fable, neither he nor Calvin really managed to break new ground, since they argued that the commission was binding on the apostles only and that the special office of apostle had been discontinued.[2] Philip Nicolai (who died in 1607) managed to "prove" that the Great Commission had indeed already been accom-

1. Gerhard Rosenkranz, *Die christliche Mission, Geschichte und Theologie* (Munich: Christian Kaiser Verlag, 1977), p. 40.

2. Harry R. Boer, *Pentecost and Missions* (London: Lutterworth, 1961), pp. 18-20.

plished.[3] When Justinian von Welz in 1664 published a plea in which he advocated, on the basis of Matthew 28:18-20, a worldwide missionary enterprise, his views were dismissed by Johann H. Ursinus as advocating interference with God's plan for the nations.[4]

William Carey was the first to make inroads into the prevalent apathy about mission in his famous *An Enquiry into the Obligations of Christians to Use Means for the Conversion of the Heathens* (1792). Carey's logic was simple: If the commission to make disciples of all nations were restricted to the apostles, then the command to baptize (Matt. 28:19) and the promise of Christ's abiding presence (Matt. 28:20) should also be subjected to this limitation! Carey won the argument, and a large-scale Protestant missionary enterprise was launched from Europe and North America. Ever since, it has been customary to base missions on the Great Commission. The Constitution of the Evangelical Foreign Missions Association in the USA explicitly affirms obedience to the Great Commission as the primary motive for mission.[5] Students who applied to attend the Student Consultation on Frontier Missions in Edinburgh in October 1980 had to sign a declaration which read, in part, "I will make the Great Commission the commanding purpose of my life for the rest of my life." These are but two of many examples of the primacy still enjoyed by the Great Commission in contemporary missionary thinking. It is indeed, in some circles, regarded as the *Magna Charta* of mission.

A Command to Be Obeyed?

Coupled with this, one frequently finds a rather one-sided emphasis on *obedience* as a motive for mission. This, too, goes back to Carey, as can be deduced from his use of the word "obligation" in the title of his 1792 publication. In addition, expressions such as "we have to obey," "it becomes us," "it behoves us," "it is incumbent upon us" occur frequently in his *Enquiry.*

Whereas such an emphasis was excusable or at least understandable in Carey's time, given the then prevailing attitude to mission, it is hardly justifiable in our day. Yet it frequently persists, and is, of course, largely due to the fact that Matthew 28:18-20 is often interpreted as a *command.* In 1890 the great Dutch theologian Abraham Kuyper declared that "mission flows from

3. Rosenkranz, *Die christliche Mission,* pp. 151-53.

4. Rosenkranz, *Die christliche Mission,* pp. 161-63.

5. Roger C. Bassham, *Mission Theology 1948-1975, Years of Worldwide Creative Tension: Ecumenical, Evangelical, and Roman Catholic* (Pasadena: William Carey Library, 1979), p. 182.

God's sovereignty, not from his love or compassion"; "all mission is obedience to God's command, and the content of the message not an invitation but a charge, an order."[6] Even John Stott said in the opening words of his treatment of the Great Commission at the Berlin 1966 World Congress on Evangelism, "In the last resort, we engage in evangelism today not because we want to or because we choose to or because we like to, but because we have been told to. The Church is under orders. The risen Lord has commanded us to 'go,' to 'preach,' to 'make disciples,' and that is enough for us."[7] Similarly, in Roman Catholic missiology the "mandatory character" of mission as an enterprise of the ecclesiastical hierarchy was traditionally identified as the main characteristic of the biblical theology of mission.[8] It tended to operate as a juridico-moral ordinance.[9]

The question whether Matthew 28:18-20 is primarily a missionary *command* will be dealt with in more detail below, when we attempt an exegesis of the passage. A few general and introductory remarks must suffice at this stage.

The first point that strikes the careful reader is that none of the passages which are usually referred to as parallels to the Matthean Great Commission (Luke 25:45-49; John 20:21; Acts 1:8) contains a *command* to do mission work. As a matter of fact, the Great Commission does not function anywhere in the New Testament. It is never referred to or appealed to by the early church. It is therefore quite clear that the early church did not embark on a mission to Jews and Gentiles simply because it had been told to do so. This would have placed mission in the context of legalism. Mission would then have been depersonalized. The "command" develops a "weight" of its own; it leads a life of its own. It becomes a marching order of a Christian militia, engaged in a holy war.[10]

Where the early Christians did indeed — albeit reluctantly at first, as far as Gentiles were concerned — embark on mission, this was simply an expression of the inner law of their lives. As Roland Allen and Harry Boer have argued cogently, the early Christian mission was an essential result of Pentecost.

6. I. P. C. van't Hof, "Gehoorzaamheid aan bet zendingsbevel," *Kerk en Theologie* 37, no. 1 (January 1980): 45. My translation.

7. John Stott, "The Great Commission," in *One Race, One Gospel, One Task,* vol. 1, ed. C. F. H. Henry and W. S. Mooneyham (Minneapolis: World Wide Publications, 1967), p. 37.

8. See, for example, Thomas Ohm, O.S.B., *Machet zu Jüngern alle Völker, Theorie der Mission* (Freiburg: Erich Wewel Verlag, 1962), pp. 407-70.

9. Fritz Kollbrunner, *The Splendour and Confusion of Mission Today* (Gwelo, Zimbabwe: Mambo Press, 1974), p. 22.

10. van't Hof, "Gehoorzaamheid aan bet zendingsbevel," pp. 45-47.

It was this event that became the driving force for mission.[11] The "debt" or "obligation" Paul had to Greeks and non-Greeks (Rom. 1:14) was the debt of *gratitude*, not of *duty*.[12] Newbigin aptly said, "We have regarded witness as a demand laid upon us instead of seeing it as a gift promised to us."[13] Or, with reference to Acts 1:8, "The word, 'You shall be my witnesses,' is not a command to be obeyed, but a promise to be trusted."[14]

A striking aspect of this promise or gift was, however, that it was only perceived as such in the process of mission. One still recognizes the element of astonished joy in Peter's words when he visited the Gentile Cornelius: "I now see how true it is that God has no favorites" (Acts 10:34, NEB). And it was only in the act of preaching the gospel to all people that Paul discovered the mystery "that through the Gospel the Gentiles are joint heirs with the Jews, part of the same body, sharers together in the promise made in Christ Jesus" (Eph. 3:6).[15]

* * *

Exposition of Matthew 28:[19-]20

"Go Ye Therefore" (?)

Within the threefold division of Jesus' words to his disciples, Matthew 28:19-20a constitutes the center. It is framed by the statement of authority (v. 18) and the assurance of Jesus' abiding presence (v. 20b). The three sections are tied together by the fourfold *all:* "all authority" (v. 18), "all nations" (v. 19), "teaching . . . all" (v. 20), and "with you always" (v. 20).

The verb *poreuthentes,* the aorist participle of *poreuomai* (to go), has been of special importance in Western missionary thinking, particularly since

11. Roland Allen, *The Ministry of the Spirit* (Grand Rapids: Eerdmans, 1962), pp. 4-5, and *Missionary Principles* (London: Lutterworth, 1968); and Boer, *Pentecost and Missions,* pp. 119, 128.

12. Paul S. Minear, "Gratitude and Mission in the Epistle to the Romans," in *Basileia: Walter Freytag zum 60. Geburtstag* (Stuttgart: Evang. Missionswerk, 1961), pp. 42-48.

13. Lesslie Newbigin, "Context and Conversion," *International Review of Mission* 271 (July 1979): 308.

14. Lesslie Newbigin, "The Church as Witness," *Reformed Review* 35, no. 1 (March 1978): 9; and Allen, *The Ministry of the Spirit,* p. 5.

15. David J. Bosch, *Witness to the World: The Christian Mission in Theological Perspective* (Atlanta: John Knox, 1980), pp. 81-83.

Carey. Says Blauw, "The fact that this *participium* is put first . . . places the emphasis on going, on traveling. One will have to pass Israel's boundaries consciously and intentionally to be able to fulfil the order."[16] Elsewhere *poreuthentes* is described as a Matthean technical term for mission.[17] Hubbard points out that it is characteristic of commissioning narratives in general.[18]

Hubbard's argument in favor of translating *poreuthentes* as an imperative verb separate from the imperative of the main verb depends, however, on the existence of a distinct commissioning *Gattung* and, as shown above, the existence of such a *Gattung* is highly doubtful. For other reasons also the translation of *poreuthentes* as an imperative "Go!" is to be questioned on two grounds.

First, we have here a construction which Matthew frequently uses and about which Schlatter says, "When two actions are connected with a single event, Matthew puts the aorist participle of the preparatory action before the aorist of the main verb. This sentence construction is so common that it may be designated a characteristic of Matthew's style."[19] This means that in Matthew 28:19 both *poreuthentes* and *mathēteusate* (make disciples) refer *to one* event.

Second, Matthew frequently uses the verb *poreuomai* (in various forms) as an auxiliary verb together with the imperative of another verb (2:8; 9:13; 11:4; 17:27; 28:7) in a *pleonastic* sense.[20] The "going" is not separate from the event expressed in the verb in the imperative mood. It does not necessarily suggest a traveling from one geographical point to another. However, this does not mean that *poreuthentes* is redundant; rather, it serves to *reinforce* the action of the main verb and adds a note of *urgency* to it.[21] This is clearly the

16. Johannes Blauw, *The Missionary Nature of the Church* (Grand Rapids: Eerdmans, 1974), p. 86.

17. Jacques Matthey, "The Great Commission According to Matthew," *International Review of Mission* 274 (April 1980): 167; and Jean Zumstein, "Matthieu 28:16-20," *Révue de Théologie et de Philosophie* 22, no. 1 (1972): 26.

18. B. J. Hubbard, *The Matthean Redaction of a Primitive Apostolic Commission: An Exegesis of Matthew 28:16-20* (Missoula, Mont.: Society of Biblical Literature, 1974), pp. 67, 83-84.

19. Adolf Schlatter, *Der Evangelist Matthäus* (Stuttgart: Calwer, 1948), p. 23. My translation.

20. See Georg Strecker, *Der Weg der Gerechtigkeit, Untersuchung zur Theologie der Mattäus* (Göttingen: Vandenhoeck & Ruprecht, 1962), p. 209; Günther Baumbach, "Die Mission im Matthäus-Evangelium," *Theologische Literaturzeitung* 92, no. 12 (1967): 890; Jack Dean Kingsbury, "The Composition and Christology of Matthew 28:16-20," *Journal of Biblical Literature* 93, no. 4 (1974): 576.

21. See P. O'Brien, "The Great Commission of Matthew 28:18-20: A Missionary Mandate or Not," *The Reformed Theological Review* 35, no. 3 (September-December 1976): 72; Cleon Rogers, "The Great Commission," *Bibliotheca Sacra* 519 (July-September 1973): 261.

case in Matthew 28:19. *Poreuthentes* serves to underline the urgency and primacy of *mathēteusate.*

Due to the standard Western translations of *poreuthentes* as "Go ye (therefore)!" and the like, a peculiar conception of mission developed. The emphasis tended to be on the "going" rather than on the "making disciples."[22] The locality, not the task, determined whether someone was a missionary; one qualified if one was commissioned by an agency in one locality to go and work in another. The greater the distance between these two places, the clearer it was that the individual was a missionary.[23] In addition, the imperative voice appealed to an activist people. It was easy to rally popular support around the vision of conquering unknown territory and pioneering on distant frontiers.[24] Chaney indicates the implications of this understanding for nineteenth-century North America: "Home missions" became a technique for maintaining Christian America. "Mission" now signified exclusively *foreign* mission, and Matthew 28:19, with its "Go ye therefore" was singled out as a proof-text. On the home front the chief concern was to check the spread of weeds. "Home missions became the great divine hoe, for keeping the garden clean."[25]

If, however, we translate *poreuthentes* not as a separate command, but as adding emphasis and urgency to *mathēteusate,* a different picture of mission emerges. It then refers to bringing people to Jesus as Lord, wherever they may be.[26] Mission then loses its preoccupation with the geographical component and becomes mission in six continents.

Make Disciples

So we move on to *mathēteusate* (make disciples), which is without doubt the principal verb in the Great Commission, as a structural analysis of the pericope shows.[27] The two modal participles "baptizing" and "teaching" (to

22. David J. Hesselgrave, "Confusion Concerning the Great Commission," *Evangelical Missions Quarterly* 15, no. 4 (October 1979): 199.

23. Bosch, *Witness to the World,* p. 46.

24. Wilbert R. Shenk, "The Great Commission," in *Mission Focus: Current Issues,* ed. Wilbert R. Shenk (Scottdale: Herald, 1980), p. 42.

25. Chaney, quoted in Bosch, *Witness to the World,* pp. 151-52.

26. O'Brien, "The Great Commission," p. 73.

27. Contra Hans Schieber, who concludes that the phrase "baptizing them in the name of the Father and of the Son and of the Holy Spirit" constitutes the center; "Konzentrik im Matthäusschluss, Ein form- und gattungskritischer Versuch zu Matt. 28, 16-20," *Kairos* 19, no. 4 (1977).

which we shall return below) are clearly subordinated to "make disciples," describing the form the disciple-making is to take.[28]

* * *

The verb *mathēteuein* (to make disciples) does not appear in the Septuagint and occurs only four times in the entire New Testament, three of which are in Matthew (13:52; 27:57; and 28:20) and one in Acts (14:21). In Matthew 27:57 it is used with reference to Joseph of Arimathea, "who had himself become a disciple of Jesus" (literally, "who had been discipled unto Jesus"). The Markan parallel (15:43) reads, "who was looking forward to the kingdom of God." Matthew wants to say materially the same as Mark, which means that he sees a close connection between the kingdom of God and Jesus.[29] In Matthew 13:52 reference is made to a scribe who "had been discipled unto the kingdom of heaven." A comparison with Matthew 27:57 once again underlines this close connection.

Whereas the verb *mathēteuein* is rare, the noun *mathētēs* (disciple) is common — at least in the Gospels and Acts — although it is not found once outside these five books. Paul never uses it. *Mathētēs* is more central in Matthew's Gospel than in the others. It occurs seventy-three times in Matthew, forty-six times in Mark, and forty-seven times in Luke. Where Mark usually refers to the small circle around Jesus as "the twelve," Matthew prefers to call them "the disciples."[30] Even where the word itself does not occur, Matthew calls attention to the *idea,* for he uses *akolouthein* (to follow) far more frequently than do the other evangelists. In Matthew 8:23, for example, Matthew explicitly mentions "and his disciples followed"; this is omitted in the parallels in Mark and Luke.[31] The English word "discipleship" is thus a correct rendering of the German *Nachfolge.*

Although there are clear parallels between being a disciple of Jesus and

28. See Ferdinand Hahn, "Der Sendungsauftrag des Auferstandenen: Matthäus 28, 16-20," in *Fides pro mundi vita: Missionstheologie heute, Hans-Werner Gensichen zum 65. Geburtstag,* ed. Theo Sundermeier (Gütersloh: Gerd Mohn, 1980), p. 35; Grant R. Osborne, "Redaction Criticism and the Great Commission: A Case Study Toward a Biblical Understanding of Inerrancy," *Journal of the Evangelical Theological Society* 19, no. 2 (1976): 79; Wolfgang Trilling, *Das wahre Israel, Studien zur Theologie des Matthäusevangeliums* (Munich: Kösel, 1964), pp. 39-40; Matthey, "The Great Commission According to Matthew," p. 168.

29. Trilling, *Das wahre Israel,* p. 29.

30. Trilling, *Das wahre Israel,* p. 30.

31. Heinrich Kasting, *Die Anfänge der urchristlichen Mission* (Munich: Chr. Kaiser Verlag, 1969), pp. 35-36.

being a disciple of a Jewish rabbi, there are also distinct differences. The disciples did not attach themselves to Jesus but were called by him. He himself, not the Torah, stands at the center of the relationship. Discipleship is therefore not a transitional stage, ending in the disciple himself becoming a rabbi (Matt. 23:8); it describes a permanent relationship with Jesus. Nowhere does Jesus debate with his disciples, only with his opponents. Ultimately the disciples would not become the transmitters of his teaching, but his witnesses.[32] To follow Jesus also suggests sharing his fate.[33]

In Matthew's time the word "disciple" and related terms had acquired a clearly circumscribed meaning for his community. It had become a major ecclesiological term, as in Acts 14:27 and 28, where "disciples" and "church" are clearly interchangeable.[34] Paul Minear is correct when he states "that in the early Church the stories of the disciples were normally understood as archetypes of the dilemmas and opportunities that later Christians experienced. Each Gospel pericope became a paradigm with a message for the Church, because each Christian had inherited a relationship to Jesus similar to that of James and John and the others."[35]

It is against this background that we have to understand Matthew's use of the verb *mathēteusate* in 28:19 — the only instance where the verb occurs in the imperative mood. In the pre-Easter period the key word was *kēryssein* (to proclaim or to preach), often linked with "the gospel (of the kingdom)," as in Matthew 4:23; 9:35; 24:14; and 26:13. It was the classical term for the ministry of Jesus, and in Matthew 10:7 also that of the disciples. Now *mathēteusate* replaces *kēryssete,* which in a way causes a stylistic unevenness, as the latter would correspond better to the object "all the nations." The substitution dramatically signals the new situation which obtains for Matthew and his community: When the Master still walked this earth, it was appropriate to speak

32. G. Bornkamm, "Enderwartung und Kirche im Matthäusevangelium," in *Ueberlieferung und Auslegung im Mattäusevangelium,* ed. G. Bornkamm, G. Barth, and H. J. Held (Neukirchen: Neukirchener Verlag, 1961), p. 37; Rogers, "The Great Commission," p. 265, quoting Rengstorf.

33. Martin Hengel, "Die Ursprünge der christlichen Mission," *New Testament Studies* 18, no. 1 (1970-71): 35.

34. See Trilling, *Das wahre Israel,* p. 31; Osborne, "Redaction Criticism and the Great Commission," p. 79; Walter Grundmann, *Das Evangelium nach Matthäus* (Berlin: Evangelische Verlagsanstalt, 1968), p. 578; Matthey, "The Great Commission According to Matthew," p. 162; Vergil Gerber, *Discipling Through Theological Education by Extension* (Chicago: Moody, 1980), pp. 36-41.

35. Paul S. Minear, *Images of the Church in the New Testament* (Philadelphia: Fortress, 1977), p. 146.

of proclaiming the kingdom or the gospel; now he is himself the Kingdom and the Gospel.[36]

The task of the disciples is no longer merely that of proclaiming, but of enlisting people into their fellowship.[37] To this end they are now empowered. To become a disciple implies a commitment both to the Master and to each other.[38] It is, moreover, no small step to take, as Matthew has already warned his readers (10:37-38). Matthew is clearly not thinking of first-level decisions only, to be followed at a later stage by a second-level decision.[39] He has no two separate stages in mind, nor two different types of Christians, one of which has only been discipled, the other already perfected. This does not mean that there is no process involved. Certainly there is. After all, following Jesus suggests a journey which, in fact, never ends in this life.[40]

Baptizing and Teaching

We have already pointed out that the phrase, "baptizing them . . . and teaching them to observe all that I have commanded you," should be read as further qualifying and describing the main verb, "make disciples," and not as independent activities. We shall now trace the consequences of this in some detail.

First, it is important to observe that the author of the First Gospel is not referring here to the catechetical training of later times which usually, in the case of converts from paganism, preceded baptism. The fact that in Matthew 28:19 the teaching is mentioned after the baptizing may therefore not be used in favor of the argument that converts should be baptized immediately and only then taught. Catechesis as an institution was not, as yet, established in Matthew's community, which was probably not at that time fully settled. Teaching here merely refers to the upbuilding of the church. The evangelist wishes only to underline the indissoluble unity of Jesus' teaching and baptism in his name; a disciple is somebody who has been incorporated into the community of believers and who keeps Jesus' commandments.[41]

36. Ernst Lohmeyer, *Das Evangelium des Matthäus* (Göttingen: Vandenhoeck & Ruprecht, 1956), p. 418.

37. Trilling, *Das wahre Israel,* pp. 47, 50.

38. Minear, *Images of the Church in the New Testament,* pp. 146-48.

39. Newbigin, "Context and Conversion," p. 310.

40. Eduard Schweizer, *Das Evangelium nach Matthäus* (Göttingen: Vandenhoeck & Ruprecht, 1973), p. 351.

41. Trilling, *Das wahre Israel,* pp. 39-40; Grundmann, *Das Evangelium nach Matthäus,*

Matthew is, once again, using the language of his own time to reflect faithfully the mind of Jesus. The Lukan parallel to Matthew's Great Commision does not mention baptism, but it does mention "repentance bringing the forgiveness of sins" which, in turn, is wanting in Matthew. That does not suggest that the first evangelist did not know about the forgiveness of sins! In fact, he early (Matt. 1:21) refers to this as the main purpose of Jesus' coming; he also adds it to the text of the institution of the Lord's Supper (Matt. 26:28). Here in chapter 28, however, Matthew uses "ecclesiastical" language: His "baptizing them" is materially the same as Luke's "proclaiming repentance and the forgiveness of sins." The practice of baptism here already suggests the institutionalized form of the exercise of the power to forgive sins. "Baptism is here a sign of the present activity of the exalted one, who even now bestows salvation on those who accept the gospel."[42]

The next participle is "teaching," which in the First Gospel is always to be distinguished from both "preaching" and "making disciples." *Didaskein* (to teach) is characteristic of Matthew, in spite of the fact that this verb occurs more frequently in Mark and Luke. We should, however, *weigh* rather than simply *count* the occurrences.[43]

"All That I Have Commanded You"

In making disciples people should be taught "to observe all that I have commanded you." Once again the language is typically Matthean. The verb *tērein* (to observe or to practice) is absent in Luke and occurs only once in Mark. Matthew uses it six times, half of these in the sense of "keeping the commandments."[44] The verb *entellesthai* (to command) that Matthew uses in 28:19 is related to the noun *entolē* (commandment) which he employs as a technical term for the commandments of the Old Testament, particularly the Torah — 5:19; 15:3; 19:17; 22:36.[45] Once again a comparison of the three Synoptic Gospels is illuminating: Luke summarizes the content of Jesus'

---

p. 579; Zumstein, "Matthieu 28:16-20," p. 27; Hahn, "Der Sendungsauftrag des Auferstandeneng," p. 36.

42. Ferdinand Hahn, *Mission in the New Testament* (London: SCM, 1965), p. 67; Trilling, *Das wahre Israel,* p. 32; Grundmann, *Das Evangelium nach Matthäus,* p. 578; Zumstein, "Matthieu 28:16-20," p. 27; Matthey, "The Great Commission According to Matthew," pp. 169-70.

43. Hahn, "Der Sendungsauftrag des Auferstandeneng," p. 42; Trilling, *Das wahre Israel,* p. 36.

44. Zumstein, "Matthieu 28:16-20," p. 27.

45. Matthey, "The Great Commission According to Matthew," p. 171.

proclamation as "repentance toward the forgiveness of sins" (24:47); Mark calls it the *euangelion* (13:10; 14:9); and Matthew refers to "that which [Jesus] has commanded."[46]

Protestant Christians, in particular, may feel embarrassed by this emphasis on commandments that have to be observed, as it suggests the possibility of salvation by works. It should, however, be pointed out that Matthew uses these expressions in a fierce polemic against (Jamnia) Pharisaism. In doing so, Matthew consciously uses the Torah according to the Jewish tradition, but in such a way that the discrepancy between teaching and doing on the part of his opponents is exposed. The issue at stake is therefore the correct interpretation of and obedience to the law: The true teacher of the law, says the author in 13:52, is one "who has been discipled unto the kingdom."[47]

The verb *entellesthai* (command) occurs here in the aorist, so the reference is not to a *new* revelation, but to what the earthly Jesus has already taught his disciples. It remains normative, now and forever. The message of the Resurrected One is the same as that of the earthly Jesus. The *Kyrios* is none other than the teacher from Nazareth.[48]

What, then, is his commandment? It is more than the moral and ceremonial law or than a purely religious, otherworldly rule of life. It is nothing less than the command to love God and people. In the story of the rich young man, Matthew has edited Mark thus: "If you would enter life, keep [*tērēson*] the commandments [*tas entolas*]" (Matt. 19:17). The words in Matthew 28 are a clear allusion to those in Matthew 19.[49] But Jesus radicalizes these commandments in a specific direction: To love one's neighbors means to have compassion on them (see also Luke's Good Samaritan) and to see that justice is done. Thus *dikaiosynē* (justice) becomes another key concept in Matthew's Gospel. The disciples are challenged to a life of righteousness (= justice) which infinitely surpasses that practiced by the Pharisees (Matt. 5:20) and to seek God's kingdom and his justice (Matt. 6:33). Justice is, as in the Old Testament, practically a synonym for compassion or almsgiving, as the famous parable in Matthew 25:31-46 demonstrates.[50]

46. Zumstein, "Matthieu 28:16-20," p. 28.

47. Bornkamm, "Enderwartung und Kirche im Matthäusevangelium," pp. 22, 28; Hahn, "Der Sendungsauftrag des Auferstandeneng," p. 306.

48. Zumstein, "Matthieu 28:16-20," p. 28; Matthey, "The Great Commission According to Matthew," p. 171.

49. Hubbard, *The Matthean Redaction*, p. 91; Hahn, "Der Sendungsauftrag des Auferstandeneng," p. 36; Bornkamm, "Enderwartung und Kirche im Matthäusevangelium," p. 28.

50. Gerhard Barth, "Das Gesetzverständnis des Evangelisten Matthäus," in *Ueberlieferung und Auslegung im Matthäusevangelium*, ed. G. Barth, G. Bornkamm, and H. J. Held (Neu-

All this has consequences for our understanding of the Great Commission and of the command to make disciples. Waldron Scott rightly sees the Great Commission within a wider context than many of his fellow-evangelicals. He says, "I am proposing that we view the larger mission, the ultimate mission, as the establishment of justice."[51] And Jacques Matthey says, "According to Matthew's Great Commission, it is not possible to make disciples without telling them to practice God's request of justice for the poor. The love commandment, which is *the* basis for the churches' involvement in politics, is an integral part of the mission commandment."[52] If this is correct — and I believe that our exegesis has proved that it is — it is evident that neither McGavran's juxtaposition of discipling and perfecting as two consecutive stages, nor his definition of making disciples as calling a people to an initial turning to Christ, is tenable. To become a disciple is to be incorporated into God's new community through baptism and to side with the poor and the oppressed. To put it differently, it is to love God and our neighbor. This is what Jesus has commanded his disciples (Matt. 28:19). And of course, for Matthew this obedience is determined not by a conformity to any impersonal commandment but by the relation to Jesus himself.[53]

All the Nations

Those who are to be made disciples are described as *panta to ethnē* (all the nations)[. . . .] *Ethnē*, in the plural, is in the Septuagint the normal rendering of *gōyim* (nations). As such, the term can have a sociological or ethnological meaning, particularly in the singular, *ethnos*. Bertram has, however, shown that in more recent parts of the Old Testament the plural *gōyim* is to be understood almost exclusively in a religioethical sense, as the collective designation not for nations but for Gentiles or pagans.[54] In this sense it was intro-

---

kirchen: Neukirchener Verlag, 1961), *passim;* Bornkamm, "Enderwartung und Kirche im Matthäusevangelium," p. 22; Schuyler Brown, "The Two-Fold Representation of the Mission in Matthew's Gospel," *Studio Theologica* 31, no. 1 (1977): 25; Hahn, "Der Sendungsauftrag des Auferstandeneng," p. 36; Matthey, "The Great Commission According to Matthew," pp. 170-73; Waldron Scott, *Bring Forth Justice: A Contemporary Perspective on Mission* (Grand Rapids: Eerdmans, 1980), pp. 164-71.

51. Scott, *Bring Forth Justice,* p. xvi.

52. Matthey, "The Great Commission According to Matthew," p. 171.

53. Blauw, *The Missionary Nature of the Church,* p. 86.

54. G. Bertram, "Ethnos, ethnikos," in *Theologisches Wörterbuch zum Neuen Testament,* vol. 2 (Stuttgart: Kohlhammer, 1935), pp. 364-66.

duced into the Septuagint and Hellenistic Judaism as *ethnē*. It became for all practical purposes a technical term for Gentiles in contrast to Jews.[55]

"Jew," too, is in this period to be understood primarily as a religious, not ethnic, designation.[56] In view of this it is unlikely that *ethnē* in Matthew 28:19 should be understood in the sense of separate ethnic units. It *could* bear that sense, but there were far more suitable Greek words to give expression to that shade of meaning: words such as *phylē* (people as a national unit of common descent), *laos* (people as a political unit with a common history; this is the Greek word most frequently used for the Jews as a people), and *glōssa* (people as a linguistic unit).[57]

When *panta* (all) is added to *ethnē,* as in Matthew 28:19, yet another nuance is created [. . . .] Within the context the emphasis is clearly on the entire world of humanity; the expression is used "in view of the worldwide mission."[58] An unbiased reading of Matthew 28:19 can therefore not take it to imply that the Christian mission is to be carried out "people by people," but that it is to reach far beyond the confines that existed up to that time[59] [. . . .] The issue behind the use of the word *ethnē* [. . .] is the issue of *salvation history:* the New Covenant is to be absolutely universal, and the only point that has to be discerned is whether the Jews are still included or not. I agree with those scholars who say they are, and that *panta ta ethnē* is to be interpreted without any restriction whatsoever.

Moreover, the tensions in the early church between Jews and Gentiles were essentially theological, not cultural. The question as to whether Gentiles should be circumcised had nothing to do with the homogeneous unit issue, as becomes clear from Paul's letters. The point he makes throughout is salvation-historical: The crucified and risen Messiah has superseded the law as the way of salvation. Some early church leaders, such as James, probably subscribed to the idea that God's eschatological community consisted of *two* peoples, namely, Israel and the new people made up of Gentiles. There were

55. Karl Ludwig Schmidt, "Ethnos," in *Theologisches Wörterbuch zum Neuen Testament,* vol. 2 (Stuttgart: Kohlhammer, 1935), p. 367; Richard R. De Ridder, *Discipling the Nations* (Grand Rapids: Baker, 1975), p. 188.

56. Bertram, "Ethnos, ethnikos," p. 362.

57. Walter Liefield, "Theology of Church Growth," in *Theology and Mission,* ed. D. J. Hesselgrave (Grand Rapids: Baker, 1978), p. 175; Hesselgrave, "Confusion Concerning the Great Commission," 200, and Letter on "Meaning of the Great Commission," *Evangelical Missions Quarterly* 16, no. 1 (January 1980): 50-51.

58. Hahn, "Der Sendungsauftrag des Auferstandeneng," p. 71; Trilling, *Das wahre Israel,* p. 31.

59. Liefield, "Theology of Church Growth," p. 176.

two different *dispensations*, and, in a way, two different but parallel ways of salvation. The Gentiles who had come to share in Israel's faith were not subject to the law and therefore not obliged to undergo circumcision. Jewish Christians, however, remained subject to both. The continuing validity of the law as a way of salvation for the Jews entailed the refusal of Jewish Christians to violate the law by sharing meals and Eucharists with Gentile Christians.[60]

However, once again, this had nothing to do with the existence of separate homogeneous units but with different understandings of salvation history; it was a matter of theology, not communications theory. Moreover, several early church leaders, Paul foremost among them, passionately opposed the theology of two separate dispensations and pleaded unceasingly for the *unity* of the church made up of *both* Jews and Gentiles. Paul still accepted the principle of division of labor as far as the mission to Jews and Gentiles was concerned (Gal. 2:7), but the salvation-historical difference between the two had been abrogated: The law was a tutor only until Christ came (Gal. 3:24). The essential difference between Jews and Gentiles was never ethnic but always salvation-historical, and even this difference had now been annulled [. . . .]

The new fellowship transcends every limit imposed by family, class, or culture. We are not winning people like ourselves to ourselves but sharing the good news that in Christ God has shattered the barriers that divide the human race and has created a new community. The new people of God has no analogy; it is a "sociological impossibility" that has nevertheless become possible.[61]

The early church gave expression to this by calling the Christians the *triton genos*, the third race next to the existing two races of Jews and Gentiles. "Beside or over against these two 'peoples' [Paul] places the church of God as a new creation . . . which is to embrace both Jews and Greeks, rising above the differences of both peoples."[62] This is the mystery revealed to Paul, "that through the gospel the Gentiles are heirs together with Israel, members together of one body, and sharers together in the promise in Christ Jesus" (Eph. 3:6, NIV).

Exclusive groupings of believers, whether around individual leaders for theological or other reasons (1 Cor 1:10-13) or around homogeneous cultural units, are unacceptable in the Christian church. Neither is the problem solved

60. Schuyler Brown, "The Matthean Community and the Gentile Mission," *Novum Testamentum* 22, no. 3 (July 1980): 208, 210-12.

61. J. C. Hoekendijk, *Kerk en volke in de duitse zendingswetenschap* (Amsterdam: Drukkerij Kampert & Helm, 1948), p. 237.

62. Adolf Harnack, *The Mission and Expansion of Christianity in the First Three Centuries* (New York: Harper & Brothers, 1961), p. 243; Hoekendijk, *Kerk en volke*, p. 237.

by regarding this as only an initial stage which will later develop into a greater openness to other Christians; the Machiavellian principle of doing evil that good may come does not work in the church. Recker, in a review of Wagner's *Our Kind of People,* thus rightly warns against "a growing virus in the body of Christ" that fosters the formation of different denominations "upon the basis of very questionable distinctives." He adds, "When individual believers refuse any longer to entertain the biblical injunction to be reconciled to their brothers but rather simply run off to find some congregation which mirrors their own foibles, fears, suspicions, prejudices, or what not in the name of feeling 'at home' or comfortable, then something is radically wrong in the body of Christ."[63]

The Promise

We now come to the final verse of the First Gospel. The promise which it contains is linked directly to the preceding commission with *kai idou* (and see) in the sense of "surely," or "therefore, be assured." The expression is once again characteristic of Matthew, as is the wording of the promise itself.

The "I am with you" theme was first broached in Matthew 1:23 ("they will call him Immanuel, which means 'God with us'") and repeated in Matthew 18:20. As we have noted earlier, the theme as such hails from the Old Testament and is related to the rabbinic concept of the *shekinah.* In the Old Testament it is used particularly when a dangerous mission is to be undertaken, as in Joshua 1:5 and Isaiah 43:2, 5. So Matthew's Gospel is to be understood as the fulfillment of the Old Testament covenant, the epitome of which was the Lord's presence with his people. Here in 28:20 Jesus promises his disciples the same assistance of which the Jews were assured by Yahweh, and he does it by virtue of the authority *(exousia)* entrusted to him and in view of the mission they have to undertake.[64]

Jesus' presence with his disciples is to last *pasas tas hēmeras heōs tēs synteleias tou aiōnos* (always, until the end of time). The expression [*hē*] *synteleia* [*tou*] *aiōnos* is found *only* in Matthew (13:39-40, 49; 24:3; 28:20). The closest parallel is *synteleia tōn aiōnōn* in Hebrews 9:26. Matthew's redactional work is therefore once again demonstrated beyond doubt.

63. Robert Recker, Review of *Our Kind of People* by C. Peter Wagner, *Calvin Theological Journal* 15, no. 2 (November 1980): 303-4.

64. Strecker, *Der Weg der Gerechtigkeit,* p. 213; Trilling, *Das wahre Israel,* pp. 40-43; Zumstein, "Matthieu 28:16-20," p. 28; O'Brien, "The Great Commission of Matthew 28:18-20," p. 77.

The first Gospel mentions neither the ascension nor the outpouring of the Holy Spirit. "The interest in [the ascension and coming of the Spirit] appears to be absorbed into the experience of the always near, comforting, and empowering presence of the Kyrios."[65] Even the delay of the parousia is not really a problem anymore: "The consciousness of the present experience of the Kyrios is so overpowering that it can embrace all future times. That which is a reality now, holds good for all time. Here the faith of the Church, not apocalyptic speculation, is speaking."[66] Thus all attention is focused on the present; there is no hint whatsoever as to the precise moment of the end. Within this context Jesus neither announces his departure nor does he actually depart; he promises, on the contrary, to remain with his disciples always. This is the overriding impression with which Matthew leaves his readers.[67] And the disciples' mission will last as long as his presence lasts: until the end of time. The mission itself thus becomes an integral part of the parousia expectation; it becomes, in effect, a "proleptic parousia."[68]

The Structure of Mission

We have come to the end. We have argued that the pericope of Matthew 28:16-20 has its foundation in tradition, though it is expressed predominantly in Matthean language. We have added that it cannot be read and understood on its own, but only against the background of the entire First Gospel and of the exigencies of the community to which the author belonged.

In the process we have exposed some weaknesses which we believe are to be detected in Church Growth missiology, particularly in its use of the Great Commission. *Hermeneutically* there is in the Church Growth movement — and surely not only there — the tendency to handle the biblical material too self-confidently and to build on one text the whole mystery of mission. *Exegetically* there is the unjustified, one-sided emphasis on *going* (which Church Growth exponents share with other evangelicals), the disjunction between discipling and perfecting, and the interpretation of *panta ta ethnē* in ethnological categories.

More *generally* there is the issue of ecclesiology and of a too narrow definition of mission. Regarding the latter it has to be pointed out that the

65. Trilling, *Das wahre Israel,* p. 43. My translation.

66. Trilling, *Das wahre Israel,* pp. 43-44. My translation.

67. Trilling, *Das wahre Israel,* p. 45; Hubbard, *The Matthean Redaction,* p. 15.

68. Osborne, "Redaction Criticism and the Great Commission," p. 82.

Church Growth movement has not yet dynamically related its missiology to the pressing problems of social ethics facing the church, notwithstanding C. Peter Wagner's attempt in *Church Growth and the Whole Gospel.*[69]

Although it would be illegitimate to erect the entire edifice of the New Testament witness concerning the church's mission on Matthew 28:16-20, we can infer some significant guidelines on the basis of our exegesis of this pericope, employing it, with all the necessary qualifications, as a paradigm for our mission today.[70]

Mission is always contextual. Mission is related to a specific time and place and situation. Thus Matthew is not simply repeating a word uttered long ago, but is reinterpreting it for his own context. The history of the Master with his disciples is foundational and paradigmatic, and as such nourishes and challenges the present. Faith is thus realized in what Kierkegaard has called *contemporaneity,* where there is, in the final analysis, no absolute discontinuity between the history of Jesus and the time of the church. By speaking of the condition and activities of those who accompanied Jesus on his way to the cross, the evangelist is speaking to the church of his own time. And it is precisely the dialectic between the history of Jesus and the existence of the believer that justifies, for Matthew, the writing of the Gospel in the way he does.[71]

A precarious existence. Matthew's community lived at a frontier. They experienced difficulty in defining their own identity in a context where they occupied the borderline between increasingly hostile Jews and as yet alien Gentiles. They experienced, to put it mildly, a crisis of identity. For us this means that mission never takes place in self-confidence and megalomania but in the knowledge of our own weakness. The missionary is no hero but stands, like the disciples in Galilee, in the dialectical tension between faith and doubt, between worship and fear (Matt. 28:17). In the midst of that tension, however, the missionary knows — by faith — that all authority in heaven and on earth has been given to Jesus. Therefore, although the missionary's own situation may be precarious, it is never hopeless.

Mission means servanthood. Although now invested with all power in the universe, the resurrected Christ is still Jesus of Nazareth who walks as a migrant through Galilee and calls his disciples to follow him to the cross. His church has to follow *that* path to glory, and *not* the alternative route suggested

69. New York: Harper and Row, 1981.

70. Matthey, "The Great Commission According to Matthew," p. 161.

71. Zumstein, "Matthieu 28:16-20," pp. 30, 33; Matthey, "The Great Commission According to Matthew," p. 162.

to him by the Devil in Matthew 4:8-9. This means that a church which wields earthly power and on that basis imposes its views on others is a church that has fallen to the Devil's temptation and is therefore disqualified from being called to the mission of Jesus. "[God] will only reach the nations if the bearers of the Gospel of the kingdom, the evangelizing disciples, come as poor, exposed, defenseless men and women, living with and not above those to whom they bring healing."[72]

Mission is incarnational. John's version of the Great Commission has Jesus saying to his disciples, "As the Father sent me, so I send you" (20:21). Thus the sending of the disciples is grounded in the sending of Jesus by the Father. Mission is *missio Dei.* Therefore baptism, the decisive act of incorporation into the church and of signifying the forgiveness of sins, takes place "in the Name of the Father and of the Son and of the Holy Spirit" (Matt. 28:19).

Incarnational mission is comprehensive in nature. Those who emulate Jesus are to be characterized by boundless compassion, fellowship, and worship.[73] They are involved in service, preaching, witness — in short, in disciple-making. The true disciple is, however, the one who is being "discipled unto the Kingdom" (Matt. 13:52), which is the same as "being discipled unto Jesus" (Matt. 27:57; notice the parallel in Mark 15:43: "who expected the kingdom of God"). It is well known that "the kingdom of heaven" occupies a key place in the First Gospel. The same is true of that other typically Matthean concept, *dikaiosynē.* This is not in every respect the same as Paul's "justification." It is, rather, justification, righteousness, and justice in one: "God's righteousness and human righteousness [= justice] do not exclude each other, but are identical."[74]

Moreover, in the First Gospel *dikaiosynē* and *basileia* (kingdom) are intimately related. Although they are not synonyms, they are mutually dependent: "The way to the *basileia* leads only via the *dikaiosynē.*"[75] When the disciples are charged to teach "all that I have commanded you" as part of the disciple-making process (Matt. 28:19), the pursuit of *dikaiosynē* lies at the center. The way of Jesus is "the way of justice" (this would be the English title of Strecker's book on Matthew). Waldron Scott is therefore correct when he relates the Great Commission to the larger mission and adds, "I am proposing that we view the larger mission, the ultimate mission, as the establishment of justice."[76]

72. Matthey, "The Great Commission According to Matthew," p. 173.

73. Bosch, *Witness to the World,* pp. 53-57.

74. Strecker, *Der Weg der Gerechtigkeit,* p. 155. My translation.

75. Strecker, *Der Weg der Gerechtigkeit,* p. 155. My translation.

76. Scott, *Bring Forth Justice,* p. xvi.

It follows from this that Christian social involvement may never be downgraded from its status as an inherent and essential part of the good news to the position of a mere adjunct of the gospel as an editorial in *Christianity Today* (1980) would have it, for "one must understand discipleship in order to make disciples, and discipleship is not fully biblical apart from a commitment to social justice."[77]

Mission (or disciple-making) avoids becoming a heavy burden, a new law, a command to obey. The disciples' involvement in mission is a *logical consequence* of their being "discipled unto Jesus" and of the "full authority" given to him (notice the "therefore" in Matt. 28:19). "You are my witnesses *because* you have been with me" (John 15:26). To be involved in mission is to receive a gift, not to obey a law; to accept a promise, not to bow to a command. Christ's promised presence (Matt. 28:10) "is not a reward offered to those who obey: it is the assurance that those who are commanded will be able to obey."[78] So the Great Commission is not a commission in the ordinary sense of the word, but rather a creative statement, in the manner of Genesis 1:3 and elsewhere, "Let there be . . ."[79]

Mission involves the church. In Matthew's understanding the church is God's chosen messenger in the world. Of course, he does not use the word "church" in the Great Commission (though he is the only evangelist who uses it at all, in Matt. 16:18 and 18:17). He talks about disciples and disciple-making, but in his thinking this is the same as "being a member of the Church" and "incorporating people into the Christian community."[80]

Discipleship ecclesiology. Matthew's "discipleship ecclesiology" highlights the fact that the believer follows a Master.[81] The *Master-disciple relationship* is prominent in the final pericope of the First Gospel. The risen Christ is still Jesus; he is thus, paradoxically, identical to the earthly Master. The same parallelism applies to the believer: the disciple in Matthew's own community is, equally paradoxically, identical to the Twelve. The intimate relationship and unconditional allegiance which applied during Jesus' earthly ministry still applies in Matthew's community.[82]

The structure of mission. Mission is indeed *structured,* not amorphous, antinomian, and purely enthusiast. On the other hand, mission should never

77. Editorial, *Christianity Today* (August 8, 1980); Scott, *Bring Forth Justice,* p. xvi.

78. Allen, *Missionary Principles,* p. 25.

79. Bosch, *Witness to the World,* p. 81.

80. Trilling, *Das wahre Israel,* p. 31; Hahn, "Der Sendungsauftrag des Auferstandeneng," p. 38; also Strecker, *Der Weg der Gerechtigkeit,* pp. 191-226.

81. Osborne, "Redaction Criticism and the Great Commission," p. 83.

82. Zumstein, "Matthieu 28:16-20," pp. 29, 31-33.

become *established,* institutionalized, ecclesiasticized. Within his community Matthew is involved in a double polemic against these two opposite heresies, embodied respectively in the early forms of Ebionitism on the one hand and enthusiastic Gentile Christianity on the other.[83]

The horizon of mission is unlimitedly universal. He who has been given all authority in heaven and on earth sends his disciples into all the world to make disciples of all nations. Nothing is said about the communication methods involved. That lies outside the scope of the Great Commission. The emphasis is entirely on the fact that the horizon has become unlimited, that the old restrictions have fallen away entirely. So the disciples see before them not so many separate tribes and tongues, but the whole of humankind that has to be discipled.

The permanence of Jesus' presence. Jesus' authority is universal ("heaven and earth"), his commission is worldwide ("all the nations"), and his *presence is permanent* ("always, until the end of time"). Ultimately, then, it is Jesus' abiding presence with his disciples "which transforms an imperative into an inspiration."[84] Even if Matthew does not mention the Holy Spirit in 28:20, Jesus' presence with his disciples is to be understood pneumatologically.

83. Zumstein, "Matthieu 28:16-20," pp. 29-31; Trilling, *Das wahre Israel,* p. 124ff.
84. Max Warren, *The Christian Imperative* (London: SCM, 1955), p. 114.

CHAPTER 7

Women and Evangelism in the Early Church

Walter L. Liefeld

A clear and balanced view of the involvement of women in the evangelistic mission of the early church requires more than the citation of a few isolated examples. The Christian mission itself was integrated with the life and growth of the church, rather than merely being one of its organizational departments. Likewise the contribution of women was not a detached phenomenon, but a major part of the total life and ministry of the church. Moreover, missionary activity in the post-apostolic period grew naturally out of the explosive missionary activity of the New Testament church.

The New Testament Period

We need, therefore, to gain an appreciation of what was transpiring during the period of Jesus' ministry and of the apostolic church. At the very beginning of the Gospel narrative the virgin Mary testifies clearly to the great things God did for her and for his people (Luke 1:49-55). Shortly after the birth of Jesus, two pious Jews, Simeon and Anna, give testimony to his messiahship (Luke 2:25-38). From what we know of the Jewish custom of that time, the establishment of evidence required two witnesses, and the witness of a woman was not acceptable. Nevertheless, at this crucial moment Luke features Anna, who proclaimed the redemption of God through the newborn Christ.

In John 4 the familiar figure of the woman at the well of Samaria reminds us of the importance of a woman's witness to Christ. "Many of the Samaritans from that town believed in him because of the woman's testimony" (John 4:39). Another testimony by a woman, however, has gone almost unnoticed. When we think of the disciples' confession of Jesus as Messiah and the Son of God, we usually call to mind Peter's theological statement, "You are the Christ, the Son of the living God" (Matt. 16:16). But Martha's confession just prior to the raising of Lazarus contains almost identical words: "I believe that you are the Christ, the Son of God . . ." (John 11:27).

Women also gave the first testimony to the resurrection of the Lord Jesus Christ. Each of the four Gospels mentions the women. Luke includes the typical male response, "But they did not believe the women, because their words seemed to them like nonsense" (24:11). Many have noted that when Paul provides a list of witnesses to the resurrection in 1 Corinthians 15, he does not mention the women. Probably this was because the testimony of women was not acceptable in Paul's world, and the Corinthians passage was intended to provide acceptable evidence. It is therefore all the more remarkable that the Gospels do relate the role of women in this first act of witness to the risen Christ.

Missionary activity, as is often emphasized, includes the work of those in supporting roles. We recall, therefore, that several women accompanied Jesus on his missionary travels and supported him financially (Luke 8:1-3).

Paul mentions a number of women who worked with him. We do not know with certainty what role these female workers had. If the names of those whom Paul said "contended" side by side with him "in the cause of the gospel" (Phil. 4:3) had been men, we would have assumed that they were co-evangelists doing the very things Paul did himself. They are mentioned "along with Clement and the rest of my fellow workers" (v. 3) and the same kind of association appears with regard to the women whom Paul mentions in Romans 16.

The high percentage of women cited along with men in Romans 16 is remarkable, especially considering the usual prominence of men over women in the society of that day. Priscilla and Aquila are mentioned together as Paul's "fellow workers in Christ Jesus" who "risked their lives for me" (vv. 3-4). One Mary "worked very hard" for the Romans, but Paul does not specify in what sense she did this (v. 6). Tryphena and Tryphosa were "women who worked hard in the Lord" (v. 12). The same is said of "my dear friend Persis, another woman who has worked very hard in the Lord" (v. 12). Again we do not know with certainty what these women were doing, but it would assuredly be wrong to settle into the assumption that they were not engaged in missionary activity along with Paul. Only a few verses later Paul speaks of "Timothy, my fellow worker," who certainly was involved in full ministry with Paul. We know that other women were also prominent in the expansion of the church. Michael Green observes that "a leading part in the spread of the gospel was undertaken by women; sometimes in public or semi-public, as in the work of a Priscilla, a Lydia, a Phoebe, a Syntyche; and sometimes in the women's quarters of the home or at the laundry."[1] Given these vignettes, we are left with no doubt that women were intensely active in the spread of the gospel during the period of the New Testament church.

Evaluating Evidence from the Early Church

As noted above, the nature and extent of women's participation in the evangelistic outreach of the early church cannot be determined merely by citations of isolated examples. This is the case no matter how glowing these examples may be in themselves. We may give several reasons for this. One is that the written records of that period are too sparse to provide a sufficient basis for sweeping conclusions. Another is that it is easily deceptive to view the early centuries from the perspective of our own times, expecting to find essentially similar modes of evangelism. This can be a problem even after discounting such obvious features of our times as radio, TV, literature, and mass crusades in great auditoriums. The differences run far deeper than that. A third reason for caution is that isolated incidents are not necessarily typical examples and therefore may not lead to a balanced conclusion as to the normal state of affairs. In short, we need to evaluate the contribution of women in terms of the way evangelism and mission were actually carried out in those times.

As regards the paucity of written records, first of all, we are unable to tell whether what has survived provides a fair and balanced picture of the contribution of women. In the early centuries, as well as throughout most of church history, it was men who authored the extant materials. Some suspect that the contributions of women were minimized. We are reluctant to offer an opinion in this regard. One aspect of this matter does, however, require comment. Some contemporary writers have suggested that the book of Acts itself minimizes the contribution of women in the New Testament church.[2] They argue that Paul's writings, despite his restrictions on women, include references to a number of women associates who are unnamed in Acts. But a comparison of Luke's Gospel with the other Synoptic Gospels shows that Luke's presentation of women, far from being inadequate or (worse) demean-

1. Michael Green, *Evangelism and the Early Church* (Grand Rapids: Eerdmans, 1970), p. 118; citing Origen, *Contra Celsum* 3.55, along with the biblical passages.

2. Elizabeth Tetlow, *Women and Ministry in the New Testament* (New York: Paulist, 1980), pp. 107-9; cf. Elizabeth A. Clark, *Women in the Early Church* (Wilmington: Michael Glazier, 1983) and Jean LaPorte, *The Role of Women in the Early Christianity* (Lewiston, N.Y.: Mellen, 1982).

ing, as has sometimes been charged, is equal to or superior to those of Matthew and Mark.[3]

If that is the case in the Gospel, where Luke can be checked, it is inappropriate to think that in Acts he deliberately skewed the narratives to obliterate traces of women's ministry. Luke's literary method involves careful focusing on specific characters. His focus on Peter and Paul, for example, may have been a reason for his giving less attention to their women associates. We cannot, therefore, assume that there were not a good number of women active in evangelism simply because they are not cited by name in Acts. By extension, we cannot assume that the records of the post–New Testament period provide us with all there is to know about women evangelists and missionaries.

The second reason for caution is our tendency to see the first centuries from a modern perspective. Was there a highly visible, unified evangelistic thrust or did the gospel spread largely through relatively simple and unspectacular ways? How would this have affected the participation of women? Balance is needed. Open-air evangelism, for example, did take place, attested to not only by the New Testament but by extrabiblical literature. Celsus's complaint, cited by Origen, was that Christians showed that they were uncouth by their street-corner approach.[4] Not incidentally, Celsus's taunt included the charge that Christians were able to convince "only the foolish, dishonorable, and stupid, and only slaves, women, and little children." The marketplace was frequented by itinerant purveyors of every sort imaginable. In addition to the outright entertainers, there were philosophers, especially the Cynics in their deliberately tattered robes, the garish cultic figures, and the crafty "religious" beggars. Christians used these opportunities, although one would be hard-pressed to name famous "evangelists" from the decades following the New Testament period.

MacMullen holds that "after Saint Paul, the church had no mission, it made no organized or official approach to unbelievers; rather it left everything to the individual."[5] These individuals, however, used every practicable means to spread the faith, and open-air evangelism was one such means. Since this was not an "organized or official" activity, however it is viewed, the church would have had no control over whether women used this opportunity. I am not aware of any evidence that they did, and the attitudes then prevailing concerning women would have made it unlikely that they would have been heard.

3. Ruth A. Tucker and Walter L. Liefeld, *Daughters of the Church: A History of Women in Ministry* (Grand Rapids: Zondervan, 1987), Excursus to Chapter One.

4. Origen, *Contra Celsum,* 3.52; cf. 7.9.

5. Ramsay MacMullen, *Christianizing the Roman Empire* (New Haven: Yale University Press, 1984), p. 34.

The Apologists are well known to us for their bold literary warfare, storming the fortresses of pagan mentality and defending the Christian faith from attack. Yet their literature did not begin to appear until a hundred years after Christ, most of it mid-second-century and later. Relatively few were involved in the literary aspect of Christian mission, but, as we shall see, women were in their number.

Apart from some outstanding instances of direct preaching and writing, however, the advance of the Christian mission seems to have been done largely by personal witnessing accompanied by the vibrant impressive testimony of moral rectitude and deeds of kindness and charity. Even the martyrs were singled out for torture not so much because they were successful evangelists, but because they were faithful witnesses. Tertullian wrote of the way in which a Christian wife of a pagan had to exercise extreme care in her relations with believers, especially men, and in her attempts to attend Christian church services.[6] This is in keeping with Peter's advice to wives as to how to win over a pagan husband by pure and reverent behavior (1 Peter 3:1-4). House churches, no doubt, were held in the larger homes, where the "household" included relatives and many slaves. A Christian hostess would have had considerable influence spiritually.

Along with public and personal methods of witness was the preaching that took place within the church itself. 1 Corinthians 14:24-25 seems to indicate that, just as Gentile "God-fearers" attended synagogues and thereby came into the Jewish faith, so, from the beginning, unbelievers could be found in Christian church services. While it was commonly argued that women should not preside over the Eucharist, there were church functions they did fulfill, including prophesying (Acts 2:17-18; 21:8-9; 1 Cor. 11:5). This fact of the multiple expression of spiritual gifts in the church, together with the 1 Corinthians 14 passage about visiting unbelievers, suggests that even within the church service, at least in the early years of house churches, the ministry of women reached unbelievers.

The third reason for caution is the problem of extrapolating a pattern of women's evangelistic activity from isolated examples. To cite a contemporary circumstance, it is possible for a Christian organization to feature in its public presentations an instance of some missionary's successful work that may not be an accurate representation of that organization's ministry as a whole. This might be useful for motivation, but it would be do insufficient basis for a historian's evaluation. Thus *Foxe's Book of Martyrs* is stirring, but not intended to be a complete, balanced picture of Christian witness in the

6. Tertullian, *Ad Uxorem,* 2.6 and 5.

early church. Nevertheless, there are some outstanding instances of women, and the adoption of a cautious attitude should not rob us of their significance.

The Post-Apostolic Church through the Fourth Century

One of the earliest testimonies to the activity of Christian women comes not from Christian sources but from an official of the Roman Empire. Pliny, governor of Bithynia, wrote the Emperor Trajan in the year A.D. 111 regarding matters in his province. He mentioned two Christian women slaves whom he had arrested. "I have judged it necessary to obtain information by torture from two serving women called by them 'deaconesses'."[7] Why did Pliny interrogate women instead of men? Did he consider them weaker and more likely to yield information? Were they well known in the community for their testimony? Were the men unavailable . . . perhaps deliberately? We do not know what was in his mind, but obviously these women were known for their Christian stand.

Their torture was equaled and surpassed by that of many women in the early church. Some years later Eusebius wrote of a woman named Blandina, who lived at about the same time as the two women just mentioned. Eusebius noted her strength in pain and of the effect of this on her captors. Finally she was hung on a stake and offered as a prey to the wild beasts, encouraging others to live and suffer for the glory of Christ.[8]

Perhaps the best-known woman martyr from the early years of the church was Vibia Perpetua. Even though the early church spawned many legends of dubious historicity, there is good reason to consider the information about Perpetua essentially reliable. Born into a wealthy family, she, her slave Felicitas, and several men were taken captive during the persecution under Septimius Severus in 202/203. The anxiety of her father, who could not identify with her strong faith, far exceeded her own self-concern. He tried by various ways to convince her that she should yield and save her life. Even more poignant, she had a baby and realized what this would mean for her child. Meanwhile, her slave Felicitas was also pregnant. Since she knew that the tormentors would not kill a pregnant woman, Felicitas prayed that the child would be born quickly. It was, and she submitted herself for execution. The account of their torture and death is vivid, including the detail that Perpetua

7. Pliny, *Letter to Trajan*, 10.96.

8. Eusebius, *Ecclesiastical History*, 5.1-61.

guided the hand of her executioner so that she would feel the pain of the sword at her throat.[9]

More stories could be related about women martyrs. One, named Quinta, refused to worship at a pagan temple and was tied by the feet and dragged "through the whole city, over the rough stones of the paved streets, dashing her against the millstones, and scourging her at the same time, until they brought her to the same place, where they stoned her."[10] Another, Saint Apollonia, had all her teeth broken out and then voluntarily jumped into the fire to her death.[11] The citation of such accounts not only celebrates the faith of these women but calls attention to the fact that, since martyrdoms were for the most part public events, spectators received an unforgettable witness to Christ.

In strong contrast to this intense, momentary declaration were the various writings that provided a continuing source of Christian teaching. A woman with great literary gift, Proba, wrote a type of literature (called a "cento") that draws on other works, in this case, that of the Roman poet Virgil. She gave testimony to Christ through such lines as:

> because Thy Son descended from the high heaven and time brought to us with our hopes at last succor and the coming of God whom for the first time a woman bearing the guises and habit of a virgin — marvelous to say — brought faith a child not of our race of blood . . . one with God, the very image of his beloved Sire.[12]

The famous Christian scholar Jerome wrote of the biblical scholarship of the devout woman Marcella. He had such confidence in her that when he went away, he directed any inquirers who needed "evidence from Scripture" to consult with her.[13] Although Marcella's name is not usually mentioned among those of the great apologists, Jerome said of her, "She was in the front line in condemning the heretics; she brought forth witnesses who earlier had been taught by them and later were set straight from their heretical error. She showed how many of them had been deceived. . . . She called upon the heretics in frequent letters to defend themselves."[14]

9. *The Martyrdom of Perpetua and Felicitas,* 5.

10. Eusebius, *Ecclesiastical History,* 6.41.

11. Eusebius, *Ecclesiastical History,* 6.41.

12. Quoted in Patricia Wilson-Kastner et al., *A Lost Tradition: Women Writers of the Early Church* (Lanham, Md.: University Press of America, 1981), pp. 45-68.

13. Jerome, *Epistle,* 127.2-7.

14. Jerome, *Epistle,* 127.10.

Another woman of whom Jerome wrote highly was Paula. She was devoted to good deeds and eventually, with Jerome, established a monastery (they were not yet called convents) for women.[15] Paula symbolizes the many women in the early church as well as throughout church history who remained virgins in order to devote themselves to God and to deeds of kindness to others. Like the Christian widows, they gave testimony by life to the reality of God's grace and the transforming power of Christ in their lives.

The influence of Augustine's mother, Monica, in turning him to Christ is well known. The great Cappadocian Father, Basil, was also influenced by a woman. His sister Macrina was concerned over his intellectual pride and directed him to a spiritual life. Their brother, Gregory of Nyssa, said of Macrina, "It was a woman who was the subject of our discourse, if indeed you can say 'a woman' for I do not know if it is appropriate to call her by a name taken from nature when she surpassed that nature."[16]

So it was that in the early years of the church's evangelistic mission, women as well as men "surpassed," in a sense, their human nature and devoted themselves spiritually to the advance of the cause of Christ. In the home, ministering in the house churches, maintaining a steadfast witness, willingly being martyred for their faith, writing and teaching the truths of the gospel, embodying the love of Christ in their practical humble deeds of charity, and influencing people in many ways to abandon lives of sin and emptiness — in all these ways and perhaps many others unchronicled for whatever reason — women participated in the fulfilling of the Great Commission.

15. Jerome, *Epistle,* 108.5-26.

16. Gregory of Nyssa, *Life of St. Macrina,* 1.6.

CHAPTER 8

Evangelism and Contemporary American Life

Bill J. Leonard

"Born Again" . . . Those words once associated in the popular mind with street preachers, holy rollers, and religious outcasts have in the last decade become the watchword of an evangelical elite in America, a thriving subculture filled with success stories, power politics, and social acceptability. Evangelism and evangelicals appear to have arrived in the American religious and political establishment. Presidents, congressional leaders, executives, and celebrities, along with multitudes of "ordinary" folks, testify to a born again experience. George Gallup, that perennial pulse-taker of the American mood, found in 1976 that 34 percent of Americans (one in three) claimed to be born again.[1] Assorted religious leaders anticipate a "third great awakening" in America as citizens return to the "old time gospel" of simple faith in Christ and the almost forsaken values of the Protestant ethic. A new generation of media evangelists challenge (at a respectful distance) Billy Graham for the office of America's chaplain while reporters offer predictions as to which "electric preacher" will receive Graham's mantle.[2] Mainline denominations, which in the 1960s appeared to reject more traditional styles of evangelical outreach, have turned their attention toward a recovery of a theology of evangelism and a style for doing evangelism in the parish and throughout the nation. "Parachurch" groups blitz college campuses and the armed services while unsuspecting travelers receive an airport witness from traditional evangelicals and cultic devotees alike.

1. George Gallup, Jr., afterword, *Religion in America: 1950 to the Present,* ed. Jackson W. Carroll, Douglas W. Johnson, and Martin E. Marty (New York: Harper & Row, 1979), p. 113.

2. Mary Murphy, "The Next Billy Graham," *Esquire,* 10 October 1978, pp. 25-32. Murphy suggests that Jerry Falwell may be the candidate. Grant Simmons, "Meet the Next Billy Graham," *Texas Business,* December 1979, pp. 25-28. Simmons suggests that Texas evangelist James Robinson will be the next.

There seems to be no shortage of evangelism or evangelicals in contemporary America. The question may better be asked: Which evangelism and which evangelicals? Is the gospel preached by so-called evangelicals in America reflective of certain biblical norms? How does it shape and how is it shaped by American culture? A number of recent works have asked those or similar questions, seeking to define evangelism and examine the state of evangelical Christianity in America.[3] This study is a brief attempt to describe certain factors which have influenced evangelism in America, to characterize various evangelical groups on the contemporary scene, and to evaluate the nature of evangelism in American religion.

Evangelism: A Working Definition

Evangelism, that word most basic to Christian faith, seems elusive in both meaning and application. At its most simple level it may be considered the proclamation that Jesus Christ lived, was crucified, and was resurrected; that he is the way of salvation for those who come to him by repentance and faith. In a classic study, *Evangelism in the Early Church,* Michael Green suggests that *kerussein* (to proclaim) is not the only meaning of evangelism. He stresses three concepts which illustrate a broader biblical and historical basis for defining the story of Jesus in its relation to the world. Those concepts are: "the gospel is good news; it is proclamation; it is witness."[4]

Briefly defined, Christian evangelism is the good news that Jesus Christ is the way to God. It is the proclamation of the story of Jesus and the call to follow him. Evangelism also involves the living out of that good news in the world. Herb Miller describes it as a threefold approach:

> (1) Being the Word — the influence of the Christian's spiritual quality and example. (2) Doing the Word — the influence of the Christian's loving acts toward other people. (3) Saying the Word — the influence of the Christian's verbal communication with those outside the church.[5]

3. David F. Wells and John D. Woodbridge, *The Evangelicals,* rev. ed. (Grand Rapids: Baker, 1977); Martin E. Marty, *A Nation of Behavers* (Chicago: University of Chicago Press, 1976); William G. McLoughlin, *Revivals, Awakenings, and Reform* (Chicago: University of Chicago Press, 1978); and Robert E. Webber, *Common Roots: A Call to Evangelical Maturity* (Grand Rapids: Zondervan, 1979).

4. Michael Green, *Evangelism in the Early Church* (Grand Rapids: Eerdmans, 1970), p. 48.

5. Herb Miller, *Evangelism's Open Secrets* (St. Louis: Bethany, 1977), p. 12.

American Evangelism: Formative Forces

Historically, the American experience has shaped significantly the directions, methods, and theology of Christian evangelism. Some of the most important influences have come from pluralism, revivalism, nationalism, and fundamentalism.

Pluralism represents a major factor in American society in general and American religion in particular. It is an obvious result of democratic government, personal liberty, and religious freedom. In religion, pluralism has meant that a number of denominations, sects, and cults could exist side by side, each free to proclaim its doctrines without coercion from the state in a society where no one church was officially dominant. Membership in each religious group was based upon the voluntary consent of the individual. Those churches wishing to grow were required to evangelize in order to secure "volunteers" for membership.[6] Evangelism, even aggressive evangelism, was therefore both a means of fulfilling a major imperative of the gospel and securing a larger number of constituents. Evangelism and church growth have seemed inseparable in American churches.

Pluralism has also meant that many groups could claim to possess the one "true" gospel without being able to impose that gospel on the entire society. Many demonstrate evangelistic zeal but not the same evangelistic message. Southern Baptists, Campus Crusaders, Full Gospel Business Men's Fellowship members, Mormons, and Moonies all demonstrate an aggressive style of evangelism, but the content of their messages is certainly not the same. Each of those groups (and a multitude of others) reflects diverse views of conversion, discipleship, and church membership. Religious freedom and its accompanying pluralism suggest that a variety of belief systems may be proclaimed as "good news," as being the most representative of biblical tradition and a variety of methods as the most reliable for winning converts.

As churches experienced the reality of pluralism, they needed a technique by which they could both fulfill the gospel command to evangelize and also attract converts to their particular view of the gospel. Revivalism became a primary method by which many American religious bodies spread the gospel and secured converts. Indeed, revivalism, as perhaps no other phenomenon, has shaped the directions of evangelical Protestantism in America.[7]

Obviously religious awakenings are not unique to the American experience. Christian history, both Protestant and Catholic, is full of accounts of

6. Sidney E. Mead, *The Lively Experiment* (New York: Harper & Row, 1963), pp. 121-22.
7. Mead, *The Lively Experiment*, pp. 122-27.

those periods when the fires of religious enthusiasm burned brightly, converts were numerous, and churches were spiritually rejuvenated. In America, however, revivalism served as both the means and the technique for fulfilling the church's call to evangelize the masses. It produced a style which dramatically influenced the content of evangelical theology.

Revivalism in many respects systematized the process of evangelism and conversion. This is reflected in the issue of "means" in revivals. Among the New England Calvinists of the First Great Awakening, the means for revival rested with God. Evangelists might preach for revival, Christians might unite in "prayer concerts" beseeching God to give revival, but ultimately only the sovereign God could grant the outpouring of revivalistic zeal. Thus Jonathan Edwards described the evangelical awakening at Northampton, Massachusetts, in the 1730s by calling it "a surprising work of God," begun and controlled entirely by the divine will.

By the Second Great Awakening of the nineteenth century, evangelists such as Charles G. Finney condemned those Christians who waited for revival while thousands remained unevangelized. Finney wrote that a revival

> is not a miracle, or dependent on a miracle, in any sense. It is a purely philosophical result of the right use of the constituted means . . . There may be a miracle among its antecedent causes, or there may not.[8]

D. L. Moody, the great evangelist of the late 1800s, elaborated on Finney's views regarding the means of evangelism. He urged any method which would lead to the conversion of a person, insisting, "It doesn't matter how you get a man to God, provided you get him there."[9] Moody and company refined Finney's new measures so that techniques for mass revivalism and personal witnessing were carefully systematized. Revival campaigns were planned in detail and Christians taught how to share their faith with "inquirers" before and after the nightly meetings.

Moody's methods continue to influence modern revivalistic evangelical techniques. Music, sermons, counselors at mass rallies, media campaigns, and training in the fine art of personal evangelism are among the major aspects of contemporary evangelical action. Revivalism has also had impact on the structure (or lack of it) in the worship services of evangelical churches. The hymns of frontier and urban revivals, spontaneous testimonies, preaching

8. Charles G. Finney, *Lectures on Revivals of Religion* (New York: Fleming H. Revell Co., 1888), pp. 12-13.

9. William J. McLaughin, *Modern Revivalism* (New York: The Ronald Press, 1959), p. 259, citing *Boston Daily Advertiser* (3 February 1877): 4.

style, and entire worship format frequently have been shaped by the revivalistic context. This is particularly true of what in many churches is the most important symbol of evangelical conversion, the invitation.

Unknown to evangelical religion before the nineteenth century, the public invitation to "come forward" and accept Christ began in the frontier camp meetings. Sinners were exhorted to enter the "anxious pens," fenced-in areas in front of the pulpits, in order to be "prayed through" to conversion. Finney perfected the process with his "anxious bench," a similar area where those seeking conversion could find support and counsel. Many questioned Finney's actions, fearing that a public response smacked of works done for salvation focusing attention on outward, not inward manifestations. Moody institutionalized the invitation or altar call by urging the unevangelized to come forward and be taken to "inquiry rooms" where trained laity and pastors spoke with each individual about specific needs.

Soon these methods had become linked inseparably to the weekly liturgy of Protestant worship. No service was concluded without an appeal to public decision. So important was this new symbol that evangelical conversion itself is often described in the language of the invitation. Believers speak of conversion as "walking the aisle" or "coming forward." So significant is the invitation, and its eternal implications, that in many churches it has become the central event of worship. If no one responds publicly, some imply that worship and sermon, pastor and people have not experienced the presence of God and that the service was less than significant. It is one of the most obvious illustrations of the way in which Christian evangelism has been shaped by American religious tradition.

The exhortation to immediate conversion and public response is also evidence of the way in which American revivalism has affected the theology of evangelism in an increasingly Arminian direction. In the period of the First Great Awakening, the evangelists were primarily Calvinistic in their theological orientation. Conversion was much more a process by which the sovereign God brought salvation to the depraved and helpless sinner. Edwards traced the steps of salvation: (1) an extreme sense of sinfulness, helplessness under the wrath of God; (2) agony over sin; (3) a time of quietness first before a "little light has risen"; (4) dawning of divine light — sometimes gradually, sometimes rapidly; (5) joy and thankfulness at the gift of redemption; (6) evidence of genuine change of heart and life.[10]

The process of conversion was often quite lengthy, extending for days.

10. Jonathan Edwards, *Distinguishing Marks of a Work in the Spirit of God,* in *The Great Awakening,* ed. Alan Heimert and Perry Miller (New York: Bobbs-Merrill, 1967), pp. 204-13.

weeks, even months, as the individual waited on God to provide the grace which produced salvation. Increasingly, however, the Calvinists themselves debated the question of human participation in the salvific process. The Edwardseans, the New Divinity men, who claimed to be the heirs of Jonathan Edwards, softened sovereignty somewhat to permit cooperation between God and those seeking conversion. They continued to insist that the chief agent in conversion was God but urged moral "duties" as a sign of true conversion.[11]

By the time of the camp meetings and the urban revivals, more democratic and Arminian ideals were claiming the support of a large number of evangelical preachers. Conversion was a process in which divine grace interacted with the free will of the individual. Indeed, no salvation could occur without the response of the human will. Grace was not irresistible; it also could be rejected or ignored by each person.

In many current evangelical communions, the sovereignty of God has been replaced by the sovereignty of the individual. Conversion is less a process of waiting on God to provide the grace for salvation than of convincing the sinner to ask God for that grace which is immediately available. Potential converts are often urged to pray a prayer and to "invite Jesus into your heart," and are assured that the moment the human will is activated, God responds. Grace is less the mysterious gift of God than the terms of a transaction which is dependent on the free will of the new believer. As H. Richard Niebuhr writes, conversion is something which happens less as process than as transaction carried out during the last hymn of the worship service.[12]

Debates over these issues illustrate one other influence of American revivalism upon evangelism. The revivals created extensive controversies among American Christians, particularly regarding the relationship of the evangelistic message to revivalistic method. Many denominations divided and new ones were formed. Often the question was not over the importance of conversion but whether or not conversion was dependent on revivalistic technique. The Regular and Separate Baptists, for example, who divided during the First Great Awakening, were both evangelical but could not agree on revivalistic method. The Regulars were suspicious of the emotionalism and sensational methods of the Separates who insisted that conversion was dramatic and, therefore, required dramatic response.

11. Sydney Ahlstrom, *A Religious History of the American People* (New Haven: Yale University Press, 1972), pp. 406-14.

12. H. Richard Niebuhr, *The Kingdom of God in America* (New York: Harper & Row, 1959), pp. 179-80.

The student of American evangelicalism should expect to find division among Christian groups regarding methods and motives related to a particular style of evangelism. The tendency to see a particular style as synonymous with proper Christian evangelism continues to be a problem which affects the evangelical efforts of many American denominations.

In addition to pluralism and revivalism, another influence on evangelicalism in America is nationalism. America's peculiar beginnings and sense of manifest destiny have been particularly significant to the evangelism promoted in many of the churches.

To varying degrees, evangelicals in America have sometimes united concepts of personal and national salvation, with particular attention to the American experience as paralleled with that of Israel. The North American continent, long unknown to the Europeans, seemed chosen by God as the place where biblical Christianity could be restored and the kingdom of God established. The idea of America as having a peculiar part in the redemptive plan was often a strong emphasis of the Puritans. Jonathan Edwards, observing the religious outpourings of the Great Awakening, saw the mass conversions as evidence of a "Golden Age," a prelude to the establishment of the kingdom. Edwards apparently believed that America had a unique role in these post-millennial preparations. He wrote:

> It is not unlikely that this work of God's Spirit, so extraordinary and wonderful, is the dawning, or at least a prelude of that glorious work of God, so often foretold in scripture . . . and there are many things that make it probable that this work will begin in America.[13]

The influence of nationalism upon American evangelicalism has been a topic of great discussion by many scholars. It is difficult to trace and generalizations are dangerous. It does seem clear, however, that certain evangelicals have united nationalistic influences with Christian evangelism. Whether in utopian sects or zealous missionaries, in American evangelists or civil religion itself, national identity has sometimes been associated with genuine Christian experience.

Perhaps no modern revivalist has so illustrated the nationalistic influence on the evangelical as William A. Sunday. For Billy Sunday, "Christianity and Patriotism are synonymous terms and hell and traitors are synonymous."[14] In Sunday's view, the best Christians were the best Americans and

13. Jonathan Edwards, "Some Thoughts Concerning the Present Revival of Religions in New England," in *God's New Israel,* ed. Conrad Cherry (Englewood Cliffs, N.J.: Prentice-Hall, 1971), p. 55.

14. McLaughin, *Modern Revivalism,* p. 444.

vice versa. In the face of massive Catholic and Jewish immigration in the early 1900s, Sunday insisted that America would accept anyone "who wants to come here and assimilate our ways and conditions." This meant a person should be "a teetotaler, a Bible-believing Protestant, and a . . . middle class citizen."[15] Obviously, Sunday's approach is extreme in some respects, but it does indicate the influence of nationalism on the proclamation of the gospel in America. The following generalizations as to nationalism and contemporary evangelicalism may be noted.

First, in the minds of some (though certainly not all) evangelicals, the possibilities for world evangelism rested upon the shoulders of American Christians. America was a "city on the hill" to give the light of the gospel to the nations. Failure to live up to that calling was to warrant the judgment of God.

Second, some evangelicals often equated evangelization with Americanization and democracy. In missionary activities at home or abroad the gift of the gospel was the gift of American culture.

Third, evangelism has sometimes been united with particular millennial views. Post-millennialists in America affirmed a sense of destiny in which they helped to convert the masses and thus bring in the kingdom of God. Both individuals and social structures could be redeemed. Pre-millenialists warned that the church should not waste time on redeeming unredeemable society but race to evangelize the nations before the second coming brought destruction to the powers of this world. Finally, some have implied that America was indeed the last best hope of church. If its message was not shared or went unheeded, the gospel was seriously threatened in the world.

In addition to pluralism, revivalism, and nationalism, the ideology of fundamentalism has had a major impact on American evangelism. Fundamentalism has been described as that movement which places emphasis on biblical inerrancy, is hostile toward modern methods of biblical and theological interpretation, and is concerned that those who reject fundamentalist doctrines are not "true Christians."[16]

It began, most agree, as a nineteenth-century reaction to liberal trends in Christian theology, closely related to certain pre-millennial groups in Britain and America and reaching giddy heights in the 1920s. Subsequent evangelicals have sometimes sought to separate themselves from the narrowness and unpopular image of fundamentalism. Some have used the phrase "neo-Evangelical" to describe conservatives who repudiated the negative image of fundamentalism but sought to remain faithful to orthodox dogma.

15. McLaughin, *Modern Revivalism*, pp. 443-44.

16. James Barr, *Fundamentalism* (Philadelphia: Westminster, 1977), p. 1.

Nonetheless, fundamentalism strongly influences many aspects of evangelism in America. First, fundamentalists agree on the need for personal conversion and on the evangelical experience of divine grace through repentance and faith. Second, they frequently relate genuine conversion, explicitly or implicitly, to certain fundamental doctrines of the faith. Such doctrines are considered non-negotiable in their relationship to Christianity. For fundamentalists, genuine conversion is intricately related to the trustworthiness of the biblical record, the legitimacy of the saving work of Christ in atonement and resurrection, his sinless nature, and the inviolability of his miracles. To certain traditional fundamentalist dogmas such as virgin birth, miracles, sacrificial atonement, bodily resurrection, and second coming, stronger statements on biblical inerrancy, the creation narratives, and a personal devil have recently been added.

Third, these doctrines often challenge the modern concern for biblical criticism, social Christianity, and ecumenical cooperation. Indeed, fundamentalists often point to the relationship between the decline of evangelism and the rise of a more liberal theological approach. They equate theological liberalism with a lack of evangelism, an evangelism often defined in terms of revivalism. They point to such modern works as *Why Conservative Churches are Growing* and insist that proper biblical authority and doctrine produces the best and most aggressive evangelism, giving preachers "something to preach" and converts something to believe.

Finally, fundamentalists sometimes mistake their orthodoxy for proper faith, indeed as the only proper evangelism. Some seem quick to call themselves "Bible-believing Christians" or "evangelicals," in contrast with "non-Bible-believing Christians" and "non-evangelicals."

Fundamentalism continues to be a powerful force in shaping church life and evangelism, as well as divisions within the denominations. With these and other influences in mind, perhaps some observations on the current state of evangelism in America may be made, both positive and negative.

American Evangelism: Its Present Shape

It is clear that the efforts to "do" evangelism in contemporary America are extremely diverse. Groups may agree on some (though not all) common principles, but differ significantly on method, doctrine, theological emphases, and practical response. In his book *Common Roots: A Call to Evangelical Maturity,* Robert E. Webber charts some fourteen different types of "evangelicals" in modern America. While not definitive, his list illustrates the great diversity which exists even among so-called "evangelicals." With those groups are other supposedly "non-evangelicals," who are castigated for their lack of direct, aggressive evangelistic work but whose concern for nurture, growth in grace, and education in the faith may also be important vehicles of Christian evangelism.[17]

Subcultural Evangelicalism

Group	Major Emphasis	Symbols
1. Fundamentalist Evangelicalism	Personal and ecclesiastical separationism; Biblicism	Bob Jones University; *Sword of the Lord*
2. Dispensational Evangeli[cali]sm	Dispensational hermeneutics; pretribulationalism and premillenarianism	Dallas Theological Seminary; Moody Bible Institute
3. Conservative Evangeli[cali]sm	Cooperative evangelism; inclusive of all evangelical groups	Wheaton College; Gordon-Conwell Seminary; *Christianity Today*; Billy Graham
4. Non-denominational Evangeli[cali]sm	Unity of the church; restoration of the church; Restoration of NT Christianity	Milligan College
5. Reformed Evangelicalism	Calvinism (some with a decidedly Puritan flavor); covenant theology and hermeneutics	Calvin College and Seminary; Francis Schaeffer
6. Anabaptist Evangelicalism	Discipleship; poverty; peace movement; pacifism	Goshen College; Reba Place Fellowship
7. Wesleyan Evangelicalism	Arminianism; sanctification	Asbury College and Seminary
8. Holiness Evangelicalism	The second work of grace	Nazarene Church
9. Pentecostal Evangelicalism	Gift of tongues	Church of God; Assembly of God
10. Charismatic Evangelicalism	Gifts of the Holy Spirit	Oral Roberts University; Melodyland School of Theology
11. Black Evangelicalism	Black consciousness	National Association of Black Evangelicals

17. Webber, *Common Roots: A Call to Evangelical Maturity* (Grand Rapids: Zondervan, 1982), p. 32.

	Group	Major Emphasis	Symbols
12.	Progressive Evangelicalism	Openness toward critical scholarship and ecumenical relations	Fuller Seminary
13.	Radical Evangelicalism	Moral, social, and political consciousness	*Sojourners; The Other Side*; *Wittenberg Door*
14.	Mainline Evangelicalism	Historical consciousness at least back to the Reformation	Movements in major denominations; Methodist, Lutheran, Presbyterian, Episcopal, Baptist

The list indicates that the evangelicals themselves are widely separated on significant issues of social action, biblical infallibility, ecumenism, gifts of the Spirit, and politics — ideas which form their basic approach to the "simple" gospel of repentance and faith.

In the face of American religious pluralism it may be too much to expect diverse groups to develop a consensus, even on evangelism, beyond very basic assertions. Diversity may help to take the gospel to a variety of persons from various strata of society. The struggle is not for a contrived consensus among different communions as much as for the responsibility of each group to be true to the biblical perspectives on evangelism.

Beyond diversity, there is no doubt that Christian evangelism is having an impact on contemporary society. The need for a personal dimension of faith and a sense of acceptance and transcendence are certainly factors which have drawn many to Christianity. The church in turn insists that the gospel is a timeless remedy for the ills of the society.

This renewed appreciation for evangelism reminds mainline churches that just as they are called to accept the social implications of the gospel, they must cultivate the evangelical dimensions as well. Both powerful forces must be kept in balance. Many established denominations are struggling with that tension today, some seeking to restate and re-emphasize their evangelical roots while retaining a commitment to the social dimension of the gospel.

Evangelism is undergoing a renewed emphasis in American churches. Whether that constitutes the much-discussed third (some say fourth) Great Awakening remains to be seen and may depend on the way the church defines evangelism.

With the renewed emphasis on evangelism have come efforts at changing the style for doing evangelism as well a concern to rethink the theology of evangelism. Both attempts illustrate the vitality and the dangers of contemporary evangelism.

The marketing of evangelism may be its most controversial aspect as different groups utilize various techniques. Some retain the older methods, calling the church to return to the "old time religion" of revivals, altar calls, evangelists, and mass conversions. The traveling professional evangelist, holding "protracted meetings" in local churches, rented halls, and football stadiums, continues to be a significant style of evangelism, particularly in the Bible Belt of the southern and southwestern United States. Thousands testify to having been converted in "crusades" led by prominent, semi-prominent, or almost unknown evangelists and their "team" of musicians, advancemen, counselors, and financial advisors. These evangelistic organizations follow the Finney-Moody-Sunday-Graham pattern of organization, conversion, counseling, and referral to local congregations. Many modern jeremiads warn that evangelism has declined as the church has turned from these time-tested, surefire methods of evangelism. Critics warn that excessive dependence on this "old time" style can lead to a trust in technique and a neglect of a biblical theology of evangelism.

Another style of contemporary evangelism provides a more "modern" approach aimed particularly at the youth culture, the secular materialists, and the unchurched. The strategy varies from group to group, reflecting the particular subculture toward which it is directed. From the ghettos of the inner city (Sojourners), to the fraternity houses of the ivy league schools (Campus Crusade), to the barracks of the Armed Forces (Navigators), to the corporate and political ghettos of business and politics (Norman Vincent Peale, Robert Schuller, and others), the gospel of Christ is couched in the language and mindset of its secular constituents. Sometimes unorthodox, sometimes culture-accommodating, usually intense and highly committed, this style of evangelism has had significant impact, person to person, on individuals often ignored or untouched by traditional evangelistic forms.

Though many others could no doubt be cited, one additional style cannot be overlooked. The old time/new time evangelism presented through the media, particularly television, is the single most influential and controversial mode of current evangelicalism in America.

Billy Graham and Oral Roberts long ago set the pattern for media evangelism. Both had their beginning in crusades televised from halls or stadiums. Graham has retained that method and is perhaps the only major figure who can still accomplish it on a national scale. Roberts set the pattern for a new generation of television evangelists, moving indoors to his own specially constructed church/stadium/studio (in this case at Oral Roberts University), where the vicissitudes of nature and electronics could be carefully controlled. Today media evangelism shapes America's perceptions of the gospel in new and uncertain ways.

Some, like Jerry Falwell and Rex Humbard, package the "old time gospel hour" into a modern media experience. Listeners are assured that the message proclaimed is that of the evangelical forefathers; the services are traditionally revivalistic, the theology unashamedly fundamentalist, and the social concerns focused primarily on issues of personal morality. Their constituency tends to be more blue-collar, working class, suburban, and rural. Others, like Robert Schuller of Garden Grove, California, preach the gospel for a more middle- and upper-middle-class constituency who appreciate the aesthetics of fountains, robed clergy, an occasional Bach chorale, and the *piece de resistance,* the magnificent sixteen-million-dollar Crystal Cathedral, dedicated in 1980, debt-free.

Still others eschew the pulpit for the talk show or variety show format of guests, music, telephone counseling, and audience participation. This style of media evangelism is evident in the phenomenal growth of the *700 Club,* the PTL (Praise the Lord) Club, and the variety show approach of Oral Roberts himself. The *700 Club* and PTL unite evangelism with Pentecostalism, playing to a cross-section of American Christians, many of whom attest to an experience of tongues and healing in addition to conversion. Numbering Baptists and Roman Catholics among its strongest supporters, the *700 Club* and its founder Pat Robertson produce a budget of fifty to sixty million dollars annually, developing the Christian Broadcasting Network with multiple programs aimed at counteracting the negative morality of the major television networks.[18]

Include in this the syndicated programs of regional evangelists and local churches, the various broadcasting efforts of major denominations, and the occasional evangelical "weirdo," and the media becomes *the major* vehicle through which many Christian groups seek to fulfill their calling to evangelize. Most of these electronic efforts preach for conversions, extol the blessings of the gospel, and plead for support (prayer and financial) in continuing and expanding the work, while claiming great statistical success in benefits to the church, the community, and the nation. They are forces to be reckoned with in the issue of gospel and culture in America.

With the influence of the American past, the successes of the present, and the complex problems of the future, those concerned to do evangelism must confront a number of important issues and questions. Some of the more crucial ones include the following.

First, American churches must struggle continually with the question of what Christian evangelism really means. For those denominations which

18. "Stars of the Cathode Church," *Time,* February 4, 1980, pp. 64-65.

seem less aggressively evangelical, an appropriate form of biblical evangelism must be discovered. If they neglect this task, they may ignore the biblical imperatives and hold to a negative view of evangelism that represents a reaction to the kind of evangelism popularized by evangelists and tent preachers. The so-called non-evangelicals, therefore, need a theology of evangelism which can be compatible with their historic traditions and which can be done with integrity, not ignored as reactionary.

The evangelicals, on the other hand, need not suppose that, because they are aggressive in their methods, they have a corner on evangelism or even that their view of evangelism is necessarily biblical. Just as it is possible "to be a bishop without being religious," it is possible to be an evangelist without being evangelical, in the New Testament sense.

This is particularly evident in the shift of many churches from an evangelism of process to an evangelism of transaction. The reaction against hyper-Calvinism has in some contexts produced a hyper-Arminianism, equally unacceptable to biblical evangelism. The danger is that modern evangelism replaces an extreme emphasis on divine sovereignty with an extreme concern for human sovereignty. There is less concern for the interaction of divine grace and free will than for grace as dominated by human freedom. "Anytime I ask," God must respond and is therefore at the mercy of the individual.

This stress on the human side of conversion can and does lead to a "transactional" view of evangelism, not as process but as single event. Once the prayer is prayed and the invitation accepted, then the transaction is over — salvation is secured and heaven achieved. Discipleship, growth, process are obscured for a one-time-does-all transaction. Thus the biblical concerns for repentance, faith, discipleship, and sanctification are minimized for an evangelism of cheap grace, easy belief, and promises of success. Indeed, the increasing effort to equate material success with Christian witness is a major problem confronting evangelism in America. The union of the gospel and the American materialistic success syndrome has seriously obscured for many upper-class congregations the biblical calling to respond to the poor and the oppressed. Ronald Sider wrote recently that evangelical Christians have practiced heresy in their blindness to the social dimensions of the gospel, the presence of God on the side of the poor and the oppressed.[19]

Second, in failing to struggle continuously with the biblical meaning of evangelism, American churches may be fooled into believing that they are acting evangelically merely because they have a style which is considered

19. Ronald J. Sider, "An Evangelical Theology of Liberation," *Christian Century,* March 19, 1980, pp. 314-18.

evangelistic. Revivalistic techniques, hucksterism, and hard-sell tactics must not automatically be equated with a valid evangelical witness. Many revivalistic methods were a way of reaching an earlier generation with the gospel, but the use of those tactics in the present day does not guarantee evangelical response. Merely to reproduce the setting of "the old time gospel hour" does not ensure that the expected spiritual results will occur. Efforts to unite revivalistic methods inseparably with evangelism itself may lead to the confusion of the gospel with particular cultural forms and social expectations. In some churches. practices identified with evangelical awakenings of the past become the only valid means for having new awakenings. Indeed, many persons may find security in the pious platitudes of an earlier generation and ignore the word of God for the present.

Finally, both the church and the individuals who seek to be evangelical must beware lest their convictions turn to arrogance and their gospel turn to dogmatism. The danger is that the church may become so proud of its evangelical responsiveness that it loses sight of its limitations, its fallibility, and its own position under the judgment of God.

Peter M. Schmiechen warns that this is particularly problematic for those modern Christians who have appropriated the name "evangelical." Clearly committed to evangelical witness, they nonetheless must avoid the temptation "to equate the gospel with characteristics of the conservative mindset and one view of the Christian faith." Schmiechen concludes that "since Christian theology is by definition evangelical, it is both naïve and arrogant to suggest that theology is evangelical only when it fits into a particular position."[20]

The identification of one segment of the Christian community as "evangelical" may imply that those without a particular philosophy or style of evangelism are not fulfilling the task to be the good news of God to the world. It may suggest that a less aggressive style is not at all evangelical and thereby obscure the heritage of many Christian groups who place evangelism within the context of nurture, teaching, and sacraments.

Clearly, American religion is experiencing, at least in certain segments, a new openness to evangelism and the church's calling to be evangelistic. As in other ages, however, Christians must never take their theology of evangelism for granted. The church must struggle continually with issues relating to evangelism, with definitions, and with action. It must seek to proclaim and live the gospel to the world, while it is itself confronted by the demands of the

20. Peter M. Schmiechen, "The Challenge of Conservative Theology," *Christian Century*, April 9, 1980, pp. 402-3.

gospel which often condemn its captivity to culture and its obsession with superficial results. The church has no choice but to respond to its evangelical calling. Later generations will decide, however, whether current American evangelism reflects that biblical imperative or is merely the product of a group of sophisticated indulgence-sellers.

CHAPTER 9

Shifting Southward: Global Christianity since 1945

Dana L. Rob

Africa
Decolonialization

From Decembe[illegible] ...ost representative meeting of world Protestantism to dat[illegible] took place in Tambaram, India. Under the gathering storm clouds of World War II, with parts of China already under Japanese occupation, Hitler triumphant in Sudetenland, and Stalinism in full swing, 471 persons from 69 different countries met at Madras Christian College for the second decennial meeting of the International Missionary Council.

For the first time, African Christians from different parts of the continent met each other. The African delegation traveled together for weeks on a steamer that proceeded from West Africa to Cape Town and around the Cape of Good Hope to India. China, besieged by Japan and torn asunder by competing warlords, nationalists, and Communists, sent forty-nine official delegates, of whom nearly two-thirds were nationals and only one-third were missionaries. The women's missionary movement, then at the height of its influence, pushed for full representation by women at Madras. Their persistence was rewarded with sixty women delegates sent by their national Christian councils, and another ten women in attendance by invitation. Europeans whose countries would soon be at war worked together in committee, as common Christian commitment overrode the tensions among Belgians, Danes, French, Germans, British, Dutch, Norwegians, and others.

The central theme that drew so many to India at a time of multiple global crises was "the upbuilding of the younger churches as a part of the historic universal Christian community."[1] With Protestant missions bearing fruit in many parts of the world, the time was ripe for younger non-Western

1. *The World Mission of the Church: Findings and Recommendations of the Meeting of the International Missionary Council, Tambaram, Madras, India, Dec. 12-29, 1938* (London: International Missionary Council, 1939), p. 7.

churches to take their places alongside older Western denominations in joint consideration of the universal church's faith, witness, social realities, and responsibilities. The roster of attendees reads like a who's who of mid-twentieth-century world Christianity.[2]

Yet the 1938 IMC conference was a gathering of visionaries, for the global Christianity it embraced was a skeleton without flesh or bulk, a mission-educated minority who were leading nascent Christian institutions. At the beginning of the twentieth century, Europeans dominated the world church, with approximately 70.6 percent of the world's Christian population. By 1938, on the eve of World War II, the apparent European domination of Protestantism and Catholicism remained strong. Yet by the end of the twentieth century, the European percentage of world Christianity had shrunk to 28 percent of the total; Latin America and Africa combined provided 43 percent of the world's Christians. Although North Americans became the backbone of the cross-cultural mission force after World War II, their numerical dominance was being overtaken by missionaries from the very countries that were considered mission fields only fifty years before. The typical late twentieth-century Christian was no longer a European man, but a Latin American or African woman.[3] The skeleton of 1938 had grown organs and sinew.

This essay paints in broad strokes the transformation of world Christianity since the Second World War — a massive cultural and geographic shift away from Europeans and their descendants toward peoples of the Southern Hemisphere.[4] The shift southward began early in the century, and the 1938 missionary conference was vivid proof of powerful indigenous Christian

2. In attendance were pioneer leaders like Bishop Azariah, the first Indian Anglican bishop, and Toyohiko Kagawa, advocate of Japanese social Christianity. There were up-and-coming theologians such as Christian Baeta of Gold Coast and D. T. Niles of Ceylon, both thirty years old. Young leaders of future social struggles included Chief Albert Luthuli, future president of the African National Congress and first African recipient of the Nobel Peace Prize in 1960, and Y. T. Wu, author of the controversial anti-Western Chinese Christian Manifesto in 1950. Women leaders included Mina Soga, social worker and the first African woman to attend an international conference, and Michi Kawai, noted Japanese educationist. For attendance list, see *The World Mission of the Church,* pp. 187-201.

3. Statistics taken from David B. Barrett and Todd M. Johnson, "Annual Statistical Table on Global Mission," *International Bulletin of Missionary Research* 24, no. 1 (January 2000): 24-25.

4. An earlier draft of this article was presented at the meeting of the American Society of Church History in Washington, D.C., on January 9, 1999. Following both the terminology of the New International Economic Order (Brandt Commission), and the geographic reality of where most churches are growing, I have chosen to speak here of Christianity in the "South." "North"/"South" nomenclature nevertheless contains imprecisions and inadequacies, as do the terms "West"/"East," "First World"/"Third World," or "First World"/"Two-Thirds World."

leadership in both church and state, despite a missionary movement trapped within colonialist structures and attitudes. But after World War II, rising movements of political and ecclesiastical self-determination materially changed the context in which non-Western churches operated, thereby allowing Christianity to blossom in multiple cultures. After examining the changing political context in which the growth of global Christianity took place, this essay will give examples of the emerging Christian movement and then comment on the challenge for historians posed by the seismic shift in Christian identity.

Christianity and Nationalism

Besides laying waste to Europe, North Africa, and western Asia, the Second World War revealed the rotten underbelly of European imperialism. In the new postwar political climate, long-simmering nationalist movements finally succeeded in throwing off direct European rule. With the newly formed United Nations supporting the rights of peoples to self-determination, one country after another reverted to local control. In 1947 India obtained its freedom from Britain, beginning a process of decolonization that continued with Burma in 1948, Ghana in 1957, Nigeria in 1960, Kenya in 1963, and on around the globe. British policies of indirect rule promoted orderly transitions in some places, but left open sores in others, for example, in Sudan, where the Islamic north was left to govern the traditionalists and Christian south in 1956. Having introduced Western democratic institutions, the United States released the Philippines in 1946. Colonial powers such as Holland, France, and Portugal resisted the nationalist tide, ultimately to no avail. The Belgians were so angry at losing their colonies that they literally tore the phones off the walls in the Congo, leaving the colonial infrastructure in ruins. The French departed Algeria after six years of fighting the independence movement. Only a coup d'état in Portugal finally persuaded the Portuguese to free Angola and Mozambique in 1975, which, like many countries, erupted into civil war once the Europeans had departed. Different ethnic and political groups that had previously cooperated in opposition to European imperialism now found themselves fighting over control of nations whose boundaries, size, and even political systems had been created by foreigners. The success of anti-imperialist independence movements, with subsequent internal struggles for control in dozens of fledgling nation-states, was the most significant political factor affecting the growth of non-Western Christianity in the decades following World War II.

To understand why decolonization profoundly affected the state of Christianity in the non-Western world, one must explore the prior ambiguous relationship between Western missions and European imperialism. On the one hand, although missionary work often predated the coming of Western control, imperialism's arrival inevitably placed missions within an oppressive political context that they sometimes exploited for their own benefit. In China, for example, the unequal treaties of 1842 and 1858 permitted missions to operate in selected port cities and to buy land. Foreign missions in China benefited from extraterritoriality, whereby they were not subject to Chinese laws and regulations. In colonial Africa, missions received land grants. For example, in 1898 Cecil Rhodes awarded 13,000 acres to American Methodists for their Rhodesian Mission. Sometimes, however, the missionaries themselves stood between the indigenous peoples and their exploitation by Europeans. French Protestant missionary Maurice Leenhardt defended the land rights of the Kanaks in face of overwhelming pressure from French colonialists in New Caledonia. Presbyterian missionaries William Sheppard and William Morrison faced trial in 1909 for exposing the atrocities perpetrated on rubber gatherers in the Belgian Congo. While courageous individual missionaries mitigated the effects of imperialism on indigenous peoples, by and large the missions benefited materially from European control. Most missionaries saw themselves as apolitical and preferred the status quo of colonialism to the uncertainties of national revolution.

Another important factor in understanding the ambiguous relationship between missions and imperialism before decolonization was the importance of missionary schools. Christian missions pioneered Western learning in the non-Western world. In 1935 missions were running nearly 57,000 schools throughout the world, including more than one hundred colleges. Mission schools promoted literacy in both European languages and vernaculars, and they spread Western ideals of democratic governance, individual rights, and the educability of women and girls. Despite their limitations, missions through education provided local leadership with the tools it needed to challenge foreign oppression. The Christian contribution to Asian nationalism was extremely significant, especially through the impact of mission schools. Korea, for example, was colonized by the Japanese in 1910. At that time, mission schools were the only form of modern education in the country. In 1911 the Japanese military police accused students at a Presbyterian school of plotting to assassinate the Japanese governor-general. The police arrested 123 Koreans for conspiracy, 105 of whom were Christian nationalists. In 1919, thirty-three Koreans signed the Korean Declaration of Independence. Fifteen signatories were Christians, even though Christians represented only 1 percent of the total population.[5] Mission education, which combined vernacular literacy with Western learning, clearly played a key role in equipping nationalist leadership.

The role of mission schools in creating nationalist leadership was important not only in Asia, but also in Africa. Missions founded schools before those of colonial governments, including the first higher education for Africans in 1827 at Fourah Bay College in Sierra Leone, and higher education for South Africans at Fort Hare in 1916. By the Second World War, mission churches in Africa had produced a Christian elite poised to found independent governments. When independence came, even though Christianity was a minority religion, its adherents played a much larger role than their numbers warranted. Most black African leaders were churchmen. Kenneth Kaunda, first president of Zambia, was the son of a Presbyterian minister. Hastings Banda, first president of Malawi, received his early education in a mission school and attended college in the United States. Kwame Nkrumah, first president of Ghana, attended Catholic mission schools and began his career teaching in them. Leopold Senghor studied for the priesthood before entering politics and becoming first president of Senegal. Similarly, Julius Nyerere, first prime minister of Tanzania, both studied and taught in Catholic mission schools. Not only did mission schools train many nationalist leaders, but church-related institutions provided opportunities for developing indigenous leadership.

After World War II, with the process from decolonization to independence in full swing, Christianity in the non-Western world faced an entirely new context. In 1954, leading East Asian Christians wrote a volume entitled *Christianity and the Asian Revolution.* Reflecting on the social convulsions of the twentieth century, the Christian leaders defined the "Asian Revolution" not only as a reaction against European colonialism, but also as a search for human rights and economic and social justice, ideas obtained from the West itself. The authors noted, "As the American colonists revolted in the name of English justice against British rule, so Asians, in the name of political and social doctrines which originated in large part in Europe and America, revolted against European colonialism."[6] The rejection of colonialism by Asian and African Christians included rejecting Western missionary paternalism, with its Eurocentrism and moral superiority. From the 1950s through the 1970s, as

5. Donald N. Clark, *Christianity in Modern Korea* (Lanham, Md.: University Press of America, 1986), pp. 8-10.

6. Rajah B. Manikam, ed., *Christianity and the Asian Revolution* (Madras: Joint East Asia Secretariat of the International Missionary Council and the World Council of Churches, 1954), p. 7.

nations shook off the legacy of European domination, churches around the world accused Western missionaries of paternalism, racism, and cultural imperialism. The refrain "Missionary, Go Home"[7] reached its peak in the early 1970s. In 1971 Christian leaders in the Philippines, Kenya, and Argentina called for a moratorium on missionaries to end the dependence of the younger churches on the older ones. In 1974 the All Africa Conference of Churches, meeting in Lusaka, Zambia, called for a moratorium on Western missionaries and money sent to Africa, because of the belief that foreign assistance created dependency and stifled African leadership.

The cries for moratorium from Latin American, Asian, and African Christians shocked the Western missionary movement. But indigenous Christian protests against Western mission were insignificant compared with the wholesale rejection of Christianity that occurred within revolutionary movements led by non-Christians. At the International Missionary Council meeting of 1938, the largest delegations of Asian Christians came from the countries with the largest Western-style Christian infrastructures: India and China. Both Indian and Chinese Christianity boasted national Christian councils under indigenous leadership; both enjoyed thriving ecumenical movements that supported organic church unions; both hosted a range of Christian colleges and hospitals. Ironically, anti-Christian backlashes raged in both countries. Because Christianity was a minority religion in both China and India, its association with European domination widely discredited it as dangerous and foreign in the eyes of the majority non-Christians. Despite a community that traced its founding to the apostle Thomas, most Indian Christians were outcastes, members of ethnic groups despised in Hindu society. Practicing a double discrimination against both Christianity and low-caste status, the postcolonial Indian government excluded Christian Dalits (outcastes) from the affirmative-action programs guaranteed to other ethnic minorities. The government of India began denying visas to missionaries in 1964, and Christians faced ongoing discrimination and intermittent persecution in both India and Pakistan.[8]

7. Wilbert R. Shenk, "Toward a Global Church History," *International Bulletin of Missionary Research* 20, no. 2 (April 1996): 51. For a discussion of the relationship between missions and nationalism, see Dana L. Robert, "Christianity in the Wider World," part 6, in *Christianity: A Social and Cultural History,* 2nd ed., ed. Howard Kee et al. (Upper Saddle River, N.J.: Prentice-Hall, 1998), pp. 563-69.

8. The rise of Hindu fundamentalism in the late 1990s increased drastically the amount of anti-Christian violence. In Gujarat alone, sixty recorded incidents occurred in the second half of 1998 until Christmas, and roughly the same number occurred in the few weeks after (Thomas Quigley, "Anti-Christian Violence in India," *America,* April 3, 1999, p. 3).

In China, the place of the largest Western missionary investment in the early twentieth century, accession to power by the Communists in 1949 condemned Christianity as the religion of the colonialist oppressor. Chinese churches became sites for Marxist struggle against the "opium of the people." In 1950 the Communist government organized Chinese Protestants into the Three-Self Patriotic Movement and Catholics into the Catholic Patriotic Association. Under theologian Y. T. Wu, who had attended the Madras IMC meeting in 1938, the Three-Self Movement published the Christian Manifesto, which stated that missionary Christianity was connected with Western imperialism and that the United States used religion to support reactionary political forces. The document called for Chinese Christians immediately to become self-reliant and separate from all Western institutions.[9] The Three-Self Movement began holding meetings at which Christian leaders were accused of betraying the Chinese people and were sent to labor camps for "reeducation." With the outbreak of the Korean War in 1950, the remaining foreign missionaries left China, for their presence was endangering the Chinese Christian community. The few missionaries who did not leave were imprisoned along with many leading Chinese Christians. The worst suffering of Chinese Christians occurred from 1966 to 1976 during the Cultural Revolution, a period in which no public worship was permitted in China. The very schools and hospitals that had seemed like the best contribution of foreign missions to China were held up as the proof of missionary imperialism and foreign domination of Christianity. Millions of Chinese died as the government encouraged the destruction of all things religious or traditional. Except for a catacombs church of unknown strength, it seemed to China watchers in the 1970s that the Communist dictatorship had destroyed Chinese Christianity.

In parts of Africa, anticolonial movements sometimes took an anti-Christian stance. Nationalist leaders accused missions of telling Africans to pray and then stealing their land while their heads were bowed. Despite having been a resident mission pupil in childhood, Jomo Kenyatta, leader of the anti-Christian, pro-independence Mau-Mau rebellion in Kenya during the 1950s and later the country's first president, accused missionaries of trying to destroy African culture. During the Mau-Mau liberation struggle, which mobilized African traditional religion against Christianity, rebels killed African Christians who refused to drink the goats' blood and other sacrifices of the pro-independence cult. During the Cold War, Marxist ideology as well as

9. "The Christian Manifesto: Direction of Endeavor for Chinese Christianity in the Construction of New China," in *Religious Policy and Practice in Communist China,* ed. Donald Macinnis (New York: Macmillan, 1972), pp. 158-60.

funding from the Soviet Union and China began playing a role in African conflicts. Following the Cuban example, Communists funded movements in Mozambique and Angola, dismantled mission schools, and attacked churches as supposed organs of capitalism and European religion.

By the 1970s, on a political and ideological level, world Christianity seemed in disarray. Although mission education, literacy training, and ideals of individual human worth had provided tools that initiated intellectual leadership of independence movements in Asia and Africa, the perceived alliance of foreign missions with European domination branded Christianity a henchman of colonialism. In the West, reacting against the colonial legacy, scholars and historians similarly indicted Christian missions as a tool of Western domination. As far as Western intellectuals were concerned, the non-Western Christian was a mercenary "rice Christian," and the missionary as outdated as a dinosaur. The teaching of missions and world Christianity began disappearing from colleges and seminaries, a casualty of the Vietnam-era rejection of "culture Christianity" and Western domination in world affairs. With indigenous church leaders calling for moratoriums on missionaries, Western mainline churches became highly self-critical and guilt-ridden. Attempting to shift from paternalistic to partnership models of mission, they began cutting back on Western missionary personnel. During the long process from decolonization to independence, scholars, politicians, and leading ecclesiastics branded both Western missions and world Christianity failures because of their perceived social, theological, and political captivity to the despised colonial interests.

Revival and Renewal in World Christianity

The irony of world Christianity from the Second World War through the 1970s was that even as scholars were writing books implicating Christianity in European imperialism, the number of believers began growing rapidly throughout Asia, Africa, and Latin America. Perhaps if historians in the sixties and seventies had been studying Christianity as a people's movement rather than a political one, they might have noticed that growth among the grassroots did not mirror the criticisms of intellectual elites. The process of decolonization and independence began severing the connection between Christianity and European colonialism. The repudiation of missionary paternalism, combined with expanding indigenous initiatives, freed Christianity to become more at home in local situations.

Another fallacy of treating Christianity as a politicized Western movement is that scholarship ignored the way in which ordinary people were receiving the gospel message and retranslating it into cultural modes that fitted their worldviews and met their needs.[10] In retrospect it is evident that even during the colonial period, indigenous Christians — Bible women, evangelists, catechists, and prophets — were all along the most effective interpreters of Christianity to their own people. The explosion of non-Western Christianity was possible because Christianity was already being indigenized before the colonizers departed.

In the uncertainty of postcolonial situations, in the midst of civil strife and ethnic tensions in emerging nations, indigenous forms of Christianity spread quietly and quickly. Even in the so-called mission denominations, native leaders took over and indigenized positions held formerly by Western missionaries. In Kenya, for example, Mau-Mau rebels targeted Anglicanism as the religion of colonizers during the 1950s. But after Mau-Mau, independence, and the subsequent instability of a struggling government, Anglicanism in Kenya emerged even stronger, with exponential growth among the Kikuyu from the 1970s onward. Not only was Anglicanism now led by Kenyan bishops and priests, but the new context transformed the liability of being an English religion under a colonial government into the advantage of being a global faith under an independent government. In the 1980s and 1990s, as political and economic institutions began collapsing under corrupt one-party dictatorships, the church became one of the few institutions with the moral authority and international connections to oppose the government, which it did on occasion. In some parts of Africa, the church's infrastructures and international connections provided more stability for supporting daily life than did the government.[11] The postindependence growth of Anglicanism occurred so steadily throughout former British colonies that Africa is now the continent with most Anglicans. At the 1998 Lambeth Conference, the highest consultative body of the Anglican Communion, 224 of the 735 bishops were from Africa, compared with only 139 from the United Kingdom and Europe.[12] Anglicans in Nigeria report 17 million baptized members, compared with 2.8 million in the United States.[13]

Given its brutal suppression under Communism after 1949, the Chinese

10. William R. Burrows, "Reconciling All in Christ: The Oldest New Paradigm for Mission," *Mission Studies* 15-1, no. 29 (1988): 86-87.

11. On the church and the nation-state, see Andrew F. Walls, "Africa in Christian History — Retrospect and Prospect," *Journal of African Christian Thought* 1, no. 1 (June 1998): 8-14.

12. "Background Briefing, Lambeth Conference at a Glance," Anglican Communion News Service LCO14, July 18, 1998.

13. Bob Libby, "How Many Anglicans Are There?" *Lambeth Daily,* August 8, 1998, p. 4.

church provides the most stirring illustration of the resilience of Asian Christianity. In 1979 five thousand Chinese Christians attended the first public worship service allowed since 1966. By suffering under Communism along with other citizens, Chinese Christians proved they were not the "running dogs" of imperialists but were truly Chinese citizens. With the end of the Cultural Revolution, Christians began reclaiming buildings that had previously been seized. The Chinese Christian Council opened thirteen theological seminaries and began printing Bibles, creating a hymnal, and training pastors for churches that had gone without resources for fifteen years. Recent scholarship estimates that on the eve of the Communist takeover, one-fourth of all Chinese Christians were already members of indigenous, independent Chinese churches.[14] It was these indigenized forms of Christianity that provided the most resistance to Communist domination of the churches. Biblically literalist, directly dependent on the power of the Holy Spirit, and emerging from the religious sensibilities of popular Chinese religion, indigenized forms of Chinese Christianity grew the most under Communist persecution. What had been 700,000 Protestants in 1949 grew to between 12 and 36 million Protestants by the end of the century.[15] In addition to government-approved churches, millions of Chinese Christians meet in house churches characterized by spontaneous spoken prayer, singing and fellowship, miraculous healing, exorcisms of evil spirits, and love and charity to neighbors.

The translation of Christianity into African cultures was most obvious in the life and work of so-called African Independent or African Initiated Churches (AICs), defined by Harold Turner as churches founded in Africa, by Africans, primarily for Africans. By 1984 Africans had founded seven thousand independent, indigenous denominations in forty-three countries across the continent. By the 1990s, over 40 percent of black Christians in South Africa were members of AICs. Chafing under white domination and racism, African-led movements began breaking off from mission churches in the 1880s. The earliest independent churches emphasized African nationalism in ecclesiastical affairs. They received the name "Ethiopian" in 1892 when a Methodist minister, Mangena Mokone, founded the Ethiopian Church in the Witwatersrand region of South Africa. Believing that Africans should lead their own churches, Mokone cited Psalm 68:31: "Ethiopia shall stretch out her hands to God."[16]

14. Daniel H. Bays, "The Growth of Independent Christianity in China, 1900-1937," in *Christianity in China: From the Eighteenth Century to the Present,* ed. D. H. Bays (Stanford, Calif.: Stanford University Press, 1996), p. 310.

15. Robert, "Christianity in Wider World," p. 570.

16. Inus Daneel, *Quest for Belonging: An Introduction to a Study of African Independent Churches* (Gweru, Zimbabwe: Mambo, 1987), p. 49.

During the early twentieth century, important African prophets and evangelists emerged throughout the continent, often to be arrested and persecuted by colonial authorities who deemed spiritual independence a dangerous precursor to political independence.

By the mid-twentieth century, the largest group of AICs were known as Spirit churches, often called Aladura in western Africa and Zionist in southern Africa.[17] Spirit churches were characterized by a prophetic leader, a high emphasis on the Holy Spirit, Pentecostal phenomena such as speaking in tongues and exorcisms, and often a holy city or "Zion" as headquarters. With Bible translation into many African languages, prophetic African leaders interpreted the Scriptures for themselves in line with African cultural practices. Zionists, for example, permit polygamy, which exists both in the Bible and in traditional African cultures. Their leaders rely on dreams and visions for divine inspiration — also both a biblical and traditional African practice. Many people are attracted to AICs because they focus on healing the body and spirit through prayers, laying on of hands, and administration of holy water and other remedies. Women healers treat barren women and other sufferers, providing respite for them in healing colonies. In Zimbabwe more than 150 indigenous churches have extended the metaphor of healing by joining in a movement to heal through planting trees — 750,000 trees in 1997 alone.[18] Spirit churches spread rapidly following political independence because they translated the Christian faith into African cultures, thereby both transforming the cultural forms and expanding the meaning of the gospel as received from Western missionaries. Spirit churches also spread because they mount vigorous missionary movements, sending out evangelistic teams that dance through the villages, singing, praying, preaching, healing, and drawing people into a vigorous worship life.

Another momentous change in the world church since the 1960s can be traced to the renewal of Catholicism, the largest branch of Christianity with approximately 980 million members in 1996. The Second Vatican Council (1962-65) brought to Rome the Catholic bishops, who together voted major changes in Catholicism's theological self-definition, customs, and attitudes. As these bishops returned to their homelands, they began putting into practice the idea of the church as the people of God, with Mass said in the vernacular and a new openness to current sociocultural realities.

17. Daneel, *Quest for Belonging,* p. 49; Deji Ayegboyin and S. Ademola Ishola, *African Indigenous Churches: An Historical Perspective* (Lagos, Nigeria: Greater Heights, 1997); John S. Pobee and Gabriel Ositelu II, *African Initiatives in Christianity* (Geneva: WCC, 1998).

18. ZIRRCON Trust, Annual Report (Masvingo, Zimbabwe: n.p., 1997).

In particular, the more than 600 Latin American bishops who attended the Vatican Council gained a new sense of their potential as the numerically largest block of Catholics in the world. Latin American bishops reflected on their common social problems — stark division between rich and poor, takeovers by military dictatorships, and a legacy of a church that took the side of the rich. At the meeting of Latin American bishops in Medellín, Colombia, in 1968, the bishops evaluated the social context of their continent and spoke with a powerful voice against the dependence of Latin America on the industrialized North — a dependence that perpetuated the poverty of the South. Calling the church to take the side of the poor, the bishops supported a new "theology of liberation."[19]

The "renewed commitment to democracy and human rights in the Catholic Church" supported a wave of democracy throughout Latin America, Eastern Europe, and the Philippines during the 1970s and 1980s.[20]

The movement toward democracy in traditionally Roman Catholic countries was not universally acclaimed by the church, as the route often entailed violent rebellion and upheaval of the status quo. The theology of liberation immediately came into conflict with powerful military dictatorships, which began persecuting the church. Militaries martyred an estimated 850 bishops, priests, and nuns in Latin America during the 1970s and early 1980s. Military governments targeted church leaders at all levels because they were conscientizing the poor — teaching them to read and defending their human rights. The Roman Catholic Church in Latin America gained a vitality it had long lacked as laypeople began meeting in Base Christian Communities, which functioned as Bible study groups that reflected on the relationship between the church as community and social injustices. But as the theology of liberation confronted the social and political power structures in Latin America, the Catholic Church became divided between those who supported liber-

19. Edward L. Cleary, O.P., *Crisis and Change: The Church in Latin America Today* (Maryknoll, N.Y.: Orbis, 1985), chap. 2.

20. Samuel Huntington, cited by Paul Marshall, *Their Blood Cries Out: The Worldwide Tragedy of Modern Christians Who Are Dying for Their Faith,* introduction by Michael Horowitz (Dallas: Word, 1997), p. 9. See specific studies, for example, Robert L. Youngblood, *Marcos Against the Church: Economic Development and Political Repression in the Philippines* (Ithaca, N.Y.: Cornell University Press, 1990); Jeffrey Klaiber, *The Church, Dictatorships, and Democracy in Latin America* (Maryknoll, N.Y.: Orbis, 1998); Enrique Dussel, "From the Second Vatican Council to the Present Day," in *The Church in Latin America 1492-1992,* ed. Dussel, *A History of the Church in the Third World,* vol. 1 (Maryknoll, N.Y.: Orbis, 1992), pp. 153-82. For the struggle within Catholicism, see Phillip Berryman, *The Religious Roots of Rebellion: Christians in Central American Revolutions* (Maryknoll, N.Y.: Orbis, 1984); Penny Lernoux, *People of God: The Struggle for World Catholicism* (New York: Penguin, 1989).

ation theology among the "people of God" and those more conservative, who felt the nature of the church was more hierarchical and otherworldly.

The renewal of Catholicism in Latin America since the Second Vatican Council underscores a major tension in the growth of non-Western Christianity since the mid-twentieth century: the forms and structures for the growth of late twentieth-century Christianity could not be contained within either the institutional or the theological frameworks of Western Christianity. The Base Christian Communities, for example, introduced Bible study and a more intense spirituality into what had been nominal Catholic practice. Faced with the severe shortage of priests, Latin American Catholics, once they became used to reading the Bible for themselves, began forming their own churches and breaking away from Catholicism. Ironically, the liberation theologies of the Base Christian Communities may have created heightened expectations that could not be fulfilled, and disillusioned Catholics began founding their own churches. Protestant growth has become so rapid in Latin America that scholars have predicted that Protestants, notably of Pentecostal persuasion, could constitute a third of the Latin American population by the year 2010, with their greatest strengths in Guatemala, Puerto Rico, El Salvador, Brazil, and Honduras.[21] These new Protestants are founding their own churches, such as the Universal Church of the Kingdom of God, a Pentecostal group begun in the late 1970s by Edir Macedo de Bezerra. By 1990 this homegrown denomination had 800 churches with two million worshipers led by 2,000 pastors throughout Latin America. Neither Catholicism nor the classic churches of the Protestant Reformation can contain the vitality of Latin American Christianity today.

Reasons for the revival and renewal of global Christianity today are too complex and diverse to be encapsulated in a brief essay. In addition to increasing indigenization within a postcolonial political framework, many sociological factors affect church growth, including urbanization, dislocation caused by war and violence, ethnic identity, the globalizing impact of cyberspace, and local circumstances. Political contexts differ widely for Christian communities around the world. Nevertheless, Christianity throughout the non-Western world has in common an indigenous, grassroots leadership; embeddedness in local cultures; and reliance on a vernacular Bible. Where Christianity is growing in the South, it supports stable family and community life for peoples suffering political uncertainty and economic hardships. The

21. Mike Berg and Paul Pretiz, *The Gospel People* (Monrovia, Calif.: MARC and Latin American Mission, 1992); Guillermo Cook, ed., *New Face of the Church in Latin America* (Maryknoll, N.Y.: Orbis, 1994).

time when Christianity was the religion of European colonial oppressors fades ever more rapidly into the past.

A Global/Local Christian Fabric

As Christianity shifts southward, the nature of Christianity itself evolves. The movement of the faith from one culture to another typically has caused a major change in the self-understanding and cultural grounding of the Christian movement.[22] Past cultural shifts occurred when Christianity moved from a Hebrew to a Greco-Roman milieu, and then from a Mediterranean to a European framework. With the voyages of discovery, Europeans began exporting their religion in the late 1400s. At that time Christian expansion was partly a function of the state, reflecting the Christendom model of church/state relations. Even the voluntarism of Protestant missions occurred within a largely Christendom model. But the end of European colonialism after the Second World War accompanied a decline of European religiosity relative to the rest of the world. The virtual destruction of Russian Orthodoxy under the Communist regime was also a major factor in the elimination of the Christendom model.

Now much of the dynamism within world Christianity is occurring below the equator. As Christianity shifts southward, the interpretations of Christianity by people in Latin America, Africa, and southern Asia are coming to the fore. This challenging face of the world church also brings new interpretive challenges for historians.

One of the knottiest interpretive problems in understanding Christianity today is the tension between a worldwide community of people who call themselves Christians and a multitude of local movements for whom Christianity represents a particular culture's grappling with the nature of divine reality. Christianity is a world religion with a basic belief that God has revealed himself in the person of Jesus Christ, whose adherents are spread throughout the globe. Yet as Lamin Sanneh has so cogently argued, by virtue of its use of the vernacular in speaking of God and in spreading the Scriptures, Christianity has translated or incarnated itself into local cultures.[23] What at first glance appears to be the largest world religion is in fact the ultimate local religion. In-

22. Andrew Walls, *The Missionary Movement in Christian History: Studies in the Transmission of Faith* (Maryknoll, N.Y.: Orbis, 1996).

23. Lamin Sanneh, *Translating the Message: The Missionary Impact on Culture* (Maryknoll, N.Y.: Orbis, 1989).

digenous words for God and ancient forms of spirituality have all become part of Christianity. Flexibility at the local level, combined with being part of an international network, is a major factor in Christianity's self-understanding and success today. The strength of world Christianity lies in its creative interweaving of the warp of a world religion with the woof of its local contexts.

The increasing cultural diversity within Christianity, with the recognition of the local within the global and the global within the local, complicates the writing of church history in the twenty-first century. The days are gone when the history of Christianity could be taught as the development of Western doctrine and institutions. Being in the middle of a large-scale transformation in the nature of Christianity, we do not yet have an adequate interpretive or even descriptive framework for what is happening. Australian historian Mark Hutchinson advocates a paradigm shift in the history of Christianity to a model of multiculturalism, a globalization of evangelicalism.[24] Others interpret worldwide growth as the spread of Pentecostalism, since the majority of growing churches today express themselves in Pentecostal worship styles.[25] A history-of-religion framework sees that the growing energy of Christianity has always been drawn from primal spirituality.[26] Sociologists have explored the spread of Christianity today as a process of modernization, a variant of the Weberian thesis in the growth of capitalism.[27] Historians influenced by liberation theology stress that the central focus of history should be the poor and marginalized rather than the ecclesiological elites of the Christendom model.[28] Liberation theology has a strong influence on the ongoing history projects of the Ecumenical Association of Third World Theologians.

24. Mark Hutchinson, "It's a Small Church After All," *Christianity Today,* November 16, 1998, pp. 46-49. Hutchinson is associate director of the Currents in World Christianity Project, funded by Pew Charitable Trusts, which seeks to understand the global spread of evangelicalism.

25. Walter Hollenweger, *Pentecostalism: Origins and Developments Worldwide* (Peabody, Mass.: Hendrickson, 1997); Harvey Cox, *Fire From Heaven: The Rise of Pentecostal Spirituality and the Reshaping of Religion in the Twenty-First Century* (Reading, Mass.: Addison-Wesley, 1994); Allan Anderson, *Bazalwane: African Pentecostals in South Africa* (Pretoria: University of South Africa Press, 1992).

26. Andrew Walls, "Origins of Old Northern and New Southern Christianity," in *Missionary Movement,* pp. 68-75. Sociologist Peter Berger of Boston University has led a research institute investigating the growth of world Protestantism as an aspect of economic culture.

27. David Martin, *Tongues of Fire: The Explosion of Protestantism in Latin America,* foreword by Peter Berger (Oxford: Blackwell, 1990).

28. Enrique Dussel, *A History of Latin America: Colonialism to Liberation (1492-1979),* trans. and rev. Alan Neely (Grand Rapids: Eerdmans, 1981); Dussel, *Church in Latin America.*

While each of these models has something to offer in helping us speak and teach about world Christianity, there is danger in the theories of globalization that skip over the painstaking historical research necessary for each local context. Global analyses need to begin with local history, with the internal criteria of each movement as the starting point of our historical musings.[29] As with the outdated nomenclature of mission history, such as "younger churches," "developing churches," the "history of the expansion of Christianity," and so on, there is a constant temptation to define the changing global patterns in relation to the European and the North American experience.

The tension between the global and the local is not merely an academic exercise but it is a struggle over identity. For example, some commentators are describing the growing world church as Pentecostal. Pentecostal and charismatic scholars want to claim the growth of world Christianity as part of their own missionary success.[30] Since Pentecostal phenomena were so derided in Western Christianity into the 1980s, it is understandable that Western Pentecostal scholars wish to include all phenomenologically similar movements as somehow related to Azusa Street. Anthropologists might similarly wish to describe new Christian movements as Pentecostal because of the prominence of common phenomena such as speaking in tongues, healing rituals, and the alleged marginalized social status of many adherents. For political liberals who look down on what they perceive to be narrow pietism, the word "Pentecostal" has been attractive as a negative descriptor, as part of an implied spillover from the Christian fight in the United States.

For historians, however, unreflective use of the term "Pentecostalism" to summarize growing world Christianity has the same problem as calling all biblical Christianity "fundamentalism." It reduces local identity to a standardized set of criteria, in this case to phenomenology. Are Pentecostal phenomena the defining mark of identity for local practitioners, or are there other theological or communal identity markers that are more meaningful for them? Do all Pentecostal phenomena worldwide have an organic connection to Azusa Street and the missionary movement that spread from there, or is Pentecostal practice reflective of indigenous cultural initiative? Is the use of the word "Pentecostal" just the latest instance of categories originating from

29. Shenk, "Toward a Global Church History," p. 56.

30. Pentecostal historian Vinson Synan told the Eighteenth Pentecostal World Conference in 1998 that more than 25 percent of the world's Christians are Pentecostal or charismatic and "the renewal will continue with increasing strength into the next millennium." "Current News Summary," available online at http://www.religiontoday.com, accessed October 5, 1998.

the North being used to explain and somehow take credit for what is going on in the South?

Non-Western historians are cautioning against blanket use of the word "Pentecostal" to describe indigenous Christianity. For example, Nigerian church historian Ogbu Kalu, head of the African history project for the Ecumenical Association of Third World Theologians, has criticized the Pentecostal terminology as reflecting the dominance of anthropology in ignoring essential historical and theological differences among current movements. Kalu insists that historians be more accurate and recognize the differences that arise within the movements themselves.[31] Inus Daneel, the leading interpreter of African Initiated Churches in Zimbabwe, argues vigorously against the label of Pentecostalism being plastered onto indigenous churches. Not only have these churches been founded by African prophets, but they have recruited their members largely from the traditional population, not from so-called mission churches. Although they emphasize the Holy Spirit, the AICs deal with issues arising from African culture, not from Western Pentecostalism. To claim that AICs are otherworldly, for instance, ignores the holism that undergirds African religions.[32]

As scholars analyze and define what is happening in world Christianity today, we must apply such globalizing concepts as "Pentecostal" only after careful research into the local contexts.[33] Historians should take the lead in acknowledging the new Christianities as radically indigenous movements, not simply Pentecostalism or primal religiosity, or perhaps not even multicultural options within a global evangelicalism. Each movement should be studied from within its own internal logic, even as the universal nature of Christianity is recognizable in the construction of local identities. Popular Korean Christianity is a case in point. David Yonggi Cho leads the largest church in the world, the Yoido Full Gospel Church in Seoul, Korea. Cho is by member-

31. Ogbu Kalu, "The Estranged Bedfellows: Demonization of the Aladura in African Pentecostalism," in *African Christian Outreach: The AIC Contribution,* ed. M. L. Daneel (Pretoria: University of South Africa Press, 2000).

32. M. L. Daneel, "African Initiated Churches in Southern Africa: Protest Movements or Missionary Churches?" paper presented at Currents in World Christianity conference, Cambridge University, July 15, 1999.

33. One possible paradigm is to distinguish between largely urban, modernizing movements, and rural, neo-traditionalist movements. In Singapore, for example, there are growing numbers of English-speaking, Internet-linked, young professional Pentecostals. These Christians are part of an international network replete with its own literature, hymnody, and global evangelistic consciousness. In rural Indonesia, however, nonliterate indigenous Christian movements, influenced by the spirit world of Javanese mysticism, are not connected to the nearby urban elites. (I am indebted to Graham Walker for this example.)

ship a Pentecostal, a minister in the Assemblies of God. Yet the emphasis of his congregation on material blessings and on such spiritualities as a prayer mountain is clearly attributable to the influence of Korean shamanism. Does the Yoido Full Gospel Church exemplify globalized Pentecostalism or localized spirit religion? As historians work within the tensions between global and the local that characterize indigenous world Christianity today, we should recognize that each form of twenty-first century Christianity represents a synthesis of global and local elements that has its own integrity.

As Christianity declines in Europe and grows in the South, historians need to recognize what the International Missionary Council saw in 1938: the future of world Christianity rests with the so-called younger churches and their daily struggles. Ultimately, the most interesting lessons from the missionary outreach during the Western colonial era are what happened to Christianity when the missionaries weren't looking, and after the colonizers withdrew. The challenge for historians lies in seeing beyond an extension of Western categories and into the hearts, minds, and contexts of Christ's living peoples in Asia, Africa, and Latin America.

PART THREE

The Study of Evangelism in the World of Theology

For the study of evangelism to offer faithful and effective resources to the church it must earnestly engage Christian theology. As noted in the two previous sections, those who seek to develop a relevant and authentic understanding of evangelism must give careful attention to the biblical foundations and the unfolding historical narrative related to the practice. Of equal importance, however, is sustained reflection upon evangelism in the larger world of theology. Among the areas of biblical, historical, and theological studies, evangelism is frequently located as a sub-discipline, often on the margins, of practical theology. However, when one considers that those who study and practice evangelism engage in reflection upon God's invitation to all people to be reconciled through Jesus Christ and to respond in faithfulness through the power of the Holy Spirit by participating in the reign of God, such a location seems desperately misplaced. The study of evangelism, to put it quite simply, is serious theological work.

Unfortunately, as a result of complex theological developments during the past several centuries — and due in large measure to the misguided bifurcation of theory and practice — theologians neglected the study of evangelism or relegated it to the margins of serious theological discourse. It is extremely difficult, in fact, to identify any major theologian, of any theological persuasion, for whom the study of mission/evangelism figures prominently in his or her theological system. More often than not theologians relegate the study of evangelism to the realm of the practitioner and thereby perpetuate these kinds of unhealthy divisions. Those approaches in which the study of evangelism remains tangential to Christian theology produce few resources of value in the life of the church. On the other hand, whenever theologians/practitioners have been intentional about bringing the study of evangelism into the center of serious theological inquiry, faithful vision and effective practice have emerged from the dynamic interaction.

All the essays in this section demonstrate the integral relationship between evangelism/mission and Christian theology. They argue that the study of evangelism is serious theological work and that theology remains deficient without attention to the mission of God; they identify the critical insights that emerge from the interface of theology and evangelism; and they explicate the missional ramifications drawn from central Christian tenets within the larger world of theology/ethics.

Stephen K. Pickard, director of St. Mark's National Theological Centre and head of the School of Theology at Charles Sturt University, teaches theology, mission, and evangelism in an Australian context. In the lead essay of this section he builds a bridge between the frequently isolated worlds of theology and evangelism. In an effort to counter their unfortunate and false separation, he develops the idea of communication as the point of contact between the two; theology and evangelism are both about speaking the gospel. Pickard constructs a foundation for evangelism upon the concept of God as logos (language). Moving beyond communication theory to a theological conception of communication, therefore, he suggests that evangelism is the compressed articulation of the more explicit work of theology. The church functions as a "sacrament of non-dominative communication"; evangelism is free and full speech about God's unrestrained love as it has been revealed in Jesus Christ. The communicative life of the church, guided by the parameters of simplicity, repetition, and wisdom, reflects the fullest possible integration of theology and evangelism for the purpose of transformation and the praise of God.

A professor of systematic theology at Lutheran School of Theology in Chicago, Carl E. Braaten locates evangelism within the context of God's universal grace as expressed in the Christian conception of the Triune God. The evangelistic imperative derives from the conception of a God who reaches out to humanity and reveals redemptive purposes through the gospel of the risen Christ in the power of the Holy Spirit. Since it is God's nature to offer the fullness of God's self in both creation and redemption, whenever the church turns in upon itself, it loses sight of the universal horizon of God's all-embracing reign. Recapturing a robust vision of the God of the Scriptures enables the community of faith to embrace a more comprehensive view of the vertical and horizontal dimensions of the gospel and the power of God's freedom and love.

Darrell L. Guder, professor of missional and ecumenical theology at Princeton Theological Seminary, draws our attention to the centrality of the incarnation to the church's evangelistic methodology in mission. Reflecting upon a critical missiological theme of the 1980s — "doing mission and evangelism in Jesus Christ's way" — he fully integrates the model of Jesus' life as the "Word become flesh" and the way in which the community of faith goes about its mission. Failure to live out the faith in an incarnational manner, he argues, has led to a separation of evangelism from "the full dimensions of gospel obedience." The doctrine of the incarnation provides the key to a necessary, but often neglected, integrative function in the theology of evangelism. In particular, it helps us to grapple with five unfortunate dichotomies frequently manifest in the life of the church: Christian faith vs. culture, evangelistic ministry vs. spiritual formation, the means vs. the end in evangelism, doing evangelism (word) vs. doing justice (deed), and the person vs. the work of Christ.

In an essay on the doctrine of salvation, Ronald J. Sider, founder of Evangelicals for Social Action, expands one particular aspect of evangelism elevated in Guder's analysis, namely, the integral nature of word and deed. After surveying five conflicting viewpoints with regard to the relationship between evangelism and social justice, he articulates a holistic conception of salvation based upon his reading of the gospel. A biblical concept of salvation, he maintains, refers as much to active social service in this world as to the winning of souls. Redemption involves the Christian in a cosmic struggle against "the principalities and powers" as well as offering forgiveness of sins to the believer. Sider concludes that evangelism and social action are inextricably interrelated. The implications of this intricate synergy in the church's evangelistic mission include emphases upon the call to repentance, the importance of the church as a signpost to the kingdom, the understanding of social action as a preparation for the gospel, and the necessity of costly discipleship.

A brief article by the well-known Duke University theologian/ethicist Stanley Hauerwas concludes this section and segues into the next section on ecclesial practices. In his "Worship, Evangelism, Ethics: On Eliminating the 'And,'" he analyzes a dominant dualistic approach that mistakenly separates theology and evangelism — "the church at worship and the church in its evangelistic mode." He employs insights from the liturgical theology of Don Saliers to explore a holistic alternative to this way of thinking/being/acting. He suggests that faithful worship of the crucified God is evangelism. Truthful worship that shapes character and celebrates the mystery of the resurrection through eucharistic action evangelizes people into a life of holiness that knows no separation of worship, evangelism, and ethics.

CHAPTER 10

Evangelism and the Character of Christian Theology

Stephen K. Pickard

Introduction

Evangelism and theology have not proved to be very compatible partners, at least in the modern period of the Christian tradition. The relationship perhaps has more the character of a stormy courtship ending in separation rather than a well-established marriage. The nature of their partnership was nicely symbolized in the August 1960 meeting between Billy Graham and Karl Barth — arguably the two greatest figures to evangelism and theology respectively in the twentieth century. The Barthian interpretation of the meeting is recorded by Barth's biographer, Eberhard Busch:

> [Barth's] son Markus brought them together in the Valais. However, this meeting was also a friendly one. "He's a 'jolly good fellow,' with whom one can talk easily and openly, one has the impression that he is even capable of listening, which is not always the case with such trumpeters of the gospel." Two weeks later Barth had the same good impression after a second meeting with Graham, this time at home in Basel. But, "it was very different when — we went to hear him let loose in the St. Jacob stadium that same evening and witnessed his influence on the masses. I was quite horrified. He acted like a madman and what he presented was certainly not the gospel. . . . It was the gospel at gunpoint. . . . He preached the law, not a message to make one happy. He wanted to terrify people. Threats — they always make an impression. People would much rather be terrified than be pleased. The more one heats up hell for them, the more they come running." But even this success did not justify such preaching. It was illegitimate to make the gospel law or to "push" it like an

> article for sale. . . . We must leave the good God freedom to do his own work.[1]

It would, of course, be interesting to hear Graham's side of the meetings and his version of what happened at the St. Jacob stadium. At any rate the story symbolizes something of the growing rift between theology and evangelism in the modern period.[2] Lamenting the steady decline in the theological competence of evangelists over the generations and the problems associated with much modern mass evangelism, William Abraham concludes that "it is not surprising if theologians prefer to pass by on the other side and leave the whole mess to whatever Samaritan may have mercy upon it."[3] Of course, given the fortunes of theology in the wake of critical Enlightenment thought, evangelists may well have felt justified in adopting a similar strategy in regard to modern theology.

Clearly there is a need for a fresh approach in which is developed "a fresh universe of discourse that will open up a critical conversation on the complex issues that relate to evangelism."[4] However, what this fresh approach might entail remains as yet undetermined. At one level there does not seem to be any shortage of published material on evangelism as such, particularly from the late 1960s. Generally speaking much of this material is preoccupied with questions of biblical foundations and principles, discussions concerned with apologetics and the developing of effective programs for evangelism.[5] In

1. E. Busch, *Karl Barth: His Life from Letters and Autobiographical Texts* (London: SCM, 1976), p. 446.

2. Thus, W. Abraham, in his recent book *The Logic of Evangelism* (London: Hodder & Stoughton, 1989), pp. 8-9, notes the decline in the theological competence of the better-known evangelists over the generations. John Wesley was steeped in the classical Anglican theological tradition. Jonathan Edwards was not only a pastor and preacher involved in the "Great Awakening" of his time — he was also one of the great theologians of the modern Christian tradition. Charles Finney, though able intellectually, was less patient with the academy and the theological tradition and more pragmatic in outlook. In later evangelists, such as D. L. Moody and Billy Sunday, there is little theological substance left. Billy Graham, while sympathetic to the task of theology in the work of evangelism, has contributed little. The new generation of television-evangelists have shown, in Abraham's view, little "serious attempt to reflect deeply about the work in which they are engaged" (p. 10).

3. Abraham, *Logic of Evangelism,* p. 10.

4. Abraham, *Logic of Evangelism,* p. 10.

5. The bibliographies of most books on evangelism will quickly bear this out. See, e.g., bibliographies in T. S. Rainer, ed., *Evangelism in the Twenty-First Century* (Wheaton, Ill.: Harold Shaw, 1989); D. J. Kennedy, *Evangelism Explosion* (London: Coverdale House, 1972): M. Green, *Evangelism in the Local Church* (London: Hodder & Stoughton, 1990).

more recent material greater attention to questions of culture and context can be discerned.[6]

Two dominant strands run through the material. One strand is associated with a strong focus on verbal proclamation and is characteristic of Protestant evangelicalism.[7] The other strand has a strong emphasis on communicating the gospel through social action. This perspective has traditionally been an important plank in the World Council of Churches' understanding of evangelism.[8] However, these two strands are increasingly difficult to disentangle, if recent statements from the Lausanne Congress and the WCC are to be taken with the seriousness they deserve.[9] It seems that with the approach of the end of the second millennium the evangelism spectrum is becoming increasingly complex and controversial. The rise of Pentecostalism in the twentieth century has played no small part in this emerging diversity.[10] Important statements from the Roman Catholic and Orthodox Churches have enriched and stimulated discussion of evangelism.[11] Consequently the old boundaries are not so easy to maintain. Evangelism is moving in new directions. What is required is a fresh willingness to listen and learn from each other, particularly those who see things differently from us but with whom is shared a common bond in communicating the mystery of the gospel. But to what extent do evangelists and theologians listen and learn from each other?

6. See, e.g., O. Costas, *Liberating News: A Theology of Contextual Evangelization* (Grand Rapids: Eerdmans, 1989); L. Newbigin, *The Gospel in a Pluralistic Society* (London: SPCK, 1989).

7. See. e.g., Kennedy, *Evangelism Explosion.*

8. For a useful discussion see, e.g., Paulos Mar Gregorios, "The Witness of the Churches: Ecumenical Statements on Mission and Evangelism," *The Ecumenical Review,* 40, nos. 3-4 (July-October 1984): 359-66.

9. The relevant documents are: *The Manila Manifesto: An Elaboration of the Lausanne Covenant Fifteen Years Later* (Pasadena, Calif.: Castle Press, 1989) and *Mission and Evangelism — An Ecumenical Affirmation* (Geneva: WCC, 1982). Both documents evidence important attempts to develop an understanding of evangelism that includes both words and deeds. The traditional emphases remain but clearly reflect the influence of each other's ecclesial orientations.

10. Any discussion of the recent history of evangelism is incomplete to the extent that it ignores the growth and impact of Pentecostalism in the twentieth century. This is well documented in the well-known authoritative work by W. J. Hollenweger, *The Pentecostals* (London: SCM, 1972). The point was well made some years ago by F. D. Bruner: "Pentecostalism and Mission are almost synonymous," in *A Theology of the Holy Spirit* (Grand Rapids: Eerdmans, 1970), p. 32.

11. See *Evangelii Nuntiandi: Apostolic Exhortation of Paul VI on Evangelization in the Modern World* (Sydney, Australia: St. Paul Publications, 1989); *Redemptoris Missio: Encyclical Letter of John Paul II On the Permanent Validity of the Church's Missionary Mandate* (Sydney, Australia: St. Paul, 1991); I. Bria, ed., *Go Forth in Peace: Orthodox Perspectives on Mission* (Geneva: WCC, 1986).

Evangelism and Theology: A Tale of Two Ships

One thing absent from the wealth of material on evangelism is any well-developed contemporary theology of evangelism that might inform the church's practice of it.[12]

In this respect, at least, the old boundaries between evangelism and theology are still firmly in place. It might be said that the good ship *Evangelism* has a lot of crew members, all of course busy at important tasks. But the ship is short of theological fuel. This fact remains hidden, at least to the upper-deck crew members. They do not know there is a shortage of fuel; they are not even aware that fuel of that kind is necessary. When they are not asleep, you can see them on deck painting, polishing, rearranging, and reorganizing.

Meanwhile, down in the engine room are to be found the engineers. They meet regularly — i.e., have conferences — to discuss the machinery of the ship. The question of fuel is an important topic on the agenda below deck. The problem is that the fuel supplied in the past no longer provides the energy the ship requires. What of course is desperately needed is new fuel, but where is it to come from?

So the good ship *Evangelism* is afloat and its crew are highly active, though if you look closely some appear a little worn. The really pressing issues about where the ship is headed, or rather how it is managing to head in a

12. Abraham's *The Logic of Evangelism* is an important recent effort to articulate a contemporary theology of evangelism with a strong ecclesiological orientation. Costas's *Liberating News* is rigorous in its approach to "contextual evangelization." The strength of both books is that they identify important issues and provide a useful frame of reference for future thinking. Abraham is well aware of the difficulties of overcoming the divide between evangelism and theological concerns. B. Johnson in *Re-thinking Evangelism: A Theological Approach* (Philadelphia: Westminster, 1987) writes out of a concern that evangelism in the mainline churches be done "with integrity" and "for the right reasons": "The starting place for this important task is theology." Accordingly his book, born of the fruit of his own experience in evangelism and teaching of theology, is an attempt to "examine the central theological categories from an evangelistic perspective." However, he seems somewhat apologetic for this approach, stressing that his real concern is that the book will enable the development of "fresh models and strategies" and the setting forth of plans to get on with the task! The pragmatic thrust is understandable but begs many questions about the relationship between theology and the evangelistic task. A more traditional reformed theological approach to evangelism is offered by R. Kolb, *Speaking The Gospel Today: A Theology for Evangelism* (St. Louis: Concordia, 1984). Again, the burden of the book is to allow evangelists and theologians to listen to each other (preface, p. 8). Green's magnum opus, *Evangelism Through the Local Church,* has a strong apologetical and practical bias. What is missing is a more theologically informed discussion of evangelism. He is more concerned with getting on with the job. But the task he envisages looks quite different from those proposed by Abraham and Costas.

number of different directions, remain high on the agenda. But alas, these matters do not seem to be any clearer for the many rounds of discussions held among engineers with occasional input from the above-deck crew. In fact, some crew members and a couple of engineers became so frustrated that they lowered a life-raft and quietly paddled off to a desert island where they could learn again about building ships, ocean currents, and how to tread water over 70,000 fathoms.

One day the crew on deck of the good ship *Evangelism* noticed a very large ship passing by, the *Charismatic Queen*. The top decks seemed filled with people throwing streamers, waving and beckoning the *Evangelism* crew to join them. It looked so inviting, even if, on closer inspection, the ship appeared to be going around in ever decreasing circles.

It is as well to note that there are other ships sailing upon this ecclesial ocean. The most impressive of these are the bulk oil tankers; in particular the 500,000-ton bulk carrier *Theological Tradition*. Oddly enough, when you inspect the various containers on such carriers you cannot find any that would seem, on first inspection at least, to provide the right kind of high-octane fuel required for the good ship *Evangelism*. This, at least, was the opinion of some of the crew of the *Evangelism* who, upon sighting the bulk carrier *Theological Tradition* (a rare occurrence), rowed over to seek help with their fuel problem. Perhaps not surprisingly, the crew were not well received.

Captain Dogmatic was clearly embarrassed at the prospect of having to welcome the *Evangelism* crew. Following a clumsy and rather condescending greeting, the crew were allowed to sniff around. But not being at all sure of what they were looking for, they soon became discouraged and left. The captain and crew of the tanker had tried to tell them that such carriers no longer serviced evangelism-class ships. In fact, it soon became apparent in the short exchange between the two crews that the tanker crew were no longer certain whom they supplied with fuel. But they were deeply committed to steaming around the ecclesial ocean, if only to meet up with other such tankers for cordial exchanges and perhaps the trade of a container or two.

To be truthful, the tanker fleet were not in good shape. More ominously, there were moves afloat to remove the enormous tanker fleet to a safe harbor just off Cape Irrelevant. This would solve the immediate problem of oil spills, which did nobody any good. In the last few decades a number of dangerous ones had occurred, which had caused a great deal of damage to the evangelism-class ships. As a result the tanker *Bultmann* had already been towed away to join the *Patristic Fleet*. The tanker *Continental Calvin* and alas, the giant tanker *Judicious Hooker*, much beloved of the tribe Anglicanus Classicus, had met a similar fate. Needless to say, the H.M.S. *Higher Criticism* had long since rusted.

Exploring the Connections: The Priority of Communication

Evangelism and theology often seem poles apart, unable and unwilling to come close, let alone join forces. The fear is loss of purity, of being contaminated by the other. Theology is frightened that in the interchange it will forfeit its academic and scholarly reputation. Evangelism might find itself being led up a dead end. But evangelism and theology need each other and — more important — their life-source is a shared one. The church's practice of evangelism and theology arises out of its life in Christ. The one-in-Christ bond is the presupposition for all ecclesial communication.

The argument that follows presupposes an interwovenness between evangelism and theology. What of course is critical is to clarify how the interdependence of evangelism and theology, which arises out their common life in Christ, actually works. This points to the importance of clarifying some of the interconnections between evangelism and theology in the church, for it is in the process of exploring the interconnections that a more adequate understanding of evangelism and theology can emerge. For this reason tight definitions are inappropriate at this stage. However, what is important is that evangelism and theology are understood to belong to the more general theme of communication. In particular it is the dynamics of communication as it relates to evangelism and theology that emerges as critical. The essay is thus about the character of communication that is "worded." From another point of view what is offered here is a rather extended comment on Ephesians 6:19 — "And in particular pray for me that utterance may be given to me as I open my mouth that I may boldly and freely make known the mystery of the gospel."

The Communicative Life

Communications is a massive area in modern life and thought. There is good reason for this: "every act, every pause, every movement in living and social systems is also a message; silence is communication; short of death it is impossible for an organism or a person not to communicate."[13]

It would seem that communication is both a condition of and essential to our humanity. Communication has been referred to as "the transmission of energy in a form."[14] This is a highly compressed definition that needs more

13. A. Wilder, *The Rules Are No Game: The Strategy of Communication* (London: Routledge & Kegan Paul, 1987), p. 124.

14. D. Hardy and D. Ford, *Jubilate: Theology in Praise* (London: DLT, 1984), p. 157.

time than can be given here. It is clear from this definition, however, that communication cannot be restricted to language. All language is communication but very little communication is language.[15]

Touch is a rich medium for communication. Visual communication is perhaps the richest of all. A traditional Chinese proverb states: "One hundred tellings are not as good as one seeing."[16] It is true that we often fail to recognize the importance and influence of other modes of communication, especially those associated with popular culture. It is also true that

> since the scientific revolution of the seventeenth century, language has been commonly identified with "thought" or "reason" and assumed to be more important or more significant than other modes of communication, such as the environment of non-verbal communication that makes thought and language possible.[17]

However, it is also the case that "there is no communication system between animals, insects, or computers that remotely approaches the complexity, flexibility, and capacities of language."[18]

We are more intimately involved in communication through language than in any other activity besides love and work — and both of these are modes of communication that usually require language. Communication is thus a general category within which language appears as a special case. An important conclusion from these brief and unsurprising comments is that language is not simply a means to another end, an instrument for other purposes. Rather, language is a medium through which the communicative life occurs. In this sense it is constitutive of human life. Human social life is formed and shaped through language. As such, language is a part of human reality rather than a copy or misrepresentation of it.[19]

15. Wilder notes in *The Rules Are No Game* that the "non-linguistic modes of communication in society include music, the visual arts, the visual aspects of film and television; kinship. status, money, sex and power, accent, height, shape and beauty; much mathematics, dreams, and fantasy; images, ideals, emotions, and desires; the production and exchange or commodities; and clan, date, race, and sex" (p. 137).

16. Wilder, *The Rules,* p. 122.

17. Wilder, *The Rules,* p. 138.

18. Wilder, *The Rules,* p. 136.

19. Wilder, *The Rules,* p. 130.

Communication and Language: Some Ecclesiological Perspectives

These general remarks about communication and language are important in considering evangelism and theology in the church. Both these themes can be treated as tasks of the church. However, as a particular task of the church, communication can be done well or poorly. What then becomes important is the improvement of communication. This involves strengthening techniques and devising more appropriate strategies. In this context those interested in evangelism might allude to the character of God's communication and spend a good deal of energy analyzing the strategies and principles that informed Jesus' evangelism.[20] This is all well and good but it does not push the discussion very far. The main problem is that in this context communication is quickly reduced to a question of method, strategy, and style. Communication is here what the church does to and for others who are unchurched. It is what the church does to achieve another end. Language is reduced to an "instrumentalist" function. A lot of modern evangelism operates within this instrumentalist framework. Evangelism in this context can too easily operate in a "tool-like" way, and become excessively manipulative.

Not surprisingly, some people find this pragmatic approach reductive and distortive of the gospel. There is, it is claimed, more to the task of communication than simply "wording truths," as if the gospel could be reduced to the delivery of certain information in a neat and pure form. Accordingly, advocates of the alternative view argue that good communication involves a self-giving which is more than merely information requiring a response. Rather, communication has the character of an open exchange in which the distance between hearer and speaker is bridged in a fulsome way which includes but goes beyond mere words. This approach has its ecclesiastical form in the history of the World Council of Churches, with its stress on social action as a necessary part of spreading the good news.

What is easily overlooked is that both the above approaches see communication as a task to be performed by the church. In other words both end up operating with an instrumentalist view of communication whether it is in evangelism through word and/or deed. This does not have to be the case but it often is.

Communication moves to a different level when it is no longer considered as simply one task among many but rather becomes a way of understanding the whole life of the church. Communication is here no longer one

20. A popular and important book in this regard is R. E. Coleman, *The Master Plan of Evangelism.* This book was originally published in 1963 and is now in its 45th printing.

church practice but concerns its very existence. The focus is the church as a communicative system. What is important in this view is the quality of the interactions occurring between texts, traditions, persons, and institutions. This approach can illuminate how communicative life is disturbed or disrupted by ideological elements. This perspective on communications can offer important insights into the structuring and activities of ecclesial life. It can provide the basis for an understanding of the church as a "sacrament of non-dominative communication."[21]

These comments link up with the earlier discussion of language and communication as constitutive of human community. Communication is not something the church does, but something it is. The critical factor is the quality of the church's communicative life. It is of high quality to the extent that it mirrors the character of God. This means it is called to be a sacrament of non-dominative communication. This essential note of the church ought ideally to be present in all its communicative tasks. Thus the wording of truth in evangelism and theological discourse ought to occur in a non-dominative way. Of course, to speak about non-dominative communication is to speak about power relations. To communicate through language is to be implicitly involved in certain power relations. The apostle Paul was acutely aware of this: "For I resolved to know nothing while I was with you except Jesus Christ and him crucified. I came to you in weakness and fear, and with much trembling. My message and preaching were not with wise and persuasive words, but with a demonstration of the Spirit's power, so that your faith might not rest on men's wisdom, but on God's power" (1 Cor. 2:2-5). If then, we are to be communicators of the gospel, the content and form of our language ought to be informed by the non-dominative ideal, through which we, as well as others, are continually surprised that through weakness God's power is manifest.

A question arises as to how this ideal feature of the church's communicative life might be reflected in the evangelistic and theological tasks of the church. Quite clearly at this level the concern is primarily with communication through language, with "wording" the truth of God. This is the domain of logos communication. There is a long tradition in Christianity of "wording" truth. It has to do with the character of God whose word is creative of light and life, whose word takes the form of Torah for the people of Israel, whose word is spoken by the prophets. Logos reality comes to its most concentrated form in Jesus Christ: "In the beginning was the word and the word was with God and the word was God . . . and the word became flesh and dwelt

21. See G. Baum and A. Greely, eds., "Communication in The Church," *Concilium* 111 (1978): 92 and 98ff.

among us," as it is written in the prologue of St. John's Gospel. It is the word of God that is preached in the early church and that expands (Acts 6:7; 12:24). The subsequent Christian theological tradition is a tradition of "wording" the truth. So in one sense it is not surprising that the Western theological tradition has been so dominated by logos theology.

The Crisis in Word Communication

There is, however, a crisis in logos communication. It has been around for some time and it will remain. People generally are suspicious of mere words. And perhaps with good reason. Lies are told by words. In many walks of life it seems that the more uncertain and insecure people become the more words are used to cover up inadequacies.

Within theology the crisis of logos communication is well established. It may be symptomatic of a deeper loss of confidence that God is really present in the community of faith.[22] Furthermore, there is at present a strong reaction against the long dominance of the word tradition in Christianity. This is evident when language is given a secondary significance, a medium for expressing something more primal.[23] Language on this account operates as means to another end. This instrumentalist view of language and thus theology is a natural reaction to a type of word communication that presupposes a tight or rigid one-to-one correspondence between human word and Divine Word. This is exemplified in modern theology by a form of doctrinalism that codifies truth in particular and fixed language forms. This form of propositional objectivity ends up codifying God, a point well appreciated by Karl Barth.[24] Human words are, on this view, no longer fed or capacitated by

22. See the discussion in E. Farley, *Ecclesial Man: A Social Phenomenology of Faith and Reality* (Minneapolis: Fortress, 1975), chap. 1.

23. This view of religious language is implicit in what has been referred to in recent theology as the experiential-expressive dimension of religion. In this view attention is focused on feelings, attitudes, existential orientations and practices rather than what happens at the level of "symbolic investigations," e.g. at the level of language which expresses experience. This powerful trend in religious understanding stands in the tradition of Schleiermacher. For further discussion, see G. A. Lindbeck, *The Nature of Doctrine: Religion and Theology in a Post-Liberal Age* (London: SPCK, 1984), chap. 1.

24. A good example of the rigid doctrinalism against which Barth so vigorously contended can be found in Barth's critique of the tradition of fundamental articles of faith. Barth linked the emergence of this notion of articulating the faith with seventeenth-century Protestant Scholasticism. Barth argued that the codification of faith into certain articles of faith which were then raised to the status of a "classic text" involved "a definition, limitation and re-

God's Word but effectively block the full and free-flowing Divine Word. Of course, the more unstable and fragmented life seems to become the tighter become the institutional controls upon the language of faith. The result is "orthodox reductionism." Full and free speech is thwarted in the interests of a false notion of purity which requires a tight one-to-one correspondence between the reality which faith witnesses to and its form in language. Naturally, logos communication of this kind will set up a counter-reaction which seeks a freer communicative life. Unfortunately this option, already mentioned above, can easily get caught in the trap of human subjectivity. It becomes unclear how human words mirror or refer to the truth of God. Evangelism might end up being merely the good news of my life rather than the good news of the life of God in which I live. Theological discourse might end up being just what I think. Ironically, anxiety over the wording of truth has contributed to a massive reductionism in evangelism and theology. This reductionism is evident both in a tight formalized "orthodox reductionism" and in an undisciplined subjectivizing of faith. What has been sacrificed in both developments is joyful praise of God through language. What has been forgotten is that the logos of God authorizes and legitimates free-flowing, abundant discourse directed by praise of the God of Jesus Christ.

What is being suggested here is that God is logos — language. Language is not merely instrumental, a means to another end. Language is a medium of God's presence and power energizing and directing all things to their truth in God. Human response to the presence and activity of God is to praise God. This praising occurs in language as it is informed by the truth of God. Such language, if it is to be the language of true praise, can be neither overformalized nor undisciplined but within the community of Jesus Christ it is constrained by the love of Christ (2 Cor. 5:14).

Dynamics of Full and Free Speech in the Church

But the critical issue now concerns the nature of that inner constraint by which the language of faith is not held back but released in order to praise God. What is thus urgently required in the church is an improved under-

---

striction of the Word of God" (p. 865). When the expression in doctrine of the church's encounter with "God in His Word" became the pretext for "the establishment of specific, irrevocable, fundamental articles" (p. 864), then the way was blocked, in Barth's view, for the free operation of the Word of God and the Church. For page references, see Karl Barth, *Church Dogmatics*, I/2 (Edinburgh: T & T Clark, 1956-78), pp. 863-66.

standing of the dynamics of full and free communication. In other words, what is happening in good communication of the truth?

There are perhaps at least three dimensions to full and free speech in evangelism and theology that ideally inform and direct the church's praise of Jesus Christ. First, full and free speech involves an implicit appeal to *simplicity.* Secondly, such communication operates with a bias toward *repetition.* Thirdly, it witnesses to the presence of *wisdom.*

It is not just any kind of simplicity, repetition, and wisdom that is needed but simplicity, repetition, and wisdom understood in quite particular ways. Our task now is to develop an understanding of how good communication occurs under or with the guidance of the above three parameters. The suggestion is that speech in the church which is constrained by the love of Christ will be speech that involves an appeal to simplicity, a bias toward repetition, and a witness to the presence of wisdom. Within each of these three dimensions of communication, evangelism and theology operate in different but complementary ways.

The Appeal to Simplicity

The first mark of full and free communication is simplicity. Jürgen Moltmann has said:

> What cannot be said simply does not need to be written at all. Simplicity is the highest challenge to Christian theology, Theology stands under the demand to speak simply because, as Christian theology, it stands or falls with the church.[25]

In the context Moltmann clearly has in mind the issue of communication in the church. His sentiments would, no doubt, find joyful approval among those involved in evangelism — though before we go any further it is also well to note that for every difficult and complex problem there is always a perfectly reasonable and simple answer that is wrong.

Nevertheless, the good news is never confusing or complicated. Neither is it simplistic. There is, it seems, a way of wording the faith — seeding the word — which communicates the mystery of the gospel with a profound simplicity. Such simplicity is not that which "boils" truth down to the bare essentials. That is a popular strategy but it is no more than that; just a useful strat-

25. Jürgen Moltmann, *The Open Church* (London: SCM, 1978), p. 9.

egy of questionable worth. It can easily lead to a "checklist" gospel, in which certain propositions are offered for assent. But there *is* a way of communicating with simplicity that has more of the character of a concentration of profundity. This might take the form of a "word in season" — that word for which Paul prays when he opens his mouth: "Pray also for me, that whenever I open my mouth, words may be given me so that I will fearlessly make known the mystery of the gospel" (Eph. 6:19, NIV). His prayer is not for "the bare essentials" but a compelling snapshot of the faith of Jesus Christ, a rich compression of the truth. It is precisely because the gospel is not simple but profound that he prays for the wisdom to put the mystery with simplicity. On this account evangelism might be understood as communicating the gospel in microcosmic form.

There are no blueprints for achieving this simple profundity in the truth. It is Spirit-led, and informed by the love of Christ. Sharpness, clarity, and depth of insight are not merely well-honed skills but capacities bestowed by God for his praise. Furthermore, in the body of Christ it should not be presumed that all these qualities will be present in the same person to the same degree. What is critical is an openness to God in order that, like Paul, utterance may be given evangelists as they open their mouths, that they may be freely released to open up the secrets of the good news of God. There is no appeal here to a ready-made plan. Rather what we find is a reliance upon God as one speaks freely and flowingly of the love of God in Christ Jesus.

I have suggested that simplicity properly understood has more of the character of concentrated abundance. It has to be like this to be the truth of God. However, precisely because the evangel is this kind of simplicity it is capable of significant expansion. In fact the compression of truth is not only capable of being "strung-out," so to speak, it has an inbuilt drive for extension. This movement to concentration points and extension in a very free-flowing and fulsome way belongs to the dynamic of truth itself.

In this compression/extension dynamic inherent in the communication of the gospel, evangelism represents a recurring moment. It belongs to a process of communication. Evangelism is not a full stop, but a comma. Theological discourse participates in this communications process as it moves beyond the comma. Theology unravels the truth further, bringing fresh illumination and sharpness to it. In this sense theological discourse is called playfully and joyfully to "string-out" the truth. The snapshot offered in evangelism now becomes the video of theology, though the analogy ought not to be pressed too far.

A good example of this dynamic between compression and systematic extension of faith is provided by the work of Paul Tillich. Tillich recognized the concentrated abundance of the gospel in relation to his own highly developed systematic enterprise: "The statement that Jesus is the Christ contains in some way the whole theological system, as the telling of a parable of Jesus contains all artistic potentialities of Christianity."[26]

Given the above formulation of simplicity as concentrated abundance in the truth it is clear that evangelism and theology are, properly speaking, complementary forms of gospel communication. Evangelism represents a concentration point — the comma in the sentence — theology represents the extended form of communication. Good communication requires both compression and extension of the truth. Evangelism and theology act as catalysts for each other in the process of communication. Precisely because such communication is dynamic, we find a multiplicity of concentration points en route to fuller communication. Free-flowing communication actually requires continual refocusing or re-concentration. Compression of the truth in a concentrated form — as in evangelism — is in fact a recurring moment in communication of the truth. This is important. It suggests a second feature of gospel communication which might be termed the bias toward repetition.

The Bias toward Repetition

Repetition is not usually treated as a theme in modern theology, though it is important in everyday life and thought, and certainly warrants serious theological consideration. Good evangelism evidences certain recurring patterns or references to God's ways with this world and human life. The history of the Christian tradition is informed by a recurring focus on the creative, redemptive, and life-giving character of the Triune God. This is the God who is praised in Jesus Christ. On this account evangelism might be understood as "the horizontal dimension of praise *repeated and explained* to others so they can join the community of praise."[27]

From this perspective it is not the fact of repetition per se but its quality that is of critical importance. Repetition in evangelism and in everyday life has both healthy energizing forms as well as more disturbed, barren, and ultimately destructive forms. Modern society is highly repetitive in its structure and routine. Negative forms of repetition abound. For many workers heavy industry is a world of repetitive and unfulfilling work practices where human beings often function in a machine-like manner. In the area of mental health

26. Paul Tillich, *Systematic Theology,* vol. 3 (London: James Nisbet, 1964), pp. 215-77.
27. Hardy and Ford, *Jubilate,* p. 19 (my italics).

the compulsion to endlessly repeat certain behavior patterns is well known. In Alzheimer's disease there is a loss of the power of recall; this loss of the capacity to remember means that those who love and care for such people are locked into repetitive communication patterns. There is the constant re-presenting of one's identity and love as well as more routine tasks.

More generally, repetition is viewed in a negative light in our society. Repetition is often associated with inauthenticity.[28] What society seems to demand is constant change, which involves discarding the past and present in the search for the totally new. Advertising is a good example of this search to overcome repetition. It is, of course, a self-defeating exercise. What becomes paramount is maximum exposure of the consumer public to the new product. Such exposure requires repetition and so the cycle is perpetuated.

The negative aspects of repetition ought not to blind us to the fact that repetition is an important and necessary feature of our everyday life. If the toothbrush and soap as well as regular and balanced food intake are to count, it is obvious that the repetition of the daily rituals associated with these things gives vitality and freshness to human life. The dream of every golfer is to develop a swing that repeats itself. Definite recurring patterns of behavior, communication, and exchange (e.g., greetings, farewells) seem to be a necessary part of the healthy ordering of human society. Not surprisingly the positive and negative aspects of repetition can be discerned in religious life, for example, in worship.[29]

28. In this respect S. Sykes, *The Identity of Christianity* (London: SPCK, 1984), p. 325, quotes and comments upon Lionel Trilling's remark, "in an increasingly urban and technological society, the natural processes of human existence have acquired a moral status in the degree that they are thwarted." Anything resembling a mechanical process, and that would include the order and repetition of a liturgy, is felt to be "inimical to the authenticity of experience and being." See Trilling, *Sincerity and Authenticity* (London, 1974), p. 128.

29. In my own tradition of Anglicanism worship was patterned liturgically around *The Book of Common Prayer.* As the title indicates it was prayer that was common to the congregation and repeated Sunday by Sunday and daily for those who said the Daily Offices. At the opposite end of the spectrum is Pentecostalism. This church life is self-consciously nonliturgical, seeking freedom and spontaneity. In between are a whole range of differing ecclesial traditions. How is repetition relevant here? It is relatively commonplace to view Anglican liturgy as unhelpfully repetitive over against more free-flowing charismatic worship. However, highly structured liturgical worship does have the capacity to generate freedom. One is mercifully relieved from what has been termed "the introspective conscience of the West." Freshness from without becomes a real possibility. But of course, it is also true that such worship can prove sleep-inducing. At the other end of the spectrum, Pentecostal worship can assume a highly predictable and structured form in which the weekly repetition of certain activities is eagerly sought for among the gathered worshipers. Music in worship is undergoing a renaissance right now. One feature of the newer forms of music is repetition. This has the capacity to completely kill

Accordingly, there is an expectation in evangelism that what is proclaimed today is the same good news that brought redemption yesterday and will do so tomorrow. Minimally, we are right to expect a recurring pattern in the proclamation of the evangel. Furthermore, earlier it was suggested that this recurring pattern will have a trinitarian form if it is to do justice to God's relation with creation. In this sense certain components or dimensions in the evangel will recur: creation, redemption, fulfillment. The challenge is to repeat the evangel in its fullness — its rich simplicity — rather than in some mutilated form. There is, at this level, good and bad evangelism.

Theological discourse participates in the dynamic of creative repetition. Here the aim is comprehensive communication of the truth of Christianity. So what ought to emerge in good theology is a fulsome opening of the gospel as it is woven into myriad themes and life situations. Furthermore, what we ought to observe and in fact can discern in the Christian tradition is a recurring engagement with a trinitarian understanding of God. Why trinitarian? Because this is the form of the God who has generated Christian worship, mission, and service in history. A recurring trinitarian pattern in theology can, of course, be linked to the very nature of the being of God. This was articulated most powerfully in the twentieth century by Karl Barth, who referred to God's threefold repetition of himself. Some notion of repetition belongs: it seems, to the structure of the being of God.[30]

However, it is precisely at this point that the problem of repetition becomes acute. Good repetition requires *freshness through sameness.*[31] What is required in good evangelism and theology is creative repetition. What this

---

the spirit or alternatively take it to new heights. It is not repetition per se that is the problem but it is quality, i.e., whether or not it mediates freshness.

30. Barth's treatment of the threefold "repetition in God" (p. 366) is highly sophisticated and programmatic for his theological enterprise. What is revealed and witnessed to in Scripture is a threefold differentiation in God in his unimpaired unity (p. 299). God repeats himself three times, in three quite "inexhangeable" modes of being: "God reveals Himself. He reveals Himself through Himself. He reveals Himself . . . this subject, God, the Revealer is identical with his act in revelation and also identical with its effect" (p. 296). For this reason the doctrine of revelation begins with the doctrine of the triune God. For page references, see *Church Dogmatics,* I/2, pp. 295-383. In Barth's theory of the repetition of God priority tends to be given to the unity rather than the threefoldness within God. This incipient modalism is succinctly put by a recent commentator. "God's triple restoration of himself is much more prominent than his relation to himself," A. C. Heron, *The Holy Spirit* (Philadelphia: Westminister, 1983), p. 167.

31. This, of course, was the burden of Barth's development of the threefold repetition in God: "Although, in keeping with God's riches, revelation is never the same but always new, nevertheless, as such it is always in all circumstances the promulgation of the logos, of the Lordship of God" (*Church Dogmatics,* I/1, p. 306).

amounts to is that there can be no such thing as simple or pure repetition. It is impossible.

Creative repetition is required by the very character of God, whose threefold repetition — Father, Son, and Spirit — is the ideal of "freshness through sameness." Creative repetition is required by the in-time-ness of human experience. Life goes on, and demands new responses. The world is becoming increasingly complex; it is not the same as it was two thousand years ago. Good repetition is not achieved by simply imprinting what was said yesterday upon a new context; that is the way of domination. Good repetition emerges through attentiveness and discernment in the contingencies of life, i.e., the context. Context is, after all, the weaving together of different textures. There are no shortcuts.

One such shortcut is implicit in the notion that the gospel is "substance-like." In this case the substance is equated with propositions of truth that are to be worded in precisely the same manner. Pure repetition is, on this view, a sign of faithfulness. Such repetition offers the illusion of security but the price is high; the truth of God is reduced to a form of doctrinal legalism. However, the real problems are transferred elsewhere, i.e., into the practical sphere concerned with the application of truth. This gives the illusion of secure foundations but such theology has forfeited freshness for a kind of sameness. Or perhaps the element of freshness is transferred to the question of application and practice of the truth. Is it any wonder that the theology soon loses its vigor and appeal? It no longer witnesses to the fresh activity of God.

Another equally dangerous shortcut is to discard the past altogether. Creativity and freshness are sought, but this is thought to require severing links with the tradition. Often this amounts to newness for newness' sake. This approach strikes a deep chord in Protestantism and produces an "occasionalism" of the Spirit. God comes and goes; continuity is hard to discern. It seems here that the idol of pure repetition has been firmly rejected. No sameness, only freshness. However, there quickly emerges another kind of repetition, via the back door, so to speak. What is repeated is often nothing more than the profundities of human subjectivity. This is characterized by a fairly directionless, free-floating Christianity which becomes curved-in on the human subject and simply repeats a range of human thoughts uninformed by God's presence. To end up communicating "just what I think," is to end up with sameness without freshness.

To conclude, what is repeated in evangelism and theology is the content of praise, repeated in such a way that others will want to join the community of Jesus Christ. We ought not to be frightened of repetition but welcome it, seek to understand what we are doing, and allow our repeating of the good news to be informed by our praise of God.

With simplicity we have identified the basic complementarity between evangelism and theology, the former representing a concentrated expression of the latter's more extended discourse. This gave rise to repetition as a feature of both modes of communication. It should not go unnoticed that the challenge of repetition — of freshness through sameness — provides a useful theological heuristic through which to reconsider context as constitutive of good communication in evangelism and theology.

However, it might fairly be asked: simplicity of what, repetition of what? Has not the discussion skirted around the main issue of the "content" of evangelism and theology? The issue of content has been implicit in what has already been said and has occasionally surfaced. It is time to treat this explicitly as an issue in communication.

The Presence of Wisdom

The question of content might be more fruitfully and adequately understood as a question of the presence and nature of wisdom. This requires some further teasing out. Earlier it was suggested that in evangelism and theology the content of praise is repeated in such a way that others join the community of Jesus Christ. What is repeated here is "the content of praise." Now "content of praise" is a fundamentally dynamic understanding of content. It can't be reduced to a static substance-like thing. What is praised in Christian worship and discipleship is not a set of propositions or certain truths. Of course, no one would actually want to say this. It is the living God. However, there is a form of doctrinalism in the church that quickly codifies the truth of the living God in such a way that the language of faith is set in certain fixed and tight forms. This is not to suggest that any language will do. But, unfortunately, the inevitable tendency to doctrinalize the truth in the above way eventually has the effect of solidifying the truth of God's dynamic presence. Belief becomes law-like; God is legalized as the lawgiver. A good test of this tendency is the prevalence of the language of "substance" in relation to the gospel. The language suggests physicality, concreteness, and fixity. More generally, this approach to content often gives the impression that the good news is "information-like" — a unique assemblage of facts. Christianity as an obediential religion fits well within this framework. The purpose of evangelism is thus reduced to the communication of certain information that will generate obedience to God.

It is true that we live in an information culture where power is vested in the holders and disseminators of information. But the "content of praise" cannot be too readily reduced to certain information now available to the world.[32] If, however, the "content of praise" is to be information, then it will have to be information of a particular kind, i.e., it will have to be such that it is capable of forming and reforming humankind in the way of godliness. What is critical here is attention to the dynamics of the presence of God forming and transforming created life. This suggests a patterning of God's life in human life. This is not merely a case of delivering information and then invoking some added-on doctrine of the Holy Spirit to do something with the information.

What we are dealing with in "the content of praise" may be information-like or knowledge-like but it is never *just* knowledge or information. Rather it is knowledge which is properly directed. It is goal seeking. Now in the Christian tradition such "content of praise" used to be referred to as wisdom. Theology was originally wisdom that bestowed illumination and salvation.[33] Such wisdom was not substance-like nor codified propositions. Rather it concerned the "enwisening" of human life with the life of God. This wisdom came to its concentration in Jesus Christ.[34] Furthermore, it was the wisdom of God in Christ crucified and risen that has been witnessed to in the evangel (1 Cor. 1:18–2:8).

It is this wisdom that is praised in the Christian community, repeated in evangelism, and meditated upon in theology. The theme of wisdom seems to be enjoying a renaissance in these last few years. But there is always a danger that overuse will lead to shallowness. It can easily become a synonym for well-honed common sense. In Christianity, however, wisdom is that which God bestows and it is that to which all things are to be assimilated, i.e., brought into relation with and changed accordingly. Wisdom as such is the dynamic activity of God's presence lifting or raising created life to the fullness of truth. I have referred to this process as the enwisening of life. It is God's Christlike

32. Interestingly, Karl Barth's massive resurrection of the Christian Tradition did not entirely escape the problem. There is a lingering sense in this great theologian's work that all that is really required — given the triumph of grace in the world in Jesus Christ — is for humankind to be informed of this event. Passing on the knowledge is what it is all about, or so it might be construed.

33. See, e.g., E. Farley, *Theologia: The Fragmentation and Unity of Theological Education* (Minneapolis: Fortress, 1983), chap. 2.

34. For a discussion of Jesus Christ as the concentration of the wisdom of God, see D. Hardy, "Rationality, the Sciences and Theology," in G. Wainwright, ed., *Keeping the Faith: Essays to Mark the Centenary of Lux Mundi* (London: SPCK, 1989), pp. 294ff.

work in the world. This is what is praised in the Christian community. This is what is repeated in its simplicity in evangelism. This is what is unraveled in its infinite richness in theological discourse.

Transformation: The Purpose of Communication

The second half of this essay has offered a brief consideration of some of the dimensions of full and free speech relevant to evangelism and theology in the church. The essential structure of the relationship between evangelism and theology was developed through the theme of simplicity. The basic dynamic calling forth and calling for continued communication — what is normally treated as a question of context — was developed under the theme of repetition. The question of content was briefly redeveloped as the presence of wisdom. Simplicity as concentrated abundance of truth, repetition as freshness through sameness, and wisdom as properly directed knowledge are the three key parameters that guide good communication in evangelism and theology. These three parameters, understood in particular ways, are present and operating as speech in the church "constrained by the love of Christ."

What happens within this communicative framework? In the Christian tradition the answer has been transformation through conversion. This points to the fact that communication involves exchange, in this case an exchange of lives. The communicative life is always a life of bestowing and receiving, i.e., a life of exchange. When this is done well, human life is built up: life is raised to its full truth in God.

This points, however, to the fundamentally expansive nature of human life. It is capable of being added to quantitatively and qualitatively. Human life is raised to its full truth. This perfecting occurs in and through communication. Good communication is the condition for fresh, expanded life possibilities. This is a process in which the past is transcended without being wasted. The old is taken up into something new (2 Cor. 5:17). In the resurrection, Jesus Christ did not leave his wounds behind (John 20:19-23). They belonged to his new life but in a new way. When we think of Christian conversion it might be helpful to consider it from the point of view of the potential of godly human communication to expand and build up human life. This happens through the bestowal of fresh understanding, energy, and direction. This is what happens when our life is assimilated to the wisdom of God who himself is the energy, order, knowledge, and purpose of all things.

Conclusion

It has been suggested that evangelism and theology are complementary forms of human response to God's communication. The further suggestion is that these forms are informed and directed according to the criteria of simplicity, repetition, and wisdom, understood in quite particular ways. These three criteria provide the conditions for faithful "wording" of the gospel. Why these three criteria? Ultimately, to be good criteria they have to be developed in relation to the truth of God. Who is God? In the Christian tradition God is praised as a being of communicative love. There is a simplicity to such a God — an abundance of richness in a highly concentrated form. This simplicity of God's being is repeated in self-differentiation — as creator, redeemer, and fulfiller. In this repetition of God's simplicity, wisdom is bestowed and created life is transformed. The communicative structure of the being of God is concentrated in Jesus Christ and overflows in the presence of the Spirit of the father's Son. This is the God who evokes human praise. When this is repeated in evangelism and theology, the outflow of God's communicative love expands and manifests itself through more open, free, and wise communicative life in human society.

Full and free communication in human life is thus a response to God's own self-communication. Evangelism and theology occur under the constraint of God's own simplicity, repeated in Jesus Christ that wisdom might be realized in human life. As evangelism and theology realize God's wisdom in human language, they praise the truth of God. So ultimately, to engage in such activities is itself a praise of God. In this context it is appropriate to refer to evangelism and theology which is praise-centered. Praise which honors the truth of God in communication is the way through which God's presence is realized and human life is built up and expanded by the truth. This is God's converting work. As such, it is salvific.

This essay has invited readers to leave their ecclesial boats, don scuba-diving gear, and explore the life of the ocean upon which so much ecclesiastical sailing takes place. Without the ocean there would be no ships. And without God's overflowing love in Jesus Christ there would be dead silence. As it is we are compelled to echo St. Paul: "And pray for us that we may be given utterance when we open our mouths that we might freely and fully communicate the mystery of the gospel."

CHAPTER 11

The Meaning of Evangelism in the Context of God's Universal Grace

Carl E. Braaten

I. The Biblical Foundations of Evangelism

The classical expression of the evangelistic task of the church is given in the Great Commission of the risen Lord, recorded in Matthew 28:19-20: "Go therefore and make disciples of all nations, baptizing them in the name of the Father and of the Son and of the Holy Spirit, teaching them to observe all that I have commanded you; and lo, I am with you always, to the close of the age." This trinitarian formula is not only a baptismal confession of the early church, it also offers a comprehensive setting for understanding the universal intention of God in his covenant with Israel, the coming of God's kingdom in the person of Jesus, and the preaching of the apostles in the power of the Spirit. The roots of world evangelization are deeply embedded in the entire history of God's revelatory activity set forth in both the Old and New Testament Scriptures and they give us a number of starting points for reflecting on the church's role in the universal scheme of God's grace.

The evangelistic activity of the early church did not start from scratch. It was a continuation of what God had already announced through the prophetic history of Israel. The call of Abraham, the father of faith, was God's way of initiating a new relationship between himself and all the nations. Here is the nucleus of the promise which the New Testament announces as the salvation to be extended to all people's through Christ Jesus. God's purpose in setting Israel apart from other nations was to prepare the way for the coming of God's rule throughout the whole world. The purpose of election was not to shower Israel with special favors for the sake of its own salvation, but strictly for the sake of witnessing to the lordship of God over all the nations of the world. It is clear that God's special relationship with Israel was not an end in itself but a means to bring about a universal relation between God and all peoples.

The root of this universal perspective of Israel's place among the nations lies in its radical monotheism. In Deuteronomy 4:39 we read: "Know therefore this day, and lay it to your heart, that the LORD is God in heaven and on the earth beneath; there is no other." If Israel's task is to witness faithfully to Yahweh as the one and only Lord of the nations, the universal horizon is clearly implied. The book of Isaiah speaks of Israel's role in terms of bringing forth "justice to the nations," (42:1) of being a "light to the nations." (42:6). In the book of Jonah it is apparent that Israel's vocation was not to be confined to itself, but included the task of proclaiming the infinite love of God among the heathen nations.

Connected with the universal scope of Israel's mission was its expectation of salvation through the future coming of the Messiah who has the power to redeem the world. Even though the time of this salvation lay in the future, Israel became engaged in direct witnessing activity. Particularly during the time between the two Testaments, the Jews of the Diaspora made efforts to convert pagans and to gain followers of the Torah. This means that when the apostle Paul and the early missionaries preached the gospel to the Gentiles, there was a considerable constituency of Gentile converts providing points of contact in the major cities of the Roman Empire. The universal thrust of biblical faith had already been put in motion by the Jewish Diaspora prior to the coming of Jesus as the Messiah and the rise of the Christian community. It is noteworthy, too, that the Greek translation of the Old Testament — the Septuagint — became the great document of Jewish mission, and thus placed a ready-made tool at the service of Paul's preaching to the Gentiles.

The Gospels picture Jesus of Nazareth as one who confined his mission to the "house of Israel." Matthew 15:24 quotes Jesus as saying: "I was sent only to the lost sheep of the house of Israel." This is illustrated by his order to the disciples: "Go nowhere among the Gentiles and enter no town of the Samaritans, but go rather to the lost sheep of the house of Israel" (Matt. 23:15). Jesus went further; he attacked the conversion efforts of the Jews of his time: "Alas for you, lawyers and Pharisees, hypocrites! You travel over sea and land to win one convert; and when you have won him you make him twice as fit for hell as you are yourselves" (Matt. 23:15, NEB).

On the other hand, Jesus is never pictured as one with narrow religious or nationalistic attitudes. He broke through Jewish particularism by freely demonstrating his openness to the Samaritans, both in his actions and in his parables. Furthermore, Jesus' proclamation of the coming kingdom embraces a future that includes Gentiles along with the Jews. Matthew 8:11 states, "I tell you, many will come from east and west and sit at the table with Abraham, Isaac, and Jacob in the kingdom of heaven." Salvation in the kingdom is open to all people, Jews and Gentiles; yet, meanwhile, Jesus and his disciples restricted their preaching to the people of Israel. But at the end of time the nations will make their way to Jerusalem, feast on Mount Zion, and worship the true God. In continuity with the Old Testament, the expectation of salvation in the Gospels is universal and eschatological. The future kingdom of God includes all nations of the world, and the special role of the Jews is to be God's chosen people serving that end.

In summary, we can say that we have not yet reached a full biblical theology of evangelism with the materials from the Old Testament, nor even with the coming of the Messiah and his proclamation of the kingdom of God. Something radically new was required to raise the evangelistic consciousness of the people of God to another plane. This new element broke through in the suffering, death, and resurrection of the Messiah Jesus.

The apostles were authorized by Jesus to be the first Christian evangelists because they were witnesses of his resurrection. As representatives of the risen Christ the apostles were commissioned to proclaim God's salvation to the uttermost parts of the world. As apostolic emissaries of Christ they became founders and leaders of new ecclesial communities. Thus, the church as the new people of God, the new community gathered around the presence of the risen Christ, is founded forever on the faith and witness of the apostles.

The church is not identical with the kingdom of God which Jesus proclaimed. Rather, the new community gathered around the name of Jesus exists in order to proclaim the good news of God's kingdom to all the nations, and to be a sign of its activity in the world. The apostles preached that Israel's hope for the coming of God's rule and kingdom was realized in the coming of Jesus as the Messiah, but not in the usual nationalistic and political terms. Instead, the coming of God's righteous rule took place in the crucifixion and resurrection of Jesus, and therefore the apostles proclaimed Jesus as the focal point of God's continuing activity in world history. The apostolic preaching of Christ became the primary means of access to the mystery of the kingdom. The great christological titles were applied to Jesus to designate the absolute meaning of his person and work. Jesus is Messiah, Son of Man, High Priest, Prophet, King, Lord, Savior, Son of God, and finally connected with the significance of all these titles, the New Testament designates Jesus as the Word of God, indeed, addresses him as "God." Jesus is the core of the apostolic message.

In the New Testament the accounts of the resurrection of Jesus and his commission to the apostles to go with the gospel to the nations appears intertwined in the same context. The gospel is the good news of what God has done to death in raising Jesus from the grave; that is the heart of the message of the apostles and to the nations. "Christ is risen!" Death has been conquered at Easter and a new ruler has been enthroned in the world. "Christ is King." The effect of this event is absolutely decisive, uniquely authoritative, and universally valid. As Matthew 28:18-20 states the matter: "All authority" has been given to Christ; "all nations" are to be made disciples and baptized in the name of the Triune God; they are to be taught "all that I have commanded you"; and Christ promises to be with his followers "always, to the close of the age." There are no qualifications, no limits bearing on time or space, geography or chronology, that could plausibly relativize the Lord's mandate for the proclamation of the gospel to all peoples, everywhere, until the end of time.

But the apostles were not given a worldwide mandate to accomplish under their own power and direction. Easter was followed by Pentecost. The apostolic witness to the risen Christ became charged with power by the outpouring of the Holy Spirit, authorized by Christ himself: "But you shall receive power when the Holy Spirit has come upon you; and you shall be my witnesses in Jerusalem and in all Judea and Samaria and to the end of the earth" (Acts 1:8).

Here we have the beginnings of world evangelization in a nutshell: the commission to preach the gospel of the risen Christ in the power of the Holy Spirit to all the nations, beginning in Jerusalem and then going to every part of the world until time runs out. The direct result of the apostolic proclamation of the gospel was the creation of a new kind of community transcending the usual distinctions between Jew and Gentile, male and female, rich and poor, etc. This new community is the body of Christ, the temple of the Holy Spirit, the new people of God, called and commissioned to preach the gospel, to cross all frontiers, and to witness to the realities of the new age that has dawned.

The apostolic pattern of being called and sent by Christ to the world continued to be valid for the generations of Christians following the apostles. Christian identity and gospel proclamation were inseparable. Christians who existed among Jews and Gentiles understood that it was the gospel that made the difference, and that belief in this gospel meant the privilege and obligation to make it known to all others. The successors of the apostles had to continue doing what the apostles had begun. How was this to be done? Through the ongoing proclamation of the word and witness of the apostles to the crucified Christ. "Faith comes from what is heard," said Paul, "and how are people to believe in him of whom they have not heard? And how are they to hear without a preacher?" (Rom. 10:14-17). All baptized believers are preachers in the sense that they are called to bear witness to the full and final revelation of the world's reconciliation through Jesus Christ our Lord.

II. The Abiding Evangelistic Task

The church in history exists between the times: the *kairos* of salvation in the person of Jesus and the final *parousia* at the end of history. As long as the kingdom of God has not yet arrived in its full power and glory, the church is called to continue in the apostolic line to spread the good news of the gospel to all people. The memory of God's victory in the death and resurrection of Jesus keeps alive the hope for history to reach its final goal, the basic transformation of the conditions of life as we know it, especially the defeat of death, and at last the eternal life in communion with God forever. In the end the world of creation will be set free from its bondage and decay and will obtain the glorious liberty of all the children of God. The final consummation will spell the removal of all evil, the overthrow of Satan and his power of destruction, and the conquest of sin and all its consequences.

But the kingdom of God is not merely future; it is also present as an offer of mercy to sinners, restoring humanity's broken relationship with God. This new relationship is experienced through repentance and faith, as the forgiveness of sins, a new life in Christ, and receiving the gifts of the Spirit, with far-reaching implications for life in all its daily aspects. This new relationship with God cannot be confined to the private sphere of life or matters of personal piety. Jesus' ministry of the kingdom showed signs of breaking into every dimension of life, healing physical illness, exorcising spirits, feeding the hungry, speaking out against corrupt officials and religious authorities, and caring for the poor and neglected.

Correspondingly, the church is to be a Christlike medium of the kingdom of God in this world, bringing its missions to the frontlines of struggle on behalf of human beings, including the battles being fought in the political, social, and economic areas of life. Through missionary service the gifts of the kingdom of God are offered to the world and distributed here and now. Yet, Christians must not be carried away into a kind of utopian enthusiasm, as though they could expect the ultimate victory over physical death, disease, destruction, and deprivation under the present conditions of existence in history. All solutions to human problems of this side of the final consummation remain partial and preliminary.

A church committed to continue the apostolic mission in the world must believe that entry into the kingdom of God is mediated by the church's proclamation of the gospel of Jesus Christ and by its administration of the sacraments. This constitutes the primary aim of the church's existence everywhere in the world. Those who are incorporated into the church through faith and baptism are ordained by the Spirit to convey the gospel of the kingdom of God to all who do not yet believe. The church continues in history under the original mandate of Jesus: "And this gospel of the kingdom will be preached throughout the whole world, as a testimony to all nations; and then the end will come" (Matt. 24:14).

God's plan of salvation includes all the nations. Until this plan is consummated the Christian church is engaged in a task that bears on the meaning and destiny of the present history of the world. Meanwhile, Jesus Christ represents the "Yes and Amen" for all the promises of God, and sets the church in motion in the power of his Spirit to proclaim and pioneer the hopes opened up for all peoples, nations, cultures, and religions. The evangelistic imperative to go and tell fades away whenever the church turns in upon itself and loses sight of the universal horizon of God's all-embracing kingdom. If the gospel has not already been preached to all nations, the church has no choice but to bring its witness wherever the name of Jesus Christ is not yet being confessed.

The church today must strive assiduously for a comprehensive view of the kingdom: the vertical dimension of the gospel which mediates the unconditional grace of God as well as the horizontal dimension in which we meet Christ and the persons of our needy neighbors; the depth dimension which deals with the universal human condition of sin and estrangement as well as the breadth dimension which struggles with demonic forces in everyday existence; the personal dimension which lifts up the absolute significance of every individual human being in the sight of God as well as the political dimension bearing on the quality of justice and liberty that prevail on earth. The comprehensive symbol of the kingdom of God includes all these dimensions, and the church is right to work for their realization as an expression of its faith in Christ in the power of the Spirit.

No matter what the social, economic, or political circumstances may be, the church still has the indispensable task of witnessing meaning and goal in life in Jesus Christ, thus bestowing on individuals here and now a sense of absolute worth in the eyes of God. Witness to individual persons with the hope of conversion — repentance and faith — is an inalienable priority of the church's total mission. Avoiding this aspect of personal evangelism is always a sign that the church has forgotten the way of the kingdom in the ministry of our Lord who touched and changed the lives of forgotten individuals, and who made God's love for the world manifest in behalf of all sorts of individuals, children, women and men, rich and poor, sick and sinful, crippled and blind.

Some Christians have wearied of the evangelistic task altogether. They may view Christianity as an appropriate religion for Western culture, but with no right to claim universal validity for all other cultures. The twin concepts of religious pluralism and historic relativism make it seemingly difficult to see how that which has occurred in one time and place can possess final meaning for all peoples and ages. Perhaps we can engage in a dialogue between religions or faiths, and benefit from the cross-fertilization of ideas. Then the aim of the church's evangelistic outreach would be more like cultural exchange than religious conversion. Others would make a case for recoiling from evangelistic activity because of its recent association with Western imperialism and expansionism. Western missions allegedly become colonial outposts of the divided churches of Europe and America. Missions supposedly became propaganda organs by which the denominations reduplicated themselves in Africa and Asia. These charges have been told over and over again, and people hold varying opinions on the success or failure of the Western missions.

Regardless of all that, theologically viewed the apostolic mission of the Messiah and God's kingdom is a continuation of the biblical history of promise, proceeding beyond the limits of Israel, reaching in principle absolutely universal dimensions. In the New Testament no limits are set to the universality of God's redemptive will. "God would have all to be saved and come to the knowledge of truth" (1 Tim. 2:4). In an ultimate sense we are not even speaking of the mission of the church and its evangelistic task. For the mission belongs to the one God, unfolding a plan for the world that emanates from the Creator of the world, the Lord of history, and the Savior of all humanity. The unique thing, however, about this biblical kind of universalism is the way it is mediated through particular events of history, beginning with the election of Israel, so that the eschatological goal of world history is carried as a promise within the concrete history of God's missionary people. In contrast, there is a gnostic type of universalism which trusts in a spiritual or mystical essence common to all religions ultimately void of all concrete symbols and historical events. What makes biblical faith into a global missionary movement is that the universal promise looks to concrete history for its future realization, and following the apostles the church believes it has been summoned and commissioned by God to serve as a particular means to the universal end.

III. The Final Hope of Biblical Universalism

Today there is a trend in both Protestant and Catholic theology to restrict the scope of biblical universalism, and to make Christ small and unimportant. The Christocentric emphasis is under attack, at least among the deans of modern liberal Protestant and Catholic progressive theology. Our biblical, evangelical,

Reformation Christology is too exclusivistic. On account of historical relativity and religious pluralism, many are challenging the place of Christ as the goal of things. Is Christ really that final, definitive, and normative?

John Hick represents a liberal Protestant view which allows Christians to hold to Christ as their unique Savior without necessarily claiming as much for others. Christ may be my personal Lord and Savior, but this does not mean that he is the only Savior or the only Lord for all other religions. To hold Christ as the final and normative Word of God is branded as "theological fundamentalism." There is room, after all, for other savior figures in other religions, at least enough to go around for everybody. To be sure, Jesus is one of the ways in which God meets the world of human experience, but it is arrogant bigotry to claim that Jesus is God's unique way of dealing with the salvation of the world.

Other voices in modern theology like Tom Driver, Rosemary Ruether, and Dorothee Sölle are claiming that the uniqueness, normativity, and finality of Jesus Christ account for the sins of Christianity, its sexism, racism, and anti-Semitism. The scandal of the particularity that insists on a once-and-for-all Christ is supposedly the breeding ground of intolerance, supremacy, imperialism, and what these theologians call "Christofascism." As Tom Driver says, "The infinite commitment of God to finitude in Jesus does not indicate something done once and once for all time."[1] What these theologians are asking for is a "paradigm shift" from a theology wherein Christ is the center to one in which he is one of the satellites in a galaxy of religious superstars. John Hick calls it a "Copernican revolution," contrasting it with the old Ptolemaic system of geocentric thinking, which imagines that the incarnate revelation of God in Christ stands at the center of the universe of world religions. Paul Knitter, a progressive Catholic, speaking in favor of this new trend, states: "We are in the midst of an evolution from Christocentrism to theocentrism."[2] James Gustafson continues the attack on Christocentricity, demanding that the homocentric view that focuses on God's humanity in the earthly Christ must give way to a theocentric perspective that fits a post-Copernican view of the universe.[3]

1. Tom Driver, *Christ in a Changing World: Toward an Ethical Christology* (New York: Crossroad, 1981), p. 65.

2. Paul Knitter, "Towards a Theocentric/Nonnormative Christology: Growing Endorsement," unpublished paper given at the American Academy of Religion at the Currents in Contemporary Christology Group, p. 11. The paper was published in an altered form in Knitter's *No Other Name? A Critical Survey of Christian Attitudes toward the World Religions* (Maryknoll, N.Y.: Orbis, 1985).

3. James Gustafson, *Ethics from a Theocentric Perspective* (Chicago: University of Chicago Press, 1981).

I agree with Paul Knitter's assessment that there is "growing endorsement" of a "nonnormative christology" both among Protestant and Catholic theologians. They are holding ranking positions in the prestigious divinity schools. However, there is a counter-offensive going on in contemporary theology sparked by interest in Karl Barth's Christocentric trinitarianism. Diametrically opposed to the anti-Christological trend is a movement to continue the Barthian initiative toward a new affirmation of the Trinity on the basis of Christology. There are new books on the Trinity by Eberhard Jüngel, Jürgen Moltmann, and Robert W. Jenson.[4] They represent a significant advance to a new conception of the Trinity, precisely at a time when most other theologians have raised the white flag of surrender.

When we stress, as we have done, a Christocentric trinitarian perspective, some liberals charge "archaism," and when we emphasize universalism some evangelicals cry "heresy." How can we have our cake and eat it too? Do we need to restrict the confidence born of hope and prayer that God will get his wish in the end that all will be saved? May we share the hope of Karl Barth? He said: "There is no good reason why we should forbid ourselves, or be forbidden, openness to the possibility that in the reality of God and man in Jesus Christ there is much more than we might expect and therefore the supremely unexpected withdrawal of that final threat, i.e., that in the truth of this reality there might be contained the super-abundant promise of the final deliverance of all men. To be more explicit, there is no good reason why we should not be open to this possibility . . . of an *apokatástasis* or universal reconciliation."[5]

We would teach a highly nuanced and qualified evangelical universalism. It is not a dogma, not a piece of knowledge, not something to which humans have a right and a claim. Yet, it is something for which we may cautiously and distinctly pray and hope, that in spite of everything that seems to point conclusively in the opposite direction, God's mercy will not cast off his world forever. Alternatives to a Christocentric universalism are Arminianism and double predestination. It should come as no surprise that a Lutheran is comfortable with neither. For us the doctrine of election means at least that those who come to faith in Jesus Christ are elected through God's grace and love. God's justice and wrath have already taken their toll in the rejection of Jesus Christ on the cross. (Shades of Barth.) God's love is not limited. It is limited neither by human freedom nor by divine wrath.

4. Eberhard Jüngel, *The Doctrine of the Trinity: God's Being Is In Becoming* (Grand Rapids: Eerdmans, 1976); Jürgen Moltmann, *The Crucified God* (New York: Harper & Row, 1981); Robert W. Jenson, *The Triune Identity* (Philadelphia: Fortress, 1982).

5. Karl Barth, *Church Dogmatics*, IV/3, first half (Edinburgh: T & T Clark, 1961), p. 478.

We cannot hold a universalism of the Unitarian kind. People are not too good to be damned. There is no necessity for God to save everybody, nor to reject anyone. God is not bound by anything outside of himself. He is not bound to give the devil his due. If we take into account God's love, he would have all to be saved. If we reckon with his freedom, he has the power to save whomsoever he pleases. This does not lead to a dogmatic universalism. But it does mean that we leave open the possibility that within the power of God's freedom and love, all people may indeed be saved in the end. This follows as a possibility from the fact that God is free from all external factors in making up his mind. Not even the human predicament, the *need* of salvation, is primarily the motive of God's love in Jesus Christ. God loves because it is his nature to love, as Anders Nygren emphasized so powerfully in *Agape and Eros*, not first because there are people in need of his love.

The other side of the possibility of universal salvation is that of reprobation. We cannot rule out the possibility of divine reprobation to those who remain in unbelief and disobedience to the end. If this is a possibility in principle that cannot be ruled out, the moment one contemplates the atonement of Jesus Christ the threat of eternal rejection is seen in a new light. The threat of eternal condemnation is real for all people. Nevertheless, there is no basis to assert that God will necessarily in the end actualize this possibility. Christians may hope and pray that all might be saved, that the distinction between those who already believe and those who do not yet believe will ultimately be destroyed by the Word of God who "is able from these stones to raise up children to Abraham" (Matt. 3:9).

The scale is tilted decidedly toward the hope of universal reconciliation on account of Christ. We agree with Barth that it cannot be denied that eternal reprobation is a possibility, but in the light of God's verdict in the victory of Jesus Christ, it becomes an "impossible possibility." Barth says, "No aversion, rebellion, or resistance on the part of non-Christians will be strong enough to resist the fulfillment of the promise of the Spirit which is pronounced over them too . . . or to hinder the overthrow of their ignorance in the knowledge of Jesus Christ . . . the stream is too strong and the dam too weak for us to be able reasonably to expect anything but the collapse of the dam and onrush of the waters. In this sense Jesus Christ is the hope even of these non-Christians."[6]

In a still more explicit passage, Barth states that the justification of the world of sinners in Jesus Christ is the content of predestination. "The exchange which took place on Golgotha, when God chose as his throne the

6. Barth, *Church Dogmatics*, IV/3, first half, pp. 355-56.

malefactor's cross, when the Son of God bore what the son of man ought to have borne, took place once and for all in fulfillment of God's eternal will, and it can never be reversed. There is no condemnation — literally none — for those that are in Christ Jesus."[7] Then he says, more boldly still, that after the coming of Jesus Christ unbelief becomes "an objective, real, ontological impossibility. . . . Faith, however has become an objective, real ontological inevitability for all, for every man."[8]

IV. Then Why Evangelize?

It is the task of the Christian community to announce to the world what God has accomplished for its salvation in Jesus Christ. The good news is that all people have been united with God in Christ. One chief difference between the Christian and non-Christian is that the one knows and the other does not yet know. That difference, of course, makes a lot of difference. The point, however, is that the Christ-event is full; there is no void which has to be filled up by the church or the world. The evangelistic task of the church is to bear witness to the word and deed of God in Jesus Christ. Christ alone is the true minister, the true missionary of God par excellence. All of us are more like acolytes assisting in the priestly and prophetic ministry of Christ.

What is the relation between Christian evangelism and the eternal destiny of all people? Evangelicals are concerned to ask whether in the end the unbelieving heathen are really saved. Barth's doctrine of justification is radically objective. "There is not one for whose sin and death He did not die, whose sin and death He did not remove and obliterate on the cross. . . . There is not one who is not adequately and perfectly and finally justified in Him. There is not one whose sin is not forgiven sin in Him, whose death is not a death which has been put to death in Him. . . . There is not one for whom He has not done everything in His death and received everything in His resurrection from the dead."[9] In the face of literally hundreds of such beautiful passages, evangelicals understandably ask: "Then what is the point of evangelism?" If the heathen are already saved in Christ, and nothing more needs to be added, then where is the urgency in world evangelization?

We are all fully aware that the majority of the world's billions do not know and believe in Christ. We also believe that what God has done objec-

7. Barth, *Church Dogmatics,* II/2, p. 167.
8. Barth, *Church Dogmatics,* IV/1, p. 747.
9. Barth, *Church Dogmatics,* IV/1, p. 638.

tively in the reconciling work of Christ must be subjectively appropriated in order to bear fruit in the lives of individuals. This subjective appropriation is the work of the Holy Spirit through his witnesses who indeed do call for existential decisions of faith. Those who proclaim Christ do intend to evoke a response of faith. Those who proclaim Christ do intend to evoke a response of faith in the hearts of those who hear the gospel. How can this paradox be resolved? God's will to save all is subjectively appropriated by only a few. The solution lies in God's hands. Meanwhile, we all live in the shadow of death. We all stand under the threat of being damned. The danger of condemnation hangs over us like a sword.[10] Haven't we all said from time to time, "Well, I'll be damned!" But Barth says, "It is God's affair whether or when He will take seriously and put into effect this insane desire."[11] God's final condemnation has not yet been pronounced on each one of us. The threat has not yet been fulfilled; the sword has not yet fallen. "The falsehood of man may be only an undertaking which finally proves impracticable."[12]

We would also end our speculation on a hopeful note. Ours is a universalism of hope and prayer, not a matter of gnostic speculation or pantheistic metaphysics. The whole sinister stream of historical events and human falsehood cannot have a meaning and a future of itself apart from the determination of God to deal with his world according to his gracious word in Jesus Christ. It is noteworthy that Barth is the only theologian in the history of Christianity who has dared to say a cautiously hopeful word for poor Judas who betrayed Jesus and destroyed himself.

10. Barth, *Church Dogmatics*, IV/3, first half, pp. 464-65.
11. Barth, *Church Dogmatics*, IV/3, first half, pp. 465-66.
12. Barth, *Church Dogmatics*, IV/3, first half, p. 466.

CHAPTER 12

Incarnation and the Church's Evangelistic Mission

Darrell L. Guder

In the ecumenical conversation about mission and evangelism in the last decade, there is frequent reference to "doing mission and evangelism in Jesus Christ's way." In 1989, the World Council of Churches (WCC) convened its conference on world mission and evangelism in San Antonio under the theme, "Your Will Be Done: Mission in Christ's Way."[1] In 1987, an international grouping of ecumenical-evangelical missiologists and church leaders met in Stuttgart to consider the forthcoming San Antonio meeting. Their purpose was to think about the evangelistic mission of the church and to prepare a statement reflecting their insights for the 1989 conference. The result was a book entitled *Proclaiming Christ in Christ's Way: Studies in Integral Evangelism.*[2] In 1982, the WCC's Commission on World Mission and Evangelism presented its major statement, *Mission and Evangelism: An Ecumenical Affirmation.*[3] It contains a section entitled "Mission in Christ's Way." The reception of this language can be traced around the world. In 1991, for example, the General Assembly of the Presbyterian Church (USA) adopted a document on mission and evangelism entitled *Turn to the Living God — A Call*

1. Frederick R. Wilson, ed., *The San Antonio Report: Your Will Be Done: Mission in Christ's Way* (Geneva: WCC, 1989); hereinafter referred to as *Your Will Be Done* (1989).

2. Vinay Samuel and Albrecht Hauser, eds., *Proclaiming Christ in Christ's Way: Studies in Integral Evangelism: Essays Presented to Walter Arnold on the Occasion of His 60th Birthday* (Oxford: Regnum, 1989); hereinafter referred to as *Stuttgart Statement.*

3. World Council of Churches, *Mission and Evangelism: An Ecumenical Affirmation* (Geneva: WCC, 1983), published with a Study Guide for Congregations by the Commission on World Mission and Evangelism and the Division of Overseas Ministries, National Councils of the Churches of Christ in the U.S.A., New York, 1983; hereinafter referred to as *Mission and Evangelism.*

To Evangelism in Jesus Christ's Way,[4] which specifically refers to the WCC statement of 1982.[5]

This imagery, "doing mission and evangelism in Jesus Christ's way," indicates a broadening ecumenical consensus about the relationship between the Incarnation — the actual way in which the Word became flesh or the model of Jesus' life — and the way in which the church goes about its mission. Such an "incarnational" approach ("incarnational" is apparently a twentieth-century neologism) raises a lot of questions, particularly at a time when, in some quarters, the Incarnation is itself the theme of heated debate. Therefore, it will be helpful to examine carefully what is occurring theologically when we talk about "mission in Jesus Christ's way."

When we go back before the appearance of the WCC 1982 document, *Mission and Evangelism: An Ecumenical Affirmation,* we enter into a period of several decades in which most Western mainline Protestant traditions tended to de-emphasize evangelism as the verbal proclamation of the gospel with the intent to draw people to personal faith in Christ. The focus was generally more upon the church's social witness and involvement with a broad agenda of justice and peace. Often evangelism was redefined as an expression of social witness, so that the word was used for almost anything a mainline denominational agency wanted to affirm. The American Presbyterian version of this process is called by Milton J. Coalter the "rethinking, retooling, and restructuring" of evangelism, which he dates from about 1963 on.[6] Throughout this period, however, thinking and writing about the mission of the church never completely disavowed the centrality of the church's evangelistic mission, as awkward as that central tenet of our confessional tradition might have been for some. The emphasis upon incarnational evangelism emerged in various attempts to define the church's witness in ways that sought to include both verbal proclamation and social witness. This approach has now established itself in the concept of "mission in Christ's way." It is a genuinely helpful way of thinking, which does not undermine the evangelistic ministry of the church, but rather strengthens it.

4. Presbyterian Church (USA), *Turn to the Living God: A Call to Evangelism in Jesus Christ's Way:* A Resolution adopted by the 203rd General Assembly (1991) for study and implementation (Louisville: Office of the General Assembly, 1991); hereinafter referred to as *Turn to the Living God.*

5. *Turn to the Living God,* p. 11.

6. Milton J. Coalter, "Presbyterian Evangelism: A Case of Parallel Allegiances Diverging," in *The Diversity of Discipleship: Presbyterians and Twentieth-Century Christian Witness,* ed. M. J. Coalter, J. M. Mulder, and L. B. Weeks (Louisville: Westminster/John Knox, 1991), pp. 33-54, especially pp. 46ff.

The emphatic use of this incarnational imagery in the 1982 WCC document *Mission and Evangelism: An Ecumenical Affirmation* shows that such language had achieved a notable ecumenical currency. Such statements emerge from long and difficult processes of drafting and editing which draw together representatives across the full spectrum of churchly traditions and cultures. When they finally agree, then we have language that we can use in the multicultural, worldwide church with some hope that we all mean the same things when we say the same words. The publication of *Mission and Evangelism: An Ecumenical Affirmation* in 1982 was a signal event for the theology and practice of mission. It represented a broad consensus of Christian thought on the church's evangelistic mission.[7] It strongly affirmed the centrality of evangelistic mission as well as defining how that mission was to be carried out. Thus, it certainly may be regarded as a corrective to American Presbyterianism's attempts to "retool and restructure" evangelism in the preceding twenty to thirty years.

The incarnational thrust is already addressed in the document's opening section on "The Call to Mission," where John 20:21 is cited: "As the Father has sent me, even so I send you." As we find often in the contemporary documents on this theme, this "as" is interpreted with a double meaning. It refers both to the fact God has sent Christ, and also to the way in which God has sent Christ, as a human among humans, in the particularity of human experience.[8] In the document's next paragraph, the incarnational linkage between Christ and the church's witness is expanded upon: "The early church witnessed to its Risen Lord in a variety of ways, most specially in the style of life of its members."[9] The wording to which later documents all would refer comes in a section entitled, "Mission in Christ's Way." It begins again with the reference to John 20:21. John's mission mandate is linked with Paul's kenotic or "self-emptying" emphasis in Philippians 2, when the document states, "As the Father has sent me, even so I send you. . . . The self-emptying of the servant who lived among the people, sharing in their hopes and sufferings, giving his life on the cross for all humanity — this was Christ's way of proclaiming the good news, and as disciples we are summoned to follow the same way."[10]

7. Even the broad consensus of evangelical thinking on mission, represented by the Lausanne Covenant of 1974, can be said to be reflected in the 1982 World Council Statement, since there is a general agreement that the World Council process was at least in part a response to Lausanne.

8. *Mission and Evangelism,* pp. 9-10, ¶3.

9. *Mission and Evangelism,* p. 10, ¶4.

10. *Mission and Evangelism,* 29, ¶28.

In 1988, the WCC sent out a preparatory booklet on the theme of the approaching San Antonio conference on world mission and evangelism. In this study booklet, the participants were asked to consider "Mission in Christ's Way," and were told that "we may trust the model of Jesus' life for our engagement in God's mission. While the good news that we proclaim as Christians is that God's grace was in Jesus Christ, we cannot credibly proclaim that by methods or actions that do not correspond to the model of Jesus' life. The incarnation . . . *is* mission. . . . The incarnational mission of Christ is thus the only model of mission."[11]

This emphatic language was subsequently developed by Emilio Castro, by then the general secretary of the WCC, in his address in San Antonio on the conference's theme. He proposed that the proclamation of "God's saving will," which "has been perfectly fulfilled in Jesus Christ," is to be guided by the "criterion" of Jesus Christ. This is what it means to "interpret [God's] will in the present." Not only do we pray "in Jesus' name" to ensure that our prayer is "purified by the Spirit," but "equally, in the other direction, when we seek to interpret God's will in the real world of history, there too the 'name' — the criterion — of Jesus Christ has to be fundamental in controlling and determining our actions."[12]

When we survey this procession of statements on the church's doing evangelism in "Jesus Christ's way," then it becomes clear that the central issue is evangelistic methodology. In none of the documents is there any argument about the possibility of the Incarnation of Jesus Christ as God's Son. Nor is there any reference to the ancient christological debates about the two natures. The deity and humanity of Jesus are assumed when we now ask, What does the Incarnation have to say about the way in which we go about the church's mission?

The reason this question is arising, I believe, is the discomfort in the Western Christian traditions that emerges when we look objectively at the history of missions and evangelism in the last two to three centuries. From the perspective of global mission, we have every reason to rejoice at the spread of Christianity and the emergence of indigenous churches in virtually every nation on earth. Yet, at the same time, we are painfully aware of the legacy of Western cultural imperialism that accompanied that missionary movement. The Hocking Report of 1930, among many twentieth-century evalua-

11. Commission on World Evangelism and Evangelism, World Council of Churches, *Your Will Be Done: Mission in Christ's Way: Study Material and Biblical Reflection* (Geneva: WCC, 1988). The first of the Bible studies in the booklet was on John 1:1-14, and by this very choice the centrality of the incarnation to one's theology of mission was brought out.

12. *Your Will Be Done,* pp. 134-35.

tions of Western mission, clearly indicts the Western churches for their "domination and cultural control" in the churches and cultures in which they have evangelized.[13] Christopher Sugden of the Oxford Centre for Missions Studies has succinctly analyzed the theological problem. He explains that we in the West have looked upon the context of missionary evangelism as neutral. "All people are sinners so all contexts are the same in what matters; . . . the message to be proclaimed is universal, [and] there is one way to salvation."[14] This approach has meant, of course, that the Western view of all contexts for mission has been governed solely by Western perspectives. Thus, we often failed to do mission "in Jesus Christ's way," because we have assumed that our way was, in fact, synonymous with Jesus Christ's way.

Similarly, in the history of American evangelistic activity, especially American revivalism, there are repeated examples of a separation of evangelism from the full dimensions of gospel obedience within our society. Faith has been reduced to a private and individual affair. There has been a persistent refusal to draw out the implications of Christ's message of the kingdom of God to every dimension of creation. This too represents a failure to grasp the incarnational nature of mission. It becomes more compellingly obvious as we learn to read the gospels self-critically, testing our own cultural assumptions and filters rigorously.[15]

As Eugene Stockwell said in San Antonio, "Often the church has in the past, and in our time, engaged in a mission that by no stretch of the imagination could seen to be 'in Christ's way.'" He illustrates this by referring to word proclamation separated from worship, deed, and life. He points to the cultural trappings that surround our witness so as to obscure Christ, and to the frequent emphasis upon numerical growth over spiritual depth.[16] Another way to formulate this critique would be to say that the dominant value system of much of Western missions and evangelism has been success measured in terms of the marketplace's value system. The emphasis upon doing mission

13. John R. Fitzmeier and Randall Balmer, "A Poultice for the Bite of the Cobra: The Hocking Report and Presbyterian Missions in the Middle Decades of the Twentieth Century," in *The Diversity of Discipleship,* pp. 105-9.

14. Christopher Sugden, "Evangelicals and Wholistic Evangelism," chap. 3, in *Stuttgart Statement,* pp. 30-31. See also David Bosch, *Transforming Mission: Paradigm Shifts in Theology of Mission* (Maryknoll, N.Y.: Orbis, 1991), pp. 1-8, for a summary of the "crisis" in missions.

15. See Ronald C. White and C. Howard Hopkins, *The Social Gospel: Religion and Reform in Changing America* (Philadelphia: Temple University Press, 1976).

16. Eugene Stockwell, "Mission Issues for Today and Tomorrow," in *Your Will Be Done,* p. 117. See also John Mackay, *Ecumenics: The Science of the Church Universal* (Englewood Cliffs, N.J.: Prentice-Hall, 1964), pp. 175-77, for a trenchant critique of Western missions.

"in Christ's way" might then be compared to our Lord's cleansing of the temple of evangelistic theory and practice in order to re-assert the biblical criterion for mission. This criterion, as was suggested by Emilio Castro, will be found in the human life and ministry of Jesus as the Incarnate Son of God. This is the energy behind the growing emphasis upon an "incarnational approach" to mission and evangelism.

A grammatical innovation is very significant in this discussion. A noun used to summarize a central fact of faith, *incarnation,* has spawned an adjective, *incarnational.* This is a recent development in English. The *Oxford English Dictionary* cannot find any use of the term before 1912. Perhaps a thorough search of the writings of the Anglican "incarnational theologians" of the late nineteenth century might turn up an earlier example, but only by a few years.[17] The adjective "incarnational" cannot be formulated in German, which has led some German theologians to doubt whether the idea is even thinkable (a not unknown tendency of German theology).

I first came upon incarnational language with regard to evangelism in working with the American para-parochial youth ministry organization Young Life. The leadership of Young Life described their approach to youth ministry and evangelism as "incarnational." What they were expressing with this term was that the communication of the gospel be appropriate to its content. The message, the messenger, and the communication of the message should be seen as a whole, based upon the life, death, and resurrection of Jesus Christ. Their own usage of "incarnational" language arose from conversations with D. Campbell Wyckoff and John Mackay at Princeton Theological Seminary. Mackay described what Young Life attempted with young people as "incarnational witness." This reference led me to look more closely at Mackay's possible contribution to the discussion of the church's mission in incarnational terms.

There is general agreement that Mackay was a major figure in the ecumenical history of the twentieth century. His importance was many-sided: he was one of the most significant missionary figures in the Latin American world; he was the president of Princeton Theological Seminary; he was a founding president of the WCC; and he was the initiator of the academic discipline of ecumenics.[18] With regard to our theme, his insights were undoubt-

17. See Robert Paul, *The Atonement and the Sacraments: The Relation of the Atonement to the Sacraments of Baptism and the Lord's Supper* (New York: Abingdon, 1960), pp. 216-27; Brian Hebblethwaite, "The Propriety of the Doctrine of the Incarnation as a Way of Interpreting Christ," *Scottish Journal of Theology,* 33, no. 3 (1980): 201-12; also in B. Hebblethwaite, *The Incarnation: Collected Essays in Christology* (Cambridge: Cambridge University Press, 1987), pp. 53ff.

18. Richard Shaull, describing John Mackay as "one of the outstanding leaders of the

edly incisive for the future development of thought about the church's mission done "in Jesus Christ's way."

He was perhaps the first English-speaking theologian to develop a theological concept of the "incarnational principle" for the church's mission, at least in print. He expounds this theme in his major work, *Ecumenics: The Science of the Church Universal,* published in 1964.[19] Building upon a classic and orthodox Christology, Mackay arrives at the key sentence: "Christ's life in the world was of such a kind as to reveal to [humanity], by words and deeds, what God is like."[20] Thus it is essential for the church's mission mandate to focus upon the humanity of Jesus. This has, as Mackay put it, "incalculable importance for our understanding of God's pattern for living. It provides the image of what men and women should be who take seriously Jesus Christ and His mission to the world."[21]

"The church's mediation of the love of God in evangelical witness" is how Mackay defines the church's mission.[22] He endorses the Anglican definition of evangelism formulated in 1918 and affirmed by the Temple Commission in 1945: "To evangelize is so to present Christ Jesus in the power of the Holy Spirit, that [all people] shall come to put their trust in God through [Jesus Christ], to accept Him as their Savior, and serve Him as their King in the fellowship of His Church."[23]

The crucial question, then, is "How to Present Jesus Christ." To expound his view, Mackay introduces here the "incarnational principle."[24] Like the "as" in John 20:21, the "so" in the Anglican definition is the crux: "To evangelize is *so* to present Christ Jesus." Mackay asks, "Taking it for granted that a faithful presentation of Jesus Christ . . . will not produce redemptive fruits except through the 'power of the Holy Spirit,' what features should mark the process whereby Christ is presented?"[25] By using the term "incarnational" for his methodological argument, Mackay clearly intended to raise the question of evangelistic method to a theological level commensurate

---

world Church today," said that he was "the missionary statesman whose insights and actions in relation to the mission of the church are constantly keeping things moving in many different areas of the Church's life," Richard Shaull, "[John Mackay] as Missionary Statesman," *The Princeton Seminary Bulletin,* 52, no. 4 (May 1959): 24.

19. Mackay, *Ecumenics.*

20. Mackay, *Ecumenics,* p. 63 (italics his).

21. Mackay, *Ecumenics,* p. 65.

22. Mackay, *Ecumenics,* p. 162.

23. Mackay, *Ecumenics,* p. 169, quoting *Towards the Conversion of England* (London: The Press and Publications of the Church Assembly, 1945), p. 1.

24. Mackay, *Ecumenics,* pp. 172ff.

25. Mackay, *Ecumenics,* p. 172.

with the content of the gospel. The medium is not to be equated with the message. Instead, the medium is to be appropriate to the message.

Mackay defined the "incarnational principle" in this way: "The evangelical word must become indigenous flesh."[26] This means that the witness must identify oneself "in the closest possible manner" with one's environment. "All mere foreignness in manner, speech, living, and sometimes dress must disappear. . . . [One] will be humble, sensitive to [people's] needs, concerned about their interests." The witness will be "in every respect a friend, [giving] concrete expression by word, act, and disposition to the reality of love, of Christian *agape,* mediating thereby the love of God in Christ Jesus."[27]

Mackay sees this principle at work in every era of Christian history where there has been a "truly redemptive effort." "People have responded to Christ and the church has been established and has grown, in the measure in which Christ's representatives ceased to be mere outsiders in the life of a people, and became, not condescendingly, but joyously and empathically, involved in their common life and concerns."[28] Based on this principle. Mackay then roundly criticizes the cultural insensitivity of much of Western missions. It has usually entailed too narrow definitions of evangelism: "There is clear evidence that whenever a Christian mission from abroad devoted itself exclusively to evangelistic activity in a narrow, technical sense, without its component members identifying themselves closely with a community and its welfare, the work became sterile."[29] Here, the humanness of Jesus, and the example of his life, are seen as paradigmatic for the mission activity of the church. In effect, the incarnational approach becomes an ethic of evangelism, based upon the humanity of Christ, whose life and actions are as much the norm of obedient Christian living as are his words.

The significance of this incarnational approach can be seen in its *integrative* function for our theology of the church's mission. This integration occurs in two major dimensions. It provides a biblically informed, theologically coherent way of drawing what, in another context, I have described as the being, doing, and saying of incarnational witness.[30] At the same time, this approach also integrates various dichotomies that are prevalent in both our thinking about and doing of mission. These dichotomies are manifestly harmful to the obedient carrying out of Christian mission.

26. Mackay, *Ecumenics,* p. 173.

27. Mackay, *Ecumenics,* p. 173.

28. Mackay, *Ecumenics,* p. 173.

29. Mackay, *Ecumenics,* p. 177.

30. D. L. Guder, *Be My Witnesses: The Church's Mission, Message, and Messengers* (Grand Rapids: Eerdmans, 1995), *passim.*

First, the incarnational approach to the church's evangelistic mission helps us to grapple with the unfortunate dichotomy often made between Christian faith and culture. The incarnational approach takes the particularity and variety of cultural settings with great seriousness. Rather than seeing a scandal or a problem in the particularity of Jesus' own Incarnation as a Jew in Palestine in the first century, one can appreciate the biblical-theological validation of the importance of context. The indigenization and contextualization of Christian witness are then rightly seen as the necessary consequence of the Incarnation of Christ. As Vinay Samuel states, "The incarnation of God's Son is the final affirmation of God's identification with human culture."[31]

A second dichotomy involves the divisions of the church. The incarnational approach to the church's evangelistic mission can be ecumenically fruitful. It opens up avenues of discourse with ancient traditions that place great value upon the doctrine and the mystical significance of the Incarnation, particularly the Orthodox and Western monastic traditions. Contemporary Orthodox and Roman Catholic missiologists have argued that the Incarnation bears a missionary character. As the Catholic scholar Gregorius has suggested, the "church as the mystical Body of Christ is the continuation of the historical Christ and his work of redemption."[32] This might prove a helpful point of departure for the current dialogue in America with the Orthodox,

31. Vinay Samuel, "Gospel and Culture," chap. 5 in *Stuttgart Statement,* pp. 75-76. See also John Mackay on "incarnational identification with the world," *Ecumenics,* pp. 141, 163-74, 176-78; *Stuttgart Statement,* pp. 214, 217 (especially 10, 11), and 218 (15); World Council of Churches, *Minutes and Reports of the Commission on World Mission and Evangelism, December 31, 1972 and January 9-12, 1973, Bangkok Assembly 1973* (Geneva: WCC, 1973), pp. 57ff., 72-73. This sensitivity for and openness to all human cultural expressions embraces the human religious experience in other faiths as well, so that we find in repeated discussions of Christian relationships with other faiths an emphasis upon respect for the "beliefs and devotion of others," upon listening as well as telling, upon recognizing the work of the Spirit in all cultures. But this open and non-judgmental openness to interaction with other faiths is not to be construed as a restriction upon Christian witness, but rather as a way of defining how that witness is to be carried out. The prevalent usage of the idea of "incarnational" evangelism does not imply that we are not to present Christ to those of other faiths, but rather defines the way in which we are to do it, modeled upon the way in which Jesus interacted with people during his life. On the insistence that openness to dialogue with and respect for other religions does not imply that the gospel is not to be proclaimed to all peoples in all cultures, see *Stuttgart Statement,* p. 222 (24 & 25); "Witness among People of Living Faiths," nos. 14-45, *Mission and Evangelism* (1983), pp. 47-48; "People of Many Religions," *Turn to the Living God,* pp. 18-19, and often elsewhere; see also Lesslie Newbigin, *The Gospel in a Pluralist Society* (Grand Rapids: Eerdmans, 1989), *passim,* but especially "The Gospel and the Religions," pp. 171ff.

32. P. Gregorius, O.F.M. Cap., "Der Missionsgedanke und die Menschwerdung Jesu Christi," *Zeitschrift für Missionswissenschaft und Religionswissenschaft,* 37, no. 4 (1953): 267.

who are having difficulties with their relationships with their Protestant sister churches. The incarnational approach might also assist in integrating more effectively the Catholic traditions of spiritual formation into the Protestant practice of evangelistic ministry.[33]

Another way in which the incarnational approach can be ecumenically integrative relates to the conservative groupings. These groupings are strongly committed to evangelism and yet struggle with issues of interpretation and authority of Scripture. The incarnational emphasis, understood as God's way of entering into human history and culture, can help those who are burdened by rigid views of particular methods of inspiration. For some who honestly agonize over the meaning and application of Scripture when bound to such a docetic view of God's revelation as represented by theories of inerrancy, it is a liberating insight to realize that God's incarnational activity must by definition involve the ambiguity of human culture. Part of the wonder of God's gracious sovereignty in revelation is his willingness to make himself known in and through frail and ambiguous humans and their experience. That frailty and ambiguity is part of the biblical witness and actually helps us to encounter God in our own humanness.

God's gracious willingness to enter into particular human experience is then grasped as good news for us. We begin to understated that, as Psalm 111 makes clear, the love and righteousness of God are made known through God's actions in history. Those actions are carried out in and through fallible human beings, portrayed with all the candor of the biblical witness. The God who has always acted incarnationally for the sake of the healing of God's rebellious creation is the God who continues to enter into our ambiguous reality as the Holy Spirit empowers our incarnational witness. Such an incarnational approach becomes a highly stimulating way to probe further the realism of the "internal testimony of the Holy Spirit" in our experience today. Critical studies of the Bible enhance our experience of God's self-disclosure as the Spirit confirms that God was at work in the revelatory events, in every stage of their witnessing and preserving, and in our hearing and obeying today.

A third type of dichotomy we find in the church's practice of evangelism and mission has to do with the separation of the means from the end in gospel proclamation. This tendency, particularly in Western evangelistic methodologies, defines a very narrow view of the end of evangelism, for example, the salvation of one's soul, and then develops whatever means will

33. It is intriguing to note that the American Presbyterian professor of evangelism Ben Campbell Johnson has published a book entitled *Speaking of God: Evangelism and Initial Spiritual Guidance* (Louisville: Westminster/John Knox, 1991).

lead to that desired end. This approach produces abuses and distortions, especially in the so-called "electronic church."[34] The incarnational model, doing evangelism in "Jesus Christ's way," forces us to take the issue of congruence between what and how we proclaim with utmost seriousness. It is patently absurd to proclaim the good news that God the Creator is God the Redeemer, that the Judge is compassionate and merciful in carrying out justice, in ways which are unloving, manipulative, insensitive, or even violent. It is equally impossible to talk about God's love for the poor, the outcast, and the marginal, and not to incarnate that love in the ways that demonstrate that God's kingdom is, in fact, coming now. One cannot communicate a gospel of love without letting that love become the dominant agenda of one's own life and the life of the community. This conviction seems to me to pervade the writings of Paul. He is constantly concerned that the quality of the community's life, whether it be in Corinth, Rome, Thessalonica, or Ephesus, will be the first evidence that the good news of the love of God in Jesus can be heard and responded to. The life of the Christian witness, in all its imperfection, is intended to incarnate the present love of God. Thus Paul can write to the Thessalonians that his ministry emerged out of his deep care for them. This resulted in his determination to share with them "*not only* the gospel of God *but also* our own selves. . . ." (1 Thess. 2:8). Such a statement leads us to recognize in Paul a profoundly incarnational approach to ministry. It also raises serious questions about another dichotomy alleged by some biblical scholars, that is, the division between the Jesus of history and the Christ of Paul. After all, it was Paul who said that the apostle was "always carrying in the body the death of Jesus, so that the life of Jesus may also be made visible in our bodies" (2 Cor. 4:10).

To use contemporary language, the incarnational principle cannot tolerate a separation between "our walk" and "our talk." The *Stuttgart Statement on Evangelism* provides one of the best summaries of incarnational witness:

> It has to be emphasized that we can only communicate the gospel to people if we open ourselves to them and enable them to open themselves to us. This means that listening to them is crucial in the sharing of the gospel with them; we cannot share the gospel without sharing ourselves. We live by the gospel of an incarnate Lord; this implies that the gospel has to become incarnated in ourselves, the "evangelists." This is not to suggest that, in our evangelism, we proclaim ourselves, but that those whom we

34. For an "incarnational critique" of evangelistic proclamation in the electronic media, see *Stuttgart Statement,* p. 214; *Your Will Be Done,* pp. 33-34; Guder, *Be My Witnesses,* pp. 157-59.

> wish to invite to faith in Christ will invariably look for signs of that faith in us. And what will happen if they do not find these? Does not the credibility of our evangelism, to some extent at least, depend on the authenticity of our own lives? Can we evangelize others without becoming vulnerable ourselves?[35]

A fourth dichotomy addressed by the incarnational approach is the distinction made between doing evangelism and doing justice. This is kin to a longstanding distinction debated in German diaconic circles between "word-proclamation" and "deed-proclamation." The incarnational approach toward gospel witness[36] must lead American Presbyterians, for example, to think through again the current definition of their church's goals. They have placed "doing evangelism" and "doing justice" next to each other, which creates the impression that they are somehow mutually distinctive. This is a friendly critique. There is no question about the fact that this definition represents a significant and risk-laden commitment of this church. Furthermore, it fairly reflects where it has come in these last decades: it has moved out of a period in which evangelism was not taken very seriously or was so redefined as not to be anything recognizably evangelistic.[37]

But we must ask what understanding of the gospel it is that separates evangelism from justice? What kind of justice are we talking about if it is not inherently linked to the mercy of God revealed in the gospel? Does not the gospel necessarily define all that we do in response to it as witness? Must not that witness include both the doing and the saying of good news, which reveals both the love and righteousness of God? The theological task in the Presbyterian Church, I would suggest, is to continue along the lines proposed by the document, *Turn to the Living God.* It must seek theological definitions that will overcome this artificial division.

Many churches and theologians have been struggling with this issue for many years, of course. We are constantly producing documents which state that it is essential to keep gospel proclamation and the witness to God's justice together.[38] It is very hard for us to do this and really believe that we have done it. We show that in the way we continue to sort each other out as being

35. *Stuttgart Statement,* p. 214.

36. I have suggested in my book *Be My Witnesses* that the New Testament word family *marturia/marturos/marturein* is the more comprehensive term for mission, encompassing verbal proclamation *(kerygma),* community *(koinonia),* and service *(diakonia).*

37. See Coalter, "Presbyterian Evangelism," pp. 45ff.

38. For an early example, see Commission on Ecumenical Mission and Relations, UPCUSA, *An Advisory Study* (New York: United Presbyterian Church [USA], 1962), pp. 45ff.

in one camp or the other. This continuing debate demonstrates how much hard theological work remains to be done and how much we need to listen to and learn from one another.[39]

The fifth and final dichotomy that the incarnational approach would overcome would be any interpretation of the Incarnation that would separate it from the atonement. This is certainly too complex a matter theologically to pursue in this essay, but it should be noted that there is a certain hesitancy in many parts of contemporary Protestantism when it comes to addressing the meaning of the cross. In *Turn to the Living God,* for instance, there is no direct reference to the cross or the work of atonement, although it is clearly implied in the document's argumentation. I can point to the space between two sentences in the section entitled, "Turn and Be Reconciled," where the atoning work of Jesus must take place, or else the argumentation does not really follow.[40] I cite this as only an example of the widespread difficulty that we sense when we turn to the theme of the cross. We are reacting for understandable reasons to the overly emotional and manipulative kind of proclamation that abuses the mysterious and awe-inspiring power of the work of the atonement. We know that the work of the cross is central. We know that the Incarnation is good news because "God so loved the world that God gave the only begotten Son. . . ." But when we stress the Incarnation in our evangelism and divorce it from the cross, then that incarnational emphasis becomes unduly moralistic and ultimately not good news at all. The humanity of Jesus is looked upon as the model or pattern for human behavior along the lines of the ethical liberalism of the nineteenth century. The problem of the human sinful condition is never really addressed, and the dimensions of God's grace and love are never fully expounded.

When we talk about doing evangelism in Jesus Christ's way, we are set-

39. Perhaps we can be instructed in this struggle by the ecumenical-evangelical missiologists who produced the *Stuttgart Statement on Evangelism* in 1987. They proposed to resolve this dichotomy with the concept of "integral evangelism." Their term is intended to address any and every attempt to detach the church's evangelistic ministry from everything else it is called to do. Their language is strong: "If the Church chooses to remain silent in the face of injustice and oppression, both in society at large and in the Church itself, it jeopardizes its entire evangelistic ministry. These concerns . . . are inseparably related to evangelism and every effort to drive a wedge between these is to be rejected as the proclamation of a spurious gospel." Christians, they say, are doing integral evangelism when they "challenge unjust structures," and "struggle for justice and peace." It is the study of Scripture that leads to such actions, and these actions are powerfully evangelistic. The Stuttgart theologians expressly call this "incarnational evangelism," which integrates *kerygma* and *diakonia.*

40. *Turn to the Living God,* p. 7; the space is between the two sentences in the penultimate paragraph.

ting out for ourselves no trivial theological agenda for our continuing work on the church's evangelistic mission. By defining that agenda in terms of the Incarnation, however, we are discovering biblical and theological resources for our work that are not only corrective of our inadequacies in both understanding and doing evangelism. This approach is also stimulating the church to move beyond our present definitions and theories to new and more inclusive theological constructions. To use Avery Dulles's language, the incarnational model for evangelism and mission is both explanatory and exploratory.[41] It can lead us into challenging insights into our mission, in terms of both the message and the way its witness is to be carried out. Like all good theology, the work on the incarnational understanding of mission and evangelism should be done modestly, critically, and rigorously. But let it also be done joyfully, with the expectation that we will discover more of what the gospel means, that good news which, as Peter Stuhlmacher constantly reminds us, "is always before us."

41. Avery Dulles, *Models of the Church* (Garden City, N.J.: Image Books [Doubleday], 1978), pp. 28ff.

CHAPTER 13

Evangelism, Salvation, and Social Justice: Definitions and Interrelationships

Ronald J. Sider

It is no secret that an extremely important and often sharp and divisive debate currently rages among Christians over both the meaning of evangelism and salvation and the relationship of evangelism to social justice. The World Council of Churches' Bangkok Consultation (Jan. 1973) on Salvation Today, the Chicago Declaration of Evangelical Social Concern (Nov. 1973), the Response to the Chicago Declaration by the Division of Church and Society of the National Council of Churches (1974), and the Lausanne Covenant (1974) all reflect this ferment. But they do not represent agreement.

What is evangelism? What is salvation? What is the relationship between salvation and social justice? When one surveys current attempts to answer these questions, one discovers at least five significantly different answers.

I. Five Conflicting Viewpoints

1. *Evangelism Is the Primary Mission of the Church*

Billy Graham is the best known representative of the view that the primary mission of the church is evangelism, the goal of which is the personal salvation of individual souls. Regenerate individuals will then have a positive influence on society. In his keynote address at the International Congress on World Evangelization at Lausanne, Graham defined evangelism as the announcement of the good news that "Jesus Christ, very God and very Man died for my sins on the cross, was buried, and rose the third day." "Evangelism and the *salvation of souls* is *the vital mission* of the church."[1] Since Graham

1. "Why Lausanne," mimeographed address of July 16, 1974, pp. 12-13. Graham's italics.

also believes that Christians have a responsibility to work for social justice, including the reform of unjust social structures, he would comment favorably on the Chicago Declaration.[2] But working for social justice is "not our priority mission."[3] And the Lausanne Covenant reflects Graham's basic view that "evangelism is primary" (section 6). For Graham, the word "salvation" connotes the justification and regeneration of individuals. Regenerate persons, of course, have an indirect influence on society, but social action undertaken by Christians is entirely distinct from evangelism, which is their primary assignment. From this perspective then, the gospel is individualistic and evangelism is primary.

2. *Evangelism Is One Basic Mission of the Church*

In his important address on evangelism at Lausanne, John R. Stott, the famous London pastor and theologian, expressed a second viewpoint which differs from Graham's in at least one significant way. Like Graham, Stott tends, at least in this address, toward an individualistic definition of the content of the good news. Evangelism is the announcement (in words and works of love, but especially in words) of the historic, biblical Christ who forgives and regenerates through the Holy Spirit. But he also emphasizes gospel *demands* in a way that some evangelicals do not. Saving faith accepts Jesus as Lord, not just as Savior. Or as the Lausanne Covenant puts it, "in issuing the gospel invitation, we have no liberty to conceal the cost of discipleship" (section 4).

What makes Stott's position significantly different from Graham's, however, is that he refuses to describe evangelism as the primary mission of the church. Rather, "evangelism is *an* essential part of the church's mission."[4] Evangelicals, Stott says, sometimes emphasize the Great Commission so much that they ignore or de-emphasize the Great Commandment. The two tasks are quite distinct and dare not be confused — therefore Stott refuses to apply the word "salvation" to sociopolitical liberation — but they are, apparently, equally important. Those who adopt this second viewpoint, then, still define the gospel individualistically, but they do not assert that evangelism is more basic for the Christian than concern for social justice.

2. See *Christianity Today,* January 4, 1974, p. 18.

3. "Why Lausanne," p. 11.

4. John R. W. Stott, "The Nature of Biblical Evangelism," mimeographed Lausanne address, p. 4. Stott's complete understanding of evangelism and salvation is undoubtedly contained only imperfectly in this short address, upon which I have relied exclusively in this typology.

3. The Primary Mission of the Church Is the Corporate Body of Believers

A third response to our question about the proper definition and relationship of salvation and social justice might be called a "radical Anabaptist" viewpoint. The good news of forgiveness and regeneration is an important part of the gospel, but not all of it. By their words, deeds, and life together, Christians announce the good news that by grace it is now possible to live in a new society (the visible body of believers) where all relationships are being transformed. The church refuses to live by the social, cultural, and economic values of the Old Age. Instead it incarnates the values of the New Age in its life together and thereby offers to the world a visible model of redeemed (although not yet perfect!) personal, economic, and social relationships. That people can live by faith in Jesus who justifies and that regenerates can enter this new community is now good news. The church then is part of the content of the gospel.

Obviously this definition of the good news overcomes the individualistic character of the first two positions. But it does not equate salvation with socio-political liberation. Sin always has and always will radically corrupt all political programs of social justice designed and implemented by men. There is a great gulf between the church and the world. The new community to be sure has relevance for social justice in the surrounding society, especially as the character of its common life provides a model for secular society. But political activity is not its primary task. As John Howard Yoder puts it, "the very existence of the church is her primary task." "The primary social structure through which the gospel works to change other structures is that of the Christian community."[5]

4. The Conversion of Individuals and the Political Restructuring of Society Are Equally Important Parts of Salvation

This fourth viewpoint is the one most common in ecumenical circles. Salvation is personal and social, individual and corporate. The salvation which Christ brings is "salvation of the soul and body, of the individual and society, mankind and the groaning creation (Rom. 8:19)."[6] The content of the gospel

5. John H. Yoder, *The Politics of Jesus* (Grand Rapids: Eerdmans, 1972), pp. 153-57.

6. Report from Section II, "Salvation and Social Justice," World Conference on Salvation Today. See *Bangkok Assembly 1973* (Geneva: WCC, n.d.), p. 88.

is that "Jesus saves." But Jesus came to save the entire created order from the power of sin. Hence salvation refers not only to the forgiveness of sins and the regenerating activity of the Spirit but also to the growth of social justice through the restructuring of economic and political institutions. Since struggles for economic justice and political freedom are part of salvation, those at Bangkok could say that "salvation is the peace of the people in Vietnam, independence in Angola, [and] justice and reconciliation in Northern Ireland."[7] Given this definition of salvation, it is obvious that one can speak of evangelizing social structures as well as individuals. Accordingly, a recent report of a working group on evangelism of the National Council of Churches USA asserts that "Evangelism may be directed to groups, to power structures, and to cultural configurations of persons as well as to individuals."[8]

If one is to understand this viewpoint it is essential to see that the individual aspects of salvation are still present. At Bangkok, there are repeated references to the fact that salvation also includes personal conversion and liberation from guilt. Political or economic justice is "not the whole of salvation. . . . Forgetting this denies the wholeness of salvation."[9] One might of course ask whether the overall emphasis and program activities of the WCC reflect this definition, but in theory at least the word "salvation" connotes both the justification and regeneration of the individual and the political restructuring of society in the interests of greater socioeconomic justice.

That this set of definitions is very widespread is hardly a secret. It constitutes the presuppositional core of the most recent theological movement, the theology of liberation, the best example of which is the extremely important recent book *A Theology of Liberation* by the Latin American theologian Gustavo Gutiérrez. More surprising, perhaps, is the fact that the nonconciliar evangelicals are adopting this terminology.

In his recent book, *Political Evangelism,* Richard Mouw chooses this broader definition of salvation and evangelism. Mouw by no means abandons or even deemphasizes the importance of calling persons to faith in the Lord Jesus who justifies and regenerates individuals. And he makes an excel-

7. *Bangkok Assembly,* p. 90.

8. David James Randolph, A Report on Evangelism USA, mimeographed paper (n.p., 1974). One of the weaknesses of this report is an inadequate emphasis on sin and repentance. To say that "the good news of the gospel is that life may be celebrated as God's gift through Jesus of Nazareth" (section F, 2) is true but incomplete. What is missing is a vigorous biblical emphasis on sin and therefore a call for repentance. Life as it is, is devastated by sin and hence cannot be celebrated apart from repentance and conversion. The same problem appears in Gustavo Gutiérrez, *A Theology of Liberation* (Maryknoll, N.Y.: Orbis, 1973), e.g., p. 152.

9. See *Bangkok Assembly,* pp. 88 and 90.

lent statement on the centrality of the church in God's plan of redemption. But salvation is not limited to these areas. The heart of the gospel is that Jesus saves. And Jesus came to save "the entire created order from the pervasive power of sin."[10]

Mouw assumes — unfortunately he never develops a biblical argument for his position — that since the redemptive work of Christ has cosmic implications, therefore all political activity is a part of evangelism.

> The *scope* of the evangelistic activity of the people of God must include the presentation of the *fullness* of the power of the gospel as it confronts the cosmic presence of sin in the created order. *Political* evangelism (i.e., political activity) then is one important aspect of this overall task of evangelism.[11]

Latin American Orlando E. Costas is another nonconciliar evangelical who has adopted this broad set of definitions. Costas quotes approvingly from Bangkok: "As guilt is both individual and corporate so God's liberating power changes both persons and structures."[12]

Since Christ is "Lord and Savior of the whole cosmos," salvation is present when oppressed people secure greater economic justice.[13] Costas, of course, is quick to point out that the salvation which emerges in the struggles for social justice is only partial and relative. It will reach its fullness only when our Lord returns. But it is part of the salvation Christ brings. According to this fourth viewpoint, then, salvation connotes both the justification and regeneration of the individual believer and also the social justice that emerges through the political restructuring of society.

5. *Evangelism Is Politics Because Salvation Is Social Justice*

The fifth and final set of definitions removes the transcendent element of salvation completely and simply equates salvation and social justice.

10. Richard J. Mouw, *Political Evangelism* (Grand Rapids: Eerdmans, 1973), p. 13.

11. Mouw, *Political Evangelism*, p. 89.

12. "Evangelism and the Gospel of Salvation," *International Review of Mission* 43 (1974). But surely this formulation is perplexing. One would expect a sentence which begins with a comment on guilt to conclude with a statement of forgiveness through the cross. Is this an example of a tendency to reduce sin to its horizontal implication?

13. "Evangelism and the Gospel of Salvation," p. 32. For a fuller statement of Costas's position, see his recently published book *The Church and Its Mission: A Sharing Critique from the Third World* (Wheaton: Tyndale House, 1974).

The secular theologies enunciated in the late 1960s by theologians such as Gibson Winter and Harvey Cox provide clear illustrations. Defining salvation as humanization, Winter asserted:

> Secularization recognizes history and its problems of meaning as the sphere of man's struggle for salvation. . . . The categories of biblical faith are freed from their miraculous and supernatural garments. . . . Why are men not simply called to be human in their historical obligations, for this is man's true end and his salvation?[14]

And a preparatory statement for the WCC's Fourth Assembly at Uppsala (1968) came dangerously close, at least, to this secularized understanding of salvation: "We have lifted up humanization as *the* goal of mission." Evangelism is politics and salvation is social justice.

That these five sets of conflicting answers to fundamental theological questions have resulted in confusion and sharp conflict in the churches is painfully clear. There are signs, however, that proponents of all these conflicting viewpoints are ready in a new way today to reexamine their positions and correct one-sided emphases. Perhaps it is at this moment of flux and reexamination that everyone can wholeheartedly resubmit cherished formulae to the authority of God's written Word. I want therefore to examine the most important relevant New Testament concepts — gospel (εὐαγγέλιον), salvation (σωτηρία), redemption (ἀπολύτρωσις), and the principalities and powers (ἀρχαὶ καὶ ἐξουσίαι) — with the expectation that the use of these terms in the New Testament will guide us toward a more helpful way to state the relationship between evangelism, salvation, and social justice.

II. New Testament Terminology

1. *The Gospel*

What, according to the New Testament, is the gospel? It is the good news about the kingdom of God (Mark 1:14-15). It is the good news concerning God's Son, Jesus the Messiah who is Savior and Lord (Rom.1:3-4; 2 Cor. 4:3-6). It is the good news about the historical Jesus — his death for our sins and his resurrection on the third day (1 Cor. 15:1-5).[15] And it is the good news about a

14. Gibson Winter, *The New Creation as Metropolis* (New York: Macmillan, 1963), pp. 60-61. For Cox, see *The Secular City* (New York: Macmillan, 1965), p. 256 and elsewhere.

15. So too Mark 14:9, where the content of the gospel is Jesus' death. See *Theological Dic-*

radically new kind of community, the people of God, who are already empowered to live according to the standards of the New Age (Eph. 3:17).

Stated more systematically, the content of the gospel is (1) justification by faith through the cross; (2) regeneration through the Holy Spirit; (3) the Lordship of Christ and (4) the fact of the church.

That the gospel includes the wonderful news of justification by faith in Christ whose death atoned for our guilt before God need hardly be argued. It is central to the argument of both Galatians (see especially 1:6-17; 2:14-21; 3:6-14) and Romans (see especially 1:16-17). Nor need we argue the fact that the good news also includes the fact that the Risen Lord now lives in individual persons who believe in his regenerating and transforming their egocentric personalities.

Anyone who proclaims a gospel which omits or deemphasizes the justification and regeneration of individuals is, as Paul said, preaching his own message, not God's good news of salvation in Jesus.

Good news, too, we all recognize, is the proclamation that this Jesus who justifies and regenerates is also Lord — Lord of all things in heaven and earth. The gospel he preaches, Paul reminded the Corinthians, was not himself, but rather "Jesus Christ as Lord" (2 Cor. 4:4-5). Seldom, however, do we appropriate the full implications of the abstract dogma. If Jesus' Lordship is part of the gospel, then so too is the radical discipleship this sovereign demands.

> If any man would come after me, let him deny himself and take up his cross and follow me. For whoever would save his life will lose it; and whoever loses his life for my sake and the gospel's will save it. (Mark 8:35; cf. 10:39)

Regeneration and discipleship are inseparable. The one who justifies and regenerates also demands that we forsake all other lords, shoulder the cross, and follow him. Accepting the evangelistic call necessarily and inevitably entails accepting Jesus as Lord of our personal lives, our family lives, our racial attitudes, our economics, and our politics. Jesus will not be our Savior if we reject him as our Lord. Too often Christians (especially evangelical Protestants in this century) have proclaimed a cheap grace that offers the forgiveness of the gospel without the discipleship demands of the gospel. But that is not Jesus' gospel. Right at the heart of the gospel is the call to a radical discipleship which makes Jesus Lord of one's entire life.

---

tionary of the New Testament, ed. Gerhard Kittel and Gerhard Friedrich, trans. G. W. Bromiley, 9 vols. (Grand Rapids: Eerdmans, 1964-74), 2:728. Hereafter *TDNT.*

The fourth element of the good news is less widely perceived to be part of the gospel. But both Jesus and Paul clearly teach that the church is part of the good news. In Ephesians 3:1-7, Paul says that he was made a minister of the gospel to announce the mystery that the Gentiles are also part of the people of God. The fact that at the cross Jesus destroyed the ancient enmity between Jews and Gentiles, thus creating a radically new visible community where all cultural, racial, and sexual dividing walls are overcome, is a fundamental part of the gospel Paul was called to preach.

According to the Gospels, the core of Jesus' good news was simply that the kingdom of God was at hand. Mark 1:14-15 reads: "Jesus came into Galilee preaching the gospel of God and saying, 'the time is fulfilled, and the kingdom of God is at hand; repent, and believe in the gospel.'" Over and over again the Gospels define the content of the good news as the kingdom which was present in the person and work of Jesus (Mark 1:14-15; Matt. 4:23, 24, 14; Luke 4:43; 16:16).

But what was the nature of the kingdom Jesus proclaimed? Was it just an invisible kingdom in the hearts of individuals? Was it a new political regime of the same order as Rome? One hesitates to simplify difficult questions about which many scholars have written learned tomes. But let me risk presumption. The kingdom became present wherever Jesus overcame the power of evil. But the way Jesus chose to destroy the kingdom of Satan and establish his own kingdom was not to forge a new political party. Rather, Jesus chose to call together a new visible community of disciples joined together by their acceptance of the divine forgiveness he offered and their unconditional submission to his total Lordship over their lives. Paul says in Colossians 1:13-14 that Jesus "has delivered us from the dominion (or kingdom) of darkness and transferred us to the kingdom of his beloved Son, in whom we have redemption, the forgiveness of sins."

That this kingdom is not just an invisible spiritual abstraction peopled with ethereal, redeemed souls is very clear in the New Testament. Jesus not only forgave sins; he also healed the physical and mental diseases of those who believed. His disciples shared a common purse. The early church engaged in massive economic sharing (Acts 4:32–5:16; 2 Cor. 8). The new community of Jesus' disciples was and is (at least it ought to be) a visible social reality sharply distinguished from the world both by its beliefs and its lifestyle.[16] His kingdom, of course, will reach its fulfillment only at his return, but right now by grace people can enter this new society where all social and economic relationships are being transformed. That an entirely new kind of

16. See Yoder, *Politics of Jesus,* chap. 2, "The Kingdom Is Coming."

life together in Jesus' new peoplehood is now available to all who will repent, believe, and obey is good news. The kingdom of heaven is not just a future, but also a present reality. The church is part of the good news.[17]

Thus far we have seen that the content of the gospel is justification, regeneration, Jesus' Lordship, and the fact of the church. But is there not a "secular" or "political" dimension to the gospel? Since Jesus said in Luke 4 that he came to free the oppressed, release the captives, and evangelize the poor, is not political activity designed to free the oppressed also evangelism?

Luke 4:18-19 is a crucial text. Reading from the prophet Isaiah, Jesus defined his mission as follows:

> The Spirit of the Lord is upon me, because he has anointed me to preach good news to the poor (εὐαγγελίσασθαι πτωχοῖς). He has sent me to proclaim release to the captives and recovery of sight to the blind, to set at liberty those who are oppressed, to proclaim the acceptable year of the Lord.

In this text Jesus identifies several aspects of his mission. He says he has been sent to release the captives, heal the blind, and free the oppressed. That this is a fundamental part of his total mission is beyond question. But he does not equate the task of helping the oppressed with preaching the gospel to the poor. Nor does he say one task is more important than another. They are both important, but they are also distinct.[18]

The same point is clear in other passages. In Matthew 11:1-6, Jesus responded to John the Baptist's question, "Are you the Messiah?" by saying:

> Go and tell John what you see and hear: the blind receive their sight and the lame walk, lepers are cleansed and the dead are raised up and the poor have good news preached to them [are evangelized].

Again, Jesus does not equate preaching the gospel to (that is, evangelizing) the poor with cleansing lepers. He does all of these things.[19] And they are all important, but one activity cannot be collapsed into another.

One final example is important. In both Matthew 4:23 and 9:35, the

17. I do not, however, equate church and kingdom. See George Eldon Ladd, *A Theology of the New Testament* (Grand Rapids: Eerdmans, 1974), pp. 57-134, especially pp. 104-19.

18. The grammar itself underlines this point. The infinitive εὐαγγελίσασθαι depends on the verb ἔχρισέν, whereas the other infinitives (κηρῦξαι and ἀποστεῖλαι) depend on ἀπέσταλκέν. Grammatically, the two statements are separate.

19. Again the grammar is relevant. All the verbs are joined by καί, which is commonly used to string together a list of distinct items or actions.

evangelist summarizes Jesus' ministry as follows: "And he went about all Galilee, teaching in their synagogues and preaching the gospel of the kingdom and healing every disease and infirmity among the people."[20] Here there are three distinct types of tasks: teaching, preaching the gospel, and healing sick people. They are not identical tasks. They should not be confused. None dare be omitted. All are crucial parts of this mission of Jesus. But for our purposes the most important conclusion is that none of these texts equates healing the blind or liberating the oppressed with evangelism. These texts in no way warrant calling political activity evangelism. There is no New Testament justification for talking about "evangelizing" political structures.[21] According to the New Testament, then, evangelism involves the announcement (through word *and deed*) of the good news that there is forgiveness of sins through the cross; that the Holy Spirit will regenerate twisted personalities; that Jesus is Lord; and that people today can join Jesus' new community where all social and economic relationships are being made new.

2. *Salvation*

What is the meaning of the word "salvation" in the New Testament? Probably the best New Testament argument for adopting a broad definition of salvation can be developed from the use of the word "save" (σῴζω) in the Synoptic Gospels. In about one of every four descriptions of Jesus' healings, the Synoptic accounts use the word "save" to describe physical healing by Jesus.[22] In Mark 6:56, the text says: "As many as touched (his garment) were healed (ἐσῴζοντο)."[23] One could cite other similar illustrations. It is quite clear, of course, that the verb "save" connotes more than physical healing. Whereas in Mark 10:52 Jesus told the blind man whom he had healed, "Your faith has saved you," in Luke 7:36-50 he spoke the identical words to the sin-

20. See also Luke 9:1-6, 11.

21. One might try to argue from Luke 4:43 ("I must preach the good news of the kingdom to the other cities also") that cities as political entities were "evangelized." But surely the text means that he wanted to *preach* to *persons* in those cities. Matt. 28:19 calls Christians to "make disciples of all nations, baptizing them. . . ." Is that a call to disciple or evangelize political structures? I think not. The text reads μαθητεύσατε πάντα τὰ ἔθνη βαπτίζοντες αὐτούς. The shift from the neuter τὰ ἔθνη to the masculine αὐτούς indicates that he is calling on us to disciple *persons*. Only individuals can respond to the gospel.

22. σῴζω is used 16 times in this way; θεραπεύω 33 times; ἰάομαι 15 times. See *TDNT*.

23. So too Mark 10:52, Mark 5:28-34, etc. So too occasionally in Acts (4:9 and 14:9) and once in James (5:15).

ful woman who anointed his feet (Luke 7:36-50), even though he had not healed her body.

Now it seems to me that it is not entirely plausible to argue that since the Gospels apply the word "save" to physical healing, it is also legitimate to extend the word to cover all kinds of activity done in the name of the Lord to liberate sick and oppressed persons. If there is a New Testament justification for using the word "salvation" to apply to political liberation, it is here.

But one must immediately point out that the usage just noted is by no means the primary usage of the terms "save" and "salvation" in the New Testament. These words, in fact, are not key words in the Synoptic tradition.[24] When they do appear elsewhere in the Synoptics, they refer to entering the kingdom or following Jesus. When Jesus informed his disciples that it is hard for a rich man to enter the kingdom, the startled disciples asked: "Then who can be saved?" Being "saved" and entering the kingdom are synonymous.[25] In light of this and similar passages, we can say that someone is saved as he enters the new peoplehood of God where all economic relationships are being transformed.

The story of Zacchaeus (Luke 19:1-10) is striking in this connection. After his encounter with Jesus, Zacchaeus repented of his sins. As a rich, corrupt tax collector who had profited from an oppressive economic structure, he repented of his "social" sins and promptly gave half of his ill-gotten gain to feed the poor. Jesus immediately assured him "today salvation has come to this house." Now, this text does not mean that wherever economic justice appears, salvation is present. Since Jesus had come to save the lost, he had sought out lost Zacchaeus (v. 10). But it was only after Zacchaeus had submitted to Jesus' message and repented of his sins that Jesus assured him of salvation. Salvation means repentance, submitting to Jesus, and entering the new community of Jesus' disciples, wherein all relationships including economic relationships are being transformed.

In Paul the usage is unambiguous. One is saved as one confesses that Jesus is Lord and believes that God raised him from the dead (Rom. 10:10-13). We obtain salvation as we hear the gospel and believe that we are justified by faith rather than works (Rom. 1:16-17). Salvation for us sinners is freedom (through the cross) from the just wrath of God: "While we were yet sinners Christ died for us. Since therefore we are now justified by his blood, much

24. "Elsewhere in the core of the synoptic tradition σῴζω and σωτηρία are very much in the background." *TDNT,* 7:991.

25. See also Luke 13:22-30, where an eschatological entry into the kingdom is clearly in view. Cf. also Mark 13:13, 20.

more shall we be saved by his life."[26] Elsewhere in the New Testament, the connotation is similar. The usual meaning of salvation in Acts is the forgiveness of sins.[27] In James, the verb "save" connotes deliverance from divine punishment at the final judgment.[28]

The author of the lengthy article on these words in Kittel's *Theological Dictionary of the New Testament* summarizes his findings in this way:

> New Testament σωτηρία does not refer to earthly relationships. Its content is not, as in Greek understanding, well-being, health of body and soul. Nor is it the earthly liberation of the people of God from the heathen yoke as in Judaism. . . . It has to do solely with man's relationship to God. . . . In the New Testament . . . only the event of the historical coming, suffering, and resurrection of Jesus of Nazareth bring salvation from God's wrath by the forgiveness of sins.[29]

One must conclude then that the dominant connotation of the words "save" and "salvation" throughout the New Testament does not encourage the adoption of a broad definition of salvation. The use of the verb "save" with reference to physical healing in one quarter of the Synoptic accounts of Jesus' healings offers the only substantial New Testament warrant for expanding the word "salvation" to refer to social justice brought about through politics. The vast bulk of the New Testament passages points in the other direction.

3. *Redemption*

Does the New Testament use of the term "redemption" (ἀπολύτρωσις) offer any additional help? Should Christians think of political activity producing "redeemed" social structures? Paul told the Christians at Rome that they were justified by God's grace through faith by the means of "the redemption which is in Christ Jesus, whom God put forward as an expiation by his blood, to be received by faith" (Rom. 3:24-25). Paul also explicitly equated redemption

26. Rom. 5:9. Quite frequently, as here, Paul speaks of salvation as something which is still partly future (cf. Eph. 2:5-8; Rom. 11:11; 2 Cor. 6:2).

27. See *TDNT,* 7:997. Frequently, too, it is a general term used to describe what happened as the church proclaimed Jesus' death and resurrection (e.g., Acts 4:12; 13:26; 16:30-31).

28. *TDNT,* 7:996. See James 5:20, 4:12. the words "save" and "salvation" are used hardly at all in the Johannine literature (*TDNT,* 7:997).

29. *TDNT,* 7:1002. Forester does go on to indicate that σωτηρία also connotes a cosmic, eschatological salvation (Rom. 8:18ff.). But the word salvation is not used in this key passage; hence I will consider it below in the discussion of *the powers.*

with forgiveness of sins. After reminding the Colossian Christians that they had been delivered from the kingdom of darkness to the kingdom of the Son, Paul added that it is in Jesus that "we have redemption, the forgiveness of sins" (Col. 1:13-14; Luke 21:28; Rom. 8:23).

There is also an important eschatological dimension to redemption. We are sealed unto the day of redemption (Eph. 1:14; 4:30; Luke 21:28; Rom. 8:23). Especially important is the fantastic Pauline vision of eschatological restoration in Romans 8:18ff. At our Lord's return, the entire creation will be set free from sin and all its consequences. Even our bodies will experience "redemption" (v. 23). The passage is crucial, but it is best discussed in detail after we have examined Paul's concept of the "powers."

When, then, is redemption? It is the forgiveness of sins offered to persons who believe that Jesus' cross is the expiation of their sins. And it is also the total reversal of all the evil consequences of sin which our Lord will accomplish at his return. Redemption is therefore not something that happens to secular economic and political structures now. It is something that happens to persons as they are in Christ.[30]

4. The Principalities and Powers

One final set of concepts must be examined. What are the implications of the Pauline conception of the "principalities" and "powers" for our search for the most helpful definition of salvation?[31]

I begin with the assumption that John Howard Yoder is basically correct when he argues that the principalities and powers are not just angelic beings which inhabit the heavens. The powers are also "religious structures (especially the religious undergirdings of stable ancient and primitive societies), intellectual structures ('ologies' and 'isms'), moral structures (codes and customs), political structures (the tyrant, the market, the school, the courts, race

30. Cf. F. Büchsel in *TDNT,* 4:354: "ἀπολύτρωσις is bound up strictly with the person of Jesus. We have it in Him, Col. 1:14; Eph. 1:7; R[om]. 3:24. By God He is made unto us ἀπολύτρωσις; 1 C[or]. 1:30. Redemption cannot be regarded, then, as a fact which He has indeed established, but which then has its own intrinsic life and power apart from His person, so that one can have it without being in personal fellowship with Him. To give to redemption this objective autonomy is to part company with Paul. For him there is redemption only within the circumference of faith in Jesus."

31. The most important texts are Rom. 8:38f.; 1 Cor. 2:8; 15:24-28; Eph. 1:20-21, 3:10, 6:12; 2:15. For an analysis of these texts, cf. Berkhof, *Christ and the Powers,* trans. John Howard Yoder (Scottsdale, Pa.: Herald, 1962), and Yoder, *Politics of Jesus,* chap. 8.

and nation)."[32] The powers are the ordered structures of society and the spiritual powers which, in some way we do not fully comprehend, lie behind and undergird religious, intellectual, socioeconomic, and political structures.

Paul makes it very clear that the powers were created through Jesus Christ. "For in Him all things created, which are in heaven and on earth, the visible and invisible, whether thrones, dominions, principalities, powers; all things are created through Him and for Him" (Col. 1:16). The powers are part of God's good creation. Unfortunately, sin has invaded this good creation and the powers have been corrupted to the point that they are now hostile toward God. At the cross, however, God disarmed the principalities and powers (Col. 2:15). The risen Lord is now Lord not just of the church but also of all rule and authority and power and dominion. Ultimately, at his return — and here the breathtaking scope of the cosmic redemption Paul envisaged comes into view — the Lord will complete his victory over the powers and reconcile all things to God (1 Cor. 15:24-26; Col. 1:20).

In light of this cosmic Pauline view of the work of Christ, we must again ask whether it is not legitimate to apply the word "salvation" to the improvement of social structures. But to answer this question, we must ask two other questions: When are the powers reconciled to God? And what does Paul say is the relationship of the church to the powers now?

The victory over the fallen powers has already proceeded so far that members of the body of believers are freed from the tyranny of powers. This is the revolutionary message of Ephesians 2. Paul refers to the powers who still try to tyrannize believers as "philosophy," "human tradition," and "elemental spirits of the universe" (v. 8). These powers foolishly demand adherence to legalistic dietary regulations and petty religious festivals (vv. 16-23). Paul's response is that precisely because Jesus is Lord of all things (and therefore Lord of the powers) and precisely because he disarmed the powers at the cross, Christians are not subject to their mistaken, tyrannical demands (vv. 9-10, 14-15).

One hardly needs to add, however, that Christ has not completed his victory over the powers, even though the church now has the power through Christ to resist their tyranny. Not until Christ's return will he complete this victory. Only at his coming will Christ totally dethrone every rule and every authority and power, thereby completing his victory over sin and all its consequences including death itself.[33] This final, cosmic restoration is so sweep-

32. Yoder, *Politics of Jesus,* p. 145. See also Berkhof, *Christ and the Powers,* chap. 2.

33. Cor. 15:20-26. This only happens "at his coming" (v. 23). See Berkhof, *Christ and the Powers,* p. 34 for the view that the best translation of καταργήση in v. 24 is "dethrone." The pow-

ing and all-encompassing that Paul can use the word "redemption" in connection with it. In the breathtaking passage in Romans 8, Paul envisions the day when the entire creation through which sin has rampaged like a global hurricane will be liberated from its bondage to sin and its consequences and will obtain the glorious liberty of the children of God. At that day we will attain the redemption of our bodies (Rom. 8:23). Presumably one can by extension speak of the eschatological redemption of the entire creation. But it is important that the only time Paul used language about salvation and redemption for anything other than the justification and regeneration and reconciliation occurring now in the church is when he discussed the eschatological restoration at our Lord's return. Sin is far too rampant to justify the use of this language in connection with the tragically imperfect human attempts to introduce social justice in the interim between Calvary and the eschaton.

This does not mean that Christ has nothing to do with the powers now. He is the Lord of the world as well as the church (Eph. 1:22). As the sovereign of the universe, he presumably is now at work doing precisely the things the prophets tell us the Lord of history does — namely destroying unjust societies and creating more just ones. But sin is still too all-pervasive to warrant the application of "salvation" language to the limited, imperfect, albeit extremely important social justice that does emerge in the time before the eschaton. Paul reserves salvation language for the redemption occurring in the church.

But what, then, is the church's relationship to the powers? Ephesians 3:10 says that through the church, the manifold wisdom of God is to be made known to the principalities and powers in the heavenly places. Does that mean we should evangelize social structures? Not really. What is the wisdom of God that is to be made known to the powers? It is the mystery of the church! It is the good news that the hostility between the Jews and Gentiles is at an end because the dividing walls that the fallen powers erect between cultures, races, and sexes have been broken down in Christ (see all of Eph. 2–3). The fact that God has decided to provide salvation through his new community which accepts Jesus as the only Lord and therefore lives now in defiance of the values, norms, and prejudices of the fallen powers is what the church makes known to the principalities and powers. As Yoder points out, this message from the church to the powers is not the equivalent of the substitute for,

---

ers are not destroyed; they are dethroned. Thus the reconciliation of all things discussed in Col. 1:20 is an eschatological reconciliation that occurs only at our Lord's return so far as the powers are concerned. Verse 20 does not mean that the powers are now reconciled or even that they are being reconciled even though God's ultimate plan is total reconciliation at Christ's return. Hence Col. 1:20 does not justify the use of "salvation" language for the emergence of social justice now.

nor the prerequisite of the evangelistic call to individuals.[34] Speaking to the powers dare not be confused with evangelism. (In real life, at least in the short run, it sometimes hinders evangelism and "church growth"!) But it is no less important because it is different and distinct. As in the other cases then, our examination of the Pauline concept of the powers leads to the same conclusion. Evangelism and social action are both important. Christians must be involved in both. But the salvation which God has chosen to provide through evangelism must not be confused with social justice.

III. A Sixth Option: Distinct Yet Equal

In light of New Testament usage it would seem that all five viewpoints outlined at the beginning of this essay are inadequate.[35] I think there is a sixth option. Evangelism and social action are equally important, but quite distinct aspects of the total mission of the church.

Evangelism involves the announcement (through words and deeds) of the good news of justification, regeneration, the Lordship of Jesus Christ, and the fact of the new community wherein all relationships are being redeemed. When individuals accept this good news, they enter into a personal relationship with the living God through faith in Jesus Christ and experience salvation. Social action involves the political restructuring of society for the sake of greater social justice. To label this increased social justice "salvation" is confusing. Until our Lord's return, all attempts to restructure society will at best produce only significantly less imperfect societies tragically pockmarked by the consequences of the Fall.

But that does not mean that evangelism is more important than social

34. "The church is under orders to make known to the Powers, as no other proclaimer can do, the fulfillment of the mysterious purposes of God (Eph. 3:10) by means of that Man in whom their rebellion has been broken and the pretensions they have raised have been demolished. This proclamation of the Lordship of Christ is not a substitute for nor a prerequisite to the gospel call directed to individuals. Nor is it the mere consequence within society of the conversion of individuals one by one. . . . That Christ is Lord, a proclamation to which only individuals can respond, is nonetheless a challenge to the Powers. It thus follows that the claims such proclamation makes are not limited to those who have accepted it." Yoder, *Politics of Jesus,* pp. 160-61.

35. The analysis of New Testament terminology is only one part of the total task. In a fuller treatment, this exegetical approach would need to be complemented by a theological section in which one could, I think, successfully argue that: (1) the broad definition of evangelism and salvation tends to obscure sin as guilt *coram Deo* (e.g. Gutiérrez; see n. 8 above); (2) the broad definition of evangelism and salvation obscures the sharp New Testament distinction between the church and the world.

action. Some will say: "Surely if unevangelized souls are going to eternal damnation, than evangelism must be our primary concern." Now, I find that a powerful concern because I believe that our Lord taught that people are free to reject his loving offer of grace and that they consequently suffer eternal separation from the presence of the living God. But our Lord was quite aware of that when he chose to devote vast amounts of his time to healing sick bodies that he knew would rot in one, two, or thirty years. The Gospels provide no indication, either theoretically or by the space devoted to each, that Jesus considered preaching the good news more important than healing sick people. He commanded us both to feed the hungry and to preach the gospel without adding that the latter was primary and the former could be done when and if spare time and money were available. Jesus is our only perfect model. If God Incarnate thought he could — or thought he must — devote large amounts of his potential preaching time to the healing of sick bodies, then surely we are unfaithful disciples if we fail to follow in his steps.

The reverse of course is equally true. Neither theoretically nor in the way we allocate personnel and funds dare the church make social action more important than evangelism. The time has come for all biblical Christians to refuse to use the sentence: "The primary mission of the church is . . ." I do not care if you complete the sentence with "evangelism" or "social action." Either way, it is unbiblical and misleading. Evangelism, social action, fellowship, teaching, worship are all fundamental parts of the mission of the church.[36] They must not be confused with each other although they are inextricably interrelated.

I have argued both that evangelism and social action are distinct and also that they are inseparable and interrelated in life. Let me conclude with a brief discussion of several aspects of their interrelationship.

In the first place, proclamation of the gospel necessarily includes a call to repentance and turning away from all forms of sin. Sin is both personal and structural. Evangelical Protestants regularly preach that coming to Jesus means forsaking pot, pubs, and pornography. Too often in this century, however, they have failed to add that coming to Jesus necessarily involves repentance of and conversion from the sin of involvement in structural evils such as economic injustice and institutional racism. Biblical evangelism will call for repentance of one's involvement in both individual and structural sins. And since the gospel also includes the proclamation of Jesus' total Lordship, biblical evangelism will clearly declare the cost of unconditional discipleship.

36. See the helpful comments by Michael Cassidy, "The Third Way," *International Review of Mission* 63 (1974): 17.

Evangelistic altar calls should remind people that Jesus demands a turning away *(conversio)* from both personal and social evil. Evangelists regularly insist that coming to Jesus excludes continued lying and adultery. If that does not compromise *sola gratia,* then neither will a biblical insistence that coming to Jesus will necessarily include repenting of one's involvement in institutional racism and economic justice and working for less racist and less unjust societies.

Second, the very existence of the church as a new community where all social relationships are being redeemed has a significant impact on society because the church offers a visible model of the way people can live in community in more loving and just ways. The church was the first to develop hospitals, schools, orphanages, etc. These all witness to the fact that living a new model in defiance of the norms and accepted values of surrounding society can in the long run have a powerful effect on the total social order.[37]

Third, social action sometimes facilitates the task of evangelism. Just as the very oppressed situation of persons trapped in unjust social structures sometimes hinders a positive response to the gospel, so too increasing social justice may make some people more open to the good news.[38] Sometimes precisely the act of working in the name of Jesus for improved socioeconomic conditions for the oppressed enabled persons to understand the proclaimed word of God's love in Christ. In that situation the act of social concern is itself truly evangelistic.[39] Furthermore, a biblically informed social action will not fail to point out that participation in social injustice is not just inhuman behavior toward the neighbor but also a damnable sin against Almighty God. Hence biblical social action will contain, always implicitly and often explicitly, a call to repentance.

Fourth, it is not helpful to use the words "the Great Commission" to connote evangelism and "the Great Commandment" to connote social concern. When, in the Great Commission, Jesus instructed his followers to make disciples of all nations, he specifically noted that this would mean baptizing new converts *and* teaching them to observe all that he had commanded his disciples to do. By both word and example, Jesus commanded his disciples to feed the hungry, release the captives, and liberate the oppressed. Failure to teach prospective believers and new converts that coming to Jesus necessarily

37. See the excellent statement on this in Mouw, *Political Evangelism,* p. 47.

38. But this is not always the case. Nor does social action depend for its validity or justification on the fact that sometimes it is "pre-evangelism."

39. But this frequent interrelationship does not mean that all social action is evangelistic, nor that it is helpful to define politics as evangelism.

involves a costly discipleship that will confront social, economic, and political injustice constitutes a heretical neglect of the Great Commission.

In the same way, the Great Command obligates the Christian to proclaim the gospel to the neighbor just as surely as it compels him to improve the neighbor's societal environment. If one loves the neighbor as oneself, one will seek eagerly for ways to tell that neighbor of him who is the Way, the Truth, and the Life.

In practice, then, evangelism and social action are intricately interrelated. They are inseparable both in the sense that evangelism often leads to increased social justice and vice versa and also that biblical Christians will, precisely to the extent that they are faithful followers of Jesus, always seek liberty for the oppressed (Luke 4:18). But the fact that evangelism and social action are inseparable certainly does not mean that they are identical. They are distinct, equally important parts of the total mission of the church.

In his discussion of the meaning of salvation, the Latin American Gustavo Gutiérrez, a leading exponent of liberation theology, adopts a broad definition of the word "salvation" so that it includes political liberation. To those like me who limit the word "salvation," he offers a dire warning. He denounces

> . . . those who in order to protect salvation (or to protect their interests) lift salvation from the midst of history where men and social classes struggle to liberate themselves from the slavery of oppression. . . . It is those who by trying to "save" the work of Christ will "lose" it.[40]

As an evangelical, I take this challenge and warning with utmost seriousness. But the best response is not to abandon a biblical definition of crucial concepts. Rather we must demonstrate by our words and our action that we have not excluded political liberation from the meaning of salvation in order to justify our affluence or past unconcern with political oppression. Only if we biblical Christians throw ourselves into the struggle for social justice for the wretched of the earth so unequivocally that the poor and the oppressed know beyond all question that we will risk all in the struggle against economic and political oppression — only then will Third World theologians be willing to hear our critique of unbiblical definitions of salvation. And only then will the oppressed of the earth be able to hear our good news about the risen Lord Jesus.

40. Gutiérrez, *Theology of Liberation*, p. 178.

IV. Concluding Undogmatic Postscript

I do not want to suggest that the sixth option presented in this essay is the only non-heretical viewpoint! Evangelicals need to approach their theological formulae with more humility than in the past. It is the scriptural Word that is infallible, not our ever-imperfect attempts to restate it in appropriate contemporary ways. I think that all but the fifth, "secular" viewpoint, which simply equates salvation with political justice, are possible positions for Christians. The broad definition of salvation (view four) does not go beyond the permissible as long as individual salvation through a personal faith in the biblical Lord Jesus receives as much emphasis as social action. But this dare not be only a verbal, theoretical equality. Programming and budgets must also reflect this equality.

But a concern to avoid dogmatism does not mean either that careful theological precision is unimportant or that the several viewpoints are equally valid. I think that the first four viewpoints outlined at the beginning of this essay are inadequate, confusing, and finally unbiblical. Hopefully the continuing debate about the definition and interrelationship of evangelism, salvation, and social justice will lead us all to a fuller appropriation of biblical truth.

CHAPTER 14

Worship, Evangelism, Ethics: On Eliminating the "And"

Stanley Hauerwas

The Background of the "And"

Tents — I think the problem began with tents. At least I know that tents created the problem for me. When I was a kid growing up in Texas, it never occurred to me that a revival could be had in the church building. You could only have a revival in a tent. You "went to church" in the church. You "got saved" in the tent. Worship was what you did in the church. Evangelism was what you did in the tent. Thus was created "the problem" of how to understand the relationship between worship, evangelism, and ethics.

I do not know if Don Saliers was a product of, or even participated in, tent evangelism, but I do know that, like me, he has benefited from but also suffered at the hands of an American form of Christianity that tents produced. That form of American Christianity is called Methodism. Moreover, like me, he has become "Catholic" — or at least our fellow Methodists often think the importance that Saliers and I attribute to "liturgy" has made us Catholic.[1] Saliers was trained to be a philosophical theologian, and I am supposed to be an ethicist. How and why did we ever become so fascinated with liturgy, not only as something the church does but as crucial for helping us better understand how theology should be done?

It would be presumptuous for me to speak for Saliers, but I suspect that he is as concerned about liturgy, and for the same reason, as I am — he is a Methodist. This may seem a strange confession, given the separation between worship and theology so often legitimated by current Methodist practice. Yet

1. The quotation marks around *liturgy* suggest the unfortunate and still all too common Protestant assumption that "liturgical" churches are Catholic. Often the worship shaped by the experience of Protestant revivalism is not thought to be liturgical.

Saliers represents personally and intellectually the Methodist refusal to separate theology and piety. Indeed, Saliers's focus on worship becomes a way to explore how the *and* might be eliminated between theology and evangelism or theology and ethics. Our difficulty, of course, is that we are members of a church whose history, particularly in America, was shaped by the tent-sanctuary divide. Currently some Methodists are even suggesting, in the interest of church growth (which has become synonymous in some circles with evangelism), that worship must be made more "user-friendly." They thus assume a tension exists between worship and evangelism.

I am not suggesting that the tensions some currently feel between worship and evangelism are due to "the tents," but I think there are analogies between then and now. Certain pictures of worship and/or evangelism hold some Christians captive, leading them to think that there must be a deep difference between the church at worship and the church in its evangelistic mode. At least some seem to think that the only kind of worship consistent with effective evangelism cannot be identified, let alone associated, with what the church understands as "traditional" Sunday morning worship.[2]

I would venture that those who have never experienced a tent revival, which includes many Methodists as well as Protestant evangelicals, associate evangelism with a Billy Graham crusade. Of course, Billy Graham just moved the venue to football stadiums, combined that move with media savvy and organizational sophistication, and got the same tent-revival results albeit on a larger scale. What some Methodists now want and have tried to do is to move the football stadium back into the church in an effort to attract the "unchurched." The tents have become the church, which makes some worry that "traditional" Methodist worship is being watered down.

That is the context within which Saliers has tried to help us recover liturgy as the locus of the theologian's work. Of course, for him the very as-

2. Of course one of the ironies of this view is that the "Sunday morning worship service" thought too "formal" for the effective evangelism is the result of past evangelistic form. For example, it is not uncommon in Methodist services that the offering is taken up before the sermon. This order is the result of revivals in which it was assumed that following the sermon some would respond and be "saved." You would not want an offering intruding between the sermon and the response of those needing to be saved. Such an intrusion would mean you might miss the emotional moment, thus letting the sinner escape. Edward Phillips notes that the revival had three distinct liturgical movements: (1) preliminaries, involving hymn singing, special music, testimonies, love offerings; (2) the message; and (3) the altar call. This pattern, he observes, "became embedded in the Protestant mind as the pattern of church meeting. The problem is that it became the pattern, not just for revivals, but for Sunday worship. Sunday worship was turned into an evangelistic service." See his "Creative Worship: Rules, Patterns, and Guidelines," *Quarterly Review* 10, no. 2 (1990): 14.

sumption that there may be a tension between worship and evangelism (or ethics) is indicative that something has gone terribly wrong. He rightly assumes that Christian worship has always been the way the church has both evangelized and gone about its moral formation. "Go therefore and make disciples of all nations" is a command of Jesus, not a suggestion about which we might make up our minds. Making disciples is the legitimating activity that makes the church the church. As Julian Hartt, another good Methodist, noted in his *Toward a Theology of Evangelism,* "Whenever the church is authentically Christian the conviction yet lives that its sole reason for existence is the preach the gospel of the kingdom in Christ."[3] There can be no such preaching without the church at worship. The way the church "wins converts," therefore, is by making us faithful worshipers of the God who alone is worthy of worship.

Truthful Worship

Saliers has tried to help Methodists recover the way worship is evangelism and ethics by reminding us how worship is about the shaping of the affections. In what I hope has been a supportive move, I have tried to help Methodists recover the social and political significance of worship by claiming that the first task of the church is not to make the world more just but to make the world the world. Such a claim is not, as is often alleged, designed to legitimate a withdrawal of the church from the world, but just the opposite. If the church's first task is to be the church, it is so because without the church the world would have no way to understand what justice entails. For as Augustine observed, "justice is found where God, the one supreme God, rules an obedient City according to his grace, forbidding sacrifice to any being save himself alone."[4] That the "cities" in which we now exist do not worship the one true God only indicates how important it is that the church be truthful in its worship.

The church's worship, therefore, is evangelism. That we Methodists thought we had to erect tents to evangelize should have suggested to us that something had gone wrong with our worship. The tents, to be sure, assumed a generalized Christian culture in which everyone, at least everyone in the

3. Julian Hartt, *Toward a Theology of Evangelism* (New York: Abingdon, 1955), p. 9. Hartt's book remains one of the finest accounts of evangelism we have. Hartt's influence at Yale Divinity was everywhere during the years Saliers and I studied there.

4. Augustine, *The City of God,* trans. David Knowles (Harmondsworth, England: Penguin, 1972), p. 890 (19.23).

South, assumed that sometime in their life they ought to be "saved."[5] This resulted in the further problem that many who "got saved" in the tent did not show up on Sunday morning with a regularity that might testify to the lasting effects of their being saved. Nonetheless, the same people got to claim the name Christian, since they had been saved. That the saved did not act like those who had been saved, moreover, was one of the reasons "ethics" became such a concern. Some hoped that if we just thought harder about something called ethics we might find a way to make people live better lives. This was a deep mistake, as it turned out.

These problems are simply reproduced by those who are currently trying to make the church the tent in order that they might reach the "seekers." They assume that what is important is that new people should come to church. As a result, they fail to see that the more important question should be, does the church to which they are coming worship God truthfully? As Saliers has insisted, in worship "form matters" for the truthful shaping of our emotions. The words we use matter.[6] That the Word should be followed by table matters if we are to be rightly formed as Christians. It matters what kind of music shapes our response to the Psalms, since what the psalm declares is not separable from how we as the church sing that declaration.[7]

5. The reason I am a theologian is that I never was able to get "saved." I understood I was a member of the church, but I also knew that I was supposed to be saved at a Sunday night service — Sunday night services were what we did between summer tent events. I wanted to be saved, but it just never happened. I finally decided somewhere around fourteen that if God was not going to save me I would "dedicate my life to Christian service" by becoming a minister. So during the sixteenth singing of "I Surrender All" — a relatively short altar call, as altar calls went on Sunday nights — I dedicated my life to God by declaring I would become a minister. That never happened, but it did result in my majoring in philosophy in college, going to seminary, doing a Ph.D. in theology, and, as they say, the rest is history.

6. The effect of the loss of eloquence in worship is a moral loss. Our lives morally depend on our being able to describe that which we do and do not do truthfully. When the language used in worship is degraded, so are our lives. For example, consider the word *just.* Often those who pray extemporaneously say, "Lord, we would ask you just to do X or Y." Not only is the use of *just* in that context ugly, but theologically it suggests, "Lord, we are really not asking for all that much given your power." I realize that often the use of *just* is meant to suggest humility, but such humility cannot help but sound like a pose. Eloquence, of course, is not achieved by using "archaic" language but by the constant attention necessary to put basic matters simply.

7. I mention the Psalms in particular because of Saliers's work to ensure their inclusion in the 1989 edition of the *United Methodist Hymnal.* It is my belief that this hymnal is the most important development in Methodism in the last fifty years. Theologians often think that what is important is what other theologians think, but much more important is what the church does. It is to Saliers's great credit that he has understood this. The time he has dedicated to help

In this respect there is an interesting parallel between liturgy and ethics as disciplines. To think liturgically and ethically is to try and help the church discover connections by developing historical analogies, exploring philosophical and theological implications, and in the process make normative recommendations. That is why, hopefully, it is hard to distinguish the work done in liturgy from that done in ethics.[8] After all, when all is said and done liturgy and ethics are just ways to do theology, and theology, so understood, might again be construed as worship.

The liturgist's concern to have the different parts of the liturgy "make sense" is quite similar to the ethicist's concern to help the church understand the relation between certain kinds of behavior and moral judgment. Adultery means having sex with someone who is not your spouse, not matter how "loving" the extramarital encounter is or may have been. "I come to the garden alone" are not appropriate words to be sung in corporate worship, no matter how meaningful some people may find the hymn.[9] Part of the diffi-

---

the church sing is not wise if you want a successful academic career, but he has rightly understood that such a career is a very small thing indeed compared to the glory of praising God.

8. This is particularly the case if you are, like me, a convinced Aristotelian. For Aristotle, what and how we "feel" when we do the virtuous thing is as important as our doing it. Aristotle says moral virtue "is concerned with emotions and actions, and it is in emotions and actions that excess, deficiency, and the median are found. Thus we can experience fear, confidence, desire, anger, pity, and generally any kind of pleasure and pain either too much or too little, and in either case not properly. But to experience all this at the right time, toward the right objects, toward the right people, for the right reason, and in the right manner — that is the median and the best course, the course that is a mark of virtue." *Nicomachean Ethics*, trans. Martin Ostwald (Indianapolis: Bobbs-Merrill, 1962), 1106b.15-24. I take it that those concerned with helping us worship God rightly do so as Aristotelians — which is to say, it is not enough that we do what we do but that we do what we do rightly. It is, of course, crucial to remember that we do not worship alone, which means that sometimes I must rely on my fellow worshipers to feel rightly for me.

9. Ed Phillips had to tell me that "In the Garden" was written not by Fanny Crosby but by Austin Miles. The problem with this beloved hymn is not, as is often suggested, the hymn's barely repressed sexual longing. There is nothing wrong with desire even if it is confused. Rather the problem with hymns like "In the Garden" is that their lyrics and music are shallow. A steady diet of worship formed by such hymns and prayers not only reflects a shallow church but also produces a shallow people. I know this seems like a harsh judgment that can also betray a "high culture" arrogance that disdains "popular religion." I have nothing but profound respect for the "country churches" that thought "In the Garden" the best hymn they sang. The problem, however, is that hymn and the worship that was shaped by it proved incapable of preparing those who sang it to recognize, much less resist, the world that increasingly made their Christian commitments unintelligible. I am well aware that many churches whose hymns and prayers are richer are often equally unprepared to challenge the world. Yet hymns like "A Mighty Fortress" have the potential to help mount a resistance that "In the Garden" can never muster.

In a letter to me about this hymn Ed Phillips — a church historian and liturgist who culty is that Protestant Christians, evangelical and mainstream alike, have lost their ability to make such judgments. They have done so, moreover, because they have debased their worship in the name of evangelism and moral uplift.

As Marva Dawn reminds us in her *Reaching Out without Dumbing Down,* worship is "for" God, which is not the same as "meaningful for us."[10] Worship that is for God is, she argues, character forming. That truthful worship of God requires that we proceed in "good order" is a reminder of the very God who alone is deserving of worship. For, as the quote from Augustine reminds us, it is not any God that Christians worship, but the God whose justice is be found in Jesus' cross and resurrection. To learn to worship that God truthfully requires that our bodies be formed by truthful habits of speech and gesture. To be so habituated is to acquire a character befitting lives capable of worshiping God.

One of the ironies of our time is that many "conservative" Christians fail to understand the relation between truthful worship and truthful living. For example, many "conservatives" became upset at women and men allegedly worshiping Sophia in the name of making liturgy "meaningful for women." Yet too often the same people who criticize the worship of God as Sophia are more than ready to distort the proper order of Christian worship in the name of evangelism. They, of course, say they use the name of Jesus, but they fail to see that *how* Jesus' name is used makes all the difference. Without the Eucharist, for example, we lack the means to know the kind of presence made possible by Jesus' resurrection.

The Eucharist is usually not considered an essential aspect of Christian worship by those concerned with church growth. Evangelism means getting people to church, because unless we go to church, it is assumed, our lives are without moral compass. Thus the assumption that lack of attendance at church and our society's "moral decay" go hand and hand. What such people fail to see is that such decay begins with the assumption that worship is about "my" finding meaning for my life rather than glorification of God. Such evangelism is but another name for narcissism. Christian worship requires that our bodies submit to a training otherwise unavailable so that we can become capable of discerning those who use the name of Jesus to tempt us to worship

---

teaches at Garrett Theological Seminary — notes that "the last stanza subverts the entire text and makes it, actually, more interesting than you might at first notice: 'I'd stay in the garden with him though the night around me be falling, but he bids me go; through the voice of woe his voice to me is calling.' In other words, we might *want* to remain 'in the garden' all day long, but Jesus says, 'get out there where the suffering is!'"

10. Marva Dawn, *Reaching Out without Dumbing Down* (Grand Rapids: Eerdmans, 1995), pp. 75-104.

foreign gods. Without the Eucharist we lose the resource to discover how these gods rule our lives.

It is important to note the problem is not whether our worship is "contemporary" or "traditional." Too often such an alternative is an attempt to make us choose hymns that were contemporary in the seventeenth century but sound "traditional" today because we no longer remember what seventeenth-century music sounded like. Nor is it a question of whether worship can be changed. Worship is always being "changed." To remain "the same" while everything around you is changing, whether you like it or not, *is* to be changed. That is why those who sometimes insist on the actual use of tents may think they are doing the same thing that was done in the past, but in fact the very consciousness required to use tents when tents are no longer necessary makes the use of these tents different.

The question, then, is not choosing between "contemporary" or "traditional," to change or not to change, but rather the faithful character of our worship, insofar as such worship shapes the truthful witness of the church to the world. The problem with churches that make "evangelism" (that is, the continuous acquisition of new members) the purpose of their worship is not whether the worship is contemporary. The question is whether they are worshiping the God of Jesus Christ. Moreover, it is not just the "church growth" churches, the Willow Creeks, that have that problem, but "normal" mainstream churches.[11]

Consider, for example, this statement on the back of the bulletin of a very "successful" Methodist church (name changed to protect the guilty): "You are welcome, just as you are, at 'Pleasant City'! Everyone is welcome

11. I may have been among the last in this society to learn that Willow Creek is the paradigm of churches that use modern marketing methods to sustain church growth. The best way to think about such "churches" is to compare them to a shopping mall where periodically the customers are gathered for a common event. Such churches seek to be full-service institutions providing athletic activities, clubs, and childcare. If such churches were more centered around determinative liturgies that were recognizably Christian they might be usefully compared to medieval cathedrals. The latter were often centers for carnival, trade, and politics, and I see no reason to be critical. The problem with churches like Willow Creek is not that they are the center of so many activities but that those activities do not require for their intelligibility the Mass. I realize such a comment will invite the charge I am romanticizing the medieval life, but I am more than willing to take that risk. For an arresting account of the vitality of religious life in late medieval culture, see Eamon Duffy, *The Stripping of the Altars: Traditional Religion in England, c. 1400-1580* (New Haven: Yale University Press, 1992), as well as David Aers's criticism of Duffy for failing to provide an adequate account of the complex social, political, and military factors shaping "religion": David Aers, "Altars of Power: Reflections on Eamon Duffy's *The Stripping of the Altars*," *Literature and History* 3, no. 2 (Autumn 1994): 90-105.

here. We particularly welcome those who have been away from church for a while, and those who are not members of any church. Whether you're married, single, divorced, or in transition, you truly matter to us because you matter to God. We would be honored to have you become a member of Pleasant City Church. Check the box on the friendship pad if you wish to discuss church membership."[12]

Is that evangelism? What would worship in such a church look like? How would anyone in that church know which god it is that seems allegedly so concerned about them? It is easy to criticize Willow Creeks, but Willow Creeks merely exemplify the loss of the Christian worship of God in the name of "more members." The difficulty with worship intentionally shaped to entertain those who are "new" is not that it is entertaining but that the god that is entertained in such worship cannot be the Trinity. For example, to worship the Trinity requires at the very least that we learn to say together the Apostles' Creed. That such a discipline has, in the name of evangelism, become odd, even for Methodists, is but an indication of how distorted our worship has become.

The heart of Saliers's work has been to try to remind his church, the Methodist Church, that faithful and truthful worship of the crucified God is evangelism. That he has done so has not won him universal acclaim among Methodists. That he insists that worship be done "right" is rightly seen by some as a threat to church growth. I suspect that Saliers does not make that erroneous assumption. The fact that large numbers of people are attracted to a church is not in itself a sign of false worship, but like me he probably thinks that if such is the case it is an indication that a close example of how that church worships is a good idea.[13] That we, moreover, feel the need for such an

12. That this invitation is particularly directed at a person's marital status is but an indication of the privatization of Christianity in liberal cultures. The church gets to claim its own peculiar jurisdiction, in this case something to do with the family, because the family is "private." Such an invitation would have been interesting if it had said, "Whether you are rich or poor, in debt or not, just out of prison or on the street, you are welcome." Such an invitation would have indicated some recognition of how class divides our churches, but to acknowledge class is even more threatening for most churches than the acknowledgment of homosexuality or racial divides. I have noticed the "higher" a church's liturgy, the more likely some recognition of class is possible. I have no strong evidence to support this generalization, nor am I sure, if it is true, why it is so. Of course, this is true mainly of Roman Catholic churches. That farm workers, for example, appear at Catholic Masses predominantly populated by middle-class people is open to many explanations. But such explanations surely must involve an account of how the liturgy offers some challenge to the power that class has over our lives.

13. To attract large numbers of people presupposes that they are coming to worship without requiring fundamental change in their own lives. There is nothing wrong in itself with worship being entertaining, but the difficulty is the kind of entertainment necessary to attract large

examination is because we are Methodists who believe that the shaping of our lives in worship is inseparable from the moral shaping of our lives — a shaping that cannot help make us appear quite odd given the assumptions about what it means to be "morally normal" in American society.

Holiness

The name we Methodists have used to indicate the inseparability of worship, evangelism, and ethics is *holiness.* We believe that God's salvation is nothing less than participation in God's very life through word and sacrament. Worship is what we do for God, but in that doing we believe our lives are made part of God's care of creation. To be made holy is to have our lives rendered unintelligible if the God who has claimed us in Jesus Christ is not the true God. To be holy is have our lives "exposed" to one another in the hope that we will become what we have been made.

From Wesley's perspective, Christian worship is evangelism because worship is converting work.[14] Though this may sound Pelagian, the work that worship does is not something we do apart from God. Worship requires that our sins be named, confessed, forgiven.[15] In worship, we discover that sin is not something we do, but rather it is a power that holds us captive.[16] The good news of the gospel, the message proclaimed to the nations, is that we are freed from sin by the God who would be honored, who would be worshiped, before all else.

From a Wesleyan perspective, to be made holy, to be made capable of accepting forgiveness for our sins so that we might worthily worship God,

---

numbers. If worship must, as is often alleged, compete with TV, the TV will always win. Our only hope is that some will find the demanding character of the worship of God so enthralling they will be drawn to it time and time again.

14. For an account of Wesley's views on these matters, see Ole Borgen, *John Wesley on the Sacraments* (Grand Rapids: Francis Asbury/Zondervan, 1986).

15. The worship service at Pleasant City had no confession of sin. Since the service from which I extracted the bulletin quote was a Fourth of July service, there were pledges made to the United States flag, the Christian flag, and the Bible. Sin was mentioned in the last pledge: "I pledge allegiance to the Bible, God's Holy Word, and will make it a lamp unto my feet, a light unto my path, and hide its words in my heart that I may not sin against God."

16. Of course, that sin names the powers does not mean that we do not sin. We confess our sins as those who have willingly sinned, but our willingness names complicity. I often think the closest paradigm we have to what it means to confess our sin is the alcoholic's confession at AA: "My name is X and I am an alcoholic." It may be that alcoholism is a power that possesses someone in such a manner that they can never remember "choosing" to be an alcoholic. Only as I confess that alcoholism is "me" is there any hope of recovery. Sin may not always be something I have "done," but it is nonetheless mine.

does not involve just "personal holiness." As Augustine suggested above, nothing is more important for a society than to worship God justly. Without such worship terrible sacrifices will be made to false gods. Contrary to the modern presumption that as enlightened people we are beyond sacrifice, few societies are more intent on sacrifice than those we call modern.[17] Societies that think they have left sacrifice behind end up basing their existence on the sacrifice of the poor in the name of human progress. Christians believe that we are the alternative to such sacrificial systems because we have been given the gift of offering our "sacrifice of thanksgiving" to the One who alone is worthy of such praise. That is what makes us a holy people, a people set apart, so that the world might know there is an alternative to murder.

That I teach "ethics" through the liturgy and Saliers refuses to do theology as if prayer does not matter is, I hope, testimony to the fact that we are Methodist "perfectionists."[18] We have staked our work and our lives on the assumption that if in some small way we can help our church recover liturgical integrity, we will not have to deal with a question about the relationship between worship, evangelism, and ethics. Of course it may still be useful to distinguish between worship, evangelism, and ethics as subjects of study, but hopefully such distinctions will be seen as part of the church's ministry reflected in a diversity of gifts. Such gifts, however, cannot become separate disciplines or realms if they are to be of service.

Yet neither of us can deny that if we do in fact worship God truthfully, we may well find the church again worshiping in tents. For such worship creates a people who by necessity are on the move, forced to wander among the nations, home nowhere yet everywhere. Such a people are bound to attract followers, because the God who has called them from the nations is so beautifully compelling. That is, after all, why we believe that there is nothing more important in a world that does not believe it has the time to worship God than to take time to worship God in truth.[19]

17. For an extraordinary account of our current sacrificial system we call America, see Gil Bailie, *Violence Unveiled: Humanity at the Crossroads* (New York: Crossroads, 1995). Bailie's analysis draws on the remarkable work of René Girard.

18. For an account of the way I teach Christian ethics at Duke Divinity School, see my *In Good Company: The Church As Polis* (Notre Dame, Ind.: University of Notre Dame Press, 1995), pp. 153-68. I confess I have no idea how much I have stolen over the years from Donald Saliers, *The Soul in Paraphrase: Prayer and Religious Affections* (New York: Seabury, 1980), but I know it is more than I have acknowledged. For example, everything I have said in this essay could be and, hopefully, will be read as a commentary on his claim that "prayer is a logically required context for the utterance of theological truths" (p. 82).

19. I am indebted to Kelly Johnson and Jim Fodor for their criticism of an earlier draft of this essay.

PART FOUR

The Study of Evangelism among the Ecclesial Practices

In recent years, from the sphere of the business world to that of religious communities, the language of "practices" has become common parlance. Social theorists have reconceived businesses and churches as "communities of practice" and have sought to demonstrate the importance of practices in the formation of those communities and their participants. The concept of practices, of course, is nothing new in the life of the church, but contemporary students of ecclesial practices are discovering much about how these activities both shape people and reflect their values and senses of meaning. Practical theologians have examined discrete areas of Christian practice for years. The Association of Practical Theology, for example, delineates a number of subdisciplines, including the practices of administration, education, homiletics, mission, pastoral care, and worship. Among these various areas of ministry, the rediscovery of the Christian practices of hospitality, discernment, forgiveness, healing, and singing, among many other activities of the faithful, promises to help people envision a more authentic way of life in Christ.

The writers featured in this section all affirm that the essential connection between their respective areas of practice and evangelism relates to the way in which these practices are actually embodied in real-life situations. The faithful and effective practice of evangelism depends not only upon the security of biblical foundations and the veracity of theological reflection, but also upon the inherent consistency of interrelated practices within the community of faith. Participating in the church's evangelistic mission entails locating the practice of evangelism within a larger network of these interconnected practices. Healthy relations among these practices support the mission of the church; inconsistency, antagonism, and reductionism inevitably impede the church's evangelistic ministry. Competition among these various areas of ministry compromises their essential interrelatedness. A recognition of the organic unity of the ecclesial practices, however, leads to a more profound recognition of interdependence in the lived practice of Christian communities. Reductionism with regard to the practice of evangelism — envisaging evangelistic practice simply as verbal proclamation, apologetics, or "invitation to decision" — leads inevitably to a truncated understanding of evangelism, perpetuates the marginalization of its serious study, and threatens the health of the community. Just as evangelism is the heart of the church's mission, so evangelism is the core of all ecclesial practices. If practices of worship, discipleship, or pastoral care are pursued without an evangelistic orientation — namely an intentional proclamation and embodiment of the gospel of Jesus Christ — then such practices not only lose their motivation and power, but arguably cease to function as Christian practice. The essays in this section, therefore, demonstrate the interdependent nature of evangelism and several relevant ecclesial practices.

Scholars and practitioners have long debated the interface of evangelism and discipleship. They tend to fall into two distinct camps. On the one hand are those who view these two aspects of the Christian life as distinct and separate. Evangelistic practice brings the new believer to a point of faith where the practices of Christian discipleship take over; a hand-off of sorts takes place between the evangelist and the pastor or community of faith. On the other hand are those who conceive discipleship as inseparable, even indistinguishable, from evangelism. No easy line of demarcation can be drawn that separates the activity of either sphere. Walter Brueggemann, noted Old Testament scholar and practical theologian, argues persuasively for a "distinct but not separate" understanding of the relationship between the two. He establishes this more synthetic approach upon the fundamental understanding of God as the One who calls and sends. Having demonstrated from both the Old and New Testaments how God calls people to praise and obedience and sends them out to bear witness to justice, mercy, and faith, he describes the way in which the interdependent practices of discipleship and evangelism draws God's children into and establish them in an alternate way of being in the world for its sake. Discipleship — manifest most fully in the four disciplines of the early church: teaching, fellowship, breaking of bread, and prayer — entails nothing less than the "resituating of our lives" in God's just and loving reign. Evangelism is God's invitation and summons to live into this reality, despite the fact that the world continues on an "anti-creation" trajectory characterized by power and injustice. Evangelism and discipleship function harmoniously to establish and sustain God's children in "the miracle of transformative goodness."

In missionary contexts it has always been common to emphasize the inseparability of evangelism (invitation to faith) and catechesis (learning the faith). Separated artificially in a Western Christendom model of the faith, the integral nature of these practices finds renewed expression in the post-Christian context of twenty-first-century Europe and America. John Westerhoff, former visionary Christian educator of Duke Divinity School, argues the importance of connecting evangelism, evangelization, and catechesis. While his definitions of these terms are rather idiosyncratic, the model of making disciples that he offers affords important insights with regard to the health of the Christian community in this new millennium. Evangelization — a process essentially lost over the course of the past several centuries, he argues — has to do with initiating persons into the faith and incorporating them into the life of the Christian community. He defines evangelism (in a conventional although more limited manner than we would wish) as proclaiming the gospel of God's salvation through word and example to those who do not know or accept it. If evangelism refers to practices at the front end of disciple-making, catechesis is "the process by which a person shows that he or she is Christian." He defines catechesis, therefore, as "the intentional, lifelong process by which Christians are made, fashioned, and nurtured." It is the process through which persons develop their faith, character, and consciousness. The missing link between evangelism and catechesis — the lost practice Westerhoff seeks to rediscover for the life of the church — is evangelization.

Paul W. Chilcote, a noted Wesley scholar, professor of evangelism, and former missionary in Africa, explores the integral nature of worship and evangelism through the lens of Methodist hymnody and practice. After laying a biblical foundation for the intimate relationship between worship and evangelism based upon Acts 2:46-47 and examining the image of *paideia* (instruction through action) in Hebrews 12:9-10 as a concept implying their integration, the author describes the liturgy of the worshiping community as the primary matrix of evangelistic ministry. Worship shapes people of faith and prepares them to be evangel-bearers in their daily lives. The call of the prophet Isaiah (6:2-8) reveals a paradigm related to worship that instructs our understanding of evangelism as well. The acknowledgment of the One we worship and the radiance of God's loving nature are the foundations of evangelistic ministry. The experience of repentance and forgiveness liberates God's people and enables them to be ambassadors of reconciliation and restoration. In the worshiping community, the servants of God proclaim the word and the whole people of God respond to God's Word in both mission and Eucharist.

Very little work has been done to explore the connections between evangelism and the practices of pastoral care. Indeed, as with regard to the other ecclesial practices we have surveyed, scholars seldom seem to connect these two spheres of action in the church. The final essay in this section, by Presbyterian pastor and pastoral theologian J. Patrick Vaughn, examines evangelism from the perspective of obligation and crucifixion, images articulated particularly and respectively in the theological writings of Don Browning and Jürgen Moltmann. Vaughn proposes that when evangelism is grounded in the suffering love of the Triune God, the image of evangelist can shape and inform the ministry of pastoral care and counseling. The cross reveals that the Triune God suffers because of human sin, in solidarity with and on behalf of humanity. This revelation is the "evangel" at the heart of all evangelistic practice. Given this cruciform foundation, Vaughn identifies at least five "obligations" for pastoral caregivers as those who bear witness to the gospel (that is, function as evangelists) in their practice of the cure of souls. He signals the importance of personal relationships; sensitivity to human experiences of need and pain; support and encouragement, particularly that which is only possible in an empathetic community of faith; respect for boundaries, always guarding against the abuse of power and coercion of any form; and confrontation of sin and evil. He echoes the sentiments of Carroll Wise, who defined pastoral care as "the art of communicating the inner meaning of the gospel." He points, in others words, to the intimate connection between evangelism and pastoral care in the community of God's people.

CHAPTER 15

Evangelism and Discipleship: The God Who Calls, the God Who Sends

Walter Brueggemann

I begin with four affirmations that I will exposit in some detail:

1. The God of the gospel is a God who calls persons and communities to God's own self, to engage in praise and obedience.
2. The God of the gospel is a God who sends persons and communities to claim many zones of the world for God's governance of "justice, mercy, and faith" (Matt. 23:23).
3. The God of the gospel lives among and in contestation with many other gods who also call and send, but whose praise and obedience are false, precisely because there is no commitment to "justice, mercy, and faith."
4. Consequently, the persons and communities called by this God for praise and obedience and sent by this God for justice, mercy, and faith also live among and in contestation with other gods, other loyalties, other authorities. Inescapably, the ones called and sent are always yet again deciding for this one who calls and sends. This endless process of deciding again is accomplished in freedom from all other calling gods and all other sending loyalties. That endless deciding, moreover, requires great passion, imagination, and intentionality.

God Calls

The God of the gospel calls to praise and obedience. This is, we confess, the one true God, who is the giver of all life and who intends that all life should gladly be lived back to God. It is God's rightful place to invite and expect such a turn back to God in joy and well-being. The characteristic response to the Creator by all creatures is to give praise (that is, exuberant, self-ceding gladness to God), and obedience (that is, active engagement in doing God's will and making the world to be the creation that God intends). The call of God, in short, is to discipleship, that is, to follow God's presence and purpose and promise with the disciplines necessary to the project.

1. The God to which the Old Testament bears testimony is a God who calls, who disrupts the lives of settled people, who gives them a vocation that marks life by inconvenience and risk. The ground of the call is the good news of the gospel that God has a powerful intentionality for the world, which, when enacted, will make a decisive difference for good in the world. Of the Old Testament's many calls to the disciplines of praise and obedience, I will mention only two.

(a) The story of Israel begins with God's abrupt address to Abraham, an address that is decisive and delivered without any forewarning. Abraham is addressed in an imperative: "Go"; and with this address Abraham's life is radically displaced. He is caught up in a world of discourse and possibility about which he knew nothing until addressed, a world of discourse and possibility totally saturated with God's good promises for him and for the world through him (Gen. 12:1). By this call Abraham is propelled into an orbit of reality that totally preempts his life and removes him completely from any purpose or agenda he may have entertained for himself before that moment. Of Abraham's answer to the address of God we are told very little. The text says only, "So Abram went" (Gen. 12:4). Later, this response is interpreted as a supreme act of faith:

> By faith Abraham, when put to the test, offered up Isaac. He who had received the promises was ready to offer up his only son, of whom he had been told, "It is through Isaac that descendants shall be named for you." He considered the fact that God is able even to raise someone from the dead — and figuratively speaking, he did receive him back. (Heb. 11:17-19)

(b) This same God also calls Moses by meeting him in the burning bush (Exod. 3:1-6). The call itself consists in three elements:

- God calls him by name, "Moses, Moses." In this address God seizes the initiative in the life of Moses. Moses is known by God from the outset in elemental ways and is called to engage the mystery of God.
- Moses is warned that he is standing on holy ground. That is, his locus is not what he thought, not simply a place for the struggle for social justice in which he was already engaged, but a zone inhabited by demanding, addressing holiness. The call is an abrupt act that displaces Moses for a world of conflict propelled by God's holiness.

- Moses is resituated in the tradition of God's people, as God recalls God's identity from the book of Genesis: "God of Abraham, God of Isaac, God of Jacob." Moses is thereby wrenched away from what he might have thought was the circumstance of his life and decisively relocated in a larger narrative about which he knew nothing until that moment of confrontation.

2. The same God, in the life and in the utterances of Jesus, makes the same claim in the New Testament. In each case the call, an authorizing imperative, is a disruption that sets lives on totally new trajectories that had not previously been in purview. The simple, uninflected imperative is "follow me," an imperative that sets folk on a new path of obedience, trailing along the path that Jesus himself walked in obedience:

- In Mark 1:16-20, immediately upon announcing the nearness of the kingdom (vv. 14-15), Jesus comes upon the four fishermen who abandon their old life for this new following.
- In Mark 8:34-38, just after announcing his own death and resurrection (v. 31), Jesus issues a call to the disciples:

  > If any want to become my followers, let them deny themselves and take up their cross and follow me. For those who want to save their life will lose it, and those who lose their life for my sake, and for the sake of the gospel, will save it. (Mark 8:34-35)

- Following Jesus leads to Jerusalem, a path that culminates in a cross, a reality that contradicts all the hopes and promises of the world into which Jesus goes, that is, into the world of settled legitimacy and power.
- In Mark 10:17-22, Jesus offers a call to the man who had kept all the commandments: "Jesus, looking at him, loved him and said, 'You lack one thing: go, sell what you own, and give the money to the poor, and you will have treasure in heaven; then come, follow me'" (Mark 10:21).

In all these cases, Jesus' claim upon people's lives places their lives in crisis; it is the same sovereign claim that is so uncompromising in the narratives of Abraham and Moses.

3. Of course, it is a huge leap from these biblical summonses to our own time, place, and circumstance. Nevertheless, we imagine that the same calling God calls "men and women of all ages, tongues, and races into his church."[1]

1. The phrasing is from the "Statement of Faith" of the United Church of Christ.

The call is not to join an institution or to sign a pledge card; it is rather to sign on for a different narrative account of reality, one that is in profound contrast to the dominant account of reality into which we are all summarily inducted.

This God of the gospel calls men and women away from the bad news of the world, away from the dominant, dehumanizing values of commodity and brutality that are all around us. The calling God means for us to disengage from the postures, habits, and assumptions that define the world of power and injustice, so devoid of mercy and compassion in every arena of life. The call is away from ordinary life, ordinary possessions, and ordinary assumptions to a way of life that the world judges to be impossible. Thus the call is, indeed, to an impossibility.

Discipleship is no easy church program. It is a summons away from our characteristic safety nets of social support. It entails a resolve to follow a leader who himself has costly habits, in order to engage in disciplines that disentangle us from ways in which we are schooled and stupefied and that introduce new habits that break old vicious cycles among us, drawing us into intimacy with this calling God. Discipleship requires a whole new conversation in a church that has been too long accommodating, at ease in the dominant values of culture that fly in the face of the purposes of God.

It is right to conclude, in my judgment, that the God who calls is the God of discipleship, the one who calls people to follow, to obey, to participate in his passion and mission. Such disciplines — in the Old Testament, in the New Testament, and now — intend and permit a drastic reorienting of one's life, an embrace of new practices and, most particularly, a departure from other loyalties that have seemed both legitimate and convenient.

God Sends

The God who calls is the God who sends. This God sends because God has compelling authority to issue imperatives that anticipate ready acceptance, and God has a compelling passion for what is to be effected and enacted in the world that this God governs.

1. The sending of Abraham (and Sarah) is perhaps the overarching missional dispatch in all of Scripture. God issues to Abraham an initial imperative: "Go." Then God makes extravagant promises to Abraham concerning land, name, and blessing. But the sending culminates with this responsibility entrusted to Abraham: "By you all the families of the earth shall be blessed" (Gen. 12:3).

Israel exists to cause a blessing that is to be widely shared. "Blessing" is not a religious or moral phenomenon in the world of Israel, but is a characteristic feature of creation that is fruitful and productive. Blessing means that the world should be generous, abundant, and fruitful, effecting generative fertility, material abundance, and this-worldly prosperity — *shalom* in broadest scope. Israel's life is to make the world work better according to the intention of the Creator.

Genesis 12:1-3 functions, on the one hand, as a hinge to what follows.[2] The passage looks forward toward the entire family of Abraham that exists in order to evoke blessing in the world. More stunning, on the other hand, is the awareness that this mandate looks back to Genesis 3–11, that is, to all the nations of the world that are under curse: Adam and Eve, Cain and Abel, the Flood, and the tower. All of these narratives tell of the families of the earth becoming alienated from God and living in contradiction to the will of God. In God's missional mandate to Abraham, Abraham is called to exist so that the general condition of curse in the world is turned to a general condition of blessing, life, and well-being. Israel's mission is to mend the world in all its parts.

Paul quotes this very text from Genesis in urging that the gospel pertains to the Gentiles: "And the scripture, foreseeing that God would justify the Gentiles by faith, declared the gospel beforehand to Abraham, saying, 'All the Gentiles shall be blessed in you'" (Gal. 3:8). The wondrous phrase of Paul, "gospel beforehand," is a recognition that from the outset the good intention of the Creator God cannot be limited to any ethnic or racial or national enclave. Here is the warrant for a vision of a community of *shalom,* rooted in God's own vision of the creation, that repudiates every death-bringing distinction and every leverage of some over against others. Moreover, the mandate in Genesis is not to make the nations over into Israelites, nor even to make them Yahwists. The focus is kept upon the improvement of the quality of life as willed by the Creator God.

2. The issue of sending is rhetorically the same in the Exodus narrative, though the effect is very different. The sending of Moses is almost a humorous rhetorical act. YHWH issues a series of first-person resolves, all concerning YHWH's intention in the face of pharaonic oppression:

> Then the LORD said, "I have observed the misery of my people who are in Egypt; I have heard their cry on account of their taskmasters. Indeed, I know their sufferings, and I have come down to deliver them from the

2. Hans Walter Wolff, "The Kerygma of the Yahwist," *Interpretation* 20 (1966): 131-58; Patrick D. Miller, "Syntax and Theology in Genesis 12:3a," in *Israelite Religion and Biblical Theology: Collected Papers* (Sheffield: Sheffield Academic, 2000), pp. 492-96.

> Egyptians. . . . The cry of the Israelites has now come to me; I have also seen how the Egyptians oppress them." (Exod. 3:7-9)

But the next verse comes as a surprise. YHWH might then have said, "I will go to Pharaoh"; but YHWH does not. Instead, Moses hears, "So come, I will send you to Pharaoh to bring my people, the Israelites, out of Egypt" (v. 10). The most difficult and most dangerous task of emancipation is not undertaken by YHWH alone, solely as divine deliverance. Rather, emancipation is a human task, to be undertaken amid the risky problematics of Pharaoh's political reality.

The mission of Moses is nothing less than the confrontation of a form of political power that no longer has anything of a human face. More than that, Moses' mandate is to confront exploitative economic power that is understood to be an embodiment of false theology, so that the task of liberation and transformation of the empire is deeply rooted in a theological conflict between the Lord of liberty and the gods that endorse and legitimate exploitative economics (see Exod. 12:12).

The mission is a human mission, with YHWH cast in a crucial but supporting role. God offers to transform the slave economy, but only in and through direct, risky human engagement. Moses immediately senses the problem and the risk of the call; consequently, we hear from him five points of resistance (Exod. 3:11–4:17). Moses does not want the mission, which is nothing less than transforming the social system of Egypt from working according to the vision of the pharaonic superpower, bringing that economy in line with a covenantal vision of reality. The mission concerns the way in which power is practiced in the world. YHWH's role is to legitimate, authorize, and support the human mission by shows of presence and power that are only available in the midst of alternative human action.

3. The sending of the disciples of Jesus concerns both walk and talk. I take Matthew 10:5-15 to be a model for Christian mission. The initial mandate to the twelve is to talk: "As you go, proclaim the good news, 'The kingdom of heaven has come near'" (v. 7). The kingdom of heaven — the rule of God — has come near. The sentence is terse and does not last long enough to say, "has come near in the life and person of Jesus." The Synoptic tradition insists that in the actions of Jesus — acts of healing, cleansing, feeding, forgiving — a new governance is now unmistakably in effect. The kingdom comes near when the creation begins to function according to the blessed intention of the Creator. God has drawn near to usher in a new reality that is to be enacted and effected by human missioners who act boldly on the basis of the proclamation that they themselves accept as true and as the basis for an alternative life in the world.

The second part of the mandate to the disciples is the walk: "Cure the sick, raise the dead, cleanse the lepers, cast out demons" (Matt. 10:8a).

The imperative to act is fourfold: cure the sick (because the sick have fallen under powers that wish them ill); raise the dead (where the spiritual force of death prevails, enact the power of life); cleanse lepers (make the unclean ritually acceptable); cast out demons (break the power that opposes the new governance). In doing this, the disciples receive the mandate to "travel light":

> You received without payment; give without payment. Take no gold, or silver, or copper in your belts, no bag for your journey, or two tunics, or sandals, or a staff; for laborers deserve their food. (Matt. 10:8b-10)

We conclude that the capacity to effect these transformative wonders requires complete reliance on the news of the new ruler; the negative counterpoint is the shunning of the resources of the status quo that will rob the disciples of power to be effective.

The mission is dangerous, because God's will for the world is in deep tension with the way the world is organized:

> See, I am sending you out like sheep into the midst of wolves; so be wise as serpents and innocent as doves. Beware of them, for they will hand you over to councils and flog you in their synagogues; and you will be dragged before governors and kings because of me, as a testimony to them and the Gentiles. When they hand you over, do not worry about how you are to speak or what you are to say; for what you are to say will be given to you at that time; for it is not you who speak, but the Spirit of your Father speaking through you. (Matt. 10:16-20)

The present population of those sick or dead, the lepers, and demon-possessed is not an accident. Rather, the present system works as it does precisely because a certain quota of lives has been "handed over" to antihuman forces, and the system prospers on their backs. The attempt to draw those "handed over" back into the realm of the human will evoke deep hostility, from wolves that, though viciously ravenous, will work by legal means under the guise of respectability. The normal state of the missioner is to be in trouble with the authorities who are characteristically defenders of systems that deny humanness.[3]

3. See C. S. Song, "The Politics of Revolution," in *Proclaiming the Acceptable Year,* ed. Justo L. Gonzalés (Valley Forge, Pa.: Judson, 1982), pp. 25-39.

Now the text moves beyond mission and picks up on our other theme of discipleship:

> A disciple is not above the teacher, nor a slave above the master; it is enough for the disciple to be like the teacher, and the slave like the master. If they have called the master of the house Beelzebul, how much more will they malign those of his household! (Matt. 10:24-25)

The people among whom Jesus is sent do not like him, so they will not like his disciples either. Clearly the mission is done by those under discipline. And perhaps the ultimate discipline is this:

> So have no fear of them; for nothing is covered up that will not be uncovered, and nothing secret that will not become known. What I say to you in the dark, tell in the light; and what you hear whispered, proclaim from the housetops. Do not fear those who kill the body but cannot kill the soul; rather fear him who can destroy both soul and body in hell. (Matt. 10:26-28)

4. Our talk of mission must, of course, pay attention to Matthew 28:16-20, verses that are commonly understood as decisive for this theme. The imperative of the risen Lord to the remaining eleven followers is clear and firm: go, make disciples, baptize, and teach.

The post-Easter company of disciples, the inchoate form of the church in this most churchy gospel, is sent. Its task is to recruit others into the counter-community of Jesus:

- To make disciples means to bring others under the disciplines that mark the followers of Jesus. It is assumed that the primal core of disciples is under discipline itself, so that its members can instruct new recruits into the practices and habits that will sustain life and mission in the counter-community.
- Baptism, reflecting a more ecclesial assumption on the part of Matthew, has become the rite of initiation into an alternative community. In the earliest church, baptism was a decisive, dramatic transfer of life into a new community with new disciplines, new loyalties, and new obligations.
- Teaching is fundamental to the missional church that is sent. The primal curriculum of the church's teaching pivots on the twin trinitarian claims that (a) the historical person of Jesus is the embodiment and disclosure of God's true character and that (b) Jesus' spirit continues to in-

fuse this community (and the world) after his departure from the earth. This mandating text at the close of Matthew already recognizes, in the earliest church, that knowledge of the tradition is fundamental to mission; ignorance of the tradition will make mission either impossible or undertaken for the wrong reasons.

5. The difficult and demanding task is to complete the sequence that extends from Old Testament to New Testament to early church by trying to line out what that sending now may mean to us in our circumstance. It is clear that the sending is not to another place, on the assumption that some places have already been "won over" and other places remain to be "taken." That, of course, was the old assumption of mission — characteristically "foreign" mission — uncritically assuming that the home base was "secure" for the gospel. Rather, this sending means to be dispatched as an alternative power in every place where anti-creation powers rule, dispatched there to talk and walk the truth that the legitimate power of governance belongs to the One who authorizes restoration of what belongs rightly — at the outset and at the finish — only to God. That is, the sending is to be understood as becoming alternative community in the midst of conventional communities:

- To enact alternative community in the midst of conventional communities is highly conflictual, as it was for Moses and for Jesus in his own life, and as it was for the early church. The powers of the conventional have acute antennas for the ways in which status quo reality is thwarted and called into question by alternative reality.
- Enactment of alternative community requires intentionality sustained by carefully embraced and regularly practiced disciplines, so that discipleship is a sine qua non for mission.
- This counter-community has as its core task the naming and confrontation of alien spiritual powers that govern the conventional society into which we are all, in many ways, inducted.[4]
- These alien spiritual powers, however, characteristically are manifested as socio-political-economic powers, so that religious and political-economic issues are always both spiritual and political-economic, never either one or the other. This both/and reality in turn means that the old quarrel between evangelism and social action is a cheap, misinformed argument. It is precisely the talk of the evangel that matches the walk of

4. See Walter Wink, *Naming the Powers: The Language of Power in the New Testament* (Philadelphia: Fortress, 1984).

action in the world on behalf of the new governance that is proclaimed in the evangel.

The news of a restored creation is counter to a system of meaning and power that I term technological-therapeutic-military consumerism — a system that in our society unrelentingly offers a total worldview that comprehends all and allows no opening for any alternative. This dominant mode of power and meaning is a way of rendering reality that silences "the news" and voids the One who is the subject of our "news":

- technological — the reduction of life's choices to technological options in which critical voices of alternative are screened out and eliminated. Thus "techno-speak" can allow no room for the slippery, dramatic Character who is at the core of the church's news.
- therapeutic — the assumption that our goal in life is to live a pain-free, stress-free, undisturbed life of convenience. Most television ads are aimed at this elusive and impossible goal, which stands deeply opposed to any news that has a cross at its center.
- military — the deployment of immense forces, funded by massive resources, to protect an entitled advantage in a world that is committed to an unsustainable standard of living.
- consumerism — the deep and unexamined assumption that "more" (of whatever) will make us safer and happier, a claim difficult to maintain when one ponders the fact that massive consumerism is matched by pervasive unhappiness and profound insecurity.

To characterize our culture as marked by an ideology of technological-therapeutic-military consumerism — to which all of us subscribe in some serious way — is to mark a primal mission context for the evangel. In that world, the mission to be enacted by those under discipline is to cure, raise the dead, cleanse, and cast out demons; to make disciples, teach, and baptize.

So consider: the calling God calls; the sending God sends. This God calls and sends because God the Creator intends that the world will again be free, able and competent to be God's abundant creation. That prospect, however, requires breaking the grip of alien powers that impede the fullness of creation. It is the intention of the Creator, we confess, that the kingdom of this world should become the kingdom of our God who is the Creator. The New Testament version of that claim is, of course, that the coming rule of our God will be the coming rule of his Messiah (Rev. 11:15).

Those called and sent in our time have a mandate not unlike that of

Abraham and Moses, and not unlike that of the disciples of Jesus, because the talk and the walk are in every time and place fundamentally the same.

Discipleship and Evangelism

This biblical background now permits us to propose certain theological presuppositions for discipleship and evangelism:

1. That God calls and sends with authority attests to our common conviction that this God is entitled to such imperatives among us, that is, that God acts with appropriate authority in calling and sending.
2. The God who calls and sends is the God of the good news, the one who created the world and calls it "good," the one who in Israel is manifested through wonders of emancipation and sustenance, wonders that constitute the dazzling miracles of Israel's doxologies; this is the one evidenced in Jesus of Nazareth, who caused the blind to see, the lame to walk, the lepers to be cleansed, the dead to be raised, the poor to rejoice (Luke 7:22). The God who calls and sends has a long history of miracles of transformative goodness.
3. This God of creation and redemption, of newness and transformation, is a God with a concrete intention for the world, an intention of well-being that is articulated in concrete mandates and commandments, one who will be obeyed by those who offer praise.
4. This God who calls and sends is the originator, sponsor, and advocate for *shalom* in all the world; God summons creatures of all sorts to join in the enactment of that *shalom.*
5. This God of the gospel, evidenced in miracles and voiced in imperatives, is a counterforce in the world, a counter to all of the powers of death and negation that operate in every zone of creaturely reality. God calls us to disengage from those powers to which we have tacitly sworn allegiance and sends us to confront, struggle with, and defeat those powers for the sake of God's counter-will in the world.
6. The calling and sending of God place us regularly in crisis because (a) we do not want to disengage from the powers of negation to which we are deeply inured, and (b) we do not want to struggle against those mighty powers. Thus a willing response to God's calling and sending, in praise and obedience, entails sustained, disciplined, concrete intentionality.

It is the character, reality, will, and purpose of God that propel us into a crisis of discipleship and evangelism. The dominant script of our society wants to silence the voice of this God of miracle and imperative. Where the dominant script succeeds in eliminating God, moreover, the possibility of discipleship and the capacity for evangelism evaporate, because it is only the option of the good news that produces ground and opportunity for either discipleship or evangelism.

Discipleship

Discipleship is not just a nice notion of church membership or church education; it entails a resituating of our lives. The disciples of Jesus are the ones who follow their master, able to do so because they have been instructed in his way of life, both his aim and his practice of embodying that aim. The disciple is one who is closely associated with the master-teacher, a profoundly undemocratic notion, for the relation consists in yielding, submitting, and relinquishing oneself to the will and purpose of another.

Discipleship fundamentally entails a set of disciplines, habits, and practices that are undertaken as regular, concrete, daily practices; such daily disciplines are neither greatly exciting nor immediately productive, but like the acquiring of any new competence, discipleship requires such a regimen — not unlike the learning of a new language by practicing the paradigm of verbs; not unlike the learning of piano by practicing the scales; not unlike the maintenance of good health by the tenacity of jogging; not unlike every intentional habit that makes new dimensions of life possible. The church is a community engaged in disciplines that make following the master-teacher possible and sustainable.

How shall we speak of such workable disciplines?

We may begin with the constants of the early church in the book of Acts: "They devoted themselves to the apostles' teaching and fellowship, to the breaking of bread and the prayers" (Acts 2:42).

The four disciplines of the early church are undertaken immediately upon baptismal entry into the alternative community; they become the basis for the startling missional activity in the narratives that follow. Thus the disciplines stand exactly between the entry of baptism and the mounting of mission. The practices are:

- Teaching: instruction into the tradition. We know from 1 Corinthians 11 and 15 that, according to Paul, the tradition to be learned and transmitted concerns especially the practices of the Eucharist and the most succinct assertion of the crucifixion and resurrection of Jesus. A baptized church is a studying church.

- Fellowship. The church is a face-to-face community of people who are together for good stretches of life, for whom company with other believers is enjoyable and important. The pragmatic reason for this practice is that resistance and alternative are not possible alone, a point long known in the twelve-step programs.
- Breaking of bread. Nothing is so elemental as solidarity in eating, where we are bodily engaged with each other.
- Prayer. Prayer is the regular communal act of ceding one's own life and our common life over to the real subject of the "news." We may imagine, further, that these prayers of the church include table prayers, the church's most intimate practice of creation theology wherein we marvel at the inscrutable production of bread, a gift freely given to us.

A second version of early church discipline is "prayer and fasting" (see Mark 9:29, marginal note). According to some manuscript traditions, fasting is a precondition of the power to heal and transform. Fasting is essentially an alien notion in much of the Reformed tradition, because we shun visible spiritual practices and because we affirm the goodness of life. If, however, we think of fasting as breaking the vicious addictive cycles of loyalty to a consumer society, then we will certainly recognize prominent forms of addiction — notably television — that may admit of disciplined disengagement.

To these I would add that in current discussion, the recovery of Sabbath as a day of disengagement from the power of production and consumption may be important. I have noted of late connections made by Jewish scholars between Sabbath and stewardship, Sabbath as relinquishment of control over my life and stewardship as a recognition that life is not our own.

The most characteristic neighbor practices of the Christian life are to be understood as acutely countercultural, especially generosity, compassion, and forgiveness. The daily commitment to such practices is grounded, I have no doubt, in study, prayer, and fellowship. The practices themselves, however, are profoundly countercultural in a society that is deeply lacking in the elemental ingredients of common humanness. These practices significantly challenge the dominant assumptions in our culture.

These disciplines, if taken seriously, are immensely inconvenient. But of course that is part of their purpose in a culture that imagines it need never be inconvenienced. The disciplines function to inconvenience us enough that we become conscious, self-conscious, and intentionally aware of who we are and what we are doing with our lives. Indeed, only those who are inconvenienced enough to be intentional will have energy for mission.

Evangelism

The term "evangel" is a rendering of "gospel" that is in turn a rendering of "news," "good news." The most succinct usages of the term in the Old Testament are in Isaiah:

> Get you up to a high mountain,
> O Zion, herald of good tidings;
> lift up your voice with strength,
> O Jerusalem, herald of good tidings,
> lift it up, do not fear;
> say to the cities of Judah,
> "Here is your God!"
>
> (Isa. 40:9)

> How beautiful upon the mountains
> are the feet of the messenger who announces peace,
> who brings good news,
> who announces salvation,
> who says to Zion, "Your God reigns."
>
> (Isa. 52:7)

The phrasing that occurs in these texts — "Here is your God" and "Your God reigns" — is gospel talk. The two statements assert that the God of Israel whom Babylon had silenced and voided is back in play. The evangel asserts the revivification of this God long dormant:

> The LORD is the everlasting God,
> the Creator of the ends of the earth.
> He does not faint or grow weary;
> his understanding is unsearchable.
>
> (Isa. 40:28)

> Now after John was arrested, Jesus came to Galilee, proclaiming the good news of God, and saying, "The time is fulfilled, and the kingdom of God has come near; repent, and believe in the good news." (Mark 1:14-15)

The talk of gospel is an announcement of new governance. The walk of gospel is to act as though the new rule of God were in effect, though there continues to be much data to the contrary. Thus the talk and the walk of the news constitute an act of resistance and the embrace of an alternative, even when the ground for the alternative is readily doubted in dominant culture. The "as though" proviso is an act of defiance and refusal, as the prophet notes:

> Though the fig tree does not blossom,
>   and no fruit is on the vines;
> though the produce of the olive fails
>   and the fields yield no food;
> though the flock is cut off from the fold
>   and there is no herd in the stalls,
> yet I will rejoice in the LORD;
>   I will exult in the God of my salvation.
>
> (Hab. 3:17-18)

As discipleship is not simply church membership, so evangelism is not simply church recruitment of new members. Evangelism is the invitation and summons to resituate our talk and our walk according to the reality of this God, a reality not easily self-evident in our society. The call of the gospel includes the negative assertion that the technological-therapeutic-militaristic consumer world is false, not to be trusted or obeyed, and the positive claim that an alternative way in the world is legitimated by and appropriate to the new governance of the God who is back in town.

We should not be too grandiose about the alternative. There are indeed occasional times appropriate to spectacular evangelical assertion. On most days and in most places, however, the talk and the walk of good news become the slow, steady engagement with and practice of God's will for generosity, compassion, and forgiveness in a world organized against those practices. Such practices are undertaken in the conviction that such acts on the spot make an important difference to the condition of the world and on the further conviction that the effect of such testimonial living is cumulative and will prevail, because such practice is rooted in the reality of the Messiah of whom we confess: "Christ has died, Christ is risen, Christ will come again."

God's call is a summons, but a summons away from a world too hard. God offers a genuine alternative to life in a distorted world, an alternative that will produce joy and well-being:

> Come to me, all you that are weary and are carrying heavy burdens, and I will give you rest. Take my yoke upon you, and learn from me; for I am

> gentle and humble in heart, and you will find rest for your souls. For my yoke is easy, and my burden is light. (Matt. 11:28-30)

God's sending is risky, and it is to be celebrated. Lest we congratulate ourselves too much on being sent, here is Jesus' word on the return of the evangelists who report success:

> The seventy returned with joy, saying, "Lord, in your name even the demons submit to us!" He said to them, "I watched Satan fall from heaven like a flash of lightning. See, I have given you authority to tread on snakes and scorpions, and over all the power of the enemy; and nothing will hurt you. Nevertheless, do not rejoice at this, that the spirits submit to you, but rejoice that your names are written in heaven." (Luke 10:17-20)

The outcome of the news is that the ones under discipline have their names written in heaven — utterly safe, utterly loved, and utterly treasured — where moths do not consume and where thieves do not break in to steal. This is a good destiny offered and promised to the ones called and sent.

CHAPTER 16

Evangelism, Evangelization, and Catechesis: Defining Terms and Making the Case for Evangelization

John H. Westerhoff

There are as many definitions of "evangelism" as there are definers. Some of these definitions focus on evangelism's message, some on its intended results, some on the recipients of its message, and some on the methods used to transmit that message. As might be expected, the differences between such definitions can be great.

Sometimes the word "evangelization" is used as a synonym for evangelism. For many, however, the word "evangelization" is unknown, and those who are familiar with it do not agree on its definition.

The word "catechesis" is similar to evangelization. That is, some are unfamiliar with it, and few agree on a definition. Further, the language of evangelization and catechesis is often confused. In light of this, I shall suggest definitions of "evangelism," "evangelization," and "catechesis" and then offer descriptions of their characteristics.

The early church understood its mission to be that of proclaiming the gospel of God's salvation through word and example to those who did not know it or had not accepted it. The objective was to attract persons to the church with its good news concerning God's reign. I call this "evangelism," and it took place in the society where people lived and worked.

Persons who were attracted to the Christian community of faith and its way of life through acts of evangelism were brought to an initial commitment to Christ and incorporated into the life of the Christian community of faith. This process I term "evangelization," and it took place within the life of the church.

Evangelization ended after a fifty-day period known as the "mystagogia," which followed baptism. However, as soon as this process was completed, another intentional, lifelong process of learning and growth, which I call "catechesis," began so that the faith of the newly baptized might be enhanced and enlivened and their Christ-like character more fully formed.

Accordingly, evangelization, along with prescribed rites, may be defined as a formative process of initiation through participation in and the practice of the Christian life of faith. It aims at conversion and the preparation of persons for baptism.

In the case of adults, evangelization precedes catechesis, just as in Jesus' words at the end of Matthew: After first saying, "Go therefore and make disciples of all nations, baptizing them in the name of the Father and of the Son and of the Holy Spirit. . . ," Jesus adds, ". . . teaching them to obey everything that I have commanded you" (Matt. 28:16-20). For children who have been baptized, the process is a bit different. Through catechesis (which has an evangelization dimension) children are led toward making a personal affirmation of faith and of commitment to the Christian way of life (understood by some as confirmation). Nevertheless, following that action, catechesis continues. Thus, catechesis is the intentional, lifelong process by which Christians are made, fashioned, and nurtured. Evangelization is a similar process engaged in by adults to prepare them for both baptism and this lifelong pilgrimage.

Historical Reflections

Christian initiation, characterized by a series of rituals and a process of evangelization to prepare adults for baptism, developed early in the church's history. By the second century it was fully established. However, by the sixth century it was no longer practiced. With the establishment of Christendom in the fourth century, infant baptism, followed by some attempts at catechesis, became normative. As time went on, catechesis in the church was increasingly neglected. It was assumed that the society would nurture Christians. During the sixteenth and seventeenth centuries, the time of the Reformation and the Enlightenment, the language of catechesis diminished among Protestants; and the language of education, with a primary concern for the acquisition of knowledge and skills, evolved. The theological concern became doctrine, believing propositional truths. The ethical concern became moral decision-making. Both were legitimate ends for education, or perhaps for better instruction, beginning with children after their baptism.

Nineteenth-century Roman Catholic missionaries sought a return to earlier expressions of evangelism and evangelization and a new commitment to the Christian initiation of adults. At the Second Vatican Council, "The Constitution on the Sacred Liturgy" established guidelines for revising initiatory practice and the restoration of an adult catechumenate. Now, as we enter what appears to be a post-Christian era, a new interest is apparent among Protestants, Roman Catholics, and Anglicans in evangelism, evangelization, and catechesis.

As this interest mounts, it is important to remember that Christianity has been a part of the fabric of Western society for so long that many, especially mainstream Protestants, have assumed Christians do not need to evangelize. Until the present, few Protestants questioned the survival and growth of Christianity in the United States. Instead, the issue was that of the survival and growth of particular denominations. As a consequence, evangelism was understood by some as church growth through the attraction of baptized Christians, faithful or lapsed, from one denomination to another. Supported by an understanding of the ecumenical movement as a blending together of various traditions, mainline Protestant denominations emphasized similarities rather than differences. The result was a loss of identity and competition for members on the basis of services offered. Somewhat embarrassed by the thought of converting adults, these denominations depended on their people having babies to baptize so as to maintain membership growth. However, their members had fewer children, and deaths soon outnumbered births. Further, insofar as growth in numbers was taken more seriously than growth in faith, many members soon became inactive, giving a false picture of numerical strength. More serious was the fact that the lives of the baptized were not significantly different from the lives of those who had never been baptized. This perhaps explains why so few non-Christians were attracted to these churches.

For what was once the mainstream of Christianity in the United States, there was a familiar pattern to life. When children were born into society, typically they were taken by the family to be baptized or, as it was sometimes called, "christened." Most often it was a private family affair, soon forgotten. Birthdays rather than the baptismal day were celebrated. It was assumed that attendance at a public school provided formation in Christian values, values synonymous with national values. Attendance at Sunday church school, typically spotty, took care of everything else necessary to be raised as Christian. Sometime during early adolescence, there was attendance at classes taught by the clergy — a sort of summary of their theological education — followed by participation in what many understood as a puberty rite, called confirmation. Following that event, youth often acted as if they had graduated from participation in the church's life. Later they would return to be married, have children, and repeat the cycle. Evangelism was at best an uncomfortable word, and evangelization unheard of. To be sure, this is a caricature, but perhaps true enough to make a point.

New Understandings

For many years, the church was divided between those who emphasized infant baptism and those who emphasized adult believers' baptism. Each had its defenders, and each position was defendable. Infant baptism testifies to the truths that the faith of the community comes before our faith; that God's action always comes prior to our human response; that baptism is something we need to grow into; and that faith is a gift, a gift that comes through participation in the sacramental life of the community.

Adult believers' baptism testifies to the truths that baptism, though a sacrament, does not give us something we do not have but makes us aware of something we already have; that God's actions toward us require a moral response and personal acceptance; that our human response needs to be a mature one that is manifested in our lives; and that faith is necessary if we are to benefit from God's actions. Typically, those who defended adult believers' baptism saw no need for evangelization. Evangelism alone was satisfactory before baptism. Education could take place later. Those who defended infant baptism also believed in education after baptism but also tended to neglect evangelism and evangelization.

Increasingly in our day, adult believers' baptism is being accepted as the norm or standard for baptism, and infant baptism is defended as a legitimate exception. In any case, baptism needs to be "lived into" through the renewal of one's baptismal covenant at numerous times in one's life. In the case of infant baptism, a personal renewal of the baptismal covenant entered into for the child by its parents needs to be made. Further, as we become increasingly aware that society does not fully support the Christian life of faith, and that there are an increasing number of unchurched, unbaptized persons, a new emphasis on adult converts and the need for evangelization has emerged.

Since we have now arrived at a point where both adult believers' and infant baptism are affirmed, and owing to our growing awareness that Christendom, as we have known it, has radically changed, new concern for evangelism and the evangelization for those who have never been baptized is on the rise. For those who have been baptized, there is a search for a new understanding of catechesis, confirmation, and baptismal renewal.

As Urban Holmes maintains in his *Turning to Christ,* there is a difference between the church's mission (to restore all people to unity with God and each other in Christ), the strategy for accomplishing that mission (the renewal of the church), and the tactic to accomplish that renewal (evangelization). Through a congregation's evangelization of adults, it can renew its own life and thereby be enabled to be faithful to its mission, which is to attract others to Christ and his church.

Aims of Evangelization and Catechesis

Christianity emerged in history as a gift. God chose to act through the life, death, and resurrection of Jesus Christ to inaugurate God's reign of justice and peace. And God called into being a community that was to be a sign and witness to that good news. It was a community with a mission: to restore all people to unity with God and each other in Christ. This was to be accomplished by attracting persons to the church; here through evangelization, they were to be prepared for baptism and thereby enter upon a new way of life, a lifelong pilgrimage of personal formation and communal reform and renewal through catechesis until God's mission was fulfilled.

Christianity is a way of life. Therefore, from the beginning it has been the responsibility of all baptized Christians to proclaim the gospel in word and example. The life of every Christian is to be under close scrutiny. The truth of the gospel is judged by the world according to the consistency between what the baptized profess and how they live. Faith and works cannot be separated. No dualism between being and doing, between who we are and how we live, is to be permitted.

This way of life is a consequence of faith, best understood as perception. Christian faith is a particular and peculiar way of perceiving life and our lives. It manifests itself in believing and thinking, in trusting and loving, in worshiping and obeying, but fundamentally it is a way of "seeing."

Christian faith manifests itself in a person's or community's character, that is, in one's sense of identity and behavioral dispositions. Early Christians were to have Christ's faith and live Christlike lives (2 Cor. 3:18; Rom. 12:1-2), that is, to share in Christ's character traits. Christian faith also makes possible a particular consciousness or the ability to be aware of God's presence and action in human life and history and to discern the interior movement of the spirits.

Evangelization and catechesis are the means by which persons develop their faith, character, and consciousness. The process of evangelization does not give faith, nor does it produce character. Faith is a gift resulting from God's action within a community of faith and our human response. Character results from our disciplined practice, but not without God's help. Evangelization plays an instrumental role in transmitting faith and influencing character during the period of Christian initiation that leads to baptism.

Evangelization and Catechesis

Evangelization is the participation in and practice of the Christian life of faith, an intentional process within a community of faith that influences the transformation of a person's faith, character, and consciousness, thereby preparing him or her to be baptized and enter upon a lifelong pilgrimage of being fashioned into Christlike persons. Evangelization is the initial stage by which persons are led step by step to a first commitment to the Christian life of faith. In the case of baptized children who cannot make a commitment of their own, there is an evangelizing dimension to catechesis, that lifelong process by which persons are fashioned as Christians.

The Christian initiation of adults, which is a series of rites and stages of preparation for baptism, is the context for evangelization. Through faithful witness to the gospel — evangelism — persons are attracted to the church. They come as inquirers. They tell their stories and listen to others tell theirs. The faithful offer hospitality and tell their stories, explaining the significance of the Christian story and the community formed by that story. During this period, those initially attracted to the Christian community are guided to examine and test their motives in order that they may freely commit themselves to pursue a disciplined participation in the Christian life of faith. They are helped to understand that Christianity is a way of life learned through practice and participation in the life of the church over a lifetime, and that the way to begin is to enter upon a process of evangelization that will prepare them for baptism.

Having expressed a desire to prepare for baptism, the candidates participate in a public liturgical act that includes being signed with the cross and begins a period known as the catechumenate. This initial period of formation includes the following: attendance at Sunday worship, engagement with the Scriptures, the development of a disciplined life of prayer, participation in the congregation's outreach programs, and other practices to be described under catechesis later in this essay. This period will continue for one or more years. To acquire a new way to perceive life and our lives; a new set of allegiances, attitudes, and values; a new identity and behavioral dispositions takes time. Personal readiness, rather than time, is the crucial factor during this period of formation and testing. While the whole community is the teacher, candidates will have sponsors to accompany them and serve as role models for the Christian life of faith.

When the community observes signs that the candidates have adopted a new way of life, they are ready for the rite of election that will make them candidates for baptism. They then enter upon a forty-day Lenten discipline of intense self-examination, fasting, and prayer to prepare themselves spiritually and emotionally for baptism. This is a period of purification and enlightenment, not study. Its aim is to lead the converts to a renunciation of the power of evil and the acceptance of Jesus Christ as Savior. It bids converts to receive the tradition of the faith and commit themselves more fully to the life of faith. It is a time for recollection and readiness. This recollection rehearses their catechumenal experience and reflects upon it so that the catechumens might begin to understand the life of faith and its requirements. This period of election culminates in the rite of initiation, or baptism, symbolizing forgiveness of sins and a new life of grace; chrismation, symbolizing being marked as Christ's own that we might share in his royal priesthood, as well as admission into the community's life in the Holy Spirit; and reception of Eucharistic bread and wine, symbolizing life in God's reign of justice and peace.

Following baptism, the newly baptized enter a final period known as the mystagogia, the great fifty days from Easter to Pentecost. The newly baptized, having experienced the great mysteries of the sacraments, gain a deeper understanding of their meaning. Further, through a series of formal and informal activities, they experience the fullness of corporate life in the church as well as a deeper understanding of daily life and work as their ministry.

Now that the newly baptized have accepted their place in the life of the Christian community of faith they begin the lifelong process of living into their baptism. Once they have came to know who and whose they are and how they are called to live through continuing participation in the life of the church and the practice of the Christian way of life, they become who they already are, namely, persons who have been incorporated into the body of Christ, infused with Christ's character, and empowered to be Christ's presence in the world.

Certain assumptions are foundational to evangelization. For one thing, evangelization is understood as a personal journey that calls for creativity, flexibility, and adaptability. It is not an institutional program that is identical for everyone. It is a person, with a personal story and life history, who is being evangelized. Evangelization, therefore, is a process that needs to be made relevant to each person. For another thing, evangelization is a process that takes place in a community of faith, a community that is continually being renewed and reformed. A community of faith orders and organizes its life around a common story and ritual. It has a common understanding of authority that informs its life of faith. It has a common purpose beyond its own life and survival. And it has a common life that is more like a covenanted family than a contractual institution. Further, evangelization assumes that its primary concerns are faith understood as perception, character understood as identity and behavioral disposition, and consciousness understood as subjective awareness. Last, evangelization assumes that conversion is a process and not an event, which involves, over a period of time, transformations in a person's faith, character, and consciousness, in a person's loyalties, convictions, and commitments. Evangelization intends to aid persons to repent, that is, to change the way they see things and therefore change the direction of their lives.

Catechesis

The third-century theologian Tertullian wrote, "Christians are made, not born" (*Apol.* xviii). Christian initiation is a process through which one goes while being transformed into a new creation and fashioned into the likeness of Christ. Christian initiation is only the beginning; it launches one on a lifelong journey of becoming the being one is made by baptism.

This process of fashioning was originally called catechesis, which means literally "to echo." When used by the early church, it implied echoing the Word, and the Word was a person, Jesus. Catechesis was the process directed at the formation of Christlike people: In English, it was called christening. Regretfully, over time, christening became associated solely with the ritual of baptism and catechesis with the memorization and repetition of words.

It has become clear in our day, however, that the making of Christlike persons is a lifelong process. In the case of adult converts, an intense process is also needed to prepare them for Christian initiation. I have called this process evangelization. As a process, it is similar to catechesis.

Catechesis comprises three deliberate (intentional), systemic (interrelated), and sustained (lifelong) processes, which I have named formation, education, and instruction. Formation is participation in and the practice of the Christian life of faith. It is both a transforming, or converting, and a conforming, or nurturing, process aimed at fashioning the faith, character, and consciousness of persons and communities.

Education is critical reflection on our lives of faith in the light of the gospel. It is a reforming process that aims at producing ever more faithful lives and communities. It implies growth and change.

Instruction is the acquisition of knowledge, such as the contents of Scripture, and skills, such as the ability to interpret Scripture. It is an informing process that provides persons with the knowledge and skills necessary to engage in critical reflection or education.

These processes are interdependent, and all are necessary; however, it is formation that is foundational to the fashioning of Christlike persons. Both education and instruction are required for faithful formation; instruction alone is inadequate.

Ritual Participation: Rituals are repetitive, symbolic actions of word and deed that manifest and express the community's sacred narrative. Participation in these actions, or rites, is the single most important factor in shaping one's faith, character, and consciousness. It is for this reason that, in the history of the church, whenever the church believed that it was not being as faithful as it should, it engaged in liturgical reform. At the heart of evangelization is faithful participation in rites that are true to the gospel.

Environment: We shape our space and what we see, hear, taste, smell, or touch within it. This space, in turn, influences our lives and how we behave. For example, arrangement of space can encourage communal or individualistic understandings of life. Pictures of women or men engaged in particular activities establish perceptions of appropriate behavior for each. Liturgical space that separates a nave for the laity and a sanctuary for clerical use may encourage a sacred-secular dualism. Proper evangelization will consider what catechumens see, touch, taste, feel, and smell in the church.

Ordering of Time: Our calendars and how we order a day, a week, and a year influence our understanding and behavior. What we remember and celebrate does the same. It is important that the church's story order our lives if that story is to be manifested in our living. If it is not, some other narrative will be. The period of evangelization needs to cover at least one yearly liturgical cycle so that the whole story can be experienced.

Organization of Life: How we are encouraged and supported to spend our time, talents, and treasures influences us greatly. It is important that we live with the realization that all we have belongs to God, that we have a right to keep very little for ourselves, and that we are obliged to use all we have in God's service for the good of all people. During evangelization, persons need to be encouraged to tithe, for the mission of the church and its ministries, their time, talents, and money.

Human Interaction: How we treat one another and how we expect persons to behave shapes our behavior. For example, do we respect the dignity of every human being, do we love others the way God loves them, and do we offer others what they need rather than what they deserve? We learn how to behave by experiencing how others behave toward us. Faithful evangelization makes certain that catechumens observe and experience the Christian life of faith.

Role Models: There are always persons whom the community establishes as role models whose lives are to be imitated. Some are living persons, such as those the community establishes as teachers. Others, such as the saints, are dead, and their lives we remember and celebrate. Evangelization requires that the church provide sponsors whose lives the catechumens can imitate.

Disciplines: Communities encourage persons to practice particular behavior, such as the making and keeping of promises, simplicity of lifestyle, caring for the natural world, regular daily prayer, and meditation on Scripture. During the period of evangelization, catechumens are to be encouraged to develop, by practicing Christlike virtues, disciplines that will shape their characters.

Language: How we talk influences how we behave. For example, when possessiveness dominates the way we speak, then we begin to believe that we can and ought to have things. How we name good and evil influences how we live. Inclusiveness of language influences how we treat each other. Thoughtful evangelization requires that we reflect on how we speak in the church so that what we say and what we do correspond to each other and are manifestations of the Christian life of faith.

Conclusions

To be baptized is to become *a* Christian; to live into that baptism is to become Christian, that is, to live a Christlike life of faith. Evangelization is the process by which a person prepares to become a Christian, and catechesis is the process by which a person shows that he or she is Christian.

If we engage in evangelization, in the Christian initiation of adults, we will need to take seriously not only evangelism — to attract persons to the Christian faith and the church — but also evangelization, to prepare them adequately for baptism.

Nevertheless, I suspect there will be obstacles to accepting evangelization that will need to be addressed. Some will say it is too impractical for our day. Some will resist it because they are unfamiliar with it and because it involves change. Others will not be comfortable with the language of formation and will insist that instruction, which is more familiar, is all that is needed. There will also be those who believe that evangelization is too difficult and too demanding to be popular. Regardless, if the church is to be faithful, it must take evangelization and catechesis seriously, for two facts cannot be doubted: (1) After almost two thousand years of proclaiming the gospel, there are still millions of people who have not accepted the gospel; and (2) after baptizing persons for the same length of time, the lives of those baptized are rarely significantly different from the lives of the unbaptized. Perhaps fact two helps to explain fact one.

Suggested Reading

William Abraham, *The Logic of Evangelism* (Grand Rapids: Eerdmans, 1989).

Richard Armstrong, *The Pastor as Evangelist* (Philadelphia: Westminster, 1984).

A. Theodore Eastman, *The Baptizing Community* (New York: Seabury, 1982).

Michael Green, *Evangelism in the Early Church* (Grand Rapids: Eerdmans, 1989).

Johannes Hofinger, S.J., *Evangelization and Catechesis* (New York: Paulist, 1976).

Urban Holmes, *Turning to Christ* (New York: Seabury, 1981).

Mark Searle, *Christening* (Collegeville, Minn.: The Liturgical Press, 1980).

Robert Webber, *Celebrating Our Faith* (San Francisco: Harper & Row, 1986).

John Westerhoff and Carolyn Hughes, *Living Into Our Baptism* (Wichita: St. Mark's Press, 1992).

CHAPTER 17

The Integral Nature of Worship and Evangelism

Paul W. Chilcote

When my family and I first arrived in Mutare, Zimbabwe, in August 1992, the entire southern region of Africa was experiencing one of the worst droughts of the century. In spite of the fact that our formal work was at Africa University and the Old Mutare Centre, Janet and I both felt called to do something to help the many hungry people that surrounded us. It did not take us long to discover that widows and children were starving within ten miles of the university. Through our contacts with the church we met Rev. Elisha Kabungaidze, pastor of the Mundenda Circuit, with responsibility for some seven churches in one of the hard-hit areas. With the help of Elisha and a devoted circle of lay leaders within his congregations, we began to identify the "poorest of the poor" within the bounds of his wide-ranging parish. Some were members of his churches; most were not. We traveled throughout the area with Elisha, delivering food and other items basic to life. It was a humbling experience, but through it all I rejoiced in the holistic vision of evangelism and its integral connection with worship, embodied in this hardworking servant of God.

Each morning of worship/evangelism/mission began with our group standing together in a circle. We greeted one another with the name of Christ. We prayed. One of our members read the Word for the day. We sang. We prayed some more, and then we set out. We had the privilege of walking from hut to hut with Elisha and his parishioners, repeating the same basic sign-act of love with him. Every day was truly sacramental. As we approached a homestead, Elisha would call out the names of the family in his deep, resonant voice and exchange the traditional greetings. "Marara ere?" "Did you sleep well through the night?" "Tarara marara o." "Yes. I slept well if you slept well." Elisha would explain to the families why we had come, for they were usually unaware of our plans to visit. He would tell them we knew that they had no food and that the love of Jesus had moved us to do whatever we could to help them in their need. Often the women would fall to the ground and weep, and then spring to their feet, dancing and singing the praises of God. The Shona of Zimbabwe have a saying: "If you can talk, you can sing. If you can walk, you can dance." And we had many opportunities to witness and to practice both. We always prayed together, and we almost always sang a song as we departed. It was a joyful song, a song of hope within the midst of suffering. More often than not it was *Makanaka Mambo Jesu, makanaka Mambo Jesu;* "Oh how good is our great chief, Jesus."

Elisha lived out a model of evangelism — a way of being in mission in the world — that struck me very deeply. His participation in God's mission reflects with integrity, I believe, what Albert Outler once described as the trio of dominical imperatives regarding evangelism, namely, heralding, martyrdom, and servanthood.[1] Before Elisha did anything, he acknowledged God's presence and adored the Triune One. Wherever he went, he announced the gospel, the good news. He boldly proclaimed the love of God for all people and pointed to the Creator, Savior, and Sustainer he had come to know through Jesus Christ. He provided witness in the sense of living out his life in solidarity with God's people. He lived the life of a servant, a life characterized by the ungrudging outpouring of himself. When I asked him on one occasion where he had learned this winsome way of life, he responded by saying, "I think it is simply in my Methodist blood."

Far from a partisan cry (hardly something I intend here), I think Elisha was directing us to an essential principle, for surely, as the Wesleys argued repeatedly, their effort was simply to rediscover "primitive Christianity." While never using the language of "evangelism," their primary project was to emulate a pattern of life in community that reflected the presence of a living Lord and a liberating/healing Spirit.[2] Implicit in my narration of life in the shadow of Elisha is the integral nature of worship and evangelism in the community of faith. I don't know if Elisha could have distinguished worship from evangelism in any sophisticated or nuanced manner. In fact, I would submit to you that the fullest possible integration of doxology and disciple-making was the key to his contagious faith. He lived what many are beginning to rediscover in post-Christian Western cultures at this very time. In the past decade or so, a growing number of church leaders and scholars have begun to address the

1. Albert Outler, *Evangelism in the Wesleyan Spirit* (Nashville: Tidings, 1971), pp. 99-104.

2. I first narrated this account at a conference on "Evangelization, the Heart of Mission: A Wesleyan Imperative," sponsored by the General Board of Global Ministries of The United Methodist Church and its Mission Evangelism Committee, January 1995.

connection between evangelism and worship, that perennial question in all ages of renewal in the life of the church.[3] In such times as these, spiritual fruit has always been abundant.

In relation to these monumental questions, therefore, my proposal is rather modest. I simply desire to explore the fundamental relationship between worship and evangelism, using the hymns and writings of Charles Wesley (the neglected brother of the founder of Methodism) as a vehicle for discovery.

I.

The terms "worship" and "evangelism" suffer from a common malady. They both defy simple definition. Both can be defined so narrowly that the profound nature of their significance is lost; they can be defined so broadly that they come to mean nothing. In common discourse within the life of the church today, "worship" can mean anything from the entirety of the Christian life to a set of praise music in the context of the Christian assembly. Likewise, "evangelism" can range in meaning from the specific act of preaching the gospel to a group of unchurched homeless men in an inner-city soup kitchen to the entirety of the Christian faith. Despite the importance of precision, I am actually quite happy, at this point, to leave us in a state of "happy ambiguity" with regard to definition, because a part of this exercise is to discern the interface of these practices in the life of the church. Defining these terms in too narrow a fashion may blind us to their broad-ranging application; applying only broad strokes may obliterate the fascinating detail that actually constitutes real life. While it will be important for me to establish some basic parameters shortly — which I hope to do more descriptively than prescriptively — I think we do well to start where Charles Wesley would have begun, namely, in Scripture.

There are many biblical texts that leap immediately to mind as we contemplate the meaning of worship or the meaning of evangelism, but one text

3. This conversation actually goes much farther back within the *oecumene* of the church, to the Second Vatican Council. But for the discussions within Protestant circles, and reflective of much more recent dialogue, consult Sally Morgenthaler, *Worship Evangelism* (Grand Rapids: Zondervan, 1995); Robert Webber, *Worship Is a Verb* (Waco: Word, 1985); Patrick Kiefert, *Welcoming the Stranger: A Public Theology of Worship and Evangelism* (Minneapolis: Fortress, 1992); Daniel Benedict and Craig Miller, *Contemporary Worship for the 21st Century: Worship or Evangelism?* (Nashville: Discipleship Resources, 1995); Leander Keck, *The Church Confident* (Nashville: Abingdon, 1993); Andy Langford and Sally Overby Langford, *Worship and Evangelism* (Nashville: Discipleship Resources, 1989).

jumps out at me as I reflect upon the integral dynamic that links the two: Acts 2:46-47.

> Day by day, as they spent much time together in the temple, they broke bread at home and ate their food with glad and generous hearts, praising God and having the goodwill of all the people. And day by day the Lord added to their number those who were being saved.

However brief this description might be, it is a fairly definitive portrait of life in Christ — a life that directly links worship and evangelism. True spiritual worship, as St. Paul made so abundantly clear in Romans 12, has to do, in fact, with every aspect of life. There can be no separation of worship or liturgy from the totality of life as we really know it. Worship, in this broad sense then, is the grateful surrender of all we are and all we have, a "living sacrifice" of praise and thanksgiving to the God of love who has created all things and bears witness with our spirits that we are the children of God. It is living in and for God and God's way in human history in all things. The ministry of evangelism in this earliest Christian community, the consequence of which was "the Lord adding to their number day by day," consisted of spending time in the communal worship and praise of God, sharing together the sacred gift of food, and offering kindness and hospitality to others. Just a few verses earlier in this chapter, of course, Luke provides a little more detail. "They devoted themselves to the apostles' teaching and fellowship, to the breaking of bread and the prayers" (Acts 2:42). There was a certain specificity with regard to the foundation of this evangelistic community in Word and Sacrament. There was a peculiar nature to the worship of God that they practiced. But all of this life together — including the sharing of personal possessions so that no one lacked the basic necessities of life — was aimed at living in and manifesting the reign of God.

It is a cliché now to describe worship, and more precisely liturgy, as "the work of the people" and to think of evangelism in similar fashion, not as the work of a single individual, but of "the whole people of God." The purpose of this corporate service — this shared labor of love — is to form us in praise and engage us in God's mission. Charles Wesley seems to have learned early in life that worship/evangelism is *paideia* — life-shaping instruction or formation through action. For the earliest Christians — like those we see in the Acts of the Apostles — this classical Greek understanding of discipline must have entailed all those things that are done in the community of faith that shape the whole person in her or his journey toward maturity in Christ. In this process, however, nothing was more critical than the words and actions of the liturgical assembly that spilled over naturally into lifestyles of good news in the world. True worship springs from the heart, but worship (defined here in the more narrow sense as the liturgy) also has the potential to shape Christlike people who become evangel-bearers for others.

The writer to the Hebrews uses the language of *paideia* to describe a vision of the Christian life: "We had human parents to discipline us, and we respected them . . . But [God] disciplines us for our good, in order that we may share his holiness" (Heb. 12:9-10). The concept of a discipline that frees the human spirit and leads the emancipated child of God into a life characterized by holiness of heart and life clearly inspired the Wesleys. Charles bears witness to the potency of the vision:

Loose me from the chains of sense,
 Set me from the body free;
Draw with stronger influence
 My unfettered soul to thee!
In me, Lord, thyself reveal,
 Fill me with a sweet surprise;
Let me thee when waking feel,
 Let me in thine image rise.

Let me of thy life partake,
 Thy own holiness impart;
O that I might sweetly wake
 With my Saviour in my heart!
O that I might know thee mine!
 O that I might thee receive!
Only live the life divine!
 Only to thy glory live![4]

Authentic evangelism both reflects and creates an "O that I might . . ." modus operandi in life and a desire to praise God in all things. So orthodoxy — the right praise of God — involves a joyful obedience and a daring surrender. It is not too much to say that the evangelistic ministry of the community of faith and the worship of the assembly — and specifically the liturgy — shape us in such a way that we believe in God (faith), desire nothing but God (love), and glorify God by offering our lives fully to Christ (holiness).

4. *The Works of John Wesley,* vol. 7: *A Collection of Hymns for the Use of the People Called Methodists,* ed. Franz Hildebrandt and Oliver Beckerlegge (Oxford: Clarendon, 1983), p. 428 (Hymn 278.4, 5) (hereinafter *Hymns* 7).

St. Paul places this concept at the center of his admonition to Christian parents in Ephesians 6:4, where he commands them to bring up their children "in the discipline and instruction of the Lord." Charles picks up this theme in one of his "family hymns" and refers to this process — in a profoundly evangelistic turn of phrase — as a means to "draw their souls to God."[5] In a hymn written for the opening of the Methodist School in Kingwood he expands the image:

Come, Father, Son, and Holy Ghost,
   To whom we for our children cry!
The good desired and wanted most
   Out of thy richest grace supply —
The sacred discipline be given
To train and bring them up for heaven.

Answer on them the end of all
   Our cares, and pains, and studies here;
On them, recovered from their fall,
   Stamped with the humble character,
Raised by the nurture of the Lord,
To all their paradise restored.[6]

The more famous fifth stanza of the hymn articulates the holistic nature of this integrative, formational process:

Unite the pair so long disjoined,
   Knowledge and vital piety:
Learning and holiness combined,
   And truth and love, let all men see
In those whom up to thee we give,
Thine, wholly thine, to die and live.

My contention here is quite simple. I believe that the Wesleys viewed the liturgy of the church — doxological evangelism, if you will — as the primary matrix in which this nurture raised and restored the children of God, both those inside, and potentially those outside the household of faith. Through Word and Sacrament, God sets us on our journey of faith, offers us spiritual nourishment, and provides the necessary guidance for us to find our way

5. *Works* 7:637 (Hymn 456.8).
6. *Works* 7:643 (Hymn 461.1, 2).

home, especially when we require the perennial reminder that home is wherever God's reign is realized in the life of the world.

II.

Another biblical text, I believe, affords a provisional lens through which to explore the integral nature of evangelism and worship.[7] In an effort to flesh out the foundational concepts of worship/evangelism as doxology and discipline I want to import a motif that is not without some dangers, but I find it helpful in exegeting the Wesleyan tradition nonetheless. I refer to the so-called "Isaiah motif" drawn from the call of the prophet in Isaiah 6:1-8, a pattern at one time fashionable for ordering the various acts of Christian worship and also explicating the evangelistic call to mission. A reminder of the text might prove helpful:

> In the year that King Uzziah died, I saw the LORD sitting on a throne, high and lofty; and the hem of his robe filled the temple. Seraphs were in attendance above him; each had six wings: with two they covered their faces, and with two they covered their feet, and with two they flew. And one called to another and said:
>
> "Holy, holy, holy is the LORD of hosts:
> the whole earth is full of his glory."
>
> The pivots on the thresholds shook at the voices of those who called, and the house filled with smoke. And I said: "Woe is me! I am lost, for I am a man of unclean lips, and I live among a people of unclean lips; yet my eyes have seen the King, the LORD of hosts!" Then one of the seraphs flew to me, holding a live coal that had been taken from the altar with a pair of tongs. The seraph touched my mouth with it and said: "Now that this has touched your lips, your guilt has departed and your sin is blotted out." Then I heard the voice of the LORD saying, "Whom shall I send, and who will go for us?" And I said, "Here am I; send me!"

The paradigm embedded in this narrative involves, at least, a fivefold progression:

7. The analysis of Isa. 6:2-8 which follows relies heavily upon my presidential address to The Charles Wesley Society, "Preliminary Explorations of Charles Wesley and Worship," at Point Loma Nazarene University, October 2004, to be published in *The Proceedings of The Charles Wesley Society.*

1) Adoration: "Holy, holy, holy is the LORD of hosts," moves the worshiper to
2) Confession: "Woe is me!" to
3) Forgiveness: "your guilt has departed and your sin is blotted out," and through
4) Proclamation: "Then I heard the voice of the LORD saying," to final
5) Dedication: "Here am I; send me!"

While there is an abiding truth in this sequence of devotion, it is dangerous to transpose it mechanically either into worship or the practice of evangelism.[8] It is always important to remember that the inbreaking Word gives and sustains life. At times God acts unpredictably. There is also a potential danger, I want to admit, in mechanically imposing this structure upon the Wesleys. But while it is artificial to choreograph God's presence and movement or to plot these serially in a service of worship or in a strategy of evangelism, much less to squeeze Wesley into this mold, there is a certain "evangelical" logic in the Isaiah motif that resonates with a Wesleyan understanding of the divine/human encounter. I think this is well worth exploring. So permit me to examine briefly these specific dimensions of Isaiah's theophany.

Adoration

The Isaiah narrative opens with an overwhelming sense of awe, majesty, and wonder. Our first response to God is acknowledgment of whom it is we worship.[9] The good news about God only becomes intelligible in this posture. Virtually every day of Charles Wesley's life began with Morning Prayer, including the words of the ancient prayer of praise, the *Te Deum:*

> We praise thee, O God: we acknowledge thee to be the Lord. All the earth doth worship thee, the Father everlasting. To thee all Angels cry aloud: the Heavens, and all the powers therein. To thee Cherubim and Seraphim continually do cry, Holy, holy, holy, Lord God of Sabaoth; Heaven and Earth are full of the Majesty of thy Glory.

8. See, in particular, the critique of the threefold pattern of vision, contrition, and commission drawn from the Isaiah text in Paul W. Hoon, *The Integrity of Worship* (Nashville: Abingdon, 1971), pp. 51, 287.

9. See Robert E. Cushman, "Worship As Acknowledgment," in *Faith Seeking Understanding: Essays Theological and Critical* (Durham, N.C.: Duke University Press, 1981), pp. 181-97.

In the 1780 *Collection of Hymns for the Use of the People called Methodists,* Wesley alludes to the Isaian *Sanctus* in at least four hymns:

Meet and right it is to sing,
  In every time and place,
Glory to our heavenly King,
  The God of truth and grace.
Join we then with sweet accord,
  All in one thanksgiving join:
Holy, holy, holy, Lord,
  Eternal praise be thine![10]

Selections drawn from his earlier collection of *Hymns on the Trinity* emphasize the awe with which one should approach God and the glory of God's tremendous and mysterious majesty:

Holy, holy, holy Lord,
God the Father and the Word,
God the Comforter, receive
Blessing more than we can give!

Thee while dust and ashes sings,
Angels shrink within their wings;
Prostrate Seraphim above
Breathe unutterable love.

Fain with them our souls would vie,
Sink as low, and mount as high;
Fall, o'erwhelmed with love, or soar,
Shout, or silently adore!

"All honor and glory to Jesus alone!" Charles cries, as he stands in beatific rapture *coram Deo* — before a "universe filled with the glory of God."[11] It is the radiance of God's nature, revealed most fully in the dual graces of creation and redemption, that overtakes the awestruck child:

Th'o'erwhelming power of saving grace,
The sight that veils the seraph's face,

10. *Works* 7:346 (Hymn 212.1). Note the explicit reference to the Communion Service of the *Book of Common Prayer* in the opening line.

11. *Works* 7:342, 344, the closing lines of Hymn 210.1 and 7.

The speechless awe that dares not move,
And all the silent heaven of love![12]

Little wonder that one of the most memorable lines in all of Charles Wesley's verses concludes his great hymn to love: "Lost in wonder, love, and praise." Is this not where true worship, where faithful evangelism, must always begin; in this posture?

Repentance and Forgiveness

The prophet can only respond: "Woe is me! I am lost, for I am a man of unclean lips, and I live among a people of unclean lips!" When we contemplate our own lives in relation to this God — or compare them with the life of Jesus — we are overwhelmed, as well, by our inadequacy, our brokenness, our fallen condition. In the Wesleyan tradition, repentance is a paramount concern because it strikes at the very heart of salvation. Confession and forgiveness are central to the Christian view of what it is we need to be saved *from* and what it is we need to be saved *into.* For Charles, no less than for his brother, salvation is both legal and therapeutic; it is related both to Christ's redemptive work *for* us and the Spirit's transforming work *in* us; it revolves around freedom from sin and freedom to love. Repentance is like the threshold of a door that opens the way to our spiritual healing. It is like the first step in a journey that leads us home.

Nowhere in Scripture is repentance and forgiveness more poignantly expressed than in Jesus' parable of the lost child in Luke 15. Stripped of dignity, value, and identity, the critical turning point for the estranged son in the story comes with these important words, "But when he came to himself . . ." Both John and Charles define repentance as "true self-understanding." The prodigal "came to himself." In the depth of his despair, he remembered who he was and to whom he belonged. Charles plays with this image in his sermon on Ephesians 5:14. As he turns directly to the text itself, he admonishes:

> Wherefore, "Awake thou that sleepest, and arise from the dead." God calleth thee by my mouth; and bids thee know thyself, thou fallen spirit, thy true state and only concern below: "what meanest thou, O sleeper? Arise! Call upon thy god . . . that thou perish not."[13]

12. *Works* 7:92 (Hymn 9.10).

13. Kenneth G. C. Newport, ed., *The Sermons of Charles Wesley* (Oxford: Oxford University Press, 2001), p. 216 (hereinafter *Sermons*). Cf. John Wesley's sermon on "The Way to the

For Charles, repentance signifies a true self-knowledge that leads to contrition and total reliance upon God's pardoning mercy in Christ.

He employs this image in a hymn celebrating God's universal grace as it is made manifest in the context of the worshiping community of God's people:

Sinners, obey the gospel word!
Haste to the supper of my Lord;
Be wise to know your gracious day!
All things are ready; come away!

Ready the Father is to own
And kiss his late-returning son;
Ready your loving Saviour stands,
And spreads for you his bleeding hands.

The Father, Son, and Holy Ghost
Are ready with their shining host;
All heaven is ready to resound:
"The dead's alive! The lost is found."[14]

In the successive stanzas Charles layers the imagery of spiritual emotion elicited from the struggle to know God and to entrust one's life to God: pardon, favor, peace; the seeing eye, the feeling sense, the mystic joys; godly grief, pleasing smart; meltings, tears, sighs; guiltless shame, sweet distress, unutterable tenderness; genuine meek humility, wonder.

A full paragraph from another of Charles Wesley's sermons is well worth quoting in its entirety at this point. It is taken from his sermon on 1 John 3:14, which Charles preached at least twenty-one times during 1738 and 1739, just at the outset of the revival and as a consequence of the brothers' shared reawakening to living faith. The sermon itself is a depiction of the three states of humanity, describing those who do not know and do not seek God, those who do not know but seek God, and those who know God. It is a compelling appeal to come to one's self so as to know God fully. Charles pleads:

Kingdom," II.1: "This is the way: walk ye in it. And first, repent, that is, know yourselves. This is the first repentance, previous to faith, even conviction, or self-knowledge. Awake, then, thou that sleepest. Know thyself to be a sinner, and what manner of sinner thou art. Know that corruption of thy inmost nature, whereby thou art very far gone from original righteousness . . ." (*The Works of John Wesley,* vol. 1: *Sermons I,* ed. Albert C. Outler [Nashville: Abingdon, 1984], p. 225).

14. *Works* 7:90 (Hymn 9.1, 2, 5).

"Therefore also now, saith the Lord, turn ye even to me with all your heart, and with fasting and with weeping, and with mourning. And rend your hearts and not your garments, and turn unto the Lord your God; for he is gracious and merciful, slow to anger and of great kindness, and repenteth him of the evil." Oh that this infinite goodness of God might lead you to repentance! Oh that any one of you would even now arise and go to his Father and say unto him, "Father, I have sinned against heaven and before thee, and am no more worthy to be called thy son!" He sees you now, while you are a great way off, and has compassion, and only awaits your turning towards him, that he may run and fall on your neck and kiss you. Then will he say, "Bring forth the best robe (even the robe of Christ's righteousness) and put it upon him, for this my son was dead and is alive again; he was lost and is found."[15]

Charles Wesley understood that worship, in all of its various dimensions, but particularly in the liturgy of the people of God, has the power to bring us into an awareness of the Holy. He also understood, it would seem, with Henri Nouwen, that forgiveness is the name of love in a wounded world. Acknowledgment and confession bring healing. Forgiveness liberates people from enslavement to sin through the power of God's love in Jesus Christ. Liturgy offers the gift of this divine forgiveness as God comes to us in Christ with "healing in his wings."[16] Wesley realized that reconciliation and restoration are only possible through the intervention of God's grace. That grace is offered, first and foremost, he believed, in the context of a worshiping community that manifests the hospitality of God and proclaims boldly to all:

His bleeding heart shall make *you* room,
   His open side shall take *you* in.
He calls you now, invites *you* home —
Come, O my guilty brethren, come![17]

Proclamation

"Then I heard the voice of the Lord, saying . . ." Charles Wesley celebrated the presence of the Word of God and trusted in its power. It is not too much to

15. *Sermons,* p. 142.

16. For Charles's multiple references to this Mal. 4:2 image, see *Works* 7:157, 252, 270, 385, 420, 530, 608, 611, and 630, in addition to "Hark, the Herald Angels Sing."

17. *Works* 7:117 (Hymn 29.6.3-6). Emphasis added.

claim that the Wesleyan revival was nothing other than a rediscovery of the sacred Christian Scriptures. "The Bible, the whole Bible, nothing but the Bible —," one Wesleyan scholar observed, "this is the theme of John Wesley's preaching and the glory of Charles's hymns."[18] It is not without value to remember that the most critical works related to Wesleyan doctrine — John's *Standard Sermons* and *Notes on the New Testament* and Charles' *Hymns* (particularly the 1780 *Collection*) — all revolve primarily around the community of God's people in worship. The proclamation of God's Word in corporate worship and the rediscovery of the "living Word" among the early Methodist people was the life force of the movement. The essential content of Charles Wesley's preaching was the inclusive love of God revealed to us in Jesus Christ. Nowhere in the Wesleyan corpus is the living encounter with this good news summarized more poignantly than in the familiar lines of his great hymn, "Wrestling Jacob":

> 'Tis Love! 'Tis Love! Thou diedst for me;
> I hear thy whisper in my heart.
> The morning breaks, the shadows flee,
> Pure Universal Love thou art:
> To me, to all, thy bowels move —
> Thy nature, and thy name, is LOVE.[19]

This inclusive, unconditional love is made known to us through the Word and the Spirit. For Wesley, the Word (Jesus Christ and the story of God's love in Scripture) is distinct from, but can never be separated from the Spirit of God. Three hymns that Charles intended for use "Before reading the Scriptures" (Hymns 85-87 from Section III, *Praying for a Blessing* in the 1780 *Collection*) and one of his most noteworthy hymns of petition that precedes them (Hymn 83, "Spirit of faith, come down") demonstrate this essential connection. He identifies the Holy Spirit as the "key" to the sacred book, the active force that opens to us the treasure of God's message of grace and love: "Come, Holy Ghost," he implores, "Unlock the truth, thyself the key, / Unseal the sacred book."[20] "Now the revealing Spirit send," he prays, "And give us ears to hear."[21] Only the Spirit is able to "Reveal the things of God" by removing the barrier to our spiritual sight.

18. *Works* 7:3.
19. *Works* 7:251 (Hymn 136.7).
20. *Works* 7:185 (Hymn 85.2.1, 3-4).
21. *Works* 7:186 (Hymn 86.3.3-4).

No man can truly say
  That Jesus is the Lord
Unless thou take the veil away,
  And breathe the living word.[22]

Or again:

While in thy Word we search for thee
  (We search with trembling awe!)
Open our eyes, and let us see
  The wonders of thy law.[23]

"Come, Holy Ghost, *our* hearts inspire," pleads Wesley, "for you are the 'Source of the old prophetic fire'."[24] His concern throughout is for a dynamic, relational, vibrant encounter with God through the Spirit, who can

  Inspire the living faith
  (Which whosoe'er receives,
The witness in himself he hath,
  And consciously believes),
  The faith that conquers all,
  And doth the mountain move,
And saves whoe'er on Jesus call,
  And perfects them in love.[25]

Dedication

On the most basic level, all worship is response to God's prevenient action, and response is the goal of all evangelistic practice. In answer to the Lord's question, "Whom shall I send, and who will go for us?" Isaiah responds by saying, "Here am I; send me!" In Charles' vision of the worshiping community, and certainly in the evangelistic practice of the early Methodist communities, God commissions the faithful as ambassadors of Christ and graciously enables each disciple to reaffirm his or her true vocation. Charles' hymns reflect a myriad of potential responses to God's call, both individual and corporate. While each deserves full attention in its own right, I will simply hint at

22. *Works* 7:182-3 (Hymn 83:1.1; 2.1-4).
23. *Works* 7:186 (Hymn 86.2).
24. *Works* 7:185 (Hymn 85.1.1, 3). Emphasis added.
25. *Works* 7:183 (Hymn 83.4).

two interrelated aspects of dedicatory response in Wesley, namely, mission and Eucharist. The former aspect, related to Wesley's missiological ecclesiology, is, most likely, immediately obvious to most; the latter, reflecting the absolute centrality of Charles' sacramental vision of life, affords, I believe, some of Wesley's most important insights and contributions to contemporary conversations about worship and evangelism.

The Imperative of Mission. Charles' hymns frequently reflect an understanding of the Christian life in which the most appropriate response to God's transforming grace is Christian outreach to the world and participation in God's mission to restore justice, peace, and love to all.[26] In one of Wesley's greatest missionary hymns, as S T Kimbrough has observed,

> there is an intermingling of praise and mission, for to follow means faithful service. How does one *know* and *feel* sins forgiven, *anticipate* heaven on earth and *own* that love, even in this world, is heaven? Through service to God and others — *by breaking out of the world of self and reaching out to others!*[27]

In Charles Wesley's vision of the church — and particularly the authentic community of faith in continuous praise of God — mission and evangelism flow directly out of our encounter with God's Word in worship. Evangelism, like worship, as we have seen, is an essential activity of the whole people of God. In imitation of Christ, and through our encounter with the living Word, we learn to woo others into the loving embrace of God and then help them to see that their mission in life, in partnership with Christ, is to be the signposts of God's reign in this world.

In his hymn, "For a preacher of the gospel," Charles Wesley reminds us of this transforming, evangelistic call of God upon our lives:

> I would the precious time redeem,
>   And longer live for this alone,
> To spend and to be spent for them
>   Who have not yet my Savior known;

26. See, in particular, the analysis of "Glory to God, and praise and love" in S T Kimbrough, Jr., *A Heart to Praise My God* (Nashville: Abingdon, 1986), pp. 17-27, where he discusses response in terms of "Outreach to the Marginalized," "Universal Outreach to All," and "Outreach to Each Individual" and Tore Meistad, who provides similar insight into the hymn in "The Missiology of Charles Wesley and Its Links to the Eastern Church," in *Orthodox and Wesleyan Spirituality,* ed. S T Kimbrough, Jr. (Crestwood, N.Y.: St. Vladimir's Seminary Press, 2002), pp. 214-18.

27. Kimbrough, *A Heart to Praise,* p. 23.

Fully on these my mission prove,
And only breathe to breathe thy love.

My talents, gifts, and graces, Lord,
Into thy blessed hands receive;
And let me live to preach thy word;
And let me to thy glory live:
My every sacred moment spend
In publishing the sinner's friend.

Enlarge, inflame, and fill my heart
With boundless charity divine!
So shall I all my strength exert,
And love them with a zeal like thine;
And lead them to thy open side,
The sheep, for whom their Shepherd died.[28]

The Imperative of Eucharist. The connection between evangelism and Eucharist is extremely intimate for Wesley, and can be discerned most clearly, I believe, in his concept of Eucharistic sacrifice. In Charles' sermon on Acts 20:7 (more properly what might be described as an introductory "treatise" to a larger, unfinished work on the sacrament) we encounter a concept of sacrifice consonant with the view he espouses in his *Hymns on the Lord's Supper* devoted to this theme. Charles views the sacrament as a "re-presentation" of the sacrifice of Christ.[29] As J. Ernest Rattenbury has demonstrated, his stress is persistently on the twofold oblation of the church in the sacrament; the body of Christ offered is not merely a sacred symbol of Christ's "once-for-all" act of redemption, but is also the living sacrifice of the people of God.[30]

The sacrificial character of the Christian life, in which the worshiper participates repeatedly at the table of the Lord, and its relationship to the sacrifice of Christ is clarified in Charles' hymns. In this regard, he follows the language of Daniel Brevint's *The Christian Sacrament and Sacrifice* very closely; namely, "The main intention of Christ herein was not the bare *remembrance* of His Passion; but over and above, to invite us to His Sacrifice":[31]

28. *Works* 7:597 (Hymn 421.3-5).

29. *Sermons,* pp. 277-86. Cf. John C. Bowmer, *The Sacrament of the Lord's Supper in Early Methodism* (London: Epworth, 1951), pp. 223-32.

30. See J. Ernest Rattenbury, *The Eucharistic Hymns of John and Charles Wesley* (London: Epworth, 1948), pp. 123-47.

31. Rattenbury, *Eucharistic Hymns,* p. 178.

While faith th'atoning blood applies,
Ourselves a living sacrifice
We freely offer up to God;
And none but those His glory share,
Who crucified with Jesus are,
And follow where their Saviour trod.

Saviour, to Thee our lives we give,
Our meanest sacrifice receive,
And to Thine own oblation join,
Our suffering and triumphant Head,
Through all Thy states Thy members lead,
And seat us on the throne Divine.[32]

Worship is recapitulation, and as we repeatedly participate in the Eucharistic actions of offering, and thanking, and breaking, and giving — the constitutive aspects of an authentic, sacrificial life — God conforms us into the image of Christ — our lives become truly Eucharistic as faith working by love leading to holiness of heart and life.

The name of Jürgen Moltmann has become synonymous with the theology of hope. I first met Professor Moltmann when I was a graduate student at Duke University. During one of his visits to campus, I very timidly invited him to lunch and we enjoyed a wonderful meal together. While introducing myself to him more fully, I explained that I was working in my doctoral studies with Frank Baker. He interrupted and said, "Oh, I'd like to share a story with you about Frank and Nellie Baker." And I sat back to take it all in.

He said that during the Second World War there was a German prisoner of war camp on the northeast coast of England. A young pastor and his wife served a small Methodist circuit close by. They felt called by God to reach out to these foreign soldiers in some way. They were filled with compassion and concern. So they went to the commander and asked permission to take a German prisoner with them to church each Sunday — to share in Word and Sacrament — and then to eat their Sunday dinner together in their home. It was agreed. So Sunday after Sunday, a steady flow of German soldiers worshiped and ate with the Bakers in their home throughout the course of the war. This world-famous theologian paused, looked at me intently, and said, "One of those soldiers was a young man named Jürgen Moltmann. And I want you to know that the seed of hope was planted in my heart around Frank and Nellie Baker's Sunday dinner table."

32. Rattenbury, *Eucharistic Hymns*, p. 236 (Hymn 128.4).

The Bakers lived the integral nature of worship and evangelism. I am absolutely sure that, if you had asked, "What are you doing?" Frank or Nellie would have said, "Well, we are simply doing what Christians do. We are spending time together in the worship of our good God, breaking bread together and eating our food with glad and generous hearts." May it be so in each of our lives, to the glory of Jesus our Lord.

CHAPTER 18

Evangelism: A Pastoral Theological Perspective

J. Patrick Vaughn

It began as an infection in her gum. Six weeks later Janice, a seventy-five-year-old member of my congregation, lay comatose in an intensive care unit. She had developed a particularly virulent strain of pneumonia, and the doctors gave her no hope of recovery. I visited her the night before she died. When I walked into the waiting room, I saw her brother and sister. I sat down and listened to their shock and dismay. Soon, I realized that the sister, Laura, had not spoken. She seemed withdrawn, and I wanted to offer her an opportunity to express herself. When I asked how she was feeling, she responded, "My eyes hurt." I inquired further. She released a heavy sigh and replied, "Too much water running." In four simple words Laura verbalized the anguish of her family.

Pastoral theology is concerned with shepherding, with the healing, sustaining, and guiding dimensions of ministry. It seeks to integrate insights and reflections gleaned from the disciplines of both the social sciences and theology in order to understand and better serve the community of faith. Unfortunately, those engaged in the ministry of shepherding have not consistently and intentionally imagined themselves to be evangelists. In this essay I propose that when evangelism is theologically grounded in the suffering love of the Triune God, the image of evangelist promises to shape and powerfully inform the ministry of pastoral care and counseling. The evangelist is the one whose primary concern is "too much water running."

Metaphors and Obligations

In *Religious Ethics and Pastoral Care* Don Browning offers a model for theological reflection that facilitates the development of a biblically faithful and theologically coherent understanding of evangelism.[1] In an attempt to reintegrate moral reasoning with the church's ministry of care, Browning suggests that ethical reflection operates on five levels. The first is termed the *metaphorical* or *symbolic* level. This is concerned with issues of ultimate reality. The second level asks questions of obligation. This is the level of *principle.*

Browning argues that level one impacts and informs level two. The manner in which a community envisions God will mold how that community understands who it is obligated to be and what it is obligated to do. A church's ministry is largely influenced by the metaphors it employs to give an image to ultimate reality. "The vision," Browning observes, "colors all that we say and do. It affects our moral thinking. Even though it does not determine it in all respects, it deeply influences the way we regard and care for one another."[2] Communities live by the way that they image ultimate reality. Their obligations to act and serve are formed by their shared vision of God.

Browning's model suggests that the ministry of evangelism begins with an inquiry concerning the very nature of God. As Terence Fretheim has noted,

> it is not enough to say that one believes in God. What is important is the *kind* of God in whom one believes. Or, to use different language, metaphors matter. The images used to speak of God not only decisively determine the way one thinks about God, they have a powerful impact on the shape of the life of the believer. They may, in fact, tend to shape a life toward unbelief.[3]

The symbols a community employs to image God powerfully shape and form the nature and practice of ministerial obligation. Pastoral theological reflection upon the ministry of evangelism begins with the very nature of God as captured and expressed in metaphor.

The Metaphor of the Cross

For Christians, the cross stands as one of the central metaphors in the faith community. Jürgen Moltmann has even suggested that it "is the test of every-

1. Don Browning, *Religious Ethics and Pastoral Care* (Philadelphia: Fortress, 1983), pp. 47-71.

2. Browning, *Religious Ethics and Pastoral Care,* p. 59.

3. Terence Fretheim, *The Suffering of God: An Old Testament Perspective* (Philadelphia: Fortress, 1984), p. 1.

thing which deserves to be called Christian."[4] The cross reveals a God whose love is so great that God experiences painful suffering in and through the divine/human relationships.[5]

The cross reveals that God suffers because of human sin. The priests and politicians, the religious community and Roman government were incredibly threatened by Jesus' life and ministry. He reached out to the poor and outcast, sat at table with tax collectors and sinners, ministered to the abused and beaten. Believed to be heretical, seditious, and dangerous, he was finally rejected even by his most trusted confidants. Human sin and rejection nailed Christ to the cross.

The cross reveals that God suffers with humanity. In his pain, brokenness, and victimization, Jesus identifies with all who experience pain, brokenness, and victimization. He aligns himself with all who know abandonment and forsakenness. Jesus is Immanuel, God with us. In short, the God who suffers with men and women is a God of *compassion.* Compassion literally means to "suffer with." Andrew Purves has noted that the Hebrew word for compassion is *rachamim.* It is

> derived from another Hebrew word, *reckem* which means womb or uterus. The literal meaning of compassion, then, is the womb pained in solidarity with suffering of another. The feeling of deep kinship with another is understood now is an intimate and physical way as the wounding of the womb. The wounded womb is the core of the biblical meaning of compassion. At its most basic, compassion represents a feminine characteristic of God.[6]

While men and women know suffering, God knows suffering in a profoundly deep and interior way.

The cross reveals that God suffers on behalf of humanity. Jesus' death brings the hope of a right and renewing relationship with God as well as with other men and women. God the Father surrendered the Son to death that he might become the Father of all people. The Father willingly endured the pain of losing a beloved Son that all men and women might become God's children. Similarly, the Son willingly entered into the suffering and death of the

4. Jürgen Moltmann, *The Crucified God* (New York: Harper & Row, 1974), p. 7.

5. Though I focus on the New Testament on the cross, it is important to remember that the Old Testament also bears witness to a God of suffering love. See Fretheim, *Suffering of God,* pp. 107-48.

6. Andrew Purves, *The Search for Compassion: Spirituality and Ministry* (Louisville: Westminster/John Knox, 1989), p. 69.

cross to be the "brother and savior of all who are condemned and accursed."[7] The cross transforms relationships that are marred by sin. It is a transformation that involves divine pain and suffering. The God of the cross is a God of suffering love.

The metaphor of the cross also captures the Trinitarian nature of God. In *The Trinity and the Kingdom,* Moltmann attempts to develop a sociological understanding of God.[8] He rejects a view of the Trinity that envisions God as either a supreme substance or absolute subject. Such interpretations narrowly view God as either an arbiter of power or an ultimate, solitary individual. In contrast, Moltmann argues that the doctrine of Trinity describes a God whose very nature is communal.

In the Western church this doctrine has traditionally been formulated as an attempt to maintain the unity of God. Moltmann believes, however, that God's unity has been so radically asserted that the inner differentiated persons of the Godhead have been virtually collapsed into a solitary entity. He argues that God's unity can be more powerfully and faithfully understood in terms of *perichoresis,* a mutual indwelling. In describing this form of unity he writes,

> An eternal life process takes place in the triune God through the exchange of energies. The Father exists in the Son, the Son in the Father and both of them in the Spirit, just as the Spirit exists in both the Father and the Son. By virtue of their eternal love they live in one another to such an extent, that they are one. It is a process of most perfect and intense empathy. Precisely through the personal characteristics that distinguish them from one another, the Father, the Son and the Spirit dwell in one another and communicate eternal life to one another. In the perichoresis, the very thing that divides them then becomes that which binds them together. . . . The trinitarian persons form their own unity by themselves in the circulation of the divine life.[9]

God is one, but not in a homogenized, monolithic, inaccessible, uniform, unvaried manner. God is one in a dynamic, passionate, relational, mutual indwelling of persons in love. The doctrine of the Trinity "describes God in terms of shared life and love rather than in terms of domineering power. God loves in freedom, lives in community, and wills creatures to live in community. God is

7. Elisabeth Moltmann-Wendel and Jürgen Moltmann, *God — His & Hers* (New York: Crossroad, 1992), p. 68.

8. Jürgen Moltmann, *The Trinity and the Kingdom* (San Francisco: Harper & Row, 1981).

9. Moltmann, *The Trinity and the Kingdom,* pp. 174-75.

self sharing, other regarding, community forming love."[10] God is not a lone monarch ruling in solitude. God is a covenantal God who governs in and through and as community, ever seeking to bring others into relationship.

In the cross of Christ the suffering love and communal being of God are supremely embodied and expressed, for "here the love of the Father which communicates itself becomes infinite pain at the sacrifice of the Son. Here the responsive love of the Son becomes infinite suffering over being rejected and cast out by the Father. What happens on Golgotha extends to the depths of the Godhead and therefore shapes the divine life forever."[11] The cross reveals the depth of God's desire to enter into community with men and women. This communal God willingly endures suffering and death so that humanity might be renewed, redeemed, and restored. The cross reveals a Triune God of suffering love. This is the evangel which evangelists seek to share.

Obligations Concerning Evangelism

Again, obligations arise out of metaphors of ultimate reality. Browning has written, "It is not only in theology but, to a surprising extent, in the modern psychologies as well that the way we metaphorically represent the world in its most durable and ultimate respects influences (although not necessarily determines in all respects) what we think we are obligated to do."[12] The cross reveals a Triune God of suffering love. I believe that this metaphor powerfully shapes the community of faith and gives birth to certain principles concerning the ministry of evangelism.

First, the metaphor of cross enlivens the community of believers to share the good news of Jesus Christ. Evangelism is born in the very nature of God, not in particular commandments or laws. The church shares the evangel because the God that she worships is a God who is community-building, other-seeking, other-affirming. The Triune God of suffering love deeply hungers for fellowship with women and men. Charles Gerkin has noted,

10. Daniel I. Migliore, *Faith Seeking Understanding: An Introduction to Christian Theology* (Grand Rapids: Eerdmans, 1991), p. 64.

11. Moltmann-Wendel and Moltmann, *God — His & Hers*, p. 68.

12. Don Browning, *Religious Thought and the Modern Psychologists* (Philadelphia: Fortress, 1987), p. 20. Browning asserts that systems of psychological investigations are not morally neutral, and he illustrates how metaphors inherent in various modern psychologies do give birth to certain obligations regarding human life. He then creatively compares such obligations with the obligations shaped by Christian faith as expressed in the theology of Reinhold Niebuhr.

> Yahweh does not choose to stay apart from the affairs of the world, but chooses rather to be actively engaged in the world of human affairs seeking to fulfill Yahweh's own purposes. The God of Israel is an active, passionate God concerned for the preservation of the community of God's people and the welfare of all. Said plainly and straightforwardly, the God Yahweh does not choose to stay aloof from the affairs of the world. Yahweh moves out from Yahweh's self in acts of compassion and justice. So also should Yahweh's people.[13]

The church is fundamentally and primarily motivated to engage in the ministry of evangelism because of who God is, a Triune God of suffering love. The very nature of God shapes the people of God into a community that ever seeks to share the good news with others.

Second, evangelical endeavors shaped by the metaphor of the cross will be personal and relational. Gimmicks, manipulation, threats, and stale, prepackaged methods of proclamation are not acceptable. The God of relationship desires relationship. This suggests that the evangelist will not share the gospel simply through direct proclamation. He or she will share the evangel with an empathic ear and a deep, compassionate willingness to listen to others. Such openness and sensitivity to the other are essential in the establishment and development of genuine community. In other words, the good news of Jesus Christ simply cannot be communicated from a distance, whether that distance is provided by a large imposing pulpit or emotional unavailability. The good news is shared through a relationship that reflects the perichoretic nature of God.

Third, the metaphor of cross suggests that evangelical endeavors will be acutely sensitive to human experience, especially the experience of pain and suffering. God so attends to the condition of men and women that God weeps when they weep and rejoices when they rejoice. People's pain and needs are important to evangelists because they are important to God. The faithful evangelist will be open to the particular plight of God's children, offering the gifts of intimacy, presence, and the willingness to suffer with another in a situation of hurt and brokenness. Even as God enters into the world of human experience, so too will faithful evangelists seek to enter more fully into that world.

Surprisingly, through faithful attempts to share the good news, the evangelist will also be nurtured, nurtured by the God who is already present in the other person's life. When Christ told his disciples that as they minis-

13. Charles V. Gerkin, *Prophetic Pastoral Practice* (Nashville: Abingdon, 1991), p. 134.

tered to the "least of these" they were ministering to him (Matt. 25:40), he was speaking from the perspective of the suffering love of the Triune God. In the relational embrace of people's hurt and pain, evangelists may hope to be embraced by the presence of the God they serve.

Fourth, because God is a communal God, the sharing of the gospel will involve the work and commitment of the fellowship of believers. It will not suffice for an individual or committee or governing body to engage in sharing God's love. Evangelism is the privilege and responsibility of the entire church. It depends upon a network of mutually supportive men and women.

Fifth, evangelism informed by the metaphor of the cross will recognize and respect limits. There is in the Godhead inner differentiation as well as love and respect for the integrity of the other persons. Personal boundaries are not transgressed. Evangelists will also respect an individual's or family's or even community's boundaries. In *Hopeful Imagination* Walter Brueggemann comments on the obligation to respect limits. He remarks,

> Those in ministry have a terrible temptation to take responsibility for others, to do for others what they will not do for themselves. We have a difficult time having enough freedom to disengage ourselves, to let others be free when they are wrong, to let others be free to fail, even when they are surely headed for destruction. . . . A ministry of vitality requires that we be deeply concerned for and utterly free from other people.[14]

Evangelical efforts may include both verbal and nonverbal invitations to relationship. Adopting biblical imagery, evangelists will knock at the door (Rev. 3:20), but, in recognizing the integrity of the boundaries of the other, the door will not be knocked down. Though perhaps not perceived or understood by the evangelist, she or he trusts that God is already in the home, abiding in rooms of pain and brokenness. When the door does not open, evangelists trust that God continues to be at work in those persons' lives. When the door does open, they trust that it is God who has turned the knob. Recognition of limits not only ensures respect for the dignity of others, it also serves to release the evangelist of unnecessary burden and responsibility. Ultimately, God is responsible for humanity not those who serve God.

Finally, since God suffers because of human sin and rejection, the witness of evangelism is obligated to confront evil and sin in the world. On a social level, evangelism involves confronting forces that dehumanize and kill, powers that seek to strip away human value and dignity (e.g., racism, ageism,

14. Walter Brueggemann, *Hopeful Imagination: Prophetic Voices in Exile* (Philadelphia: Fortress, 1986), p. 51.

militarism). On a personal level, this involves gently, relationally, and firmly holding people responsible for their lives, enabling them to recognize, face, and repent of the pain they have inflicted upon themselves, upon others, and even upon God. As Ben Johnson has written, "The church, because it is the body of Christ, must always concern itself with mission and evangelism, because Christ came to save lost persons and to redeem the world."[15] The metaphor of cross thus calls the evangelist to resist the polarization of social activism and personal commitment.

Pastoral Caregivers as Evangelists

Perhaps out of concern for therapeutic neutrality, those who seek to serve as shepherds have seemed reluctant to image themselves as evangelists.[16] This is understandable given the distorted view of evangelism in popular culture and in certain expressions of the faith community.[17] Yet, this is also sad and unfortunate. Because the evangelist is the one who bears the good news of the Triune God of suffering love, the image of evangelist offers to shape and inform powerfully the ministry of pastoral care and counseling.

As evangelists, pastoral caregivers are obligated to be concerned with developing personal relationships. The shepherd knows his or her flock by name (John 10:3). The essence of any pastoral encounter is the establishment and nurture of a personal relationship. This is *perichoresis* in action. In the homes of parishioners, in hospital rooms, and in the counseling office, it is this appreciation and deepening of relationship that offers the hope of healing and restoration.

As evangelists, pastoral caregivers are obligated to be sensitive to human experience, particularly need and pain. Pastoral care and counseling are inherently evangelical because they are forms of ministry that tend to brokenness. Shepherds care for their lost and wounded sheep. As a friend of mine is fond of remarking, "Personal hurts require personal healing." When we ministers listen to the agonizing cries of the sick, the dying, the divorced, the depressed, the grieving, we are not simply being kind or polite. Through

15. Ben C. Johnson, *Rethinking Evangelism* (Philadelphia: Westminster, 1987), p. 79.

16. I certainly do not intend this to be a categorical statement. However, in reading, training, and conversations with pastoral counselors and chaplains, I am impressed by the lack of the intentional and consistent appropriation of the image of evangelist.

17. Ben Johnson has observed that certain interpretations of the meaning and practice of evangelism focus on "saving souls from hell." He terms this "evangelicalism." It is actually a perversion of evangelism. See *Rethinking Evangelism,* pp. 15-19.

our care and sensitivity we are sharing the suffering love of the Triune God. We are, indeed, serving as evangelists.

As evangelists, pastoral caregivers are obligated to be involved in communities that offer mutual support and encouragement. Pastors, chaplains, and pastoral counselors are not Lone Rangers. Our ministry is vitally dependent upon fellowship with our brothers and sisters. The Association for Clinical Pastoral Education and the American Association of Pastoral Counselors, for example, are organizations that seek to offer guidance, consultation, supervision, and support in an attempt to serve the people of God as faithfully as possible. This is not simply psychologically prudent but theologically mandated.

I think it is important to note that such community involves not only caregivers, but extends to care receivers as well. In my opening illustration I described the anguish of a grieving family. The sister lamented that her eyes hurt because of "too much water running." Through our sharing we formed a community; I believe that I was only able to reach out to them in their brokenness because of my own personal experience of a sustaining community. I have several colleagues with whom I regularly meet to share my joys and sorrows. I also shared this particular pastoral encounter with my Clinical Pastoral Education group. They listened and helped me to tend to my own sense of loss. The metaphor of the cross reminds us shepherds that it is only as we are engaged in mutually fulfilling and supporting communities that we are enabled to reach out to our wounded and hurting sheep. In short, this metaphor issues serious challenges to individualistic approaches to pastoral care and counseling.

As evangelists, pastoral caregivers demonstrate a respect for boundaries and limits. Emotional defenses are respected. A counselor, chaplain, or pastor does not force someone to share areas of life that he or she may want to protect. Daniel Migliore has defined sin as both pride and self-rejection.[18] Both reflect a lack of respect for limits. In the former the boundaries of the other are neglected. In the latter the boundaries of the self are neglected. Engaging self, neighbor, and God in deeper and more fulfilling ways is made possible only through struggling with one's limits and boundaries.

As evangelists, pastoral caregivers confront sin and evil. Since such confrontation is generally associated with social action and social causes, it might well be asked if this is really possible in a hospital room, a counseling center, or the front porch of a parishioner. The answer is unequivocally affirmative. In these very places self-destructive and/or suicidal impulses are confronted,

18. Migliore, *Faith Seeking Understanding*, pp. 130-35.

the physical and emotional abuse of spouses and children is challenged, the lack of concern for oneself or others is contested, and the gods who deny pain and relationship are defied.

I have long been uncomfortable with and suspicious of those who call themselves evangelists. As I have allowed the metaphor of the cross to touch and move me, however, I have discovered a deeper appreciation for evangelism. I now feel comfortable with the role of evangelist. While certainly appreciating and using insights gleaned from the social sciences, the role of evangelist reminds me that pastoral care and counseling are fundamentally shaped and informed by the faith community. It is as an evangelist of the cross that I offer empathy to a woman grieving the death of a sister or listen to the anger of a woman who has been abused, or reach out to a child who has a serious illness. It is as an evangelist of the cross that I participate in community that I may engage others in community. It is as an evangelist that I lift up the hope of God's presence in the midst of the brokenness and pain and suffering of human life. In short, the role of evangelist has moved me to reclaim and deepen my appreciation for our theological heritage.

In addition, I believe that those of us engaged in the ministry of pastoral care and counseling have an important word to offer the church. We can challenge the church when it settles for slick marketing techniques and avoids the suffering love of the cross. We can question the church when it engages in evangelism as monologue instead of dialogue. We can remind the church that healing comes not through assent to a particular doctrine but through the struggle and development of a caring relationship. We can model for the community of faith a form of evangelism that strives to be responsive to the metaphor of the cross. As evangelists we hold forth good news for the church!

Carroll Wise has defined the ministry of pastoral care as "the art of communicating the inner meaning of the gospel to persons at the point of their need."[19] This is the essence of evangelism. My hope is that those of us engaged in the ministry of pastoral care and counseling will more and more image ourselves as evangelists. Who is an evangelist? Quite simply, she or he is the one who seeks to share the good news of Jesus Christ by tending to the experience of those who cry out, "Too much water running!"

19. Carroll Wise, *The Meaning of Pastoral Care* (New York: Harper & Row, 1966), p. 8.

PART FIVE

Evangelism in Diverse Ecclesiastical and Ecumenical Settings

In this section we juxtapose a set of contrasting views or images with regard to the practice of evangelism. The study of evangelism has suffered in the past from a failure to engage in dialogue across ecclesial boundaries. Particularly in North America, one segment of the evangelical Protestant tradition has shaped the popular conception of evangelism and rendered other viewpoints unintelligible to those both inside and outside the church. The present situation calls for a greater appreciation of the gifts and insights brought to the table of conversation by diverse traditions within the Christian family and by contemporary ecumenical partnerships.

Our commitment to listen to divergent voices simply reflects the fact that all theological reflection is contextualized within specific traditions of thought and practice. The way in which Methodists, Roman Catholics, and Pentecostals practice evangelism, for example, reflects the biblical hermeneutics, theological emphases, and methodological commitments peculiar to these respective traditions. While such particularity often leads to distinctive interpretations, and even controversy, the contexts and theological traditions within which these interpretations and practices are formed provide important resources for the study and practice of evangelism within the larger community of faith. The essays in this section represent a spectrum of Christian traditions, therefore, including Orthodox, Pentecostal, Evangelical, Roman Catholic, and conciliar Protestant voices. They demonstrate the complex theological landscape related to the study of evangelism in diverse ecclesiastical and ecumenical settings, but their juxtaposition contributes hopefully to the mapping of this landscape and moves us in the direction of greater understanding.

Particular attention has been given to the way in which these essays have been ordered. The two opening selections stand in stark contrast with one another, drawn as they are from opposite poles in the spectrum of the Christian family, namely, the Orthodox and Pentecostal traditions. While both maintain a strong pneumatological core and claim an apostolic inheritance, the spiritual ethos, liturgical life, and practices of these traditions represent a study in contrasts. The authors of the remaining essays reflect upon the three most critical documents related to evangelism in the second half of the twentieth century: the Lausanne Covenant of the International Congress on World Evangelization (1974); *Evangelii Nuntiandi* (Evangelization in the Modern World), the Apostolic Exhortation promulgated by Pope Paul VI (1975); and "Mission and Evangelism: An Ecumenical Affirmation," approved by the World Council of Churches' Commission on World Mission and Evangelism (1982). The discussion of these remarkable documents reflects the fertile, yet volatile, nature of the last quarter of the century in particular as Catholic and Protestant theologians struggled with the topic of "mission and evangelism" at the approach of the new millennium.

Alexander Veronis, founder of the Orthodox Christian Mission Center, interprets evangelism and mission in light of the historic witness of the saints through the ages. The primary mandate of the church is to preach the good news of Jesus Christ to all humanity. But countless luminaries of the Orthodox heritage demonstrate how this proclamation involves attention to the physical as well as the spiritual needs of persons. As one might imagine, ecclesiology figures prominently in the attempt of the Orthodox to articulate a theology of evangelism. The cosmic mission of the church, the centrality of the bishop, and the Eucharistic character of Christian life demonstrate the impossibility of real evangelism devoid of an ecclesial base. In addition to the many active forms of evangelism within his tradition, Veronis elevates "passive mission" as the essence of the Orthodox way. This form of evangelism attracts people to the gospel, rather than taking the gospel to them. It consists primarily of praying without ceasing and permitting one's light of faith to shine in the daily round of Christian living.

Pentecostalism defies easy definition. Unlike a denomination that maintains its identity by means of confessional statements, articles of religion, or liturgical practices, this movement within the global community of faith differs widely from one context to another. Samuel Palma Manriquez represents the Pentecostal tradition as manifest in his native Chile. His understanding of evangelism reflects the particularities of this context: Pentecostalism is a religion of the poor, characterized by poverty as a way of being in society. Feeling lost in the world, Chilean Pentecostals understandably orient life around religious conversion as recuperation. This experience happens in what Manriquez describes as "affective communities." Evangelism is a communal reality in which broken persons experience healing and affirmation, receive a new identity, and are incorporated into a new culture. Service functions as an extension of the community of the saved, reaching into those communities most directly affected by political persecution and economic crisis.

During the last quarter of the twentieth century, as we have seen, conversations — sometimes heated debates — about evangelism escalated dramatically within the Roman Catholic tradition and between two ecumenical bodies, the World Council of Churches (consisting of conciliar Protestants) and the Lausanne Committee (consisting of evangelical Protestants). The International Congress on World Evangelization, held at Lausanne in the summer of 1974, was one of the most remarkable events of the late twentieth century. Gathering together nearly three thousand participants from over 150 countries (half of which were from the so-called "third world" of that time), the conference recaptured some of the excitement and euphoria of earlier ecumenical assemblies, but with an amazing spirit of humility, liberation, and seriousness. John Stott, chief architect of the Lausanne Covenant, the landmark document on world evangelization that emerged from this congress, reflects upon the significance of this statement and the event as a whole. Responding to the Bangkok Report of the World Council of Churches (1972) that elevated the importance of sociopolitical salvation, Lausanne emphasized the balance of personal salvation and social responsibility. In its clarification of the concept of "mission," however, it maintained the priority of evangelism, and the practice it envisaged was fourfold: biblically grounded, ecclesially oriented, culturally sensitive, and cosmically engaged. With regard to the goal of world evangelization, the conference recovered a confidence, according to Stott, "in the truth of God's Word and in the power of God's Spirit."

Nearly simultaneous to this development within the evangelical world, Pope Paul VI promulgated one of the most important doctrinal statements of his pontificate, the Apostolic Exhortation on "Evangelization in the Modern World." According to Jerry Persha, Maryknoll theologian, in this document the pope attempted to develop an adequate and comprehensive understanding of evangelization for the post–Vatican II Roman Catholic community. The essence of the exhortation is the simple statement that "the church exists to evangelize." Persha examines the holistic vision of Pope Paul VI — a vision at once personal, social, and cultural — under the broad themes of the content of evangelization, the identity of the church in relation to that content, and the manner of communicating it. With regard to content, the pope defines the gospel by renaming it in terms of the reign of God as experienced and manifest in Jesus Christ and lived out in the community of faith in the paschal mystery of grace. The identity of the church is bound inextricably to Jesus' own mission to proclaim and enact the reign of God. The church community, the creation of the Holy Spirit, offers to the world a sign of reconciliation by means of its own cruciform character, patterned after the life and ministry of Jesus. The first means of evangelization, therefore, is an authentic life of Christian witness. This living testimony must include genuine dialogue that gives primacy to the world of the other, but seeks to clarify a gospel characterized by faith, hope, and love.

African theologian and ecumenical stateswoman Mercy Amba Oduyoye interprets the significance of the WCC statement "Mission and Evangelism: An Ecumenical Affirmation," the third document in this trilogy of essential late twentieth-century reading, in light of the prior and widely acclaimed Faith and Order publication *Baptism, Eucharist and Ministry.* The "Mission and Evangelism" affirmation assimilates the missiological developments of a half century, including the groundbreaking work of Lausanne and Pope Paul VI. It is a call for action at a time of urgency and reflects a growing consensus about the foundation of the church's mission in the world: the universal need of conversion, the subordination of power to love, the holistic nature of the gospel, and the essential need for dialogue among other principles. The affirmation maintains that evangelism is inextricably bound to baptism and Eucharist, the sign of incorporation into the body of Christ and the means to authentic discipleship and mission. "Mission and Evangelism" affirms that evangelism is a missional practice of the whole people of God.

CHAPTER 19

Orthodox Concepts of Evangelism and Mission

Alexander Veronis

His name was Archimandrite Chrysostomos Papasarantopoulos; he was born in 1902 and buried in 1972. He was short and bald with a white beard, pleasant, but not striking in appearance. He had an intensity about him that caught one's attention. He had fire in his heart, fire that kindled with faith in Jesus Christ. After meeting him, one would not easily forget Fr. Papasarantopoulos. A priest for many years, situated in the comfortable city of Athens, Greece, it was not until he was in his middle fifties that he found the opportunity to receive a theological education. He obtained a degree from the University of Athens School of Theology, and shortly thereafter felt the call of Christ to "go . . . and make disciples of all nations" (Matt. 28:19).

At the university Fr. Papasarantopoulos met African students from Uganda, where for some years a small Orthodox mission had existed. They represented the first native Orthodox Christians from Uganda to be formally educated in the Orthodox faith. One of these fellow students, Theodore Nankyamas, would later play a prominent role and become one of the first Orthodox bishops in East Africa. Another, Demetrios Mumbale, would become the first Orthodox physician and founder of an Orthodox medical clinic in Uganda. So it was to Uganda that Fr. Papasarantopoulos went in 1960 at the age of 58 to begin his missionary work. (No official missionary society existed in Greece at the time.) Like the apostle Paul, Fr. Papasarantopoulos ventured forth in full confidence that the God who called him would also provide for his needs and support. He was not to be disappointed. So much did Fr. Papasarantopoulos operate on faith that when an aspiring missionary wrote him years later inquiring about the health conditions, the climate, the job description of a missionary, and a host of other questions about East Africa, he replied characteristically: "My brother, since you heard an inner voice, crush your doubts, close your ears to what others tell you. Make the sign of the cross and begin your journey. As for the rest, leave all in the hands of our heavenly Father. . . ."[1]

For the next twelve years, until his death in 1972, Fr. Papasarantopoulos carried on an amazingly productive ministry among the neophyte Orthodox missions of Uganda, Kenya, Tanzania (Tanganyika), and Zaire. Numerous obstacles confronted him: racism, language barriers, primitive living conditions, lack of funds, limitations imposed upon him by superiors, ill health, poor diet, etc. Not one to despair easily, Fr. Papasarantopoulos looked upon each obstacle as a challenge and managed "with God's help," as he was accustomed to saying.

Slowly his perseverance and pure faith began to reap a plentiful harvest. He learned Swahili and translated portions of the Scriptures and church services into the language of his listeners. In a whirlwind of activity, he traveled incessantly from village to village, preaching, teaching, baptizing, building small churches, establishing new parishes, and bringing the holy mysteries (sacraments) of the Orthodox Church to thousands of Africans. He kept up a vigorous correspondence with his friends in Europe and the United States and regularly published an informative "Newsletter" of the Metropolis of Irinoupolis in East Africa which he addressed to Orthodox Christians everywhere in the ecumene. He urged men and women to come to Africa to help labor in the plentiful harvest he found there. And those who could not come and be missionaries (ἱεραπόστολοι) he urged to become senders of missionaries (ἱεραπόστολεις). "I beseech you," he wrote near the end of his life, "since I have been brought to the midst of the sea, pray and implore that our 'fishing for people' may not tarry to fill nets."[2] His zealous ministry attracted other missionaries to East Africa from Greece and America. One month before his death he wrote a letter from Zaire, a new area where he went to spend the final two years of his life: "I love the Africans and am fully convinced that the Lord has brought me here. I hope to use the few remaining days of my old age preaching and teaching here. The place I am now located in is a large city (Kanaga) of 50,000 people near the central part of the Congo (Zaire). The people are eager to learn about Orthodox Christianity. But I am old and alone and my capacities are now limited. I don't know how I'll manage, but the Lord Jesus will show me, as he always has in the past. Remember me in your prayers."[3]

The missionary work of Fr. Papasarantopoulos points to some traditional concepts of Orthodox evangelism and missions.

1. Newsletter of the Metropolis of Irinoupolis in East Africa, November 12, 1967.

2. Letter, June 28, 1971 to Alexander Veronis.

3. Letter, November 5, 1972 to Alexander Veronis.

The Gospel

Fr. Papasarantopoulos's urgent concern to preach "the evangelion," the good news of Jesus Christ, to all humanity stresses a basic concept of Orthodox who see this as a primary mandate of the Lord. Orthodox believe that the Lord's gospel releases captives from sin and corruption, provides understanding to the spiritually blind, sets at liberty those who in any way are oppressed, brings spiritual renewal and new life from above, provides abundant living, sanctifies believers, and leads to deification and salvation (Luke 4:18; 2 Cor. 5:17; John 3:3, 16; 10:10, Eph. 5:26; 1 Cor. 6:11; 2 Peter 1:4). They see the gospel as God's truth which he wants humanity to hear and accept for all to live in his eternal kingdom of agape (love) (1 Tim. 2:4; John 14:6). A famous Greek evangelist/missionary/teacher, Kosmas Aitolos (1713-1779), exemplifies the zeal of many Orthodox missionaries in preaching the gospel when he says:

> If it were possible for me to ascend to the sky and cry with a loud voice and preach to the whole world and say that our Christ is the Son and Logos of God and true God of true God, and the life of all, I would do so. But inasmuch as I cannot do that great thing, I do this small one, and walk from place to place and teach my brethren according to my power.[4]

Social Concerns

Orthodox understand the gospel as a message to the total person, physically as well as spiritually. They see Christ's teaching about healing the sick, feeding the hungry, caring for the widow and orphan, uplifting the disinherited, supporting the oppressed, fighting injustice, and making life in this world hospitable for all as part of the complete gospel message. Well known in history are the Christian examples of luminous church fathers, preachers, and missionaries who combined social concerns with their preaching of the gospel. Let us consider some examples.

John Chrysostom (347-404), considered by some as the Church's greatest preacher, was born in wealth which he renounced early in life to take up an ascetic Christian lifestyle of simplicity, prayer, and philanthropy. Although he reached the highest office of the Church as patriarch of Constantinople, his unceasing railings against the rich and support of the poor eventually led him

4. Constantine Cavarnos, *St. Kosmas Aitolos* (Belmont: Institute for Byzantine and Modern Greek Studies, 1971), p. 20.

to martyrdom. His moral teachings and writings are still widely read and are an inspiration for philanthropy.

Basil the Great (329-378), the Cappadocian church father, brought the gospel to many and founded monasteries, orphanages, and old age homes, becoming a champion of the world's dispossessed. His description of, and appeals on behalf of, the hungry sound like a contemporary appeal against world hunger:

> Hunger is the most pitiable of all ills, the worst of miseries, the most fearful of deaths. The point of the sword brings death quickly; raging fire puts an end to life suddenly; the teeth of wild beasts put an end to the miseries of men much sooner. Hunger is a long, slow punishment, an endless martyrdom. It is like a creeping disease with death ever imminent, but always delayed. It drains the natural moistures of the body; it chills the body heat; it consumes the flesh and gradually exhausts the strength. The flesh, all colour gone, clings to the bone like spider webs. As the blood diminishes, the skin loses its lustre and turns black and dries up; and this poor livid body is of a mingled wan and sick colour. The knees no longer support the body; they are moved only when force is used on them. The voice grows reedy. Weak eyes lie useless in hollow sockets, like nuts in dried-up shells. The hollow stomach contracts, shapeless, shrunken, cleaving to the spine. What kind of punishment do you think is deserved by a man who passes the hungry without giving them a sign?[5]

Sergios of Radonezh (1314-1392) lived in extreme simplicity, thus identifying with the poor peasants of Russia. He conducted a vigorous monastic ministry of evangelism, missionary work, and social welfare among pagan tribes of the forest in the northern regions of Russia. He and his disciples founded fifty Christian communities which spread as far as the White Sea and the Arctic Circle. His life and ministry introduced two centuries of Russian spirituality (1350-1550) known as a golden age in Russian Orthodox history.[6]

Twice a year, on July 1 and November 1, the Orthodox Church commemorates the healing ministry of two third-century "holy, unmercenary" physician brothers, Kosmas and Damian, whose reputations spread throughout Cilicia in Asia Minor during the third century. They were noted for their benevolent Christian ministry in caring for the sick in the name of Christ, to whom they also preached. Both died as martyrs in 303, victims of the Diocletian persecutions.

5. Robert Payne, *The Holy Fire* (London: Harper, 1958), p. 149.

6. Timothy Ware, *The Orthodox Church* (Baltimore: Penguin, 1963), p. 94.

Kosmas Aitolos, the eighteenth-century preacher quoted above, whom some consider the greatest missionary of modern Greece, is credited with founding two hundred elementary schools and ten high schools in eighteenth-century Greece because "the school," he believed, "opens churches and monasteries. It is at school that we learn what God is, what the angels are, what the demons, paradise, hell, virtue, vice, the soul, and the body are."[7]

Kosmas's achievements become more amazing when one considers the historical conditions of his time. Greece was undergoing a dark age in its Christian development. The Ottoman Turks, Muslims by faith, imposed numerous religious restrictions upon the areas of the Byzantine Empire which they conquered and controlled for almost four centuries, even though they permitted Orthodox Christians to exercise their faith within limitations. Kosmas, for example, constantly encountered red tape from local Turkish authorities in order to receive permission to preach and teach the gospel. Even with permission, he was warned against converting Muslims and had to confine his evangelism to the Orthodox. At the age of sixty-six his life ended in martyrdom at the hands of the Turks.

The monastic community in Orthodox history contributed significantly to both the preaching of the gospel and to showing social concern. In a revealing study on Orthodox social welfare and philanthropy during the Byzantine Empire's illustrious era, which lasted over eleven centuries, Constantelos remarks:

> As a result of the monastic philanthropy of love and service to mankind, monasteries became centers of hospitality, almsgiving, and care for the sick, the pilgrims, and the wayfarers. . . . Basil counseled the members of his monastic city to work not only to keep the body under subjection, but to provide their institutions with sufficient goods to feed those in want. . . . Monasteries were usually havens for travelers, strangers, and the poor. . . . Charities were to be performed with compassion and love as if being offered to Christ.[8]

A contemporary Orthodox monastic, Mother Maria of Paris, supports this tradition of the social gospel when she writes:

> The bodies of our fellow human beings must be treated with more care than our own. Christian love teaches us to give our brethren not only

7. Cavarnos, *St. Kosmas Aitolos,* pp. 13, 17.

8. Demetrius Constantelos, *Byzantine Philanthropy and Social Welfare* (New Brunswick: Rutgers University Press, 1968), pp. 89-90.

> spiritual gifts, but material gifts as well. Even our last shirt, our last piece of bread must be given to them. Personal almsgiving and the most wide-ranging social work are equally justifiable and necessary.
>
> The way to God lies through love of other people, and there is no other way. At the Last Judgment I shall not be asked if I was successful in my ascetic exercises or how many prostrations I made in the course of my prayers. I shall be asked, did I feed the hungry, clothe the naked, visit the sick and the prisoners: that is all I shall be asked.[9]

The Use of the Vernacular

Historically, Orthodox missionaries have followed the example of Fr. Papasarantopoulos and have learned first the language of the people they are trying to reach with the gospel. In Orthodox history books Cyril and Methodios, the renowned Greek brothers of the ninth century who created "Church Slavonic" through the use of the Cyrillic alphabet, usually get credit for epitomizing this concept. Before they left Thessalonika to become "apostles to the Slavs," they translated the Scriptures and liturgical services of the Orthodox Church into the vernacular. In Moravia (modern Czechoslovakia), where they and their disciples preached the gospel, Cyril and Methodios encountered overt hostility from Frankish missionaries who believed that only three sacred languages should be employed for Scripture and worship in the Christian faith: Hebrew, Greek, and Latin. The persistence of Cyril and Methodios in using the vernacular eventually enabled all the Slavic nations (Bulgaria, Serbia, Russia, etc.) to read the Scriptures and to worship in a language they could understand.[10]

There were other prominent Orthodox missionaries who followed in this tradition. The Russian Stephen of Perm (1340-1396) translated the gospel into the language of the Zyrians. Makary Glukharev (1792-1849) mastered the language and culture of the nomadic tribes in the Altai Mountains of Central Siberia, where he translated the Bible and liturgical books into the Telengut dialect and conducted services in the vernacular. His disciples Landishev and Vladimir continued his mission, converting 25,000 of the 45,000 inhabitants of the Altai region to Christianity.[11] John Veniaminov (Bishop Innocent, 1797-1879), missionary to Alaska, translated and wrote for the native Alaskans (Aleuts, Tlingits,

9. Ware, *The Orthodox Way,* pp. 52-53.

10. See Francis Dvornik, *Byzantine Missions among the Slavs* (New Brunswick: Rutgers University Press, 1970), for a detailed account of this point.

11. Nicholas Zernov, *Eastern Christendom* (New York: Readers Union, 1961), p. 181.

Eskimos). And Nicholas Kassatkin (1836-1912), a Russian missionary to Japan, translated the Bible and church service books into Japanese.

In Orthodox history these various missionaries have been canonized and are not only looked upon as saints, a title not easily won in the Orthodox Church, but also as individuals identified with the nations they evangelized. Thus, the Church speaks of Saints Cyril and Methodios as Apostles to the Slavs, Saint Innocent as Apostle to America, Saint Nicholas (Kassatkin) as Apostle to Japan, Saint Herman of Alaska, etc.

One example of how "indigenization" occurred as Orthodox missionaries went to different lands is given by the account in Japan of a meeting between the famous nineteenth-century missionary, Archbishop Innocent (John Veniaminov), and Nicholas Kassatkin, a young Russian Orthodox priest who was serving as a chaplain of the Russian consulate in Tokyo at the time. Innocent saw great potential for missionary work among the Japanese and exhorted Kassatkin "to stop reading French and German books" and "to study Japanese diligently in order to bring Christianity to the people of that country."[12] Kassatkin zealously undertook the challenge and eventually translated the Scriptures and liturgical services into Japanese. Within his lifetime, Kassatkin's Japanese mission had founded an Orthodox seminary for the training of indigenous clergy and catechists, had erected the Orthodox Cathedral of the Resurrection in Tokyo, had won many Japanese to Christianity (35,000 by the end of his life), and had trained converts to work on the translation of church books into Japanese.[13]

Ecclesiology

Orthodox perceive their church as "the household of God built upon the foundation of the apostles and prophets, Christ Jesus himself being the cornerstone" (Eph. 2:19, 20); as the original Eucharistic community of faith instituted by Christ (1 Cor. 10:16-27; John 6:53-58); as the "one, holy, catholic, and apostolic Church" (Nicene Creed); as the church of the seven ecumenical synods (325-787); and as the visible witness on earth of Christ and his gospel with an unbroken "sacred tradition" lasting almost two thousand years in which the gospel message has been preserved in its pristine state. The church,

12. Paul D. Garrett, *St. Innocent, Apostle to America* (New York: St. Vladimir's Seminary, 1979), p. 267.

13. Bolshakoff, *Orthodox Missions Today,* as quoted in C. S. Calian, *Icon and Pulpit* (Philadelphia: Westminster, 1968), p. 54.

Christ's body, has the cosmic mission of the Lord himself "to unite all things in him (Christ), things in heaven, and things on earth" (Eph. 1:10). It is all-inclusive because in Christ "there is neither Jew nor Greek, there is neither slave nor free, there is neither male or female" (Gal. 3:28; Matt. 19:13-14; James 2:2-7), rich or poor, adult or child. As per "Ignation theology," the bishop brings unity to the visible church in Christ's place. Ignatios, a first-century church father, speaks of the "one altar" behind which sits "the one bishop in the place of God," surrounded by the presbyters and deacons in the presence of the people of God (laity), all together symbolizing the unity of the church.[14] Thus, the place of the bishop in the church becomes crucial to the maintenance of its unity and for the preservation of the faith. His authority protects the catholicity of the church, as well, not only in its universal connotation as the body of Christ encompassing all people in all places for all time with the full gospel, but also in its parochial setting. When the presbyter, acting in the bishop's place, unites the local people of God in the Eucharist, he is expressing the catholicity of the church parochially. This unity is envisioned as a christological reality. At the celebration of every Eucharistic service, the whole Christ is revealed, as well as "the ultimate eschatological unity of all in Him" which this gathering implies.[15] Orthodox express their unity at every liturgy with the faithful of all generations in a prayer of the liturgy that is read immediately following the consecration:

> We offer unto Thee this reasonable service for those who have fallen asleep in the faith: forefathers, fathers, patriarchs, prophets, apostles, preachers, evangelists, martyrs, confessors, ascetics, and every righteous spirit in faith made perfect.[16]

There are obvious implications concerning the importance of apostolic succession in the Orthodox Church's ecclesiology. Since the bishop preserves and perpetuates the faith from one generation to another, Orthodox consider apostolic succession as part of the sacred tradition of the church's nearly two thousand-year history.

The necessity for a clearly stated ecclesiology as a prerequisite to any type of theology of evangelism or missionary endeavor is expressed as follows by Nikos Nissiotis who compares the Orthodox viewpoint to that of conservative evangelical Protestant theology:

14. See Ignatios of Antioch as quoted by John D. Zizioulas, "The Eucharistic Community and the Catholicity of the Church" in *The New Man* (Atlanta: Standard, 1973), pp. 115-16.

15. Zizioulas, "The Eucharistic Community," pp. 115ff.

16. *The Divine Liturgy,* Greek Orthodox Archdiocese of North and South America, 24.

> . . . there is a great difference between the Orthodox and the conservative evangelical attitude. This difference consists in that in any kind of evangelistic theology an Orthodox would begin from a sound ecclesiology, that is, from the Church as the focus, means, and sign of the regathering of the whole world into fellowship with God — the historical, visible, and institutional Church, which cannot be separated from the event in Christ. This strong ecclesial basis, which is a *sine qua non* for the Orthodox understanding and practise of evangelism, is lacking . . . in both the radical (pro-secularist) and the conservative evangelical theology of the non-Orthodox churches (and also in the works of certain radical Roman Catholic theologians). . . . It is not sufficient to preach Christ alone, lest He become the intellectual, monistic principle of an individual faith. Christ must be preached within His historical reality, His body in the Spirit, without which there is neither Christ nor the gospel. Outside the context of the Church, evangelism remains a humanism or a temporary psychological enthusiasm.[17]

Nissiotis, in discussing contemporary, radical, pro-secularist trends, as well as those of the conservative evangelicals, concludes his observations with this remark: "The purpose of my observations is less to criticize the modern trends in evangelism than to contribute to them the conviction that real evangelism is impossible without an ecclesial basis."[18]

The Effects of a Living Mission

As with all preachers of the gospel, the full results of Fr. Papasarantopoulos's missionary efforts in Africa will be known only to the Lord of the church. Orthodox history teaches that like prayer, the life of "a righteous man has great power in its effect" (James 5:16). However, the seemingly humble ministry of this one missionary, advanced in age before he began, has had a direct effect on the Orthodox Church in both Greece and the United States. Shortly after his departure for Africa from Athens, a new missionary movement began in Greece in 1961 called "The Inter-Orthodox Missionary Center" under the aegis of the Pan-Orthodox Youth Movement, Syndesmos. Its stated goals are: (1) revival of the missionary spirit in the Orthodox Church, (2) study of theoretical and practical problems in missionary activity, (3) preparation of work-

17. "An Orthodox View of Modern Trends in Evangelism," *The Ecumenical World of Orthodox Civilization* 3 (1974): 187-91.

18. "An Orthodox View," p. 190.

ers for Orthodox missions, and support of the Orthodox in East Africa, Alaska, and Korea.[19] A new journal entitled *Porefthentes (Go Ye),* edited by Anastasios G. Yannoulatos, accompanied this movement. Through the writings and influence of Yannoulatos, now a bishop and professor at the University of Athens, and this new movement, interest in missions has greatly expanded in Greece over the past twenty years. Today there are at least three missionary societies in that country operating out of Athens, Thessalonike, and Patras, all of which publish journals on missions. There were no such official organizations existing in modern Greece prior to Fr. Papasarantopoulos's venture of faith in Africa. It is noteworthy that all developed almost immediately after Fr. Papasarantopoulos's correspondence from the mission field began to ignite the faith of his friends and supporters in Greece.

A similar phenomenon occurred in the United States. Although the Greek Orthodox Archdiocese of North and South America was founded in 1921,[20] it took until 1964 for its Biennial Clergy-Laity Congress to present its first official report on foreign Orthodox missions.[21] In 1966, when the second such report was presented, part of the terminology used was that coined by Fr. Papasarantopoulos in his correspondence when he urged Orthodox Chris-

19. *Porefthentes* 10 (April-September 1968): 24.

20. George Papaioannou, *From Mars Hill to Manhattan* (Minneapolis: Light and Life, 1976), p. 33. This excellent study of the Greek Orthodox Church in America shows the enormous struggles the church underwent to establish itself in America among the waves of immigrants who arrived from Greece in the first half of the twentieth century. Squabbles over language, politics, authority, schisms, ecclesiastical procedures, ethnicity, etc., created numerous internal problems that literally consumed all the attention and energy of the church leadership. The fruitful reign of Archbishop Athenagoras (1930-48), who finally brought unity and order to the Greek Orthodox Archdiocese of North and South America, was actually a period of evangelism and mission. Athenagoras was establishing Greek Orthodoxy in a unique setting never encountered before by the church. He was bringing the gospel to a free country without a state church, already Christianized in large part by Protestants and Catholics, and had the tremendous task of organizing a poor, ill-educated, immigrant population which knew virtually nothing of American culture, custom, language, etc. The success of this mission is attested to today by the fact that sixty years later, the Greek Orthodox Archdiocese of North and South America under Archbishop Iakovos (1959-present) enjoys unity, eleven bishops, 425 well-established parishes serving a thriving community of over 2,000,000 Greek Orthodox Christians, a theological school and college, and a synod of bishops guiding the church through the traditional Orthodox synodal system of administration.

21. Bishop Athenagoras of Elaias, dean of the Holy Cross Orthodox Theological School of Brookline during my student days, started an Orthodox Missionary Society in 1956 within the seminary. He also brought foreign students for study at Holy Cross. Our Missionary Society began correspondence with Orthodox missions. These were the seeds planted which blossomed into a fuller national outreach in foreign missions from our archdiocese during the mid-1960s.

tians throughout the world to become "senders of missionaries," especially if they could not become missionaries themselves.[22] The Greek Archdiocese of North and South America, originally a mission itself to immigrants of Greece, accepted the challenge of Fr. Papasarantopoulos and, in 1967, initiated an annual national Lenten Offering Card project to raise support for foreign missions. The following year Archbishop Iakovos established a Foreign Missions Office in the Archdiocese for the first time with the appointment of a bishop (Silas of Amphipolis) as its head.[23] Interest in missions has expanded since then so that today the Archdiocese supports modest foreign missions in Uganda, Kenya, Ghana, Tanzania, Alaska, Korea, Mexico, and Latin America. Among the factors that have contributed to this progress, one must certainly mention the impact of Fr. Papasarantopoulos's ministry in Africa.

A similar influence occurred upon the Russian Orthodox Church when in 1874 the first Orthodox Missionary Society in modern Russia was established in Moscow, following the illustrious ministry to Alaska and the Orient of the Russian missionary John Veniaminov (Bishop Innocent). The metropolitan of Moscow in 1870, under whom the Missionary Society began, was none other than John Veniaminov himself, who had attained this high position in the Russian church during the final years of his life!

Mission through Personal Sanctity

Whereas Papasarantopoulos's mission of incessant activity and movement represents one type of evangelism common in Orthodox history, there exists another extremely effective kind of mission which is more passive and which attracts more people to the gospel, rather than taking the gospel to them. This second type of mission follows the biblical teachings of praying without ceasing and letting one's light of faith shine before men (see 1 Thess. 5:17; Matt. 5:14-16). Seraphim of Sarov expresses it well when he says, "Acquire inward peace, and thousands around you will find their salvation."[24]

Normally, passive mission means people remain in one place, trying through prayer and a simple, holy lifestyle to achieve advanced dimensions of discipleship and spirituality. The holy, Christ-centered, Spirit-filled life which results not only attracts the attention of many, but brings observers

22. See article "Ierapostelefs," in *The Religious and Ethical Encyclopedia* 6 (Athens, 1965), p. 763.

23. Alexander Veronis, "Greek Orthodox Foreign Missions," *The Orthodox Observer,* September 1969, p. 12.

24. Ware, *The Orthodox Way,* p. 118.

into an acceptance of the Christian gospel which they credit for producing such holy people. This is a common phenomenon in Orthodoxy. I shall cite several examples:

Anthony the Great (251-356) is well known as a holy ascetic and hermit. During his long pursuit of God in the Egyptian desert, Anthony attracted multitudes of disciples, who in turn brought thousands to a knowledge and acceptance of the gospel. Athanasios the Great, the champion of Christ's divinity against Arios at the Ecumenical Synod of Nikaia (325), acknowledged the deep influence of Anthony upon his own spiritual life.[25] Though a contemplative monk, Anthony did not hesitate to temporarily reenter the secular world, along with his monastic followers, to help defeat the Arian heresy in Alexandria. Anthony's example in living the gospel continues to highly motivate contemplative monastics.

Seraphim of Sarov (1759-1833) is one of the most revered holy men of modern Russia. Seraphim lived most of his life as an extreme ascetic and contemplative hermit. At one time he stood on a rock for three years praying incessantly day and night. During another period of time he maintained complete silence for thirteen years (1807-1820). A monk of the monastery at Sarov for most of his life, Seraphim often remained in a nearby hermitage praying, reading, and working in his garden. He had frequent visions of the Virgin Mary Theotokos, the apostles, and Christ. In 1825, at the age of sixty-six, he finally felt led by God to become a starets (spiritual guide). During his last nine years of life, unending streams of people, sometimes thousands in one day, came to see Seraphim for spiritual guidance, healings, prophecy, and matters related to the gospel. His influence upon people of all social classes, from the aristocracy to peasants, was immense. Austere with himself, Seraphim manifested astounding love and profound compassion toward others. People saw the radiance and joy of the Holy Spirit in him, a fact not surprising from one who taught that

> When the Spirit of God descends upon a man and overshadows him with the fulness of his outpouring, then his soul overflows with a joy not to be described, for the Holy Spirit turns to joy whatever he touches.[26]

The numerous healings of the deaf, the blind, the lame, the mentally ill, etc., attributed to Seraphim include his cure of Nicholas Motovilov, who later wrote a book entitled *Conversation of Saint Seraphim on the Aim of Christian*

25. See *St. Athanasius: The Life of St. Antony,* ed. Robert T. Meyer (New York: Paulist, 1950).

26. *St. Athanasius,* p. 118.

Life, from which comes an often quoted teaching of Seraphim's on the Holy Spirit's centrality in the Christian life:

> Prayer, fasting, vigils, and all other Christian practices, however good they may be in themselves, certainly do not constitute the aim of our Christian life; they are but the indispensable means of attaining that aim. For the true aim of the Christian life is the acquisition of the Holy Spirit of God.[27]

Paissy Velichkovsky (1722-1794) was a Russian monk at Mount Athos who went to Romania in 1763 and who became abbot of a monastery which he developed into a powerful spiritual haven with over five hundred monks. This community devoted itself to translating spiritual writings into Slavonic. Among their works were the first Slavonic edition of the *Philokalia* (1793), a massive anthology of spiritual writings from the fourth to fifteenth centuries mostly on the subject of prayer. Velichkovsky initiated a monastic revival across Romania and Russia which brought an era of widespread spiritual revival.[28]

Herman of Alaska (1756-1837), a Russian monk, was living in the Russian Valaam Monastery of Finland as a hermit in 1793 when he was selected by his abbot, the Elder Nazary, to go on a mission to Kodiak, Alaska, along with nine other monks. It took this missionary team 293 days of difficult traveling by land and ship over a distance of 7,327 miles to reach their Kodiak mission! Initially, the mission met with success with the conversion of several thousand native Alaskans to Christianity. Harsh conditions in Alaska, plus a fatal shipwreck carrying the mission's new bishop and his co-workers, diminished the mission until only Herman survived. The simple monk Herman, who had a limited education, spent over forty years in Alaska living in his New Valaam hermitage, built with his own hands on Spruce Island. His life of holiness, simplicity, teaching, example, and kindness to the native Aleuts won many converts to Christianity. He became a protector of the Aleuts against the cruel exploitation of Russian traders, who treated the native Indians as animals. Along with the Aleuts, Herman, too, suffered persecution and mistreatment. Herman's holiness kept attracting followers not only during his lifetime, but long afterward. His memory increased with time, and in 1867, Bishop Peter of Sitka began a formal inquiry into the life of Fr. Herman. In 1970, the Orthodox Church formally canonized him as "Saint Herman of Alaska," the first Orthodox saint of the American continent and whose life motto was, "From

27. Ware, *The Orthodox Church,* pp. 131, 235.
28. Ware, *The Orthodox Church,* p. 130.

this day, from this hour, from this minute, let us strive to love God above all else and fulfill his holy will."[29]

Canonization, which all three of the above-mentioned "passive missionaries" received, means that they are considered "holy" men by the Orthodox Church and worthy of inclusion in the canon (list) of saints. Thus, their names are commemorated formally by the church in services on certain days. The Orthodox Church does not make saints. It simply recognizes officially as saints certain individuals whom the faithful of the church already regard as "holy" men and women of the past. Orthodox ask saints, who now live in the church triumphant, for their prayers, just as they ask friends of the church militant to pray on their behalf. Further evidence of the effective witness to the gospel of the passive missionaries of the church lies in the very fact of their canonization.

Proselytism

Orthodox believe that they have preserved the gospel message intact, without deletion or addition from the inception of the church at Pentecost. When historical circumstances have permitted, as the evidence shows, Orthodox have conducted vigorous missions among non-Christians. Political conditions, on the other hand, created relatively arid periods of missionary activity. Such, for example, were the two-and-a-half centuries (1240-1480) when Russia lived under the Mongol yoke, the eight centuries in which the Ottoman Empire destroyed Byzantium and subjugated the Orthodox Church in the Balkans and the Near East (thirteenth to early twentieth centuries), and the communist yoke of our own time which controls all the Orthodox nations of Europe except Greece, severely discriminating against religious worship and overtly persecuting Orthodox Christians.

Orthodox resist and find offensive those efforts of other Christian communities who attempt to proselytize Orthodox Christians. Traditionally, Orthodox missions have taken place among non-Christian people of the world, not among Protestant and Catholic believers. That is why missionaries of these latter two traditions are usually strenuously opposed by Orthodox when attempts of "sheep-stealing" are made from their flocks. The hostility generated over the past five centuries between Orthodox and Roman Catholics over the "Uniate issue" created by the Jesuit proselytization of Orthodox in the then-kingdom of Poland through the Council of Brest-Litovsk (1596),

29. Bishop Peter of Sitka, "Canonization of Saint Herman of Alaska" (1970), pp. 32, 66.

offers but one illustration. The Orthodox Church of Greece, too, strongly opposes efforts of evangelical Protestant groups who enter Greece with attempts to evangelize Greek Orthodox Christians with the "true gospel" message. On the other hand, the Orthodox bishops welcome non-Orthodox Christian service groups who offer technical assistance to underdeveloped provinces of their dioceses. The Mennonites, who established a model farm in the rural diocese of Kisamou-Selinou of Crete, Greece, in the 1960s (in which they taught advanced agricultural methods to the peasants), were heartily welcomed and supported by Bishop Irenaios of that diocese. These Mennonites left a lasting impression upon the Orthodox of the island through their example of loving service. Orthodox find such missions far more illuminating and helpful than evangelists or missionaries who attempt to change their faith.

"Our presence ought to be positive, not aggressive against others," writes Bishop Yannoulatos. And Fr. Kassatkin, who worked among the non-Christians of Japan, practiced the same irenic approach to missions: "Believe, if you will, without any polemics or critique of the other confessions; and avoid attacks against others, even against Buddhism and Shintoism. Christ himself, the fullness of truth, did not win souls save in peace."[30]

30. Anastasios G. Yannoulatos, "Initial Thoughts toward an Orthodox Foreign Mission," *Porefthentes* 10 (April-September 1968): 21.

CHAPTER 20

Religion of the People and Evangelism: A Pentecostal Perspective

Samuel Palma Manriquez

General Description

Pentecostalism in Chile started in 1909. It first emerged as a search for religious renewal, limited to a small group of people within the Methodist Church. At the time, such a search was not seen as part of the normal life of that church and the group met with hostility; finally it was expelled. Since then Pentecostalism has grown rapidly and expanded all over the country, reaching between 15 and 20 percent of the total population, and nearly 30 percent of the inhabitants of poor areas. In this sense, in terms of its social composition, it could be said that Chilean Pentecostalism has become the "popular religion of Protestantism," and at the same time it has become a "religion of the poor." This means that Pentecostalism has been able to appeal to the poor by responding to some of their needs and demands that have not been met by either the Catholic Church or the traditional Protestant churches.

From the point of view of its organization, Pentecostalism in Chile is divided into thousands of large and small denominations, most of which are local autonomous churches. Such division has been the result of a continuous process of fragmentation in which any time a group within a church disagrees with that church's major decisions it can leave and create a new church. This means that the basic structures of the Pentecostal churches are rather weak and depend on the consensus of the members for their operation. It also means that such a consensus is not easy to reach within Pentecostal churches.

Although there are some branches of North American and Swedish Pentecostalism in Chile, most of it appears as a national phenomenon, which means that Chilean Pentecostalism has been able to organize and develop itself as a basically national religion, at least in institutional terms. This does not necessarily mean, however, that Pentecostalism shares a nationalistic view of the society, either in historical or in geographical terms; rather, it means that it feels proud of being self-sufficient and self-sustaining, in opposition to the so-called "historical churches," which are seen as national sections of international institutions.

Given that most Pentecostals come from a previous religious experience in the Catholic Church, and that they have become "converted" precisely because they felt their church did not respond to their religious needs, Pentecostalism as such has generally been strongly influenced by an anti-Catholic feeling. This feeling has also been deepened by a somewhat arrogant attitude toward Pentecostals by the hierarchy of the Catholic Church. Therefore, the relationships between Pentecostalism and Catholicism have been mostly rather difficult, conflicting, and mutually competitive.

The majority of the members in Pentecostal churches are women, but normally they do not occupy higher positions in the hierarchical structure of the churches, except in a few churches in which they can become pastors, or even members of the denominational leadership. Women generally perform the tasks associated with service to the sick, the poor, or the weakest among the members of the church. In the case of those churches involved in community work, the women are usually the ones playing the most important role in serving the poor and relating to other community organizations.

In many communities of aboriginal people some Pentecostal churches have had and still have a rather divisive influence, both in terms of commanding the people not to take part in their traditional rituals and celebrations and in terms of weakening their collective capacity to resist the cultural dominance and struggle for their rights. However, other Pentecostal churches are trying to develop new ways of relationship with the aboriginal communities, supporting their cultural resistance while making it possible for them to improve their living conditions and incorporate tools and technologies that could help such purposes.

The social and political participation of Pentecostals traditionally has been limited to casting a vote in the polls, while the leaders and pastors usually command the members to abstain from taking active part in workers' organizations or political parties. In this sense, Chilean Pentecostalism — at least in institutional terms — historically has been in a sort of "social strike," as such social behavior was once defined. Many individual Pentecostals did take part in the social process of structural changes that took place in the late 1960s and early 1970s, especially as leaders of rural workers. After the military coup of 1973, many Pentecostal churches became involved in social and political issues, both supporting the poor in their struggle for physical and psychological survival and in their efforts to organize themselves and win back democracy. Other churches, however, especially their main leaders, actively supported the military regime.

The society in which Pentecostalism exists and operates is a rather secularized one. Though the majority of the people are Catholic in culture, there is also a strong nonreligious cultural orientation that has been developed under the influence of a traditionally lay state and the communist and socialist parties and organizations. Historically, the workers' organizations and trade unions have been independent of religious influence, normally being influenced by the state and the leftist political parties.

Pentecostalism: A "Religion of the Poor"

When Pentecostalism began in Chile there existed a deep and increasing feeling of social crisis. At the beginning of the twentieth century, the production and export of nitrate — used as a fertilizer in the agricultural industry — began to decline because of German production of synthetic nitrate. A few years earlier, after a great increase in the wheat production and export to the United States and Australia, those markets had suddenly broken down, with the result that agricultural activities in Chile decreased. This meant, therefore, that thousands of workers and their families were forced to leave the mining towns and the countryside, settling in the cities, which became overrun with poor and jobless people who then invaded urban lands and installed themselves in precarious shanty towns.

Such a situation led to social unrest and conflicts that eventually caused thousands of people to be killed by the police or the army. In such a context appeared Pentecostalism. The years that followed were marked by the deep structural crisis caused by the "great depression" of the world economy in the 1920s and 1930s, and the efforts of the national state to reorganize the economy along import substitution industrialization policies and the creation of an internal market. This meant also a process of rapid and increasing proletarianization of peasants, artisans, and other independent workers. And these were the people to whom Pentecostalism appealed.

To understand why these people become Pentecostals I suggest looking at two basic vital experiences of those poor who become Pentecostal: the experience of poverty as a "life experience" and the "experience of Pentecostal religious conversion."

Poverty as a "Life Experience"

To the poor, poverty means more than scarcity of goods or lack of access to basic services; poverty is a way of being in society; it is a biographical experience, a "life experience." Insofar as poverty is a "life experience," it has to do with the relationships that a poor person establishes with him/herself — his/her body, biography, wishes, and so on — and with others. In other words, the poor person lives poverty as an experience of relating to him/herself and relating with others in a way in which his/her life does not seem to belong to him/her and does not seem to have any value either for him/herself or for others.

In turn, relationships with oneself and with others are properly group relationships. In the historical context in which Chilean Pentecostalism first appeared and developed, the poor did not have the conditions necessary for formulating groups. Their homes were usually overcrowded, suffused with noise and bad odors, and exposed to invasion by delinquents and police. For the poor, the availability of space for one person very often competes with another's need of space; too often the weakest members are forced out on to the streets, or else the streets become more attractive than home as a place to be.

Such conditions are particularly onerous for women, who, confined to cramped living quarters, are condemned forever to the effort of making the home an intimate and caring place for the family. Among the poor in Chile, women suffer a higher frequency of depression and mental torment than men do, the most frequent causes of which are the lack of intimacy and of trustful relationships, as well as the responsibility of caring for a large number of children and the lack of income from jobs outside the home.

The Experience of Pentecostal Religious Conversion

Most testimonies of Pentecostal religious conversion follow a similar pattern: A person is born into a Catholic family and home; early in childhood he/she learns about God and the values and norms one is expected to follow. Suddenly the child's security is destroyed by the death of one of the parents, or the need to leave home to earn his/her own bread; the affective bonds are missed and the child or teenager has to "go out into the world." Once far away, he/she must take any job that is available, usually the hardest and least remunerative. He/she meets other people in a like situation and they become a "marginal group." The group thus founded generally engage themselves in "wine-drinking practices," or become involved in illegal activities.

The young person feels marginalized, guilty, and alone. He/she takes part in the group but cannot identify with it. Rather, he/she recalls the "old days" at home, the affection experienced there and the values and norms learned. He/she feels "lost in the world" and wishes to go back to the former times and the affective and normative experiences associated with home. At that point, he/she is open and ready for the experience of Pentecostal religious conversion.

The pattern described above does not mean that the Holy Spirit is absent or indifferent in the process of conversion. Rather, it means that the Holy Spirit operates through the entire human and biographical experiences of the poor.

From this point of view, Pentecostal conversion can be seen as a religious response to a deep emotional need, one that appears to be associated with a feeling of having transgressed from the early affective order learned in childhood. Therefore, conversion could be seen as a way of trying to recuperate, at least figuratively, the early order and a pattern of relationships in which affection is lively and real.

The Experience of an Affective Community

The Pentecostal community usually offers itself as a place in which the poor can find a group of equals. The newcomer is welcomed, accepted, valued, and understood in his/her shame, guilt, and solitude. He/she is called "brother" or "sister"; is incorporated into the group and thereby is given confidence, declared useful, and invited to become a permanent member. The person's needs are considered and some urgent support is provided. Incorporated into the collective rituals of the community, he/she can sing aloud without risking the ridicule of neighbors, relatives, or friends (in Chile people only sing aloud when they are alone or drunk); he/she can share a collective prayer while praying alone during the service (which means speaking aloud without any restriction or shame), and so on. The totality of such an experience is a "healing" action by the community toward the newcomer, providing the conditions for the affirmation of a new identity and the incorporation into a "new culture."

The "healing" experience gives way to a deep feeling of belonging to a "community of equals," characterized by the expression of affection and the adoption of a specific language (the bad words are left behind and the language of the community is learned) and a particular set of behaviors (more or less opposite to the behavior the person used to display when he/she was "lost in the world").

Given that the members of the Pentecostal group are normally poor, they have many needs that must be met. If a member needs food somebody will provide it; if he/she is ill or dies, the community will assist and support; if the person is unemployed, somebody will share information about jobs available, or will ask his/her boss to provide a job for the "brother" or "sister," being willing to vouch for that person. Therefore, the Pentecostal community operates as an instrumental group in which the basic needs of the poor are met in one way or another.

The Relationships between Pentecostalism and the People's Culture

Whatever the definition of "people's religiosity," there is a basic feature that is common to them all: the idea of "spontaneity" as opposed to that of "institutionalization." In other words, the underlying issue behind the people's religion is the possibility to express in it or through it the totality of the subjective experiences of the people in their everyday lives, which are normally hidden, blocked, or ignored. This means that its meanings are closely associated with their experiences of life but also that such experiences do not have alternative ways to be elaborated or incorporated into their biographies as collective or social experiences. Moreover, one may say that the "people's religiosity" is a way of making collective or social or public the experiences of everyday life that are lived individually and privately. In this sense, Pentecostalism offers the opportunity to manifest what is hidden, repressed, or ignored each day or night, every week, every month, and every year: sin, fear, guilt, shame, pain, hope, expectation, and so on. In other words, it offers an opportunity to openly express feelings, emotions, and sentiments; namely, to express the entire basic affection and disaffection of the poor.

However, the fact that Pentecostalism is a religion of the poor implies that it is also a powerless religion. It is the religion of those who are not allowed to express themselves openly in their private or public lives. Therefore, it is not surprising that Pentecostalism usually appears to be a protective and defensive religion: its members are powerless in social, economic, political, and cultural terms. For any group to take action on any given issue it must have some kind of power (call it energy, strength, control, power, and so on); if the members of that group are powerless they will not take any action unless they somehow change their condition. Moreover, if such a group is constantly disturbed and harassed by its environment it will retreat and avoid any active contact with the outside world.

At the same time, if the group members are linked by the very subjective experience of being a community, and they accept and operate their organization within the limits that are permitted to keep the balance between spontaneity and institutionalization, then such a group will tend to avoid innovation both in terms of its internal structures and in terms of their tasks or activities. And this is exactly the case of the Pentecostal groups. In order to resist, survive, and develop, the group tends to make a radical separation and distinction between "inside" and "outside" the community.

As will be demonstrated later, however, the Pentecostal group itself is also changing with time, showing a clear evolution in the ways in which it relates to society and to the people's culture.

"Evangelization" as a Way of Relationship with the Society

The most generalized and traditional type of relationship between Pentecostalism and society has been the "evangelization" approach. At a group level it is usually carried out in the form of "preaching in the open air," while at an individual level it adopts the form of "personal preaching."

Of course, in social and cultural terms, the only people to whom the Pentecostal groups can address their message are the poor. The experience that Pentecostalism offers comes out of and goes back to the poor; therefore, it can be meaningful only to them (though it should also be said that the Pentecostal message may be meaningful as well to impoverished or suffering people even if they belong to middle-class groups). Given that the Pentecostal group sees itself as a powerless group (in social, cultural, economic, and political terms; it sees itself as "powerful" in religious terms), those called by its message are invited to "leave the world" and join the "community of the saved."

This implies also a characterization of the society and a definition of the basic relationship with it: the society is seen from the point of view of those who become "converted" and therefore generalized as "the world." The relationship with it is one of "leaving the world," namely, those who are "lost" must leave the world to find a "road to salvation." (The notion of "world" is distinct from the notion of "society"; the former indicates a subjective experience of the conditions in which the poor lives his/her life; the latter indicates an objective category that defines the historical conditions in which the people interact).

However, given that most Pentecostals come from a previous religious experience of Catholicism, the invitation to "leave the world" normally represents also an invitation to leave Catholicism. Thus Catholicism becomes identified with the "world" in which people are lost, and therefore, Catholicism also becomes a major contradictor of Pentecostalism. (Chilean Pentecostalism is highly reactive to any contact with the Catholic Church, which, in turn, appears highly reactive to Pentecostalism and normally calls it a "sect," or treats it as such).

The invitation to leave the world is not limited to alternative religious possibilities but includes any other "way out of the world" offered by the society. This means that Pentecostalism usually rejects both the political projects that offer a "new world" and the possibility of changing one's lot through "lucky strikes" (gambling, betting, and so on). In the case of indigenous people whose "world" is formed by their own deteriorated culture (often exposed to economic exploitation and social discrimination and to the invasion of social vices such as drunkenness, prostitution, drug addiction, and so on), Pentecostalism usually calls the people to "leave their own world," which includes their culture, traditions, and identities. However, this should not be seen as an attempt to destroy the native culture but as a self-protecting reaction of those who become converted against their own previous religious or social and cultural experience. Of course, many Pentecostal churches readily activate such self-protective reaction of the "converted" so as to reinterpret it along unrecognized racist lines: they are induced to adopt the lifestyle of the majority within the Pentecostal community as part of the normal common "witness" of the "saved."

Nevertheless, such "leaving the world" is always a relative way of abandoning some of the tempting and risky aspects of the life of poverty but it does not necessarily mean leaving the society or the community. Such a way would be impossible in practical terms and, after more than eighty years of continued growth and increasing institutionalization, Pentecostals know it.

"Service" as an Extension of the "Community of the Saved"

There are many ways in which the Pentecostal community actually takes care of the needs of the poor: they visit those who are ill at home or in hospital; support those who are in jail; assist the neighbors when a member of their families dies or visit them in case of major accidents; sometimes they feed the beggars and blind people, and so on. Each one of these forms of service is normally understood as a way of "extending the community of the saved" and is basically a specific way of evangelizing through different means.

For many Pentecostal churches this is the only legitimate way of serving the poor and the only one that is "according to the true gospel." Those who are served are normally seen as having above all "spiritual needs," which are satisfied together with their material needs. At the same time, they are seen as "humble" in need or in trouble, a category that does not imply any political or social opposition, likely to be activated as conflicting interests (the opposite to the category of "humble" is a rather ambiguous category that indicates individual and not structural attributes: arrogant, brave, and so on).

For a church whose members are poor and see themselves as powerless, such a way of serving the poor — with the categories it activates, avoiding political, social, or cultural conflicts — could be seen rather as a limited but valuable way of relating to the society. However, provided that the Pentecostal churches go through some process of internal change — as will be seen later on — it could also be seen as a symptom of a wider problem: the inability to learn to cope both with its internal changes and with the changes in the society as a whole.

"Service" as a Normal Relationship between the Pentecostal Community and the Poor

Since the decade of the 1960s, and in a more active way during the years of the military government (1973-90), many Pentecostal groups and churches started to implement special programs designed to serve the needs of those who were persecuted for political reasons or those who were most affected by the economic crisis that came out of the deep structural adjustments implied in the neo-liberal conversion imposed on the Chilean society.

To carry out such programs requires knowledge of the actual needs of the poor, and the best ways of coping with them. It also requires coordinating with the local or community organizations in order to make them part of the decision-making process, to organize together activities aimed at educating and training teams of people — both church members and leaders or members of social organizations. Very often the local churches became part of a network of local organizations, assuming different roles and performing various tasks within those networks.

In realizing those programs the members of the Pentecostal communities usually met different people, many of them belonging to Catholic grassroots communities or political parties. The experience of working together led to a new practice of ecumenism based on the will to serve the poor. Any theological or social reflection soon started to include both biblical and political elements, creating new opportunities for developing a common understanding of the situations they were concerned with and the meaning of their work.

Those who were served were seen as "poor" (instead of "humble") and their needs were seen as both "basic needs" and "spiritual needs." However, the latter were not necessarily nor exclusively associated with the "need of salvation," but rather their needs were associated with their search for recognition as human beings, acceptance, participation, and freedom of expression.

In turn, the category of "poor" appears opposite to the category of "rich," and both of them appear dialectically related in structural terms. In order to get out of the condition of being poor it is necessary to modify the structural relationships with the rich, and such relationships are more properly social relations. The poor should became a "subject" of their own liberation and societal change and, for the poor, it meant creating and developing their own organizations and defining their own ways of action. The role of the church then became the role of "accompanying" the poor in their own efforts to change their situation and build up their own future.

The Internal Changes within Chilean Pentecostalism and the Possibility for New Relationships with the Poor

After more than eighty years of active presence in society, Chilean Pentecostalism has become a major religion among the poor. During that time its own composition has also changed, in both social and generational terms, and those changes somehow tend to change the relationship between Pentecostalism and society and with it the relationship between Pentecostalism and the people's culture.

Social Mobility and Internal Differentiation

In social terms, the children or the grandchildren of those who were converted directly from the "world" are now rather "middle-class" people. This does not mean, however, that Pentecostalism in Chile as a whole is becoming a "middle-class" religion.

There are two main factors that seem to preclude such a possibility. On the one hand, in spite of the increasing institutionalization of many churches, the most generalized pattern of relationship among the members is that described above, namely, they tend to operate as an "affective community," establishing horizontal relations among themselves. On the other hand, in most of the churches there is always an ongoing process of incorporation of new members or new "converted" who are poor, and they normally constitute the bulk of the members of the church.

Therefore, the process of becoming middle-class people appears also as a selective one, not available for everybody but for those who are able to "make the most" of the opportunities that Pentecostalism offers its members: for instance, leaving behind alcoholism and nicotine addiction and their effects on attitudes toward work or toward the management of the household. This internal social differentiation appears as a pattern that tends to reproduce itself so as to keep the Pentecostal churches as "churches of the poor," in spite of the social mobility of some individual members.

Nevertheless, those young people who are likely to take on the new leadership within the Pentecostal churches are precisely the children of those members who have become more influential in both social and institutional terms. Because of the intensive interaction with the poor within their churches, however, these young people tend to identify themselves with the poor, both within and outside their churches.

Generational Differences

In generational terms, these young Pentecostals have built up their own ways of relating to the society. They have not had the experience of their parents and therefore for them the "world" does not appear as something to "leave," but rather it is their normal lifestyle. They have gone to school, have become professionals, technicians, or specialized workers. They have established diverse forms of social relations with people who do not belong to the church, and therefore have different cultural and social practices. Interacting with them thus requires different degrees of adaptation and tolerance.

In this sense, they do not have the problem of protecting themselves from the "world" in the same way as their parents did, though in cultural terms they may feel that there are many aspects of the social and cultural life of the society that should be kept away. It is not unlikely that they will slowly open their churches and communities to new and more significant ways of relationship with the poor, and through the poor, with the entire society.

The question remains, however, as to how they will elaborate the theological and biblical implications of their faith and their understanding and experience of society. They have learned to relate differently to society through secular ways — education, social mobility, labor or professional relationships, and so on — in social and cultural terms, but they have not necessarily learned to do it in religious terms. Therefore, there is something missing, a gap to be filled. The question is one of how to do it in a "Pentecostal way." My hope is that these lines will contribute to the working out of such a way.

CHAPTER 21

The Significance of Lausanne

John Stott

The International Congress on World Evangelization which took place at Lausanne from July 16 to 25, 1974, was on any showing a remarkable if not actually unique gathering. Of the 2,700 participants from over 150 nations, approximately 50 percent came from the Third World; they also represented a wide diversity of denominational backgrounds from both inside and outside the WCC. *Time* magazine referred to the Congress as "a formidable forum, possibly the widest-ranging meeting of Christians ever held."

The Spirit of Lausanne

The "spirit of Lausanne," though more tangible than most spirits, is difficult to describe. My analysis would be threefold. The first element was a welcome humility (we evangelicals tend to be more cocksure than humble), as penitence replaced triumphalism. Secondly, the bracing winds of freedom were blowing. Although we were united in our basic evangelical faith and commitment, especially in our common submission to the supreme authority of Scripture, there was no party line laid down by committee which the rest of us were expected to toe. Rather the contrary. The Planning Committee had the courage to invite speakers whose views were known to be controversial and made no attempt to censor them. As a result there were tensions and there was lively argument. Issues were faced and not swept under the carpet. Frankly, this was a sign of maturity not always evident in evangelical assemblies. We had debate and disagreement, but without discord.

Thirdly, there was a conspicuous air of seriousness. Here were not hardened and rather blasé professional conference-goers, but a meeting of Christians who believed in God and meant business with God. Having read both

John Mott's and Temple Gairdner's accounts of Edinburgh 1910, I would guess that something of the excitement and euphoria of Edinburgh were recaptured at Lausanne. We separated in a mood of expectation, determined under God that the vision of Lausanne should be fulfilled and the dream of world evangelization come true. This resolve was expressed in the Lausanne Covenant, which concludes: "We enter into a solemn covenant with God and with each other to pray, to plan and to work together for the evangelization of the whole world." The fact that without any pressure (indeed, rather the reverse) over 2,000 had signed the Covenant before leaving the Congress is a mark of the earnestness and solidarity of the participants.

Clarification of "Mission"

Perhaps the first major achievement of the Congress lies in our clarified understanding of the mission of the people of God. Philip Potter told the WCC Central Committee at its meeting in Crete in 1967 that "ecumenical literature since Amsterdam has used 'mission,' 'witness' and 'evangelism' interchangeably." The same could be said of evangelical literature. But now there is a willingness among evangelicals to accept that if mission (which is God's first and the church's second) is what God sends his people into the world to do, then it includes social as well as evangelistic activity. Samuel Escobar's paper on "Evangelism and man's search for freedom, justice, and fulfillment" put the cat among the pigeons. But, though not everybody would accept his precise formulation, I judge that the great majority endorsed the thrust of his argument. He warned against the danger of mutilating the gospel by eliminating the demands for the fruit of repentance in concrete social and ethical terms. He emphasized that "God's salvation transforms man in the totality of his life," and that we must renounce "a false and anti-biblical dichotomy between evangelism and social action."

So the final draft of the Lausanne Covenant brought the two topics into juxtaposition, paragraph four being entitled "The Nature of Evangelism" and paragraph five "Christian Social Responsibility." Both paragraphs need to be studied with care, so that unjustified deductions are not drawn from them. Paragraph five, for example, specifically disassociates itself from several recent ecumenical positions. It affirms that "reconciliation with man is not reconciliation with God, nor is social action evangelism, nor is political liberation salvation." That is to say, although recognizing the indispensability of both parts of these three pairs, it repudiates all attempts to identify them. This is, of course, an allusion to Bangkok. True, the Bangkok Report speaks of "salvation in four dimensions" (economic, political, social, and personal), and adds that "our concentration upon the social, economic and political implications of the gospel does not in any way deny the personal and eternal dimensions of salvation." Nevertheless, the impression the report gives is that the really important kind of contemporary "salvation" is sociopolitical; only a rather grudging assent seems to be given to personal salvation. Certainly no clarion call to evangelism was sounded at Bangkok. So Lausanne both denied that socio-politico-economic liberation is "salvation" in biblical terms (this hermeneutical question between Geneva and Lausanne still needs to be faced) and insisted that liberation and salvation are two distinct works of God. The confusion of creation and redemption, common grace and saving grace, the reformation of structures and the regeneration of persons seems to lie at the heart of current ecumenical-evangelical tensions.

Evangelicals and Social Action

But paragraph five of the Lausanne Covenant is not just negative. It expresses penitence "both for our neglect and for having sometimes regarded evangelism and social concern as mutually exclusive," and affirms that "evangelism and socio-political involvement are both part of our Christian duty." Then it goes on to ground our duty in doctrine. It touches on four biblical doctrines. First, the doctrine of God: "we affirm that God is both the Creator and Judge of all men" and that we should share "his concern for justice and reconciliation throughout human society and for the liberation of men from every kind of oppression." Secondly, the doctrine of man: "Because mankind is made in the image of God, every person, regardless of race, religion, colour, culture, class, sex or age, has an intrinsic dignity because of which he should be respected and served, not exploited." Thirdly, the doctrine of salvation: "The message of salvation implies also a message of judgment upon every form of alienation, oppression and discrimination, and we should not be afraid to denounce evil and injustice wherever they exist." Further, "the salvation we claim should be transforming us in the totality of our personal and social responsibilities. Faith without works is dead." Fourthly, the doctrine of the kingdom: "When people receive Christ they are born again into his Kingdom and must seek not only to exhibit but also to spread its righteousness in the midst of an unrighteous world."

It should be remembered that Lausanne was a Congress on *World Evangelization*. It is striking, therefore, that Christian social responsibility should have been discussed at all, let alone so much. When the Lausanne

Continuation Committee met in Mexico City in January this year, there was some uncertainty whether the mandate given by the Congress to the Committee was restricted to evangelism or included the wider concerns expressed in the Covenant. In practice, each regional group will doubtless make up its own mind on this issue. Certainly, evangelicals have only begun to theologize their newly recovered awareness of sociopolitical obligation. There is need for a deeper and clearer understanding ourselves, and for theological debate with the liberation school. It may be of interest that a European Conference of Evangelical Theologians is planned for August 1976, and that its topic will be "The Kingdom of God and Modern Man."

The Priority of Evangelism

While recognizing that the Christian mission in the world embraces both social and evangelistic action, the Covenant explicitly states that "in the church's mission of sacrificial service evangelism is primary" (paragraph six). It is on this subject, therefore, that the Congress and the Covenant concentrate. Moreover, if within our mission priority should be given to evangelism, then also within evangelism priority should be given to those who have never heard, or never truly heard, the gospel. Before the Fourth Assembly of the WCC Dr. Donald McGavran of the Fuller School of World Mission and Institute of Church Growth wrote an outspoken article entitled: "Will Uppsala Betray the Two Billion?" I myself have vivid memories of the discussions which took place in Section II ("Renewal in Mission") as we were locked in a rather fruitless confrontation and somehow never managed to secure a true meeting of minds or clarification of issues. In the end the report contained a mention of the world's two billion unevangelized. But Uppsala gave no urgent summons to world evangelization such as Alan Walker of Sydney tells me he has urged the World Council to issue since New Delhi 1961. Now, however, Lausanne has issued such a call. "More than 2,700 million people, which is more than two-thirds of mankind, have yet to be evangelized. We are ashamed that so many have been neglected; it is a standing rebuke to us and to the whole Church" (paragraph nine). The same paragraph, borrowing a phrase of Dr. McGavran's, went on to state that "there is now . . . in many parts of the world an unprecedented receptivity to the Lord Jesus Christ," as a result of which "this is the time for churches and para-church agencies to pray earnestly for the salvation of the unreached and to launch new efforts to achieve world evangelization."

What sort of evangelism was envisaged at Lausanne? Four chief aspects of it may be selected, and will be illustrated by quotations from the Covenant.

Biblical Faith

The first is an uncompromising commitment to the biblical gospel. We who were at Lausanne believe that evangelism must be defined primarily in terms of the evangel. It is not the results so much as the message by which evangelism is constituted. To be sure, we expect results, for we believe in God and are seeking to "persuade men" (2 Cor. 5:9). Nevertheless, to quote from Dr. J. I. Packer's well-known essay: "The way to tell whether in fact you are evangelizing is not to ask whether conversions are known to have resulted from your witness. It is to ask whether you are faithfully making known the gospel message."[1] We are aware, of course, that many modern theologians will retort that there is no gospel in the New Testament, but rather a whole series of distinct gospels. We venture to disagree. Although indeed the New Testament contains a variety of emphases (so that Paul could write of "my gospel"), some historical development, and different evangelistic approaches according to the situation, yet at the same time "there is only one Saviour and only one gospel" (paragraph three). So the Covenant includes unequivocal statements on biblical inspiration, truthfulness, and authority (paragraph two) and on "the uniqueness and universality of Christ" (paragraph three). The latter paragraph rejects both universalism and syncretism as "derogatory to Christ and the gospel," and affirms that "Jesus Christ, being himself the only God-man, who gave himself as the only ransom for sinners, is the only mediator between God and man."

The Centrality of the Church

The second aspect of evangelism as set forth at Lausanne is the centrality of the church in the purpose of God and in evangelism. Evangelicals have often seemed (and indeed been) rugged individualists with a low, rather pragmatic view of the church. It is heartening, therefore, to read the assertion that "the church is at the very centre of God's cosmic purpose," as is clear from Ephesians, and is "his appointed means of spreading the gospel" (paragraph six). There can be no evangelism without the church. This immediately raises the questions of co-operation and renewal. On cooperation, the Covenant accepts that "evangelism . . . summons us to unity" and that "disunity undermines our gospel of reconciliation" (paragraph seven). At the same time, be-

1. J. I. Packer, *Evangelism and the Sovereignty of God* (Downers Grove, Ill.: InterVarsity Press, 1961), p. 41.

cause evangelism involves the evangel, one hopes that our friends in the ecumenical movement will at least understand our conscientious problem when we are asked to engage in cooperative evangelistic endeavor with those who seem to us to have compromised the integrity of the gospel. Of course we accept that there is room for disagreement on secondary issues, but not on the fundamentals of historic, biblical Christianity. We believe that the very church which is God's agent in evangelism "becomes a stumbling block to evangelism when it betrays the gospel" (paragraph six). There is some hope, however, that "we who share the same biblical faith," and yet have separated from one another unnecessarily, will now be more "closely united in fellowship, work and witness." Indeed, "we confess that our testimony has sometimes been marred by sinful individualism and needless duplication" (paragraph seven). So the Lausanne Continuation Committee has been given a mandate to develop regional and functional cooperation. This should include strategic regional planning not only between Western missions (whose "dominant role . . . is fast disappearing," paragraph eight) and Third World missions ("a great new resource for world evangelization"), but also in "a growing partnership of churches" and of parachurch agencies.

The concept of the church renewed for mission is hardly novel in the ecumenical movement, but Lausanne saw evangelicals recognizing in healthy self-criticism the need for the spiritual and moral renewal of their own churches. "A church which preaches the cross must itself be marked by the cross" (paragraph six). It is not only a doctrinal betrayal of the gospel which becomes a stumbling block to evangelism, but also a lack of faith or of love or of "scrupulous honesty in all things including promotion and finance." The church must also become immersed in secular society, and not stand aloof from it. Both "presence" and "dialogue" are indispensable to evangelism, not as an alternative to proclamation, but as providing the only context within which the proclamation may be made with Christian sensitivity.

Culture and the Gospel

Thirdly, Lausanne emphasized the need to take culture seriously. The relation of culture to evangelism was a major topic of debate. Although there is still hesitation among us about contemporary references to black theology, African theology, etc., the Covenant does recognize that our cultural background is bound to affect our perception of the gospel and that the Holy Spirit "illumines the minds of God's people in every culture to perceive its truth (*sc.* of God's revelation) freshly through their own eyes" (paragraph two). There is also a frank confession that "missions have all too frequently exported with the gospel an alien culture" (paragraph ten). It was Dr. René Padilla of Argentina who popularized the expression "culture Christianity." He referred to the Spanish conquest of Latin America and to nineteenth-century European colonialism. But his main example (which caused much offense to some) was the equation with Christianity of the American way of life, including its emphasis on technology and methodology. I gather that Dr. Padilla's strictures were taken as a veiled critique of the Church Growth School, although he made no mention of this. Yet the Church Growth pioneers will have read the criticisms of Professor Orlando Costas in his recent *The Church and Its Mission: A Shattering Critique from the Third World.* I find myself hoping that critics and the criticized will have the courage to face each other. The dialogue was only begun at Lausanne; its continuance could be fruitful in mutual understanding and correction.

Cosmic Conflict

A fourth aspect of Lausanne's presentation of evangelism was the recognition of a cosmic conflict. Evangelism is not a merely human activity, a question of perfecting techniques. We believe that unseen intelligences are arrayed against us. However much the wise and sophisticated may smile at our naïveté, we are convinced that "we are engaged in constant spiritual warfare with the principalities and powers of evil, who are seeking to overthrow the church and frustrate its task of world evangelization" (paragraph twelve). This paragraph of the Covenant goes further and identifies some of the areas in which we detect the activity of our enemy. It speaks on the one hand of false ideologies outside the church and on the other of false gospels inside it. For the devil is an arch-deceiver. But we do not imagine that we ourselves are immune to the temptations and deceptions of the devil. On the contrary, we are aware of the subtle kinds of worldliness to which we evangelicals are prone.

So we need the armor of God. More than that, we believe in the power of the Holy Spirit, and we acknowledge that "without his witness ours is futile" (paragraph fourteen). Every stage of the process of conversion and sanctification — conviction of sin, faith in Christ, new birth, and Christian growth — is *his* work. The paragraph refers both to the fruit of the Spirit and to the gifts of the Spirit. To some extent the challenge posed by the charismatic movement was faced at Lausanne. Both charismatics and non-charismatics, together with people who have a foot in both camps, not to mention members of mainline Pentecostal churches, were given a fair share of the platform and of the subsidiary meetings. There was discussion and disagreement, but again no really fundamental disunity. For all of us are united in our conviction that what the Church needs most of all is "a visitation of the sovereign Spirit of God."

Perhaps if we who were at Lausanne are asked what above all else we want to say to the rest of the church, our message would concern the Word and the Spirit. To us the major conditions of true evangelism, and therefore of the evangelization of the world, are a recovery of confidence both in the truth of God's Word and in the power of God's Spirit.

CHAPTER 22

Toward Developing an Adequate and Comprehensive Understanding of Evangelization

Jerry Persha

The evangelizing mission of the church is at the heart of the Christian community's saving identity and purpose in the world. The church exists to evangelize.[1] All of its internal life, its organizational structure, liturgical celebration, and communal service, together with its external life of witness and dialogue in the world, is for the purpose of leading people into the good news which Jesus Christ represents. The church is simply called to celebrate through worship, to witness by life and deed, and to interpret by word the good news of Jesus Christ for human life in all aspects: personal, social, and cultural.

It is this definition of evangelization which will be the object of our following reflections. To develop an adequate and comprehensive understanding of the evangelizing mission of the church entails, therefore, at least three distinct but inseparable dimensions: the content of evangelization, the identity of the church in relationship to that content, and the manner of communicating it. All three dimensions are intimately related and will mutually influence one another. Let us turn to the first, the content of evangelization.

The Content of Evangelization

Paul VI in his Apostolic Exhortation, *Evangelii Nuntiandi,* has succinctly summarized the heart of evangelization as that of communicating the good news of Jesus Christ for human life to all peoples. In his exhortation, Paul VI attempts to define the good news by renaming it after the central mystery

1. Paul VI, *On Evangelization in the Modern World* (Washington, D.C.: United States Catholic Conference, 1976), art. 14, p. 12.

which consumed all of Jesus' historical life, ministry, and message: the kingdom or reign of God.[2] He affirms that the church is called principally, and before all else, to proclaim the saving character of God's reign. In fact, all else is relative to this mystery. Everything else becomes "the rest," given in addition.[3] To know, therefore, the content and dimensions of the good news first implies understanding the intrinsic meaning of God's reign which initially unfolded in the life and person of Jesus Christ as he moved and mingled with humanity in the Jewish society of his day.

The Meaning of the Reign of God in Jesus' Life

Much has been written in recent years about the meaning of the reign of God from scholarly exploration of the New Testament writings — particularly the three Synoptic Gospels. We will not attempt to explore the vast literature on the subject, but rather, from that literature, try to offer a synthetic portrait of the saving character of the mystery of God's reign as the mystery interpretatively expressed itself in Jesus Christ. It is hoped we will be faithful to the consensus that is being reached by scholars on this subject.

Two inseparable dimensions of God's reign continuously seem to emerge from Jesus' message and life. One involves Jesus' personal experience of God's sovereignty over him. "Abba" is the name Jesus gives to God. The other dimension is Jesus' enactment of that very experience through his life and ministry. Both dimensions offer us clear avenues for understanding the meaning of the reign of God, which was the heart of Jesus' mission.

Let us turn to the first: Jesus' particular experience of God's sovereignty. For the Jewish people, God's kingdom first meant the revelation of him who refuses to abdicate his sovereignty over human life and creation. "You shall do homage to the Lord your God and worship him alone." The first commandment of the Decalogue always remained the enduring test of every Jew and of the Jewish nation as a whole. God's sovereignty contradicts everything which comes on the scene in its own name, for its own glory, and by its own power. Not to recognize and live obediently under that sovereignty was to fall into the sin of idolatry — the primal sin of humanity. Idolatry, after all, is human life addicted to and ruled by another sovereignty, fashioned from the seductive attractions of the finite things of this world.

The Gospel accounts leave little doubt that Jesus radically accepted the

2. Paul VI, *On Evangelization,* art. 8, p. 10.

3. Paul VI, *On Evangelization,* art. 8, p. 10.

first commandment of the Decalogue in his own life; that acceptance alone would lead him to the cross. Yet it is also apparent from the Gospels that Jesus' experience of God's sovereignty was not one of distance or detachment but of confident trust and childlike abandonment. God was Abba to Jesus, God was also Abba to all of human life, compassionate, generous, and forgiving. Jesus' very words and deeds suggest this. Three dimensions of his ministry prominently stand out as interpreting for us the meaning of God's sovereignty over human life. One is that Jesus appears "to ritualize" the saving rule of Abba through his cures and exorcisms, and especially through his table fellowship with outcasts and the poor. All these actions manifest not only the indiscriminate character of his Abba's generosity and compassion but God's actual preoccupation and preference for the abandoned of society. "Abba" first implies compassionate and merciful justice. Jesus' own actions and behavior prominently attest to this. And yet no one in principle was excluded from God's reign. The terrorist (Zealot) and the traditionally faithful, the collaborator (tax collector) and the intellectual (scribe), the social outcast and the prominent — all were invited to trust God's sovereignty as interpretatively expressed in the actions of Jesus. Universal inclusion appears to be a characteristic feature of God's reign.

A second dimension of Jesus' ministry articulating the meaning of God's sovereignty was his prophetic preaching, which frequently took the form of parables. Many of these parables tend to evoke a vision of God's presence at work in the ordinary events of men and women. They often reflect experiences of lavish, unexpected generosity. They invite reflection upon qualities of life shared by all: vulnerability, dependency, and need. Some parables, moreover, manifest a distinct quality of offensiveness because they demand a reversal of priorities: the poor and outcasts are now blest, the last are first, one saves life by squandering it. Through his prophetic teaching, Jesus will critique the socioreligious establishment of his day by insisting that human life and well-being, justice and forgiveness, genuine care and concern take precedence over everything. These are the very values and interests which the sovereignty and life of Abba imply. Consequently, all idolatrous pursuits of power and greed, all relationships of oppression and inhuman dependency must be given up. For inclusion into God's reign, personal and social conversion is therefore necessary.

The third prominent manner in which Jesus expresses the meaning of God's sovereignty is conversion. Conversion and repentance, in fact, describe the style through which God's reign is to be lived and shared with others in history. Jesus' life and ministry are a call to conversion, to a life of childlike faith and trust in the unbelievable closeness, generosity, and forgiveness of

Abba. Such conversion implies letting go of false securities which push people to grasp at life and others. Repentance is the painful yet joyous recognition that human life has only one center, the sovereign grace and rule of Abba. And it was precisely to this center which Jesus gave witness through the praxis of his life. At root, conversion is turning toward, living from, and serving God's sovereignty in this world. It therefore implies the rejection of idolatry in one's personal life and a commitment as well to expose the idolatry of society. Both require suffering. That is why the reign of God has a profoundly paschal character.

The Paschal Character of the Reign of God

The Gospel portrait of Jesus clearly suggests that, as a creature, he resisted idolatry in his personal life. He did not live as if he himself were the center of his own life. He lived from and for the grace of God. He never denied his creatureliness and the limitations which his human life implied. Jesus accepted his finitude; he suffered and overcame its inherent threat by opening himself up in faith to something greater than death itself. That is why Jesus never appeared to hide from his creatureliness through rebellious pride, lust, or power. That is also why Jesus never sought to circumvent suffering, pain, and persecution as he ministered to the sovereignty of Abba in the society of his day. He was reconciled to his human condition. Unlike the old Adam, he did not grasp at equality with God, but humbly accepted his creatureliness in obedience and love. He therefore lived humanly, and to live humanly is to suffer.

Fidelity to God in his sovereignty also impelled Jesus to expose the idolatry of his society. This too implied suffering. He was not afraid to confront injustice, authoritarianism, and the idolatrous use of power and wealth. He resisted the destructive influences of society which sought to derail him from his mission. Society frequently makes uncompromisingly good individuals suffer violently and undergo martyrdom. Jesus' very death expressed his willingness to accept even imposed suffering and persecution rather than to be unfaithful to his Abba. To live humanly is to suffer, but to bear one's humanity faithfully, serving God's sovereignty in a society ruled by other interests, is to suffer greatly.

Jesus' death on the cross, therefore, tells us what authentic human life looks like when lived in obedience to God within a social environment saturated by sin. Jesus' free and voluntary acceptance of death was his supreme act of fidelity, his deepest conversion experience. The cross adequately summarizes what his entire life was about; unflinching service and obedience to the truth, goodness, and sovereignty of Abba. And by transcending his fear of suffering and death through faith-filled obedience, Jesus encountered the fullness of life and glory. His resurrection proclaimed and witnessed to this fact. The mystery of the reign of God, therefore, is the mystery of God's transforming life encountered through obedience unto suffering and death. It implies fidelity to the gracious sovereignty of God and therefore to our human condition as creatures. But it also implies the fidelity of serving and ministering to that sovereignty in society. The resurrection of Jesus proclaimed that all such cruciform fidelity is the doorway leading to life, indeed, to the fullness of life and glory.

The Reign of God Becomes the Reign of the Risen Lord

To know, therefore, the shape and content of the reign of God and its good news for human life is to know Jesus Christ. That is why Paul VI could affirm in his Apostolic Exhortation that Jesus Christ himself is the good news of God for humanity. In him is found everything that humankind is groping for concerning God, the meaning and purpose of life and death, and humanity's final destiny and truth.[4] Our knowledge of the reign of God, however, is not merely confined to the historical Jesus. After all, the earliest Christian communities continued to experience in faith Jesus Christ as risen and present among them. In fact, it was the experience of Jesus as the risen one that enabled them to remember and interpret the meaning of his historical life and ministry. And it is this experience of Jesus as risen that can deepen our understanding of God's reign.

Outside the Synoptic Gospels, reference to the reign of God markedly thins out in the preaching and teaching vocabulary of the church in the New Testament. The early Christian communities do not appear to preach the kingdom but Jesus Christ himself. The Pauline Epistles call others not to the kingdom of God as such but to Jesus Christ, the exalted Lord of the whole world and of the church. Ephesians (1:20-21) celebrates the risen one who has been enthroned at God's right hand in the heavenly realm. First Corinthians (15:24-25) speaks of him who is destined to reign until God has put all enemies under his feet. Believers are called into union with Christ, to be in Christ. For Paul, God's reign is now the reign of the risen Jesus. The same can be said of the Johannine writings. The book of Revelation (11:15) perhaps best sums it up: "The sovereignty of this world has passed to our Lord and his Christ and he shall reign forever and ever."

4. Paul VI, *On Evangelization,* art. 53, p. 36.

For the early church there is no divine reign of which Jesus of Nazareth is not the center. Christ himself replaces the kingdom terminology in the church's faith and preaching vocabulary. The deeper significance of the mystery of God's reign is now realized in terms of the living presence of the risen Christ, reigning over all creation and his church. And it is this reign of the risen Lord which can offer us a greater understanding and appreciation of the universality of Jesus Christ himself.

The Universality of Jesus Christ

The resurrection was a new and creative event which fully exalted Jesus into the mystery of God by totally filling and transforming him with the Spirit of God, so that he in turn could share that Spirit with others. The writings of both Luke and John make clear that through his resurrection and exaltation, Jesus, the man born of, and empowered by, the Spirit, now becomes Lord of the Spirit — the one who bestows the Spirit on creation (cf. Acts: 2:33; John 15:26). Jesus, therefore, through his resurrection, begins to share in God's own prerogative as the Giver of the Spirit.[5] Paul in his writings can even name the Spirit "the Spirit of Christ" (Rom. 8:9), "the Spirit of God's Son" (Gal. 4:6), and "the Spirit of Jesus Christ" (Phil. 1:19). The reign of God is now the reign of the crucified and risen one who seeks to rule over creation through the power and presence of his Spirit.

Here the universality of Christ can best be appreciated. By virtue of his resurrection, Jesus is no longer bound by time, history, or culture. He becomes, in fact, the totally *transcultural* one, present to all of creation through the grace of his Spirit. Wherever and whenever men and women consciously or unconsciously abandon themselves in obedience to the influence of that gift, present to them in the depths of their humanity, their lives will bear the paschal stamp and direction of the life of Jesus Christ himself. Life lived in the Spirit assumes a "Christologic" shape — a life of obedience and service, likened to that of Jesus Christ, which refuses to bypass Golgotha but chooses instead to enter the likeness of his suffering and death and thereby also experience the power of his resurrected life. As we shall explore below, the evangelizing mission of the church will demand a profound fidelity and sensitivity to the life of this paschal mystery of grace expressing itself in the lives, societies, cultures, and religions of all people. Wherever that life is unfolding, there also the sovereignty of the crucified and risen Lord is being expressed in history.

5. James D. G. Dunn, *Christology in the Making* (Philadelphia: Westminster, 1980), p. 142.

The Identity of the Church in Relationship to the Cosmic Reign of Christ

We have already mentioned that the evangelizing mission of the church is at the heart of the Christian community's saving identity in the world. Just as the central focus of Jesus' own mission was the proclamation and enactment of the reign of God, so too the heart and purpose of the church's mission cannot be otherwise; it must be intimately related to that reign, deriving its particular identity and mission from it. That reign, however, has assumed the name of the crucified and risen one who exercises God's sovereignty over creation through the gift of his Spirit. The saving mission of the church, therefore, rests upon its unique relationship to the Spirit of Jesus Christ. Only by specifying this relationship can the church's identity and importance to humanity be properly clarified.

The Church Community: The Creation of the Spirit

The ecclesial community itself is the creation of the Spirit of the risen Christ. Through his resurrection, Jesus is totally transformed and becomes himself "life-giving Spirit" to others. Through the experience of the risen Lord's gift of the Spirit among them, the first disciples became a proclaiming and witnessing body of believers. What founds the church, therefore, is the action of God who raised Jesus Christ from the dead through the power of the Spirit. Through that Spirit an assembly of people is gathered from the various nations to share a common life flowing from the event of the new creation, the resurrection of Jesus. The church itself is the beginning of the new creation in time, anticipating and heralding the destiny to which all of human history is summoned.

What properly distinguishes the church community, however, cannot simply be the life of the Spirit, since that very Spirit has been poured out over all flesh. All of humanity has been graced by its presence and, consequently, interiorly invited to pattern its life after the paschal and transformative character of Jesus' own life.[6] What distinguishes the church, more particularly, is its explicit faith in Jesus Christ — a faith which acknowledges his universal lordship over creation. The one advantage that the church has over the rest of humanity is that there has been granted to it the faith to recognize and to acknowledge the cosmic reign of Jesus Christ in the Spirit. Through the ecclesial

6. Walter M. Abbott, S.J., *The Documents of Vatican II* (New York: American Press, 1966), pp. 221-22.

body that reign achieves a unique specificity. The church is that sphere or portion of the world wherein Christ's universal rule in the Spirit is openly confessed and celebrated in faith, consciously lived in a community of shared life, and publicly witnessed to in the world through a life of transforming service. The church does not in any way confine Christ's lordship, but rather signifies its meaning and purpose by living the gift of his Spirit in obedient acknowledgment. Herein lies the importance of the church for humanity.

The Importance of the Church for Humanity

Because of its faith in Jesus Christ, the church knows the destiny and goal to which all of human history is summoned. Everything under the heavens is to be reconciled and united in and through Christ (Eph. 1:9-10). He is the mystery hidden for all ages, the goal toward which all of creation tends. Christ's work is the reconciliation of the universe through the gift of the Spirit. The church, therefore, must become in its own life and body a definition and sign of the reconciliation which the Spirit effects. In this way Christ's lordship becomes concretized through it and signified to the world.

The church, moreover, knows the paschal shape of human life responding to the Spirit. The reign of Christ cannot be manifested in the life of the ecclesial body if pain, struggle, and suffering are bypassed. The sign of reconciliation which is offered to the world is cruciform in character, patterned after the life and ministry of Jesus. The church is called to become the place where paschal liberation and deliverance are being realized and where, therefore, authentic reconciliation and peace are engendered through the obedient and worship-filled acceptance of the Spirit's life. Only in this way does the church become sacrament of the transforming life of the Spirit — the reflectively Christified portion of the universe wherein God's universal self-offer is not only consciously acknowledged and celebrated but sealed through the actual life of its members and visibly signified to the world.

And yet if the church is called to be sacrament of Christ's reign in the Spirit, it is also called to serve the reconciling life of Christ's Spirit in the world. It is both sacrament to that life and servant in the world for its continual attainment. Indeed, Christ is head of the church as Lord of the universe, and as Lord of the universe he continually reminds the ecclesial body of its mission of service to him in the world in the work of reconciliation.[7] That

7. Donald Senior and Carroll Stuhlmueller, C.P., *The Biblical Foundations for Mission* (Maryknoll, N.Y.: Orbis, 1983), p. 202.

very mission of service will reflect two prominent ways in which the good news is communicated: witness and dialogue.

The Mission of the Church: Communicating the Content of the Good News

The church's mission to the world is to minister to the reconciling work of Christ. It is an inherently communitarian mission of service which must express the life of the Spirit as well as seek to promote it in the world at the same time. The ministry which the church renders the world, therefore, must itself give witness to God revealed by Jesus Christ.[8] The first means of evangelization must always be an authentic life of Christian witness.[9] People, after all, are much more prone to listen to the witness of a genuine life of service and love than to the words of a proclaimer. And if they do listen to the latter, it is because the proclaimer is a witness.[10] The church's mission of witness in fact becomes the *silent* proclamation of the good news.[11] It is the first and most important way of evangelizing.

Paul VI insists, however, that a life of witness is incomplete without the clarifying word of the gospel message.[12] Nonetheless, the gospel message is not something to be inflicted or imposed on others. The conscience and convictions of all must be deeply respected. Authentic Christian witness will often provoke friendship, questioning, conversation, and even admiration among people. It may, in fact, initiate a dialogue in the lives of others concerning the meaning and purpose of the witness. Opportunities will be provided to name the mystery of Jesus Christ, but according to the rhythm, pace, and conversation of others and always in relationship to their life. Dialogue, therefore, will give primacy to the world of the other. It will seek to conform itself to the contours of that world so that the message of the good news can speak vitally to human life and also adequately interpret the often inarticulate aspirations of sincere inquirers. In this way, the Christian message itself will be more deeply understood.

Witness and word of dialogue are the two indispensable ways in which the content of the good news is communicated. Both are necessary in the invitation to others to consider the meaning of Jesus Christ. Witness without

8. Paul VI, *On Evangelization,* art. 26, p. 20.
9. Paul VI, *On Evangelization,* art. 41, p. 28.
10. Paul VI, *On Evangelization,* art. 41, p. 28.
11. Paul VI, *On Evangelization,* art. 21, p. 17.
12. Paul VI, *On Evangelization,* art. 22, p. 18.

interpretation, unaccompanied by word of dialogue, can remain ambiguous or unclear for the other. But equally so, word of dialogue without witness is empty. Both must complement one another.

If dialogue and witness are the two primary ways of communicating the content of the good news, they, nevertheless, can only be properly exercised through a deep sensitivity to the life of the Spirit, the grace mystery, expressing itself in the personal, social, and cultural life of the people. Evangelization at heart is the creative conjoining and interplay between God's outward word expressed in Jesus Christ with God's inward word of the Spirit. It is the grace that is already present encountering the grace that has come in the message and life of Jesus Christ. The Spirit, as it expresses itself through the personal lives, societies, cultures, and even religions of people, does not lead beyond Christ but ever deeper into the mystery of Christ. Through a deep sensitivity to the diverse expressions of the life of the Spirit, insights and challenges can be received that would lead in turn to a deeper understanding of the mystery of Christ himself. Let us turn once again to the life of transformation that manifested itself in Jesus Christ to discern more clearly the fundamental characteristics and shape of the Spirit's life. The church's witness and dialogue are intimately related to that life and can be clarified through it.

Transforming Characteristics of the Life of the Spirit

The mystery of God's universal self-communication is, of course, the mystery of grace offered to, and present in, the lives of men and women everywhere. We have named this mystery of grace more particularly the Spirit of Jesus Christ. As bestower of the Spirit, the risen Lord's presence and rule over creation can be thought of in terms of the Spirit's life. As Jesus' own life makes clear, the Spirit engenders a life of paschal transformation in human beings wherever and whenever it is accepted and embraced in obedience and abandonment. Jesus himself is the fullest description of what the transforming life of the Spirit both looks like and invites humanity to become.

The life of transformation that expressed itself in Jesus Christ can perhaps best be described by three commonplace but nonetheless exceedingly important realities, faith, hope, and love. If we analyze carefully the Synoptic Gospels, we find all three thoroughly present in the historical life of Jesus. Each will be characteristic of the transforming life of the Spirit.

First of all, there can be no question from the Gospel portrait of Jesus that he confidently trusted in the goodness and nearness of this Abba. In fact it appears that his deep human faith in God enabled him to embrace suffering and death responsibly and kept him thereby from swerving in his loyalty, devotion, and obedience to his God. He never tried to become as creature what he was not: the source and center of life. He always lived from and for the grace of Abba. Even more, he personally accepted in confidence and trust the violent death of persecution that society imposed upon him. He transcended his fear of suffering and death through faith in God. He did not let fear of suffering, pain, and death derail his journey of obedience. Through faith, he entered fully into his humanity and creatureliness and bore the suffering involved with living human life authentically, even when made more difficult by a sinful social order.

The Spirit likewise invites all humanity to a way of life characterized by faith. Whenever men and women transcend their fear of suffering and death as they authentically struggle to live and share their humanity with others, there the life of the Spirit is unfolding. For implied in that struggle is confidence and trust, faith in the intrinsic worthiness of their efforts. Even if such faith is not explicitly articulated or even directed toward a transcendent reality, only the Spirit, the divine self-gift, can engender such magnanimous and risky trust. Implied here is the inarticulate movement of men and women transcending themselves and the condition of their life through suffering and pain toward some ultimate and lasting meaning both for themselves and for others. Genuine human faith is the work and movement of grace in the life of humanity.

Closely allied to faith was Jesus' hope. The Synoptic Gospels also record some of the defeats, disappointments, and failures of his mission. And yet there is no note of fatalism or despair on Jesus' part. Without hope in the truth and value of his mission and therefore in his Abba, Jesus could have exercised no responsible movement of his freedom toward others in obedience to his God. Human freedom cannot act responsibly without hoping in the intrinsic worthiness and importance of its efforts. Without hope, freedom becomes more than static; it falls into despair, indifference, and apathy. Certainly none of these qualities emerge from the life and actions of Jesus recorded in the Gospels. And unless we want to assume that Jesus, in dying, suffered a moral breakdown, we may suppose that he went to his death in love, offering himself for others and hoping that God's future, always greater than the present, would be gracious, responsive, and vindicating. Through hope even in the face of hardship and disappointments — even in the face of threatening death — Jesus is inspired to creative fidelity, to continue his journey of obedience. He did not succumb to the illusion of progress or instant success but clung to his experience of God through which he enacted a new vision of humanity based on the interests and life of his Abba. Hope, therefore, was another transforming dimension which characterized his human life. Through it, he risked himself for a better future, struggling to bring about a state of affairs not yet existing.

It is likewise the Spirit's involvement with men and women everywhere that enables humanity to hope and continue patiently its efforts to construct a better world, to realize a history of human solidarity together — even in the face of bitter disappointment, failure, and death. Here, too, even if such hope is not explicitly directed toward some transcendent reality, it nevertheless is religious, for only the Spirit, the divine presence, can keep humanity from despairing about its frequently felt experiences of incompleteness and failure. It is through hope that men and women can break the shackles of fatalism and transcend their egotistical fears which close the future to the status quo of their present securities and condition. Genuine hope is the movement of transcendence, the fruit of the Spirit, whereby people everywhere can risk themselves and their lives to construct a world which mirrors a vision of a better future for the life of humanity.

The third transforming element that defines Jesus' life was love. Jesus had a deep sense of being loved and cherished by his Abba. Unlike the old Adam, he expresses and lives his true self — a self convinced of being God's beloved, a self borne by that love, and, therefore, a self no longer shaped and dominated by fear but freed to love in return. Jesus was the true image of God who patterned his conduct on the graciousness and generosity of his Abba, never revolting against or tiring of that dependency. His life was the expression of humanity fully reshaped to the image of God — a self so consumed by, and convinced of, God's love that Jesus could engender that capability in others by expressing it himself.

Again it is the Spirit's presence and involvement with humanity which provokes in the lives of men and women self-acceptance and the conviction of the importance and absolute value of every human being. Without self-acceptance and a deep appreciation for the lives of others, the human family could not construct a community of service and love together. Only the Spirit, the divine self-presence, could relieve the burden of human guilt, convince people that they are loved and forgiven, and provoke in them through that very conviction, the movement of their freedom toward others in unselfish service. Through the Spirit, men and women are enabled to transcend themselves by going out of themselves and, in that exodus, express their often inarticulate longings to be lastingly united to others.

This paschal and transformative pattern of life lived in faith, hope, and love is the deepest expression of the life of the Spirit. Wherever this pattern is present in the lives of peoples, cultures, and religions, there the reign of Christ is unfolding. Indeed, the ultimate mystery of life itself, experienced by all the religious faiths of the world, can perhaps best be appreciated by its power to unleash a similar pattern of living in the lives of believers everywhere. The church's very dialogue and witness in the world, therefore, must be deeply sensitive to this inward word of the Spirit expressing its life through the rich cultural and religious texts and lives of people. That very sensitivity will, in turn, enrich its dialogue and witness in the world.

The Church's Mission of Dialogue

Through dialogue the church is first called to learn from, to acknowledge, and to receive the rich insights arising from the cultural and religious traditions and lives of people. Such insights may confirm, nuance, perfect, and even challenge its own understanding of the human mystery revealed in Jesus Christ. In this way a deeper understanding of God's involvement with humanity can be gained, which in turn can enrich and complement the life and message of Jesus Christ himself. Jesus Christ, after all, was an historical being bound to one culture and one society in a given time and moment of history. Because of that, he could not have possibly expressed the mystery of grace in all its historical unfolding and multifaceted dimensions. He could only have expressed the meaning of God's involvement with humanity through the limits of his culture, language, and symbols. Everything, in fact, that the early Christians themselves learned of God in Jesus Christ was shaped by the linguistic, moral, social, political, and psychological structures of their time-bound, spatially situated condition in history. Through dialogue, the church can grow in deeper respect for the illuminating insights and even challenges which God's inward word of the Spirit is expressing through the life of humanity. Through these insights the gospel message itself is clarified and known more profoundly.

The life of the Spirit does not, however, totally relativize the revelation of Jesus Christ. He still remains for the church the normative expression of the mystery of God found and articulated in human life. In him is revealed the origin and destiny of human life. In him is also revealed the transformative and paschal pattern of life responding to the sovereignty of God's presence and grace. Jesus Christ is the way — but a way that is open to all truth and goodness. And it is the life of the Spirit in the world that must continually illumine and guide the church ever more deeply into the inexhaustible meaning and truth of Jesus Christ.

The Church's Mission of Witness

The church's mission to the world, however, cannot consist solely in words of dialogue. God also calls the church to manifest the vision of human life which it has received from Jesus Christ. That vision cannot remain abstract but must serve human beings in a concrete manner. That is why the church must officially commit itself to serving justice and the cause of social solidarity. Through such commitment, the ecclesial community visibly advocates God's plan of salvation for the whole of the human family: the realization of human communion through the power and grace of the Spirit.

Witnessing to and enacting that vision in the world, however, are full of risk and tension because the terrain of concrete history is always shaky and ambiguous. No one particular solution to the problems of the human family is ever infallible or lasting. This in itself can never excuse the church from plunging into history, for it is only through history that its vision of faith can be witnessed to and lived. The church is called, therefore, to choose among the relative options of history and through them, help serve the cause of human reconciliation. Such options can take a whole variety of forms: social and educational programs, hospital services, political and economic assistance, and diverse works of charity and human promotion. If the church is to minister to the cosmic rule of Christ, it can do so only by incarnating itself in the world, utilizing its resources. The church must even at times offer critical political support to that which it judges to be in the best interests of human well-being — especially when such support is demanded to safeguard the transcendence of human life in the face of despotism, cruelty, and exploitation.

The criteria, however, which the church employs to choose its historical options in the service of justice and human solidarity must not be arbitrary or capricious. Like Jesus Christ, the ecclesial community must stand on the side of the poor and oppressed. It must first sensitize itself to human life, read and interpreted from the needs and plight of the oppressed. With an open and discerning heart, it must then reflect upon reality in light of the vision of human life it has received from Jesus Christ. And in its reflections, the church is called at times to employ the help of the human sciences to understand more deeply the social, economic, and political circumstances of peoples and nations, and to be informed ahead of time about realistic possibilities for the future. Its options, however, will always remain relative. They can never be absolutized. And yet it is precisely through them that the church ministers to the Spirit's work of reconciliation in the world.

What the church offers then to humanity through its witness and dialogue is service to a reality larger than itself. And it must continue to offer this service not because humanity will be condemned without it, but rather because the human world needs this witness and dialogue if it is to grow toward its true destiny and full measure of life: the kingdom of Christ.

CHAPTER 23

Unity and Mission: The Emerging Ecumenical Vision

Mercy Amba Oduyoye

Introduction

From both the biblical witness and the history of the church it seems quite obvious that the unity and the mission of the church belong together. The social and ethical implications of the basic texts reinforce the need to hold the two visions of the church together and to work at them simultaneously, since a manifestation of the unity of the church is itself a witness to the mission with which the church is entrusted. "Keep them one," Jesus prayed to God, "that the world may believe that you sent me" (cf. John 17:21). Whatever the perspective from which we read the Scriptures, common sense and experience have demonstrated that the disunity of Christians and of churches generates cynicism toward the gospel and limits the effectiveness of the proclamation which we make to the world.

However we understand the origin, period, and context of Jesus' missionary command in Matthew 28, the fact is that from the earliest Christian communities on there has been the proclamation of the gospel, the baptizing of those who believed (and their households), and the coming together of communities of believers. It makes sense for those who believe that they belong to a common ancestor to meet together and to attempt to talk with one voice and work for their mutual good, demonstrating their common identity and acting toward their common goal. The church has seen itself from its inception as a new community of humanity founded on the Christ-event. Being one, being seen as one, and acting together as one have all been marks of the church to which the churches still strive to be faithful.

Two Ecumenical Statements

The two statements on which this essay is based — *Baptism, Eucharist and Ministry* and *Mission and Evangelism: An Ecumenical Affirmation*[1] — come from the Commission on Faith and Order and the Commission on World Mission and Evangelism (CWME) of the World Council of Churches. The WCC is made up of over more than 300 member churches "committed to close collaboration in Christian witness and service. At the same time, they are also striving together to realize the goal of visible church unity" (BEM, Preface, p. vii). These two WCC Commissions represent different approaches to attaining the ecumenical vision but they are one in centering their quest on the *faith* and the *witness* of the church. Thus unity and mission are central to these two Commissions; and this essay is an attempt to hold their statements together within a common vision.

BEM is the result of half a century of study of three theological issues upon which the churches need to reach consensus if they are to manifest the unity of the church more visibly. ME has a more recent history, but is by its very nature a distillation of what the missionary movement of the church, the IMC and the WCC have believed in, and has informed the work of CWME long before it came to be encapsulated in print. ME was issued at the request of the Central Committee meeting that followed Nairobi in 1976. Melbourne's (1980) theme, "Your Kingdom Come," generated reflection on our missionary obedience. Meanwhile the Central Committee itself was calling the attention of member churches to "the confessing character of every local community." Witnessing to the faith and being in mission were being seen together not only by the WCC but by its member churches. Studying the two texts, one is struck by the common themes that the twin foci of unity and mission generate. These include the need to come to some understanding of the nature of the church; the identity of those to whom the mission has been entrusted; and the relevance and effectiveness of the mission in each place and in each context.

There is, of course, a difference in tone and thrust between the two texts. It is not entirely accidental that BEM is frequently referred to as a "document," while ME identifies itself as an "affirmation."

In addition, the two texts approach their common themes differently: one focuses on what the churches have themselves said, and the other on what

1. *Baptism, Eucharist and Ministry,* Faith and Order Paper no. 111 (Geneva: WCC, 1982), hereinafter BEM; *Mission and Evangelism: An Ecumenical Affirmation,* Mission Series no. 4 (Geneva: WCC, 1983), hereinafter ME.

they need to agree to say together. Thus BEM focuses on the "institutional church," and seeks to outline the consensus that may be reached on the key issues of baptism, Eucharist, and ministry. It relates these to the unity and mission of the church which, it says, will be promoted by the churches' mutual recognition. ME urges the church, both as a body and as persons, to recognize the urgency of the work of mission and to face the task on the basis of the level of consensus we already have (while we continue to search for further theological grounds for our unity in mission and the relation between unity and mission). Thus it is a call to the churches to *act* in mission in accordance with what they *say* about mission. The complementarity and interdependence of the two approaches is inescapable; a creative tension exists between them, and this could lead to the fashioning of a "cutting edge" for common work which could inspire many Christians and contribute to fulfilling the church's mission of being Christ to the world. These fresh articulations of the ecumenical vision may serve to promote and revitalize the churches' commitment to ecumenism.

Thus the two texts must be accepted as complementary approaches to themes of common and critical concern. It belongs to our "celebration of diversity" that Faith and Order and CWME both belong to the same Program Unit (Faith and Witness) of the WCC. Just as the WCC as a whole, both Faith and Order and CWME would affirm that the "unity we look for is not uniformity but the multiple expression of a common faith and a common mission" (ME, p. 27).

Points of Contact

At several points in BEM mission and unity are directly linked. This is hardly surprising; the bylaws of Faith and Order refer to the churches' "common life in Christ, in order that the world might believe" (Section 2). Throughout BEM Jesus Christ is emphasized as both the source of the church's mission and the foundation of its unity (Ministry, p. 12).

The call to mission in ME opens with a reminder that "the present ecumenical movement came into being out of the conviction of the churches that the division of Christians is a scandal and an impediment to the witness of the church" (p. 1).

The churches are described as being on a pilgrimage toward unity under the missionary vision of John 17:21. The one church of Christ is "a *sent* body" and *togetherness* marked the existence of the apostolic church as evidenced in the New Testament. It is a sobering thought to consider the possibility that some may have rejected Jesus Christ because of what they saw in the lives of Christians (ME, p. 13). But even more frightening is the thought that perhaps the church is part of the "powers of this world" that promote division (ME, p. 23). ME is insistent on doing mission *together.* The churches are to announce together, and clearly, their common hope and common calling (ME, p. 23).

Despite the diversity of the church's self-expression, the worldwide mission is conceived of as one. As a result of a deeply ecumenical perception of the Christian mission, the churches seek to undertake together the work of announcing the reign of God. Oneness of the mission of the church is buttressed by an ecumenical consensus that the unity we look for is not uniformity, but the multiple expressions of our common faith and common mission (ME, p. 27).

Different Approaches

There is, says "Mission and Evangelism," an inextricable link between unity and mission: ME strikes one as a lament on disunity, seeking urgently to transcend it for the sake of mission. It is a call to mission that passionately depicts disunity as a scandal and an impediment. Ecumenism and evangelism are linked in the prayer of John 17, which is a fundamental text for both the Faith and Order and the missionary-related movements.

The difference in approach of BEM to the issue of unity and mission has to do with the working methods used to arrive at its statements. BEM is part of Faith and Order's effort to provide "theological support to the efforts the churches are making towards unity" and has been described by the commission as signifying a *kairos* of the ecumenical movement, given that "sadly divided churches have been enabled to arrive at substantial theological agreements" (BEM, p. x). The document is the product of generations of researchers and drafters whose work has been tested and complemented by plenary commission members, local steering groups, and consultations on specialized problem areas. This multilateral study is complemented by the studies of bilateral conversations of confessional families which have flowed into it.

From the several issues that Faith and Order and, more recently, the bilaterals have attempted to explicate, the areas of baptism, Eucharist, and ministry emerged as central to the search for that mutual recognition by the churches which is so necessary for the visible unity of the church. The three issues were also seen to be closely related to the mission of the church; disagreements in these areas are special barriers to mission. How was the church to call for the unity of the human community, and to carry out its mission to the world with conviction, when it is so visibly divided on these fundamentals of belief and practice? Here of course there is complete agreement with "Mission and Evangelism," which affirms in its section on ecumenical convictions that the churches have to recognize each other as participants in the one worldwide missionary movement and covenant to work together.

BEM seeks theological means to enable the churches to achieve a genuine and clear recognition of each other. The necessity of returning to the tradition of the gospel was identified as a key point; strategies were debated and sketched for seeking convergences in these three areas, always aiming to arrive at commonalities in the understanding of the faith amid theological divergences.

In this process Faith and Order has helped the churches reclaim the richness of our common heritage in the gospel, that gospel we are to preach to the ends of the world as the one body of Christ. Mutual recognition of baptism, Eucharist, and ministry will be a witness to the unity of the church and give credibility to its proclamation.

BEM therefore is a challenge to the churches to take the causes of their division seriously, to analyze them, to separate the fundamental issues from the peripheral ones that have accrued over the years, and to ask: "How much diversity is tolerable within the unity which is God's gift to us?"

ME offers its own challenge: to announce the reign of God which alone is the ground of hope in this world. Though BEM is not oblivious to the real world in which the church exists, an awareness of this context dominates the ME document. It derives directly from the existential experience of churches in concrete situations of mission around the world. The world of our contemporary experience is one that heightens the need to call all peoples to repentance. Thus the orientation of ME is more "people-centered," and demands personal involvement and response. The call to proclamation and witness insists that "those who are considered to be nothing are precious in God's eyes" (1 Cor. 1:26-31).

ME is based on certain ecumenical convictions (§§9-45), reflecting a growing consensus about the foundation on which the churches might covenant to work together for the kingdom. These common convictions include the following:

all persons and peoples are to be called to conversion;
the gospel is to touch all realms of life;
common witness should be the natural consequence of our unity with Christ in his mission;
when mission is "in Christ's way," power is subordinate to love;

the church belongs to that movement of God's love shown in Christ who went to the periphery of life (Heb. 13:12);
good news is to be proclaimed together;
the mission is in, and to, the whole world ("mission in and to six continents");
the church's mission includes witnessing among people of other living faiths.

ME has adopted the liberation methodology of seeing action and reflection as belonging together, thereby freeing us to celebrate and evaluate critically our mission and unity. But the fact that the BEM process yielded the Lima liturgy, an ecumenical (though of course unofficial) celebration of the Eucharist, demonstrates that this more "formal" approach can also have very practical results for the churches. The two approaches are not antithetical. As we work together within the one WCC, both statements provide a means of identifying areas of joint research and collaboration in processes of ecumenical formation within the member churches of the WCC.

The issue of ecclesiology is central to both BEM and ME It is the *church's* unity and mission that is at stake; baptism, Eucharist, and ministry are "institutions" of the church. From both statements it becomes clear that further work on ecclesiology is necessary. But both texts reflect the present ecumenical climate: both are permeated by a concern for visible church unity and the need for a relevant and effective mission; and both show a heightened sensitivity to "the other" in dialogue, and a certain wariness toward once-for-all statements and "frozen truths." This gives both documents the potential to be groundbreaking instruments for living in a global world of mutual interdependence and mutual ecumenical learning.

The three specific issues of baptism, Eucharist, and ministry provide a structure for reviewing the common ground between the two documents. "You will be baptized with my baptism," Jesus told them, ". . . and you will do the work (the *mission*) that I do." He himself in his lifetime instituted the common meal (the Eucharist). Indeed, not much can be said about the church's unity and mission without taking these fundamental realities into account.

Baptism

ME views evangelism as bringing persons to a personal encounter with Christ; it sees baptism as honoring the individuality of persons within the community. The gospel call is intended to elicit a personal response, namely, personal repentance and personal forgiveness. Christ's calling was a personal one; the emphasis on the personal reality of baptism is an effective antidote to anonymity, and a recognition of the importance of a personal commitment to Christ. Since faithfulness to the gospel call means also ultimately faithfulness to the human community, baptism gives the church an opportunity to demonstrate our communal responsibility to nurture those seeking to be faithful to God's call. BEM emphasizes this in its discussion on the baptism of infants (Commentary, p. 12).

Baptism is understood in both BEM and ME as a unique act marking one's belonging to God and incorporation into the body of Christ. This carries with it the demand to be in mission. Furthermore, baptism implies liberation and renewal, it symbolizes and effects the transcending of divisive human barriers. Our common baptism, uniting us to Christ in faith, is a basic bond of unity (see Baptism, pp. 6, 10). We are constituted into "one people called to confess and serve One Lord in each place and in all the world." This is why at public baptism the church as a body publicly renews its pledge to be "an environment of witness and service."

BEM confirms the suitability of the baptism of persons of all ages, provided that the church as a *community* takes itself and the implications of baptism seriously. Questions still arise, however, in areas where our practice differs. Should all the baptized participate in the Eucharistic meal? Should baptized women who feel called to "ordained ministry" be excluded? Are the churches manipulating this symbol (consciously or unconsciously) in order to perpetrate the visible disunity of the church? Do these differing positions signify our refusal to accept the gift of unity being presented in God's outstretched hands? These and other questions in regard to baptism need further work.

Meanwhile, we affirm that baptismal unity will be "a genuine Christian witness" to the healing and reconciling love of God. Recognition of the one baptism puts the churches on the way to overcoming divisions, and to manifesting their fellowship more visibly and more effectively. Such an orientation can only support our work toward common witness and common service as further expressions of the unity of the church.

The Eucharist

ME emphasizes that the church is a community whose author and sustainer is the Holy Spirit, and that as a communion of the Spirit the church finds its primary aim and ultimate purpose in the Eucharist celebration and the glorification of the Triune God (see Appendix, p. 7). Thus the Eucharist is placed in the center of the church's existence, confirming and affirming BEM's search for ecumenical convergence in this area.

It has become an ecumenical truism that our separation at "the Lord's Table" is a scandal. That we cannot easily gloss over centuries of disagreements on the Eucharist is also being constantly reiterated — to the point of paralyzing all attempts at rapprochement. Yet the inextricable link between the Eucharist and a convincing witness to the gospel is endorsed by all churches which participate in this sacrament. ME notes that "the celebration of the Eucharist is the place for the renewal of the missionary conviction at the heart of every congregation"; it quotes Paul (1 Cor. 11:26) to the effect that in the Eucharist, Christ is proclaimed (p. 21). In the Eucharistic liturgy the whole world is raised to God in thanksgiving for its redemption, and intercessions are made for the fuller realization that the world is in the presence of God and under God's loving rule. Such lofty global statements — which we all accept — "fall flat" as we *live* our inability to sit at one table together. Both texts are aware that this undermines the credibility of our witness to Christ. Thus "there are times and places where the very act of coming together to celebrate the Eucharist can be a public witness" (ME, Appendix, p. 7).

The water of baptism and its rehearsal of the passing through the water of the Exodus are echoed in the understanding of the Eucharist as deliverance from bondage. In this it is symbolic of the church's mission to those who participate in the celebration, as well as to those who observe it from the outside. BEM affirms that the Eucharist is a proclamation of God's rule of justice, love, and peace (see especially pp. 20-26). In it the church is presented as a "servant of reconciliation in the world." As a "community of the New Covenant" the church invokes the Holy Spirit for its sanctification and renewal that it may be "led into all justice, truth and unity" and empowered to fulfill its mission in the world. This Eucharistic community when fully constituted becomes a manifestation of God's people. The Eucharist is the church's common witness to God and thanksgiving on behalf of itself and the whole world. BEM and ME share the conviction that the Eucharist is the meal of the people in mission. The very celebration of the Eucharist is the church's participation in God's mission to the world.

Virtually all the statements on the Eucharist are geared toward the church's mission and unity. BEM affirms that the church proves inconsistent if we are not participating in the restoration of the world situation and human condition (Eucharist p. 20), thus articulating equally the evangelistic concern of ME. BEM warns that we are under judgment as long as unjust relationships of any kind prevail in society (Eucharist, p. 20). One could almost say that in many places BEM is itself a "proclamation," a *mission movement* to the churches decrying the "obstinacy of unjustifiable confessional oppositions within the body of Christ" (Eucharist, p. 20) which prevents the churches from celebrating the Eucharist "as a universal communion in the body of Christ." Our proclamation and celebration of God's work in the Eucharist is tarnished by our lack of responsible care for the "other" and for the world with its suffering, injustice, and want.

That the very celebration of the Eucharist is a *proclamation* is highlighted in both statements. It witnesses to the joy of the resurrection while signifying that the world is to become an offering to God and a hymn to the Creator (Eucharist p. 5). Jesus said: "You shall know them by their fruits" (Matt. 7:20). BEM affirms that the Eucharist transforms Christians into the image of Christ and therefore makes them effective witnesses; and in the Eucharist, we are nourished and strengthened for confession by word and action so that those beyond the visible Eucharistic community might be gathered in (cf. Eucharist, pp. 22-26, ME p. 2, and Appendix p. 7).

Ministry and Mission

Evangelism understood as conversion to Christ and the inculturation of human cultures expresses part of the mission of the church. But so does the building up of "cells" of Christian believers in the midst of human communities. Once such cells have been formed and named church, they see themselves as called "to proclaim and to prefigure" the kingdom of God. They undertake the proclamation of the kingdom of God in deed and word. They announce the gospel to all realms of life and become, by their very existence, a witness to Christ in their environment. Each and every member of each and every cell of Christ-believers is in mission, confessing the faith, giving an account of the hope that sustains them, and witnessing by caring for and loving the neighbor.

Both BEM and ME reflect the growing ecumenical agreement on the calling of the people of God to mission. The term "priesthood of all believers" is endorsed by all the churches, as is the need to recognize the diversity of gifts within the church. The need to speak and act in terms of a diversity of ministries is not in dispute; the question is how it operates in concrete situations. It is in this connection that BEM poses the question: "How, according to the will of God and under the guidance of the Holy Spirit, is the life of the church to be understood and ordered, so that the gospel may be spread and the community built up in love?" (Ministry, p. 6). Mission is the practice of the whole church and all members of the believing community are inter-related. The issue is how this interrelationship is ordered and what effect that has on the church's mission.

Both BEM and ME show how difficult it is to put our eloquent language about the priesthood of all believers into praxis. Both texts reflect a fundamental tension: on the one hand, the church is called to convey to the world the image of a new humanity (BEM, Ministry, p. 18); on the other, it often mirrors the structures of the human community, and succumbs to what ME describes as the powers that promote division (p. 24).

As many of the responses to BEM have pointed out, its ministry section focuses on the ordained ministry, its authority, forms, and succession. This has the danger of reinforcing an image of the church as consisting of the clergy — who are also the persons charged with being in mission. The aim is the unity of ministry, but in fact what is developed is the unity of the *ordained* ministry. Thus the common witness of both ordained and other members of the church is an area that calls for intensive common reflection by both Faith and Order and CWME.

ME notes that "common witness should be the natural consequence of the church's unity with Christ in his mission" (p. 23). But serious issues are raised by the fact that the church's mission crosses national frontiers, and touches a vast diversity of cultures and socioeconomic and political situations. That this calls for a variety of ministries is obvious. But what kinds of ministries? How can the churches be mutually accountable for their ministry and forms of mission and witness? What about cases where the ultimate unity of the church and its mission is being denied by the very form and style of "mission" as practiced by individuals, groups, or even churches? What does the ecumenical movement do when faced by "missions" which are deliberately divisive and anti-ecumenical? What about missions which have reversed the old ecumenical principle, and have done together only what they could not in conscience do separately?

Without a better understanding of the church we cannot talk of the unity and renewal of the church, nor live it in a way that makes the church "Christ in the world." There is consensus that we owe a missionary obedience in and to all the six continents and all realms of life, until Christ comes. But many are reluctant to recognize that within the so-called "evangelized places" there are vast numbers of unevangelized persons — and structures, i.e., institutions that create or preserve injustice. We are all agreed that we shall preach, but the question of what we should preach will only be adequately answered as we study together, and learn to state more clearly the fundamentals of our faith. It is, ultimately, the joint proclamation of that common faith which will project the unity of the church as founded on Christ who is both the source of the church's mission and foundation of its unity.

Promoting the Convergences

What emerges from the texts is the need to listen more carefully to what the various sub-units of the WCC, the various streams of the ecumenical movement, and the various churches have to tell of their experiences and experiments in these areas. We are being called to "see the ecumenical movement whole." Unity and mission are *constituent images* of the ecumenical vision and no single movement, institution, or church can claim a monopoly or exclusive expertise in either one of them. There are indications at several points that joint study and action by Faith and Order and CWME will be of mutual edification and improve the quality of each Commission's own specialized work. Respect for the differences in approaches, and a keen sense of what method best achieves results in specific realms and issues, will promote that mutual respect for "the other" on which the very existence of the ecumenical movement depends.

The insight that visible church unity is a *necessary condition* for the credibility of our message, and that unity is *in itself* mission, should go some way toward promoting the churches' ecumenical resolve. Faith and Order has served the vision of church unity. The call of the International Missionary Conference was for cooperation and avoidance of competition, overlapping and wastage of resources; anything that fed the visible disunity of the church was to be avoided. It was stimulated by an ecumenical vision of unity and mission. The unity in mission that inspired the coming into being of the WCC has been well served by the participation of the International Missionary Council and its successor commissions of the WCC. It is now time to move into a period of deeper reflection, to move toward the inevitable interpenetration of the mission/unity of the church.

It is also necessary to be realistic about the "images" which both Faith and Order and CWME have presented. Theology has often been pursued as an abstract, elitist discipline, and this has meant that the work of Faith and Order has not influenced the churches as deeply and widely as it could have done. Its work has been revered, praised, widely distributed, and implemented without, however, really affecting the attitude of the whole people of God. The broad popular response to BEM is a step in the right direction; but this should now affect all the work of Faith and Order. The challenge to Faith and Order is to ask: "How do the specialized articles which we write become part of the faith by which the whole people of God live day-by-day?" Or even more sharply: "What are the theological implications of the fact that a response to BEM is requested from the highest level of ecclesiastical decision-making?" (Preface, p. x). This is understandable in a document directed officially to member churches of the WCC. But it raises the question of whether the teaching authority of the church derives ultimately from the whole people of God or from the institutional structures of the churches.

The challenge to CWME is to sharpen and deepen its theological reflection. Its commitment focuses on concrete situations; this is natural since, although what constitutes mission and evangelism has constant parameters, their actual practice is contextual. The solid theological work toward the ME statement is a step in the right direction. And this is part of the mission experience itself, as those whose ecumenical commitment is worked out through participation in evangelism constantly find themselves asking theological questions, having to articulate their faith over against specific challenges of contemporary life, and in the dialogue with people of other living faiths.

I believe that the clearest imperative coming from a common reading of BEM and ME is the need to develop and strengthen the mission of the whole people of God. This means those who do not wear the title "theologian," "missionary," "pastor," or "evangelist" but are still members of the body of Christ and who care for the united mission of the church, and its effectiveness in this world for which Christ died.

If I may close on a personal note, my first involvement in a WCC consultation was at the Boldern Academy in March 1967. The title of the consultation report, "Ecumenical Commitment and Christian Education," has made a profound impact on me. BEM and ME are a fresh call and challenge to our ecumenical commitment and, I hope, will lead to our being "educated" to a united mission by a united church.

PART SIX

Evangelistic Praxis in Diverse Cultural Contexts

Throughout the ages, the followers of Christ have bound themselves intimately to the contexts in which they have lived, in ways that both challenge and embrace the cultural forces that characterize their time. Rooted initially in the rich soil of Hebraic religion and culture, early Christian missionaries, such as St. Paul and those who followed in his succession, felt compelled by the mandate of the gospel to transplant this "way of life in Christ" into new and diverse cultural contexts. Portions of the New Testament recount the difficulties inherent to this process of indigenization, and the history of the church is the epic story of this process of translation, but the successful movement of Christianity from one cultural context into another foreign to it represents one of its most unique characteristics. There is no Christianity other than contextual Christianity. Whether described as transplantation, indigenization, or translation, this process both defines and shapes evangelistic praxis. Perhaps nothing is more complex than the way in which Christian people have sought to express their faith in Jesus Christ in, through, and among different cultures. The cultural context of a Christian community shapes the practice of evangelism just as much as the historical context and theological ethos of a denomination determines its distinctive missiological frame of reference.

Concern about the relationship between Christians and their cultures dominates much of the current literature on mission and evangelism. This is most certainly true of those traditions and contexts in which Christian people feel increasingly alienated from the mainstream of the cultural tide. But whether held captive by an idealized vision of Christianity divorced from the particularities of any time or place — or whether held captive by an attitude of cultural superiority that fails to distinguish the Christian faith from its cultural context and thereby breeds imperialistic practice — the perennial danger of the well-intentioned Christian committed to evangelistic ministries is the illusion that we have everything to give and nothing to receive. If evangelism is a way of life for the baptized within communities of faith, then the translation of the gospel from community to community must not only acknowledge the complexities of the process involved with humility, but must allow for at least two further components: (1) attentiveness to the other and receptivity to the rediscovery of the gospel through those we seek to serve, and (2) acknowledgment of the role of the Holy Spirit in this dynamic work of God.

As the essays in this section demonstrate, such a dynamic process is not only complex, but often difficult. Evangelism as translation involves more than language or simple ritual differences in cultures. More than anything else it requires attentiveness, and in a world in which the Christian center of gravity has shifted southward, this requires a particular sensitivity among the Christians of the North and the West. Having assumed a posture of cultural superiority and privilege in the past, it is now important for those Christians who live in post-Christian contexts to listen anew to voices from Africa, Asia, and Latin America, where Christianity is growing and thriving. The question of culture remains perennial. But careful processes of discernment guided by the Holy Spirit make faithful and effective responses to the Christian gospel possible within and among diverse cultural contexts.

An excerpt from Lesslie Newbigin's book *Foolishness to the Greeks* introduces the issue of the relationship between Christianity and culture. The noted missionary theologian argues his preference for the concept of the "contextualization of the gospel" over other alternatives that fail to capture the dynamic involved in placing the gospel in the total context of a culture at a particular moment in time. He defines "culture" as "the sum total of ways of living developed by a group of human beings and handed on from generation to generation." Carefully avoiding any hint of a "pure gospel" unadulterated by any cultural accretions, he describes speaking the gospel as "the announcement that in the series of events that have their center in the life, ministry, death, and resurrection of Jesus Christ something has happened that alters the total human situation and must therefore call into question every human culture." Communication of the gospel across cultural frontiers must necessarily entail issues of language, the challenge of conversion, and reliance upon the gracious work of God.

J. N. K. Mugambi, professor of philosophy and religious studies at the University of Nairobi in Kenya, takes "A Fresh Look at Evangelism in Africa." He suggests that the modern missionary enterprise in Africa has been insensitive to the cultural integrity of the African peoples. He calls for a conversion of attitude in order to help African Christians regain a sense of dignity and integrity within the life of the church. A theology of evangelism and cultural alienation that demanded the total rejection of the African cultural heritage as a prerequisite to the acceptance of Christ created a form of Christianity in Africa that is superficial, formal, and frequently suspended in the normal round of life for African Christians. In reaction against this oppressive missiology, just as liberation became the dominant theme of Latin America in its post-colonial experience, inculturation has become a major theme in African missiology, particularly in Catholic circles. Effective evangelization, argues Mugambi, must include knowledge of the core of the gospel, effective rather than exploitative methods of communication, and attentiveness to and appreciation for the cultural context. Culture-sensitive evangelism in Africa, he maintains, is only possible when those involved in the communication of the gospel are willing to be changed by those they seek to change.

Those people evangelized within the Asian context experienced the same mission scenario as their African counterparts, attempting today to discover what it means to be truly Asian and truly Christian in a post-colonial, post-imperialist situation. Hwa Yung, director of the Centre for the Study of Christianity in Asia at Trinity Theological College in Singapore, explores strategic issues related to mission and evangelism from an Asian perspective. He describes the shift of the center of gravity in global Christianity in the direction of the non-Western world (as explored in this volume by Dana L. Robert), the reverse flow of mission and evangelism toward the West, and the contemporary "clash of civilizations" theory of Harvard scholar, Samuel Huntington, which is shaping missiology. In addition to these three trends, he identifies three issues of particular import for Asia, namely, an increasing crisis in leadership in the churches, a truncated and distorted gospel inheritance, and the presentation of a Jesus alien to Asian culture. In response to these three trends and three issues particular to Asia, Yung offers five proposals related to evangelization in the future, focusing on questions of indigenization, holism, contextualization, and potential synergy between Western and Asian forms of the Christian faith.

In his discussion of evangelism in a Latin American milieu, Mortimer Arias, former Methodist bishop in Bolivia and renowned missiologist, argues for a paradigm of contextualization that reflects the perennial dynamic and dialectic relationship between gospel and culture. Recounting the long history of evangelization in South and Central America, he establishes a cartography of mission, identifying phases and paradigms: Catholic conquest with its civilizing evangelization, Protestant transplantation with its missionary evangelization, Pentecostal growth with its indigenous evangelization, and the more recent development of various programs of professional evangelization. The Second Vatican Council and the Medellín Conference of Roman Catholic Bishops in the 1960s revolutionized understandings of evangelism in Latin America and turned greater attention to the church itself and the need to rediscover Christian authenticity from the inside out. Other indigenous theologians, such as Orlando Costas and José Míguez Bonino, added their voices to this chorus and emphasized the need to reclaim a holistic vision of the church's mission in the world. Arias issues a clarion call for "prophetic contextualization," consisting of a "costly evangelization" that is conflictive, engaged, and emancipatory.

CHAPTER 24

Foolishness to the Greeks

Lesslie Newbigin

There is, of course, nothing new in proposing to discuss the relationship between gospel and culture. We have Richard Niebuhr's classic study of five models of relationship in his book *Christ and Culture.* We have had the massive work of Paul Tillich, who was so much concerned with what he called, in the title of his first public lecture, the "theology of culture." But this work has mainly been done, as far as I know, by theologians who had not had the experience of the cultural frontier, of seeking to transmit the gospel from one culture to a radically different one.

On the other hand, we have had a plethora of studies by missionaries on the theological issues raised by cross-cultural missions. As Western missionaries have shared in the general weakening of confidence in our modern Western culture, they have become more aware of the fact that in their presentation of the gospel they have often confused culturally conditioned perceptions with the substance of the gospel, and thus wrongfully claimed divine authority for the relatives of one culture.

For some on the liberal wing of Protestantism, such as W. E. Hocking, Christian missions were to be almost absorbed into the worldwide spread of Western culture, and this was quite explicit. But those on the opposite end of the spectrum, the conservative evangelicals, were often unaware of the cultural conditioning of their religion and therefore guilty, as many of them now recognize, of confusing the gospel with the values of the American way of life without realizing what they were doing. In the last couple of decades there has been a spate of missionary writings on the problem of *contextualization.* This has been preferred to the terms *indigenization* and *adaptation,* earlier much used by Protestants and Catholics respectively. The weakness of the former was that it tended to relate the Christian message to the traditional cultural forms — forms that belonged to the past and from which young people were turning away under the pervasive influence of "modernization." The effect was to identify the gospel with the conservative elements in society. The weakness of the latter term, *adaptation,* was that it implied that what the missionary brought with him was the pure gospel, which had to be adapted to the receptor culture. It tended to obscure the fact that the gospel as embodied in the missionary's preaching and practice was already an adapted gospel, shaped by his or her own culture. The value of the word *contextualization* is that it suggests the placing of the gospel in the total context of a culture at a particular moment, a moment that is shaped by the past and looks to the future.

The weakness, however, of this whole mass of missiological writing is that while it has sought to explore the problems of contextualization in all the cultures of humankind from China to Peru, it has largely ignored the culture that is the most widespread, powerful, and persuasive among all contemporary cultures — namely, what I have called the modern Western culture. Moreover, this neglect is even more serious because it is this culture that, more than almost any other, is proving resistant to the gospel.

Let us begin with some preliminary definitions. By the word *culture* we have to understand the sum total of ways of living developed by a group of human beings and handed on from generation to generation. Central to culture is language. The language of a people provides the means by which they express their way of perceiving things and of coping with them. Around that center one would have to group their visual and musical arts, their technologies, their law, and their social and political organization. And one must also include in culture, and as fundamental to any culture, a set of beliefs, experiences, and practices that seek to grasp and express the ultimate nature of things, that which gives shape and meaning to life, that which claims final loyalty. I am speaking, obviously, about religion. Religion — including the Christian religion — is thus part of culture.

In speaking of "the gospel," I am, of course, referring to the announcement that in the series of events that have their center in the life, ministry, death, and resurrection of Jesus Christ something has happened that alters the total human situation and must therefore call into question every human culture. Now clearly this announcement is itself culturally conditioned. It does not come down from heaven or by the mouth of an angel. The words *Jesus Christ* are the Greek rendering of a Hebrew name and title, *Joshua the Messiah.* They belong to and are part of the culture of one part of the world — the eastern Mediterranean — at one point in history when Greek was the most widespread international language in the lands around the Mediterranean Sea. Neither at the beginning, nor at any subsequent time, is there or can there be a gospel that is not embodied in a culturally conditioned form of words. The idea that one can or could at any time separate out by some process of distillation a pure gospel unadulterated by any cultural accretions is an illusion. It is, in fact, an abandonment of the gospel, for the gospel is about the word made flesh. Every statement of the gospel in words is conditioned by the culture of which those words are a part, and every style of life that claims to embody the truth of the gospel is a culturally conditioned style of life. There can never be a culture-free gospel. Yet the gospel, which is from the beginning to the end embodied in culturally conditioned forms, calls into question all cultures, including the one in which it was originally embodied.

I begin by looking at what is involved in the cross-cultural communication of the gospel. The New Testament itself, which chronicles the movement of the gospel from its origin in the cultural world of Judaism to its articulation in the language and practice of Greek-speaking Gentile communities, provides us with the models from which to begin. As a starting point, I find it illuminating to consider Paul's speech in the presence of King Agrippa and his court (Acts 26). The cultural setting is that of the cosmopolitan Greek-speaking world of the eastern Roman Empire. Paul is speaking in Greek. But at the decisive point of his story he tells the court that when God spoke to him it was not in Greek but in Hebrew: "I heard a voice speaking to me in the Hebrew language," the language of the home and the heart, the mother tongue. Paul is a citizen of that cosmopolitan Greek-speaking world. But the word that changed the course of his life was spoken in Hebrew, the language of his own native culture.

But — and this is equally important — that word spoken to his heart, while it accepts that language as its vehicle, uses it not to affirm and approve the life that Saul is living but to call it radically into question: "Why do you persecute me?" It is to show him that his most passionate and all-conquering conviction is wrong, that what he thinks is the service of God in fighting against God, that he is required to stop in his tracks, turn around, and renounce the whole direction of his life, to love what he had hated and to cherish what he had sought to destroy.

And — this is my third point — a voice that makes such a demand can only be the voice of the sovereign Lord himself. No one but God has the right and the power to contradict my devotion to God. "Who are you?" is Paul's trembling question. It is the same as Moses' question at the burning bush: "What is your name?" The answer, "I am Jesus," means that from henceforth Saul knows Jesus as simply and absolutely Lord.

We have here, I suggest, a model of what is involved in the communication of the gospel across a cultural frontier. (1) The communication has to be in the language of the receptor culture. It has to be such that it accepts, at least provisionally, the way of understanding things that is embodied in that language; if it does not do so, it will simply be an unmeaning sound that cannot change anything. (2) However, if it is truly the communication of the gospel, it will call radically into question that way of understanding embodied in the language it uses. If it is truly revelation, it will involve contradiction, and call for conversion, for a radical *metanoia,* a U-turn of the mind. (3) Finally, this radical conversion can never be the achievement of any human persuasion, however eloquent. It can only be the work of God. True conversion, therefore, which is the proper end toward which the communication of the gospel looks, can only be a work of God, a kind of miracle — not natural, but supernatural.

This pattern is brilliantly exemplified in the Johannine writings. "John" freely uses the language and the thought-forms of the religious world for which he writes. Much of it is suggestive of the sort of worldview that is often very imprecisely called "Gnosticism" and has obvious affinities with Indian thought. For this reason the Fourth Gospel was early suspected of Gnostic tendencies and has later been eagerly welcomed by Hindus as placing Jesus firmly within a typically Indian worldview. Yet "John" uses this language and these thought-forms in such a way as to confront them with a fundamental question and indeed a contradiction. The *logos* is no longer an idea in the mind of the philosopher or the mystic. The *logos* is the man Jesus who went the way from Bethlehem to Calvary. In my own experience I have found that Hindus who begin by welcoming the Fourth Gospel as the one that uses their language and speaks to their hearts end by being horrified when they understand what it is really saying. And so, logically, we move to the third point to which "John" gave equal emphasis: that — as Jesus puts it in the sixth chapter — "No one can come to me unless the Father draws him" (John 6:44). The radical conversion of the heart, the U-turn of the mind which the New Testament calls *metanoia,* can never be the calculable result of correct methods of communication. It is something mysterious for which we can only say that our methods of communication were, at most, among the occasions for a miracle.

The same threefold pattern is exemplified in the experience of a missionary who, nurtured in one culture, seeks to communicate the gospel among people of another culture whose world has been shaped by a vision of the totality of things quite different from that of the Bible. He must first of all struggle to master the language. To begin with, he will think of the words he hears simply as the equivalent of the words he uses in his own tongue and are listed in his dictionary as equivalents. But if he really immerses himself in the talk, the songs and folktales, and the literature of the people, he will discover that there are no exact equivalents. All the words in any language derive their meaning, their resonance in the minds of those who use them, from a whole world of experience and a whole way of grasping that experience. So there are no exact translations. He has to render the message as best he can, drawing as fully as he can upon the tradition of the people to whom he speaks.

Clearly, he has to find the path between two dangers. On the one hand, he may simply fail to communicate: he uses the words of the language, but in such a way that he sounds like a foreigner; his message is heard as the babblings of a man who really has nothing to say. Or, on the other hand, he may so far succeed in talking the language of his hearers that he is accepted all too easily as a familiar character — a moralist calling for greater purity of conduct or a guru offering a path to the salvation that all human beings want. His message is simply absorbed into the existing worldview and heard as a call to be more pious or better behaved. In the attempt to be "relevant" one may fall into syncretism, and in the effort to avoid syncretism one may become irrelevant.

In spite of these dangers, which so often reduce the effort of the missionary to futility, it can happen that, in the mysterious providence of God, a word spoken comes with the kind of power of the word that was spoken to Saul on the road to Damascus. Perhaps it is as sudden and cataclysmic as that. Or perhaps it is the last piece that suddenly causes the pattern to make sense, the last experience of a long series that tips the scale decisively. However that may be, it causes the hearer to stop, turn around, and go in a new direction, to accept Jesus as his Lord, Guide, and Savior.

The Jesus whom he thus accepts will be the Jesus presented to him by the missionary. It will be Jesus as the missionary perceives him. It is only necessary to look at the visual representation of Jesus in the art of different people through the past eighteen centuries, or to read the lives of Jesus written in the past 150 years, to understand that Jesus is always perceived and can only be perceived through the eyes of a particular culture. Think of the Christ of the Byzantine mosaics, a kind of super Emperor, the Pantocrator; the Christ of the medieval crucifix, a drooping, defeated victim; the Christ of liberal Protestantism, an enlightened, emancipated, successful member of the bourgeoisie; or the Christ of the liberation theologians portrayed in the likeness of Che Guevara. It will inevitably be the Christ of the missionary to whom, in the first instance, the new convert turns and gives his allegiance. This may express itself in the adopting styles of worship, dress, and behavior copied from the missionary — sometimes to the embarrassment of the latter.

But this will be only the first expression of it. The matter will not stop there, for the new convert will begin to read the Bible for himself. As he does so, he will gain a new standpoint from which he can look in a new way both at his own culture and at the message he has received from the missionary. This will not happen suddenly. It is only as the fruit of sustained exposure to the Bible that one begins to see familiar things in a new light. In this light the new convert will both see his own traditional culture in a new way and also observe that there are discrepancies between the picture of Jesus that he (from within his culture) finds in the New Testament and the picture that was communicated by the missionary. From this point on, there are various possible developments. The convert, having realized that much of what he had first accepted from the missionary was shaped by the latter's culture and not solely by the gospel, may in reaction turn back to his own culture and seek, in a sort of hostile reaction to the culture that had invaded his own under the cloak of the gospel, to restate the gospel in terms of his traditional culture. Some of what is called Third World theology has primarily this negative orientation, rather than being primarily directed toward the communication of the gospel to those still inhabiting the traditional culture. What can also happen is that the missionary, and through him the church he represents, can become aware of the element of syncretism in his own Christianity, of the extent to which his culture has been allowed to determine the nature of the gospel he preaches, instead of being brought under judgment by that gospel. If this happens, great possibilities for mutual correction open up. Each side, perceiving Christ through the spectacle of one culture, can help the other to see how much the vision has been blurred or distorted. This kind of mutual correction is at the very heart of the ecumenical movement when it is true to itself.

But even where this mutual correction does begin to take place, it is still — in the modern world — under the shadow of the overwhelming predominance of modern Western culture. All the dialogue is conducted in the languages of Western Europe, and this in itself determines its terms. Only those who have had what is called a modern education are equipped are take part in it. That is to say, it is confined to those who have been more or less co-opted into the predominant modern Western culture. Most of the missionary outreach across cultural boundaries still comes from churches that are part of this culture. How, then, can there be a genuine encounter of the gospel with this culture, a culture that has itself sprung from roots in Western Christendom and with which the Western churches have lived in a symbiotic relationship ever since its first dawning? From whence comes the voice that can challenge this culture on its own terms, a voice that speaks its own language and yet confronts it with the authentic figure of the crucified and living Christ so that it is stopped in its tracks and turned back from the way of death? One might think that the vision of the mushroom cloud that has haunted the mind of modern Western people ever since it first appeared over Hiroshima would be enough. But we know that fear does not bring deliverance. From whence can the voice, not of doom but of deliverance, be spoken so that the modern Western world can hear it as the voice of its Savior and Lord?

CHAPTER 25

A Fresh Look at Evangelism in Africa

J. N. K. Mugambi

Introduction

My intention in this essay is to review the relationship between gospel and cultures in the process of evangelization in contemporary Africa, discerning the achievements and the shortcomings of the missionary enterprise in this process, and anticipating the future of the Christian faith in Africa within a challenging context characterized by rapid social change.[1] The essay suggests that in general, the modern missionary enterprise, despite great achievements in translation of the Bible and liturgical literature into African languages, has been insensitive to the cultural integrity of African peoples, and that this attitude of insensitivity should change to one of appreciation and sensitivity if African Christians are to regain their dignity and integrity within the Church universal, and within the family of nations.[2] The bibliographical index of the

1. This essay builds on the research published in five of my earlier books: *The Biblical Basis for Evangelization* (Nairobi: Oxford University Press, 1989); *The African Heritage and Contemporary Christianity* (Nairobi: Longman, 1989); *African Christian Theology: An Introduction* (Nairobi: Heinemann, 1989); *Critiques of Christianity in African Literature* (Nairobi: East African Educational Publishers, 1992); *From Liberation to Reconstruction: African Christianity after the Cold War* (Nairobi: East African Educational Publishers, 1995). It also draws on insights from the African Christianity Series as documented in note 22 below.

2. Lamin Sanneh has highlighted the great achievement of the modern missionary enterprise in making the Christian Scriptures available in African languages; see his *Translating the Message* (Maryknoll, N.Y.: Orbis, 1989) and *Encountering the West* (London: Marshall Pickering, 1993). Ironically, however, this achievement has not yielded appreciation and respect of the African cultural and religious heritage in Europe and North America. Instead, a great deal of prejudice is still perpetuated both in the media and in academic institutions. That African traditional religion is still described as "animism" in the media and evangelical literature, shows that attitudes toward African religion and culture have not changed much in the North Atlantic since

International Review of Mission can serve as one indicator of missionary attitudes toward the African cultural and religious heritage: there is no index for African religion, African culture, or African religious heritage. The predominant attitude has been that African peoples have no culture or religion worth indexing — except as primal worldviews which could as well apply to the peoples of other cultures.[3]

The invasion of Africa's living rooms and villages by the mass media from the affluent nations of Europe and North America makes it difficult for the people of Africa, both young and old, to affirm their cultural integrity. Newspapers, radio, television, and Internet — these media are, generally speaking, driven by one theme alone: profit. In these media, culture is useful only if it promotes consumerism. Advertisements are the driving force of the media, no matter how committed the owners might be to educate, inform, and entertain their respective audiences. The days when culture was the manifestation of a people's integrity are gone. Today, culture is what the transnational corporations say it is: buying and selling goods and services in the name of progress and civilization. Christian evangelism is caught up in this web of consumerism. Evangelists find it difficult to avoid the temptation to sell the gospel the way business enterprises do — through aggressive marketing. If the gospel is a commodity for sale — like cars, or color television, or the Internet — what is the role of the Holy Spirit?

Church membership is rapidly growing in those countries and regions (especially in Africa) which are becoming more and more *pauperized,* as affluence becomes chronic in Europe and North America. Through tourism, African culture has become a commodity for curio trade and exhibition, alongside wild flora and fauna. Evangelism in Africa has become a form of Christian tourism, in which itinerant preachers come for seasonal crusades, combining their preaching with tourism and sunbathing. Missionary Christianity has yet to present African culture as the way of life of a people created in the image of God. In Catholic circles, *inculturation* has became a dominant theme in African missiology, just as *liberation* has been the dominant theme in Latin America. African expressions of Christianity have yet to penetrate the core of Christian worship in Europe and North America. To be theologi-

---

the nineteenth century. The prejudice arises largely from the condescending attitude which missionaries have portrayed in their ethnographic monographs of the African peoples.

3. Kwame Bediako, *Christianity in Africa: The Renewal of a Non-Western Religion* (Edinburgh: Edinburgh University Press, 1995), pp. 91-108; J. V. Taylor, *The Primal Vision* (London: SCM, 1963); J. B. Taylor, ed., *Primal World Views: Christian Involvement in Dialogue with Traditional Thought Forms* (Ibadan: Daystar, 1976).

cally consistent, inculturation has to be reciprocal within the global Christian community. If inculturation is another word for cultural liberation, then evangelization in Africa must be culturally liberating in order to be consistent with the gospel. The fact that "inculturation" became one of the themes of the 1994 African Synod at the Vatican indicates that cultural insensitivity in Christian missiology continues to be a thorny challenge.[4] How can we, as Christians, evangelize the people of other cultures without denigrating their cultural and religious integrity? Jesus proclaims that he has come to fulfill, not to destroy. St. Paul follows this principle in his missionary work, and fulfills Greco-Roman culture by showing the relevance of the Christian faith for the Romans, Corinthians, Galatians, Thessalonians, Ephesians, Colossians, and so on.[5]

Cultural Insensitivity and the Modern Missionary Enterprise

Cultural depreciation and insensitivity in the modern missionary enterprise has arisen from an erroneous theology of mission, which presupposes that the acceptance of Christianity necessarily demands total rejection of the African cultural and religious heritage and adoption of the culture of the missionary without question or criticism. The consequence of this missiological error has been a superficial acceptance of Christianity, which is displayed in *formal,* ecclesial settings, and suspended in the *normal,* daily life of the majority of African Christians. For this type of Christianity, J. V. Taylor used the phrase "classroom religion." Reflecting on Christianity in Uganda in 1963, Taylor wrote:

> For forty years and more the advance of the Christian Church in tropical Africa has depended more upon her virtual monopoly on Western education than upon any other factor. Today secular governments are taking that monopoly from her and it is a bitter irony that the factor which seemed to be Christianity's greatest strength in Africa threatens to prove its heaviest liability. For to a great extent it has become a classroom religion.[6]

4. On inculturation, see Aylward Shorter, *Toward a Theology of Inculturation* (London: Chapman, 1988); J. M. Waliggo and others, *Inculturation: Its Meaning and Urgency* (Nairobi: St. Paul Publications Africa, 1986).

5. 1 Cor. 9:19-22.

6. Taylor, *Primal Vision,* p. 12.

Taylor's observation is as relevant today as it was half a century ago, Leopold Sedar Senghor in Senegal,[7] and Okot p'Bitek[8] in Uganda, poetically commented on the superficiality of African Christianity, highlighting the popular impression which the modern missionary enterprise created, that Christianity is a Euro-American religion which Africans can adopt only after they have become "civilized." The complaint against the superimposition of Christianity over the African cultural and religious heritage has been partly the result of the close association of "evangelization" with "Europeanization," to the point where both terms have become interchangeable. Taylor continues:

> It is bad enough that religious pictures, films, and film-strips should have almost universally shown a white Christ, child of a white mother, master of white disciples; that he should be worshipped almost exclusively with European music set to translations of European hymns, sung by clergy and people wearing European dress in buildings of an archaic European style; that the form of worship should bear almost no relation to traditional African ritual nor the content of the prayers to contemporary African life; that the organizational structure of the Church and its method of reaching decisions should be modeled ever more closely on Western concepts rather than deviating from them. But in the last resort these are all merely outward forms that could quite easily give place to others. They are serious because they are symptoms. They persist because they are the school uniform of a classroom religion reflecting a worldview that is fundamentally European.[9]

The consolidation of "world confessional families," which incorporate the "younger churches" but control them from metropolises in Europe or North America, has not made the cultural emancipation of African Christianity possible. Whereas the European Reformation emancipated European Protestantism from the cultural domination of Rome, such a Reformation has yet to bear fruit in Africa — even though the signs of it are evident in the African Instituted Churches.[10] Within the churches of the missionary enterprise, especially in the Roman Catholic Church, there is much talk about

7. Leopold Sedar Senghor, cited by Taylor, *Primal Vision,* p. 13.

8. Okot p'Bitek, *Song of Lowino and Song of Ocol* (Nairobi: East Africa Publishing House, 1981).

9. Taylor, *Primal Vision,* pp. 13-14.

10. David B. Barrett, *Schism and Renewal in Africa* (London: Oxford University Press, 1968). In this book, Barrett viewed African Independent Churches as indications of an African Reformation.

"inculturation," but this talk is largely one-way.[11] In practice, "inculturation" refers to the appropriation in African Christianity of established doctrinal and ecclesial teachings and practices, as transmitted through the modern North Atlantic missionary enterprise. It does not reciprocally include the appropriation of African theological insights into the core of doctrinal and ecclesial teachings and practices of Euro-American Christianity.[12] The missiological error mentioned above could be summarized under the following presuppositions:

a) *Unsuitability of African heritage for mediation of the gospel:* The modern missionary enterprise has presupposed that the African cultural and religious heritage is an unsuitable vessel with which to receive the gospel (2 Cor. 4:7). To use another metaphor, the modern missionary enterprise has presupposed that the African cultural and religious heritage is an unsuitable rootstock on which to graft the gospel (Rom. 11:17-21). Thus the African has been considered a cultural blank on which anything could be written. Hence the competition among many missionary agencies for the African soul.

b) *Cultural superiority of sending churches and agencies:* It has been taken for granted that the missioner (bearer of the good news) is always culturally superior and fulfilled, while the African convert (recipient of the good news) is always culturally inferior and depraved. This attitude of cultural superiority is often echoed not only in evangelistic campaigns, but also in sermons throughout the continent. This pharisaical attitude alienates many Africans who would otherwise be willing to join the pilgrimage to discover more of the joys of Christian discipleship.

c) *Novelty as good news:* It is also taken for granted, especially in missionary circles, that the missioner (evangelizer) is always the welcome bearer of good news, and the role of the convert is to accept this good news with gratitude and without criticism. When prospective converts reject the offer of conversion, it is rare for the missioners to review their missionary methods and try a different approach. Good news is such that it cannot be concealed. When missionaries are expelled, as has happened in some countries in Africa and Asia, the fault is always traced to the regimes in power rather than to the failure of missionaries to communicate effectively in the countries where they

11. Shorter, *Theology of Inculturation.*

12. Throughout the history of Christian Mission, very few missionaries could be credited with following the example of Paul, to be all things to all people in order to win as many as possible for the sake of the gospel (1 Cor. 9:19-22). See Roland Allen, *Missionary Methods: St. Paul's or Ours,* 2nd ed. (London: Lutterworth, 1968). Also, Vincent Cronin, *Wise Man from the West* (London: Rupert Davies, 1955).

are guests. Unfortunately, some of the message that has reached Africa in the name of Christianity has been culturally so alienating as to become terribly bad news. When a young person is taught that everything his parents and ancestors have taught him is wrong, how is he expected to consolidate his personal identity? In his study of the British missionary enterprise in Kenya, A. J. Temu writes:

> Almost all Protestant missionaries to Kenya viewed all native customs and traditions with abhorrence. They saw nothing good in African dances, music, or in such important African traditions as circumcision and initiation ceremonies. They lumped them together as heathen and immoral without trying to understand them, what they were for and what significance they had in the life of the people to whom they had come to teach Christianity. No African, according to the missionaries, could become Christian before giving up his old, treasured customs. Invariably they used moral reasons for political ends.[13]

There is hardly anything that is "Christian" about the Greek and Latin classics which have formed the foundation of European "Christian" education.[14] Should African "Christian" education be founded on Greco-Roman classics or on African cultural and religious heritage? That this question should be raised indicates the degree of cultural alienation the missionary enterprise has achieved in its good work of schooling in Africa.[15] It is clear that cultural alienation was the preferred strategy of the modern missionary enterprise in Africa. This strategy suited the colonial regimes, because it facilitated the convergence between the projects of "evangelization" and "civilization."[16]

13. A. J. Temu, *British Protestant Missions* (London: Longman, 1972), p. 155.

14. Lesslie Newbigin, *Honest Religion for Secular Man* (London: SCM, 1964), pp. 23-26.

15. I have been directly involved in debate and dialogue with missionary friends and colleagues on cultural education policy and planning in East Africa. Invariably, cultural insensitivity has been so rampant among them that on many occasions we, their hosts, have been made to feel as strangers in our own cultural home. This policy dialogue culminated in revision of the Religious Education Curriculum in Kenya, whose remarkable innovation was the introduction of the African religious heritage as integral part of Christian teaching — in the same way that the Greco-Roman classics form the foundation of Christian theological training in Europe and North America. To provide a textbook for the new edition, I coauthored, with N. Kirima, *The African Religious Heritage* (Nairobi: Oxford University Press, 1976).

16. David Livingstone campaigned for the European support of Christian mission in Africa, arguing that such support would promote "Christianity" and "legitimate commerce." Legitimacy was, of course, understood from the perspective of British mercantilism, not from the interests of Africans themselves. On this point, see Roland Oliver, *The Missionary Factor in East Africa,* 2nd ed. (London: Longman, 1970).

d) *Hermeneutic authority of the missionary:* The modern missionary enterprise has presupposed that the teaching of the missionary is always consistent with biblical teaching. In general, the modern missionary enterprise has presupposed a literal interpretation of the Bible.[17] Africans have taken great interest in the Christian Scriptures. When they read the Bible for themselves, they find other texts which are of greater relevance. The clash of literal interpretations has led to the rise of thousands of independent churches — more than anywhere else in the world.

e) *Paternalism and condescension:* It has been taken for granted that the missioner (evangelizer) has responsibility over his converts, and that the converts (as recipients) of missionary generosity and philanthropy have hardly anything to offer in return. This presupposition has been exaggerated by the financial and material power of the sending agency, which puts the recipients in a relationship of dependence. Henry Venn, who was CMS general secretary in 1840-72, viewed the objective of mission as the establishment of self-supporting, self-propagating, and self-governing churches. As soon as such communities came into being, the missionary had a duty to proceed to a new place, leaving the local community to grow under inspiration of the Holy Spirit. In 1912, Roland Allen published his famous book, *Missionary Methods: St. Paul's or Ours,* in which he echoed the principles articulated by Venn.[18] Unfortunately, these noble principles do not seem to have permeated the missionary community.

These presuppositions are so prevalent that any cultural critique of the missionary enterprise is often viewed as ingratitude on the part of those to whom the gospel has been preached. However, as Cecil McGarry has observed, Jesus of Nazareth is the man of all cultures who immediately captures the attention of individuals and communities in every culture and every occupational situation.[19] This immediate appeal often becomes blurred and confused by the missionary mediation of the gospel.[20] The challenge, then, is to communicate the gospel in such a way that missionary interpretations do not hinder the convert's response to it. Translating the Bible and making it available to the people is the best way to meet this challenge. However, the appropriation of the Bible in particular cultural contexts, without missionary mediation, often yields forms of Christianity with which missionary agencies

17. Norvald Yri, *Quest for Authority* (Nairobi: Evangel, 1978).

18. Allen, *Missionary Methods.*

19. Cecil McGarry, Preface to *Inculturation,* p. 8. See also Mugambi, *From Liberation to Reconstruction,* pp. 90-106.

20. On the blurring of the gospel by missionary mediation, see Kosuke Koyama, *Waterbuffalo Theology* (London: SCM, 1974).

are uncomfortable, because they do not fit the cultural mold of the missionary establishment. In Africa, David Barrett has shown that church independency is most likely in areas where the Bible is available in local languages.[21]

Tropical Africa seems to be the only place where the Christian missionary enterprise has destroyed the confidence of people in their own cultural and religious heritage. In general, missionary policy with regard to traditional African religion and culture has been that African converts should abandon their cultural and religious heritage in order to become accepted into the Christian faith. The consequences of this policy has been *cultural schizophrenia.* As John V. Taylor observed, Christianity has become a Sunday affair, in which Africans do one thing on Sunday in church, and for the rest of the week they continue with business as usual. Perhaps this is one way of explaining the fact that countries which boast a majority of membership in Christian denominations could suffer as much devastation as Rwanda did in 1994. Christianity proclaims peace on earth and goodwill among humankind. In a country that boasts to be 90 percent Christian, how could its Christian citizens became so embroiled in conflict? What went wrong in the process of evangelizing such countries? Questions such as these have no ready answers, but they indicate that at the cultural level the missionary enterprise has not penetrated the African psyche. Africans have appropriated the gospel, but very much as an appendix to their cultural and religious identity. This double-mindedness, which the missionary enterprise has encouraged, is the root of the crisis in contemporary African Christianity.[22]

Conceptual Clarifications

The Christian faith is a missionary faith. This statement suggests that it is part of the definition of Christianity, that it is outward bound to win converts to its fold. Jesus commands all his followers to go out into all the world and make disciples of all humankind. There is a wide variety of ways of implementing this command, each of which is appropriate in particular circum-

21. Barrett, *Schism and Renewal.*

22. The crisis in contemporary African Christianity is documented in the series published by the Ecumenical Symposium of Eastern African Theologians, edited by J. N. K. Mugambi and Carroll Houle: *Jesus in African Christianity* (Nairobi: Acton, 1989 and 1998); *The Church in African Christianity* (Nairobi: Acton, 1990 and 1998); *Moral and Ethical Issues in African Christianity* (Nairobi: Initiatives, 1992); *Mission in African Christianity* (Nairobi: Uzima, 1993); *Pastoral Care in African Christianity* (Nairobi: Acton, 1994); *The Bible in African Christianity* (Nairobi: Acton, 1998); *Worship in African Christianity* (Nairobi: Acton, 1998).

stances. No method of proclaiming the Word of God is appropriate for all situations. Knowledge of the core of the message, principles of effective communication, and the cultural context in which the message is communicated — all these are essential requirements for effective evangelization.

Much of evangelical work today involves persuading — sometimes bribing — Christians to leave one denomination and join another. The missionary or evangelist in such cases believes that he or she has a fuller understanding of the gospel than those of other denominations. Before the tragic war in Rwanda in 1994 there were eight Christian denominations, of which three were the most significant. Ninety percent of Rwanda was Christian. Today there are more than fifty denominations. What does "evangelism" mean in such a country? One of the most scandalous evangelistic tensions in some countries, such as Ethiopia and Russia, arises because missionaries from the North Atlantic are trying to "convert" people who are already Christians into their own denominations. If the aim of "evangelism" is to convert the world to Christ, it makes sense to concentrate on converting non-Christians. The process of winning Christians from one denomination to another is called proselytism, and there is too much of it going on today in Africa under the banner of evangelism.

Cultural pharisaism is partly responsible for proselytism. When a person believes that his or her culture is superior to all others, and when this attitude is reinforced with the religious conviction that this "superior" culture is ordained by God, the logical outcome of such bigotry is cultural imperialism. Exposure to other cultures at an early age may help to relativize one's cultural parochialism depending on the educational process which one undergoes to internalize that exposure. Young colonial *subjects* are exposed to the imperial culture, but the educational process they undergo compels them to view their own culture as inferior and that of their masters as the ideal to which to aspire. Only through a process of liberation do colonial subjects emerge from this subjugation. This point has been lucidly elaborated by Paulo Freire.[23]

Conversely, young imperial *citizens* are brought up to believe that their culture is the best, and that imperial prowess is confirmation of the dictum that might is right. It matters very much whether a person is brought up as a *cultural subject* or as a *cultural citizen*. This differentiation is evident in the socialization of St. Paul, in contrast with that of St. Peter and the other apostles. As a Roman *citizen* St. Paul could appeal to Caesar, while St. Peter and the others, as Roman *subjects*, could not. Evangelism is colored very much by these cultural distinctions. Can evangelism be culturally liberating? Biblical

23. Paulo Freire, *Pedagogy of the Oppressed* (London: Penguin, 1996).

literalism is often associated with "evangelical" Christianity. There is a tendency to avoid the challenges of cultural diversity by hiding behind biblical literalism. Yet every Christian must relate the gospel to his or her own culture. Conversely, each convert must approach the gospel from the perspective of his or her own cultural and religious heritage. Biblical literalism cannot eradicate the fact that the Church of Jesus Christ is constituted by people of diverse cultures, diverse nations, diverse races, diverse histories. This diversity ought to be reflected in the life of the church. In practice, however, one culture tends to be superimposed upon others, and this superimposition is dehumanizing.

How can evangelism accommodate cultural diversity? This question is directly related to cross-cultural relations. Christians are at the same time citizens. They share the attitudes and prejudices of their fellow citizens. The gospel should help Christians to rise above cultural prejudice, but more often than not we, as human beings, are conformed to the norms of this world rather than transformed by the gospel.

Challenges

This section outlines some reflections on what I consider to be urgent challenges for the church in tropical Africa on the eve of the twenty-first century.

a) *Prosperity for a pauperized continent:* From an "evangelical" perspective, there is much rejoicing that tropical Africa is increasingly becoming a "Christian" region. At the same time, from an economic perspective the region is becoming increasingly pauperized almost to its total exclusion from participation in world trade and industry. This region contributes less than 2 percent of world trade, and less than 1 percent of world industry. Yet the missionary enterprise is largely responsible for the "modernization" and "Europeanization" of tropical Africa. What is the connection between Africa's pauperization and Africa's evangelization?

b) *Turning stones into bread:* As a region, tropical Africa has ample fertile land, much rain, many freshwater lakes, some of the longest rivers. Yet the region is a net importer of basic food. Most of its agricultural activity is directed toward producing cash crops for the luxurious consumption of the affluent nations. In return, the people of tropical Africa are fed with relief food from the surpluses stored in the industrialized countries. Is this situation irreversible? What does evangelism have to say about this situation? The sight of military cargo planes dropping relief food to destitute Africans has become familiar on the world's television screens. The impression created by these pictures is that of a continent that is abandoned to the mercy of the principalities and powers of this world. Feeding the hungry has become the work of non-governmental agencies and military contingents from the affluent nations. What is the meaning of Matthew 25:14-31 in this context?

c) *A minority religion in the midst of cultural and religious pluralism:* Numerically, Christianity is a minority religion in the world. It may be a significant minority, but it is a minority all the same. Although in "evangelical" circles it is often stated that Africa is increasingly becoming a "Christian" continent, the desire to turn Africa into a "Christian" continent ought to be balanced with the fact that Africa is culturally and religiously a pluralistic continent. Africans themselves take this fact for granted.

Throughout Africa, it is common to have in the same family a Muslim, Catholic, Anglican, Methodist, Presbyterian, Pentecostal, and others. Likewise, it is common for one person to be exposed to a wide range of religious backgrounds, an exposure which establishes a much wider frame of cultural and religious reference than that of the missionaries who have come to Africa. It is important to respect and appreciate the religious heritage of those Africans who are not Christians, and of those African Christians who do not belong to your denomination or mine. In such a context, what does evangelism mean? For me, it means appreciating that God, in his infinite wisdom, has left himself with many witnesses, and it is our responsibility to discern that wisdom from others before we begin to pour our own ignorance upon them.

d) *Swords into plowshares:* The quest for peace in Africa is the yearning of all people throughout this continent. In our mission schools we were taught that Christianity brought peace in Africa. Yet there have been many bloody wars arising from interreligious and interdenominational conflict. Uganda, Sudan, and Rwanda are notable examples. How can evangelism promote harmonious cultural and religious coexistence, rather than war and strife?

e) *From the cities back to the villages:* The influx of Africa's population is from rural areas toward the towns and cities. Yet these urban centers are incapable of providing the facilities and amenities for a decent livelihood for all those migrating from their rural homes. Urbanization in Europe and North America was sparked by industrialization. In Africa, urbanization is sparked by the deterioration of living conditions in the rural areas, but it is not matched by the industrialization of towns and cities. The majority of urban populations in Africa live in shanties and peri-urban settlements, without basic sanitation, lighting, and transport infrastructures. How can evangelism respond to this situation? The challenge is how to reverse the influx of population from urban to rural areas, and retain rural populations within the rural areas. The church is well placed to respond to this challenge, but to do so will require a reorientation of its ministry.

f) *Moral anarchy and political democracy:* After the end of the Cold War, Africa was bombarded with campaigns for democratization. Why were the North Atlantic countries interested in the democratization of Africa only after the Cold War? Did Africans not need democracy in the 1960s and 1970s? What political process was put in place during the Cold War? Despite the "democratic" constitutions which were endorsed in the European capitals during the process of "decolonization" Africa was subjected to "autocratization" during the 1960s and 1970s. The Cold War encouraged, and even staged, coups and counter-coups, as the superpowers and their allies wrestled for influence in Africa. The end of the Cold War has brought a new situation, during which the reigning ideology is asserting its hegemony over the whole continent.

During the late 1980s and early 1990s, democracy was equated with multiparty politics and parliamentary elections. Compliance with these two principles did not synchronize African politics with liberal economics, and multiparty politics did not yield political stability. Autocratization seems to be condoned again, in which military rulers, after usurping political power, convert themselves into politicians and seek election as civilians. In Africa it appears that anarchy is confused with democracy. With military rulers on political thrones the meaning of democracy in Africa remains an open question.

What can evangelism mean in these circumstances? For a while churches have been involved in "democratization." Yet the process of democratization is neither politically nor culturally neutral. Africa has yet to experience its own cultural renaissance, without turning for advice to its former colonial masters. Will evangelism be part of the solution to Africa's quest for cultural identity, or part of the problem?

g) *Economic prosperity and spiritual bankruptcy:* It is often suggested that Africa is "economically poor" and "spiritually rich," whereas the North Atlantic countries are "spiritually poor" and "economically rich." From an evangelical perspective, is this a situation to rejoice about? The history of Christian mission shows that surplus capital is needed to finance Christian mission. St. Paul was able to spread the gospel in the Mediterranean region because he had the financial means to do so. The modern missionary enterprise from Europe and North America to other parts of the world was possible because of the surplus capital which the age of empire accumulated. How can Africa, which now has a significant Christian population, participate in the re-evangelization of post-Christian Europe and North America? The answer does not lie in donations to host "reverse missionaries" from Africa.

Rather, the answer is to be found in revitalizing the African economy, so that surplus capital may be accumulated for a new era of Christian missions from Africa to other parts of the world.

h) *Industrialization without inventiveness:* Two of the most industrialized African countries are those which suffered economic and military sanctions when they were under institutionalized racism: South Africa and Zimbabwe. The sanctions forced the people of these countries to rely on their own brains to solve their own technological problems. When the *moratorium* debate erupted in the ecumenical movement, there was vehement opposition to it. How can African churches promote inventiveness and creativity while instant formulae, quick-fix solutions, and fast foods are dumped on the continent without restriction? How can unrestricted and uncontrolled liberalization enhance creativity and inventiveness in Africa, when the restrictions against African products are increasing in Europe and North America? Protectionism is condemned in Africa, but condoned in the OECD countries. Without political clout and economic bargaining power, how can African countries resist becoming a dumping ground for garbage and toxic waste from the OECD countries?

i) *Economics and evangelism:* The total number of European and North American missionaries operating in Africa runs into hundreds of thousands. Thus the missionary enterprise is a significant job market for the North. If all these missionaries returned home immediately, there would be a significant increase in unemployment at home. It is important to appreciate this fact so that we do not moralize evangelism at the expense of Africa's human integrity.

j) *Missions to post-Christian Europe and North America:* Post-Christian Europe and North America are as much a mission-field as pre-Christian Africa. The Church in Africa should take it as a burden to evangelize Europe and North America. However, Africa does not have the surplus capital needed for a reverse missionary enterprise. It is ridiculous for the post-Christian North to allocate its own surplus capital for its own re-evangelization. The challenge lies in enabling Africa to become economically prosperous, in the hope that its surplus capital might eventually become available for the re-evangelization of Europe and North America. In recent years in Africa I have encountered Christian missionaries from South Korea, Japan, and India. This is possible only because the per capita incomes of these countries have recently risen to levels where surplus capital is available for tourism, international investment and missionary expansion. African economies will have to grow considerably before African churches can send missionaries abroad at their own expense.

Role of the Electronic Media

John Bachman has raised the important question as to whether, from the perspective of Christian evangelism, the mass media should be viewed as "wasteland" or "wonderland." In his book *Media: Wasteland or Wonderland,* he observes that both views have their advocates.[24] His own view is that mass media need not be culturally and morally destructive. He challenges Christians to develop a constructive attitude toward the mass media, taking into consideration that the electronic age has penetrated all aspects of industrial society. In the African context, manipulation of the electronic media by owners and sponsors is so rampant that it is difficult for Africans to discern truth and value from radio, television, and film. In a setting where only a small elite has access to the electronic media, these channels of communication have become instruments of propaganda — for the peddling of particular ideologies. It is for this reason that the state in Africa has taken an interest in the religious press and religious broadcasting.

The electronic media are coming to Africa and are being seen as exciting channels of communication which amplify, modify, and even transform the traditional media — oral, ritual, and symbolic. The excitement evoked by these electronic media often leads to emotional responses with dramatic consequences, both religious and secular. It has become common for rural congregations to purchase and install public address systems even in small sanctuaries which would be much better off without electronic amplification. Such installations serve more than a communication function — they are status symbols, which indicate that the congregations are entering the electronic age, even though their utility is questionable. In urban centers, evangelistic rallies and campaigns have become commonplace, more as show business than as missionary endeavors.

Throughout tropical Africa, evangelistic rallies are being organized with ever-increasing frequency in sports fields, theaters, recreation parks, and on street corners. These rallies feature American and European missionary-tourists who visit Africa on holiday for a few days or weeks before returning to their affluent countries. They spend only a fraction of their visit in these evangelistic campaigns, while the rest of their time is spent watching wildlife, collecting African curios, and sunbathing on the tropical beaches. They preach a message promising prosperity in the midst of mass poverty, and often demand tithes from the already pauperized audience whom they hypnotize with theatrical tactics and musical enticement.

24. John W. Bachman, *Media: Wasteland or Wonderland* (Minneapolis: Augsburg, 1984).

The old image of a foreign missionary resident at a rural mission station is rapidly being replaced by the image of the missionary-tourist who periodically comes to preach for a few afternoons while spending the rest of his holiday in the game parks and tourist resorts. Between these periodic visits, local entertainers are equipped with public address systems to preach at street corners, car parks, road reserves, and other open spaces, advertising themselves as proclaimers of the good news. Poverty continues to bite, but there is no interest in relating the pauperization of Africa with this kind of preaching which promises "pie in the sky when we die, by and by." Secular non-governmental organizations are replacing the old missionary societies and their serene mission stations.

In the past, the foreign missionary would set up camp in the midst of rural communities, and expect the rural neighbors to come to him for "conversion." If they came, he would mold them in his own image. Today, the non-governmental organizations perform this function, and missionary work has been edged from humanitarian service to spiritual evangelism. Whether mission is "religious" or "secular," Africa as a region continues to recede to the abyss of destitution. The secular NGOs, which are funded to focus on the "alleviation of poverty" through entrepreneurial projects, leave the structures of world economy intact, with the consequence that the poor hardly emerge from their poverty and the poor countries become ever poorer, while the affluent countries become ever more affluent.

The association of evangelism with show-biz certainly shifts Christian mission from ecclesiology to the entertainment industry. Here is an illustration. At Jeevanjee Gardens in the center of Nairobi, loudspeakers begin blaring at full volume at about noon every working day. They play prerecorded audio cassettes as the evangelists await the lunch hour. When people leave their offices for the lunch break, teams of "evangelical" dancers mount the platforms, and the musicians take to their instruments. The park, which was designed for quiet meditation and rest, has become a daily musical extravaganza, where several so-called "Christian" bands play simultaneously at full volume, all preaching the gospel and competing for audience from the passersby, who seem helpless in the midst of the din.

Paul Gifford has documented this phenomenon with a wide range of research covering many African countries. In his book, *The Religious Right in Southern Africa,* he has illustrated the abuse of evangelism for ideological purposes, particularly in dampening the struggle against apartheid during the 1980s.[25] In 1992 he edited an anthology of research papers extending this

25. Paul Gifford, *The Religious Right in Southern Africa* (Harare: Baobab, 1988).

research to the rest of Africa, published under the title *New Dimensions in African Christianity,* under the auspices of the All Africa Conference of Churches.[26] These works show that evangelism in contemporary Africa has tended to hinder Africa's liberation rather than support it. If Jesus came so that we might have life in abundance, and if he came to proclaim liberation to those who are not free, how can one explain an approach to evangelism which negates these values? In every period of church history, the missionary enterprise has risked becoming engulfed in the reigning ideology. Evangelism today is not exempt from this risk.

When Marshall McLuhan declared that radio and television had reduced literacy to obsolescence, many of his critics thought he had exaggerated the negative impact of electronic media.[27] McLuhan had emphasized that the medium (radio and television) is the message, in the sense that we understand the message that is being communicated only through the medium that communicates it. In the context of missiology, we could say, with McLuhan, that the gospel is understood only through the medium in which it is conveyed. The missionary enterprise has packaged the gospel in a wide variety of brands so that the recipients understand it only within the framework of those brands. It is very difficult for individuals to have the privilege of exposure, to stand outside the missionary packages and view the gospel from a wider panorama than the narrow missionary brands.

The ecumenical movement, in principle, was established to provide this wide frame of reference, but it is limited and contradicted by the self-centeredness of the "world confessional families," or Christian World Communions as they are known today. Pierre Babin, reflecting on McLuhan's Theory of Communication, observes:

1. The message of faith is not first and foremost information affecting my understanding. It is the effect produced in me by the whole complex known as the medium. In the communication of faith, the message is my conversion.
2. The message is not first and foremost the material vehicle of communication. The message is the whole complex of ministries and conditions that are required for an effect to be produced. In the communication of faith, it is the church, the places of communication, the face, the gestures, and even the clothes of the religious educator. The message is the

26. Paul Gifford, ed., *New Dimensions in African Christianity* (Nairobi: AACC, 1992).

27. For a study of McLuhan, see Jonathan Miller, *Marshall McLuhan* (London: Collins, 1971); R. Rosenthal, ed., *McLuhan Pro and Con* (New York: Penguin, 1969).

interrelation of the print media, the electronic media, the use of live drama, and the preached word. It is also the forms of financing, both the marketing and the administration associated with faith. All this is part of the medium that is communicating. All these conditions lead to faith development and conversion.

3. The content of the faith message is not primarily the ideas or the teaching, but rather the listeners themselves insofar as they are affected by the medium. In the communication of faith, the content is not first and foremost the teaching of Christ. Rather, it is those who are being taught, insofar as they are reached by Christ and his church; again, insofar as they are affected by the medium.[28]

The use of mass electronic media for evangelization in tropical Africa has considerably changed the content of the evangelistic message. Radio programs can include only sketchy information, which leaves the listener to interpret the programs as he or she chooses. The live sermon which is delivered every Sunday by the parish priest or catechist in a local church is very different from the radio or television sermon. It is different from the theatrically managed sermon delivered at a cinema theater or in a soccer stadium. The televangelist is much more an actor than an orator. The live preacher in a local church is much more an orator than an actor.

In his book *Amusing Ourselves to Death,* Neil Postman aptly explains the crisis to which the world has been plunged by electronic media.[29] He contrasts the works of two critics of North Atlantic culture, George Orwell and Aldous Huxley. Orwell wrote *1984* to warn against the curtailing of freedom by dictatorship, whereas Huxley wrote *Brave New World* to warn against voluntary enslavement under the power of technology.

> Contrary to common belief even among the educated, Huxley and Orwell did not prophesy the same thing. Orwell warns that we will be overcome by an externally imposed oppression. But in Huxley's vision, no Big Brother is required to deprive people of their autonomy, maturity and history. As he saw it, people will come to love their oppression, to adore the technologies that undo their capacities to think.[30]

28. Pierre Babin, *The New Era in Religious Communication* (Minneapolis: Fortress, 1991), pp. 6-7.

29. Neil Postman, *Amusing Ourselves to Death: Public Discourse in the Age of Show Business* (New York: Penguin, 1985).

30. Postman, *Amusing Ourselves to Death,* p. vii.

Electronic media have become so pervasive that ordinary people can hardly escape from the propaganda perpetrated through radio, television, newspapers, and the Internet. Ordinary people are no longer encouraged to think for themselves. The owners of the media determine what the public should know and what they should not. Journalists are employed to implement that policy and if they do not comply, they are sacked. There are so many radio and television channels that the ordinary members of the public can hardly distinguish truth from falsehood, facts from propaganda, theology from ideology. Formal education is shifting from the classroom and the textbook to the television and computer screen. The role of the teacher and the preacher is being reduced to irrelevance, especially among the rich elite. In a world where public opinion is shaped by the electronic media, how can Africans respond to international opinion which portrays nothing constructive or positive from their continent?

The fact that Africa is negatively portrayed in the North Atlantic media is evidence of the editorial policy of those media with regard to this continent. Positive reporting on Africa would go against the policy to depict Africa as a continent which does not function. Any success stories in Africa are either suppressed or edited to reflect this policy. North Atlantic religious media, in general, is no exception. The gospel proclaims a message of hope. Yet the media, both religious and secular, continues to portray Africa as a region without a future and without hope. The media portrays Europe and North America as the places from where the salvation of Africa will come, despite the fact that strangulating bilateral and multilateral debts are largely responsible for Africa's pauperization.

It appears that North Atlantic media rejoice in "amusing to death" their audiences who are obsessed by a craving for entertainment. Postman continues:

> What Orwell feared were those who would ban books. What Huxley feared was that there would be no reason to ban a book, for there would be no one who wanted to read one. Orwell feared those who would deprive us of information. Huxley feared those who would give us so much that we would be reduced to passivity and egoism. Orwell feared that the truth would be concealed from us. Huxley feared the truth would be drowned in a sea of irrelevance. Orwell feared we would become a captive of culture. Huxley feared we would become a trivial culture, preoccupied with some equivalent of the feelies, the orgy porgy, and the centrifugal bumblepuppy. As Huxley remarked in *Brave New World*, the civil libertarians and rationalists who are ever on the alert to oppose tyranny "failed to take account of man's almost infinite appetite for distractions." In *1984*,

> Huxley added, people are controlled by inflicting pain. In *Brave New World,* they are controlled by inflicting pleasure. In short, Orwell feared that what we hate will ruin us. Huxley feared that what we love will ruin us. This book is about the possibility that Huxley, not Orwell, was right.[31]

Many European and North American radio and television channels beam their programs to African audiences. Some of them have already established FM stations and contracted to beam their television news within local channels. There is no reciprocation of African news in Europe and North America. The flow of information should be two-way. If a European or North American country is allowed a channel in one African country, there should be a reciprocal arrangement whereby the African country also be allowed a channel in Europe and North America. If the channel is based in the capital city, then so should the other channel be based in the capital city also. This is the only way to ensure fair coverage and fair reporting. The church should participate in the negotiations that make this possible.

Implications

Pierre Babin in his book *The New Era in Religious Communication* writes:

> . . . it is only possible to understand a person of another culture when one begins to understand oneself. One can begin to understand God by rousing the dormant aspects of one's own personality and by eliminating the foreign aspects that keep one closed to other cultures and other peoples. Any deeper encounter with people of other cultures is a very special way of knowing God in the twentieth century, a century of travel and international exchange.[32]

I remember vividly an insight Professor Kosuke Koyama shared with me when he visited Nairobi in the mid-1980s. He expressed disappointment that, in spite of traveling thousands of miles from New York to Nairobi, culturally he had not moved at all. He had expected to experience some cultural movement, but in the plane he was served the same meals, hotels were culturally the same, and the language was English wherever he went. He raised the question: How can we talk of cultural diversity in a world where everyone is expected to become incorporated into the one North Atlantic culture? This is

31. Postman, *Amusing Ourselves to Death,* pp. vii-viii.
32. Babin, *Religious Communication,* p. 16.

a difficult challenge for Christianity at the beginning of the twenty-first century. Culture-sensitive evangelism is possible only if and when those involved in it are willing and ready to be changed by those whom they go to change. This willingness and readiness grows out of an attitude of acceptance, appreciation, and respect for the people of other cultures, to the extent of becoming empathetically immersed in those cultures. Empathy has been a rare virtue in the modern missionary enterprise. Sympathy and pity, though plentiful, have produced condescension and ridicule.

Bishop Mvume Dandala of the Methodist Church in South Africa reminds us:

> Spirituality, as I understand it, includes a satisfying explanation of who we are, where we come from, where we are going and how we can get there. In Africa today we have a very real crisis of spirituality, and genuine liberation will not come until Africa is able to define itself and find joy in itself without seeking the approval of big brother. One always hurts inside when non-Africans speak derogatively of Mwalimu Julius Nyerere's failed *ujamaa* experiment; for they are laughing at Tanzania's failure to control its destiny on the basis of its understanding of its origins and its destiny.
>
> Until Africa finds a spirituality with which it is comfortable, within which it can search for meaning in life, from which it will seek to understand creation and its fellow human beings from beyond Africa, inculturation will not happen. If some such spiritual base is to be found, it is essential that African theologians, pastors and people have the freedom to explore and search unhindered.
>
> Perhaps the task of those who are now being called to the leadership of the church should be to protect the right of Africans to do this rather than to preserve the established conventions of the church and the Christian faith. For without this freedom, inculturation of anything religious will be only another form of playing the same old game, on the basis of the same old rules, clothed in the niceties of accommodation.[33]

These are useful insights with which to conclude. Over twenty-five years ago David Barrett projected that by the year 2000, Africa would be the "most Christian continent" in the world. Since then, this observation has been echoed many times.[34] It is echoed as a positive expectation. At the same time, it is

33. Bishop Mvume Dandala, Presiding Bishop of the Methodist Church in South Africa, in *ANITEPAM Newsletter* (April 1998): 2.

34. David B. Barrett, ed., *World Christian Encyclopedia* (London: Oxford University Press, 1982).

widely accepted that the modern missionary enterprise in Africa has been the most significant agent of social change on this continent. Evangelization and civilization have been inseparable.

During the past thirty years, the economy of Africa has deteriorated at the same inverse proportion as church membership has grown. The more Christian the continent becomes, the more pauperized it is increasingly becoming. Is this a fact for Christians to rejoice about? If not, it is a challenge which we have to take seriously. Some of the converts being won to Christianity are drawn to the church by evangelists who preach material prosperity as the reward for becoming Christians. At the beginning of his public ministry, Jesus had to face the temptation of turning stones into bread to feed the hungry. This temptation is more real in Africa today than ever before. "If you are the son of God, turn these stones into bread, so that these hungry people may eat." During the Cold War there was much talk in North America about using food as a political weapon. Will people "worship" those who feed them in times of destitution, or will God the Creator sustain them despite the *pauperization* they continue to suffer?

Most of Africa's people living beyond ten degrees north of the Equator are Muslims. This represents a large population. Africa should be considered as one whole — a whole region. It is important to appreciate that many African Muslims are not Arabs, and that Islam is as much at home in Africa as in Arabia and Indonesia. As the twenty-first century draws near, the conflict in Sudan signals the next challenge that Africa must deal with, after colonialism, racism, and the Cold War: that is, the challenge of *religious bigotry.* If rational discussion of culture-sensitive evangelism within the ecumenical movement can help Africa to resolve this challenge peacefully, it should be encouraged and promoted in every church and nation. May God help us to remove the huge logs in our own eyes so that we might be able to see the tiny specks in the eyes of our neighbors. This principle can go a long way towards facilitating culture-sensitive evangelism.

Equipping for Culture-Sensitive Evangelism

In view of the foregoing elaboration we can ask: What should be done to enhance culture-sensitive evangelism? Among others, the following are suggestions which can be implemented at relatively little cost, if there is the will to do so:

a) *Education for culture-sensitive evangelism:* There is need for Christians to engage in cross-cultural interaction, especially to correct the prejudices perpetrated in the mass media. To be effective, such education should start in the seminaries, inculcating the appreciative attitudes among the younger generation of clergy in training.

b) *Knowledge sharing for culture-sensitive evangelism:* In his recent book *Whose Reality Counts?* Robert Chambers has observed that much of the knowledge that circulates in Europe and North America about other regions is obtained and packaged from the North Atlantic perspective.[35] Consequently, there is hardly any cross-cultural exchange of knowledge. It would be worthwhile sharing African theological knowledge with the North Atlantic in a structured way, through facilitation of the flow of theological literature from Africa to Europe and North America. As the flow of knowledge is currently only one-way, a two-way flow should be developed. The ecumenical movement could be a useful instrument for this process.

c) *Alternative video and audio media:* There are many success stories in Africa which never reach the audiences of Europe and North America. The church could facilitate the production of documentary audio and video cassettes which express the experiences of Africa and Africans from the perspective of Africans themselves.

If these measures are carefully coordinated, they may contribute to a change of attitude in the North Atlantic toward an appreciation of Africans and their cultural heritage. As long as superiority and inferiority complexes clog relationships between Christians of various cultures, culture-sensitive evangelism will be impossible. In Christ all social distinctions, though, become irrelevant — not because they are glossed over but because they are taken seriously. The tragedy of Christian mission is that converts have been molded not in the image of Christ but in the image of the evangelizer. Both the missionary and the convert become pilgrims toward the kingdom of God and the distinction between them vanishes when the Holy Spirit binds their relationship.

35. Robert Chambers, *Whose Reality Counts?* (London: ITDG, 1997).

CHAPTER 26

Strategic Issues in Missions — An Asian Perspective

Hwa Yung

Some time ago, while spending a few months in Britain, I met a dignified Chinese lady in the kitchen of our hostel. A full professor from a Chinese university in a highly specialized field of information technology, she was doing some advanced research at the local university, one of the most prestigious in the country. Here was a person who epitomizes the future of China. On finding out that I teach theology, she said: "You people must come to China and preach the gospel." Startled by her statement, I asked her whether she was a Christian. I was even more amazed when she said, "No." I then asked her why she said what she did. Her answer stunned me. She replied: "China needs God. If China does not know God, there is no hope for her future."

I must confess that I have still not quite gotten over the conversation. It was a Macedonian call to the church worldwide. But before we rush to China with all the missionaries and resources at our disposal, we need to ponder for a moment the words of John Sung, the greatest evangelist and revivalist of twentieth-century China. Sung was not unappreciative of the sacrificial labor of many Western missionaries who gave their lives to bring the gospel to China. Nevertheless, by the 1920s and 1930s, he noted that often it was missionary control and dependency on Western funds that prevented the Chinese church from growing. Repeatedly he urged the budding Chinese church to cut its apron strings and move on toward independence and maturity. Asked shortly before his death in 1944 about the future of the Chinese church, Sung revealed that God had showed him that a great revival was coming. But the missionaries would all have to leave first. The history of the last fifty years shows that this was the most profound prophecy concerning the Chinese church in the twentieth century.[1]

1. William E. Schubert, *I Remember John Sung* (Singapore: Far Eastern Bible College

Asia, with some 3.7 billion people and less than 9 percent of whom are Christians, clearly needs the gospel. But Sung's prophetic statement reminds us that we cannot go on doing things in the same old manner. What then is the way forward? For what it is worth, here are some thoughts on the matter.

Three Trends and Three Issues Affecting Asian Missions

To begin with, those wanting to think strategically about Asian missions should note three important global trends. First, sometime in the 1980s, the number of Christians in the non-Western world exceeded that in the West for the first time in modern history. Figures given by David Barrett show that in A.D. 2000, the number of Christians in Europe and North America was about 750 million (39 percent), compared to almost 1.2 billion (61 percent) for the whole non-Western world. This shift of the center of gravity of the church from the Western into the non-Western world is not merely demographic. It is also reflected in the vitality and growing influence of non-Western Christianity. One can see these in the joy of African Christian worship, the fervency of Korean church prayer life, and the dynamism of evangelism in Latin American Pentecostalism, Indian rural house churches, etc. Parallel to this is the perceived decline of Western Christianity, in the face of powerful secularist and liberal pressures within an increasingly post-Christian milieu.

Perhaps the clearest illustration of this two-sided trend is Lambeth 1998, when Anglican bishops from all over the world met together. The burning issue then was whether homosexuality is an acceptable Christian moral alternative. In the end, this was overwhelmingly rejected because almost all the African and Asian bishops opposed it. The *Times of London* (August 6, 1998) commented:

> Yesterday's resolution, adopted by an overwhelming majority, was a surprising and uncharacteristically trenchant dismissal of the liberal position . . . But the outcome also reflects the growing weight at Lambeth of doctrinally conservative Third World bishops.

Lambeth 1998 may well mark a watershed in global Christianity. It was probably the first time in modern history, at a Christian gathering of interna-

Press, 1976), pp. 65-66. See also John Sung, *The Diaries of John Sung — An Autobiography,* trans. Stephen L. Sheng (Brighton, Mich.: Luke H. Sheng & Stephen L. Sheng, 1995), pp. 34, 183, and 198-99.

tional significance, that an agenda strongly driven by Western churches was decisively rejected by the whole body under the influence of non-Western leadership.

A second observable trend is the changing shape of the international cross-cultural missions force. The following summarizations are based on the total number of missionaries from Protestant, Anglican, and independent churches given in the last two editions of *Operation World.*[2]

By A.D. 2000, the numbers from the non-Western world had overtaken those from the Western world. Other evidences further support this pattern. For example, North American missions appear to be facing a serious problem today of not having enough recruits to replace those who are retiring. At the same time, Urbana 2000, a traditionally predominantly white American conference in the past, saw the presence of at least 26 percent of the twenty thousand or so students made up of Asian Americans or Asian nationals studying in North America.

Much of the energy for Christian missions in the twenty-first century will probably come from the non-Western world. In the West, the liberal churches will become increasingly irrelevant. Evangelical and Pentecostal-charismatic churches will continue to contribute, but even so it will not be like what it was before. Living in an increasingly post-Christian environment, much of their spiritual energy will be sapped by having to face an increasingly hostile spiritual and social environment outside the church, and the growing problem of moral compromise within.

The third trend concerns how the wold is being reshaped today. Harvard professor Samuel Huntington, in *The Clash of Civilizations,* argues that fundamental realignments are taking place in the post–Cold War era.[3] In the past, the battles were fought first between kings, then later between nation states, and finally between ideologies in the Cold War period. Now in the post–Cold War period, the clashes will be largely between civilizations, of which he identifies eight major ones: Western, Orthodox or Slavic, Latin American, Sinic or Confucian, Islam, Hindu, Japanese, and African. Huntington's thesis has been seriously discussed and critiqued by many. But after the terror attacks of September 11, 2001, even skeptics have to admit its validity to some degree.

In other words, civilizational patterns of thinking and action will drive

2. Patrick Johnstone, *Operation World* (Carlisle: OM Publishing, 1993), pp. 643ff.; and Patrick Johnstone and Jason Mandryk, *Operation World* (Carlisle: OM Publishing, 2001), pp. 747ff.

3. Samuel Huntington, *The Clash of Civilizations and the Remaking of World Order* (London: Simon & Schuster, 1997).

much of the world in the next few decades. This has tremendous ramifications for missions. For example, the last couple of decades have witnessed the increasing resurgence of all the traditional religious-cultural groupings, including radical Islam with groups like al-Qaeda, and fundamentalist Hinduism with India's BJP, among others. Invariably, this means that pressures on Christians in places where they are minorities will increase rather than decrease. Thus the empowerment and sustenance of persecuted churches will become an increasingly important missions agenda.

Apart from these three trends, the Asian church also faces three serious issues. To begin with, the rapid growth of non-Western Christianity in the last half-century does not mean that everything is well. In many places in Asia, serious problems exist. For example, in spite of the wildfire church growth, especially in 1960s and 1970s, Protestant churches in South Korea are facing a crisis today. Church growth began slowing in the 1980s, and plateaued or began declining in the early 1990s. Contributory factors suggested include divisions, lack of social involvement, overemphasis on megachurches, inadequate pastoral oversight, distrust of leadership, and nominalism.[4] In the last few years, charges of autocratic leadership, nepotism, and misuse and embezzlement of church funds have not helped to arrest the declining pastoral image. Clearly, in many parts of the non-Western church, Christian fundamentals are not in place, especially in relation to commitment, holiness, and character formation.

Secondly, the gospel for too long has been proclaimed in a truncated form. This problem did not begin with the fundamentalist-modernist debates of the early twentieth century, which led to the sharp dichotomy between evangelism and sociopolitical concerns. The roots go back to the domestication of Christian theology by Greek philosophy, which underlies the dualistic distinctions between soul and body, spirit and matter, and evangelism versus sociopolitical action.

Consequently, the gospel is often presented in a distorted manner, with half of it being proclaimed at best. For example, in the 1920s, precisely at a time when China was opened to foreign influence for the first time in hundreds of years, many intellectuals rejected Christianity. China was looking for national salvation. But the conservatives preached a gospel that promised only spiritual salvation, never mind the plunder and destruction of China through Western and Japanese imperialism in the nineteenth and twentieth centuries. On one

4. See, e.g., Bong Rin Ro, "The Korean Church: Growing or Declining?" *Evangelical Review of Theology* 19, no. 4 (October 1995): 336-53; and Yonggi Hong, "Nominalism in Korean Protestantism," *Transformation* 16, no. 4 (1999): 135-41.

hand, Chinese leaders saw the gospel as yet another superstition, totally irrelevant to the future of China. On the other, the modernists' social gospel offered much in terms of education, science, medicine, and the modernization of China. But it had no real answer for China's spiritual need, and therefore lacked the power to effect moral transformation and cultural rejuvenation. Hence that too was rejected. So long as we fail to show that the gospel speaks holistically to all of life, many in Asia will simply deem it irrelevant.

China's rejection of the gospel in the 1920s also illustrates a third missiological problem, that of an alien Jesus. Whenever the gospel is presented in a manner that the hearer cannot understand, because of the foreignness of the language and thought forms, and in ways that fail to address the felt needs of the hearer or a culture, then an alien Jesus is being proclaimed. Apart from a truncated gospel, other illustrations can easily be found. For example, many missionaries working in Asia today still have real problems with the supernatural and miraculous realm. They find it difficult to comprehend that almost everywhere in the non-Western world where the church is growing rapidly, the form of Christianity found in those places tends to take signs and wonders and deliverance ministries seriously. In their negative response to such manifestations of spiritual power, these missionaries often forget that their own versions of the gospel are products of Enlightenment Christianity, which Charles Kraft has described as "powerless."[5] If Asia is to hear and understand the gospel, then we need to ask how we can avoid presenting a Jesus who is alien.

Five Proposals for the Way Forward

How are we to respond to the above trends and issues? I suggest that we need to consider seriously five things in our missions agenda.

1. *Empowering the indigenous churches.* We must use all means possible to empower indigenous churches. The goal is to enable them to move on toward genuine independence so that they can take their place as equal partners in the global Christian community. The reasons are obvious. For a start, given the growing importance of non-Western churches, helping them to move toward increasing effectiveness would be one sure way to advance world missions. Further, it is also the best method to tackle the continuing problem of paternalism in missions. The latter unfortunately is still very much alive in various places, with complaints directed not just against some Western mis-

5. Charles Kraft, *Christianity with Power* (Ann Arbor, Mich.: Servant Books, 1989).

sionaries, but also against many from the newer sending churches in Asia. So long as this persists, the Holy Spirit will not be free to do his work and indigenous churches cannot mature. The prophecy of John Sung about widespread revival coming to the Chinese church only after all missionaries have left should serve as a sharp reminder to all. Missionaries — whether Western or Asian — must stop overestimating their own sense of self-importance so that the Spirit can have his way.

2. *Challenging indigenous leaders on the issues of discipleship and character.* Crucial to the growth and maturity of the indigenous churches is the need for leaders with genuine Christian commitment and character. In many parts of Asia, the churches are not short of leaders, but rather the right kind. The Korean church was probably the most vibrant in Asia in the last few decades. Yet we saw that even there the gospel fundamentals are often not in place. The failure usually begins at the leadership level. Thus, perhaps more than anything else, the great need in the Asian church today is for able leaders who also embody Christian character and exemplify servanthood. Here Asian Christians can learn much from the best of the West.

Certainly, scandals among church leaders and shallowness of Christian discipleship and holiness are also found in the Western church. Nevertheless, it needs to be said that Christian character takes time to grow. Thus in the best of the Western tradition, where holiness of life and Christian commitment have been nurtured over generations, we often find wonderful examples of Christian character. For example, we know of many Western families who have modeled missionary commitment and sacrificial service over several generations. Such things are far less common in the non-Western world, simply because there has not been the same long years of Christian traditioning and nurture. The implication here for our Western friends is clear. Guard against paternalism at every point. But do not be afraid to exemplify for us discipleship, commitment, holiness and character, if these have been granted to you.

3. *Recovery of a holistic gospel.* Earlier we noted that the underlying dualism of Western theology produced a truncated gospel. Indeed, David Bosch notes that since the time of Augustine, the individualization and spiritualization of salvation have become endemic in Western theology. This, he says, "could not but spawn a dualistic view of reality, which became second nature in Western Christianity — the tendency to regard salvation as a private matter and to ignore the world."[6] This was the particular weakness of evangelical Christianity which Lausanne II in Manila (1989) sought to address, when it took the phrase, "the whole gospel for the whole world," as part of its theme.

6. David Bosch, *Transforming Mission* (Maryknoll, N.Y.: Orbis, 1991), p. 216.

The recovery of a holistic gospel will require us first to exorcise Greek dualism from our thinking. As Francis Schaeffer noted,

> True Christianity is not Platonic. Much, however, of what passes for Christianity does have the ring of Platonic thinking in it . . . the body is bad and is to be despised. The only thing that matters is the soul. But the Bible says God made the whole man, the whole man is to know salvation, and the whole man is to know the Lordship of Christ.[7]

The gospel is holistic because biblical Christianity speaks to every human need.

Secondly, in our theological formulations, we need to reclaim "kingdom" categories. The central theme of Jesus' preaching in the Gospels is the "kingdom of God," and the central theme of the rest of the New Testament is that "Jesus is Lord/King." We need, therefore, to reconceptualize or, at least, reemphasize mission as the proclamation of Jesus' lordship over all of life — individuals, as well as whole communities; in every sphere of human life, be it spiritual, psychological, socioeconomic, or ecological; and both now and in the world to come! It is interesting that one mission leader, who has been visiting churches all over Asia, told me recently that the one word that increasingly sums up the mission task for many Asian church leaders is "transformation." And transformation it seems, is exactly what the Chinese professor mentioned earlier is also seeking.

4. *Contextualizing the gospel.* Unless genuine efforts are made at contextualizing the proclamation of the gospel and the practice of the faith, Christianity will continue to be widely perceived as a Western religion. This matter has been discussed repeatedly, yet much of Asian Christianity remains in Western captivity. This can be seen in the Gothic cathedrals in downtown Seoul, in tribal Christians in rural Malaysia worshiping God dressed up like American "angels" dancing with tambourines, in seminary training based almost entirely on Western textbooks and methodologies rooted in Enlightenment rationalism, and so forth. We seem to misunderstand the protest of the anti-Christian intellectuals of China in the 1920s when they screamed, "One more Christian, one less Chinese!" We have not heeded the plea of Sadhu Sundar Singh, possibly the most influential Indian Christian who ever lived, when he said that his people needed the "water of life" but "they do not want it in European vessels."[8]

However, if Huntington's thesis on the intensification of civilizational

7. Francis Schaeffer, *Death in the City* (London: InterVarsity, 1969), p. 74.
8. R. H. S. Boyd, *An Introduction to Indian Christian Theology* (Madras: CLS, 1975), p. 109.

clashes in the coming years is correct, then the issue of contextualization must indeed be addressed with greater urgency and at greater depth. Because, to think in civilizational terms invariably means to think contextually. We cannot go into the details of contextualization here, but some examples will help.

First, we must begin with the everyday concerns of the church, such as its hymns and worship, evangelistic and pastoral methods, architecture, etc. Second, it would require us to be sensitive to cultural and civilizational tensions in our missionary approaches. A good example of such sensitivity is found in the approach being taken by one established Western mission agency. One of their leaders mentioned in conversation that they are building a third missionary training college in Hong Kong. But why Hong Kong? His reply is instructive. Their deep concern for Muslims has led them to conclude reluctantly that the thousand-plus years of conflict between the Western and Muslim civilizations means that any breakthrough among Muslims is unlikely to come from the West.

Thirdly, Asia includes four of the largest mission fields today — the Buddhist, Confucian, Hindu, and Islamic worlds. Yet, to this day, there are relatively little serious apologetics, theologies, and ethical discussions formulated in response to the challenges of these cultures and worldviews. Unless we do our homework here, it is difficult to see how major evangelistic breakthroughs can occur. Tom Houston, the former international director for Lausanne, appears to be making a similar point in an unpublished paper entitled "Mobilizing a Church on the Move — Global Clashes: Global Gospel." Houston was making a missiological response to Huntington. He notes that the church became universal in Europe and North America because whole civilizations became Christian, not just individuals and small pockets of believers here and there. If Huntington is correct that civilizational consciousness will predominate, then similarly we need to think in terms of evangelizing whole civilizations to bring them under the Lordship of Christ. This means that we cannot continue preaching a merely Western gospel. Rather we must empower Christians from every civilization to go back to their own peoples in culturally appropriate ways. "They are the only ones who will be able to take the imperialist face away from evangelization."[9]

5. *Developing genuine partnership between Western and non-Western churches.* The centers of Christian growth are now largely found in the non-Western world. Yet despite this fundamental shift, for the moment the centers

9. Tom Houston, "Mobilizing a Church on the Move — Global Clashes: Global Gospel," unpublished manuscript, n.d., p. 19.

of power remain largely in the West: denominational and organizational structures, institutions and established mission agencies, publishing houses, academically trained personnel, and, above all, money. This imbalance can grossly distort our perceptions of the global church realities, and consequently the way we work.

For example, in almost every global ecclesiastical and missiological gathering, Western participants are in the majority. This gives the impression that Westerners are the key players, when in reality the recent growth of non-Western churches has come largely through national initiative and leadership. Thus the old paternalism is perpetuated in another guise. Sometimes, this is clumsily insensitive. One major international organization, in planning a major missiological conference, states that it wants a majority of participants to come from the non-Western world. Yet, the same pamphlet shows that almost all the organizing committee members are Western. And when the fees of such gatherings are set at levels which only the rich can afford, it ensures that the participants, agendas, perspectives, and ultimately the conclusions will be largely Western. Consequently, we remain blinded to changing global realities and locked into outmoded courses of action.

To address adequately the issue of partnership would require us to seriously deal with a whole range of questions. For example, in terms of finance and trained personnel, how and what can the West contribute to augment the meager resources of many non-Western churches? At the same time, how can this be done without giving rise to a dependency mentality on the one hand, and the perpetuation of missionary control on the other. With respect to developing leadership for non-Western churches up to the highest levels, what can we learn form John Stott's work through the Langham Trust of training national scholars with Ph.D.s? And would international agencies, traditionally under Western control, dare to incorporate non-Westerners fully into their leadership on the basis of genuine mutuality?

Moreover, we must resist the temptation to think that benefits flow only one way. Thus, we must also pursue questions like how can missionaries (not merely immigrants) from the non-Western world help revitalize moribund Western churches? How can the example of Lambeth 1998 be a model of action for non-Western churches to help Western churches fight the increasingly tough doctrinal and moral battles in a post-Christian environment? How can insights from non-Western Christianity help to reshape Western Christian thinking, at times distorted by Greek dualism, Enlightenment rationalism, and cultural biases, in a more biblical direction?

In a globalized world, the days of parochial thinking and action in world missions are clearly over. Moreover, the task is far too big for any one group to dare think that they can manage it all on their own. The way forward has to be one of genuine Christian partnership between Western and non-Western churches, and between the rich and the poor, whether materially or spiritually. The key question is how can the vast resources of the Western church on the one hand, and the vitality and dynamism of non-Western Christianity on the other, be fused together into a powerful synergistic whole for world evangelization? As we ponder the possibility that the twenty-first century may indeed be the "great century" for the advance of the gospel of Christ in the world, it is surprising that this question has occupied so little space in our deliberations. But this may well be the most important and urgent issue on the global missions agenda today.

CHAPTER 27

Contextual Evangelization in Latin America: Between Accommodation and Confrontation

Mortimer Arias

I shall attempt to describe the Latin American evangelistic experience in terms of contextualization of the gospel. A friend of mine, an engineer by trade, reminded me a few days ago that "contextualization" belongs to the technical jargon of theologians and seminaries. True, it probably originated in the hermeneutical distinction between text and context.

I have found a parable by the late D. T. Niles very helpful in understanding the concept of contextualization: the parable of the seed and the flowerpot. The gospel, according to this great Methodist preacher from Sri Lanka, is like a seed, and you have to sow it. When you sow the seed of the gospel in Palestine, a plant that can be called Palestinian Christianity grows. When you sow it in Rome, a plant of Roman Christianity grows. You sow the gospel in Great Britain and you get British Christianity. The seed of the gospel is later brought to America, and a plant grows of American Christianity. Now, said Dr. Niles, when the missionaries came to our lands they brought not only the seed of the gospel, but their own plant of Christianity, flowerpot included! So, he concluded, what we have to do is break the flowerpot, take out the seed of the gospel, sow it in our own cultural soil, and let our own version of Christianity grow.

This has been called *indigenization* in missionary theory, and it is what *contextualization* is all about. The fact is as old as Christianity itself, because the gospel doesn't come in a vacuum. Already in the New Testament what we have is not a pure gospel but a contextualized gospel, Jewish or Hellenistic, and in the distinguishable versions from Peter, Paul, or John. The New Testament record is both a *witness to* the gospel and an *appropriation of* the gospel. Some Latin American theologians are saying today that what we have in the New Testament is a "first reading of the gospel" and that we have to do our own reading today from our own context, in a dynamic interaction between text and context. Rafael Avila, a Catholic lay theologian from Colombia, has put it this way: "We have to look at Latin America with the eyes of the Bible and we have to look at the Bible with the eyes of Latin America." In the same way, each generation has to appropriate and contextualize the gospel received in the flowerpots from former generations.

When we recognize that the gospel has to be contextualized, that evangelization has to be contextual, then our troubles begin. Contextualization may become mere accommodation, acculturation, domestication, or absorption of the gospel as in syncretism or culture religion. The relationship between the gospel and culture has to be dynamic and dialectic, just like the seed that grows, taking from the soil and selecting the nutritious elements that are congenial with the life of the plant, without losing its very nature. The gospel, says Jesus, is also like leaven in the dough, like salt in the earth, like new wine. There is, then, an explosive, renewing, subversive, revolutionary power in it. This is why true contextualization also implies confrontation.

It is interesting to see how this principle is working in some of the most original theologizing being done in the Third World. Dr. Shoki Coe from Taiwan, the former director of the Theological Education Fund, is very clear on this point:

> A careful distinction must be made between authentic and false forms of contextualization. False contextualization yields to uncritical accommodation, a form of culture faith. Authentic contextualization is always prophetic, arising always out of a genuine encounter between God's Word and his world, and moves toward the purpose of challenging and changing the situation through the rootedness in and commitment to a given historical moment.[1]

To use Shoki Coe's words, we want to ask if Latin American contextualization of the gospel has been *prophetic contextualization,* "a genuine encounter between God's Word and his [Latin American] world, . . . challenging and changing the situation through *rootedness in* and *commitment to* a given historical moment." And, in Kosuke Koyama's words, we will ask ourselves whether Latin American evangelization has been "easy accommodation" or "prophetic accommodation."[2]

Of course, this question has to be put to evangelization in the United

1. Quoted in Gerald H. Anderson, ed., *Asian Voices in Christian Theology* (Maryknoll, N.Y.: Orbis, 1976), p. 4. See also Rafael Avila, *Teologia, Evangelización y Liberación* (Bogotá: Ed. Paulinas, 1973).

2. Anderson, *Asian Voices,* p. 5.

States as well, or to evangelization in any other part of the world and at any given time. While I am trying to describe and interpret what has happened in Latin America, you can try to translate or to compare it with what has happened or is happening in your own country.

We shall look at our subject from a historical perspective and in a very preliminary and tentative way.

I. The Catholic Conquest: Civilizing Evangelization

The first evangelistic penetration in Latin America came with the Spanish conquest in the sixteenth century, which is considered "one of the most important events in the whole history of Christian expansion."[3] The missionaries — priests and friars of the Franciscan and Dominican orders — came on the wave of the explorers, conquistadors, and colonizers. Evangelization was the spiritual side of the conquest. The Spanish crown had been entrusted by the pope with the responsibility of evangelizing the New World. (The same was true of the kingdom of Portugal in their part of the new lands.) The cross and the sword, Christ the King and the king of Spain, came together.[4] The Indians were supposed to be evangelized by persuasion and, if necessary, by force.[5] Slavery was prohibited by the Spanish crown, and the conversion and teaching of the Indians were entrusted to the colonizers by means of the *encomiendas,* land grants for those in charge of the Indians' evangelization and education.[6] Some of the missionaries, such as Father Antonios Montesinos and Fray Bartolomé de las Casas,[7] protested against the abuses and were able to secure protective legislation for the Indians, but it was seldom observed. There were many missionaries who went to the Indians peacefully, and not a few died as martyrs: but, in general, when the evangelizers appealed to the natives "to forsake their false gods" and to worship "the true God who is in heaven," they had all the power and superiority of the conqueror behind them. "Obedience to the great king of Spain and submission to

3. Justo González, *Historia de las Misiones* (Buenos Aires: La Aurora, 1970), p. 140.

4. See John A. Mackay, *The Other Spanish Christ* (London: SMC Press, 1932), pp. 24 and 33; José Míguez Bonino et al., *Jesús mi Vencido mi Monarco Celestial* (Buenos Aires: Tierra Nueva, 1977); Jordan Bishop, "The Church in Latin America," in *Shaping a New World: An Orientation to Latin America,* ed. Edward L. Cleary (Maryknoll, N.Y.: Orbis, 1971), p. 256.

5. González, *Historia de las Misiones,* p. 143, n. 21.

6. González, *Historia de las Misiones,* pp. 144-45.

7. Fray Bartolomé de las Casas, *Apologética Historia de las Indias* (Madrid, 1909) and *Del Unico Mod de Atraer a todas los Pueblos al Verdadera Religión* (Mexico, 1942).

the King of heaven were demanded as one single act."[8] This was *conquering evangelization.* And it raises the obvious question: Can the conquerors authentically and efficaciously evangelize the conquered? (Can the rich evangelize the poor? Can the whites evangelize the blacks in a situation of racial domination? Can the Anglos evangelize the Hispanics in a situation of social and economic superiority? Can suburbia evangelize the inner city?)

But it was, as well, *civilizing* and *colonizing evangelization.* The religious orders brought with them new livestock and new seeds, new techniques in agriculture and crafts, European arts and literate skills. (In the Southwest of the present-day United States, they were more successful in transplanting culture than in transplanting the gospel.)[9] The Jesuits made an outstanding civilizing work through the *reducciones* (Christian villages) where the natives received instruction in European mores and Catholic religion and developed new skills and industries. This civilizing task, however, implied a paternalistic attitude and in most cases the destruction of the original Indian cultures. "Spanish-ization" became synonymous with Christianization, and evangelization became colonization. (The same is true of a whole period in U.S. mission history, when Americanization was the content and intent of evangelization.)[10]

This conquering evangelization pretended to transplant the Spanish version of Christianity, the flowerpot included. The flowerpot involved not only Catholic dogmas, liturgy, and ethics, but also the Spanish hierarchy, the foreign priesthood, and even the Inquisition. The cultural genocide, however, would never be completely accomplished. The old Indian cultures — some of them widely developed — would prove to be resilient, and the old religion survived under the mantle of Christianity and with Christian names, such as the worship of the Mother Earth or the fertility deity in the imported worship of the Virgin Mary. This fact of cultural resistance and survival added to mass conversions and mass baptisms without Christian instruction, plus the short-

8. José Míguez Bonino, *Doing Theology in a Revolutionary Situation* (Philadelphia: Fortress, 1975), p. 5.

9. Mortimer Arias, "El Papel de la Iglesia en la Comunidad Meijico-Americana del Sudoeste," mimeographed paper (Dallas: Perkins School of Theology, Southern Methodist University, 1976), p. 6.

10. See Walter Vernon, *Some Thoughts on the Historic Methodist Mission to Mexican Americans* (Dallas: Perkins School of Theology, Southern Methodist University, February 1975), pp. 11ff.; R. Douglas Breckenridge and Francisco O. Garcia-Treto, *Iglesia Presbiteriana* (San Antonio: Trinity University Press, 1974), pp. 127ff., 143. A good example of the Americanization ideology in evangelism is Bishop Warren A. Candler's *Great Revivals and the Great Republic* (1904). For "Spanish-ization," see González, *Historia de las Misiones,* pp. 151 and 159.

age of clergy and the great distances to be traveled, would issue in a *syncretistic* type of Christianity, the worst kind of accommodation. In this way, we can say that conquering evangelization became conquered evangelization, another instance of the historical fact of the "conquered conquerors."

After the first impact of the conquest, in the following four centuries, evangelization would be reduced to *sacramentalization:* baptism at the entrance door to the church, and to society, attendance at the Mass and religious feasts as the main Christian activity, marriage and burial ceremonies by the Church. "Christians of the three contacts" — baptism, marriage, and funeral — were legion. Catechetical instruction, when it existed, was memoristic and moralistic.[11] But millions never had an option for a personal experience of Jesus Christ, and the Bible was both unknown and prohibited. Christ was known as the powerless, dying man on the crucifix, or the patronized baby in his mother's arms.[12] The Christ of the Gospels, the man between the manger and the cross, had not yet arrived in Latin America, except, perhaps, for a very small Christian elite. Latin America, after three centuries of evangelistic sacramentalization, remained a mission field.[13] (This is equally true of the so-called "Christian countries," or wherever Christianity is reduced to sacramentalization and discipleship is so confined to church attendance or affiliation. And it is the reason I dare to say that this area is one of the most difficult mission fields in the world.)

As the Catholic bishops in Medellín recognized in 1968, "Latin American evangelization had remained incomplete,"[14] and Latin America was ripe for a new attempt at evangelization, this time by the coming of the Protestant version of the gospel.

11. Bishop Samuel Ruiz G., exposing the position of the Medellin Episcopal Conference, "La Iglesia el Problema Indigena," in *Religiosidad Popular,* ed. Equipo Seladoc (Salamanca: Sigueme, 1976), p. 65.

12. Mackay, *The Other Spanish Christ.*

13. This was disputed before but not after Medellin. See Enrique Dussel, *Sintesis para una Historia de la Iglesia en América Latina* (Barcelona, 1967), pp. 159ff., esp. n. 14.

14. Consejo Episcopal Latinoaméricano (CELAM), *La Iglesia en la Actual Transformación de América Latina a la luz del Concilio* (2a. Conf. Gral.), 2 vols. (Bogotá: CELAM, 1967). Cf. Orlando Costas, *Theology of the Crossroads in Contemporary Latin America* (Amsterdam: Editions Rodopi, 1976), pp. 69-72. José Comblin refers to "a world still unevangelized, a young continent remaining un-Christianized." See his "Medellin: Problemas de Interpretación," *PASOS* 64 (August 1973): 3 (quoted by Costas, *Theology of the Crossroads,* p. 72, n. 53).

II. The Protestant Transplant: Missionary Evangelization

The second evangelistic penetration in Latin America came in the wave of Protestant missionaries from the Anglo-Saxon countries in the second half of the nineteenth century,[15] particularly Methodist, Baptist, and Presbyterian missionaries from the United States.[16]

The seed of the gospel in its Protestant version was strongly biblical, Christocentric, ethical, and individualistic. This would become the novelty and the fertilizing value of the Protestant missions, in contrast to traditional Roman Catholicism, which was biblically illiterate, centered on Mary and the saints, liturgical and superstitious, and strongly authoritarian.

But *the seed* would prove to be resistant. The Roman Catholic hierarchy would fight by all means and on grounds this "intromission" of Protestantism in what was considered Roman Catholic territory. Everything would be used to stop this "foreign invasion:" law and repression, social and political pressure, physical violence against persons and places of worship, even murder. Not a few of the sowers of the seed, the witnesses of the new faith, would die like grains of wheat to bring forth fruit.[17] Gradually and painfully, the Protestant missionary evangelization was getting a foothold in this missionary field in an officially Christian land. At the beginning of this century there were barely 50,000 Protestants, mostly artisans and immigrants, less than one per thousand inhabitants.[18]

The first method used by Protestants to sow the seed of the gospel was the *distribution of the Bible.* The pioneers in this apparently stony field were the American Bible Society. The forerunner was James Thomson, a Scottish preacher who distributed the Bible and started Lancasterian schools, using the

15. There were immigrant churches from Germany, Great Britain, Holland, etc. They were not there to evangelize but to preserve their faith in a Catholic land. Cf. González, *Historia de las Misiones,* chap. 9.

16. José Míguez Bonino, "The Political Attitude of Protestants in Latin America," tr. James and Margaret Goff in *Noticiero de Fe* 37, no. 9 (July 1972): 2; "It was this Protestantism — anti-clerical, liberal-capitalist (the sectarian and the American heritages), which came to our countries in the second half of the last century with Baptist, Methodist and other missions."

17. There are Protestant martyrs in almost every Latin American country. In Bolivia there are 17; the last 8 (including a Canadian Baptist missionary, a national pastor, and 6 Indian believers) were killed in 1949. In Colombia, during "the Violence" of 1948-58, there were 1,869 recorded cases of violence against Protestant persons on religious grounds (649 arrested, 38 tortured, 22 put to forced labor, 493 injured, 126 murdered, 423 families forced to flee because of persecution). See James Goff, *Protestant Persecution in Colombia, 1948-1958* (Cuernavaca, Mexico: CIDOC, 1965).

18. P. Damboriena, *El Protestantismo en América Latina,* 2 vols. (Friburgo, 1962).

Bible as the textbook, with the support of the heroes of independence of the new nations.[19] Almost every Latin American nation has stories of people converted by the reading of the Bible and giving birth to new congregations. The second method was *preaching* — first by missionaries, and soon by national and lay preachers, who put the fluency and beauty of the Spanish language and the fervor of their personal conversion to Christ at the service of communicating the good news. Very often this preaching was polemic and anti-Roman Catholic, using all the biblical ammunition against that religious-social system. A third approach to evangelization was through *educational institutions,* used to educate Protestant children in freedom, to reach the elite of the country and to motivate and train prospective Christian workers. Distribution of tracts and circulation of *Christian literature* was also a favorite instrument of evangelization until the coming of the *radio,* which became the principal medium of verbal proclamation for the Protestant groups.[20]

Of course, the Protestant seed came with its *flowerpot* — denominational doctrines and church structures, liturgy and hymnology, ethics and style of life, architecture, and even clerical composition! But there were also the cultural components of the flowerpot — the worldview, the ethos, and the ideology of the prospering and expanding capitalistic Anglo-Saxon countries, the image of democracy, progress, education, freedom, and material development. And it was this flowerpot, and not the seed itself, that the liberal politicians, the members of the Masonic lodges, and the young Latin American elite were looking at. In the nineteenth century, the old Spanish colonialism was being replaced by the commercial and diplomatic neocolonialism of Great Britain, and later on of the United States of America. Protestantism arrived in Latin America when our countries were engaged in the "age of modernization."[21] Latin American intellectuals looked at the Anglo-Saxon world as their model and to Protestantism as a timely ally.

José Míguez Bonino, the Argentinian Methodist theologian, puts it this way:

> It hardly comes as a surprise that the men engaged in this struggle felt attracted by what they thought were the social, economic and political con-

19. See González, *Historia de las Misiones,* pp. 333ff. There are two classic biographies of colporteurs in Spanish: Claudio Celada, *Francisco Penzzotti, un Apóstol Contemporáneo;* Andrés Milne, *Del Cabo de Hornos a Quito con la Biblia* (Buenos Aires, La Aurora).

20. In 1964 there were 23 Protestant broadcasting stations in Latin America — 18 in Spanish, 1 in English, and 4 in Portuguese — besides thousands of programs from commercial stations in every country (DIA, Monthly summary, May-June 1964).

21. Míguez Bonino, *Doing Theology,* p. 8.

> sequences of the religion of the Anglo-Saxon countries: Protestantism. They were not so attracted to it as a personal religion — very few became Protestants themselves. Rather they saw in it, as in the first place, an ally in the struggle against clerical domination. . . . On the other hand, Protestantism (they referred mostly to Puritanism) had helped to shape the virtues needed for the modern world: freedom of judgment, reliability, a pioneering and enterprising spirit, moral seriousness. It was the religion of activity, culture and life as opposed to ritualism, idle speculation, and the next world. Under the auspices of these men, conditions were created for the introduction of Protestant missions in Latin America. . . .
>
> Democracy, freedom, moral uprightness, science, and culture: these are the goals that the new religion is supposed to serve. As one follows the evangelical congresses and the accounts of missionaries, it becomes clear that *Protestantism accepted this function*. . . .
>
> Protestantism, in terms of its historical origin, of its introduction to Latin America, and of its ethos, came into our world as the *religious accompaniment of free enterprise,* liberal, capitalistic democracy.[22]

In summary, for the Methodist theologian from Argentina, as *Catholicism* "played the role of legitimizing and sacralizing the social and economic structure implanted in America" of the "*conquest* and *colonization* in the sixteenth century." *Protesantism* "played a minor but significant role in the liberal-modernistic project" of the "*neocolonialism* in the nineteenth."[23] The intention was evangelization, but, consciously or unconsciously, Protestantism fulfilled an ideological function. In one sense, it was confrontation, prophetic accommodation, in relation to the old social order, but it became accompaniment, simple accommodation, in relation to the neocolonial modernistic society in the making. Though many of us would celebrate with the gratitude the coming of the Protestant version of Christianity, which made possible for us a personal and transforming confrontation with the gospel of Jesus Christ, we have to accept the ambiguity of the Protestant presence in our historical situation.

In the twentieth century new missions were coming in, and a flood of missionaries from the United States entered after the Second World War. Protestantism began to grow steadily, particularly after 1930. While at the time of the Panama Congress of Protestant Missions in 1916 the Protestant community was 500,000, by 1936 it had jumped to 2,400,000. And while the population has been growing by 3 percent annually, the evangelical member-

22. Míguez Bonino, *Doing Theology,* pp. 10-22 (emphasis added).

23. Míguez Bonino, *Doing Theology,* pp. 4, 7, and 12.

ship has been growing by 10 percent, doubling every 10 years. In 1973, the Protestant community was estimated at over 20,000,000, between 7 and 8 percent of the total population. When we break these figures down we discover a few interesting facts. First, 65 percent of the Protestants in Latin America are in Brazil, where there is also the largest Catholic Church in the world. Second, the mainline Protestant churches, which are the oldest, represent 25 percent of the total evangelical community in all of Latin America. Third, the conservative evangelical and faith missions, with a huge deployment of missionary force (over 10,000 missionaries as compared with 750 from the mainline Protestant bodies), reach a modest 3 percent of the total Protestant membership in Latin America. Fourth, the Pentecostals, who work without foreign missionaries and without financial support from outside, constitute two-thirds of the Protestant community in Latin America.[24]

III. The Pentecostal Sprout: Indigenous Evangelization

The Pentecostal movement in Latin America was one of the "multiple centers of the worldwide explosion of Pentecostalism" at the turn of the century, but it has become "the only authentic South American form of Protestantism," according to the French sociologist Christian Lalive d'Epinay.[25] There are some Pentecostal missions (Assemblies of God and others) from the United States and Sweden, but the bulk of the movement belongs to those indigenous forms of Pentecostalism having no connection with or dependence on outside churches or mission boards. *Chilean Pentecostalism,* for instance, was a sprout of Pentecostal experience inside the Methodist Church under the leadership of missionary pastor Willis C. Hoover.[26] After condemnation by the Methodist Annual Conference in 1910, the movement expanded to a membership of over half a million in its several branches. The Methodist Church in Chile has retained membership numbering only 1 percent of the Pentecostal total. In Brazil, a Swedish missionary founded the Assemblies of

24. See William R. Read, Victor M. Monterroso, and Harmon A. Johnson, *Latin American Church Growth* (Grand Rapids: Eerdmans, 1969), pp. 33-60. Also W. Richey Hogg, "The Church in Latin America: An Introductory Overview," paper given at the Forum on Latin American Christianity, Perkins School of Theology, March 1, 1973.

25. Christian Lalive d'Epinay, *Heaven of the Masses* (London: Lutterworth, 1969), pp. 7, 139-40, and 223. Spanish edition, *El Refugio de las Masas* (Santiago de Chile: Editorial del Pacifico, 1968), pp. 37, 175, and 273.

26. See d'Epinay, *Heaven of the Masses,* chap. 1 and González, *Historia de las Misiones,* pp. 365ff.

God in 1910, and in the same year an Italian member of a Presbyterian church in Chicago started the Christian Congregation of Brazil. The Assemblies of God planted churches in every state in Brazil, through the work of consecrated laymen, becoming the largest evangelical church in Latin America with a membership of 1,500,000. The Congregation of Brazil had half a million members in 1967. Mancel de Mello started with a congregation in São Paulo twenty years ago, and today his Brazil for Christ Church has more members than all the historical Protestant churches together.[27]

This fantastic growth and the particularities of the movement have intrigued sociologists, missiologists, church executives, and experts from Catholic, Protestant, and secular circles. How is this phenomenon to be explained? Some give a *spiritiual* reason: the free action of the Holy Spirit. Some find *anthropological* roots: people's hunger for God. Others offer a *sociological* explanation: the Pentecostal movement, in replacing the "hacienda" social pattern, responds to the need for belonging, support, and authority for those coming from the rural areas to the insecurity and anonymity of the big cities. Others find the answer in an appropriate *pastoral methodology:* lay participation, common people communicating the good news to common people in their own situation and on their own terms; the practical training and selection of pastors through a long on-the-job process; and sound principles of self-support, self-government, and self-propagation. There are also *psychological* explanations: the freedom of expression in worship and charismatic type of authority of leaders and pastors. Finally, the *cultural* dimension: the use of popular music and instruments, the indigenization of worship. Probably each one of these explanations has relevance, but one thing is clear: here we have an evangelistic movement thoroughly contextualized.

The question is whether this is prophetic contextualization or mere accommodation. In one sense, at the individual level, there is undoubtedly a dimension of confrontation. Individuals are called to make a break with their former style of life, to "leave the world" and "follow the Lord," to become sober and honest, to put themselves and their families in order, and to "serve the Lord," preaching and witnessing in the streets. There is a definite sense of liberation from fear, loneliness, guilt, sickness. There is, as well, a social integration at the level of the congregation. But a lack of prophetic understanding of the gospel is apparent. The Pentecostal vision of the world is dualistic and pessimistic. Its ethics are very conventional and individualistic. There is a

27. Read, *Latin American Church Growth,* pp. 65ff., 101ff., and 313ff. See also Walter Hollenweger, *El Pentecostalismo* (Buenos Aires: La Aurora, 1976), chaps. 8-10.

lack of concern for society at large, though there is a concern for "the household of faith." Lalive d'Epinay, after two years of study of the Pentecostal movement in Chile, says that the Pentecostals live in a state of "social strike,"[28] a withdrawal from the world. Certainly the great challenge for the future of Pentecostalism is to find a prophetic contextualization of the gospel.

IV. The Seasonal Vintage of Revival: Professional Evangelization

Organized revival was not a spontaneous product in Latin America as it was on the North American frontier. To be sure, it has been tried for a long time in the Latin American churches that have retained the annual or semiannual "evangelistic campaign." But it has died a natural death in many churches, and in others it is merely another instrument in the permanent task of witnessing and communicating the gospel.

Latin America has proved to be a fertile or at least open field, however, for parachurch groups from the United States such as the Billy Graham organization to experiment with interdenominational evangelistic campaigns. Crusades have been held by Billy Graham himself in Buenos Aires and São Paulo, and by some of his associates in other Latin American cities, following the pattern of businesslike multimedia organization with interdenominational participation. Several "mini-Billy Grahams" have appeared in Latin America in the last twenty years. Another type of mass evangelization, very successful in terms of mass movements, has been campaigns of the faith healers.

By far the most comprehensive and best-organized effort at professional evangelization has been Evangelism-in-Depth (EID), originated in Latin America by the creative work of Kenneth Strachan of the Latin American Mission.[29] Its aim is to mobilize the whole people of God — all Christians, all churches, all methods — for evangelization during a whole year of concerted effort and pooling of resources. ("Key 73" was a mild adaptation in

28. d'Epinay, *Heaven of the Masses,* pp. 128ff. Cf. Emilio Williams, *Followers of the New Faith* (Nashville: Vanderbilt University Press, 1967), pp. 163ff.; and C. Peter Wagner, *Look Out! The Pentecostals are Coming* (Carol Stream, Ill.: Creation House, 1973).

29. See W. Dayton Roberts, *Revolution in Evangelism* (Chicago: Moody Press, 1967); Ray S. Rosales, *The Evangelism-in-Depth Program of the Latin American Mission* (Cuernavaca, Mexico: CIDOC, 1966); Wilton M. Nelson, "Panorama Histórico de la Evangelización," in *Hacia una Teologia de la Evangelización,* ed. Orlando E. Costas (Buenos Aires: La Aurora, 1973). See a reappraisal of Orlando E. Costas, "La Evangelización en los Arios Setenta: La Búsqueda de Totalidad," mimeographed paper (San José, Costa Rica CELEP, 1977); also J. D. Douglas, ed., *Let the Earth Hear His Voice* (Minneapolis: World Wide, 1975), pp. 675ff., 211ff.

the United States of this type of "saturation evangelism.")[30] It has been more effective in small countries where the evangelical community is in a minority situation, e.g., Nicaragua, Guatemala, Venezuela, Bolivia. It has not been tried in the big countries like Brazil, Argentina, and Mexico. The great values in this coordination of resources and methodologies are the mobilizing of the churches in an intentional effort for a sustained period of time, on-the-job training of laity and clergy in methods, development of national leadership, cooperation among evangelical churches, and improved public image of the evangelical community. Thousands of prayer cells, visits, tract distributions, participants in parades, and professions of faith are reported, but the results in terms of effective church growth have not been conclusive.[31]

Professional evangelization of this type stirs the congregations a bit, produces a brief public impact, and probably attracts a few people from the margins of the church. But, as Professor Rudolf Obermuller has said, the task is not "revival," because "revival" presupposes a certain knowledge of the Church and the Bible, and this is precisely what the masses do not have in Latin America![32]

What can we say of professional evangelization in terms of our inquiry? Is it prophetic contextualization? Hardly. In spite of all the modernization in terms of the media, the theology is as old-fashioned as it can be — almost a carbon copy of the mini-theology developed in the American revivals 150 years ago, docetic, individualistic, otherworldly, emotional, socially conservative, politically blind, escapist. To be prophetic you have to take the whole biblical message and history seriously. That means taking seriously the context and *people in their context.* Revivalistic preaching is the same everywhere — in New York or Nairobi, in Rio de Janeiro or Singapore — it is disincarnated, timeless, ahistorical. The advocates of Evangelism-in-Depth tried to be more inclusive in their approach and more sensitive to human needs in a given context, incorporating Good Will Caravans, for instance, as they did in Bolivia. But they have to work with and through the churches as they are, so they have to compromise on a "lowest common denominator," and this is always the fundamentalistic, conservative understanding of the gospel and evangelization.

Efforts of the movement to obtain public sympathy and support from

30. A brief introduction to "Key 73" is in Harold K. Bales, ed., *Bridges to the World* (Nashville: Tidings, 1973), article by Ted Raedeke. For a critical evaluation, see Deane A. Kemper, "Another Look at Key 73," in *Mission Trends No. 2,* ed. Gerald H. Anderson and Thomas F. Stransky (Grand Rapids: Eerdmans, 1975), pp. 126-35.

31. See George W. Peters, *Saturation Evangelism* (Grand Rapids: Zondervan, 1970), pp. 72ff.; and C. Peter Wagner, *Frontiers in Missionary Strategy* (Chicago: Moody Press, 1971).

32. Rudolf Obermuller, *Evangelism in Latin America* (London: Lutterworth, 1957).

the government made it very unlikely that the evangelistic message would become specific about the situation in a given country. Actually, most of the Presidential Breakfasts at the conclusion of the EID programs have hosted presidents who held their people in oppression and repression. The evangelizers wouldn't dare "to mention the rope in the house of the hanged," as we say in Spanish. And the reports usually celebrate the mere fact that the president came, said a few pious words, and commended the EID program. In this way they show awareness of one context — the power of government — but not of the other context of suffering, oppression, injustices, discrimination, exploitation, of the poor. They are thus alienated from the vast majority of the population to whom we are supposed to bring the good news. The organized revival is like a rake, gathering what is on the surface and piling it up as "the seasonal vintage of revival."

V. Time of Pruning: Crisis in Traditional Evangelization

In one way or another, through sowing and planting, by raking and seasonal harvesting, by transplant or indigenous sprouting, the plant of Christianity has been unevenly growing in Latin America. But now the time of pruning has come. This is much more than metaphor in our lands — it is a painful and dramatic process in the daily life and struggle of the Christian church. In the area of evangelization this means a crisis in the traditional approach and methodology. It is happening simultaneously in the Roman Catholic Church, in the Protestant community, and, to a certain degree, in the family of Pentecostal churches.

The Second Vatican Council and the Medellín Conference of Bishops in 1968 marked the turning point for the Roman Catholic Church. It was clear to the Latin American fathers that they had been engaged for a long time in a "pastoral" of conservation and sacramentalization rather than a "pastoral" of evangelization. They were aware that Catholic people were being baptized but going "through life without being truly converted to the gospel, without a personal encounter with and commitment to Jesus the Savior."[33] They saw that it was time for a radical revision and a new evangelization for the masses and the elite.[34] The task was one of evangelizing the baptized, calling the Christian

33. CELAM, *The Church in the Light of the Council*, Documents 1 (Bogotá, 1970); Seladoc, *Religiosidad Popular* (Salamanca: Sigueme, 1976), pp. 15ff., 21ff., 26ff.; Costas, *Theology of the Crossroads*, p. 346.

34. CELAM, *The Church*, Documents 1, Conclusions II.

people "to *a fuller experience of the gospel* and to *re-conversion* or, better, to a *permanent conversion*." The Dominican Jordan Bishop put it this way:

> The first task of the dynamic nucleus — priests, religious and lay people — in a Latin American parish today, would be the evangelization of the practicing Catholics in the parish. . . . *Evangelization is not a matter of statistics; above all, it is a matter of Christian authenticity.*[35]

Religious syncretism is rejected as a false incarnation, but there is a clear call to the church to incarnate itself in the life of the people in Latin America, assuming their hopes, sufferings, and struggles. This incarnation would be much more than cultural contextualization; it would be an option for the poor and oppressed, as evidenced by the mushrooming of documents, movements, declarations, confrontations, and deadly struggles triggered by the Medellín Conference.[36] The Church had discovered the neighbor, the poor on the other side of the road, and had rediscovered the gospel of human liberation in the Bible. Evangelization could never be the same. It had to be humanizing, conscientizing, and liberating.[37]

A similar process has been taking place among Latin American Protestants since the early 1960s.[38] The Central Conference of the Methodist Church in Latin America in 1960 called the churches to "an *incarnation* in the suffering and hopes of the society in which they live."[39] The Latin American Evangelical Conference in 1961 called the churches and Christians to overcome the traditional spiritualistic individualism and to assume their responsibilities in the dramatic situation of the Latin American continent, marked

35. Jordan Bishop, "The Formation of Evangelizing Communities," *Orientation Course on Latin America* (La Paz, Bolivia: Ibeas, 1968), p. 347 (emphasis added).

36. Ronaldo Muñoz, in his *Nueva Conciencia de la Iglesia en América Latina* (Salamanca: Sigueme, 1974), analyzes 169 different documents from the year 1969 only.

37. This is the way we define evangelization in our "Bolivian Thesis on Evangelization in Latin America Today," *A Monthly Letter About Evangelism* 2 (February 1975).

38. The Church and Society movement gained momentum in the 1960s and was one of the catalytic agents in sensitizing the social conscience among Protestants. For a review and evaluation of the movement, see Costas, *Theology of the Crossroads*, chap. 9. The ISAL (Iglesia y Sociedad en América Latina) consultation at El Tabo, Chile, in 1965, was the turning point. See the report and interpretation of that event in *América Hoy* (Montevideo: ISAL, 1966). A critical analysis of ISAL is "Igelsia y Sociedad en América Latina" by C. René Padilla in the volume he edited, *Fe Cristiana y Latinoamérica Hoy* (Buenos Aires: Ediciones Certeza, 1974), pp. 121-53. Other documents of this process: *América Latina: Movilización Popular y Fe Cristiana* (Montevideo: ISAL, 1971) and the collection of the magazine *Cristianismo y Sociedad.*

39. "La Iglesia y el Mundo Latinoaméricano," message from the tenth Central Conference of the Methodist Church in Lima, Peru, August 1960.

by population explosion, malnutrition, infant mortality, illiteracy, poverty, exploitation, rising expectations, and shaken by galvanizing efforts of the Cuban Revolution. "The problem is not one of growth," said Thomas J. Liggett, a missionary of the Disciples of Christ, after reporting the amazing growth of the evangelistic churches. "The problem is what are we going to do? Have we a word to say? Are we prepared for the necessary changes in the church and society? Our danger is not to be few, but not to be creative."[40] Gonzalo Castillo-Cárdenas, a Presbyterian from Colombia, told the World Conference on World Mission and Evangelism in Mexico, 1963, that the demand made of the Church is a *kenosis* and *incarnation* in the new Latin American situation.[41] "The fundamental task of Latin America Protestantism, is one of conversion to the world" said José Míguez Bonino to the Student Christian Movement Congress in Córdoba, 1964, *"a growing incarnation in Latin America."*[42] The social context had become increasingly the agenda of the church when the Methodists met in Cochabamba, Bolivia, in 1966 for a Consultation on "Evangelization and Revolution in Latin America."[43]

In the 1970s, the "new evangelical generation," particularly the leadership that had been working in the InterVarsity Movement in Latin America, was catching up and trying to respond to the challenge of prophetic contextualization.[44] Typical of this new approach is the following statement of Orlando E. Costas, the first Latin American missiologist from the Protestant ranks:

> Just as the gospel arises from within a concrete historical situation, so its communication takes place in a particular context. To evangelize one needs to understand the world of those who are to be evangelized. . . .
>
> This is precisely the tragedy of evangelism in the Latin American

40. Thomas J. Liggett, "La Situación Actual la Obra Evangélica en América Latina," second Conferencia Evangélica Latinoamérican Huampani, Peru, 1961. See *Cristo la Esperanza para América Latina* (Buenos Aires: Conf. Evangélica del Rio de la Plata, 1962).

41. Gonzalo Castillo Cárdenas, "El Cristianismo Evangélico en América Latina," mimeographed paper (Mexico: CWME, December 1963), p. 3.

42. José Míguez Bonino, "Corrientes del Pensamentio del Protestantismo en América Latina" (Cordoba, Argentina: *MEC,* July 1964), S/10/7.

43. Mortimer Arias, ed., *Evangelización y Revolución en América Latina* (Montevideo, 1969), p. 17.

44. See Samuel Escobar, "La Responsabilidad Social de la Iglesia," in *Acción en Cristo para un Continente en Crisis,* ed. CLADE (San José, Costa Rica: Ed. Caribe, 1970); Victor Araya G., "Tensiones Histórico-Teológicas en la Evangelización," in Costas, *Hacia una Teologia de la Evangelización,* pp. 177ff.; Ruben Lores, "Secularización y Evangelización en la Contexto Latinoamericano," in Costas, *Hacia una Teologia de la Evangelización,* pp. 235ff.; C. René Padilla, ed., *Fe Cristiana y Latinoamérica Hoy;* C. René Padilla, ed., *El Reino de Dios y América Latina* (Casa Bautista de Publicaciones, 1975).

> world. On the one hand, *the gospel has not been proclaimed to its fullness.* . . . The gospel has been separated from the kingdom, redemption from creation, salvation from history. The work of evangelism has been limited, accordingly, to the sphere of the privatistic, I-Thou relationship. Congruent with the latter is the fact that the proclamation *of the gospel has not been adequately validated by efficacious historical signs.* The church in Latin America has not shown the marks of the cross of unconditional engagement in the struggles and agonies of the suffering, oppressed minorities. To be able to fulfill its evangelistic task today, the Latin American Church needs, in consequence, not only *to recover the fullness of the gospel,* but, especially, *to authenticate its truth and power* in the life of unconditional obedience.
>
> If we, as Latin Americans, are to undertake seriously and efficaciously the evangelistic challenge which our world poses *today,* we have *to start evangelizing the church,* i.e., calling her to experience a new *conversion to the Christ who stands alongside of the oppressed and exploited.*[45]

This is the kind of message that the so-called "conservative evangelical" young leaders carried to the International Congress on World Evangelization in Lausanne, one that would make its impact on the whole congress and radically affect the content of the Lausanne Covenant.[46]

For José Míguez this process of pruning, of repentance and conversion, must take the shape of very concrete, risky, and painful options for the Protestant community. Prophetic contextualization obliges Protestants to reverse the accompanying role of the "modernization project" of a former generation. Says the dean of studies of the Superior Institute of Evangelical Theological Studies of Buenos Aires:

> Protestantism can overcome its crisis of identity and mission only if it can *recapture the "subversive" role* it once played, but doing so from within the radically different situation in which we find ourselves today. That means it would work to overcome the very historical movement in which it previously participated. To do this, it must intensify, interpret, and articulate anew the basic evangelical concepts of newness, repentance, transformation, new life, and the new man. This *reinterpretation* must be *based on the whole dimension of biblical witness,* be articulated *in relation to existing*

45. Orlando E. Costas, "Evangelism in Latin American Context," *CELEP Occasional Essays* 4, nos. 1-2 (January 1977): 12ff. (emphasis added).

46. See C. René Padilla, *Fe Cristiana y Latinamericaco Hoy* and *El Reino de Dios y América Latina.*

> *conditions* in our countries, and emphasize the necessity of internal and external liberation.[47]

Even Pentecostalism shows signs of being deeply affected by the human situation in Latin America. Juan Carlos Ortiz from Argentina, the representative of one of the charismatic renewal streams, bluntly says that is not a "spiritual gospel" and a "social gospel" but just one gospel, which includes the spiritual, the social, and the material. Ortiz is meanwhile experimenting with a community of sharing in his own growing church in Buenos Aires.[48] Manoel de Mello, the founder and leader of Brasil para Cristo, puts bread "as a priority" together with the gospel and proclaims a gospel that includes the denunciation of injustices. He has undertaken a multifaceted ministry for the "whole person" in his huge church in Sao Paulo, has joined the World Council of Churches, and attests to his conviction with a good record of arrests.[49] The limitation of this contextualization is that it is not prophetic enough. As Orlando E. Costas says:

> The individualism of the Pentecost service shows up even where the emphasis is as communitarian as in the renewed (charismatic) worship service. Here there is a strong consciousness of the neighbor. It is evident in a preoccupation with the individual needs of the members of the community of faith, and the visitors and near neighbors. But a concern for the structural problems of society is conspicuously absent. . . .
>
> Though it is true that the Pentecostal service reflects a strong autochthonous Protestantism, it is also true that it reflects an egocentric church . . . a church sociologically and theologically naïve, unaware of the fact that society is much more than the sum of individuals. . . . In this way, it becomes one of the main agents of *status quo* in a contingent where change is not a luxury but an unavoidable necessity.[50]

Protestantism in Latin America, in trying to be faithful to the gospel and to the Latin American person, in its evangelical witness, oscillates between accommodation and confrontation.

47. Míguez Bonino, "Political Attitude of Protestants in Latin America," p. 2 (emphasis added).

48. Juan Carlos Ortiz, "Iglesia y Sociedad," in Padilla, *Fe Cristiana y Latinoamérica Hoy,* pp. 185ff. See also J. C. Ortiz, *Call to Discipleship* (Plainfield, N.J.: Logos International, 1975).

49. Robert Barboza, "The Gospel with Bread: An Interview with Brazilian Pentecostal Manoel de Manella," in *Mission Trends No. 2,* pp. 145-54.

50. Orlando E. Costas, "The Reality of the Latin American Church," in Padilla, *Fe Cristiana y Latinoamérica Hoy,* pp. 56, 66.

VI. Prophetic Contextualization: Costly Evangelism

I want to conclude with a brief note on a new phenomenon in Latin American Christianity: the emergence of what could be called prophetic contextualization. As has been said, "The future Church historians will be puzzled in studying this period of the Church in Latin America, because, suddenly, Christians began to act out of character."[51] For centuries the church has been the supporter of the status quo. But when Nelson Rockefeller visited Latin America and made his report to President Nixon, he pointed to the Church as one of the main forces for change in the continent.[52] Strange as it may sound, the title of a recent release from the Latin American Press is quite true to the facts: "Right-wing dictators fear Christianity more than Marxism."[53] These Christians, however, are not using *Capital* or the *Communist Manifesto*. They are using their Bible, and releasing its liberating message. Not all Christians, but a growing and decisive minority, including laywomen and laymen, young people, pastors, priests, friars, nuns, and quite a few bishops, are trying to respond prophetically to "the cry of my people"[54] as Yahweh asked Moses to respond.

In one sense we are seeing the greening of the Church in Latin America. Springtime has come and a revitalizing breeze is blowing. The Roman Catholic Church has jumped over four centuries, assuming finally the Reformation of the sixteenth century and embracing the impetus of the revolution of the twentieth century. Protestants are finally overcoming their reductionistic individualism and spiritualism, and they are gradually liberating themselves from their inherited cultural hang-ups. Pentecostalists are experimenting with a growing awareness of human needs and affirming the one gospel, including the material and spiritual. There is a converging thrust to recover the whole gospel, for the whole person, and for the whole of Latin American society.[55] The Bible is being read anew in thousands of small grassroots communities ("comunidades de base") in the Roman Catholic Church.[56] The com-

51. José Míguez Bonino, "The Present Crisis in Mission," in *Mission Trends No. 1*, ed. Gerald H. Anderson and Thomas F. Stransky (Grand Rapids: Eerdmans, 1974), p. 45.

52. "Informe Rockefeller" (Buenos Aires: Tierra Nueva). The famous report was presented to President Nixon in August 1969.

53. *Latin American Press* 9, no. 26 (June 30, 1977): 1.

54. "I Have Heard the Cry of my People," a message from the Bishops of Northeastern Brazil, May 6, 1973.

55. Orlando E. Costas, "La Evangelización en los Sententa: La Búsqueda de Totalidad," in Padilla, *Fe Cristiana y Latinoamérica Hoy*, chap. 2.

56. Jetter Pereira Ramalho, "Algunas Notas sobre dos Perspectivas de Pastoral Popular: la de Las Communidades Ecclesiasticas de Base y la de los Grupos Evangélicos Pentecostales," *Cristianisma y Sociedad* 51 (1977).

mon people are commenting upon it from their own situation, and letting it speak to that situation, after generations for whom it was a sealed book.[57] Christ is being met again — as he wants to be met and served — in the neighbor, in the man on the road. Christians are discovering the neighbor — individually and socially — and they are discovering that the good news is really "*good news* to the poor" in our context. And from this discovery a new style of life, a new theology, and a new evangelization are emerging.[58]

Springtime, alas, brings not only breezes but thunderstorms, tempests, and hurricanes. There are tensions, conflicts, and divisions within the church. Even those who share a common commitment to the liberation of the oppressed and to the change of an inhuman and unjust society do not agree on tactics or methods. The old divisions along confessional and theological lines have receded into the background, and new gap is separating Christians along social and ideological lines.[59]

There are also conflicts with the sectors of society resisting change, particularly the rich and the powerful, and there is resistance even from those who gather the crumbs from the banquet of life. The Church is becoming, like her Master, a sign of contradiction. As our Bolivian Thesis on Evangelization in Latin America Today says:

> The gospel is not *neutral.* Because of its contents, its essence and its goal, evangelism is *conflictive.* It creates a conflict in the hearer, in the witness and in society. Evangelization is not identical with any party program, nor does it present the Church as an alternative power. But in announcing God's Word, and in projecting its light on human history, it inevitably has political repercussions. Even if the Church does not want to be involved in politics, politics will involve the Church. Was not Jesus falsely accused, persecuted, brought to judgment, punished, condemned and executed by political authorities and on political charges? Will the servant be cleverer than his Lord (Luke 23; John 15:18-20; Acts 19; Rev. 12; Matt. 10:16-39)?
>
> Evangelism is *engagement.* We are involved in a solidarity with other men through what we do and through what we fail to do. There is in the gospel no place for opting out. Jesus brought a dividing sword. It is impossible to serve two masters. There can be no neutrality in relation to the oppressed and the oppressor. Jesus Christ has come to liberate the oppressor and the oppressed from the sin that enslaves all men. But the an-

57. Ernesto Cardenal, *The Gospel in Solentiname* (Maryknoll, N.Y.: Orbis, 1976).

58. Gustavo Gutiérrez, "Praxis de Liberación y Fe Cristiana," *Cristianismo y Sociedad* 40/41, nos. 2-3 (1973): 110-36.

59. See Costas, *Theology of the Crossroads*, pp. 120ff.

nouncement of liberation cannot take the same expression for those who suffer oppression and for those who practice it (Matt. 10:34, 25:24-30, 6:24; Luke 1:52-53).

The announcement of the gospel implies the denunciation of everything that is not in agreement with the gospel. No evangelism is authentically evangelical if it is not at the same time prophetic. The Church cannot make compromise with any force that oppresses or dehumanizes man. It cannot name Jesus Christ if it does not name also the idols and the demons that must be cast out from the inner life of man and from the structures of society (Luke 3:1-20, 6:20-23; Matt. 23).[60]

These declarations were anticipations of what was going to happen and a description of what has been happening in the 1970s in Latin America. Most of the Latin American countries are under military regimes that have adopted a line of economic development, stability at all costs, coinciding with an anticommunist, antisocialist, fascistic type of ideology. They are using all their repressive power to kill any dissension, any protest, any alternative to the official ideology, and are ready to crush the most elementary human rights. The churches in this situation have become the "voice of the voiceless," but they are paying a price for it.[61] Pastors and professors who have been engaged in refugee programs have been arrested and have disappeared. Others have been imprisoned for months on the basis of rumors and anonymous accusations. Hundreds — including priests and nuns — have been expelled or exiled. Fifteen bishops of the Catholic Church were arrested, imprisoned for twenty-four hours, and expelled from Ecuador. Monsignor Dom Helder Camara is not allowed to speak by radio, television, or the press in his country, Brazil, but there is freedom to attack him. He and other bishops who have been denouncing the injustices, tortures, and violence, and speaking for the peasants and the workers, have been accused of being communists. Dom Helder's secretary, Father Pereria Neto, was brutally assassinated and the episcopal building was machine-gunned. A paramilitary group in Argentina repulsed a terrorist action against a general of the army by murdering three priests and two seminarians who were moderates and had nothing to do with the terrorists' action. A priest who went to the police to accompany two women and their children presenting a complaint about their lands being invaded by the big corporations in Matto Grasso, Brazil, was killed by those police. When a guerilla group in El Salvador executed the minister of foreign affairs held in hos-

60. Mortimer Arias, "Tesis Boliviana," *A Monthly Letter about Evangelism* 2 (February 1975): 18-20.

61. See monthly reports in *Latin American Press.*

tage, a rightist group, The White Warriors Union, assassinated Jesuit priest Alfonso Navarro Oviedo on May 12, 1977. Two months before, unidentified persons ambushed and killed Father Rutilio Grande and two campesinos who were with him. Between February and May, fifteen foreign priests, seven of them Jesuits, were expelled from El Salvador. The latest news is that the White Warriors Union, a paramilitary rightist organization, has threatened to kill all the Jesuits who do not leave the country within thirty days. Father César Jerez, Jesuit provincial, said: "We are going to continue to be faithful to our mission until we fulfill our duty or are liquidated."[62]

These are just a few examples of what is becoming a sort of pattern in Latin America. This new generation of Christians is discovering again that when faithfulness to the gospel and to people is at stake, there is no easy prophetism. They are learning that Christian evangelization is not cheap, verbal proclamation of evangelical propaganda. The gospel is free, but it is not cheap. Grace is free, but not cheap. Both discipleship and evangelism are costly.

But we have no right to complain. Jesus told us so. He warned us, "Beware when all men speak well of you" (Luke 6:26). "Blessed are you when you are persecuted . . . because in this way they persecuted the prophets before you" (Matt. 5:10-12). Prophetic contextualization is always risky and costly; but it is faithful and fruitful.

> In truth, in very truth I tell you,
> a grain of wheat remains a solitary grain
> unless it falls into the ground and dies;
> but if it dies, it bears a rich harvest.
>
> (John 12:24)

If this is so, the best still is to come.

62. *Latin American Press* 9, no. 26 (June 30, 1977).

AFTERWORD

Continuing Conversations and New Trajectories in the Study of Evangelism

The future of the study of evangelism depends upon attentiveness to the biblical and theological foundations of the practice and to the activity of the Spirit of God that always leads the community of faith into new avenues of witness and service. Continuing conversation about authentic manifestations of this missional practice (as well as its counterfeits) must be linked inextricably to new trajectories of Christian vocation in an increasingly complex and fractured world. This volume helps to demonstrate the substantial attention given to foundational questions in the study of evangelism: How does one come to know God in Christ? How does the disciple of Christ engage culture? How does the Spirit work through both moments of crisis and processes of spiritual discovery in the Christian journey? What is the role of the community in discipling? Questions like these focus upon the *content* of the gospel and *practices* that faithfully communicate God's good news in Jesus Christ. Indeed, in the selection of material for this collection, we have focused intentionally upon the historical and theological underpinnings of the practice rather than upon techniques or specific strategies. We have also attended to the crucial issue of diversity through the exploration of a wide variety of ecclesial and cultural contexts. The contributors to this book offer groundbreaking insights into the ministry of evangelism and deepen our appreciation of the complex and shifting horizons of the study of evangelism.

Collaboration and interdisciplinarity must characterize the work of the church and the academy concerning evangelism as practitioners and scholars alike address all of the attendant concerns of the practice. The basic questions are perennial: What is evangelism? What is the relationship of the evangel-bearing community to the particular, historical context in which it is immersed? How do individuals and communities partner with God in the process of forming people into authentic disciples of Christ? What practices constitute the *missio Dei* and how are all persons welcomed most effectively into the alternative community of God's beloved children? What approaches to this missional practice are sufficiently attuned to present global and cultural realities that they open doors and expand horizons, not with coercive force but through winsome engagement, bringing the gospel story into dialogue with the hopes and dreams of the struggling human family? Certainly these are some of the most pressing theological questions of any age, and this theological frame of reference for the study and practice of evangelism acknowledges the centrality of relationship to God and to others.

Theology shapes practice and practice shapes theology. The future calls for tremendous versatility in the effort to live in this dynamic tension, perhaps more so today than ever before. Despite the fact that there may be distinctive readings of biblical texts and historical contexts and that the implications drawn from this witness may differ from one setting to the next, those engaged in evangelistic ministry must take these foundations seriously nonetheless, embracing God's desire to be in relationship with all human beings and our more hesitating quest to be in relationship with each other. Our best efforts must start within the community of faith. Engagement with people within the Christian tradition who represent a multiplicity of cultural and ecclesial contexts enriches our understanding of God's good news in Jesus Christ and expands our vision of evangelistic praxis. Faithful and effective evangelism in the future will empower those who have been formed by the gospel to cross boundaries that often function as dividing walls between people.

As the essays in this concluding section demonstrate, scholars and practitioners committed to the study of evangelism must not only construct their vision proactively around foundational principles drawn from the Christian heritage, but they must also be willing to consider systemic sins such as racism, sexism, and materialism that mitigate against an authentic Christian witness. No one can offer guidance and leadership to Christian communities concerning evangelistic practice apart from a serious engagement with issues such as these. These are some of the most critical cutting edges in the study of evangelism today. The edges are sharp and painful, to say the least, but confronting our failure to be an obedient church in such matters with genuine humility and repentance affords a unique opportunity for the people of God to live into the vision of beloved community and offer it as a living hope more effectively.

We live in an age of global angst — a time in which the brokenness of the world intrudes upon our illusions of sanctuary, peace, and quiet. "Tribalisms" of various orders, concerns about religious pluralism and fundamentalism, and manifestations of racism dominate the news. What does it mean to be an evangel-bearer at a time such as this? Another question looms large in our time as well: Where are the women in the study of evangelism? And what about the other "marginalized" peoples of the Christian family? What sources need to be recovered and developed so that all might hear these voices more clearly? Finally, many of the essays in this volume argue and demonstrate that evangelism is a missional practice of the whole people of God. One of the most dynamic expressions of this vision is linked to the rediscovery of hospitality as a practice constitutive of the church. While many other issues and concerns will emerge to create alternative trajectories related to evangelism and its study in the future, these three areas — the healing of racial/ethnic animosity, the recovery of women's perspectives, and the practice of hospitality — are particularly noteworthy as we contemplate the way in which the church is called to serve the present age.

In his essay on "God's Justice and Good News," Otis Turner, a Presbyterian specialist in the area of racial justice, explores the inextricable link between evangelism and antiracism. Racism within the life of the church is far more complex and intertwined with the structures and values of society than many would like to believe. For the church to become an authentic expression of God's vision for the human community, the church must embrace the connection between evangelism and antiracism, functioning as an agent of change in the realization of a community that is fair, just, and sustainable.

Letty M. Russell, East Harlem pastor and Yale theologian, elucidates the interrelationship of evangelization and liberation from biblical, ecumenical, and feminist perspectives. The feminist vision within which she stands maintains a holistic understanding of the saving mission of God, involving proclamation, partnership, service, and celebration. Russell guards against lopsided views of both evangelism and liberation by emphasizing God's traditioning action, the goal of which is always shalom for all humanity. The feminist perspective, in her view, avoids the dangers of proselytism by pointing all persons to God's new creation through a *liberating* evangelism; it avoids the dangers of secularism by pointing to Jesus Christ as the One through whom God's Good News is experienced as *evangelical* liberation.

In his groundbreaking study of evangelism as a "centripetal mission" in the life of the church, Mortimer Arias identifies hospitality as the "almost forgotten Christian virtue" essential to the church's evangelistic ministry. He reverses the traditional image of evangelism as a "centrifugal mission" — going from the center to the periphery of the world — and advocates a "come and see" centripetal approach that emphasizes the authenticity of the Christian life as the essential and decisive core of evangelism. Arias's rediscovery of hospitality as the primary practice of evangelistic ministry challenges the radical individualism of Western Christianity and elevates this indispensable dimension of Christian authenticity.

The gospel reveals that God's purpose is reconciliation — from the restoration of each person to a loving relationship with God through Christ to the realization of God's reign in human history through the inbreaking of God's Spirit of shalom. Commitment to this vision of life enabled by God's grace necessitates simultaneous focus, therefore, upon the particular and the global in the ministry of evangelism. As the geographic centers of Christianity continue to shift, the study of evangelism requires greater recognition of the impact globalization is having upon the missional practices of the church. Missiologists of the rising generation, and many of them representing the non-Western world, alert us to the emerging particularities that constitute global Christianity and the way in which they extend our horizons beyond the strategies and methodologies defined by the mentors and practitioners of Western Christendom. The integrity of the church's mission will also depend increasingly upon the evangelist's serious engagement with issues of injustice in the world. The deepening shadows of war and violence, exploitation and oppression, hunger and poverty, mock the message of peace on earth and good will to all — the Good News made known in the life, death, and resurrection of Jesus. The message of personal salvation in Christ and freedom in God's grace must be complemented with a cloud of witnesses who embody the thirst for justice and model ways of compassionate service in Christ's way.

Evangelism is the heart of mission, and the heart of evangelism is love. The extension of God's love through the community of faith, not only to friends and those easily loved, but also to strangers both far and near, and even to enemies, is the true test of the church's evangelistic mission. Evangelism will continue to place great demands upon our imagination as we seek to realize the daunting vision of justice and peace for all in every aspect of life. Love, however, breeds creativity, and the desire to share God's love with others will be the renewing force that flows into new methods, larger dreams, and greater solidarity in Christian witness. Our fervent prayer is that the essays you encounter in this collection provide an impetus for you to dedicate yourself anew to this vision and the thoughtful and rigorous study of evangelism. We are convinced that God delights in every rediscovery of this missional practice in the church and that the loving actions of those who bear the gospel in Christ's way glorify God.

CHAPTER 28

God's Justice and Good News: Looking at the Intertwined Dynamics of Evangelism and Antiracism

Otis Turner

The Presbyterian Church (U.S.A.) has set a goal of increasing the percentage of racial ethnic membership to 20 percent by the year 2010. One factor that influenced the church to choose 20 percent as the benchmark is that the percentage of racial ethnic people in the United States is approximately 26 percent and rising, while racial ethnic people comprise about 6 percent of Presbyterian membership. Thus there was a perceived need to place more emphasis on racial ethnic evangelism so that the composition of the church will be more reflective of the population of the nation. Another factor is a strong desire to reverse the membership decline that has plagued the denomination for decades.

In 1965, membership in the PCUSA was estimated to be 4.2 million; in 2001, membership was estimated to be 2.5 million. The emphasis on racial ethnic church growth is part of a broader churchwide emphasis on evangelism that is intended to reverse the membership decline. The 1996 General Assembly recognized that if such an ambitious goal is to be achieved, an intentional strategy must be developed that takes into consideration the distinctive needs of the varied racial ethnic constituencies in light of their historic experiences. A churchwide strategy for racial ethnic church growth was adopted by the 210th General Assembly (1998). Implementation of the strategy has begun. But it faces some formidable challenges.

One of the challenges is awareness. According to the November 2000 Presbyterian Panel, only 7 percent of the membership is aware of the denominational goal for racial ethnic membership, although 66 percent of pastors are aware of it. That is a significant gap in awareness between clergy and laypeople. While such difference in awareness exists around other issues, it is particularly significant here as an indicator of points of resistance that we must overcome. Additionally, approximately three-fourths of the membership do not believe that the goal is likely to be achieved.

Funding is another challenge. The Panel indicates that 46 percent of the membership is opposed to using significantly more funding in an effort to raise racial ethnic membership to 20 percent by 2010. Nevertheless, funding is a critical barrier that we must overcome if the Presbyterian Church is to have a reasonable chance of achieving its racial ethnic membership goals. Funding must be significantly increased, not just for racial ethnic evangelism, but also in racial justice and antiracism work, because the most significant barrier to increasing racial ethnic membership in the denomination is still racism. The 1998 General Assembly affirmed this reality when it adopted the report on racial ethnic church growth. It said:

> Given the well-documented racial problems that dominate our culture, it is difficult for us to truly serve the interests of a multicultural society without some form of social intervention. Enhanced efforts to achieve racial ethnic church growth must employ intervention methods such as antiracism training to effect necessary reform of institutional behavior that historically has prevented the church from including people of color. Systematic racism, discrimination, prejudice, disempowerment, and cultural depreciation all serve to inhibit racial ethnic church growth. Racial ethnic church growth is inextricably linked to the struggle for racial justice. Thus, as the church invests resources in racial ethnic church growth strategies, it must also invest in the struggle against racism and other social injustice. To do one without the other is a prescription for failure. Racial justice implies pluralism, cultural diversity, and a more equitable distribution of economic, political, and social power. Justice also leads to the achievement of group dignity and social affirmation. If the church recognizes these crucial connections and strengthens its investment in programs like antiracism training, it is more likely to achieve its racial ethnic church growth goals as it moves into the next century.[1]

The Assembly recognized that there are crucial connections between evangelism and racism. However, according to the Presbyterian Panel, an awareness of these connections is very low in the denomination. While more than 80 percent of the membership believes that the church should be in the forefront of efforts to fight racism, 46 percent of the membership is opposed to using significantly more resources to achieve racial ethnic membership goals set by the denomination. This is an anomaly that reflects a lack of awareness of the connections between evangelism and racism. As noted by the 1998 General Assembly, a failure to recognize the connection between

1. *Minutes,* Part 1, 1998, p. 414.

evangelism and racism and provide adequate funding to deal effectively with both is a prescription for failure.[2]

Dealing with racism and doing racial ethnic evangelism are complex and challenging matters. One of the complicating factors is rapidly changing demographics. Some predictions suggest that by the middle of this century a majority of the U.S. population will be comprised of people that the PCUSA refers to as racial ethnic. Whether such predictions are accurate is academic. As a practical matter, the racial profile of the United States is changing and a lot of people are having difficulty dealing with it.

The change in immigration patterns is one thing that is driving the demographic shift. In 1940, an estimated 70 percent of immigrants who came to the United States were from Europe. By 1990, immigration from Europe had dropped to an estimated 15 percent, with the remaining 85 percent coming from Asia, Latin America, the Caribbean, and Africa. This has resulted in some major demographic shifts with which many Americans are still struggling, engendering such phenomena as the English-only initiatives, regressive immigration policies, and resurgent xenophobia. While these reactions are condemned by the social policies of the Presbyterian Church, some disconnects in denominational awareness are problematic. For example, the Presbyterian Panel reveals that the least preferred strategy for racial ethnic church growth is "encouraging white congregations to make greater efforts to reach out to racial ethnic persons." This includes 27 percent of members, 32 percent of elders, and 51 percent of pastors.

What is the reason for such resistance to reaching out to racial ethnic people? Could it be a fear that such efforts would change the profile of white congregations? Could it be that if white congregations reached out to people of color, they would not come? Could it be that if racial ethnic people did join white congregations in significant numbers, it would change the power relationships in the congregations? Is it the result of unresolved racial tension that lurks beneath the surface? I suggest that it is all of these and others. After all, 11 A.M. on Sunday remains the most segregated hour in the nation. That is no accident of history. As a practical matter, it is an indication of where some of the difficult points of resistance are.

Those whose sense of personhood is grounded in the notion that the United States must remain a predominantly white nation, or that white hegemony must remain normative, will have some identity-shaking experiences as diversity in the United States increases. This will not be limited to fringe or reactionary elements associated with hate groups. It will involve people of

2. *Minutes,* Part 1, 1998, p. 414.

goodwill as well. Through no fault of their own, a larger segment of the nation's population will encounter more difficulty making the transition to a racially diverse and inclusive community than we might expect. White flight is not a phenomenon of the political or religious right. It involves liberals, moderates, conservatives — that is, the whole spectrum.

The church will be no exception. This is not because of ill will. People of goodwill have long recognized that eradicating the sin of racism from church and society is a high priority. However, the church is now aware that the phenomenon of racism is far more complex and intertwined with the structures, culture, and values of society than was originally thought. The church also recognizes that eradicating racism will be a long journey that requires discernment, prayer, and worship-based action. These realizations, nudged by changing demographics, have pushed many local communities and congregations to struggle with the growing problem of racism. The 1998 General Assembly said,

> Enhanced efforts to achieve racial ethnic church growth must employ intervention methods such as antiracism training to effect necessary reform of institutional behavior that historically has prevented the church from including people of color.[3]

This is why the connection between evangelism and antiracism is so crucial to the life of the church.

The church is confronted with an unprecedented opportunity — and it also faces an unprecedented pitfall. More people are affirming the value of diversity than ever before. We have created a diversity table[4] and can see how valuable diversity is for the mission of the church. Although many people think that the diversity table is the solution to the race problem, it is not. Therein lies the danger. The diversity table is the place where answers can be found. It is a place where we can figure out how to transform institutions, structures, and values that sustain racism. We must be mindful of the fact that we do not have an adequate value infrastructure to sustain a multicultural and multiracial society or church relatively free of social conflict. That is a foundation that we must build.

We have achieved a level of tolerance that will enable us to come to-

3. *Minutes*, Part 1, 1998, p. 414.

4. "Diversity Table," as used here, refers to those places in church and society where people of different racial and cultural backgrounds can share a common space with a sufficient degree of civility to permit dialog to take place. Multicultural churches, workplaces, and educational institutions are examples.

gether at a multicultural table and engage in dialogue. However, we must remember that we bring to the table that which will destroy it. We bring the self-interest of all competing groups, including a legacy of racism. However, as we engage in dialogue, competing self-interest can be transformed into a common self-interest wherein the needs of all are met. Martin Luther King Jr. points out that, in order for a common self-interest to have permanence and loyalty, the multicultural elements must have goals from which they benefit but which are not in fundamental conflict to each other. Although King speaks in terms of the formation of an alliance, his fundamental point is precisely the one I seek to make with regards to multiculturalism. Quoting King:

> A true alliance is based upon some self-interest of each component group and a common interest into which they merge. For an alliance to have permanence and loyal commitment from its various elements, each of them must have a goal from which it benefits and none must have an outlook in basic conflict with the others.[5]

Finding the common denominator is the critical task: it must be the norm of the value infrastructure that will emerge when we are able to deconstruct and transform institutions and structures that are racially biased and oppressive. This is what antiracism is designed to achieve.

An antiracism methodology has been developed for the Presbyterian Church and is in the process of being refined. It is a change process that will help us make the transition from where we are to where we need to be if the goal of racial ethnic church growth is to be achieved.

The Changing Process

The change process has several stages.

Deconstruction. It begins with deconstruction, wherein we become aware of and unlearn the complex array of myths and misinformation that constitute the foundation of prejudice. Oppression begins with misinformation that takes on the appearance of truth and is codified in traditions and policies that structure society, that inform and shape institutional and personal behavior. Misinformation functions to justify a network of institutions that create advantages for some while discriminating against others. Deconstruction addresses the fundamental basis of prejudice and incorrect informa-

5. Martin Luther King Jr., *Where Do We Go From Here: Chaos or Community* (Boston: Beacon, 1967), p. 151.

tion that has been passed from generation to generation. As we begin to understand the nature of prejudice and the false premise upon which it is built, we become more aware of the learned behavior that is reinforced and acted out as discrimination.

Behavior analysis. The second stage is behavior analysis, which addresses the constellation of social forces that shape the social behavior of oppressors and the oppressed. It is well known that the behavior of oppressors must be a target of change. Much of the work on breaking down oppression has focused on the privilege of oppressors. However, such writers as Paulo Freire and Franz Fanon point out that we have seriously underestimated the degree to which the adaptive behavior that the oppressed is forced to learn and internalize in order to survive is a contributing factor.[6] When change takes place, the learned behavior of the oppressors and oppressed must be taken into consideration.

Power analysis. The third stage in the change process is power analysis. Here we come to understand the role of social power in establishing and maintaining systems of oppression. It is social power — the capacity to control and manipulate resources to achieve a desired end — that transforms prejudice into racism. Societies structure their common life, create and perpetuate institutions and the values that undergird them, distribute goods and services, and determine their goals and aspirations by the exercise of power. If we are going to dismantle racism, we must first understand the power arrangements that perpetuate and sustain it. Only then will we get a sense of how it can be dismantled. We must also know what sources of power can be used to bring about change. It is important to note that racial oppression results from an abuse of power. A right use of power results in justice.

Visioning. The fourth step is visioning. This begins with imagining what the church or society would be like if it were not affected by racism. That seems easy enough. However, the problem with visioning has to do with the degree to which our imagination is tied to current reality. Imagining specific realities that are different are often difficult, because the most common image that we have of change in race relations is a mere reversal of present power relationships. This is particularly true for those who have histories of power and privilege. The inability to imagine a positive alternative engenders fear and resistance to change.

Visioning is not about trading places; it is about imagining a church and a society free of the barriers that keep us from appreciating and living

6. Paulo Freire, *Pedagogy of the Oppressed* (New York: Continuum, 1999); Franz Fanon, *The Wretched of the Earth* (New York: Grove Press, 1963).

into the diversity of God's creation and realizing our oneness in Jesus Christ. It is about creating a community where all can realize the full extent of their God-given talents.

Reconstruction. The fifth and final stage in the change process is reconstruction, implementing a new vision in concrete terms. This is the point at which we are able to take the learnings derived from social analysis and theological reflection and build strategic bridges to positive social change. We change policies and procedures; we share power; we cultivate new values; we reshape and remake institutions and systems where racial justice and equality are normative. The racial justice policies of the PCUSA have addressed dismantling racism for decades. What has been missing for decades is a methodology that will enable us to do that and the will to implement it.

Racism is a social construction; as such, it can be deconstructed and unlearned. If we have the courage to do it, we can build the beloved community. This is what antiracism is about. It is designed to change individuals and the interaction of individuals within the context of community. Personal transformation alone is not the answer. Personal transformation must result in changed behavior and changed institutions.

The ultimate goal of antiracism is to create a community that is fair, just, and sustainable. We now know that such a goal is attainable. Antiracism can empower the Presbyterian Church (and other faith communities that engage in similar processes) to be a vital part of a growing movement that seeks to build a racially just society. It is a long journey from where we are to the beloved community. But with courage, determination, and faith-based action, we can get there.

Racial ethnic evangelism and antiracism are inextricably linked. If the church does not recognize this connection, its efforts at racial ethnic church growth will fail.

CHAPTER 29

Liberation and Evangelization — A Feminist Perspective

Letty M. Russell

It is vital for the task of Christian mission in our time to catch a vision of the unity and interrelationship of liberation and evangelization in the work of the gospel. The two are very much related from a biblical, ecumenical, and feminist perspective. So much so that I would say that liberation is one shorthand description of what the good news is that we have to "show and tell." Sometimes we fail to see the interrelation because we spend so much time trying to exclude the perspective of "others" that we fail to pay attention to the way God's arithmetic bids us share the good news in many unexpected ways.

I. Perspectives on Interrelationship

There are many perspectives from which to approach our subject and each is colored by our own context, our own life story, and the ways in which we struggle together with others to live out the gospel message. The ultimate meaning of liberation or evangelization is not determined, however, by one's perspective, be it feminist, black, Third World, or whatever. The meaning comes from the biblical story of what God is doing in bringing about New Creation in Jesus Christ. Yet that meaning must be interpreted in relation to our various "worldviews" and "church views." Three perspectives which are important for me are *biblical, ecumenical,* and *feminist.*

Biblical perspective. Liberation and evangelization are interrelated because of the *freedom of God:* from us and for us. God has chosen to be with us as a sending God, one who sends prophets, Son, apostles, and us to be part of God's mission of bringing New Creation to fulfillment (Isa. 43:18-21). As Creator, God chooses to be free from us and from all of creation; free from our manipulation or easy formulas. Yet as liberators, God chooses to be free for us and the world in order to liberate us from our own individual and collective sin and oppression. The freedom of God allows us to be part of God's continuing story by sharing the good news of God's liberating and saving actions with humanity.[1]

One of the problems that Christians face in bridging their theological differences is that there is often confusion in the meaning and traditions of certain words. One of these English words is *salvation.* In the Bible there is no one meaning for this word. It has a wide spectrum. In the Old Testament one of the most important words for the goal of salvation is *shalom:* a social event, a venture in co-humanity which cannot be reduced to a formula. The word represents a summary of all the gifts of God to humanity and all creation. God's promised gifts are to be fulfilled in the coming of the Prince of Peace to "establish it . . . with justice and with righteousness" (Isa. 9:6-7; Ps. 85:8-13). In the Old Testament two of the key motifs of salvation overlap and converge in the meaning of *shalom:* liberation as deliverance, and blessing as total spiritual and physical wholeness and well-being.

In the Gospels the two overlapping motifs of *shalom* appear in the One who came to fulfill the promise of salvation (Luke 2:14; John 14:27). In Paul's writings and in the later Epistles, however, the word most often used to connote salvation, *soteria,* deals mainly with the divine-human relationship and not with social relationships. In early church history we discover a tendency to reduce and narrow the broader understanding of *shalom* even further in the light of the Hellenistic view of the separation of body and soul. The Latin word *salus* became focused on one aspect of liberation — that of the eternal destiny of the soul-in-afterlife that was to be saved through the church.[2]

In struggling to represent the wholeness of the biblical perspectives it is important that the good news we share be as much as possible "the whole gospel for the whole world." In the view of most liberation theologies the two overlapping motifs of *shalom* often appear as a description of this good news. Liberation is seen as a gift of God's action in history, as well as the agenda of those who join together in community to share in transformation of the world. Blessing is often described as the process of humanization, the setting free of all humanity to have a future and a hope (cf. Jer. 29:11).

Ecumenical perspective. In the perspective of Christian response to God's

1. Letty M. Russell, "The Freedom of God," *Enquiry,* United Presbyterian Church, USA (September 1975), p. 26.

2. Letty M. Russell, *Human Liberation in a Feminist Perspective — A Theology* (Philadelphia: Westminster, 1974), pp. 106-8.

oikonomia, or stewardship of the world, there has always been a certain tension among various views of the ways in which the church should carry out its task by participating in God's mission.[3] In recent ecumenical history we can remind ourselves that the World Council of Churches (WCC) emerged in 1948, in part, because of the need for unity in mission and evangelism among the churches. In order to establish what might be an area of common understanding, the WCC undertook a ten-year study that concluded in 1959 with the publication of what Hans Hoekendijk has called a sort of "first ecumenical consensus" on the work of evangelism. Evangelism was understood as a sharing of words and worlds and included a threefold aspect of *kerygma, koinonia,* and *diakonia.* Emphasis was placed on our post-Christendom situation; on situational realism, or what we call today "contextualism"; and on the laity as the people of mission.[4]

The New Delhi Assembly in 1961 singled out the "Missionary Structures of the Congregation" for further investigation, and a report on this study in 1967 hoped to establish a sort of "second ecumenical consensus on the work of evangelism." The report contained clues for structures that emerged from six perspectives: God-World-Church; History as Self-Understanding; Participation in God's Mission; Humanization; Laity — Reference Group for Mission; and Pluriformity of Structures.[5]

The result of this ongoing work seems to have been that many persons within and outside World Council churches were alienated by the second attempt at consensus and denounced both the report and the WCC. This is, of course, ancient history for us. A proposal was made to begin yet a third study at the Uppsala Assembly that could go more deeply into the meaning of humanization and mission. Task forces were begun in various concrete situations where they could begin to test out some of the understandings of evangelism in relation to the theme "Christians in Changing Institutions." This study reached conclusion and was reported in 1974 but nothing even approaching consensus was attempted. Emphasis had shifted toward Christians in all parts of the world finding their way to witness to the gospel in their own setting.[6]

Perhaps our study here is part of a new stage in the discussion. At least we look with renewed hope for unity in mission, for much has happened in the last ten years to show that division between social action and evangelization is not made so easily. So-called "young evangelicals" are pointing to

3. Ernst Käsemann, "The Beginnings of Christian Theology," in *Apocalypticism,* ed. Robert W. Funk (New York: Herder and Herder, 1969), pp. 17-46.

4. "A Theological Reflection on the Work of Evangelism," *The Bulletin,* WCC Division of Studies, 5, nos. 1-2 (November 1959).

5. *The Church for Others and the Church for the World* (Geneva: WCC, 1967).

6. "Caught in a Web," *Risk,* WCC, 10, no. 3 (1974), entire issue.

evangelical views of social concern. Christians in Third World contexts are beginning to speak of "salvation today" as a continuing effort to understand salvation as a social as well as an individual event. As Gutiérrez puts it:

> Salvation — the communion of . . . [people] with God and the communion of . . . [people] among themselves — is something which embraces all human reality, transforms it, and leads it to its fullness in Christ.[7]

A truly global dialogue, giving voice to the many voiceless, is beginning to emerge. Liberation theologies are joining in that dialogue, helping us to see the way actions of evangelization may be truly part of God's liberating purpose and the way struggles for liberation may be truly part of God's mission.

Feminist perspective. Among other liberation theologies that work to reflect upon the experience of oppression in the light of their participation in God's liberating actions in creating a more human society, feminist theologies share in this concern to give an account of the hope that is in us (1 Peter 3:15). Feminists are advocates of equality of the sexes. Feminist Christians join other Christians in sharing their experience of God's love so that our theological understanding of God's purpose and will may be increased.

There are three themes of feminist theologies that seem to be related to our present task. One is the emphasis on *collective efforts* at doing theology. Much theology emerges out of group consciousness and struggle and is not necessarily written by experts to be "handed down" to the nonprofessionals. Another is the serious effort to see ways in which *consciousness raising* can be used as a tool for reflection and action in searching for ways to work together for social and personal conversion. Lastly, and perhaps most important, there is a strong *rejection of either/or,* dualistic categories of any sort, and a search for holistic ways of understanding the dimensions of our human existence.[8] These perspectives are shared with many liberation theologies in their *praxis* methodology that leads them to "do and tell liberation."[9]

II. Liberation and Evangelization

Participation in God's liberating and blessing action in the world leads to a sharing of the good news of God's liberation in Jesus Christ or to the word/act

7. Gustavo Gutiérrez, *A Theology of Liberation* (Maryknoll, N.Y.: Orbis, 1971), p. 151.

8. Rosemary Ruether, *Liberation Theology* (New York: Paulist, 1972), pp. 16-22.

9. Gabriel Fackre, *Do and Tell: Engagement Evangelism in the 70s* (Grand Rapids: Eerdmans, 1973), p. 15.

of evangelization. Action coupled with reflection is not a program to be accomplished and forgotten. It is an evangelical attitude toward life itself; an attitude that looks at what is going on in situations of oppression, trying constantly to see the problems and to work out the way in which God's will of liberation can be done, only to begin again with the next set of problems and consequent actions.[10]

Christian communities continue to witness to the sending and saving mission of God through proclamation, partnership, service, and celebration.[11] These overlapping dimensions of communicating the gospel are very much a part of God's liberating action. However, the dimensions are distorted when one aspect is emphasized at the expense of another and may become one-sided in respect to evangelization or to liberation.

One-sided views of evangelization. One of the ways of seeking to prevent the various dimensions of evangelism from becoming one-sided in the life of the church is to remember that the work of evangelization is derived not primarily from our own actions alone, but from God's traditioning action whose goal is *shalom* for all humanity. The church's role is to point to Christ in the world and not to itself. Another way is to remember that evangelization includes the totality of God's concern for liberation and blessing in all aspects of human life. It is also helpful to remember that the gospel is contextual and situation-variable. In each situation the meaning of the good news speaks concretely about particular needs for liberation and speaks in the language, lifestyle, and social structures of that particular place (1 Cor. 9:19-21).

Liberation theologies can be helpful in maintaining the full dimensions of evangelization. They begin from a theocentric basis as reflection on the liberating action of God, and seek by means of praxis to focus on social as well as individual needs of persons and groups. Above all, liberation theologians are committed to share in the situations of oppression in order to make hoping and planning a means of bringing new life and freedom. Ahron Sapezian points to this when he says,

> If rootedness is the starting point, *commitment* to the dispossessed in their struggle for emancipation is the basic *ethical stance* in the "theology of liberation."[12]

10. Russell, *Human Liberation,* pp. 125-30.

11. Robert McAfee Brown, *Is Faith Obsolete?* (Philadelphia: Westminster, 1974), p. 19.

12. Ahron Sapezian, "Theology of Liberation — Liberation of Theology: Education Perspectives," *Theological Education* 9, no. 4 (Summer 1973): 259.

For liberation theologians the key issue is not *orthodoxy* but *orthopraxy.*[13] Without denying the importance of disciplined, logical, and documented reflection on the meaning of biblical and ecclesial tradition, it is basically concerned not with reformulation of doctrines, but with the challenge of giving form to the message of the gospel as a praxis of liberation.

One-sided views of liberation. The dangers of one-sidedness are also present in liberation theologies when they make use of ideologies in such a way that the gospel message is obscured. Just as evangelism can degenerate into narrow proselytism, which sees its purpose solely as recruitment of members, liberation theologies sometimes become focused *only* on mobilization of people for a particular cause. They tend to forget that ultimately the cause is transcended by God's cause of eschatological mission. In the same way, the practice of evangelism has sometimes become a form of propaganda designed to create people in our own image instead of letting the love of God become incarnated into people's own lifestyles and culture. Liberation theologies have this same tendency when their social concern degenerates into a form of ideology which all people are supposed to accept.

It helps to avoid these dangers when we remember that traditioning itself has a double meaning. The handing over *(paradidonai)* of Christ can mean betrayal to the cross as well as sharing God's victorious love with others. Participation in God's traditioning of Christ calls for constant care not to betray the tradition by false methods of handing over, which become barriers to the hearing and living out of the good news.

III. God's Arithmetic and the Good News

In seeking to move beyond the false dichotomy of liberation versus evangelization, it may help us to remember that God works in many unexpected ways to bring about the new age. Sometimes, when we least expect it, small numbers of people are very important in representing the larger whole of humanity in God's purpose. At other times there is a multiplication of gifts when we least expect it, or an inefficient use of time and resources affords the most openness to God's love and concern. Three such clues about God's arithmetic may be helpful to us in keeping our concern for the importance of either evangelization or liberation in perspective: representative numbers; minus situation; and multiplication tables.

Representative numbers. Hans-Ruedi Weber has pointed out in his arti-

13. James H. Cone, *God of the Oppressed* (New York: Seabury, 1975), pp. 36-38.

cle on "God's Arithmetic" that, in both the Old and New Testaments, "It is not the many who become the agents of God's mission of reconciliation for all, but the few who are so weak that they must put all confidence in God's strength."[14] Redemption of the world comes through the history of a tiny nation and then through the One member of that nation chosen to give his life as a ransom for all (Mark 10:45).

In God's eschatological arithmetic the increase in numbers is seen as a qualitative sign of the New Age, not as a quantitative validation of God's plan of salvation or of the plans of human beings who consider themselves to be God's "ground personnel." Mission is much more directly connected with sacrifice, rather than statistics. "Numbers and growth are important in God's arithmetic: not necessarily large and increasing numbers, but representative numbers and growth in grace."[15]

Minus situation. The uniqueness of our participation in God's mission is, strangely enough, not tied to the superiority of the work we perform in God's eschatological arithmetic. Its uniqueness stems from its representation of God's presence in Christ in the world and also from the fact that is often not as "successful" as the work of others. We find ourselves in a minus situation in regard to working for justice, for we are tied to ecclesial and economic institutions that owe their survival to the perpetuation of injustice and unequal distribution of wealth and power in the world.[16] We also appear to be in a growing minus situation in regard to the proportion of Christians in relation to the world population.

The strength of our situation in the service of the Lord is that often we have opportunity to provide space for others to participate and share the work, growing in the use of their own gifts, simply by exercising a "minus virtue" of *calculated inefficiency.* In this type of efficiency we search for ways to invest ourselves with the outcasts and marginal people of any society, sharing in the ministry of Christ.[17]

Multiplication tables. God's strange arithmetic leads us in many directions in relation to our sharing in the task of liberation and evangelization. Although representative numbers and calculated inefficiency sometimes lead to lack of "worldly success," still there is also a marvelous multiplication table in the way God works in the world. God sometimes adds to the number of those who are being saved (Acts 2:47). For, when there is a new focus of rela-

14. Hans-Ruedi Weber, "God's Arithmetic," in *Mission Trends No. 2*, ed. Gerald H. Anderson and Thomas F. Stransky (Grand Rapids: Eerdmans, 1975), p. 65.

15. Weber, "God's Arithmetic," p. 66.

16. José Comblin, *The Meaning of Mission* (Maryknoll, N.Y.: Orbis, 1977), pp. 80-81.

17. Hans Hoekendijk, *Horizons of Hope* (Nashville: Tidings, 1970), p. 33.

tionship in Jesus Christ, the one becomes twelve, becomes five hundred, becomes five thousand, and so on!

If we are confident that "God is an equal-opportunity provider" then we are called to make the resources of God's creation and God's will for justice and liberation available to all humanity.[18] We are commissioned to accept responsibility for the many failures and problems of our work and that of our partners in Christian community, but at the same time to rejoice when multiplication signs of justice and peace are discovered. When our partnership in liberation and evangelization is lived to expectancy of God's creative and redemptive love, we will often find that the gifts and talents of people are multiplied like loaves and fishes in places where we might least expect them.

Perhaps the reminder of such clues as these about the strange ways in which God is at work will help us to keep our perspective focused on what God is about to do in God's New Creation and not upon our own plans and purposes (2 Cor. 5:17). In God's eschatological arithmetic, false dualisms between liberation and evangelization are overcome in many unexpected ways. J. C. Hoekndijk reminds us of this when he says,

> To let Christian hopes determine our evangelism means that we move forward in a world with unlimited possibilities, a world in which we shall not be surprised when something unforeseen happens, but shall, rather, be really surprised at our little faith, which forbids us to expect the unprecedented.[19]

We may be able to avoid the dangers of proselytism through a *liberating evangelization* that points toward God's New Creation. We may be able to avoid the dangers of secularism through an *evangelical liberation* that points toward the good news of Jesus Christ. Liberation and evangelization belong together. Evangelization is a *praxis* of liberation, for it is in the doing and telling of the good news of Jesus Christ that we are set free. This liberation will always be one shared with others and understood from many perspectives, as we journey together on the road to freedom — with others, for others, toward God's future.

18. Term used by Charles V. Willie in a sermon entitled "The Priesthood of All Believers," preached at the Ordination Service of Episcopal Women, Philadelphia, July 24, 1974.

19. J. C. Hoekendijk, *The Church Inside Out,* ed. L. A. Hoedemaker and P. Tijmes (Philadelphia: Westminster, 1966), p. 23.

CHAPTER 30

Centripetal Mission, or Evangelization by Hospitality

Mortimer Arias

One day last summer I visited an English-speaking church in Vienna where the American pastor preached on Titus 1:5-16. His reference to the importance of hospitality for Christian leaders and their witness (1:8) was seed sown for later reflections on what I thought might be called "evangelization by hospitality."

The fact that I am living the experience of a privileged guest in the United States, enjoying the wonderful hospitality of the American church, made the subject of hospitality especially meaningful to me. I think hospitality should be seen as an important part of the ongoing mission of the church.

The Scriptural Emphasis on Hospitality

Hospitality is becoming an almost forgotten Christian virtue in our style of life today, particularly in big cities with their rampant crime on the streets, their locked-in apartments, and all their affluent, urban, and bourgeois devices which attempt to create privacy in our homes and our lives.

In the New Testament, however, hospitality was a distinctive mark of Christians and Christian communities. "Open your homes to strangers," says Paul, in describing the Christian lifestyle (Rom. 12:13). "Welcome one another," he continues, "as Christ welcomed you" (15:17). A few lines later when introducing the deaconess Phoebe to the Romans, Paul again suggests hospitality, "Please, give her a Christian welcome" (16:2). But the apostle has not finished with the subject. He again reminds the Christians of the Empire's capital about "Gaius, my host and the host of the whole congregation" (16:23). A remarkable number of hospitality instructions in a single letter!

Bishops, elders, and widows are summoned to hospitality in the Pastoral Letters (1 Tim. 3:2; 5:9; Titus 1:8). The apostle Peter considered hospitality the right and normal thing for Christians to do: "Open your homes to each other, without complaining" (1 Peter 4:9). And the Letter to the Hebrews elaborates further the potential meaning of hospitality, raising it to a very privileged duty for the rank-and-file Christians: "Remember to welcome the strangers in your homes. There are some who did it and welcomed angels without knowing it" (Heb. 13:2).

Where did such a high esteem for hospitality come from? Of course there was a long-honored tradition of hospitality both among the Orientals and the Greeks. The Old Testament recounts the memorable experience of Abraham and Sarah in hosting the messengers of the Lord (Gen. 18:1-8; cf. 19:1-3). And hospitality was essential in the beginning of the Christian mission and the expansion of the emergent church in the New Testament through homes of Christians and well-disposed friends (Acts 1:13; 2:46; 5:42; 9:43; 12:12-17; 1 Cor. 16:19; Col. 4:15). It has been suggested that the transmission of the materials that became incorporated in our present Gospels first circulated through Christian travelers and in the atmosphere of hospitality.[1] The house church model continued beyond the second century, in times when Christians had no temples or public buildings available.[2] Gradually an effective network of communication spread all over the Roman Empire through the modest means of hospitality.

The instructions of the New Testament on hospitality go beyond mere necessity and strategy. There were deep spiritual and theological foundations, as Paul suggests with his exhortation: "Receive one another as Christ received you." I dare to believe that hospitality was rooted finally in Jesus' own teaching and command:

> I was a stranger and you received me in your homes . . . Indeed, whenever you did this for one of the least of these, . . . you did it for me: Whoever welcomes you, welcomes me; and whoever welcomes you, welcomes the one who sent me. (Matt. 25:35, 40, 43; Mark 9:37, Luke 9:48)

For the temporary mission of the Twelve, hospitality was an indispensable component:

1. Donald Wayne Riddle, "Early Christian Hospitality: A Factor in the Gospel Transmission," *Journal of Biblical Literature* 7, no. 2 (1938): 141-54.

2. Floyd V. Filson, "The Significance of the Early House Churches," *Journal of Biblical Literature* 8, no. 2 (1939): 105-12.

> When you come to a town or village, go in and look for someone who is willing to welcome you, and stay with him until you leave the place. (Matt. 10:11ff.)

But it is not only a provisional missionary device. In the Gospel of John it becomes a solemn affirmation, a sort of universal principle:

> I tell you the truth; whoever receives anyone I send, receives me also; and whoever receives me, receives him who sent me. (John 13:20)

Can we see, then, how the matter of hospitality is intimately related to Christian life and mission? It seems obvious that here hospitality is quite inclusive: it has to do with brothers and sisters in the faith, with Christian leaders and congregations, with children, with missionaries, with the "least one of these," the needy neighbor, whoever this may be, and specifically when it is a foreigner, a stranger.

For centuries Christians have discussed the sacraments — as mediators of God's presence, as "the real presence" of the Lord in the elements of the Eucharist. Perhaps we need to discuss the sacrament of welcoming the neighbor! God comes to us in the disciples, the missionaries, children, and the "least one of these" — especially the needy neighbors.

Hospitality Evangelization

In hospitality there is much more than Christian politeness and civilized behavior. It may not be out of order to think in terms of hospitality evangelization! I would venture the hypothesis that hospitality was an effective evangelistic instrument during the Middle Ages, considering the historical role of convents, hostels, and places of refuge for travelers, pilgrims, or runaways. "Hospital" is a word and an institution born precisely out of Christian hospitality.

Any missionary or seminary teacher worth their salt could tell us the decisive role hospitality played in their ministry. It is in the atmosphere of a real home where Christians can be better known and where both hosts and guests can share their needs, their pains, their hopes, their faith. Is it surprising that today, despite our big buildings and our sophisticated means of communication, we come once again to house churches, neighborhood cells, and base Christian communities as vital instruments for the renewal of the church, for evangelization and for church growth?

As there are hospitable homes there are hospitable churches. In recent years Christians concerned with the division between confessions at the Lord's table have suggested the need for "Eucharistic hospitality" — offering an open table to Christians of other denominations or confessions. But a hospitable church is much more than an eventual open table to other Christians — it is an open church, a welcoming church.

How hospitable are our churches? This amounts to asking, how evangelistic are they? I cannot forget the story of Mahatma Gandhi who during his younger years in South Africa approached a Christian church where he was rejected at the door because of his color. That was the last opportunity any Christian church had to welcome Mahatma Gandhi!

Some churches have a selective hospitality. Some time ago I went to visit the new Hispanic pastor and congregation of an Anglo church in California which had begun Spanish services. I approached one building where a woman was preparing refreshments. Her radiant smile faded as soon as I asked in my Spanish-accented English for the Spanish-speaking worship service. Pointing her chin, she said in a disappointed tone, "There!"

A person can be made to feel welcome in obvious and subtle ways, not only through signs and formal greetings of the ushers, but in the attitude of the whole congregation, in the style of worship, and in the way the local church relates to the surrounding community.

National Hospitality

There is also the hospitality of countries and societies. We in South America grew up with the idea that our countries were very hospitable, with open doors for immigrants who came from Europe in the years past "to win America" *(hacerse la America)*. But we have been discovering that ours was also a selective hospitality. It took the Asians to remind us of the closed policy of immigration in Latin American countries (despite vast reserves of land) in relation to the land-hungry peoples of Asia. Also hundreds of thousands of Latin Americans have discovered that their own countries were not hospitable to their own people who have been expelled from their homelands because of need, oppression, repression, and persecution. What used to be "lands of refuge" became hunting grounds of political prisoners, nonconformists, and those suspected of independent ideas and wrong associations. The recent drama of El Salvadorian peasants killed in their own land, in their own huts, and pushed across frontiers by army helicopters is just one more chapter of this sad story.

The United States, too, was born out of this great idea of being a hospitable country: "the land of the free, the home of the brave." Engraved on Bartholdi's Statue of Liberty in New York's harbor are the memorable words,

> Give me your tired, your poor,
> your huddled masses yearning to breathe free . . .
>
> Send these, the homeless, tempest-tossed to me.

I have experienced this hospitality myself, and for this I am deeply grateful. When I was forced into exile from my own adoptive country, when other Latin American countries were tightening their laws in relationship to those from neighboring countries, I was graciously received in this nation. I have a job, I have a church, I have friends, I have a host country which has become my interim home. Even though I hope eventually to return to my country, I can say that in many ways this has been for me "the land of the free."

There are others who have a different experience and tell another story, like the original Mexicans who lost their lands after the vast Southwest became part of this expanding country. There are contradictions, here as elsewhere, between our conscious ideals and our unconscious attitudes. While the United States is sending its young people to "defend freedom" in Europe, Korea, or Vietnam, it may be denying that freedom at home. This was evident in the action of angry Ku Klux Klan members who burned Vietnamese fishing boats in Galveston, Texas. When asked by reporters about the human rights and the freedom of enterprise of these Vietnamese immigrants, one answered, "They have no rights here! They have left their rights when they left their country." I wondered at the time if this angry Texan had sent a son or a nephew to fight in Vietnam for the freedom of that faraway people who was being denied the freedom of competition upon arrival in Texas.

I knew that both my positive experience — shared by millions and desired by many others — as well as the sad experiences of some Cubans in recent migrations, as well as the dreadful experience of Haitians in the last months, and those Salvadorians repatriated to their land of violence, fear, and misery — all have direct and indirect implications for evangelization, for the authentic and efficacious sharing of the good news of Jesus Christ.

Personal hospitality, church hospitality, and the hospitality of the society at large are all inseparable in the genuine evangelization of peoples coming to our doorstep. This brings me to another side of these reflections to what is being called "centripetal mission."

Centripetal Mission

Christian mission from its beginning has been centrifugal mission — going from the center to a periphery in the world. Mission cannot remain at any center, it has to move to new boundaries and frontiers: "to all peoples everywhere"; "to the whole world"; "to the whole creation"; "to the end of the earth"; and "to the end of time."

When we think of mission or evangelization we think of going. And yet there is another dimension of mission which is the Old Testament pattern — centripetal mission. Israel is the missionary people of God, "the light of the nations," whose primary mission is not to go but to be the people of God. After the resurrection and Pentecost the pattern changes radically, but it does not mean that there is no longer any place for centripetal mission — by attraction, by incarnation, by being. Jesus himself called his disciples to be the salt of the earth, the light of the world, the city upon a hill, the leaven in the dough — all images of incarnational Christian witness.

Dr. Waldron Scott, in his last book on mission perspectives, *Bring Forth Justice*, has raised the point forcefully, relating the centripetal dimension in mission to authenticity and effectiveness:

> The centripetal mission of the Old Testament was always linked with a call to Israel to be *authentic* in [its] life before God. This emphasis is still relevant to us today. The insoluble link between authenticity of life and efficacy of witness was surely in Peter's mind when he wrote: "But you are a chosen race, a royal priesthood, a holy nation, God's own people, that you may declare the wonderful deeds of him who called you out of darkness into his marvelous light."[3]

In this perception centripetal mission is a permanent and essential dimension of mission; it has to do with quality, with authenticity, with being. This dimension tends to be a priority in those countries traditionally considered the *sending centers* of mission — where Christian presence is visible and dominant. This is particularly true of those places like Europe and the United States that have become a window to the world and a center of attraction for the peoples of the earth.

The former president of the World Fellowship of Evangelicals continues his reflections on this point, with this warning,

3. Waldron Scott, *Bring Forth Justice* (Grand Rapids: Eerdmans, 1980), p. 80. The quote references 1 Peter 2:9.

> Within our societies, evangelical churches must be foremost in the pursuit of the justice of God. The failure of the churches to be sensitive and obedient to the demands of the gospel within their own culture greatly enfeebles their witness when they move across cultural frontiers, as many a modern missionary has discovered to his or her dismay.[4]

So the future of missions will not depend only on what cross-cultural missionaries do "out there" in the considered peripheries of the world or on the mission fields, but by what Christians do in their sending centers. It is a fact of life today that President Reagan's statements about the Third World, and the military-industrial complex's actions regarding the world arms race and nuclear weapons, have evangelistic and missionary implications — for better or for worse.

Migrations and Mission

Another fact to be remembered is that the "world out there" suddenly is right here at our doorstep — legally or illegally — by the millions. The Hispanic population alone is estimated at more than 20 million, and this has been called the "decade of the Hispanics." There are thousands more "out there" applying in American consulates around the world for entrance to the United States as tourists, students, migrant-workers, or immigrants. Thousands are venturing everything they have and risking their lives in precarious boats, trying to reach the shores of hope (although some of them may end up in a concentration camp or be expelled back to the sea).

Surely the United States cannot solve the problem of all migrants and refugees (estimated by some to number today some 14 million people). All countries need to have laws concerning immigration, but nothing will stop this pressure and the continuous flow of people from all over the world, however it may be limited and controlled. The economic centers of the world, with their higher standards of living and more opportunities for work, are the poles of attraction to the impoverished of the world.

A friend of mine who is a Latin American bishop spoke clearly to this point. When I remarked that the United States could not handle all the people who want to come here, he said, "That is the price you pay for being the head of the Empire!" Some might protest the use of the word, "empire," but we must be realistic. The country, which has more than two hundred mili-

4. Scott, *Bring Forth Justice*, p. 80.

tary bases around the world; which inundates with its mass media production through millions of TV sets, newspapers, magazines, books, and thousands of cultural centers; which is the main supplier of arms in the world; which wants to have access and freedom of enterprise on its own terms in every market around the globe; which consumes 40 percent of all the natural resources of the earth; which considers itself the defender of "freedom and democracy" on six continents; which looks at Korea, the Persian Gulf, or El Salvador as its own zone of "national security" — that nation cannot expect to remain isolated and to keep its frontiers closed to that world that it is pretending to lead!

However we interpret these facts, they have an evangelistic dimension and pose an inescapable missionary challenge: namely, centripetal mission, or evangelization by hospitality. How are we in the church going to deal with the many migrants "invading" our cities and towns? Are we going to see them as "problems" or as missionary opportunities?

Perhaps we need to study migrations not only for their economic, social, and political implications, but also in terms of missionary strategy. The only church I know which has a migrant policy is the Roman Catholic Church. It is even more important to understand the place of migrations in God's plan for humanity and his kingdom. The Bible is a book full of migrations. God is the God of the migrants, the pilgrim people. The people of God were borne on the shoulders of the Father of Migrants, Abraham, "who went out not knowing where he was going," and ended with only a grave in a garden. It was sheer hunger, and the abundance of Egypt's grain silos, which pushed Jacob and his family from their native land to that affluent center. And it was the gigantic network centered in Rome that decided the future of the Christian church in the Roman Empire.

Can we see in the faces of contemporary Asians, Latin Americans, and Africans, pushed from their lands and attracted to our shores, the potential glow of the angel of the Lord — the Lord of migrants who transforms and moves history through migrant peoples, and raises his own people as a pilgrim church among many diverse peoples?

To Reach or to Receive?

Christian strategists are rightfully concerned with "reaching the unreached." The United States is the great reservoir of missionary force in the world with more than 35,000 missionaries in over a hundred countries. The great problem for these strategists is how to raise witnesses inside the thousand different "peoples" of the world where no Christian presence or symbol now exists.[5]

But how about those "hidden places" who are within our reach, who have an excess of Christians, churches, and TV religious programs around them? The question here is not how to reach the unreached but how to receive the newcomers, how to testify authentically to the overreached.

The United Methodist Church, like other mainline churches in the United States, has been passing through a decline in membership for several years. Now there are some signs of recovery and growth. New congregations are beginning every week, but most of them are among migrant minorities, especially Korean.

The Southern Baptists have discovered this fertile missionary frontier some time ago. M. Wendell Belew, in his presidential address at the American Society of Missiology last June, had this to say,

> While our Foreign Mission Board works in about 100 nations in the world, we work in 77 here in the United States. The two largest Laotian Baptist churches in the world are here. There are twice as many Vietnamese Baptist churches here than there ever were in Vietnam. There are more Spanish-speaking Baptist churches than in all the rest of the world.[6]

I talked personally with this Southern Baptist missionary executive about the way they carry out their international mission in the United States. He told me they simply care about the newly arriving population. They begin by getting information from the Census Bureau, and then try to make contacts. First they look for Christians, no matter what denomination they may originally come from. Sometimes they find lay leaders, even pastors, who have not been in touch with any other church, and then they offer to help start meetings and congregations, training leaders, providing literature, doing whatever they can to promote an evangelistic outreach.

Belew is enthusiastic about the strategic meaning of this centripetal mission, which eventually may become centrifugal:

> As missiologists we have an opportunity to rediscover North America. As part of the world scope of missions we should notice that God has placed many nations in our nation which can be recipients of our "internship"

5. See the Pattaya Consultation on World Evangelization, World Council of Churches, *Your Kingdom Come* (Geneva: WCC, 1980).

6. M. Wendell Belew, "American Missiology: Context and Challenge," *Missiology* 9, no. 1 (January 1981).

for the fields of the world. One day these churches will send out their indigenous witness to the nations of the world.[7]

"Come and See"

This centripetal approach has its problems and challenges. The authenticity of our Christian life becomes essential and decisive. As many as are attracted may also be repelled by our style of life and our attitudes. It is one thing to go "out there" and tell the people "the old, old story"; it is another to bring them here and show them how Christians live. Our affluent style and our permissive society may attract those ready to incorporate our standards and our style, but this probably will not lead to an authentic Christian commitment.

In the Gospel of John, evangelization was done through witness more than by proclamation. It is interesting to see how many times the expression "come and see" is the clue for the evangelistic event. These were the words Jesus said to his first disciples. Philip said them to Nathaniel. The Samaritan woman used them in her decisive witness, which brought a whole town to Jesus (John 1:39, 46; 4:29, 42).

This is a risky type of evangelization. Can we safely, or hopefully, invite the new populations at our doorstep saying, "Come and see"? Come and see our lives, our church, our society? I agree with Waldron Scott that this is a fundamental challenge to our evangelization, the indispensable dimension of authenticity.

The Other Side: From the Periphery to the Center

There is another side to this subject which I have not seen in any church growth strategies: putting ourselves on the receiving end of this missionary experience. Is it possible that God wants to give us new dimensions to our understanding of the gospel through these populations coming to us?

Belew speaks of an "internship" that may enable these Christians to go as "indigenous missionaries" to their own countries of origin. Cannot they be missionaries to this country and to our churches? Is it not a fact that there are already quite a few leaders in many denominations who originally came from the so-called "ethnic" churches?

Hospitality is a two-way street. In Christian terms, to reach is to be

7. Belew, "American Missiology."

reached. To evangelize is to be evangelized. Simon Peter might tell us that he learned a great deal about God's strategy through his encounter with Cornelius and his family. Peter even had to update his orthodoxy (Acts 10).

It is a great thing to provide logistic support to migrant groups to enable them to evangelize among themselves, among "their own kind," but we should not avoid the missionary opportunity God is giving us by bringing the world to our doorstep. Our congregations should offer themselves in a give-and-take relationship to Christians from other cultures. The Jewish-Greek congregation in Antioch, the most missionary-minded church in the New Testament, apparently had evangelistic insights which the apostolic church in Jerusalem was not aware of.

Orlando Costas, in his recent lecture on "Evangelism in the Eighties: Witnessing to a New World Order," summarizes the American society in the 1980s in a masterful way. He says it appears it will be "a decade of gloom" and forecasts rough days ahead — economically, socioculturally, politically, and militarily. Costas believes, however, that this decade will provide a new opportunity for evangelization. The present mood of pessimism will be our opportunity to announce a gospel of life, joy, and hope — the gospel of the kingdom of God.

> In the gloomy climate of American Society in the '80s, where false dreams and deadly illusions cover up a perplexed, confused, humiliated, lonely and deeply saddened population, full of anxieties and broken in spirit, the church needs to emphasize the joy and gladness of the gospel. In so doing it will provide a challenging alternative to a schizophrenic style of life, organized on one side around wealth, power, pleasure and fun, and on the other, around a growing psychological and sociological impoverishment, a dreadful fear of becoming politically, economically and militarily weak, full of self-defeating guilt feelings and in a melancholic and insensitive mood.[8]

Now, where are the signs of this new evangelism in the '80s? Surprisingly, Costas doesn't find it in the "center" as much as in the "periphery" of the American society and the American church.

> It is a fact that, at a time when important sectors of mainline Christianity have become stagnant and dry, and when leading sectors of the evangelical, fundamentalist and charismatic movements have embarked on a

8. Orlando E. Costas, "Evangelism in the Eighties: Witnessing to a New World Order," mimeographed paper (1981), p. 16.

> neo-Christendom project, and have incorporated the illusion of a Pax Americana, and an exclusivistic, revived "American Dream," large sectors of the church of the poor and disenfranchised are bearing a vigorous witness to the gospel — without fanfare, financial resources or academically-qualified personnel. Black, Hispanic, Asian and Native American churches and Christians, in partnership with a minority from the mainstream society which has identified itself with the poor, the powerless and the oppressed of the land, are witnessing to the new world order announced in the gospel — outside the realm of economic wealth, military might and political power, and inside the world of millions who are being wasted by numerous forms of social, economic and political evils.[9]

This is what Costas calls "the other American Church," "from the underside of the American history," which is "growing numerically by leaps and bounds" and experiencing "the gospel as life and joy in an environment of death and misery," that "knows how to sing the songs of Sion in a strange land." And he believes that if mainstream Christians "start a teach-in of their minority counterparts" and "apply their model of evangelization," this country could see a transformation in personal and collective lives as never before.

I personally would like to know more about what is going on at the periphery. It may well be, as the Melbourne Conference on Missions and Evangelism said, that the Christ who moves to the peripheries of life and society, may speak to us from there in a new and powerful way.[10] This could also be the meaning of centripetal mission and evangelization by hospitality.

9. Costas, "Evangelism in the Eighties," p. 16.
10. WCC, *Your Kingdom Come.*

Further Reading

Part One: Defining the Ecclesial Practice and Theology of Evangelism

Abraham, William J. *The Logic of Evangelism.* Grand Rapids: Eerdmans, 1989.

Barrett, David B. *Evangelize! A Historical Survey of the Concept.* Birmingham, Ala.: New Hope, 1987.

Bashford, Robert. *Mission and Evangelism in Recent Thinking, 1974-1986.* Oxford: Latimer House, 1990.

Boff, Leonardo. *New Evangelization: Good News to the Poor.* Maryknoll, N.Y.: Orbis, 1991.

Bosch, David J. *Transforming Mission: Paradigm Shifts in Theology of Mission.* Maryknoll, N.Y.: Orbis, 1991.

Braaten, Carl E., and Robert W. Jenson, eds. *The Strange New Word of the Gospel: Re-evangelizing in the Postmodern World.* Grand Rapids: Eerdmans, 2002.

Brennan, Patrick J. *Re-Imagining Evangelization: Toward the Reign of God and the Communal Parish.* New York: Crossroad, 1995.

Coleman, Robert E. *The Master Plan of Evangelism.* Rev. ed. Westwood, N.J.: Fleming H. Revell, 2006.

Costas, Orlando. *Liberating News: A Theology of Contextual Evangelization.* Grand Rapids: Eerdmans, 1989.

Fox, H. Eddie, and George Morris. *Faith Sharing: Dynamic Christian Witnessing by Invitation.* Rev. ed. Nashville: Discipleship Resources, 1996.

Glasser, Arthur F., ed. *Crucial Dimensions in World Evangelization.* South Pasadena, Calif.: William Carey Library, 1976.

Greinacher, Norbert, ed. *Evangelization in the World Today.* New York: Seabury, 1979.

Gumbel, Nicky. *Telling Others: The Alpha Initiative.* Eastbourne: Kingsway, 1994.

Hacker, Paul. *Theological Foundations of Evangelization.* St. Augustine: Steyler, 1980.

Johnson, Ben Campbell. *An Evangelism Primer: Practical Principles for Congregations.* Atlanta: John Knox, 1983.

Jones, Scott. *The Evangelistic Love of God and Neighbor.* Nashville: Abingdon, 2003.

Kolb, Robert. *Speaking the Gospel Today: A Theology of Evangelism.* St. Louis: Concordia, 1984.

McGavran, Donald A. *Understanding Church Growth.* 3rd ed. Grand Rapids: Eerdmans, 1990.

Marshall, Michael. *The Gospel Connection: A Study of Evangelism for the Nineties.* London: Darton, Longman & Todd, 1990.

Neave, Rosemary. *Gossiping the Gospel: Women Reflect on Evangelism.* Auckland, New Zealand: The Women's Resource Center, 1992.

Newbigin, Lesslie. *The Open Secret: Sketches for a Missionary Theology.* Rev. ed. Grand Rapids: Eerdmans, 1995.

Pippert, Rebecca Manley. *Out of the Saltshaker and into the World: Evangelism as a Way of Life.* Rev. ed. Downers Grove, Ill.: InterVarsity, 1999.

Poe, Harry L. *The Gospel and Its Meaning: A Theology for Evangelism and Church Growth.* Grand Rapids: Eerdmans, 1996.

Poterski, Donald C. *Reinventing Evangelism: New Strategies for Presenting Christ in Today's World.* Downers Grove, Ill: InterVarsity, 1989.

Rainer, Thom S., ed. *Evangelism in the Twenty-First Century: The Critical Issues.* Wheaton, Ill.: Harold Shaw, 1989.

Robert, Dana. *Evangelism as the Heart of Mission.* Mission Evangelism Series, no. 1. New York: GBGM, 1997.

Samuel, Viney, and Albrecht Hauser, eds. *Proclaiming Christ in Christ's Way: Studies in Integral Evangelism.* Oxford: Regnum, 1989.

Scherer, James A., and Stephen B. Bevans, eds. *New Directions in Mission and Evangelization.* Vol. 1. *Basic Statements 1974-1991.* Maryknoll, N.Y.: Orbis, 1992.

Stone, Bryan P. *Evangelism After Christendom: The Theology and Practice of Christian Witness.* Grand Rapids: Brazos, 2006.

Towns, Elmer L., ed. *Evangelism and Church Growth: A Practical Encyclopedia.* Ventura, Calif.: Regal, 1995.

Webber, Robert E. *Ancient-Future Evangelism: Making Your Church a Faith-Forming Community.* Grand Rapids: Baker, 2003.

Part Two: Biblical and Historical Sources for the Study of Evangelism

Arias, Mortimer. *Announcing the Reign of God: Evangelization and the Subversive Memory of Jesus.* Philadelphia: Fortress, 1984.

Arias, Mortimer, and Alan Johnson. *The Great Commission: Biblical Models for Evangelism.* Nashville: Abingdon, 1992.

Barrett, David B. *Cosmos, Chaos, and Gospel: A Chronology of World Evangelization from Creation to New Creation.* Birmingham, Ala.: New Hope, 1987.

Barrett, David B., and James W. Reapsome. *Seven Hundred Plans to Evangelize the World: The Rise of a Global Evangelization Movement.* Birmingham, Ala.: New Hope, 1988.

Beidelman, T. O. *Colonial Evangelism: A Socio-Historical Study of an East African Mission at the Grassroots.* Bloomington: University of Indiana Press, 1982.

Brueggemann, Walter. *Biblical Perspectives on Evangelism: Living in a Three-Storied Universe.* Nashville: Abingdon, 1993.

Fung, Raymond. *The Isaiah Vision: An Ecumenical Strategy for Congregational Evangelism.* Geneva: WCC, 1992.

Green, Michael. *Evangelism in the Early Church.* Grand Rapids: Eerdmans, 1970.

Hardman, Keith J. *Seasons of Refreshing: Evangelism and Revivals in America.* Grand Rapids: Baker, 1994.

Hunter, George G., III. *The Celtic Way of Evangelism: How Christians Can Reach the West . . . Again.* Nashville: Abingdon, 2000.

———. *Radical Outreach: The Recovery of Apostolic Ministry and Evangelism.* Nashville: Abingdon, 2002.

Klaiber, Walter. *Call and Response: Biblical Foundations of a Theology of Evangelism.* Trans. Howard Perry-Trauthig and James A. Dwyer. Nashville: Abingdon, 1997.

McQuilkin, J. Robertson. *The Great Omission: A Biblical Basis for World Evangelism.* Grand Rapids: Baker, 1984.

Maynard-Reid, Pedrito U. *Complete Evangelism: The Luke-Acts Model.* Scottsdale, Pa.: Herald, 1997.

Mead, Loren B. *The Once and Future Church: Reinventing the Congregation for a New Mission Frontier.* Bethesda, Md.: Alban Institute, 1991.

Mugambi, J. N. K. *The Biblical Basis for Evangelization: Theological Reflections Based on an African Experience.* Nairobi, Kenya: Oxford, 1989.

Payne, Bishop Claude E., and Hamilton Beazley. *Reclaiming the Great Com-*

mission: A Practical Model for Transformating Denominations and Congregations. San Francisco: Jossey-Bass, 2001.

Pope-Levison, Priscilla. *Turn the Pulpit Loose: Two Centuries of American Women Evangelists.* New York: Palgrave Macmillan, 2004.

Rudnick, Millton K. *Speaking the Gospel through the Ages: A History of Evangelism.* St. Louis: Concordia, 1984.

Senior, Donald and Carroll Stuhlmueller. *The Biblical Foundations for Mission.* Maryknoll, N.Y.: Orbis, 1983.

Terry, John M. *Evangelism: A Concise History.* Nashville: Broadman, 1994.

Tuttle, Robert G. *The Story of Evangelism: A History of the Witness to the Gospel.* Nashville: Abingdon, 2006.

Part Three: The Study of Evangelism in the World of Theology

Bradshaw, Bruce. *Bridging the Gap: Evangelism, Development and Shalom.* Monrovia, Calif.: MARC, 1993.

Chapman, John. *Know and Tell the Gospel: The Why and How of Evangelism.* Sydney: Hodder & Stoughton, 1981.

Conn, Harvie M. *Evangelism: Doing Justice and Preaching Grace.* Grand Rapids: Zondervan, 1982.

Costas, Orlando. *Christ Outside the Gate.* Maryknoll, N.Y.: Orbis, 1982.

Dawn, Marva. *Reaching Out Without Dumbing Down.* Grand Rapids: Eerdmans, 1995.

Drummond, Lewis. *The Word of the Cross: A Contemporary Theology of Evangelism.* Nashville: Broadman, 1992.

Guder, Darrell L. *Be My Witnesses: The Church's Mission, Message, and Messengers.* Grand Rapids: Eerdmans, 1985.

———. *The Continuing Conversion of the Church.* Grand Rapids: Eerdmans, 2000.

Hauerwas, Stanley, and William H. Willimon. *Preaching to Strangers: Evangelism in Today's World.* Louisville: Westminster/John Knox, 1992.

Johnson, Ben Campbell. *Rethinking Evangelism: A Theological Approach.* Philadelphia: Westminster, 1987.

Kallenberg, Brad J. *Live to Tell: Evangelism in a Postmodern World.* Grand Rapids: Brazos, 2002.

McGavran, Donald A. *Effective Evangelism: A Theological Mandate.* Phillipsburg, NJ: Presbyterian and Reformed, 1988.

Marshall, Michael. *The Gospel Conspiracy: Unlocking the Church for Renewal and Evangelism.* Eastbourne: Monarch, 1992.

Nichols, Bruce, ed. *In Word and Deed: Evangelism and Social Responsibility.* Grand Rapids: Eerdmans, 1986.

Packer, J. I. *Evangelism and the Sovereignty of God.* Downers Grove, Ill.: InterVarsity, 1961.

Pickard, Stephen K. *Liberating Evangelism: Gospel Theology and the Dynamics of Communication.* Harrisburg, Pa.: Trinity, 1999.

Pope-Levison, Priscilla. *Evangelization from a Liberation Perspective.* New York: Peter Lang, 1991.

Shepherd, Norman. *The Call of Grace: How the Covenant Illuminates Salvation and Evangelism.* Philipsburg, N.J.: Presbyterian and Reformed, 2001.

Sider, Ronald J. *Evangelism, Salvation and Social Justice.* Bramcote: Grove, 1977.

———. *One-Sided Christianity: Uniting the Church to Heal a Lost and Broken World.* Grand Rapids: Zondervan, 1993.

Sider, Ronald J., Philip N. Olson, and Heidi R. Unruh. *Churches that Make a Difference: Reaching Your Community with Good News and Good Works.* Grand Rapids: Baker, 2002.

Stott, John R. W., ed. *Evangelism and Social Responsibility.* London: Paternoster, 1982.

Wallis, Jim. *The Call to Conversion.* San Francisco: Harper, 1981.

Wells, David. *God the Evangelist: How the Holy Spirit Works to Bring Men and Women to Faith.* Grand Rapids, Eerdmans, 1987.

Part Four: The Study of Evangelism among the Ecclesial Practices

Armstrong, Richard Stoll. *The Pastor-Evangelist in Worship.* Philadelphia: Westminster, 1986.

———. *Service Evangelism.* Philadelphia: Westminster, 1979.

Arn, Win, and Charles Arn. *The Master's Plan for Making Disciples.* Pasadena, Calif.: Church Growth, 1982.

Arnold, Jeffrey. *Small Group Outreach: Turning Groups Inside Out.* Downers Grove, Ill.: InterVarsity, 1998.

Augsburger, Myron S., et al. *Mastering Outreach and Evangelism.* Portland, Ore.: Multnomah, 1990.

Benedict, Daniel T., and Craig Kennet Miller. *Contemporary Worship for 21st Century: Worship or Evangelism?* Nashville: Discipleship Resources, 1994.

Crandall, Ron. *The Contagious Witness: Exploring Christian Conversion.* Nashville: Abingdon, 1999.

———. *Witness: Exploring and Sharing Your Christian Faith.* Nashville: Discipleship Resources, 2001.

Croft, Steven. *Growing New Christians: Developing Evangelism and Nurture in the Local Church.* London: Marshall Pickering, 1993.

Dunnam, Maxie D. *Congregational Evangelism: A Pastor's View.* Nashville: Discipleship Resources, 1992.

Escamilla, Roberto. *Come to the Feast: Invitational Evangelism.* Nashville: Discipleship Resources, 1998.

Green, Michael. *Evangelism Through the Local Church.* Nashville: Nelson, 1990.

Hofinger, Johannes. *Evangelization and Catechesis: Are We Really Proclaiming the Gospel?* New York: Paulist, 1976.

Holash, Lise M. *Evangelization: The Catechumenate and its Ministries.* Dubuque, Iowa: William C. Brown, 1983.

Hunter, George G., III. *The Contagious Congregation.* Nashville: Abingdon, 1979.

Johnson, Ben Campbell. *Speaking of God: Evangelism as Initial Spiritual Guidance.* Louisville: Westminster/John Knox, 1991.

Johnson, Ron, and Leonard Sanderson. *Evangelism for All God's People: Approaches to Lay Ministries in the Marketplace.* Nashville: Broadman, 1990.

Keifert, Patrick R. *Welcoming the Stranger: A Public Theology of Worship and Evangelism.* Minneapolis: Fortress, 1992.

Kincaid, Ron. *A Celebration of Disciple-Making: How Church-centered Evangelism Can Excite Your Congregation to Growth.* Wheaton, Ill.: Victor, 1990.

Langford, Andy, and Sally Overby. *Worship & Evangelism.* Nashville: Discipleship Resources, 1989.

Larsen, David. *The Evangelism Mandate: Recovering the Centrality of Gospel Preaching.* Wheaton, Ill.: Crossway Books, 1992.

Mittelberg, Mark. *Building a Contagious Church: Revolutionizing the Way We View and Do Evangelism.* Grand Rapids: Zondervan, 2000.

Morgenthaler, Sally. *Worship Evangelism: Inviting Unbelievers into the Presence of God.* Grand Rapids: Zondervan, 1999.

Peace, Richard V. *Small Group Evangelism: A Training Program for Reaching Out with the Gospel.* Downers Grove, Ill.: InterVarsity, 1985.

———. *Holy Conversation: Talking About God in Everyday Life.* Downers Grove, Ill: InterVarsity, 2006.

Pierson, Robert D. *Needs-Based Evangelism: Becoming a Good Samaritan Church.* Nashville: Abingdon, 2006.

Richards, Elton P., Jr. *Outreach Preaching: The Role of Preaching in Evangelism.* Minneapolis: Augsburg, 1987.

Senn, Frank C. *The Witness of the Worshiping Community: Liturgy and the Practice of Evangelism.* New York: Paulist, 1993.

Sorenson, Stephen W. *Like Your Neighbor? Doing Everyday Evangelism on Common Ground.* Downers Grove, Ill.: InterVarsity, 2005.

Southard, Samuel. *Pastoral Evangelism.* Louisville: John Knox, 1981.

Swanson, Roger, and Shirley Clement. *The Faith-Sharing Congregation.* Nashville: Discipleship Resources, 1999.

Webber, Robert E. *Celebrating Our Faith: Evangelism through Worship.* San Francisco: Harper, 1986.

———. *Journey to Jesus: The Worship, Evangelism and Nurture Mission of the Church.* Nashville: Abingdon, 2001.

Wright, Tim. *Unfinished Evangelism: More Than Getting Them in the Door.* Minneapolis: Augsburg Fortress, 1995.

Part Five: Evangelism in Diverse Ecclesiastical and Ecumenical Settings

Armstrong, Richard S. *Faithful Witnesses: A Course in Evangelism for Presbyterian Laity.* Philadelphia: Geneva, 1987.

Bliese, Richard H., ed. *The Evangelizing Church: A Lutheran Contribution.* Minneapolis: Augsburg Fortress, 2005.

Boyack, Kenneth, ed. *The New Catholic Evangelization.* New York: Paulist, 1992.

Briese, Russell. *Foundations of a Lutheran Theology of Evangelism.* Frankfurt: Peter Lang, 1994.

Burt, Robert L., ed. *Affirming Evangelism: A Call to Renewed Commitment in the United Church of Christ.* Cleveland: UCCBHM, 1993.

Coalter, Milton J. and Virgil Cruz, eds. *How Shall We Witness? Faithful Evangelism in a Reformed Tradition.* Louisville: Westminster/John Knox, 1985.

Collins, Kenneth J., and John H. Tyson. *Conversion in the Wesleyan Tradition.* Nashville: Abingdon, 2001.

Fung, Raymond, ed. *Evangelistically Yours: Ecumenical Letters on Contemporary Evangelism.* Geneva: WCC, 1992.

———, ed. *Not a Solitary Way: Evangelism Stories from around the World.* Geneva: WCC, 1992.

Gunter, W. Stephen, and Elaine Robinson. *Considering the Great Commission: Evangelism and Mission in the Wesleyan Spirit.* Nashville: Abingdon, 2005.

Hunter, George G., III. *To Spread the Power: Church Growth in the Wesleyan Spirit.* Nashville: Abingdon, 1987.

John, Jeffrey, ed. *Living Evangelism: Affirming Catholicism and Sharing the Faith.* London: Darton, Longman & Todd, 1996.

Knight, Henry H., III. *Transforming Evangelism: The Wesleyan Way of Sharing Faith.* Nashville: Abingdon, 2006.

Linn, Jan G. *Reclaiming Evangelism: A Practical Guide for Mainline Churches.* St. Louis: Chalice, 1998.

Logan, James C., ed. *Theology and Evangelism in the Wesleyan Heritage.* Nashville: Kingswood, 1994.

———, ed. *Christ for the World: United Methodist Bishops Speak on Evangelism.* Nashville: Kingswood, 1996.

Lovell, Arnold. *Evangelism in the Reformed Tradition.* Decatur, Ga.: CTS, 1990.

Nichols, Alan, ed. *The Whole Gospel for the Whole World: Story of Lausanne II Congress on World Evangelization, Manila 1989.* Charlotte, N.C.: Lausanne Committee, 1989.

Outler, Albert C. *Evangelism in the Wesleyan Spirit.* Nashville: Discipleship Resources, 1971.

Padilla, C. René. *The New Face of Evangelism: An International Symposium on the Lausanne Covenant.* Downers Grove, Ill.: InterVarsity, 1976.

Paul VI, Pope. *Evangelization in the Modern World (Evangelii Nuntiandi).* New York: USCCB, 1976.

Wills, Dick. *Waking to God's Dream: Spiritual Leadership and Church Renewal.* Nashville: Abingdon, 1999.

World Council of Churches. *Mission and Evangelism: An Ecumenical Affirmation.* Geneva: WCC, 1982.

Part Six: Evangelistic Praxis in Diverse Cultural Contexts

Amaladoss, Michael. *Making All Things New: Dialogue, Pluralism, and Evangelization in Asia.* Maryknoll, N.Y.: Orbis, 1990.

Bate, Stuart C. *Evangelisation in the South African Context.* Rome: EPUG, 1991.

Bebbington, David W. *Evangelism in Modern Britain.* London: Cambridge University Press, 1992.

Croft, Steven, et al. *Evangelism in a Spiritual Age: Communicating Faith in a Changing Culture.* London: Church House, 2005.

Deck, Allan Figueroa. *The Second Wave: Hispanic Ministry and the Evangelization of Cultures.* New York: Paulist, 1989.

Guder, Darrell L., ed. *Missional Church: A Vision for the Sending of the Church in North America.* Grand Rapids: Eerdmans, 1999.

Hedlund, Roger E. *Evangelization and Church Growth: Issues from the Asian Context.* Madras: McGavran Institute, 1992.

Hunsberger, George, and Craig Van Gelder. *The Church between Gospel and Culture.* Grand Rapids: Eerdmans, 1996.

Hunt, Stephen. *The Alpha Enterprise: Evangelism in a Post-Christian Era.* Burlington, Vt.: Ashgate, 2004.

Hunter, George G., III. *Church for the Unchurched.* Nashville: Abingdon, 1996.

———. *How to Reach Secular People.* Nashville: Abingdon, 1992.

Joe-Adigwe, Hypolite A., ed. *Women, Justice and Evangelisation.* Onitsha, Nigeria: Archdiocesan Secretariat, 1980.

June, Lee N., ed. *Evangelism and Discipleship in African-American Churches.* Grand Rapids: Zondervan, 1999.

Kavunkal, Jacob. *To Gather Them into One: Evangelizatioin in India Today.* Indore, India: Satprakashan Sanchar Kendra, 1985.

Kew, Richard, and Cyril C. Okorocha. *Vision Bearers: Dynamic Evangelism in the 21st Century.* Harrisburg, Pa.: Morehouse, 1996.

Kochuparampil, Xavier. *Evangelization in India.* Kerala, India: OIRSI, 1993.

Mayers, Marvin K. *Christianity Confronts Culture: A Strategy for Crosscultural Evangelism.* Rev. ed. Grand Rapids: Zondervan, 1987.

Mroso, Agapit J. *The Church in Africa and the New Evangelisation.* Rome: EPUG, 1995.

Newbigin, Lesslie. *Foolishness to the Greeks: The Gospel and Western Culture.* Grand Rapids: Eerdmans, 1986.

———. *The Gospel in a Pluralist Society.* Grand Rapids: Eerdmans, 1989.

Rhodes, Stephen. *Where the Nations Meet: The Church in a Multicultural World.* Downers Grove, Ill.: InterVarsity, 1998.

Sanneh, Lamin. *Translating the Message: The Missionary Impact on Culture.* Maryknoll, N.Y.: Orbis, 1991.

Shorter, Aylward. *Evangelization and Culture.* London: Geoffrey Chapman, 1994.

Sigmund, Paul E., ed. *Religious Freedom and Evangelization in Latin America: The Challenge of Religious Pluralism.* Maryknoll, N.Y.: Orbis, 1999.

Smith, Glenn C., ed. *Evangelizing Blacks.* Washington: Paulist National Catholic Evangelization Assoc., 1988.

Snyder, Howard. *Global Good News.* Nashville: Abingdon, 2001.

Stewart, Carlyle F. *African American Church Growth: 12 Principles of Prophetic Ministry.* Nashville: Abingdon, 1994.

Stewart, Carlyle F., ed. *Growing the African American Church.* Nashville: Abingdon, 2006.

Ukpong, Justin S., ed. *Evangelization in Africa in the Third Millennium.* Port Harcourt, Nigeria: Catholic Institute of West Africa, 1992.

Webber, Robert, and Rodney Clapp. *People of the Truth: A Christian Challenge to Contemporary Culture.* Harrisburg, Pa.: Morehouse, 1993.

Wilson, Jacqueline E., ed. *Our Roots and Gifts: Evangelization and Culture, An African American Catholic Perspective.* Hyattsville, Md.: Archdiocese of Washington, 1990.

Name Index

Subject Index